READINGS IN MEDIEVAL HISTORY

JONATHAN F. SCOTT
Late of New York University

ALBERT HYMA
The University of Michigan

ARTHUR H. NOYES
Late of Ohio State University

NEW YORK

APPLETON-CENTURY-CROFTS, INC.

5108-8

MANUFACTURED IN THE UNITED STATES OF AMERICA

DEDICATED TO THE MEMORY OF
DANA CARLETON MUNRO

DEDICATED TO THE MEMORY OF
DANA CARLETON MUNRO

PREFACE

The general plan of this volume is similar to that of Scott and Baltzly's *Readings in European History since 1814,* the principal purpose of the compilers being to provide selections likely to stimulate the interest of college students in the reading and study of history. Excerpts have been made both from primary sources and secondary works. Very little documentary material, however, has been included. Such material is of course readily available in a number of source books on medieval history.

It is a pleasure to acknowledge the indebtedness of the compilers to those who have been kind enough to aid them in their work. Useful suggestions have been made by Professor André Beaumont, Miss Margaret S. Scott of the Brearley School, and Dr. Henry Noss of New York University. The assistance of Miss Margaret Walker, Secretary of the Department of History at Washington Square College, has been invaluable in connection with the correspondence involved in the preparation of the book. The compilers take this occasion to thank all of these, as well as authors and publishers who have given permission to reprint material, for their generous coöperation.

CONTENTS

READINGS IN MEDIEVAL HISTORY

READINGS IN MEDIEVAL HISTORY

1. THE LOT OF THE COMMON MAN UNDER THE EARLY ROMAN EMPIRE AND TODAY. A COMPARISON [1]

It is generally admitted that the civilization of the early Middle Ages was greatly inferior to that of the Romans in the time of Augustus Caesar. Whether or not Roman civilization at its best was superior to our own, however, is a question not easily answered.

Those who take it for granted that there has been distinct progress since the days when Rome was in her glory are apt to be thinking of the remarkable development of pure and applied science in modern times. On the other hand those who maintain that Roman civilization was of a higher type than ours are quite likely to be thinking in terms of the culture of the upper classes then and today.

The author of the following selection makes no pretense of giving a final answer to this moot question. He is inclined to believe, however, that at least the lot of the common man is somewhat better than it was at the opening of the Christian era.

A glowing faith in progress characterized the nineteenth century. New inventions and a new industrial organization were increasing production with marvelous rapidity. Comforts multiplied. Wealth grew by leaps and bounds. Kings were toppled from their thrones and in their places came democratic governments, winning popular support with magical promises of better times. Systems of universal, compulsory education were set up in all of the most enlightened states. The benevolent spirit of humanitarianism set itself zealously to care for the weak, the distressed and the handicapped. Here and there a Karl Marx might cry out that if the rich were growing richer the poor were growing poorer, and that some day a terrible class revolution would ensue. But his voice was lost in the chorus of praise for the blessings of democracy and industrial evolution.

Today, however, in the wreckage of a post-war world, amid nations armed to the teeth and glaring at one another with fear and suspicion, in the midst of world-wide economic depression, disillusioned men may well ask whether nearly two thousand years of Christian history have accomplished anything worth while for humanity, whether the lot of the common

[1] Jonathan F. Scott, "The World Today and at the Time of the First Christmas." The New York *Herald Tribune,* December 20, 1931.

man today is any better than it was at the time that Christ was born in Bethlehem of Judea.

The greatness and glory of the Roman world into which the humble Jesus was born still grip the imagination. On the imperial throne at Rome sat the divine Augustus, whose praises were sung by Vergil and Horace, greatest of the Roman poets. The vast empire over which he ruled, some 2,000 miles in breadth and 3,000 in length, encircled the Mediterranean Sea. Scattered far and wide throughout these dominions were many fair cities, with well paved streets, shady porticos, graceful triumphal arches, beautiful temples and monuments, well built houses, often centrally heated and amply supplied with running water brought within the city wall by scientifically constructed aqueducts. Connecting these cities and running in straight lines were the best built roads the world has ever known.

The reign of Augustus marked the beginning of an era of peace after centuries of unremitting warfare, a peace that was to last nearly 200 years. With unexampled peace came unexampled prosperity. For the bold and the shrewd the opportunities for making money were enormous. Senators, knights and ex-slaves engaged eagerly in the engrossing pursuit, some buying and selling vast tracts of land, some trading on a huge scale within the empire in oil, wine, grain or slaves, some purchasing shares in ships that sailed the distant seas, bringing, it might be, tin from Britain or silks, spices and precious gems from India and China.

Making money quickly, these adventurous capitalists spent lavishly. In the cities they built magnificent palaces. These palaces, "extending almost over the area of a town, were adorned with marbles from the quarries of Paros, Laconia, Phrygia or Numidia, with gilded ceilings and curious panels . . . with hundreds of tables of citrus-wood, resting on pillars of ivory, each costing a moderate fortune, with priceless bronzes and masterpieces of ancient plate." In the country, at the seashore or in the mountains, these same men built themselves spacious villas, sparsely furnished in accord with the prevailing taste, but beautifully decorated. In city palace and rural villa the Roman magnate entertained his friends and hangers-on on a magnificent scale. Games, recitations, music, theatrical displays, all helped to entertain the guests. Hours were dawdled away in the luxurious, sumptuously decorated baths, to which were devoted sometimes as many as twenty rooms, and at costly banquets which, among the grosser sort, often degenerated into orgies of gluttony and drunkenness. Always hordes of slaves were on hand to minister to every want of master and guest. Such luxury naturally dissipated quickly many fortunes and men once wealthy groaned under heavy burdens of debt.

Of all this luxury the Roman writers have much to say; of the life of the common man exceedingly little. Like their wealthy patrons, these authors were little interested in the masses of the people, whom they held to be vicious and degraded and on whom they often looked down with the utmost contempt. Certain Christian historians, however, lacking adequate information, have used their imaginations. Looking at ancient civilization through the spectacles of prejudice they have depicted the Roman Empire as a sink of iniquity and the masses of the people, free and slave, as ground down into abject misery under the oppression of a hard-hearted debauched aristocracy of birth and money. This prejudiced view modern classical scholarship has done much to correct. Painstakingly poking into the nooks and crannies of available source material it has reached the conclusion that the condition of the common man at and around the time of Augustus Caesar was not as black as it has so often been painted. The proportion of slaves to freemen was apparently not as great as was once supposed. Many slaves were treated with genuine kindness by their masters, were allowed to accumulate money and were sometimes made their owners' heirs. Over and over again slaves were freed.

Nor were the masses of the freemen completely lacking in the amenities of life. In the cities there were a number of public buildings for the use of citizens. There were theaters and circuses, buildings for exercise and sport, and last, but not least, great public baths, "enabling every citizen to have his daily bath." The imperial government, and some at least of the wealthy citizens, were not without a sense of obligation toward the unfortunate. "Under the influence of the stoic teaching of the brotherhood of man and the duty of mutual help," says Samuel Dill, "both private citizens and the benevolent princes . . . created charitable foundations for the orphan and the needy. Public calamities were relieved again and again by imperial and private charity. The love of wealth was strong, but a spirit of benevolence was in the air." Fear, no doubt, was often a motive in this giving, as well as benevolence. This is probably especially true in the case of the free bread and the free games, "bread and circuses," which the imperial government was constrained to dole out to the masses of Rome. But, whatever the motives of giving, the condition of the people evidently was not always one of unrelieved misery.

Despite such evidence, however, showing that the common man was not as badly off at the opening of the Christian era as was once supposed, there is a darker side to the picture. Whatever may be said of the kindness of individual masters, slavery was a dreadful curse. On the great estates which were spreading over parts of the empire, some of them worked by tenants and slaves, the slaves, cultivating the fields in gangs, were often chained together. At night, still in chains, they were thrust into subterranean slave prisons, virtually dungeons, and locked in. Even in Rome it was customary in Augustus's time in private houses to chain the porter. In the great slave markets the slaves could be stripped naked, handled and hustled about like cattle. To recruit the slave markets freemen within the empire were often kidnaped and prisoners of war were sold into slavery. Julius Caesar sold 53,000 prisoners into slavery at one stroke. Slaves at Rome who were ill were often put out to recover or die on an island in the Tiber River. Evidently the system made possible fiendish exploitation and abuse of slaves by masters who so chose.

Nor was the lot of the poorer freemen an enviable one. In the country the small farms of the peasants were being rapidly swallowed up by the great estates and the peasants themselves were sinking into the position of landless laborers, serfs (coloni) or even slaves. In the cities the proletarians, despite their public baths, their theaters, their bread and circuses, were but wretchedly housed. Only the wealthy and well-to-do had houses of their own. Poor people lived in great barrack-like structures known as insulae (islands). "The common lodging-house," says a modern writer, "must have been simply a rabbit-warren, the crowded inhabitants using their rooms only for eating and sleeping, while for the most part they prowled about, either idling or getting such employment as they could, legitimate or otherwise." In such places there could have been but little family life. To make matters worse not infrequently the wretched structures caught on fire or came tumbling down on the heads of those within. It seems probable that families not infrequently had no homes at all. There were schools for the well-to-do but not for the poor. Nor was there adequate police protection for the masses of the people of Rome, no machinery for holding in check assault, burglary and murder in the lower quarters of the city. Life was cheap in the slums of cities all over Italy. Moreover, the poor were liable to be swept away in droves by famine and pestilence, twin scourges whose visits to the empire were as frequent as they were unwelcome.

Today, with millions out of employment, industries striving to keep their heads above water, the financial structure of the world dislocated, prices falling, banks failing, savings disappearing and bread lines forming, the condition of the common man in Europe and America may seem hard enough and the outlook bleak. But it would be unfair to judge the civilization of today wholly on the basis of the situation at the moment. Normally the common man of today is clearly better off than his prototype in the Roman Empire at the opening of the Christian era. He is better clothed, better housed, he has better food, more education and more diversified recreation. He has more freedom and is less subject to ill treatment by those more fortunately placed than he. Even in these abnormal times, though exploitation persists slavery has disappeared from Europe and America and with it those terrible abuses from which men of the ancient world so often suffered.

Crowded tenements still exist, some of them jerry-built, but no longer do city proletarians live habitually in rabbit-warrens, many of them liable to collapse at any time. Gangsters still rob and kill, but the life and goods of the common man are far safer than they were in imperial Rome. The rich still sometimes look down on the poor but there is little of that vast contempt for the masses that was normal in the days of the Caesars. Poverty there is today in abundance but not that persistent poverty of Roman times that depended constantly on doles of bread. Hunger there is but famine on a large scale has disappeared from our Western world. Ignorance there is but schools are open for all or nearly all. Sickness there is but not the devastating plagues of 2,000 years ago.

Finally, if we compare the general spirit of Roman times with the spirit of today it would seem that there has been a substantial gain in good will. Nothing indicates a certain fundamental hardness of heart among the Romans of Augustus's day better than the gladiatorial combats. It was partly of these that H. G. Wells was thinking when he wrote in his "Outline of History": "Every now and then the reader of Roman history, reading in terms of debates and measures, policies and campaigns, capital and labor, comes upon something that gives him much the same shock he would feel if he went down to an unknown caller in his house and extended his hand to meet the hairy paw of Homo Neanderthalis and looked up to see a chinless, bestial face." "This organization of murder as a sport and show," he adds, "serves to measure the great gap in moral standards between the Roman community and his own." We turn with a shudder of horror from the thought of the audience in a Roman amphitheater deciding with a careless signal of thumbs whether or not the life of a gladiator should be spared.

This good will is evident, too, in the far greater sense of social responsibility that exists today than in Roman times. Rome had some charitable institutions, and rich men sometimes gave largess freely. But in those days, says Professor Fowler, "there were no insurance offices, no benefit societies, no philanthropic institutions to rescue the suffering from undeserved misery." Today in New York City there are hundreds of social agencies to help the underprivileged and the otherwise unfortunate and to do so more by helping them help themselves than by that indiscriminate distribution of charity which leads to pauperism. In an emergency such as exists today through the economic depression the Roman government and the more responsible men of wealth would very likely have done something to alleviate misery, but there would not have been then, as there are now, widespread giving and businesslike organization of whole-hearted efforts to relieve suffering. It is in this spirit of good will and in the widespread sense of social responsibility, perhaps more than anything else, that America today stands ethically head and shoulders above the Roman Empire.

In the development of this good will, Christianity, organized in the Church, has played a greater part for nearly 2,000 years than any other influence. The Church of the past and present is today subjected to severe criticism. Historians point to the corruption that infected so many of the clergy of early times, to the intolerance that marred the spirit of Christianity, to the bloody religious wars that not so many centuries ago divided Europe. Contemporary writers criticize the churches of today for timidity, futility and exhibitions of an un-Christian spirit. Such critics are likely to forget the great services the churches have rendered to struggling humanity. They are likely to forget that when the proud Roman Empire crumbled and fell the burden of salvaging civilization fell largely on the shoulders of the Christian clergy. Bishops assumed the work of governing and of administering justice when municipal magistrates and other officials failed. The clergy, secular and regular, conducted the only significant schools of the early Middle Ages. The monks were the first doctors, the first lawyers of medieval times. Monasteries were the first inns. The clergy established the first hospitals. Charitable work was almost entirely in the hands of the clergy. Many of these and other services are still being carried on in a more restricted field, but perhaps with greater efficiency by the Catholic and Protestant churches of today. Some of the burden has been assumed by governmental and private organizations. Whatever criticisms may be made of organized Christianity the debt of our civilization to it is enormous.

2. *SALVIAN CRITICIZES THE ROMANS*[1]

Salvian was born among the Gauls at the close of the fourth century. He belonged to a prominent family and was brought up in or near Trier in what is now western Germany, where he received an excellent education. At an early age he became a devout Christian; he sold his possessions and distributed the proceeds among the poor. For a period of six years he led the life of a monk and about the year 426 he removed to Marseilles, where he acquired the reputation of a great saint. Although he never filled a bishop's chair, remaining simply a priest, he was often called "Master of the Bishops." Among his numerous writings the most important is De Gubernatione Dei, *or* On the Government of God, *also named* On the Providence of God. *It consists of eight books, dealing with the history of western Europe and northern Africa during the decline of Rome. His criticism of the Romans is a little too severe, but it does give the modern reader a clear picture of the moral decadence of the Roman Empire in the fifth century.*

What we have said, at the end of the preceding book, about the feebleness and the misery of the Romans, might seem to be disparaging to the subject

[1] Salvian, *De Gubernatione Dei,* book VII, the opening paragraphs.

we are treating. It is easy, I know, to raise this objection: that which proves above all that God does not pay any attention to human affairs is the fact that when the Romans were idolatrous they conquered and ruled, whereas now, when they are Christians, they are conquered and enslaved. In order to overrule this objection it will no doubt suffice to repeat what has been said already about almost all the pagan nations, that those men are more guilty who knowingly transgress the divine law than those who do this without knowing it.

. . . .

How are we now to account for these disorders I have mentioned before, this union of misery and luxury? I maintain that these are the vices of the happy (although no one can be at the same time happy and criminal, since true happiness cannot be found where there is no real virtue), but they are also the vices of a long peace and of a secure opulence. Why, I ask, are these disorders seen where there is no peace now, nor any security? For peace and security have vanished from the whole Roman Empire. Why do only the vices remain? Who could maintain in a poor man a wanton desire for pleasure? For a luxurious poverty is more criminal, and the wretch who devotes himself to frivolity becomes more odious. The whole Roman world is both luxurious and miserable. Where is the man, I pray, who is at the same time poor and dissipated? Where is the man who, expecting captivity, dares to think of the arena (circus)? Where is the man who fears death and yet laughs? We, though afraid of captivity, play; though fearful of death, we laugh. You might say that the whole Roman people is saturated with sardonic herbs. It is dying and yet it laughs. And therefore, in nearly all parts of the world, our smiles will be followed by tears. Today, then, has been manifested to us the word of our Lord: "Woe unto you who laugh, for you shall weep." [1]

3. EVIDENCES OF THE DECAY OF ANCIENT CIVILIZATION [2]

Historians sometimes neglect to bring out with sufficient emphasis and clearness the nature of the decay of Roman civilization. Consequently many students who can discuss intelligently the possible causes of the decline of the Roman Empire not infrequently have but a hazy impression of the characteristics of that decline. In the following selection, however, the distinguished historian, Professor Rostovtzeff of Yale University, shows in concrete terms what the decay of Roman civilization meant.

[1] Luke VI, 25.

[2] M. Rostovtzeff, *The Social and Economic History of the Roman Empire,* Oxford. At the Clarendon Press, 1926, pp. 453–454; 477–480 (slightly condensed).

Thus arose the state of Diocletian and Constantine. In organizing it the emperors did not have a free hand. They took over a heavy heritage from the third century, to which they had to conform. In this heritage there was almost nothing positive except the fact of the existence of the Empire with all its natural resources. The men who inhabited it had utterly lost their balance. Hatred and envy reigned everywhere: the peasants hated the landowners and the officials, the city proletariat hated the city *bourgeoisie,* the army was hated by everybody, even by the peasants. The Christians were abhorred and persecuted by the heathens, who regarded them as a gang of criminals bent on undermining the state. Work was disorganized and productivity was declining; commerce was ruined by the insecurity of the sea and the roads; industry could not prosper, since the market for industrial products was steadily contracting and the purchasing power of the population diminishing; agriculture passed through a terrible crisis, for the decay of commerce and industry deprived it of the capital which it needed, and the heavy demands of the state robbed it of labour and of the largest part of its products. Prices constantly rose, and the value of the currency depreciated at an unprecedented rate. The ancient system of taxation had been shattered and no new system was devised. The relations between the state and the taxpayer were based on more or less organized robbery: forced work, forced deliveries, forced loans or gifts were the order of the day. The administration was corrupt and demoralized. A chaotic mass of new government officials was growing up, superimposed on and superseding the former administrative *personnel.* The old officials still existed but, foreseeing their doom, strove to avail themselves to the full of their last opportunities. The city *bourgeoisie* was tracked out and persecuted, cheated, and maltreated. The municipal aristocracy was decimated by systematic persecution and ruined by repeated confiscations and by the responsibility imposed on it of ensuring the success of the organized raids of the government on the people. The most terrible chaos thus reigned throughout the ruined Empire. In such circumstances the task of any reformer would be to reduce the chaos to some sort of stable order, and the simpler and more primitive the methods, the better. The more refined system of the past was utterly destroyed and beyond restoration. What existed was the brutal practice of the third century, rude and violent as it was. That practice was to a certain extent created by the situation, and the simplest way out of the chaos was to fix and stabilize it, reducing it to a system and making the system as simple and as primitive as possible. The reform of Diocletian and Constantine was the legitimate offspring of the social revolution of the third century, and was bound to follow in the main the same lines.

. . . .

The social revolution of the third century, which destroyed the foundations of the economic, social, and intellectual life of the ancient world, could not produce any positive achievement. On the ruins of a prosperous and well-organized state, based on the age-old classical civilization and on the self-government of the cities, it built up a state which was based on general ignorance, on compulsion and violence, on slavery and servility, on bribery and dishonesty. Have we the right to accuse the emperors of the fourth century of having deliberately and of their own choice built up such a state, while they might have taken another path and have constructed, not the slave-state of the late Roman Empire, but one free from the mistakes of the early Empire and yet not enshrining the brutal practice of the revolutionary period? It is idle to ask such a question. The emperors of the fourth century, and above all Diocletian, grew up in the atmosphere of violence and compulsion. They never saw anything else, they never came across any other method. Their education was moderate, and their training exclusively military. They took their duties seriously, and they were animated by the sincerest love of their country. Their aim was to save the Roman Empire, and they achieved it. To this end they used, with the best intentions, the means which were familiar to them, violence and compulsion. They never asked whether it was worth while to save the Roman Empire in order to make it a vast prison for scores of millions of men. . . .

The decline and fall of the Roman Empire, that is to say, of ancient civilization as a whole, has two aspects: the political, social, and economic on the one hand, and the intellectual and spiritual on the other. In the sphere of politics we witness a gradual barbarization of the Empire from within, especially in the West. The foreign, German, elements play the leading part both in the government and in the army, and settling in masses displace the Roman population, which disappears from the fields. A related phenomenon, which indeed was a necessary consequence of this barbarization from within, was the gradual disintegration of the Western Roman Empire; the ruling classes in the former Roman provinces were replaced first by Germans and Sarmatians, and later by Germans alone, either through peaceful penetration or by conquest. In the East we observe a gradual Orientalization of the Byzantine Empire, which leads ultimately to the establishment, on the ruins of the Roman Empire, of strong half-Oriental and purely Oriental states, the Caliphate of Arabia, and the Persian and Turkish empires. From the social and economic point of view, we mean by decline the gradual relapse of the ancient world to very primitive forms of economic life, into an almost pure "house-economy." The cities, which had created and sustained the higher forms of economic life, gradually decayed, and the majority of them practically disappeared from the face of the earth. A few, especially those that had been great centers of commerce and industry, still lingered on. The complicated and refined social system of the ancient Empire follows the same downward path and becomes reduced to its primitive elements: the King, his court and retinue, the big feudal landowners, the clergy, the mass of rural serfs, and small groups of artisans and merchants. Such is the political, social, and economic aspect of the problem.

From the intellectual and spiritual point of view the main phenomenon is the decline of ancient civilization, of the city civilization of the Greco-Roman world. The Oriental civilizations were more stable: blended with some elements of the Greek city civilization, they persisted and even witnessed a brilliant revival in the Caliphate of Arabia and in Persia, not to speak of India and China. Here again there are two aspects of the evolution. The first is the exhaustion of the creative forces of Greek civilization in the domains where its great triumphs had been achieved, in the exact sciences, in technique, in literature and art. The decline began as early as the second century B.C. There followed a temporary revival of creative forces in the cities of Italy, and later in those of the Eastern and Western provinces of the Empire. The progressive movement stopped almost completely in the second century A.D. and, after a period of stagnation, a steady and rapid decline set in again. Parallel to it, we notice a progressive weakening of the assimilative forces of Greco-Roman civilization. The cities no longer absorb—that is to say, no longer Hellenize or Romanize—the masses of the country population. The reverse is the case. The barbarism of the country begins to engulf the city population. Only small islands of civilized life are left, the senatorial aristocracy of the late Empire and the clergy; but both, save for a section of the clergy, are gradually swallowed up by the advancing tide of barbarism.

Another aspect of the same phenomenon is the development of a new mentality among the masses of the population. It was the mentality of the lower classes, based exclusively on religion and not only indifferent but hostile to the intellectual achievements of the higher classes. This new attitude of mind gradually dominates the upper classes, or at least the larger part of them. It is revealed by the spread among them of the various mystic religions, partly Oriental, partly Greek. The climax was reached in the triumph of Christianity. In this field the creative power of the ancient world was still alive as is shown by such momentous achievements as the creation of the Christian church, the adaptation of Christian theology to the mental level of the higher classes, the creation of a powerful Christian literature and of a new Christian art. The new intellectual efforts aimed chiefly at influencing the mass of the population and therefore represented a lowering of the high standards of city civilization, at least from the point of view of literary forms.

We may say, then, that there is one prominent feature in the development of the ancient world during the imperial age, alike in the political, social, and economic and in the intellectual field. It is a gradual absorption of the higher classes by the lower, accompanied by a gradual levelling down of standards. This levelling was accomplished in many ways. There was a slow penetration of the lower classes into the higher, which were unable to assimilate the new elements. There were violent outbreaks of civil strife: the lead was taken by the Greek cities, and there followed the civil war of the first century B. C. which involved the whole civilized world. In these struggles the upper classes and the city civilization remained victorious on the whole. Two centuries later, a new outbreak of civil war ended in the victory of the lower classes and dealt a mortal blow to the Greco-Roman civilization of the cities. Finally, that civilization was completely engulfed by the inflow of barbarous elements from outside, partly by penetration, partly by conquest, and in its dying condition it was unable to assimilate even a small part of them.

4. *THEORIES OF THE CAUSES OF THE DECAY OF ANCIENT CIVILIZATION*[1]

No one knows with certainty just what caused Roman civilization to go to pieces, but many historians have attempted to find out. In the following selection Professor Rostovtzeff sets forth the views of a number of historians on the subject, criticizes these views, and then suggests a possible cause that seems to him to be perhaps more fundamentally significant than any other.

The main problem which we have to solve is this. Why was the city civilization of Greece and Italy unable to assimilate the masses, why did it remain a civilization of the *élite,* why was it incapable of creating conditions which should secure for the ancient world a continuous, uninterrupted movement along the same path which our modern world is traversing again? Various explanations have been suggested, and each of them claims to have finally solved the problem. Let us then review the most important of them. They may be divided into four classes.

(1) The political solution is advocated by many distinguished scholars. For Beloch the decay of ancient civilization was caused by the absorption of the Greek city-states by the Roman Empire, by the formation of a world-state which prevented the creative forces of Greece from developing and consolidating the great achievements of civilized life. There is some truth in this view. It is evident that the creation of the Roman Empire was a

[1] M. Rostovtzeff, *The Social and Economic History of the Roman Empire,* Oxford. At the Clarendon Press, 1926, pp. 480–487 (slightly condensed).

step forward in the process of levelling, and that it facilitated the final absorption of the higher classes. We must, however, take into consideration that class war was a common feature of Greek life, and that we have not the least justification for supposing that the Greek city-community would have found a solution of the social and economic problems which produced civil war in the various communities. Further, this view suggests that there was only one creative race in the ancient world, which is notoriously false. Another explanation, tending in the same direction, has been put forward by Kornemann. He regards as the main cause of the decay of the Roman Empire the fact that Augustus reduced the armed forces of the Empire, and that this reduction was maintained by his successors. The suggestion lays the whole emphasis on the military side of the problem, and is therefore a return to the antiquated idea that ancient civilization was destroyed by the barbarian invasions, an idea which was dropped long ago by the best scholars and cannot be resuscitated. Besides, the maintenance of a comparatively small army was imperatively imposed by the economic weakness of the Empire, a fact which was understood by all the emperors. Still less convincing is the idea of Ferrero, that the collapse of the Empire was due to a disastrous event, to an accident which had the gravest consequences. He holds that by transmitting his power to his son Commodus instead of to a man chosen by the senate, M. Aurelius undermined the senate's authority on which the whole fabric of the Roman state rested; that the murder of Commodus led to the usurpation of Septimius and to the civil war of the third century; and that the usurpation and the war destroyed the authority of the senate and deprived the imperial power of its only legitimacy in the eyes of the population which was its main support. Ferrero forgets that legally the power of the emperors in the third century was still derived from the senate and people of Rome, that it was so even in the time of Diocletian, and that the same idea still survived under Constantine and his successors. He also forgets that the subtle formula of Augustus, Vespasian and the Antonines was incomprehensible to the mass of the people of the Empire, and was a creation of the upper classes, completely outside the range of popular conceptions. Finally, he fails to understand the true character of the crisis of the third century. The struggle was not between the senate and the emperor, but between the cities and the army—that is to say, the masses of peasants—as is shown by the fact that the lead in the fight was taken not by Rome but by the cities of the province of Africa. A deeper explanation is offered by Heitland. He suggests that the ancient world decayed because it was unable to give the masses a share in the government, and even gradually restricted the numbers of those who participated in the life of the state, ultimately reducing them to the emperor himself, his court, and the imperial bureaucracy. I regard this point as only one aspect of the great phenomenon which I have described above. Have we the right to suppose that the emperors would not have tried the plan of representative government if they had known of it and believed in it? They tried many other plans and failed. If the idea of representative government was foreign to the ancient world (and as a matter of fact it was not), why did the ancient world not evolve the idea, which is not a very difficult one? Moreover, the question arises, Can we be sure that representative government is the cause of the brilliant development of our civilization and not one of its aspects, just as was the Greek city-state? Have we the slightest reason to believe that modern democracy is a guarantee of continuous and uninterrupted progress, and is capable of preventing civil war from breaking out under the fostering influence of hatred and envy? Let us not forget that the most modern political and social theories suggest that democracy is an antiquated institution, that it is rotten and corrupt, being the offspring of capitalism, and that the only just form of government is the dictatorship of the proletariat. Did not the peasants of the Roman Empire act subconsciously on the same principle?

(2) The economic explanation of decay of the ancient world must be rejected completely. In speaking of the development of industry in the ancient world, I have dealt with the theory of the Marxians, as adapted to our problem by K. Bücher, M. Weber, and G. Salvioli. If the theory fails to explain even this minor point, much less will it serve to explain the general phenomenon. The Marxians forget that the ancient world went through many cycles of evolution, and that in these cycles there occur long periods of progress and other long periods of return to more primitive conditions, to the phase of economic life which is generally described as "house-economy." It is true that the ancient world never reached the economic stage in which we live, the stage of industrial capitalism. But in the history of the ancient world we have many epochs of high economic development: certain periods in the history of many Oriental monarchies, particularly Egypt, Babylonia, and Persia; the age of the highest development of the city-states, especially the fourth century B.C.; the period of the Hellenistic monarchies, where the climax was reached in the third century B.C.; the period of the late Roman Republic and of the early Roman Empire. All these periods show different aspects of economic life and different economy of capitalism. In none of them did the forms of house-economy prevail. We may compare the economic aspects of life during these periods to that of many European countries in the time of the Renaissance and later, although in no case would the comparison be perfect, as there is no identity between the economic development of the modern and that of the ancient world. According to the different economic conditions of these several periods in the history of the ancient world, the relations between house-

economy and capitalistic economy varied, and they frequently varied not only in the different periods but also in different parts of the ancient world during the same period. The ancient world was in this respect not unlike the modern world. In the industrial countries of Europe, such as England and more parts of Germany and France, economic life nowadays is by no means the same as it is in the agricultural countries, like Russia and the Balkan peninsula and large parts of the Near East. The economic life of the United States of America is not in the least identical with the economic life of Europe or of the various parts of South America, not to speak of China, Japan, and India. So it was in the ancient world. While Egypt and Babylonia had a complex economic life, with a highly developed industry and wide commercial relations, other parts of the Near East lived a quite different and much more primitive life. While Athens, Corinth, Rhodes, Syracuse, Tyre, and Sidon in the fourth century B.C. were centres of a developed commercial capitalism, other Greek cities lived an almost purely agricultural life. In the Hellenistic and Roman periods it was just the same. The main fact which has to be explained is why capitalistic development, which started at many times and in many places, and prevailed in large portions of the ancient world for comparatively long periods, yielded ultimately to more primitive forms of economic life. Even in our own times it has not completely ousted those forms. It is evident that the problem cannot be solved by affirming that the ancient world lived throughout under the forms of primitive house-economy. The statement is manifestly wrong. We might say exactly the same of large areas of the modern world, and we are not at all sure that a violent catastrophe might not bring the modern capitalistic world back to the primitive phase of house-economy, as has happened in Russia since the Bolshevik revolution.

To sum up what I have said, the economic simplification of ancient life was not the cause of what we call the decline of the ancient world, but one of the aspects of the more general phenomenon which I am trying to explain. Here, just as in the other spheres of human life, the political, social, intellectual and religious, the more primitive forms of life among the masses were not absorbed by the higher forms but triumphed over them in the end. We may select one of these phenomena and declare it to be the ultimate cause; but it would be an arbitrary assumption which would not convince any one. The problem remains. Why was the victorious advance of capitalism stopped? Why was machinery not invented? Why were the business systems not perfected? Why were the primal forces of primitive economy not overcome? They were gradually disappearing; why did they not disappear completely? To say that they were quantitatively stronger than in our own times does not help us to explain the main phenomenon. That is why many economists, who are aware that the usual explanation only touches the surface and does not probe the problem to the bottom, endeavour to save the economic explanation, and the materialistic conception of historical evolution in general, by producing some potent physical factor as the cause of the weakness of the higher forms of economic life in the ancient world. Such a factor has been found by some scholars in the general exhaustion of the soil all over the ancient world, which reached its climax in the late Roman Empire and ruined the ancient world. I have dealt with this theory above. There are no facts to support it. All the facts about the economic development of the ancient world speak against it. Agriculture decayed in the ancient world just in the same way and from the same causes as the other branches of economic life. As soon as the political and social conditions improved in the various parts of the Empire, the fields and gardens began to yield the same harvests as before. Witness the flourishing state of Gaul in the time of Ausonius and of Sidonius Apollinaries; witness the fact that in Egypt, where the soil is inexhaustible and those parts of it which are not flooded are very easily improved by the most primitive methods, agriculture decayed in the third and fourth centuries, just as in the other provinces. It is plain that the economic explanation does not help us, and that the investigations of the economists reveal, not the cause of the decline of the ancient world, but merely one of its aspects.

(3) The rapid progress of medicine and of biological science has had its influence on the problem of the decay of ancient civilization. A biological solution has been often suggested, and the theories of degeneration and race-suicide have been applied to the ancient world. The biological theory supplies us with an apparently exhaustive explanation of the decline of the assimilative forces of the civilized upper classes. They gradually degenerated and had not the power to assimilate the lower classes but were absorbed by them. According to Seeck, the cause of their degeneration and of their numerical decline was the "extermination of the best" by foreign and civil wars. Others, like Tenney Frank, think of the contamination of higher races by an admixture of the blood of inferior races. Others, again, regard degeneration as a natural process common to all civilized communities: the best are neither exterminated nor contaminated, but they commit systematic suicide by not reproducing and by letting the inferior type of mankind breed freely. I am not competent to sit in judgement on the problem of degeneration from the biological and physiological point of view. From the historical point of view, I venture to remark against Seeck that in wars and revolutions it is not only the best that are exterminated. On the other hand, revolutions do not always prevent the succeeding period from being a period of great bloom. Against Frank I may suggest that I see no criterion for distinguishing between inferior and superior races. Why are the Greek and Latin races considered the only superior races in the

Roman Empire? Some of the races which "contaminated" the ruling races, for instance, the pre-Indo-European and pre-Semitic race or races of the Mediterranean, had created great civilizations in the past (the Egyptian, the Minoan, the Iberian, the Etruscan, the civilizations of Asia Minor), and the same is true of the Semitic and of the Iranian civilizations. Why did the admixture of the blood of these races contaminate and deteriorate the blood of the Greeks and the Romans? On the other hand, the Celts and the Germans belonged to the same stock as the Greeks and the Romans. The Celts had a high material civilization of their own. The Germans were destined to develop a high civilized life in the future. Why did the admixture of their blood corrupt and not regenerate their fellow Aryans, the Greeks and the Romans? The theory of a natural decay of civilization by race-suicide states the same general phenomenon of which we have been speaking, the gradual absorption of the upper classes by the lower and the lack of assimilative power shown by the upper. It states the fact, but gives no explanation. The problem this theory has to solve is, Why do the best not reproduce their kind? It may be solved in different ways: we may suggest an economic, or a physiological, or a psychological explanation. But none of these explanations is convincing.

(4) Christianity is very often made responsible for the decay of ancient civilization. This is, of course, a very narrow point of view. Christianity is but one side of the general change in the mentality of the ancient world. Can we say that this change is the ultimate cause of the decay of ancient civilization? It is not easy to discriminate between causes and symptoms, and one of the urgent tasks in the field of ancient history is a further investigation of this change of mentality. The change, no doubt, was one of the most potent factors in the gradual decay of the civilization of the city-state and in the rise of a new conception of the world and of a new civilization. But how are we to explain the change? Is it a problem of individual and mass psychology?

None of the existing theories fully explains the problem of the decay of ancient civilization, if we can apply the word "decay" to the complex phenomenon which I have endeavoured to describe. Each of them, however, has contributed much to the clearing of the ground, and has helped us to perceive that the main phenomenon which underlies the process of decline is the gradual absorption of the educated classes by the masses and the consequent simplification of all the functions of political, social, economic, and intellectual life, which we call the barbarization of the ancient world.

The evolution of the ancient world has a lesson and a warning for us. Our civilization will not last unless it be a civilization not of one class, but of the masses. The Oriental civilizations were more stable and lasting than the Greco-Roman, because, being chiefly based on religion, they were nearer to the masses. Another lesson is that violent attempts at levelling have never helped to uplift the masses. They have destroyed the upper classes, and resulted in accelerating the process of barbarization. But the ultimate problem remains like a ghost, ever present and unlaid: Is it possible to extend a higher civilization to the lower classes without debasing its standard and diluting its quality to the vanishing point? Is not every civilization bound to decay as soon as it begins to penetrate the masses?

5. *THE EARLY GERMANS*[1]

Our sources of information about the early Germans are very scanty. The best contemporary account that has come down to us, unfortunately all too brief, is the Germania *of the Roman historian, Tacitus, written at the end of the first century A.D. Later research has revealed in it some errors. Nevertheless its importance is such that, as Professor Lynn Thorndike has said, "every student of the Middle Ages should read for himself the dozen of its pages that deal with the traits and institutions of the Germans as a whole, and get a first-hand knowledge of this original source which forms the basis of all modern accounts of the early Germans."*[2]

I. Germany proper is separated from the Gauls, the Rhaetians and the Pannonians by the Rhine and the Danube, from the Sarmatians and Dacians partly by the mountains, partly by their mutual fears. The ocean washes its other boundaries, forming deep bays and embracing large islands where various tribes and their kings have become known to us through the disclosures of recent war. The Rhine takes its rise in the steep and inaccessible fastnesses of the Rhaetian Alps, and, bending slightly to the west, flows into the northern ocean. The Danube, pouring down from the gently sloping ridge of Mount Abnoba, passes the borders of many nations, and finally forces its way through six outlets into the Black Sea; a seventh channel is swallowed up by the marshes.

II. I should say that the Germans themselves were an indigenous people, without any subsequent mixture of blood through immigration or friendly intercourse; for in ancient times it was by sea and not by land that those who wished to change their homes wandered, and the ocean, hostile, as it were, and of boundless extent on the further side, is rarely traversed by

[1] Extracts from Tacitus' Germania. University of Pennsylvania, Translations and Reprints from the Original Sources of European History. Published for the Department of History of the University of Pennsylvania by the University of Pennsylvania Press, Philadelphia. Vol. VI, No. 3, pp. 4–16 (A. C. Howland, Editor).

[2] History of Medieval Europe, p. 41.

ships from our part of the world. And not to mention the danger of the terrible and unknown sea, who indeed would leave Asia or Africa or Italy to seek Germany with its wild scenery, its harsh climate, its sullen manners and aspect, unless, indeed, it were his native country? They tell in their ancient songs, the only kind of tradition and history that they have, how Tuisto, a god sprung from the earth, and his son Mannus were the originators and founders of their race. Mannus is supposed to have had three sons from whose names those nearest the ocean are called *Ingaevones,* those in the middle country, *Hermiones,* and the others, *Istaevones.* Certain people assert with the freedom permitted in discussing ancient times that there were many descendants of the god, and many tribal names, such as *Marsi, Gambrivii, Suebi, Vandilii,* and that these were their true and ancient names. But the name Germany, they say, is modern and of recent application, since those who first crossed the Rhine and expelled the Gauls, and who are now called *Tungri,* were then named Germans; thus what had been a tribal, not a national name, spread little by little, so that later they all adopted the newly-coined appellation that was first employed by the conquerors to inspire fear and called themselves Germans.

III. They say that Hercules himself once visited them, and when about to go into battle they sing of him as the first of all heroes. They have also certain songs, by the intonation of which (*barditus,* as it is called) they excite their courage, while they divine the fortune of the coming battle from the sound itself. They inspire or feel terror according to the character of the cheering, though what harmony there is in the shouting is one of valor rather than of voices. The effect they particularly strive for is that of a harsh noise, a wild and confused roar, which they attain by putting their shields to their mouths so that the reverberation swells their deep, full voices. Ulysses, too, is thought by some to have reached this ocean in those long and fabulous wanderings of his, and to have been cast upon the shores of Germany. They say he built and named Asciburgium, a town on the banks of the Rhine still inhabited; nay even that an altar consecrated by him and inscribed with the name of his father Laertes has been found at the same place, and that certain monuments and tombs with Greek letters on them still exist within the confines of Germany and Rhaetia. I have no mind to argue either for or against the truth of these statements; let each one believe or reject them as he feels inclined.

IV. I myself subscribe to the opinion of those who hold that the German tribes have never been contaminated by intermarriage with other nations, but have remained peculiar and unmixed and wholly unlike other people. Hence the bodily type is the same among them all, notwithstanding the extent of their population. They all have fierce blue eyes, reddish hair and large bodies fit only for sudden exertion; they do not submit patiently to work and effort and cannot endure thirst and heat at all, though cold and hunger they are accustomed to because of their climate.

V. In general the country, though varying here and there in appearance, is covered over with wild forests or filthy swamps, being more humid on the side of Gaul but bleaker toward Noricum and Pannonia. It is suitable enough for grain but does not permit the cultivation of fruit trees; and though rich in flocks and herds these are for the most part small, the cattle not even possessing their natural beauty nor spreading horns. The people take pride in possessing a large number of animals, these being their sole and most cherished wealth. Whether it was in mercy or wrath that the gods denied them silver and gold, I know not. Yet I would not affirm that no vein of German soil produces silver or gold; for who has examined? They do not care for their possession and use as much as might be expected. There are to be seen among them vessels of silver that have been presented as gifts to their ambassadors and chiefs, but they are held in no more esteem than vessels of earthenware; however those nearest to us prize gold and silver because of its use in trade, and they recognize certain of our coins as valuable and choose those. The people of the interior practice barter and exchange of commodities in accordance with the simple and ancient custom. They like the old and well known coins, those with milled edges bearing the stamp of a two-horse chariot. They are more anxious also for silver coins than for gold, not because of any special liking, but because a number of silver coins is more convenient in purchasing cheap and common articles.

VI. Not even iron is abundant, as is shown by the character of their weapons. Some few use swords or long spears, but usually they carry javelins, called in their language *framea,* tipped with a short narrow piece of iron but so sharp and so easy to handle that as occasion demands they employ the same weapon for fighting at close range or at a distance. A horseman is content with a shield and a javelin, but the footmen, either nude or lightly clad in a small cloak, rain missiles, each man having many and hurling them to a great distance. There is no particular adornment to their weapons except that their shields are distinguished by the most carefully chosen colors. A few wear cuirasses, but hardly any have helmets of metal or leather. Their horses are noted neither for their beauty nor their speed, nor are they trained to perform evolutions as with us. They move straight ahead or make a single turn to the right, the wheel being executed with such perfect alignment that no man drops behind the one next to him. One would say that on the whole their chief strength lies in their infantry. A picked body of these are chosen from among all the youth and placed in advance of the line where they fight mixed with the horsemen, since their swiftness makes them fully equal to engaging in a cavalry contest. Their number is fixed; there are a hundred from each canton, and from this circumstance they take their name among their own people, so that what was at first a number is now become an appellation of honor. The main body of troops is drawn up in wedge-shaped formation. To yield ground, provided you press forward subsequently, is considered a mark of prudence rather than a sign of cowardice. They carry off the bodies of the fallen even where they are not victorious. It is the greatest ignominy to have left one's shield on the field, and it is unlawful for a man so disgraced to be present at the sacred rites or to enter the assembly; so that many after escaping from battle have ended their shame with the halter.

VII. They choose their kings on account of their ancestry, their generals for their valor. The kings do not have free and unlimited power and the generals lead by example rather than command, winning great admiration if they are energetic and fight in plain sight in front of the line. But no one is allowed to put a culprit to death or to imprison him, or even to beat him with stripes except the priests, and then not by way of a punishment or at the command of the general but as though ordered by the god who they believe aids them in their fighting. Certain figures and images taken from their sacred groves they carry into battle, but their greatest incitement to courage is that a division of horse or foot is not made up by chance or by accidental association but is formed of families and clans; and their dear ones are close at hand so that the wailings of the women and the crying of the children can be heard during the battle. These are for each warrior the most sacred witnesses of his bravery, these his dearest applauders. They carry their wounds to their mothers and their wives, nor do the latter fear to count their number and examine them while they bring them food and urge them to deeds of valor.

VIII. It is related how on certain occasions their forces already turned to flight and retreating have been rallied by the women who implored them by their prayers and bared their breasts to their weapons, signifying thus the captivity close awaiting them, which is feared far more intensely on account of their women than for themselves; to such an extent indeed that those states are more firmly bound in treaty among whose hostages maidens of noble family are also required. Further, they believe that the sex has a certain sanctity and prophetic gift, and they neither despise their counsels nor disregard their answers. We ourselves in the reign of the divine Vespasian saw Valaeda, who was considered for a long time by many as a sort of divinity; and formerly also Albruna and many others were venerated, though not out of servility nor as though they were deified mortals.

IX. Among the gods they worship Mercury most of all, to whom it is lawful to offer human sacrifices also on stated days. Hercules and Mars they placate by the sacrifice of worthy animals. Some of the *Suebi* sacrifice to Isis. The reason for this foreign rite and its origin I have not discovered, except that the image fashioned like a galley shows that the cult has been introduced from abroad. On the other hand they hold it to be inconsistent with the sublimity of the celestials to confine the gods in walls made by hands, or to liken them to the form of any human countenance. They consecrate woods and sacred groves to them and give the names of the deities to that hidden mystery which they perceive by faith alone.

X. They pay as much attention as any people to augury and lots. The method of casting lots is uniform. They cut off a branch from a fruit-bearing tree and divide it into small wands marked with certain characters. These they throw at random on a white cloth. Then the priest of the tribe, if it is a matter concerning the community, or the father of the family in case it is a private affair, calling on the gods and keeping his eyes raised toward the sky, takes up three of the lots, one at a time, and then interprets their meaning according to the markings before mentioned. If they have proven unfavorable there can be no further consultation that day concerning that particular matter; but if they are favorable, the confirmation of auspices is further demanded. Even the practice of divination from the notes and flight of birds is known; but it is peculiar to this people to seek omens and warnings from horses also. These sacred animals are white and never defiled by labor, being kept at public expense in the holy groves and woods. They are yoked to the sacred chariot by the priests and the king or chief of the tribe, who accompany them and take note of their neighing and snorting. In no other kind of divination is there greater confidence placed either by the common people or by the nobles; for the priests are considered merely the servants of the gods, but the horses are thought to be acquainted with their counsels. They have another sort of divination whereby they seek to know the result of serious wars. They secure in any way possible a captive from the hostile tribe and set him to fight with a warrior chosen from their own people, each using the weapons of his own country. The victory of the one or the other is accepted as an indication of the result of the war.

XI. Concerning minor matters the chiefs deliberate, but in important affairs all the people are consulted, although the subjects referred to the common people for judgment are discussed beforehand by the chiefs. Unless some sudden and unexpected event calls them together they assemble on fixed days either at the new moon or the full moon, for they think these the most auspicious times to begin their undertakings. They do not reckon time by the number of days, as we do, but by the number of nights. So run their appointments, their contracts; the night introduces the day, so to speak. A disadvantage arises from their regard for liberty in that they do not come together at once as if commanded to attend, but two or three days are wasted by their delay in assembling. When the crowd is sufficient they take their places fully armed. Silence is proclaimed by the priests, who have on these occasions the right to keep order. Then the king or a chief addresses them, each being heard according to his age, noble blood, reputation in warfare and eloquence, though more because he has the power to persuade than the right to command. If an opinion is displeasing they reject it by shouting; if they agree to it they clash with their spears. The most complimentary form of assent is that which is expressed by means of their weapons.

XII. It is also allowable in the assembly to bring up accusations, and to prosecute capital offenses. Penalties are distinguished according to crime. Traitors and deserters are hung to trees. Weaklings and cowards and those guilty of infamous crimes are cast into the mire of swamps with a hurdle placed over their heads. This difference of penalty looks to the distinction that crime should be punished publicly while infamy should be hidden out of sight. Lighter offenses also are punished according to their degree, the guilty parties being fined a certain number of horses or cattle. A part of the fine goes to the king or the tribe, part to the injured party or his relatives. In these same assemblies are chosen the magistrates who decide suits in the cantons and villages. Each one has the assistance of a hundred associates as advisers and with power to decide.

XIII. They undertake no business whatever either of a public or a private character save they be armed. But it is not customary for any one to assume arms until the tribe has recognized his competence to use them. Then in a full assembly some one of the chiefs or the father or relatives of the youth invest him with the shield and spear. This is the sign that the lad has reached the age of manhood; this is his first honor. Before this he was only a member of a household, hereafter he is a member of the tribe. Distinguished rank or the great services of their parents secure even for mere striplings the claim to be ranked as chiefs. They attach themselves to certain more experienced chiefs of approved merit; nor are they ashamed to be looked upon as belonging to their followings. There are grades even within the train of followers assigned by the judgment of its leader. There is great rivalry among these companions as to who shall rank first with the chief, and among the chiefs as to who shall have the most and the bravest followers. It is an honor and a source of strength always to be surrounded by a great band of chosen youths, for they are an ornament in peace, a defence in war. It brings reputation and glory to a leader not only in his own tribe but also among the neighboring peoples if his following is superior in numbers and courage; for he is courted by embassies and honored by gifts, and often his very fame decides the issue of wars.

XIV. When they go into battle it is a disgrace for the chief to be outdone in deeds of valor and for the following not to match the courage of their chief; furthermore for any one of the followers to have survived his chief and come unharmed out of a battle is life-long infamy and reproach. It is in accordance with their most sacred oath of allegiance to defend and protect him and to ascribe their bravest deeds to his renown. The chief fights for victory; the men of his following, for their chief. If the tribe to which they belong sinks into the lethargy of long peace and quiet many of the noble youths voluntarily seek other tribes that are still carrying on war, because a quiet life is irksome to the Germans and they gain renown more readily in the midst of perils, while a large following is not to be provided for except by violence and war. For they look to the liberality of their chief for their war-horse and their deadly and victorious spear; the feasts and entertainments, however, furnished them on a homely but liberal scale, fall to their lot as mere pay. The means for this bounty are acquired through war and plunder. Nor could you persuade them to till the soil and await the yearly produce so easily as you could induce them to stir up an enemy and earn glorious wounds. Nay even they think it tame and stupid to acquire by their sweat what they can purchase by their blood.

XV. In the intervals of peace they spend little time in hunting but much in idleness, given over to sleep and eating; all the bravest and most warlike doing nothing, while the hearth and home and the care of the fields is given over to the women, the old men and the various infirm members of the family. The masters lie buried in sloth by that strange contradiction of nature that causes the same men to love indolence and hate peace. It is customary for the several tribesmen to present voluntary offerings of cattle and grain to the chiefs which, though accepted as gifts of honor, also supply their wants. They are particularly delighted in the gifts of neighboring tribes, not only those sent by individuals, but those presented by states as such,—choice horses, massive arms, embossed plates and armlets. We have now taught them to accept money also.

XVI. It is well known that none of the German tribes live in cities, nor even permit their dwellings to be closely joined to each other. They live separated and in various places, as a spring or a meadow or a grove strikes their fancy. They lay out their villages not as with us in connected or closely-jointed houses, but each one surrounds his dwelling with an open space, either as a protection against conflagration or because of their ignorance of the art of building. They do not even make use of rough stones or tiles. They use for all purposes undressed timber, giving no beauty or comfort. Some parts they plaster carefully with earth of such purity and brilliancy as to form a substitute for painting and designs in color. They are accustomed also to dig out subterranean caves which they cover over with great heaps of manure as a refuge against the cold and a place for storing grain, for retreats of this sort render the extreme cold of their winters bearable and, whenever an enemy has come upon them, though he lays waste the open country he is either ignorant of what is hidden underground or else it escapes him for the very reason that it has to be searched for.

XVII. Generally their only clothing is a cloak fastened with a clasp, or if they haven't that, with a thorn; this being their only garment, they pass whole days about the hearth or near a fire. The richest of them are distinguished by wearing a tunic, not flowing as is the case among the Sarmatians and Parthians, but close-fitting and showing the shape of their limbs. There are those, also, who wear the skins of wild beasts, those nearest the Roman border in a careless manner, but those further back more elegantly, as those do who have no better clothing obtained by commerce. They select certain animals, and stripping off their hides sew on them patches of spotted skins taken from those strange beasts that the distant ocean and the unkown sea bring forth. The women wear the same sort of dress as the men except that they wrap themselves in linen garments which they adorn with purple stripes and do not lengthen out the upper part of the tunic into sleeves, but leave the arms bare the whole length. The upper part of their breasts is also exposed. However, their marriage code is strict, and in no other part of their manners are they to be praised more than in this. For almost alone among barbarian peoples they are content with one wife each, excepting those few who because of their high position rather than out of lust enter into more than one marriage engagement.

XVIII. The wife does not bring a dowry to the husband, but the husband to the wife. The parents and relatives are present at the ceremony and examine and accept the presents,—gifts not suited to female luxury nor such as a young bride would deck herself with, but oxen, a horse and bridle and a shield together with a spear and sword. In consideration of these offerings the wife is accepted, and she in her turn brings her husband a gift of weapons. This they consider as the strongest bond, these as their mystic rites, their gods of marriage. Lest the woman should think herself excluded from aspiring to share in heroic deeds and in the dangers of war, she is admonished by the very initiatory ceremonies of matrimony that she is becoming the partner of her husband's labors and dangers, destined to suffer and to dare with him alike in peace and in war. The yoke of oxen, the caparisoned horse, the gift of arms, give this warning. So must she live, so must she die. What things she receives she must hand down to her children worthy and untarnished and such that future daughters-in-law may receive them and pass them on to her grandchildren.

XIX. Thus they live in well-protected virtue, uncorrupted by the allurements of shows or the enticement of banquets. Men and women alike know not the secrecy of correspondence. Though the race is so numerous, adultery is very rare, its punishment being immediate and inflicted by the injured husband. He cuts off the woman's hair in the presence of her kinsfolk, drives her naked from his house and flogs her through the whole village. Indeed, the loss of chastity meets with no indulgence; neither beauty, youth nor wealth can procure the guilty woman a husband, for no one there laughs at vice, nor is corrupting and being corrupted spoken of as the way of the world. Those tribes do better still where only the virgins marry and where the hope and aspiration of married life is done with once for all. They accept one husband, just as they have one body and one life, that they may have no thought beyond this, no further desire; that their love may be as it were not for the married state, but for the husband. To limit the number of children or to put any of the later children to death is considered a crime, and with them good customs are of more avail than good laws elsewhere.

XX. In every household the children grow up naked and unkempt into that lusty frame and those sturdy limbs that we admire. Each mother nurses her own children; they are not handed over to servants and paid nurses. The lord and the slave are in no way to be distinguished by the delicacy of their bringing up. They live among the same flocks, they lie on the same ground, until age separates them and valor distinguishes the free born. The young men marry late and their vigor is thereby unimpaired. Nor is the marriage of girls hastened. They have the same youthful vigor, the same stature as the young men. Thus well-matched and strong when they marry, the children reproduce the robustness of their parents. An uncle shows the same regard for his sister's children as does their own father. Some tribes consider this relationship more sacred and binding than any other, and in taking hostages lay special stress upon it on the ground that they secure thus a stronger hold on the mind and a wider pledge for the family. A man's heirs and successors, however, are his own children, and no wills are made. If there are no children the next heirs are the brothers, then come the paternal and maternal uncles. The more relatives a man has and the greater the number of his connections, the more honored is his old age. Childlessness has no advantages.

XXI. A German is required to adopt not only the feuds of his father or of a relative, but also their friendships, though the enmities are not irreconcilable. For even homicide is expiated by the payment of a certain number of cattle, and the whole family accept the satisfaction, a useful practice as regards the state because feuds are more dangerous where there is no strong legal control.

No other race indulges more freely in entertainments and hospitality. It is considered a crime to turn any mortal man away from one's door. According to his means each one receives those who come with a well-furnished table. When his food has been all eaten up, he who had lately been the host becomes the guide and companion of his guest to the next house, which they enter uninvited. There is no distinction between guests; they are all received with like consideration. No one makes any difference between friend and stranger so far as concerns the rights of hospitality. If the guest on going away asks for any gift, it is customary to grant it to him, and the host on his side feels the same freedom from constraint in making a request. They take great pleasure in presents, but they do not reckon them as favors nor do they put themselves under obligations in accepting them.

XXII. As soon as they awake from sleep, which they prolong till late in the day, they bathe, usually in warm water as their winter lasts a great part of the year. After the bath they take food, each sitting in a separate seat and having a table to himself. Then they proceed to their business or not less often to feasts, fully armed. It is no disgrace to spend the whole day and night in drinking. Quarreling is frequent enough as is natural among drunken men, though their disputes are rarely settled by mere wrangling but oftener by bloodshed and wounds. Yet it is at their feasts that they consult about reconciling enemies, forming family alliances, electing chiefs, and even regarding war and peace, as they think that at no other time is the mind more open to fair judgment or more inflamed to mighty deeds. A race without natural or acquired cunning still continues to disclose the secret thoughts of the heart in the freedom of festivity. Therefore at such a time the minds of all are free and unconstrained. On the next day the matter is reconsidered and a particular advantage is secured on each occasion. They take counsel when they are unable to practice deception; they decide when they cannot be misled.

XXIII. A liquor for drinking bearing a certain resemblance to wine is made by the process of fermentation from barley or other grain. Those next the border also buy wine. Their food is of a simple kind, wild fruit, fresh game or curdled milk. They satisfy their hunger without elaborate preparation and without the use of condiments. In the matter of thirst they do not use the same temperance. If you should indulge their love of drink by furnishing them as much as they wanted, they might be conquered more easily by their vices than by arms.

XXIV. As to games, but one and the same kind is seen in all their gatherings. Naked youths who make profession of this exhibition leap and dance among swords and spears that threaten their lives. Constant practice has given them skill, skill has given grace. Still they do not indulge in this pastime with a view to profit. The pleasure of the spectators is the reward for their recklessness, however daring. They indulge in games of chance, strange as it may seem, even when sober, as one of their serious occupations, with such great recklessness in their gains and losses that when everything else is gone they stake their liberty and their own persons on the last and decisive throw. The loser goes into voluntary slavery. Though he may be the younger and stronger of the two, he suffers himself to be bound and led away. Such is their stubbornness in a bad practice. They themselves call it honor. They sell slaves of this description to others that they may not feel the shame of such a success.

XXV. But they do not employ slaves as we do with distinct functions prescribed throughout the establishment. Each has his own domicile and rules his own house. The lord exacts a certain amount of grain or cloth or a certain number of cattle as in the case of a tenant and this is the extent of his servitude. Other duties, those of the household, are performed by the lord's wife and children. To beat a slave or to punish him with chains and task work is rare. They occasionally kill one, not in the severity of discipline but impetuously and in sudden wrath as they would kill an enemy, except that the deed goes without punishment. Freed men do not rank much above slaves; they are not of much account in the household and never in the state, except only in those tribes that are ruled by kings. For there they are elevated above the free born and the nobles. The inferior position of the freedman elsewhere is the mark of the free state.

XXVI. To trade with capital and to let it out at interest, is unknown, and so it is ignorance rather than legal prohibition that protects them. Land is held by the villages as communities according to the number of the cultivators, and is then divided among the freemen according to their rank. The extent of their territories renders this partition easy. They cultivate fresh fields every year and there is still land to spare. They do not plant orchards nor lay off meadow-lands nor irrigate gardens so as to require of the soil more than it would naturally bring forth of its own richness and extent. Grain is the only tribute exacted from their land, whence they do not divide the year into as many seasons as we do. The terms winter, spring and summer have a meaning with them, but the name and blessings of autumn are unknown.

XXVII. There is no pomp in the celebration of their funerals. The only custom they observe is that the bodies of illustrious men should be burned with certain kinds of wood. They do not heap garments and perfumes upon the funeral pile. In every case a man's arms are burned with him, and sometimes his horse also. They believe that stately monuments and sculptured columns oppress the dead with their weight; the green sod alone covers their graves. Their tears and lamentations are quickly laid aside; sadness and grief linger long. It is fitting for women to mourn, for men to remember.

Such are the facts I have obtained in general concerning the origin and customs of the Germans as a whole.

6. *HUNS AND VISIGOTHS*[1]

"The Origin and Deeds of the Goths" was written by Jordanes, secretary of a Gothic chieftain, about the middle of the sixth century. It is really little more than a condensation of a considerably larger work by the famous Cassiodorus, secretary of Theodoric the Great, King of the Ostrogoths. In fact Cassiodorus' history is said to have been written at the express command of Theodoric himself. Unfortunately it was lost.

Jordanes was uncritical and credulous, blithely interspersing legend with fact. Yet his little history is of real value, since he is the earliest Gothic historian whose work has come down to us and since his account contains information about the Goths not to be found in any other source.

XXIV. After a short space of time, as Orosius relates, the race of the Huns, fiercer than ferocity itself, flamed forth against the Goths. . . .

This cruel tribe, as Priscus the historian relates, settled on the farther bank of the Maeotic swamp. They were fond of hunting and had no skill in any other art. After they had grown to a nation, they disturbed the peace of neighboring races by theft and rapine. At one time, while hunters of their tribe were as usual seeking for game on the farthest edge of Maeotis, they saw a doe unexpectedly appear to their sight and enter the swamp, acting as guide of the way; now advancing and again standing still. The hunters followed and crossed on foot the Maeotic swamp, which they had supposed was impassable as the sea. Presently the unknown land of Scythia disclosed itself and the doe disappeared. Now in my opinion the evil spirits, from whom the Huns are descended, did this from envy of the Scythians. And the Huns, who had been wholly ignorant that there was another world beyond Maeotis, were now filled with admiration for the Scythian land. As they were quick of mind, they believed that this path, utterly unknown to any age of the past, had been divinely revealed to them. They returned to their tribe, told them what had happened, praised Scythia and persuaded the people to hasten thither along the way they had found by the guidance of the doe. As many as they captured, when they thus entered Scythia for the first time, they sacrificed to Victory. The remainder they conquered and made subject to themselves. Like a whirlwind of nations they swept across the great swamp and at once fell upon the Alpidzuri, Alcildzuri, Itimari, Tuncarsi and Boisci, who bordered on that part of Scythia. The Alani also, who were their equals in battle, but unlike them in civilization, manners and appearance, they exhausted by their incessant attacks and

[1] Jordanes, *The Origin and Deeds of the Goths*. Translated by Charles C. Mierow. Princeton, Princeton University Press, 1908, pp. 38–44 (slightly condensed).

subdued. For by the terror of their features they inspired great fear in those whom perhaps they did not really surpass in war. They made their foes flee in horror because their swarthy aspect was fearful, and they had, if I may call it so, a sort of shapeless lump, not a head, with pin-holes rather than eyes. Their hardihood is evident in their wild appearance, and they are beings who are cruel to their children on the very day they are born. For they cut the cheeks of the males with a sword, so that before they receive the nourishment of milk they must learn to endure wounds. Hence they grow old beardless and their young men are without comeliness, because a face furrowed by the sword spoils by its scars the natural beauty of a beard. They are short in stature, quick in bodily movement, alert horsemen, broad shouldered, ready in the use of bow and arrow, and have firm-set necks which are ever erect in pride. Though they live in the form of men, they have the cruelty of wild beasts.

When the Getae beheld this active race that had invaded many nations, they took fright and consulted with their king how they might escape from such a foe. Now although Hermanaric, king of the Goths, was the conqueror of many tribes, as we have said above, yet while he was deliberating on this invasion of the Huns, the treacherous tribe of the Rosomoni, who at that time were among those who owed him their homage, took this chance to catch him unawares. For when the king had given orders that a certain woman of the tribe I have mentioned, Sunilda by name, should be bound to wild horses and torn apart by driving them at full speed in opposite directions (for he was roused to fury by her husband's treachery to him), her brothers Sarus and Ammius came to avenge their sister's death and plunged a sword into Hermanaric's side. Enfeebled by this blow, he dragged out a miserable existence in bodily weakness. Balamber, king of the Huns, took advantage of his ill health to move an army into the country of the Ostrogoths, from whom the Visigoths had already separated because of some dispute. Meanwhile Hermanaric, who was unable to endure either the pain of his wound or the inroads of the Huns, died full of days at the great age of one hundred and ten years. The fact of his death enabled the Huns to prevail over those Goths who, as we have said, dwelt in the East and were called Ostrogoths.

(*The Divided Goths: Visigoths*)

XXV. The Visigoths, who were their other allies and inhabitants of the western country, were terrified as their kinsmen had been, and knew not how to plan for safety against the race of the Huns. After long deliberation by common consent they finally sent ambassadors into Romania to the Emperor Valens, brother of Valentinian, the elder Emperor, to say that if he would give them part of Thrace or Moesia to keep, they would submit themselves to his laws and commands. That he might have greater confidence in them, they promised to become Christians, if he would give them teachers who spoke their language. When Valens learned this, he gladly and promptly granted what he had himself intended to ask. He received the Getae into the region of Moesia and placed them there as a wall of defense for his kingdom against other tribes. And since at that time the Emperor Valens, who was infected with the Arian perfidy, had closed all the churches of our party, he sent as preachers to them those who favored his sect. They came and straightway filled a rude and ignorant people with the poison of their heresy. Thus the Emperor Valens made the Visigoths Arians rather than Christians. Moreover, from the love they bore them, they preached the gospel both to the Ostrogoths and to their kinsmen the Gepidae, teaching them to reverence this heresy, and they invited all people of their speech everywhere to attach themselves to this sect. They themselves as we have said, crossed the Danube and settled Dacia Ripensis, Moesia and Thrace by permission of the Emperor.

XXVI. Soon famine and want came upon them, as often happens to a people not yet well settled in a country. Their princes and the leaders who ruled them in place of kings, that is Fritigern, Alatheus and Safrac, began to lament the plight of their army and begged Lupicinus and Maximus, the Roman commanders, to open a market. But to what will not the "cursed lust for gold" compel men to assent? The generals, swayed by avarice, sold them at a high price not only the flesh of sheep and oxen, but even the carcasses of dogs and unclean animals, so that a slave would be bartered for a loaf of bread or ten pounds of meat. When their goods and chattels failed, the greedy trader demanded their sons in return for the necessities of life. And the parents consented even to this, in order to provide for the safety of their children, arguing that it was better to lose liberty than life; and indeed it is better that one be sold, if he will be mercifully fed, than that he should be kept free only to die.

Now it came to pass in that troublous time that Lupicinus, the Roman general, invited Fritigern, a chieftain of the Goths, to a feast and, as the event revealed, devised a plot against him. But Fritigern, thinking no evil, came to the feast with a few followers. While he was dining in the praetorium he heard the dying cries of his ill-fated men, for, by order of the general, the soldiers were slaying his companions who were shut up in another part of the house. The loud cries of the dying fell upon ears already suspicious, and Fritigern at once perceived the treacherous trick. He drew his sword and with great courage dashed quickly from the banqueting-hall, rescued his men from their threatening doom and incited them to slay the Romans. Thus these valiant men gained the chance they had longed for—to be free to die in battle rather than to perish of hunger—and immediately took arms to kill the generals Lupicinus and Maximus. Thus that day put an end to the famine of the Goths and the safety of the Romans, for the Goths no longer as strangers and pilgrims, but as citizens and lords, began to rule the inhabitants and to hold in their own right all the northern country as far as the Danube.

When the Emperor Valens heard of this at Antioch, he made ready an army at once and set out for the country of Thrace. Here a grievous battle took place and the Goths prevailed. The Emperor himself was wounded and fled to a farm near Hadrianople. The Goths, not knowing that an emperor lay hidden in so poor a hut, set fire to it (as is customary in dealing with a cruel foe), and thus he was cremated in royal splendor. Plainly it was a direct judgment of God that he should be burned with fire by the very men whom he had perfidiously led astray when they sought the true faith, turning them aside from the flame of love into the fire of hell. From this time the Visigoths, in consequence of their glorious victory, possessed Thrace and Dacia Ripensis as if it were their native land.

XXVII. Now in the place of Valens, his uncle, the Emperor Gratian established Theodosius the Spaniard in the Eastern Empire. Military discipline was soon restored to a high level, and the Goth, perceiving that the cowardice and sloth of former princes was ended, became afraid. For the Emperor was famed alike for his acuteness and discretion. By stern commands and by generosity and kindness he encouraged a demoralized army to deeds of daring. But when the soldiers, who had obtained a better leader by the change, gained new confidence, they sought to attack the Goths and drive them from the borders of Thrace. But as the Emperor Theodosius fell so sick at this time that his life was almost despaired of, the Goths were again inspired with courage. Dividing the Gothic army, Fritigern set out to plunder Thessaly, Epirus and Achaia, while Alatheus and Safrac with the rest of the troops made for Pannonia. Now the Emperor Gratian had at this time retreated from Rome to Gaul because of the invasions of the Vandals. When he learned that the Goths were acting with greater boldness because Theodosius was in despair of his life, he quickly gathered an army and came against them. Yet he put no trust in arms, but sought to conquer them by kindness and gifts. So he entered on a truce with them and made peace, giving them provisions.

XXVIII. When the Emperor Theodosius afterwards recovered and learned that the Emperor Gratian had made a compact between the Goths and the Romans, as he had himself desired, he took it very graciously and gave his assent. He gave gifts to King Athanaric, who had succeeded Fritigern, made an alliance with him and in the most gracious manner invited him to visit him in Constantinople. Athanaric very gladly consented and as he entered the royal city exclaimed in wonder "Lo, now I see what I have often heard of with unbelieving ears," meaning the great and famous city. Turning his eyes hither and thither, he marvelled as he beheld the situation of the city, the coming and going of the ships, the splendid walls, and the people of divers nations gathered like a flood of waters streaming from different regions into one basin. So too, when he saw the army in array, he said "Truly the Emperor is a god on earth, and whoso raises a hand against him is guilty of his own blood." In the midst of his admiration and the enjoyment of even greater honors at the hand of the Emperor, he departed this life after the space of a few months. The emperor had such affection for him that he honored Athanaric even more when he was dead than during his life-time, for he not only gave him a worthy burial, but himself walked before the bier at the funeral. Now when Athanaric was dead, his whole army continued in the service of the Emperor Theodosius and submitted to the Roman rule, forming as it were one body with the imperial soldiery. The former service of the Allies under the Emperor Constantine was now renewed and they were again called Allies. And since the Emperor knew that they were faithful to him and his friends, he took from their number more than twenty thousand warriors to serve against the tyrant Eugenius who had slain Gratian and seized Gaul. After winning the victory over this usurper, he wreaked his vengeance upon him.

7. *THE GENERAL CHARACTER OF THE GERMANIC INVASIONS*[1]

After reading about numerous tribes of warriors roaming about Europe and northern Africa in the fourth, fifth, and sixth centuries, about battles, massacres, plundering, devastations, and barbarism in general, one turns with relief from the multitude of names and detailed incidents to a description of the movement as a whole. The brilliant analysis of Samuel Dill which follows here forms a useful complement to the narratives presented elsewhere.

No part of the inner life of the fifth century should, in the mind of an intelligent student, excite greater curiosity than the attitude of the Romans of the West to the invaders, and their ideas as to the future of Rome. As he reads the meagre chronicles of the times, he can hardly help asking himself, What did these men think about the real meaning of the sack of Rome by Alaric and by Genseric; of the devastation of the provinces; of the settlement of Visigoths, Burgundians, Sueves, and Vandals in regions which, in

[1] Samuel Dill, *Roman Society in the Last Century of the Western Empire.* 2nd ed. revised London, 1925, Macmillan and Co. Book IV, Chapt. I, pp. 285–294. By permission of The Macmillan Company, publishers.

spite of temporary incursions, had for centuries enjoyed the Roman peace? Was the end indeed come, the end of so much effort, of so many glories, of that great history of civil and military virtue which had given uniform law and culture to the realms of Alexander as well as to the countries bordering on the inland and the western seas? Or, were the calamities of the time, crushing as they were to individual citizens, only temporary and limited in their range, such as the Empire had often before suffered, without serious and lasting effects on the general organisation of society? And as to the causes of the calamity, were they the decline of Roman virtue and skill in statecraft, or were they the anger of the old gods of Rome for the desertion of their altars, or the punishments sent by the Christians' God for luxury and oppression of the weak? Finally, what was to be the relation of the Empire, if it was to continue, to these strange immigrants into her territory, and how were they going to behave to the power which had so long kept them at bay?

We propose to collect, from the literary remains of the period, various answers to these questions. But before doing so, there are some general considerations as to the character of the invasions of the barbarians in the fifth century, and their settlement in the provinces, which it will be well to bear in mind in the review which we propose to make. The modern, who has only the popular conception of the events of that time, is apt to think that the Western Empire succumbed to an overpowering advance of whole tribes and peoples, animated by hatred of Rome, sweeping away the remains of an effete civilisation, and replacing it, in a sudden and cataclysmal change, by a spirit and by institutions of a perfectly different order. Yet, if such were a true account of the fall of the Roman Empire, the tone and behaviour of many of the Romans of that time would be inexplicable. Here and there there are cries of horror at the havoc and slaughter which were caused by some violent incursion. And, undoubtedly, the capture of the city gave for the moment a terrible shock to the ancient faith in the strength and stability of Rome. But this was only a transitory feeling. Confidence soon returned. The cities and regions, which are said to have been desolated and ravaged, reappear with apparently few traces of any catastrophe. The government betrays no sign of confusion or despair. Individual observers may have their doubts and questionings about the course of events, but few seem absolutely dismayed, and some display a confidence and hopefulness which would be quite astonishing, if the old popular conception of the barbarian onslaughts were the true one.

A very cursory glance at the history of the Empire reveals the secret of this *insouciance*. The invasions of the fifth century were nothing new, nor was there anything very startling in the settlement of Germans on Roman soil. From the times of Marius not a century had passed without some violent inroad of German hosts. The myriads annihilated on the field of Aquae Sextiae were but the advance guard of a mighty movement, which was always pressing on to the West or South. Julius, Augustus, Tiberius, had all to throw back successive attacks on the frontier of the Rhine. Marcus Aurelius spent eight campaigns in a struggle with a vast confederacy on the Danube. In the third century almost every province, and even Italy itself, was ravaged, and the Goths, a comparatively new horde, who had worked their way from Scandinavia to the Ukraine, swept the Euxine in thousands of vessels, and harried the towns of Asia Minor and Greece. In the reign of Probus, the Germans captured and pillaged sixty towns in Gaul, and overran the whole province. Another formidable irruption took place in the middle of the fourth century. Enormous numbers of Franks, Alemanni, and Saxons passed the Rhine. A great part of Gaul was overrun, and forty towns along the Rhine were sacked. Once more the invaders were driven back with enormous loss.

The invasions of the third and fourth centuries, in respect to the numbers and impetuosity of the assailants, seem to us now to have been almost overwhelming. The Gothic host of the reign of Claudius is said to have numbered 320,000 men. The Germans who spread over the whole of Gaul in the reign of Probus must have been even more numerous if that emperor slaughtered 400,000 of them, as he is said to have done. Yet it does not appear that, at crises so appalling, the Romans ever despaired of the safety of the State. The letter of Probus to the Senate, to which we have referred, rather expresses an almost exuberant confidence. The invaders, however numerous, are invariably driven back, and in a short time there are few traces left of their ravages. The truth seems to be that, however terrible the plundering bands might be to the unarmed population, yet in a regular battle the Germans were immensely inferior to the Roman troops. Ammianus, who had borne a part in many of these engagements, says that, in spite of the courage of the Germans, their impetuous fury was no match for the steady discipline and coolness of troops under Roman officers. The result of this moral superiority, founded on a long tradition, was that the Roman soldier in the third and fourth centuries was ready to face almost any odds. In 356 an immense multitude of the Alemanni inundated Eastern Gaul. Julian, the future Emperor, who was then a mere youth, with no previous training in the art of war, was in command of only 13,000 men, of whom few were veteran troops. Yet in a very short time not an enemy was left in Gaul, and the victors were carrying the war far into the heart of Germany. There must undoubtedly have been much loss of life and property in some of these raids. Yet a very few years after the ravages which were checked by Julian, the valley of the Moselle is described to us by Ausonius as a paradise which shows no trace of the hand of the spoiler. Comfortable granges and luxurious villas look down from every height. The vineyards rise in terraces along the banks, and the yellow corn-lands can vie even with the fertility of the poet's native Aquitaine. The population are prosperous and happy. There is even an air of rustic jollity and gaiety over the scene from which all thoughts of past suffering or coming danger seem to be banished.

Of the same character were the great invasions of the opening years of the fifth century. A great army under Radagaisus, which, according to the lowest estimate, numbered 200,000 men, crossed the Alps and penetrated into Etruria. That the government regarded the danger as serious, may be inferred from the edict which called the slaves to arms. Yet Stilicho, with a force of only 30,000 regular troops, and some Hun and Alan auxiliaries, signally defeated that great host, and the prisoners taken were so many that they were sold for a single *aureus* apiece. In the beginning of the year 406 a horde of Alans, Sueves, and Vandals crossed the Rhine, from which the garrisons had been withdrawn to meet the danger in Italy. The invaders caused great consternation, and undoubtedly inflicted much damage and suffering in their passage through Gaul. But the districts and cities, which they are said to have plundered and destroyed, within a generation are found to be once more flourishing and prosperous.

In the fragmentary annals of the fifth century there is no sign that the generals of the Empire felt any fear of an overwhelming superiority on the side of the invaders. In 426 the city of Arles was attacked by a powerful force of Goths; but they were compelled by Aetius to retire with heavy loss. Two years later, the same great general recovered the Rhineland from the Franks. In 435 he inflicted a crushing defeat on the Burgundians, and compelled them to sue for peace. In the following year Litorius, the lieutenant of Aetius, by a rapid movement, relieved the town of Narbonne, when it was hard pressed by famine and the Gothic army. And although Litorius soon afterwards was taken captive by the hands of the Goths, the annalist expressly says that it was the result of reckless ambition and superstitious credulity, not of any inferiority of force. The invasion of Attila in 451 was probably the most appalling danger, in respect to the numbers of his motley host, which the Romans had had to face for ages. Aetius had only a handful of troops under his command, and although he was able to rally to his support Visigoths, Franks, Burgundians, and Saxons, yet the credit of defeating that fierce and crafty power, which had reduced all central Europe to vassalage, must be awarded to Roman daring and organisation. In the last days of the independence of Auvergne and of the Western Empire, a mere handful of troops under the gallant Ecdicius, and raised by his own resources, kept the Visigothic army for months at bay, and the Roman showed in this final struggle an almost contemptuous recklessness.

The Germans then were not superior to the Romans in military skill and courage. Nor were they animated by any common purpose or hatred of Rome. So far from having any common purpose, they were hopelessly divided among themselves, and are as often found fighting for the Empire as against it. The Franks on the Rhine were champions of Rome when they were overwhelmed by the invaders in 406. Stilicho had Alan and Hun auxiliaries in his great battle with Radagaisus. It was with Hun cavalry that Aetius and Litorius strove to check the advance of the Visigoths in Southern Gaul. It was with the aid of Visigoths, Franks, Saxons, and Burgundians that Aetius defeated the army of Attila on the Catalaunian plains. Again and again the Visigoths of Toulouse lent their forces to support the Roman power in Spain against the Sueves. The Romans of Auvergne, when they were deserted in its weakness by the imperial government, received help and encouragement in their last struggles against Euric from the Burgundians. It is clear from these facts that the Empire was not an object of hatred to the barbarians. Indeed they were often eager to be taken into its service; and many of their chiefs, like Alaric or Ataulphus, had no higher ambition than to be appointed to high military command. On the other hand, there was a corresponding readiness on the Roman side to employ barbarian forces in war. From the earliest days of the Empire these auxiliaries appear on the army lists. Germans are found in the bodyguard of Augustus. They fought under Vitellius in the foremost ranks at the battle of Cremona. Vespasian had special confidence in the loyalty of the Sueves, and had two of their chiefs in his service. Marcus Aurelius formed some corps of Germans for his war with their countrymen on the Danube. In the third century, the tendency becomes even more marked. . . .

Some of these barbarian troops took service voluntarily under an express agreement, stating the conditions on which they served. Others were compelled to join the standards as the result of defeat in battle. Some of them received regular pay and rations; others received grants of land, which were held on condition of military service, and which passed to their sons on the same condition. A page of the Notitia contains a list of more than twenty corps of these military colonists, under the name Sarmatae Gentiles, who were settled at various places from Bruttium to the Alps. Similar German corps, under the name of Laeti, had lands assigned to them in almost every part of Gaul. The Gallo-Roman population had been long accustomed to the residence of these bands on their soil. . . .

We shall see, in a subsequent chapter, that the establishment of the Germans in the south and east of Gaul disturbed and alarmed the Romans of the province far less than we should have expected. In a short time the intruders were accepted as more or less friendly neighbours. Here again the past history of the Empire will be found to have prepared men's minds for what, taken by themselves, would have seemed stupendous changes. Just as there were countless incursions for plunder before the Sueve and Vandal irruption of 406, so there were many cases of barbarians seeking and obtaining a peaceful settlement within the frontier before the Visigoths settled on the Garonne, and the Burgundians on the Upper Rhine and the Rhone. Augustus, on receiving the submission of the Ubii and Sicrambri, assigned them lands on the left bank of the Rhine. Tiberius transported 40,000 Germans into the same region. The Germans seem to have been seldom unwilling to enter the circle of the pax Romana. For instance the Batavians, driven from their own country by civil war, crossed the frontier and settled down as subjects of Rome, and for ages the Batavian cavalry had a brilliant reputation in the Roman army. In the third century Probus is said to have Germanised the provinces. He gave a settlement in Thrace to 100,000 Bastarnae, who, we are told, proved themselves loyal subjects of the Empire. A similar experiment, in the case of the Vandals and Gepidae, seems to have been less successful. A body of Franks, who had obtained from the Emperor a settlement somewhere in the eastern Mediterranean, proved even less worthy of his generosity. They got a fleet together, spread havoc and confusion through the whole of Greece, wrought great slaughter in an attack on Syracuse, and finally, having been repelled from the walls of Carthage, returned to their homes. The Salian Franks, who had been driven from their old seats and had occupied the region between the Scheldt and the Meuse, were, after some hard fighting, recognised as Roman subjects by Julian. The most striking example of the eagerness of the Germans to be received on Roman territory was the famous petition of the Goths to the Emperor Valens in 376, to be allowed to place the broad waters of the Danube between them and the terrible Huns, who were then advancing from the East. Probably a million of men, women, and children were transported across the swollen river. They came not as conquerors, but as suppliants for food and shelter, under the protection of Rome. No reader of Gibbon needs to be told the tragic tale of what followed that great migration. It was a turning-point in history.

8. THE EMPEROR CONSTANTINE AND HIS RECOGNITION OF CHRISTIANITY [1]

Eusebius Pamphilus, bishop of Caesarea in Syria, was a friend of Emperor Constantine and in that capacity wrote his Life of Constantine the Great, *a valuable biography, but too favorable to the emperor. In this work*

[1] Eusebius, *Life of Constantine,* translated by Ernest Cushing Richardson, published in *A Select Library of Nicene and Post-Nicene Fathers of the Christian Church,* second series, vol. 1, New York, The Christian Literature Co., 1890, pp. 488, 489–490, 492—493. Reprinted by permission of Charles Scribner's Sons.

the faults of Constantine have been minimized and his virtues overestimated. Nevertheless it is a source of the highest importance, inasmuch as Eusebius was an eye-witness of many of the events described by him, while Constantine himself, as his trusted friend, provided him with innumerable data on his life.

Some students hold that Constantine's recognition of Christianity was primarily a matter of political expediency. It is evident that Eusebius does not share this view.

Chapter xx

Flight of Constantine to his Father because of the Plots of Diocletian.

The emperors then in power, observing his manly and vigorous figure and superior mind, were moved with feelings of jealousy and fear, and thenceforward carefully watched for an opportunity of inflicting some brand of disgrace on his character. But the young man, being aware of their designs, the details of which, through the providence of God, more than once came to him, sought safety in flight; in this respect again keeping up his resemblance to the great prophet Moses. Indeed, in every sense God was his helper; and he had before ordained that he should be present in readiness to succeed his father.

Chapter xxii

How, after the Burial of Constantius, Constantine was proclaimed Augustus by the Army.

Nor did the imperial throne remain long unoccupied: for Constantine invested himself with his father's purple, and proceeded from his father's palace, presenting to all a renewal, as it were, in his own person, of his father's life and reign. He then conducted the funeral procession in company with his father's friends, some preceding, others following the train, and performed the last offices for the pious deceased with an extraordinary degree of magnificence, and all united in honoring this thrice blessed prince with acclamations and praises, and while with one mind and voice, they glorified the rule of the son as a living again of him who was dead, they hastened at once to hail their new sovereign by the titles of Imperial and Worshipful Augustus, with joyful shouts. Thus the memory of the deceased emperor received honor from the praises bestowed upon his son, while the latter was pronounced blessed in being the successor of such a father. All the nations also under his dominion were filled with joy and inexpressible gladness at not being even for a moment deprived of the benefits of a well ordered government.

In the instance of the Emperor Constantius, God has made manifest to our generation what the end of those is who in their lives have honored and loved him.

Chapter xxvi

How he resolved to deliver Rome from Maxentius.

While, therefore, he regarded the entire world as one immense body, and perceived that the head of it all, the royal city of the Roman empire, was bowed down by the weight of a tyrannous oppression; at first he had left the task of liberation to those who governed the other divisions of the empire, as being his superiors in point of age. But when none of these proved able to afford relief, and those who had attempted it had experienced a disastrous termination of their enterprise, he said that life was without enjoyment to him as long as he saw the imperial city thus afflicted, and prepared himself for the overthrowal of the tyranny.

Chapter xxvii

That after reflecting on the Downfall of those who had worshiped Idols, he made Choice of Christianity.

Being convinced, however, that he needed some more powerful aid than his military forces could afford him, on account of the wicked and magical enchantments which were so diligently practiced by the tyrant, he sought Divine assistance, deeming the possession of arms and a numerous soldiery of secondary importance, but believing the co-operating power of Deity invincible and not to be shaken. He considered, therefore, on what God he might rely for protection and assistance. While engaged in this enquiry, the thought occurred to him, that, of the many emperors who had preceded him, those who had rested their hopes in a multitude of gods, and served them with sacrifices and offerings, had in the first place been deceived by flattering predictions, and oracles which promised them all prosperity, and at last had met with an unhappy end, while not one of their gods had stood by to warn them of the impending wrath of heaven; while one alone had pursued an entirely opposite course, who had condemned their error, and honored the one Supreme God during his whole life, had found him to be the Saviour and Protector of his empire, and the Giver of every good thing. Reflecting on this, and well weighing the fact that they who had trusted in many gods had also fallen by manifold forms of death, without leaving behind them either family or offspring, stock, name, or memorial among men: while the God of his father had given to him, on the other hand, manifestations of his power and very many tokens: and considering farther that those who had already taken arms against the tyrant, and had marched to the battlefield under the protection of a multitude of gods, had met with a dishonorable end (for one of them had shamefully retreated from the contest without a blow, and the other, being slain in the midst of his own troops, became, as it were, the mere sport of death); reviewing, I say, all these considerations, he judged it to be folly indeed to join in the idle worship of those who were no gods, and, after such convincing evidence, to err from the truth; and therefore felt it incumbent on him to honor his father's God alone.

Chapter xxviii

How, while he was praying, God sent him a Vision of a Cross of Light in the Heavens at Mid-day with an Inscription admonishing him to conquer by that.

Accordingly he called on him with earnest prayer and supplications that he would reveal to him who he was, and stretch forth his right hand to help him in his present difficulties. And while he was thus praying with fervent entreaty, a most marvelous sign appeared to him from heaven, the account of which it might have been hard to believe had it been related by any other person. But since the victorious emperor himself long afterwards declared it to the writer of this history, when he was honored with his acquaintance and society, and confirmed his statement by an oath, who could hesitate to accredit the relation, especially since the testimony of after-time has established its truth? He said that about noon, when the day was already beginning to decline, he saw with his own eyes the trophy of a cross of light in the heavens, above the sun, and bearing the inscription, CONQUER BY THIS. At this sight he himself was struck with amazement, and his whole army also, which followed him on this expedition, and witnessed the miracle.

Chapter xxix

How the Christ of God appeared to him in his Sleep, and commanded him to use in his Wars a Standard made in the Form of the Cross.

He said, moreover, that he doubted within himself what the import of this apparition could be. And while he continued to ponder and reason on its meaning, night suddenly came on; then in his sleep the Christ of God appeared to him with the same sign which he had seen in the heavens, and commanded him to make a likeness of that sign which he had seen in the heavens, and to use it as a safeguard in all engagements with his enemies.

Chapter xxx

The Making of the Standard of the Cross.

At dawn of day he arose, and communicated the marvel to his friends: and then, calling together the workers in gold and precious stones, he sat in the midst of them, and described to them the figure of the sign he had seen, bidding them represent it in gold and precious stones. And this representation I myself have had an opportunity of seeing.

Chapter xxxviii

Death of Maxentius on the Bridge of the Tiber.

And already he was approaching very near Rome itself, when, to save him from the necessity of fighting with all the Romans for the tyrant's sake, God himself drew the tyrant, as it were by secret cords, a long way outside the gates. And now those miracles recorded in Holy Writ, which God of old wrought against the ungodly (discredited by most as fables, yet believed by the faithful), did he in every deed confirm to all alike, believers and unbelievers, who were eye-witnesses of the wonders. For as once in the days of Moses and the Hebrew nation, who were worshipers of God, "Pharaoh's chariots and his host hath he cast into the sea, and his chosen chariot-captains are drowned in the Red Sea,"—so at this time Maxentius, and the soldiers and guards with him, "went down into the depths like stone," when, in his flight before the divinely-aided forces of Constantine, he essayed to cross the river which lay in his way, over which, making a strong bridge of boats, he had framed an engine of destruction, really against himself, but in the hope of ensnaring thereby him who was beloved by God. For his God stood by the one to protect him, while the other, godless, proved to be the miserable contriver of these secret devices to his own ruin. So that one might well say, "He hath made a pit, and digged it, and is fallen into the ditch which he made. His mischief shall return upon his own head, and his violence shall come down upon his own pate." Thus, in the present instance, under divine direction, the machine erected on the bridge, with the ambuscade concealed therein, giving way unexpectedly before the appointed time, the bridge began to sink, and the boats with the men in them went bodily to the bottom. And first the wretch himself, then his armed attendants and guards, even as the sacred oracles had before described, "sank as lead in the mighty waters." So that they who thus obtained victory from God might well, if not in the same words yet in fact in the same spirit as the people of his great servant Moses, sing and speak as they did concerning the impious tyrant of old: "Let us sing unto the Lord, for he hath been glorified exceedingly: the horse and his rider hath he thrown into the sea. He is become my helper and my shield unto salvation." And again, "Who is like unto thee, O Lord, among the gods? who is like thee, glorious in holiness, marvelous in praises, doing wonders?"

Chapter xxxix

Constantine's Entry into Rome.

Having then at this time sung these and such-like praises to God, the Ruler of all and the Author of victory, after the example of his great servant Moses, Constantine entered the imperial city in triumph. And here the whole body of the senate, and others of rank and distinction in the city, freed as it were from the restraint of a prison, along with the whole Roman populace, their countenances expressive of the gladness of their hearts, received him with acclamations and abounding joy; men, women, and children, with countless multitudes of servants, greeting him as deliverer, preserver, and benefactor, with incessant shouts. But he, being possessed of inward piety toward God, was neither rendered arrogant by these plaudits, nor uplifted by the praises he heard: but, being sensible that he had received help from God, he immediately rendered a thanksgiving to him as the Author of his victory.

9. *THE PERSECUTION OF THE CHRISTIANS AND THE SO-CALLED EDICT OF MILAN.*[1]

Lactantius, narrates in his De Mortibus Persecutorum *the ill fortune of Emperor Galerius, who, struck by a terrible malady, is said to have repented of his hostility toward the Christians, and in the year 311 issued the "Edict of Galerius," preserved in its original form by Lactantius. It is reproduced below.*

Lactantius has also given an interesting account of the conversion and victory of Emperor Constantine. He claims that Constantine saw a vision in a dream at night and in his presentation Lactantius differs from the description by Eusebius, the celebrated church historian of the fourth century. Although the story of Eusebius has become the traditional view of the Church, the account presented by Lactantius is worthy of careful study.

Furthermore, Lactantius transmitted another important imperial decree

[1] Lactantius, *De Mortibus Persecutorum,* translated by William Fletcher in Ante-Nicene Christian Library: Translations of the Fathers down to A. D. 325. Vol. XXII, Edinburgh, 1871, pp. 194–198; 201–209.

to posterity, entitled the Edict of Milan. The official document itself is no longer extant, and it is not known whether the two emperors, Constantine and Licinius, issued the edict in Milan or not.

We merely have a letter addressed by Licinius to a prefect in the year 313, in which letter Licinius refers to an edict promulgated by him or by him and Constantine jointly. Judging from the way Lactantius speaks of this edict, it seems that the two emperors discussed the advisability of issuing an edict while they were in Milan, but that the decree itself was promulgated by Licinius in Nicomedia. Hence the so-called Edict of Milan should rather be styled the Edict of Nicomedia by Licinius.

Chapter xxxiii

And now, when Galerius was in the eighteenth year of his reign, God struck him with an incurable plague. A malignant ulcer formed itself low down in his secret parts, and spread by degrees. The physicians attempted to eradicate it. . . . [*But the disease grew worse.*]

. . . .

These things happened in the course of a complete year; and at length, overcome by calamities, he was obliged to acknowledge God, and he cried aloud, in the intervals of raging pain, that he would re-edify the Church which he had demolished, and make atonement for his misdeeds; and when he was near his end, he published an edict to the tenor following:

Chapter xxxiv

"Amongst our other regulations for the permanent advantage of the commonweal, we have hitherto studied to reduce all things to a conformity with the ancient laws and public discipline of the Romans.

"It has been our aim in an especial manner, that the Christians also, who had abandoned the religion of their forefathers, should return to right opinions. For such wilfulness and folly had, we know not how, taken possession of them, that instead of observing those ancient institutions, which possibly their own forefathers had established, they, through caprice, made laws to themselves, and drew together into different societies many men of widely different persuasions.

"After the publication of our edict, ordaining the Christians to betake themselves to the observance of the ancient institutions, many of them were subdued through the fear of danger, and moreover many of them were exposed to jeopardy; nevertheless, because great numbers still persist in their opinions, and because we have perceived that at present they neither pay reverence and due adoration to the gods, nor yet worship their own God, therefore we, from our wonted clemency in bestowing pardon on all, have judged it fit to extend our indulgence to those men, and to permit them again to be Christians, and to establish the places of their religious assemblies; yet so as that they offend not against good order.

"By another mandate we purpose to signify unto magistrates how they ought herein to demean themselves.

"Wherefore it will be the duty of the Christians, in consequence of this our toleration, to pray to their God for our welfare, and for that of the public, and for their own; that the commonweal may continue safe in every quarter, and that they themselves may live securely in their habitations."

Chapter xxxv

This edict was promulgated at Nicomedia on the day preceding the kalends of May (30th of April), in the eighth consulship of Galerius, and the second of Maximin Daia. Then the prison-gates having been thrown open, you, my best beloved Donatus, together with the other confessors for the faith, were set at liberty from a jail, which had been your residence for six years. Galerius, however, did not, by publication of this edict, obtain the divine forgiveness. In a few days after he was consumed by the horrible disease that had brought on an universal putrefaction. Dying, he recommended his wife and son to Licinius, and delivered them over into his hands. This event was known at Nicomedia before the end of the month (May). His vicennial anniversary was to have been celebrated on the ensuing kalends of March (1st of March following).

Chapter xxxvi

Daia, on receiving this news, hasted with relays of horses from the East, to seize the dominions of Galerius, and, while Licinius lingered in Europe, to arrogate to himself all the country as far as the narrow seas of Chalcedon. On his entry into Bithynia, he, with the view of acquiring immediate popularity, abolished Galerius' tax, to the great joy of all. Dissension arose between the two emperors, and almost an open war. They stood on the opposite shores with their armies. Peace, however, and amity were established under certain conditions. Licinius and Daia met on the narrow seas, concluded a treaty, and in token of friendship joined hands. Then Daia, believing all things to be in security, returned (to Nicomedia), and was in his new dominions what he had been in Syria and Egypt. First of all, he took away the toleration and general protection granted by Galerius to the

Christians, and, for this end, he secretly procured addresses from different cities, requesting that no Christian church might be built within their walls; and thus he meant to make that which was his own choice appear as if extorted from him by importunity. In compliance with those addresses, he introduced a new mode of government in things respecting religion, and for each city he created a high priest, chosen from among the persons of most distinction. The office of those men was to make daily sacrifices to all their gods, and, with the aid of the former priests, to prevent the Christians from erecting churches, or from worshipping God either publicly or in private; and he authorized them to compel the Christians to sacrifice to idols, and, on their refusal, to bring them before the civil magistrate; and, as if this had not been enough, in every province he established a superintendent priest, one of chief eminence in the state; and he commanded that all those priests newly instituted should appear in white habits (that being the most honourable distinction of dress). And as to the Christians, he purposed to follow the course that he had followed in the East, and, affecting the show of clemency, he forbade the slaying of God's servants, but he gave command that they should be mutilated. So the confessors for the faith had their ears and nostrils slit, their hands and feet lopped off, and their eyes dug out of the sockets.

Chapter xxxvii

While occupied in this plan, he received letters from Constantine, which deterred him from proceeding in its execution, so for a time he dissembled his purpose; nevertheless any Christian that fell within his power was privily thrown into the sea. Neither did he cease from his custom of sacrificing every day in the palace.

. . . .

Chapter xlii

At this time, by command of Constantine, the statues of Maximian Herculius were thrown down, and his portraits removed; and, as the two old emperors were generally delineated in one piece, the portraits of both were removed at the same time. Thus Diocletian lived to see a disgrace which no former emperor had ever seen, and, under the double load of vexation of spirit and bodily maladies, he resolved to die. Tossing to and fro, with his soul agitated by grief, he could neither eat nor take rest. He sighed, groaned, and wept often, and incessantly threw himself into various postures, now on his couch, and now on the ground. So he, who for twenty years was the most prosperous of emperors, having been cast down into the obscurity of a private station, treated in the most contumelious manner, and compelled to abhor life, became incapable of receiving nourishment, and, worn out with anguish of mind, expired.

Chapter xliii

Of the adversaries of God there still remained one, whose overthrow and end I am now to relate.

Daia had entertained jealousy and ill-will against Licinius from the time that the preference was given to him by Galerius; and those sentiments still subsisted, notwithstanding the treaty of peace lately concluded between them. When Daia heard that the sister of Constantine was betrothed to Licinius, he apprehended that the two emperors, by contracting this affinity, meant to league against him, so he privily sent ambassadors to Rome, desiring a friendly alliance with Maxentius; he also wrote to him in terms of cordiality. The ambassadors were received courteously, friendship established, and in token of it the effigies of Maxentius and Daia were placed together in public view. Maxentius willingly embraced this, as if it had been an aid from heaven; for he had already declared war against Constantine, as if to revenge the death of his father Maximian. From this appearance of filial piety a suspicion arose, that the detestable old man had but feigned a quarrel with his son that he might have an opportunity to destroy his rivals in power, and so make way for himself and his son to possess the whole empire. This conjecture, however, had no foundation; for his true purpose was to have destroyed his son and the others, and then to have reinstated himself and Diocletian in sovereign authority.

Chapter xliv

And now a civil war broke out between Constantine and Maxentius. Although Maxentius kept himself within Rome, because the soothsayers had foretold that if he went out of it he should perish, yet he conducted the military operations by able generals. In forces he exceeded his adversary; for he had not only his father's army, which deserted from Severus, but also his own, which he had lately drawn together out of Mauritania and Italy. They fought, and the troops of Maxentius prevailed. At length Constantine, with steady courage and a mind prepared for every event, led his whole forces to the neighbourhood of Rome, and encamped them opposite to the Milvian bridge. The anniversary of the reign of Maxentius approached, that is, the sixth of the kalends of November (27th of October), and the fifth year of his reign was drawing to an end.

Constantine was directed in a dream to cause the heavenly sign to be delineated on the shields of his soldiers, and so to proceed to battle. He did as he had been commanded, and he marked on their shields the letter X, with a perpendicular line drawn through it and turned round at the top, this being the cipher of Christ. Having this sign, his troops stood to arms. The enemies advanced, but without their emperor, and they crossed the bridge. The armies met, and fought with the utmost exertions of valour, and firmly maintained their ground. In the meantime a sedition arose at Rome, and Maxentius was reviled as one who had abandoned all concern for the safety of the commonweal; and suddenly, while he exhibited the Circensian games on the anniversary of his reign, the people cried with one voice, "Constantine cannot be overcome!" Dismayed at this, Maxentius burst from the assembly, and having called some senators together, ordered the Sibylline books to be searched. In them it was found that "on the same day the enemy of the Romans should perish." Led by this response to the hopes of victory, he went to the field. The bridge in his rear was broken down. At sight of that the battle grew hotter The hand of the Lord prevailed, and the forces of Maxentius were routed. He fled towards the broken bridge; but the multitude pressing on him, he was driven headlong into the Tiber.

This destructive war being ended, Constantine was acknowledged as emperor, with great rejoicings, by the senate and people of Rome. And now he came to know the perfidy of Daia; for he found the letters written to Maxentius, and saw the statues and portraits of the two associates which had been set up together. The senate, in reward of the valour of Constantine, decreed to him the title of *Maximus* (the Greatest), a title which Daia had always arrogated to himself. Daia . . . when he heard of the decree of the senate, . . . grew outrageous, avowed enmity towards Constantine, and made his title of the *Greatest* a theme of abuse and raillery.

Chapter xlv

Constantine having settled all things at Rome, went to Milan about the beginning of winter. Thither also Licinius came to receive his wife Constantia. When Daia understood that they were busied in solemnizing the nuptials, he moved out of Syria in the depth of a severe winter, and by forced marches he came into Bithynia with an army much impaired; for he lost all his beasts of burden, of whatever kind, in consequence of excessive rains and snows, miry ways, cold and fatigue. [*Later he was defeated by Licinius.*]

. . . .

Chapter xlviii

Not many days after the victory, Licinius, having received part of the soldiers of Daia into his service, and properly distributed them, transported his army into Bithynia, and having made his entry into Nicomedia, he returned thanks to God, through whose aid he had overcome; and on the ides of June (13th June), while he and Constantine were consuls for the third time, he commanded the following edict for the restoration of the Church, directed to the president of the province, to be promulgated:—

"When we, Constantine and Licinius, emperors, had an interview at Milan, and conferred together with respect to the good and security of the commonweal, it seemed to us that, amongst those things that are profitable to mankind in general, the reverence paid to the Divinity merited our first and chief attention, and that it was proper that the Christians and all others should have liberty to follow that mode of religion which to each of them appeared best; so that that God, who is seated in heaven, might be benign and propitious to us, and to every one under our government: and therefore we judged it a salutary measure, and one highly consonant to right reason, that no man should be denied leave of attaching himself to the rites of the Christians, or to whatever other religion his mind directed him, that thus the supreme Divinity, to whose worship we freely devote ourselves, might continue to vouchsafe His favour and beneficence to us. And accordingly we give you to know that, without regard to any provisos in our former orders to you concerning the Christians, all who choose that religion are to be permitted, freely and absolutely, to remain in it, and not to be disturbed any ways, or molested. And we thought fit to be thus special in the things committed to your charge, that you might understand that the indulgence which we have granted in matters of religion to the Christians is ample and unconditional; and perceive at the same time that the open and free exercise of their respective religions is granted to all others, as well as to the Christians: for it befits the well-ordered state and the tranquillity of our times that each individual be allowed, according to his own choice, to worship the Divinity; and we mean not to derogate aught from the honour due to any religion or its votaries. Moreover, with respect to the Christians, we formerly gave certain orders concerning the places appropriated for their religious assemblies; but now we will that all persons who have purchased such places, either from our exchequer or from any one else, do restore them to the Christians, without money demanded or price claimed, and that this be performed peremptorily and unambiguously; and we will also, that they who have obtained any right to such places by form of gift do forthwith restore them to the Christians: reserving always to such persons, who have either purchased for a price, or gratuitiously acquired them, to make application to the judge of the district, if they look on themselves as entitled to any equivalent from our beneficence.—All those places are, by your intervention, to be immediately restored to the Christians. And because it appears that, besides the places appropriated to religious worship, the Christians did possess other places, which belonged not to individuals, but to their society in general, that is, to their churches, we comprehend all such within the regulation aforesaid, and we will that you cause them all to be restored to the society or churches, and that without hesitation or controversy: Provided always, that the persons making restitution without a price paid shall be at liberty to seek indemnification from our bounty. In furthering all which things for the behoof of the Christians, you are to use your utmost diligence, to the end that our orders be speedily obeyed, and our gracious purpose in securing the public tranquillity promoted. So shall that divine favour which, in affairs of the mightiest importance, we have already experienced, continue to give success to us, and in our successes make the commonweal happy. And that the tenor of this our gracious ordinance may be made known unto all, we will that you cause it by your authority to be published everywhere."

Licinius having issued this ordinance, made an harangue, in which he exhorted the Christians to rebuild their religious edifices.

And thus, from the overthrow of the Church until its restoration, there was a space of ten years and about four months.

10. THE PERSECUTION OF THE CHRISTIANS UNDER THE ROMAN EMPIRE[1]

It was in the eighteenth century that Edward Gibbon wrote his Decline and Fall of the Roman Empire. *No chapters in his famous work aroused more controversy in his own time or later than those dealing with the early history of Christianity, the fifteenth and sixteenth. While still a boy Gibbon had been converted from Protestantism to Roman Catholicism and as a consequence had not only incurred the displeasure of his father but had been forced to leave Oxford where he had been a student. A few years later he returned to Protestantism and subsequently became a skeptic. This skepticism colors his account of early Christianity, in the treatment of which he employs irony with telling effect. "Had I believed that the majority of English readers," he wrote in his Memoirs, "were so fondly attached even to the name and shadow of Christianity, had I foreseen that the pious, the timid, and the prudent would feel, or affect to feel, with such exquisite sensibility,*

[1] E. Gibbon, *The History of the Decline and Fall of the Roman Empire*. With notes by Dean Milman, M. Guizot, and Dr. William Smith, 6 vols. New York, Harper and Brothers (no date). Vol. II, chapter XVI, pp. 186–203 (condensed).

I might perhaps have softened the two invidious Chapters, which would create many enemies and conciliate few friends."

Under the reign of Trajan the younger Pliny was intrusted by his friend and master with the government of Bithynia and Pontus. He soon found himself at a loss to determine by what rule of justice or of law he should direct his conduct in the execution of an office the most repugnant to his humanity. Pliny had never assisted at any judicial proceedings against the Christians, with whose name alone he seems to be acquainted; and he was totally uninformed with regard to the nature of their guilt, the method of their conviction, and the degree of their punishment. In this perplexity, he had recourse to his usual expedient, of submitting to the wisdom of Trajan an impartial, and in some respects a favorable, account of the new superstition, requesting the emperor that he would condescend to resolve his doubts and to instruct his ignorance. The life of Pliny had been employed in the acquisition of learning and in the business of the world. Since the age of nineteen he had pleaded with distinction in the tribunals of Rome, filled a place in the senate, had been invested with the honors of the consulship, and had formed very numerous connections with every order of men, both in Italy and in the provinces. From *his* ignorance, therefore, we may derive some useful information. We may assure ourselves that when he accepted the government of Bithynia there were no general laws or decrees of the senate in force against the Christians; that neither Trajan nor any of his virtuous predecessors, whose edicts were received into the civil and criminal jurisprudence, had publicly declared their intentions concerning the new sect; and that, whatever proceedings had been carried on against the Christians, there were none of sufficient weight and authority to establish a precedent for the conduct of a Roman magistrate.

The answer of Trajan, to which the Christians of the succeeding age have frequently appealed, discovers as much regard for justice and humanity as could be reconciled with his mistaken notions of religious policy. Instead of displaying the implacable zeal of an inquisitor anxious to discover the most minute particles of heresy, and exulting in the number of his victims, the emperor expresses much more solicitude to protect the security of the innocent than to prevent the escape of the guilty. He acknowledges the difficulty of fixing any general plan; but he lays down two salutary rules, which often afforded relief and support to the distressed Christians. Though he directs the magistrates to punish such persons as are legally convicted, he prohibits them, with a very humane inconsistency, from making any inquiries concerning the supposed criminals. Nor was the magistrate allowed to proceed on every kind of information. Anonymous charges the emperor rejects, as too repugnant to the equity of his government; and he strictly requires, for the conviction of those to whom the guilt of Christianity is imputed, the positive evidence of a fair and open accuser. It is likewise probable that the persons who assumed so invidious an office were obliged to declare the grounds of their suspicions, to specify (both in respect to time and place) the secret assemblies which their Christian adversary had frequented, and to disclose a great number of circumstances which were concealed with the most vigilant jealousy from the eye of the profane. If they succeeded in their prosecution, they were exposed to the resentment of a considerable and active party, to the censure of the more liberal portion of mankind, and to the ignominy which, in every age and country, has attended the character of an informer. If, on the contrary, they failed in their proofs, they incurred the severe, and, perhaps, capital penalty which, according to a law published by the Emperor Hadrian, was inflicted on those who falsely attributed to their fellow-citizens the crime of Christianity. The violence of personal or superstitious animosity might sometimes prevail over the most natural apprehensions of disgrace and danger; but it cannot surely be imagined that accusations of so unpromising an appearance were either lightly or frequently undertaken by the pagan subjects of the Roman empire.

. . . .

Punishment was not the inevitable consequence of conviction, and the Christians whose guilt was the most clearly proved by the testimony of witnesses, or even by their voluntary confession, still retained in their own power the alternative of life or death. It was not so much the past offence as the actual resistance which excited the indignation of the magistrate. He was persuaded that he offered them an easy pardon, since, if they consented to cast a few grains of incense upon the altar, they were dismissed from the tribunal in safety and with applause. It was esteemed the duty of a humane judge to endeavor to reclaim, rather than to punish, those deluded enthusiasts. Varying his tone according to the age, the sex, or the situation of the prisoners, he frequently condescended to set before their eyes every circumstance which could render life more pleasing or death more terrible, and to solicit—nay, to entreat—them that they would show some compassion to themselves, to their families, and to their friends. If threats and persuasions proved ineffectual, he had often recourse to violence; the scourge and the rack were called in to supply the deficiency of argument, and every art of cruelty was employed to subdue such inflexible, and, as it appeared to the pagans, such criminal obstinacy. The ancient apologists of Christianity have censured, with equal truth and severity, the irregular conduct of their persecutors, who, contrary to every principle of judicial proceeding, admitted the use of torture in order to obtain, not a confession, but a denial, of the crime which was the object of their inquiry.

. . . .

It is not improbable that some of those persons who were raised to the dignities of the empire might have imbibed the prejudices of the populace, and that the cruel disposition of others might occasionally be stimulated by motives of avarice or of personal resentment. But it is certain, and we may appeal to the grateful confessions of the first Christians, that the greatest part of those magistrates who exercised in the provinces the authority of the emperor or of the senate, and to whose hands alone the jurisdiction of life and death was intrusted, behaved like men of polished manners and liberal educations, who respected the rules of justice, and who were conversant with the precepts of philosophy. They frequently declined the odious task of persecution, dismissed the charge with contempt, or suggested to the accused Christian some legal evasion by which he might elude the severity of the laws. Whenever they were invested with a discretionary power, they used it much less for the oppression than for the relief and benefit of the afflicted Church. They were far from condemning all the Christians who were accused before their tribunal, and very far from punishing with death all those who were convicted of an obstinate adherence to the new superstition. Contenting themselves, for the most part, with the milder chastisements of imprisonment, exile, or slavery in the mines, they left the unhappy victims of their justice some reason to hope that a prosperous event—the accession, the marriage, or the triumph of an emperor—might speedily restore them by a general pardon to their former state. The martyrs devoted to immediate execution by the Roman magistrates appear to have been selected from the most opposite extremes. They were either bishops and presbyters, the persons the most distinguished among the Christians by their rank and influence, and whose example might strike terror into the whole sect; or else they were the meanest and most abject among them, particularly those of the servile condition, whose lives were esteemed of little value, and whose sufferings were viewed by the ancients with too careless an indifference. The learned Origen, who, from his experience as well as reading, was intimately acquainted with the history of the Christians, declares, in the most express terms, that the number of martyrs was very inconsiderable. His authority would alone be sufficient to annihilate that formidable army of martyrs whose relics, drawn for the most part from the catacombs of Rome, have replenished so many churches, and whose marvelous achievements have been the subject of so many volumes of holy romance. But the general assertion of Origen may be explained and confirmed by the particular testimony of his friend Dionysius, who, in the immense city of Alexandria, and under the rigorous persecution of Decius, reckons only ten men and seven women who suffered for the profession of the Christian name.

During the same period of persecution, the zealous, the eloquent, the ambitious Cyprian governed the Church, not only of Carthage, but even of Africa. He possessed every quality which could engage the reverence of the faithful or provoke the suspicions and resentment of the pagan magistrates. His character as well as his station seemed to mark out that holy prelate as the most distinguished object of envy and of danger. The experience, however, of the life of Cyprian is sufficient to prove that our fancy has exaggerated the perilous situation of a Christian bishop; and that the dangers to which he was exposed were less imminent than those which temporal ambition is always prepared to encounter in the pursuit of honors. Four Roman emperors, with their families, their favorites, and their adherents, perished by the sword in the space of ten years, during which the Bishop of Carthage guided by his authority and eloquence the councils of the African Church. It was only in the third year of his administration that he had reason, during a few months, to apprehend the severe edicts of Decius, the vigilance of the magistrate, and the clamors of the multitude, who loudly demanded that Cyprian, the leader of the Christians, should be thrown to the lions. Prudence suggested the necessity of a temporary retreat, and the voice of prudence was obeyed. He withdrew himself into an obscure solitude, from whence he could maintain a constant correspondence with the clergy and people of Carthage; and, concealing himself till the tempest was past, he preserved his life, without relinquishing either his power or his reputation. His extreme caution did not, however, escape the censure of the more rigid Christians, who lamented, or the reproaches of his personal enemies, who insulted, a conduct which they considered as a pusillanimous and criminal desertion of the most sacred duty. The propriety of reserving himself for the future exigencies of the Church, the example of several holy bishops, and the divine admonitions which, as he declares himself, he frequently received in visions and ecstasies, were the reasons alleged in his justification. But his best apology may be found in the cheerful resolution with which, about eight years afterwards, he suffered death in the cause of religion. The authentic history of his martyrdom has been recorded with unusual candor and impartiality. A short abstract, therefore, of its most important circumstances will convey the clearest information of the spirit and of the forms of the Roman persecutions.

When Valerian was consul for the third, and Gallienus for the fourth time, Paternus, Proconsul of Africa, summoned Cyprian to appear in his private council-chamber. He there acquainted him with the imperial mandate which he had just received, that those who had abandoned the Roman religion should immediately return to the practice of the ceremonies of their ancestors. Cyprian replied without hesitation that he was a Christian and a bishop, devoted to the worship of the true and only Deity, to whom he offered up his daily supplications for the safety and prosperity of the two emperors, his lawful sovereigns. With modest confidence he pleaded the privilege of a citizen in refusing to give any answer to some invidious, and, indeed, illegal questions which the proconsul had proposed. A sentence of banishment was pronounced as the penalty of Cyprian's disobedience, and he was conducted without delay to Curubis, a free and maritime city of Zeugitana, in a pleasant situation, a fertile territory, and at the distance of about forty miles from Carthage. The exiled bishop enjoyed the conveniences of life and the consciousness of virtue. His reputation was diffused over Africa and Italy; an account of his behavior was published for the edification of the Christian world; and his solitude was frequently interrupted by the letters, the visits, and the congratulations of the faithful. On the arrival of a new proconsul in the province, the fortune of Cyprian appeared for some time to wear a still more favorable aspect. He was recalled from banishment, and, though not yet permitted to return to Carthage, his own gardens in the neighborhood of the capital were assigned for the place of his residence.

At length, exactly one year after Cyprian was first apprehended, Galerius Maximus, Proconsul of Africa, received the imperial warrant for the execution of the Christian teachers. The Bishop of Carthage was sensible that he should be singled out for one of the first victims, and the frailty of nature tempted him to withdraw himself, by a secret flight, from the danger and the honor of martyrdom; but, soon recovering that fortitude which his character required, he returned to his gardens and patiently expected the ministers of death. Two officers of rank who were intrusted with that commission placed Cyprian between them in a chariot, and, as the proconsul was not then at leisure, they conducted him, not to a prison, but to a private house in Carthage, which belonged to one of them. An elegant supper was provided for the entertainment of the bishop, and his Christian friends were permitted for the last time to enjoy his society, whilst the streets were filled with a multitude of the faithful, anxious and alarmed at the approaching fate of their spiritual father. In the morning he appeared before the tribunal of the proconsul, who, after informing himself of the name and situation of Cyprian, commanded him to offer sacrifice, and pressed him to reflect on the consequences of his disobedience. The refusal of Cyprian was firm and decisive, and the magistrate, when he had taken the opinion of his council, pronounced with some reluctance, the sentence of death. It was conceived in the following terms: "That Thascius Cyprianus should be immediately beheaded, as the enemy of the gods of Rome, and as the chief and ringleader of a criminal association, which he had seduced into an impious resistance against the laws of the most holy emperors Valerian and Gallienus." The manner of his execution was the mildest and least painful that could be inflicted on a person convicted of any capital offence; nor was the use of torture admitted to obtain from the Bishop of Carthage either the recantation of his principles or the discovery of his accomplices.

As soon as the sentence was proclaimed, a general cry of "We will die with him!" arose at once among the listening multitude of Christians who waited before the palace gates. The generous effusions of their zeal and affection were neither serviceable to Cyprian nor dangerous to themselves. He was led away under a guard of tribunes and centurions, without resistance and without insult, to the place of his execution, a spacious and level plain near the city, which was already filled with great numbers of spectators. His faithful presbyters and deacons were permitted to accompany their holy bishop. They assisted him in laying aside his upper garment, spread linen on the ground to catch the precious relics of his blood, and receive his orders to bestow five-and-twenty pieces of gold on the executioner. The martyr then covered his face with his hands, and at one blow his head was separated from his body. His corpse remained during some hours exposed to the curiosity of the Gentiles, but in the night it was removed, and transported, in a triumphal procession and with a splendid illumination, to the burial-place of the Christians. The funeral of Cyprian was publicly celebrated without receiving any interruption from the Roman magistrates; and those among the faithful who had performed the last offices to his person and his memory were secure from the danger of inquiry or of punishment. It is remarkable that of so great a multitude of bishops in the province of Africa, Cyprian was the first who was esteemed worthy to obtain the crown of martyrdom.

. . . .

The sober discretion of the present age will more readily censure than admire, but can more easily admire than imitate, the fervor of the first Christians, who, according to the lively expression of Sulpicius Severus, desired martyrdom with more eagerness than his own contemporaries solicited a bishopric. The epistles which Ignatius composed as he was carried in chains through the cities of Asia breathe sentiments the most repugnant to the ordinary feelings of human nature. He earnestly beseeches the Romans that, when he should be exposed in the amphitheatre, they would not, by their kind but unseasonable intercession, deprive him of the crown of glory; and he declares his resolution to provoke and irritate the wild beasts which might be employed as the instruments of his death. Some stories are related of the courage of martyrs who actually performed what Ignatius had intended, who exasperated the fury of the lions, pressed the executioner to hasten his office, cheerfully leaped into the fires which were kindled to consume them, and discovered a sensation of joy and pleasure in the midst of the most exquisite tortures. Several examples have been preserved of a zeal impatient of those restraints which the emperors had provided for the security of the Church. The Christians sometimes supplied by their voluntary declaration the want of an accuser, rudely disturbed the public service of paganism, and, rushing in crowds round the tribunal of the magistrates, called upon them to pronounce and to inflict the sentence of the law. The behavior of the Christians was too remarkable to escape the notice of the ancient philosophers, but they seem to have considered it with much less admiration than astonishment. Incapable of conceiving the motives which sometimes transported the fortitude of believers beyond the bounds of prudence or reason, they treated such an eagerness to die as the strange result of obstinate despair, of stupid insensibility, or of superstitious frenzy. "Unhappy men!" exclaimed the proconsul Antoninus to the Christians of Asia—"unhappy men! if you are thus weary of your lives, is it so difficult for you to find ropes and precipices?" He was extremely cautious (as it is observed by a learned and pious historian) of punishing men who had found no accusers but themselves, the imperial laws not having made any provision for so unexpected a case: condemning, therefore, a few as a warning to their brethren, he dismissed the multitude with indignation and contempt. Notwithstanding this real or affected disdain, the intrepid constancy of the faithful was productive of more salutary effects on those minds which nature or grace had disposed for the easy reception of religious truth. On these melancholy occasions there were many among the Gentiles who pitied, who admired, and who were converted. The generous enthusiasm was communicated from the sufferer to the spectators, and the blood of martyrs, according to a well-known observation, became the seed of the Church.

11. THE CITY OF GOD BY ST. AUGUSTINE[1]

In the fifth century, when the Roman Empire was gradually crumbling to pieces and Rome itself (the so-called Eternal City) was twice sacked by barbarians, the Christians were wont to contrast the capital of the temporal world with the City of God in heaven. There was only one eternal city, so they argued, and that was Jerusalem above, so graphically described in the Apocalypse *by St. John. Hence we find Augustine, or St. Augustine, the*

[1] Translated by the Rev. Marcus Dods, the Rev. George Wilson, and the Rev. J. J. Smith, Edinburg, T. and T. Clark, 1878. Vol. I, pp. 1-2, 45, 47, 71-72, 91–92, 135–137, 436–437.

most influential writer among the church fathers, devoting thirteen years (413 to 426) of his busy life as Bishop of Hippo in Northern Africa to the composition of a very famous book, entitled The City of God, *in which he severely condemned the pagan religion of ancient Rome. He also explained at great length how the God of the Jews and the Christians had created the world and had controlled from the beginning of time the destinies of all nations. The selections given below present in part a list of topics discussed by the celebrated author.*

Book I. The Preface.

The glorious city of God is my theme in this work, which you, my dearest son Marcellinus, suggested, and which is due to you by my promise. I have undertaken its defence against those who prefer their own gods to the Founder of this city,—a city surpassingly glorious, whether we view it as it still lives by faith in this fleeting course of time, and sojourns as a stranger in the midst of the ungodly, or as it shall dwell in the fixed stability of its eternal seat, which it now with patience waits for, expecting until "righteousness shall return unto judgment," and it obtain, by virtue of its excellence, final victory and perfect peace. A great work this, and an arduous; but God is my helper. For I am aware what ability is requisite to persuade the proud how great is the virtue of humility, which raises us, not by a quite human arrogance, but by a divine grace, above all earthly dignities that totter on this shifting scene. For the King and Founder of this city of which we speak, has in Scripture uttered to His people a dictum of the divine law in these words: "God resisteth the proud, but giveth grace unto the humble." But this, which is God's prerogative, the inflated ambition of a proud spirit also affects, and dearly loves that this be numbered among its attributes, to

"Show pity to the humbled soul,
And crush the sons of pride."

And therefore, as the plan of this work we have undertaken requires, and as occasion offers, we must speak also of the earthly city, which, though it be mistress of the nations, is itself ruled by its lust of rule.

Chapter 33. That the overthrow of Rome has not corrected the vices of the Romans.

Oh infatuated men, what is this blindness, or rather madness, which possesses you? How is it that while, as we hear, even the eastern nations are bewailing your ruin, and while powerful states in the most remote parts of the earth are mourning your fall as a public calamity, ye yourselves should be crowded to the theatres, should be pouring into them and filling them; and, in short, be playing a madder part now than ever before? This was the foul plague-spot, this the wreck of virtue and honour that Scipio sought to preserve you from when he prohibited the construction of theatres; this was his reason for desiring that you might still have an enemy to fear, seeing as he did how easily prosperity would corrupt and destroy you. He did not consider that republic flourishing whose walls stand, but whose morals are in ruins. But the seductions of evil-minded devils had more influence with you than the precautions of prudent men. Hence the injuries you do, you will not permit to be imputed to you; but the injuries you suffer, you impute to Christianity. Depraved by good fortune, and not chastened by adversity, what you desire in the restoration of a peaceful and secure state, is not the tranquillity of the commonwealth, but the impunity of your own vicious luxury. Scipio wished you to be hard pressed by an enemy, that you might not abandon yourselves to luxurious manners; but so abandoned are you, that not even when crushed by the enemy is your luxury repressed. You have missed the profit of your calamity; you have been made most wretched, and have remained most profligate.

Chapter 36. What subjects are to be handled in the following discourse.

But I have still some things to say in confutation of those who refer the disasters of the Roman republic to our religion, because it prohibits the offering of sacrifices to the gods. For this end I must recount all, or as many as may seem sufficient, of the disasters which befell that city and its subject provinces, before these sacrifices were prohibited; for all these disasters they would doubtless have attributed to us, if at that time, our religion had shed its light upon them, and had prohibited their sacrifices. I must then go on to show what social well-being the true God, in whose hand are all kingdoms, vouchsafed to grant to them that their empire might increase. I must show why He did so, and how their false gods, instead of at all aiding them, greatly injured them by guile and deceit. And, lastly, I must meet those who, when on this point convinced and confuted by irrefragable proofs, endeavour to maintain that they worship the gods, not hoping for the present advantages of this life, but for those which are to be enjoyed after death. And this, if I am not mistaken, will be the most difficult part of my task, and will be worthy of the loftiest argument; for we must then enter the lists with the philosophers, not the mere common herd of philosophers, but the most renowned, who in many points agree with ourselves, as regarding the immortality of the soul, and that the true God created the world, and by His providence rules all He has created. But as they differ from us on other points, we must not shrink from the task of exposing their errors, that, having refuted the gainsaying of the wicked with such ability as God may vouchsafe, we may assert the city of God, and true piety, and the worship of God, to which alone the promise of true and everlasting felicity is attached. Here, then, let us conclude, that we may enter on these subjects in a fresh book.

Book II

Chapter 3. That we need only to read history in order to see what calamities the Romans suffered before the religion of Christ began to compete with the worship of the gods.

But remember that, in recounting these things, I have still to address myself to ignorant men; so ignorant, indeed, as to give birth to the common saying, "Drought and Christianity go hand in hand." There are indeed some among them who are thoroughly well educated men, and have a taste for history, in which the things I speak of are open to their observation; but in order to irritate the uneducated masses against us, they feign ignorance of these events, and do what they can to make the vulgar believe that those disasters, which in certain places and at certain times uniformly befall mankind, are the result of Christianity, which is being everywhere diffused, and is possessed of a renown and brilliancy which quite eclipse their own gods. Let them then, along with us, call to mind with what various and repeated disasters the prosperity of Rome was blighted, before ever Christ had come in the flesh, and before His name had been blazoned among the nations with that glory which they vainly grudge. Let them, if they can, defend their gods in this article, since they maintain that they worship them in order to be preserved from these disasters, which they now impute to us if they suffer in the least degree. For why did these gods permit the disasters I am to speak of to fall on their worshippers before the preaching of Christ's name offended them, and put an end to their sacrifices?

Chapter 19. Of the corruption which had grown upon the Roman republic before Christ abolished the worship of the gods.

Here, then, is this Roman republic, "which has changed little by little from the fair and virtuous city it was, and has become utterly wicked and dissolute." It is not I who am the first to say this, but their own authors, from whom we learned it for a fee, and who wrote it long before the coming of Christ. You see how, before the coming of Christ and after the destruction of Carthage, "the primitive manners, instead of undergoing insensible alteration, as hitherto they had done, were swept away as by a torrent; and how depraved by luxury and avarice the youth were." Let them now, on their part, read to us any laws given by their gods to the Roman people, and directed against luxury and avarice. And would that they had only been silent on the subjects of chastity and modesty, and had not demanded from the people indecent and shameful practices, to which they lent a pernicious patronage by their so-called divinity. Let them read our commandments in the Prophets, Gospels, Acts of the Apostles, or Epistles; let them peruse the large number of precepts against avarice and luxury which are everywhere read to the congregations that meet for this purpose, and which strike the ear, not with the uncertain sound of a philosophical discussion, but with the thunder of God's own oracle pealing from the clouds. And yet they do not impute to their gods of luxury and avarice, the cruel and dissolute manners, that had rendered the republic utterly wicked and corrupt, even before the coming of Christ; but whatever affliction their pride and effeminacy have exposed them to in these latter days, they furiously impute to our religion. If the kings of the earth and all their subjects, if all princes and judges of the earth, if young men and maidens, old and young, every age, and both sexes; if they whom the Baptist addressed, the publicans and the soldiers, were all together to hearken to and observe the precepts of the Christian religion regarding a just and virtuous life, then should the republic adorn the whole earth with its own felicity, and attain in life everlasting to the pinnacle of kingly glory. But because this man listens, and that man scoffs, and most are enamoured of the blandishments of vice rather than the wholesome severity of virtue, the people of Christ, whatever be their condition—whether they be kings, princes, judges, soldiers, or provincials, rich or poor, bond or free, male or female—are enjoined to endure this earthly republic, wicked and dissolute as it is, that so they may by this endurance win for themselves an eminent place in that most holy and august assembly of angels and republic of heaven, in which the will of God is the law.

Book III

Chapter 1. Of the ills which alone the wicked fear, and which the world continually suffered, even when the gods were worshipped.

Of moral and spiritual evils, which are above all others to be deprecated, I think enough has already been said to show that the false gods took no steps to prevent the people who worshipped them from being overwhelmed by such calamities, but rather aggravated the ruin. I see I must now speak of those evils which alone are dreaded by the heathen—famine, pestilence, war, pillage, captivity, massacre, and the like calamities, already enumerated in the first book. For evil men account those things alone evil which do not make men evil; neither do they blush to praise good things, and yet to remain evil among the good things they praise. It grieves them more to own a bad house than a bad life, as if it were man's greatest good to have everything good but himself. But not even such evils as were alone dreaded by the heathen were warded off by their gods, even when they were most unrestrictedly worshipped. For in various times and places before the advent of our Redeemer, the human race was crushed with numberless and sometimes incredible calamities; and at that time what gods but those did the world worship, if you except the one nation of the Hebrews, and, beyond them, such individuals as the most secret and most just judgment of God counted worthy of divine grace? But that I may not be prolix, I will be silent regarding the heavy calamities that have been suffered by any other nations, and will speak only of what happened to Rome and the Roman empire, by which I mean Rome properly so called, and those lands which already, before the coming of Christ, had by alliance or conquest become, as it were, members of the body of the state.

Book IV

Chapter 1. Of the things which have been discussed in the first book.

Having begun to speak of the city of God, I have thought it necessary first of all to reply to its enemies, who, eagerly pursuing earthly joys, and gaping after transitory things, throw the blame of all the sorrow they suffer in them—rather through the compassion of God in admonishing, than His severity in punishing—on the Christian religion, which is the one salutary and true religion. And since there is among them also an unlearned rabble, they are stirred up as by the authority of the learned to hate us more bitterly, thinking in their inexperience that things which have happened unwontedly in their days were not wont to happen in other times gone by; and whereas this opinion of theirs is confirmed even by those who know that it is false, and yet dissemble their knowledge in order that they may seem to have just cause for murmuring against us, it was necessary, from books in which their authors recorded and published the history of bygone times that it might be known, to demonstrate that it is far otherwise than they think; and at the same time to teach that the false gods, whom they openly worshipped, or still worship in secret, are most unclean spirits, and most malignant and deceitful demons, even to such a pitch that they take delight in crimes which, whether real or only fictitious, are yet their own, which it has been their will to have celebrated in honour of them at their own festivals; so that human infirmity cannot be called back from the perpetration of damnable deeds, so long as authority is furnished for imitating them that seems even divine. These things we have proved, not from our own conjectures, but partly from recent memory, because we ourselves have seen such things celebrated, and to such deities, partly from the writings of those who have left these things on record to posterity, not as if in reproach, but as in honour of their own gods. Thus Varro, a most learned man among them, and of the weightiest authority, when he made separate books concerning things human and things divine; distributing some among the human, others among the divine, according to the special dignity of each, placed the scenic plays not at all among things human, but among things divine; though, certainly, if only there were good and honest men in the state, the scenic plays ought not to be allowed even among things human. And this he did not on his own authority, but because, being born and educated at Rome, he found them among the divine things. Now as we briefly stated in the end of the first book what we intended afterwards to discuss, and as we have disposed of a part of this in the next two books, we see what our readers will expect us now to take up.

Chapter 2. Of those things which are contained in Books Second and Third.

We had promised, then, that we would say something against those who attribute the calamities of the Roman republic to our religion, and that we would recount the evils, as many and great as we could remember or might deem sufficient, which that city, or the provinces belonging to its empire, had suffered before their sacrifices were prohibited, all of which would beyond doubt have been attributed to us, if our religion had either already shone on them, or had thus prohibited their sacrilegious rites. These things we have, as we think, fully disposed of in the second and third books, treating in the second of evils in morals, which alone or chiefly are to be accounted evils; and in the third, of those which only fools dread to undergo—namely, those of the body or of outward things—which for the most part the good also suffer. But those evils by which they themselves become evil, they take, I do not say patiently, but with pleasure. And how few evils have I related concerning that one city and its empire! Not even all down to the time of Caesar Augustus. What if I had chosen to recount and enlarge on those evils, not which men have inflicted on each other, such as the devastations and destructions of war, but which happen in earthly things, from the elements of the world itself?

Book XI

Chapter 1. Of this part of the work, wherein we begin to explain the origin and end of the two cities.

The city of God we speak of is the same to which testimony is borne by that Scripture, which excels all the writings of all nation by its divine authority, and has brought under its influence all kinds of minds, and this not by a casual intellectual movement, but obviously by an express providential arrangement. For there it is written, "Glorious things are spoken of thee, O city of God." And in another psalm we read, "Great is the Lord, and greatly to be praised in the city of our God, in the mountain of His holiness, increasing the joy of the whole earth." And, a little after, in the same psalm, "As we have heard, so have we seen in the city of the Lord of hosts, in the city of our God. God has established it for ever." And in another, "There is a river the streams whereof shall make glad the city of our God, the holy place of the tabernacles of the Most High. God is in the midst of her, she shall not be moved." From these and similar testimonies, all of which it were tedious to cite, we have learned that there is a city of God, and its Founder has inspired us with a love which makes us covet its citizenship. To this Founder of the holy city the citizens of the earthly city prefer their own gods, not knowing that He is the God of gods, not of false, *i.e.* of impious and proud gods, who, being deprived of His unchangeable and freely communicated light, and so reduced to a kind of poverty-stricken power, eagerly grasp at their own private privileges, and seek divine honours from their deluded subjects; but of the pious and holy gods, who are better pleased to submit themselves to one, than to subject many to themselves, and who would rather worship God than be worshipped as God. But to the enemies of this city we have replied in the ten preceding books, according to our ability and the help afforded by our Lord and King. Now, recognising what is expected of me, and not unmindful of my promise, and relying, too, on the same succour, I will endeavour to treat of the origin, and progress, and deserved destinies of the two cities (the earthly and the heavenly, to wit,), which, as we said, are in this present world commingled, and as it were entangled together. And, first, I will explain how the foundations of these two cities were originally laid, in the difference that arose among the angels.

12. AN EXTRACT FROM THE CONFESSIONS OF ST. AUGUSTINE[1]

Augustine, or St. Augustine, enjoys the distinction of being the writer whose works have been more widely read in the Middle Ages than the compositions of any other man, excepting parts of the Bible. It is very fortunate that this writer left a sort of autobiography, which enables the modern reader to get a reasonably accurate picture of his life and character. Augustine is very frank in telling us of the sins of his youth, and he shows little hesitation in setting forth his other failings. Being a most religious person, he devoted a large part of his Confessions *to an account of his struggle with the flesh and sin, and he naturally dwelt at length on the story of his conversion. In the two chapters given here he discusses these matters and mentions an intimate friend, Alypius. He also informs us that his pious mother, who had long prayed for his conversion, was a witness to this conversion before she died.*

Book Eight

Chapt. XI.—*In what manner the Spirit struggled with the flesh, that it might be freed from the bondage of vanity.*

Thus was I sick and tormented, accusing myself far more severely than was my wont, tossing and turning me in my chain till that was utterly broken, whereby I now was but slightly, but still was held. And Thou, O Lord, pressedst upon me in my inward parts by a severe mercy, redoubling the lashes of fear and shame, lest I should again give way, and that same slender remaining tie not being broken off, it should recover strength, and enchain me the faster. For I said mentally, "Lo, let it be done now, let it be done now." And as I spoke, I all but came to a resolve. I all but did it, yet I did it not. Yet fell I not back to my old condition, but took up my position hard by, and drew breath. And I tried again, and wanted but very little of reaching it, and somewhat less, and then all but touched and grasped it; and yet came not at it, nor touched, nor grasped it, hesitating to die unto death, and to live unto life; and the worse, whereto I had been habituated, prevailed more with me than the better, which I had not tried. And the very moment in which I was to become another man, the nearer it approached me, the greater horror did it strike into me; but it did not strike me back, nor turn me aside, but kept me in suspense.

[1] *The Confessions of St. Augustine,* translated by J. G. Pilkington. New York, Horace Liveright, 1927, pp. 183–187.

The very toys of toys, and vanities of vanities, my old mistresses, still enthralled me; they shook my fleshly garment, and whispered softly, "Dost thou part with us? And from that moment shall we no more be with thee for ever? And from that moment shall not this or that be lawful for thee for ever?" And what did they suggest to me in the words "this or that?" What is it that they suggested, O my God? Let Thy mercy avert it from the soul of Thy servant. What impurities did they suggest! What shame! And now I far less than half heard them, not openly showing themselves and contradicting me, but muttering, as it were, behind my back, and furtively plucking me as I was departing, to make me look back upon them. Yet they did delay me, so that I hesitated to burst and shake myself free from them, and to leap over whither I was called,—an unruly habit saying to me, "Dost thou think thou canst live without them?"

But now it said this very faintly; for on that side towards which I had set my face, and whither I trembled to go, did the chaste dignity of Continence appear unto me, cheerful, but not dissolutely gay, honestly alluring me to come and doubt nothing, and extending her holy hands, full of a multiplicity of good examples, to receive and embrace me. There were there so many young men and maidens, a multitude of youth and every age, grave widows and ancient virgins, and Continence herself in all, not barren, but a fruitful mother of children of joys, by Thee, O Lord, her Husband. And she smiled on me with an encouraging mockery, as if to say, "Canst not thou do what these youths and maidens can? Or can one or other do it of themselves, and not rather in the Lord their God? The Lord their God gave me unto them. Why standest thou in thine own strength, and so standest not? Cast thyself upon Him; fear not, He will not withdraw that thy shoulders fall; cast thyself upon Him without fear, He will receive thee, and heal thee." And I blushed beyond measure, for I still heard the muttering of these toys, and hung in suspense. And she again seemed to say, "Shut up thine ears against those unclean members of thine upon the earth, that they may be mortified. They tell thee of delights, but not as doth the law of the Lord thy God." This controversy in my heart was naught but self against self. But Alypius, sitting close by my side, awaited in silence the result of my unwonted emotion.

Chap. XII.—*Having prayed to God, he pours forth a shower of tears, and, admonished by a voice, he opens the book and reads the words in Rom. XIII. 13; by which, being changed in his whole soul, he discloses the divine favour to his friend and his mother.*

But when a profound reflection had, from the secret depths of my soul, drawn together and heaped up all my misery before the sight of my heart, there arose a mighty storm, accompanied by as mighty a shower of tears.

Which, that I might pour forth fully, with its natural expressions, I stole away from Alypius; for it suggested itself to me that solitude was fitter for the business of weeping. So I retired to such a distance that even his presence could not be oppressive to me. Thus was it with me at that time, and he perceived it; for something, I believe, I had spoken, wherein the sound of my voice appeared choked with weeping, and in that state had I risen up. He then remained where we had been sitting, most completely astonished. I flung myself down, how, I know not, under a certain fig-tree, giving free course to my tears, and the streams of mine eyes gushed out, an acceptable sacrifice unto Thee. And, not indeed in these words, yet to this effect, spake I much unto Thee,—"But Thou, O Lord, how long?" "How long, Lord? Wilt Thou be angry for ever? Oh, remember not against us former iniquities;" for I felt that I was enthralled by them. I sent up these sorrowful cries,—"How long, how long? To-morrow, and to-morrow? Why not now? Why is there not this hour an end to my uncleanness?"

I was saying these things and weeping in the most bitter contrition of my heart, when, lo, I heard the voice as of a boy or girl, I know not which, coming from a neighbouring house, chanting, and oft repeating, "Take up and read; take up and read." Immediately my countenance was changed, and I began most earnestly to consider whether it was usual for children in any kind of game to sing such words; nor could I remember ever to have heard the like. So, restraining the torrent of my tears, I rose up, interpreting it no other way than as a command to me from Heaven to open the book, and to read the first chapter I should light upon. For I had heard of Antony, that, accidentally coming in whilst the gospel was being read, he received the admonition as if what was read were addressed to him, "Go and sell that thou hast, and give to the poor, and thou shalt have treasure in heaven; and come and follow me." And by such oracle was he forthwith converted unto Thee. So quickly I returned to the place where Alypius was sitting; for there had I put down the volume of the apostles, when I rose thence. I grasped, opened, and in silence read that paragraph on which my eyes first fell,—"Not in rioting and drunkenness, not in chambering and wantonness, not in strife and envying; but put ye on the Lord Jesus Christ, and make not provision for the flesh, to fulfil the lusts thereof." No further would I read, nor did I need; for instantly, as the sentence ended,—by a light, as it were, of security into my heart,—all the gloom of doubt vanished away.

Closing the book, then, and putting either my finger between, or some other mark, I now with a tranquil countenance made it known to Alypius. And he thus disclosed to me what was wrought in him, which I knew not. He asked to look at what I had read. I showed him; and he looked even further than I had read, and I knew not what followed. This it was, verily, "Him that is weak in the faith, receive ye;" which he applied to himself, and discovered to me. By this admonition was he strengthened; and by a good resolution and purpose, very much in accord with his character (wherein, for the better, he was always far different from me), without any restless delay he joined me. Thence we go in to my mother. We make it known to her,—she rejoiceth. We relate how it came to pass,—she leapeth for joy, and triumpheth, and blesseth Thee, who art "able to do exceeding abundantly above all that we ask or think;" for she perceived Thee to have given her more for me than she used to ask by her pitiful and most doleful groanings. For Thou didst so convert me unto Thyself, that I sought neither a wife, nor any other of this world's hopes,—standing in that rule of faith in which Thou, so many years before, had showed me unto her in a vision. And thou didst turn her grief into gladness, much more plentiful than she had desired, and much dearer and chaster than she used to crave, by having grandchildren of my body.

13. THE ARIAN QUESTION AND THE COUNCIL OF NICAEA[1]

Eusebius, as was indicated above (see p. 39), wrote the Life of Constantine. *In this work he gives an account of the spread of Arianism, which is reproduced below. He also tells how it was decided to hold a general church council at Nicaea in Bithynia, a province in Asia Minor. Among the numerous questions that came up there for discussion was the teaching of Arius. The decision reached by the leading ecclesiastics is set forth in the letter by Constantine to the Church of Alexandria.*[2] *These two sources clearly show that the consensus of opinion among the prominent men in the Church was antagonistic toward the belief of Arius.*

Arius lived in Alexandria during the third decade of the fourth century A. D. *Here he taught that God the Father alone was eternal, and that neither the Son (Christ) nor the Holy Ghost was of the same substance as was the Father. This doctrine of his is commonly called Arianism.*

[1] Eusebius, *Life of Constantine,* translated by Ernest Cushing Richardson, *Nicene and Post-Nicene Fathers,* second series, Vol. I, pp. 515–518, 521. Reprinted by permission of Charles Scribner's Sons.

[2] Constantine, *Letter to the Church in Alexandria.* Translation published in James T. Shotwell and Louise Ropes Lewis, *The See of Peter,* New York, Columbia University Press, 1927, pp. 487–488.

A. Book II

Chapter lxi.—How Controversies originated at Alexandria through Matters relating to Arius.

In this manner the emperor, like a powerful herald of God, addressed himself by his own letter to all the provinces, at the same time warning his subjects against superstitious error, and encouraging them in the pursuit of true godliness. But in the midst of his joyful anticipations of the success of this measure, he received tidings of a most serious disturbance which had invaded the peace of the Church. This intelligence he heard with deep concern, and at once endeavored to devise a remedy for the evil. The origin of this disturbance may be thus described. The people of God were in a truly flourishing state, and abounding in the practice of good works. No terror from without assailed them, but a bright and most profound peace, through the favor of God, encompassed his Church on every side. Meantime, however, the spirit of envy was watching to destroy our blessings, which at first crept in unperceived, but soon revelled in the midst of the assemblies of the saints. At length it reached the bishops themselves, and arrayed them in angry hostility against each other, on pretense of a jealous regard for the doctrines of Divine truth. Hence it was that a mighty fire was kindled as it were from a little spark, and which, originating in the first instance in the Alexandrian church, overspread the whole of Egypt and Libya, and the further Thebaid. Eventually it extended its ravages to the other provinces and cities of the empire; so that not only the prelates of the churches might be seen encountering each other in the strife of words, but the people themselves were completely divided, some adhering to one faction and others to another. Nay, so notorious did the scandal of these proceedings become, that the sacred matters of inspired teaching were exposed to the most shameful ridicule in the very theatres of the unbelievers.

Chapter lxii.—Concerning the Same Arius, and the Melitians.

Some thus at Alexandria maintained an obstinate conflict on the highest questions. Others throughout Egypt and the Upper Thebaid, were at variance on account of an earlier controversy: so that the churches were everywhere distracted by divisions. The body therefore being thus diseased, the whole of Libya caught the contagion; and the rest of the remoter provinces became affected with the same disorder. For the disputants at Alexandria sent emissaries to the bishops of the several provinces, who accordingly ranged themselves as partisans on either side, and shared in the same spirit of discord.

Chapter lxiii.—How Constantine sent a Messenger and a Letter concerning Peace.

As soon as the emperor was informed of these facts, which he heard with much sorrow of heart, considering them in the light of a calamity personally affecting himself, he forthwith selected from the Christians in his train one whom he well knew to be approved for the sobriety and genuineness of his faith, and who had before this time distinguished himself by the boldness of his religious profession, and sent him to negotiate peace between the dissentient parties at Alexandria. He also made him the bearer of a most needful and appropriate letter to the original movers of the strife: and this letter, as exhibiting a specimen of his watchful care over God's people, it may be well to introduce into this our narrative of his life. Its purport was as follows.

Chapter lxiv.—Constantine's Letter to Alexander the Bishop, and Arius the Presbyter.

"Victor Constantinus, Maximus Augustus, to Alexander and Arius.

"I call that God to witness, as well I may, who is the helper of my endeavors, and the Preserver of all men, that I had a twofold reason for undertaking that duty which I have now performed.

Chapter lxv.—His Continual Anxiety for Peace.

"My design then was, first, to bring the diverse judgments formed by all nations respecting the Deity to a condition, as it were, of settled uniformity; and, secondly, to restore to health the system of the world, then suffering under the malignant power of a grievous distemper. Keeping these objects in view, I sought to accomplish the one by the secret eye of thought, while the other I tried to rectify by the power of military authority. For I was aware that, if I should succeed in establishing, according to my hopes, a common harmony of sentiment among all the servants of God, the general course of affairs would also experience a change correspondent to the pious desires of them all.

Chapter lxvi.—That he also adjusted the Controversies which had arisen in Africa.

"Finding then, that the whole of Africa was pervaded by an intolerable spirit of mad folly, through the influence of those who with heedless frivolity had presumed to rend the religion of the people into diverse sects;

I was anxious to check this disorder, and could discover no other remedy equal to the occasion, except in sending some of yourselves to aid in restoring mutual harmony among the disputants, after I had removed that common enemy of mankind who had interposed his lawless sentence for the prohibition of your holy synods.

Chapter lxvii.—That Religion began in the East.

"For since the power of Divine light, and the law of sacred worship, which, proceeding in the first instance, through the favor of God, from the bosom, as it were, of the East, have illumined the world, by their sacred radiance, I naturally believed that you would be the first to promote the salvation of other nations, and resolved with all energy of thought and diligence of enquiry to seek your aid. As soon, therefore, as I had secured my decisive victory and unquestionable triumph over my enemies, my first enquiry was concerning that object which I felt to be of paramount interest and importance.

Chapter lxvii.—Being grieved by the Dissension, he counsels Peace.

"But, O glorious Providence of God! how deep a wound did not my ears only, but my very heart receive in the report that divisions existed among yourselves more grievous still than those which continued in that country! so that you, through whose aid I had hoped to procure a remedy for the errors of others, are in a state which needs healing even more than theirs. And yet, having made a careful enquiry into the origin and foundation of these differences, I find the cause to be of a truly insignificant character, and quite unworthy of such fierce contention. Feeling myself, therefore, compelled to address you in this letter, and to appeal at the same time to your unanimity and sagacity, I call on Divine Providence to assist me in the task, while I interrupt your dissension in the character of a minister of peace. And with reason: for if I might expect, with the help of a higher Power, to be able without difficulty, by a judicious appeal to the pious feelings of those who heard me, to recall them to a better spirit, even though the occasion of the disagreement were a greater one, how can I refrain from promising myself a far easier and more speedy adjustment of this difference, when the cause which hinders general harmony of sentiment is intrinsically trifling and of little moment?

Chapter lxix.—Origin of the Controversy between Alexander and Arius, and that these Questions ought not to have been discussed.

"I understand, then, that the origin of the present controversy is this. When you, Alexander, demanded of the presbyters what opinion they severally maintained respecting a certain passage in the Divine law, or rather, I should say, that you asked them something connected with an unprofitable question, then you, Arius, inconsiderately insisted on what ought never to have been conceived at all, or if conceived, should have been buried in profound silence. Hence it was that a dissension arose between you, fellowship was withdrawn, and the holy people, rent into diverse parties, no longer preserved the unity of the one body. Now, therefore, do ye both exhibit an equal degree of forbearance, and receive the advice which your fellow-servant righteously gives. What then is this advice? It was wrong in the first instance to propose such questions as these, or to reply to them when propounded. For those points of discussion which are enjoined by the authority of no law, but rather suggested by the contentious spirit which is fostered by misused leisure, even though they may be intended merely as an intellectual exercise, ought certainly to be confined to the region of our own thoughts, and not hastily produced in the popular assemblies, nor unadvisedly intrusted to the general ear. For how very few are there able either accurately to comprehend, or adequately to explain subjects so sublime and abstruse in their nature? Or, granting that one were fully competent for this, how many people will he convince? Or, who, again, in dealing with questions of such subtle nicety as these, can secure himself against a dangerous declension from the truth? It is incumbent therefore on us in these cases to be sparing of our words, lest, in case we ourselves are unable, through the feebleness of our natural faculties, to give a clear explanation of the subject before us, or, on the other hand, in case the slowness of our hearers' understandings disables them from arriving at an accurate apprehension of what we say, from one or other of these causes the people be reduced to the alternative either of blasphemy or schism.

Chapter lxx.—An Exhortation to Unanimity.

"Let therefore both the unguarded question and the inconsiderate answer receive your mutual forgiveness. For the cause of your difference has not been any of the leading doctrines or precepts of the Divine law, nor has any new heresy respecting the worship of God arisen among you. You are in truth of one and the same judgment: you may therefore well join in communion and fellowship.

Chapter lxxi.—There should be no Contention in Matters which are in themselves of Little Moment.

"For as long as you continue to contend about these small and very insignificant questions, it is not fitting that so large a portion of God's people should be under the direction of your judgment, since you are thus divided between yourselves. I believe it indeed to be not merely unbecoming, but positively evil, that such should be the case. But I will refresh your minds by a little illustration, as follows. You know that philosophers, though they all adhere to one system, are yet frequently at issue on certain points, and differ, perhaps, in their degree of knowledge: yet they are recalled to harmony of sentiment by the uniting power of their common doctrines. If this be true, is it not far more reasonable that you, who are the ministers of the Supreme God, should be of one mind respecting the profession of the same religion? But let us still more thoughtfully and with closer attention examine what I have said, and see whether it be right that, on the ground of some trifling and foolish verbal difference between ourselves, brethren should assume towards each other the attitude of enemies, and the august meeting of the Synod be rent by profane disunion, because of you who wrangle together on points so trivial and altogether unessential? This is vulgar, and rather characteristic of childish ignorance, than consistent with the wisdom of priests and men of sense. Let us withdraw ourselves with a good will from these temptations of the devil. Our great God and common Saviour of all has granted the same light to us all. Permit me, who am his servant, to bring my task to a successful issue, under the direction of his Providence, that I may be enabled, through my exhortations, and diligence, and earnest admonition, to recall his people to communion and fellowship. For since you have, as I said, but one faith, and one sentiment respecting our religion, and since the Divine commandment in all its parts enjoins on us all the duty of maintaining a spirit of concord, let not the circumstance which has led to a slight difference between you, since it does not affect the validity of the whole, cause any division or schism among you. And this I say without in any way desiring to force you to entire unity of judgment in regard to this truly idle question, whatever its real nature may be. For the dignity of your synod may be preserved, and the communion of your whole body maintained unbroken, however wide a difference may exist among you as to unimportant matters. For we are not all of us like-minded on every subject, nor is there such a thing as one disposition and judgment common to all alike. As far, then, as regards the Divine Providence, let there be one faith, and one understanding among you, one united judgment in reference to God. But as to your subtle disputations on questions of little or no significance, though you may be unable to harmonize in sentiment, such differences should be consigned to the secret custody of your own minds and thoughts. And now, let the preciousness of common affection, let faith in the truth, let the honor due to God and to the observance of his law continue immovably among you. Resume, then, your mutual feelings of friendship, love, and regard: restore to the people their wonted embracings; and do ye yourselves, having purified your souls, as it were, once more acknowledge one another. For it often happens that when a reconciliation is effected by the removal of the causes of enmity, friendship becomes even sweeter than it was before.

Chapter lxxii.—The Excess of his Pious Concern caused him to shed Tears; and his Intended Journey to the East was postponed because of These Things.

"Restore me then my quiet days, and untroubled nights, that the joy of undimmed light, the delight of a tranquil life, may henceforth be my portion. Else must I needs mourn, with constant tears, nor shall I be able to pass the residue of my days in peace. For while the people of God, whose fellow-servant I am, are thus divided amongst themselves by an unreasonable and pernicious spirit of contention, how is it possible that I shall be able to maintain tranquillity of mind? And I will give you a proof how great my sorrow has been on this behalf. Not long since I had visited Nicomedia, and intended forthwith to proceed from that city to the East. It was while I was hastening towards you, and had already accomplished the greater part of the distance, that the news of this matter reversed my plan, that I might not be compelled to see with my own eyes that which I felt myself scarcely able even to hear. Open then for me henceforward by your unity of judgment that road to the regions of the East which your dissensions have closed against me, and permit me speedily to see yourselves and all other peoples rejoicing together, and render due acknowledgment to God in the language of praise and thanksgiving for the restoration of general concord and liberty to all."

Chapter lxxiii.—The Controversy continues without Abatement, even after the Receipt of This Letter.

In this manner the pious emperor endeavored by means of the foregoing letter to promote the peace of the Church of God. And the excellent man to whom it was intrusted performed his part not merely by communicating the letter itself, but also by seconding the views of him who sent it; for he was, as I have said, in all respects a person of pious character. The evil, however, was greater than could be remedied by a single letter, insomuch that the acrimony of the contending parties continually increased, and the effects of the mischief extended to all the Eastern provinces. These things jealousy and some evil spirit who looked with an envious eye on the prosperity of the Church, wrought.

Book III

Chapter vi.—How he ordered a Council to be held at Nicaea.

Then as if to bring a divine array against this enemy, he convoked a general council, and invited the speedy attendance of bishops from all quarters, in letters expressive of the honorable estimation in which he held them. Nor was this merely the issuing of a bare command, but the emperor's good will contributed much to its being carried into effect: for he allowed some the use of the public means of conveyance, while he afforded to others an ample supply of horses for their transport. The place, too, selected for the synod, the city Nicaea in Bithynia (named from "Victory"), was appropriate to the occasion. As soon then as the imperial injunction was generally made known, all with the utmost willingness hastened thither, as though they would outstrip one another in a race; for they were impelled by the anticipation of a happy result to the conference, by the hope of enjoying present peace, and the desire of beholding something new and strange in the person of so admirable an emperor. Now when they were all assembled, it appeared evident that the proceeding was the work of God, inasmuch as men who had been most widely separated, not merely in sentiment, but also personally, and by difference of country, place, and nation, were here brought together, and comprised within the walls of a single city, forming as it were a vast garland of priests, composed of a variety of the choicest flowers.

B. Constantine, Letter to the Church of Alexandria

Constantine Augustus to the catholic church of Alexandrians, greeting, beloved brethren.

At the command of God, the splendor of truth has dissipated and overwhelmed those dissensions, schisms, tumults and, so to speak, fatal poisons of discord. Now we all worship by name the one God and believe that he is. But in order that this might come to pass, I assembled, by God's direction, at the city of Nicaea a great number of bishops, in company with whom I myself also, who am but one of you and who rejoice exceedingly to be your fellow-servant, undertook to investigate the truth. So all points which seemed by their ambiguity to furnish excuse for disputation we have discussed and clearly explained. . . . When, then, more than three hundred bishops, renowned for their wisdom and acumen, had confirmed one and the same faith, which according to the true and unerring law of God is the faith, it was discovered that Arius alone was deceived by the machinations of the devil and was the disseminator of mischief by his impious opinions, first among you and later among others also. . . . Now that which has proved itself acceptable to the three hundred bishops is no other than the doctrine of God. . . .

14. THE WEST AND GREGORY THE GREAT[1]

Among the leading authorities in this country on church history F. J. Foakes Jackson occupies a high rank. He is especially well qualified to speak on the early Christian Church and the Church Fathers. He writes, moreover, in such a clear style that the following selection by him on the Western Church and Gregory the Great will need no further introduction.

While ecclesiastical dogma was being hardened into a definite creed the Roman world was slowly dissolving. The battle of Hadrianople, where the Emperor Valens and his army were annihilated in 378, was in a sense the beginning of the end. The victorious Goths then reached the suburbs of Constantinople but advanced no further. During the reign of Theodosius the Great, the barbarians, on the whole, respected the frontiers of the empire. The crisis came about 410, when the Visigothic King Alaric captured Rome. The Roman legions were withdrawn from Britain, and the island was left to intestine discord and foreign invasion. The Goths, a Teutonic people, set up kingdoms in Gaul and Spain. Then came the terrible Vandal invasion of Africa and the establishment of the pirate kingdom of Carthage. In 455 Genseric the Vandal took Rome. But before this a more terrible enemy had appeared, in Attila and the Huns, wild Mongolian horsemen, whose fast hordes from a world unknown to the Romans carried ruin and desolation far and wide. Under the feeble rule of Theodosius II Attila's progress was unchecked, but when his sister Pulcheria raised her husband Marcian to the purple manlier counsels prevailed, and the Huns were defeated by the Roman general, Aetius, and the Visigothic king, Theodoric, at the great battle of Châlons in the year 451.

In the west the empire was in the throes of dissolution—Africa, Spain, and Britain were lost. In Italy barbarian generals set up puppet emperors only to dethrone them. At last in 476 Odoacer, a barbarian chief, the real master of Italy, deprived Romulus Augustulus of the imperial dignity, sending the insignia of the empire to the Eastern emperor, Zeno, with a message that one ruler of the Roman world was sufficient. From this time a barbarian king ruled with an authority nominally delegated to him by the emperor at Constantinople. Odoacer was supplanted by Theodoric the Ostro-

[1] *An Outline of Christianity,* New York, Bethlehem Publishers, 1926, vol. II, pp. 149–158. This section is by F. J. Foakes Jackson. Reprinted by permission of Bethlehem Publishers, Inc., and Dodd, Mead & Co.

goth, under whom civilization was for a time fostered and preserved in Italy, but whose glorious reign was succeeded by a period of uninterrupted misery and disaster.

From 476 to 521 the world was almost entirely under the sway of Arians. All the barbarians, Visigoths, Ostrogoths, and Vandals professed Arianism. Not that they could appreciate the intricate subtleties of the Greek language or the technical terms which separated those who held the Creed of Nicaea from the followers of Arius, but because they had received their Christianity from Arian missionaries, and perhaps because they disdained to worship with the despised Roman provincials. In Africa the orthodox were subjected to a cruel persecution by their Vandal overlords. Roman orthodoxy was isolated from the Christianity professed in the East as well as from that of the barbarians, till it received the support of an uncivilized race hitherto almost unknown.

On the northern frontier of Gaul the Franks were ruled by a ferocious and very able king named Clovis, who accepted baptism (496) at the hands of an orthodox bishop, St. Remigius, Bishop of Rheims, and was admitted by him to the Church with the words: "Bow thine head, Sicambrian, adore what thou hast burned, and burn what thou hast adored."

Clovis embraced the faith with ardor. When he heard the story of the Passion and Crucifixion, he exclaimed: "Had I and my Franks been there, it never would have happened!" He resolved to become the champion of the true faith. "It is a cause of great sorrow to me that these Arians should possess the best part of Gaul," he declared; "come, and with God's help, we will drive them out." He went forth conquering and to conquer, and in the end established the great kingdom of the Franks. The Goths, Eastern and Western, had disappeared. The Franks were the one barbarian nation destined to survive the chaos which followed the fall of the Western empire. That they did so was due to the close and lasting alliance which they formed with Roman Christianity.

In recalling the empire's misfortunes in the West, it must not be forgotten that in the East it retained its inherent vitality for centuries, and when all seemed lost it was capable of suddenly asserting its strength. The genius of Diocletian, and after him of Constantine, was displayed in their recognizing that the heart of the empire was no longer in Italy but in Asia Minor, and when Constantine made Byzantium impregnable as Constantinople, he thereby saved civilization for centuries. Under a vigorous administration Constantinople was capable of dominating the Mediterranean seaboard; this was proved by the long reign of Justinian, the builder of the Church of St. Sophia and the man who has left an imperishable memorial in the consolidation of Roman law familiarly known as the Code of Justinian. Under Justinian the Persians were confined to the frontier, Africa was recovered from the Vandals, and Italy from the Ostrogoths, and his reign was made glorious by the exploits of Belisarius, one of the greatest of Roman generals. For though much has been written of the degeneracy of the Roman armies, then and for generations to come, when properly led, they were more than a match for any barbarian force however numerous.

The war between the Romans of Constantinople and the Ostrogoths proved the ruin of Rome and of Italy. Rome was taken and retaken by Belisarius and the barbarian kings; the aqueducts were destroyed, and Rome was at one time left without a single inhabitant. The city remained with its splendid edifices deserted even though not demolished. Italy, except for the cities in the south and on the Adriatic coast, had become almost desolate; nor were matters improved when it was restored to the empire, and what the barbarian had spared became the prey of the imperial tax-gatherer. It was left open to another barbarian incursion—that of the Lombards, who like the Franks became a powerful influence on the destinies of Europe.

In these days of misery and desolation Italy produced two men who may justly be considered the founders of medieval Christian civilization; first the monk, St. Benedict of Nursia, and two generations afterwards, the pope, Gregory the Great. Never, either in the days of its greatest glory in the past or in the splendid future which lay before it, did the soil of Italy give birth to men who more powerfully affected the destiny of the world.

About 520, Benedict, a mere youth, accompanied by his faithful nurse, fled to the deserted country where the ruins of Nero's summer palace were still standing. Living as a hermit, he attracted first the admiration and finally the enmity of the monks of the neighborhood. Seven monasteries were founded by him; and for these he provided his famous Rule as to how monks should live. Severe and almost impossible to observe according to modern standards, his regulations were neither inhuman nor unreasonable. Benedict discouraged fantastic austerities. He combined strenuous work with constant devotion; he advocated cheerfulness and contentment. His monks were to cultivate the soil and to employ themselves in such work as they had been accustomed to by their earlier training. Other monasteries adopted the Rule, and before long learning as well as manual labor was encouraged under it. The Benedictines have maintained their ascendancy as the most learned as well as the most ancient order in the West to this day. Their Rule became the basis of all subsequent monastic regulations, and all later Western orders were the legitimate outcome of the work of Benedict.

Across the Alps was the great Frankish kingdom, orthodox in faith if not in practice. The successors of Clovis seem to have combined the worst features of Teutonic barbarism and Roman civilization. Their record is one of savage warfare among brothers who partitioned the dominion, of repeated acts of brutality, and ferocious reprisals in which the women of the family showed the same bloodthirst as the men. By degrees the descendants of Clovis, or Merovingians, as they were called, from their remote ancestor, the sea-monster Merovich, sank to being kings in name only, and the real power was exercised by their chief ministers, who bore the title of Mayor of the Palace.

But a real Christian civilization was developing in a country to which the Roman conqueror had never penetrated; men in Ireland were rivalling Benedict himself in their monastic zeal. The Scots—for by this name the inhabitants of the island were then generally known—had already filled their land with monks, many of whom were distinguished by their love of learning, the fostering of an art of their own, and above all for their missionary zeal. Irish monks, such as St. Columban and St. Gall, were to be found throughout Europe; Irish missionaries, notably St. Columba of Iona, were planting their settlements about Scotland as well as in the Orkney Islands and the Hebrides. From their island home at Hii (Iona) men were preparing to convert the Anglian kingdoms of northern England. The Christianity of the Irish was in many respects of native growth; it differed from that of the rest of Christendom in trifling, but to the men of that age important, observances, but its fervor was as unquestionable as its learning was superior to that of the rest of the West.

Towards the close of the sixth century the Roman Church was ruled by Gregory I, a pope (590–604) who, if his personal character and the circumstances of his age be taken into account, is perhaps the greatest of all those who filled the chair of St. Peter. Judged by the most modern standard Gregory was a true saint. Here and there his judgment may have been at fault, and he may have displayed an excess of credulity. But if fervent devotion, humility combined with dignity, purity of life and intention, delicate consideration for the feelings of others, unbounded charity, missionary zeal, and the gift of ruling men by love, make a saint, Gregory the Great is a saint indeed.

Gregory's early life qualified him for the part he had to play in the world, not only as pope but as statesman. He was by birth a Roman noble and filled the high office of prefect of the city. Fired with enthusiasm for the monastic life, he sold his property and devoted himself to religion in his own monastery dedicated to St. Andrew on the Coelian Hill. But his abilities were too great to allow him to remain in obscurity, and he was sent to represent the Roman Church in Constantinople. There he gained his experience of the government of the empire at headquarters and saw the magnificent ecclesiastical life in New Rome in marked contrast with the poverty of his native city. On his return to Italy he was elected pope. Rome was in a sad plight, ravaged by the plague and exposed to constant danger by the Lombard invaders of Italy. Gregory's first task was to save the inhabitants. Like a true Roman he provided the same remedy for the plague as his ancestors had done in the days of the republic. He decreed a ceremony which in ancient days would have been called a *supplicatio,* only with him the solemn procession was from one Christian church to another. A popular legend says that as Gregory passed the Arch of Trajan he was reminded that the emperor had once put off starting on his campaign to hear a widow's complaint. With the instinct of a genuine Roman Gregory admired so fine an act of justice. But he knew that Trajan as a pagan was a lost soul, and full of compassion he prayed to God to save him. His prayer was heard, but he was warned not to intercede for a heathen again. This story is alluded to by Dante, who discovered Trajan in heaven among the just rulers of the world.

In dealing with the Lombards who had invaded Italy after the expulsion of the Ostrogoths, Gregory was in a difficult position. The imperial government at Constantinople was powerless to protect Rome against the barbarians and at the same time jealous of any interference with its prerogatives. Gregory incurred the enmity of the Emperor Maurice (582–602) by arranging a truce which saved the city. The fact is that Gregory had, long before the popes received temporal dominion, become the real mouthpiece of Roman civilization in Italy.

Necessity also compelled him to take the place of the ancient emperors in providing food for the people. Rome was now surrounded by uncultivated lands and had no industries. The population was largely clerical, and religion was the only attraction which drew people within its walls. The population, meager indeed compared to the days of prosperity, had to be fed, and the pope was the only person who could find it sustenance. The estates of the Church were immense and lay in all parts of the empire, but it taxed all Gregory's prudence to make their income sufficient to meet the necessary expenditure. A great part of his correspondence, which has survived, relates to the administration of the papal properties. In this the pope is revealed as a man of affairs. He is careful to see that the Church is not defrauded, and equally solicitous for the welfare of its tenants. The smallest details do not escape his notice, and his letters show him careful in his management as well as thoughtful for the needs of others.

With all his wisdom, Gregory represents not only the piety but the superstition of his age. One of his best-known works is the "Dialogues." The book opens with the Deacon Peter finding the pope in his garden, wearied with the business of the day. In their conversation Peter adverts to the evil days into which the Church is fallen. Gregory cheers him by relating wonders which God has wrought, even in the not-distant past. The "Dialogues" is a series of miraculous stories, visions, supernatural cures, punishments, blessings, and the like. The pope had a firm belief in relics and their efficacy, and as custodian of some of the most precious in the world he dispensed fragments of them to kings, princes, and bishops with pious parsimony. The power of a relic, like the chain which bound St. Peter, was as great to injure the profane as to benefit the devout. Once the empress asked of Gregory to send her no less a relic than the head of the Apostle Paul, and Gregory replied that it was impossible to remove so sacred an object without danger of vengeance from the saint. The great pope in this respect represented his age and influenced posterity. . . .

It was incumbent on every pope to assert the dignity of the Roman See. The pride of Constantinople caused Gregory no little anxiety when its patriarch styled himself Universal (ecumenical) Bishop. Gregory considered it wrong for any bishop to assert so much superiority over his brethren —and reproved John the Faster, for so the Bishop of Constantinople, who assumed the title, was called. It is interesting to notice that Gregory refused to be thus designated, though his successors did not hesitate to assert their right to the epithet Universal. The fact is Gregory was too great a ruler to care for what men styled him. He was concerned with weightier matters, as is seen in his successful scheme to add a new country to the Christian world, his greatest exploit being the founding of the Anglo-Saxon Church.

The story of the conversion of the Teutonic invaders of England is one of the most instructive in the whole of missionary enterprise. Two forms of Christianity, widely separated from one another, the Roman and the Celtic, working independently, succeeded in making the whole island Christian. Columba (521–597), who founded the monastery of Iona, created a center from which the Celtic missionaries were later destined to begin the work in northern England. He died the very year in which Gregory's monks settled at Canterbury to commence their evangelistic efforts.

According to the beautiful story related by the Venerable Bede in his "History of the Nation of the Angles," Gregory, before he became pope, had seen boys from Deira (Yorkshire) in the slave-market of Rome. He asked who they were; and when he heard they were "Angles," "Not Angles but Angels," was his reply.

His next question was, "Whence come they?"

"From Deira."

"Then," said Gregory, "they shall be delivered from God's anger (*de ira Dei*)." He asked the name of their king, and hearing it was "Aella," said, "Then Alleluia shall be sung in his land."

The mission was as carefully planned as it was poetically conceived. Gregory had intended to go himself to this almost unknown island, but as he was starting he saw a locust. He interpreted this as a divine warning, for the Latin *locusta* stands for *loco sta* (stay where you are). It was not till the sixth year of his pontificate that Gregory chose Augustine, prior of his own monastery on the Coelian Hill, to lead the expedition. Augustine and his companions began badly. Having heard an evil report of the incurable barbarism of the islanders, they turned back.

Gregory's elevation of character is conspicuous from his next step. Instead of reproaching Augustine he promoted him to be an abbot, bade him go forth on his mission armed with full authority over his companions, and furnished him with letters of introduction to the princes and bishops of Gaul.

The missionaries landed on the Island of Thanet to find a more promising state of affairs than they had anticipated. Ethelbert, the king of the Jutish Kingdom of Kent, was acknowledged to be the Bretwalda, that is, the most powerful in Teutonic Britain. He had married Bertha, a Frankish princess who was a Christian and still practised her religion. The mission reached Britain at Easter 597, and by Whitsuntide Ethelbert and his followers received baptism.

The Gospel at first spread rapidly: bishoprics were established at Canterbury, Ethelbert's capital, at Rochester, at London. The Roman monks pushed northward among the East Angles and finally reached Yorkshire, or Deira, the southern province of the Northumbrian Angles.

Till his death in 604 Gregory was the inspiration and director of the missionaries. He had already planned for the complete subjugation of the island to the dominion of Christ. Two new provinces were to be added to the Church, with an archbishop in the two chief cities, London and York. It was only because Augustine was given a settlement in Canterbury that it became a metropolitan see. The pope watched the growth of the native Church with anxious solicitude, constantly sending letters, books, and relics, and reinforcing it with more missionary monks. He expressed his desire that the new Church should develop on lines of its own, exhorting Augustine to introduce all those customs which he found worthy of imitation in the different churches he had visited in his travels.

But the fair prospects of the Roman mission soon became overcast. After Augustine's death in 616, London and the East Saxons apostatized, and in 633 Northumbria, which had been converted by Paulinus in 627, was lost. Gregory's mission was thus practically confined to the Kingdom of Kent. Then followed a new era of missionary enterprise. The Scottish (or Irish) monks of the north poured into Teutonic Britain; a new Roman mission led by Birinus converted the West Saxons; Felix, a Burgundian bishop, established himself at Dunwich in East Anglia.

In this way heathenism was being assailed in the island from all quarters, and within a century of Augustine's arrival Britain was at least professedly an entirely Christian land. Ireland was a veritable nursery of saints, scholars, and missionaries. Thus amid all the decay of the Roman Empire in the West, in the days in which it appeared that civilization was on the verge of hopeless dissolution, the bounds of the Christian empire were being enlarged, and one of the greatest of the Roman pontiffs had laid the foundations of medieval civilization.

15. THE RISE OF THE PAPACY. GREGORY THE GREAT.[1]

Gregorovius was a learned German historian, the distinguished author of the History of the City of Rome in the Middle ages. *One of the most illuminating sections in this monumental work is that which deals with the career of Gregory the Great, who is referred to in the foregoing selection and who was elected bishop of Rome in the year 590. The story told below not only gives an excellent description of the eminent church father, but graphically depicts conditions in the city of Rome at the close of the sixth century.*

On the death of Pelagius[2] the unanimous choice of both clergy and people fell on Gregory, a man whose memory has ever been deservedly cherished as that of one of the greatest of Popes. A member of the ancient house of the Anicii, the leading family in Rome during the later days of the Empire, he was the grandson of Pope Felix and the son of Gordianus. His mother, Silvia, owned a palace beside S. Saba on the Aventine. Two of his aunts on his father's side had entered a convent; a third sister remained, however, to enjoy the pleasures of the secular life. Gregory had grown up in an age, the most terrible of any in the city's history, when, his native country being held in subjection by the Lombards, the barbarians had appeared before the very gates of Rome, and the last remains of Latin civilisation had been sacrificed to their wild thirst for destruction. Destined in youth for a political career, Gregory had acquired all the rhetorical and dialectic education which could be furnished by Rome, where, however, the schools once protected by Theodoric can scarcely still have existed. He filled the city prefecture, an office which yet lingered on; but what could a high-minded Roman effect in the State in a time such as this? to what post of honour could he rise in the republic? The highest aim which could allure a descendant of the Anicii was the bishop's chair. Repelled by the political circumstances of the time, Gregory, like Cassiodorus, sought refuge in the habit of monasticism. "The man who had formerly been accustomed to

[1] Ferdinand Gregorovius, *History of the City of Rome in the Middle Ages*. Translated from the fourth German edition by Annie Hamilton, 8 Vols. London, George Bell and Sons, 1894, Vol. II, pp. 29–38, 40–45, 53–59. Used by permission.

[2] Pope Pelagius II, who ruled from 578 to 590 (Ed.).

parade the city in splendid silken raiment, glittering with jewels, now dedicated himself to the service of the Lord in a mean cowl." We have already heard how he spent his wealth in founding monasteries. Six he built in Sicily, a fact which proves that his family must have possessed considerable property on the island. Pelagius consecrated him deacon, and made him Nuncio at Constantinople, and Rome with unanimous voice now elected him Pope.

No one seemed better qualified to guide the Church in her distress than the most eminent and benevolent citizen and former prefect of Rome. The Pope designate, however, sought to escape his high calling, and by letter requested the Emperor Maurice (with whom he stood on friendly terms) not to ratify the election. The letters were, however, intercepted by Germanus, the City Prefect and others, containing urgent entreaties that the Emperor would confirm the election, substituted in their stead. During the vacancy of the sacred chair the administration of the Church lay in the hands of the arch-presbyter, the arch-deacon and the primicerius of the notaries, but since before being consecrated Gregory commanded a delay of three days for penitential processions to invoke Heaven for deliverance from the pestilence, it would appear that on this occasion the duty of representing the bishop devolved on him alone. The plague still continued its ravages. Gregory himself, in the penitential sermon which he delivered in S. Sabina on the 29th August, asserted that the Romans died in great numbers, and that the houses remained desolate. The procession was ordered in the following manner. The population was divided into seven groups, according to age and class. Each division assembled in a different church, and thence made a pilgrimage to one common goal, the Basilica of S. Maria (Maggiore). . . . The whole population thus joined in penitential procession, and while they marched among the ruins of the deserted city, and made the air re-echo with their solemn chants, they seemed to bear the phantom of ancient Rome herself to the grave, and to inaugurate the dreary centuries which were now to follow. The procession of 590 may in truth be regarded as the beginning of Rome's Middle Ages.

Pestilence accompanied the procession. Men fell to the earth dead. A supernatural vision, however, put an end to both litany and plague. As Gregory, heading the train of penitents, reached the bridge on the way to S. Peter's, a heavenly vision greeted the eyes of the people. The Archangel Michael descended, and, hovering over Hadrian's mausoleum, placed a flaming sword in its sheath—a sign that the plague was stayed. As early as the tenth century the mausoleum received the name of S. Angelo, in memory of this beautiful legend. The chapel on its summit, however, dedicated to S. Michael, had been of earlier origin, having been built probably in the eighth century. The bronze figure of the Archangel sheathing his sword still hovers, with outstretched wings, over Hadrian's tomb, the most wonderful of all earthly monuments.

Other legends ascribe the cessation of the pestilence to a portrait of the Virgin borne by the Pope in the procession. Of the seven pictures of the Madonna, which we owe to no less an artist than the Apostle Luke, Rome possesses four, of which that of Ara Coeli is esteemed the earliest. The silver doors of the shrine, which once enclosed the sacred picture within the Church, were likewise engraved with a representation of the legend. This work belongs to the fifteenth century, but a picture on slate, representing a procession in the act of carrying a bier across a bridge, where the fortress towers in the background, is of a later date.

The ratification of the election arrived from Constantinople, but Gregory shrank in dismay from the high mission which lay before him. He himself admits that he sought to avoid it by flight, and legend in the ninth century related that he had caused himself to be conveyed secretly from Rome by some merchants, and hidden in a wooded ravine. The citizens who followed in search were guided to his retreat by a radiant dove, or a column of light, and the reluctant candidate was led back in triumph to S. Peter's, and there consecrated Pope, 3rd Sept. 590. He found the Church, to use his own expression, an old wreck, swept by the waves on every side, and whose timbers, shaken by the storm, threatened immediate dissolution.

The desperate straits to which the city was reduced afforded him material for his first sermon. When at this moment the Roman bishop (in the truest sense of the term the priest and father of his people) ascended the pulpit, the words to which he gave utterance were indeed historic actuality. Gregory summoned the remnant of the citizens to S. Peter's and the degenerate descendants of Cicero, crowded together in the gloomy basilica, listened in feverish suspense as their forefathers had listened to the orators in the Temple of Concord.

"Our Lord," so spoke the dejected bishop, "desires to find us ready, and shows us the misery of the wornout world, in order to divert our love from it. You see how many storms have heralded its approaching overthrow. If we do not seek God in quiet, trials the most dreadful will teach us to fear His judgments. In the extract of the Gospel we have just heard, the Lord forewarns us that nation shall prevail against nation, and kingdom against kingdom, and that earthquakes, famine and pestilence, horrors and signs from heaven are in store for us. We have already been visited by some of these disasters and of others remain in dread. For that nation rises against nation and subdues the land by fear, our own experience, more forcibly than even gospel history, might have taught us. We have heard from other quarters that countless cities are destroyed by earthquakes; while we ourselves suffer incessantly from pestilence. True, we do not yet perceive signs in the sun, moon or stars, but changes in the atmosphere lead us to suppose that such signs are near at hand. Fiery swords, reddened with the blood of mankind, which soon after flowed in streams, were seen in the heaven before Italy became a prey to the Lombards. Be alert and watchful! Those who love God should shout for joy at the end of the world. Those who mourn are they whose hearts are rooted in love for the world, and who neither long for the future life, nor have any foretaste of it within themselves. Every day the earth is visited by fresh calamities. You see how few remain of the ancient population; each day sees us chastened by fresh afflictions, and unforeseen blows strike us to the ground. The world grows old and hoary, and through a sea of troubles hastens to approaching death."

Gregory's first sermon reflects the temper of his time, when Rome and mankind, although bearing within themselves so many germs of new life, were yet unable to perceive anything beyond the accumulated ruin of the Empire. In the midst of that ruin, as if waiting for death, stood the effete and worn-out Romans, but the same bishop who enjoined his flock to familiarise themselves with the idea of destruction, provided at the same time for their escape. The welfare of the city was his first care, and the times were of such a nature that the bishop was obliged to regard himself as its true regent. In the universal distress there was but one asylum, the Church, and but one helper and saviour, the Pope. Famine ruled in the deserted city; Gregory wrote to Justin, the Praetor of Sicily, which still remained the granary of Rome, for an immediate supply of grain. A small portion of this supply may have been furnished by the Emperor, but the greater part was provided by the Church from the resources of her own estate. Famine was, however, more easily averted than the terror of the enemy. . . .

The approach of the Lombards interrupted Gregory in his public explanation of Ezekiel. He himself informs us that the sight of men who had suffered mutilation, and the news of the imprisonment and deaths of others, had caused him to forsake his studies. These sermons, preached under the influence of contemporary disaster, although tinged with the colouring of rhetoric, faithfully depict the historic conditions of the time, and in the eighteenth Homily more especially we possess a picture of the period of inestimable value.

"What is there in the world," exclaims Gregory, "to gladden us? All around is mourning; all around is sighing. Cities are destroyed; fortresses levelled to the ground; farms laid waste; the earth reduced to a desert. No husbandman is left in the fields, scarcely a dweller remains in the towns, and still the small remnant of mankind is daily stricken. The chastisement of heaven is not satisfied, because the debt of sin, even under such punishments, is not wiped away. We see some led into captivity, some maimed, others put to death. We are forced to recognise the position to which Rome, once the mistress of the world, is reduced. She is bowed down by pain unfathomable, by depopulation, by the assaults of the enemy and the weight of her own ruins, so that in her seems to be fulfilled the fate which the prophet Ezekiel predicted for Samaria: 'Set on the pot, set it on, I say, and also pour water into it: gather the pieces thereof into it'; and further, 'it seethed and boiled, and its bones were cooked.' And again, 'Heap up the bones together that I may kindle them with fire; the meat shall be consumed, and the whole mass shall be cooked, and the bones shall dissolve. Set the empty pot also over the faggots, that it may become hot and that its brass may be molten.' Yes, the pot was set up for us when Rome was founded, and when people collected in the city from every quarter of the earth, and their actions seethed within her, even as hot water within the pot. Therefore, it is excellently said: 'It seethed and bubbled, and the bones were cooked in the midst thereof.' The desire for earthly glory first seethed strongly within her; although the glory itself disappeared with those who sought after it. The bones signify the powerful ones of the earth; the flesh, the nations; since as the meat is borne by the bones, so will the weakness of nations be governed by the mighty ones of the earth. But see! how all the men of the world are taken from her; the bones thereof have been dissolved. The nations have revolted; the flesh also is consumed. . . . Where is the Senate? Where is the people? The bones are dissolved, the flesh consumed. All the glory of earthly dignity has expired within the city. All her greatness has vanished, and yet the few of us that remain are daily oppressed by the sword and afflictions innumerable. Therefore it may be said: 'Set up the empty pot upon the coals thereof.' For because there is no Senate the people perished, and since the trouble and sighing of those that remain wax daily, so does the empty city already burn. But why do we speak thus of men when we see the very buildings themselves fall to pieces? Therefore of the already deserted city it is seasonably added: 'Let her become hot and her brass shall dissolve.' Already the pot, in which flesh as well as bones have previously been consumed, is itself in process of dissolution, for after the inhabitants have perished, the walls themselves fall in. Where are those who once delighted in the glory of Rome? Where is their pomp? Where their pride? Where their frequent and unmeasured delight? In them is fulfilled the saying of the prophet against Nineveh that was destroyed: 'Where is the dwelling of the lion and the feeding-place of the lion's whelps?' Were not your generals and princes the lions, who, bloodthirsty and greedy of gain, overran the whole earth in search of plunder? The young lions found their food when boys and youths, children of the worldly-minded, gathered from all sides eager to secure their temporal fortune. Behold, therefore! now is the city deserted; now is she destroyed and weighed down with groaning. None any longer hasten to her to seek their fortune in this world. No mighty men: no oppressor. Of such as acquired booty by violence, not one remains behind. Wherefore we ask, 'Where is the dwelling of the lion and the food of the young lion?' It has befallen Rome even as the prophet said of Judaea: 'Her baldness spreads like that of the eagle.' The baldness of man is confined to the head, but that of the eagle extends over the whole body, since when the eagle grows old his plumes and feathers fall from him. And like the eagle bereft of its plumage, is the baldness of the city deprived of its inhabitants. The pinions on which it was wont to fly in search of prey have fallen, now that all the heroes, by whose means the city despoiled her enemies have passed away."

The Romans, amongst whom aged men, born in the golden days of Theodoric, still lingered, must have felt their hearts fail them in despair as they listened to these utterances of pain, amid the solemn silence of the basilica, and in presence of the saints, whose stern likenesses looked down upon them from the walls. The desperate fate of the city stood like a fulfilled prophecy before their eyes. We have no more terrible picture of the condition to which Rome was reduced at the end of the sixth century than this assemblage of her citizens and the sermon of the Pope; the magnificent imagery of which, allying, as it does, the history of the capital of the Roman Empire to the prophecies of the Jews, arouses a feeling of sadness utterly tragic. It was the funeral oration pronounced by the bishop beside the grave of Rome. This bishop was her noblest patriot, the last scion of an ancient and illustrious house, and his words were instinct with the very breath of Roman patriotism.

Agilulf besieged Rome, but without energy; else were it impossible that the city could have withstood the attack, when, according to Gregory's assertion, "being thinly populated and devoid of military aid," it was thrown on the protection of S. Peter or of God. As the Pope mounted to the battlements of the now tottering walls of Aurelian and Belisarius he beheld with his own eyes Roman citizens, coupled together like dogs, led captive by the Lombards, to be sold as slaves in Gaul, and while the Prefect Gregory and the Magister Militum Castorius, the only Imperial officials of rank in the city, conducted the doubtful defence, the repeated assaults against the gates may well have struck him with dismay. Neither to the vigilance of the defenders, nor to the endurance of the citizens, but to the coffers of the Church was due the withdrawal of the enemy, and Gregory, writing later to the Empress Constantina, terms himself with an ironical sigh, "the paymaster of the Lombards, under whose swords the Roman people only preserved its life thanks to the daily ransom paid by the Church."

. . . .

Gregory's influence far outweighed the power of the Imperial officials, the Romans reverencing their master and preserver in a Pope who united in his person the episcopal dignity and the renown of illustrious descent. Since the fall of the Gothic kingdom had extinguished the last remains of public life in the city, Rome had suffered a complete transformation. Neither consuls, senate, nor games recalled the temporal dominion; the patrician families had almost entirely disappeared. Gregory's letters seldom speak of any of the wealthy houses of ancient descent, except of such as had removed to Constantinople, while time-honoured names are discovered connected with estates which already belonged to the Church. Religious interests had completely thrust civic affairs into the background, and as we have already seen, the Roman people had adopted an entirely spiritual garb. There were no longer any public festivals but those of the Church. The only events which occupied the minds of the indolent people were of a spiritual nature The Church had already become a great asylum for society. Under the influence of natural disasters, hitherto unparalleled, and of the horrors of war, the belief in the approaching end of the world had gained universal acceptance, and the crowd of men anxious to enter convents and the ranks of the priesthood assumed overwhelming proportions. The needy there found food and shelter; the ambitious, dignity and rank, in an age when the titles of deacon, presbyter and bishop had become for the Romans what those of praetor, tribune and consul had formerly been esteemed. Even soldiers deserted their colours for the tonsure, and the candidates for ecclesiastical offices were in all classes so numerous, that Gregory strove to enforce some restraint, while the Emperor Maurice, by an edict of 592, forbade soldiers from entering the cloister and civil officials from being nominated to ecclesiastical offices. Roman poverty did not stretch out its hands in vain for the treasures of the Church. The times when the consul scattered gold among the people, when the prefect provided for the public distributions of corn, meat, oil and lard from the coffers of the State, no longer existed, and the cry of the people for *"Panem et Circenses"* made itself half-heard. They desired bread, and the Pope gave it abundantly. Even as a monk in his cell on the Clivus Scauri Gregory had daily fed the poor; as Pope he still ministered to their necessities. At the beginning of every month he distributed corn, clothes, and gold to the needy, and at each of the great festivals bestowed gifts on the Church and on charitable institutions. Like Titus, he held the day lost on which he had not satisfied hunger and clothed nakedness, and once, hearing that a beggar had died in the streets, he shut himself up, filled with remorse, and did not venture to approach the altar, as priest, for several days.

The public distribution of corn had in ancient times been made from porticos, theatres, and the granaries of the State. The Romans now thronged to the porches of convents and basilicas to receive food and clothing from spiritual officials. The crowds of pilgrims from beyond the seas found the ancient house in Portus, erected for their use by the Senator Pammachius, the friend of S. Jerome, ready for their reception, and on reaching Rome, whether as pilgrims or as fugitives seeking protection from the Lombards, received food and lodging in the hospitals, or in quarters provided for the purpose. Christian benevolence exercised true charity in the relief of genuine distress.

The property which gradually accrued to the Church in gifts and legacies from private individuals was conscientiously devoted by Gregory to charitable objects. And the ecclesiastical possessions were already so vast and numerous that the Pope, if not as yet wielding authority over dukedoms, had at least become the richest landowner in Italy. Possessor of the estates which the Church inherited in the peninsula, and exercising over them a definite though limited jurisdiction, he appeared in the light of a great temporal prince. The property of the Roman Church, assigned to the Apostle Peter, was scattered over various countries. It consisted of vast patrimonies or domains in Sicily and Campania, over the whole of Southern Italy, in Dalmatia, Illyria, Gaul, Sardinia, Corsica, Liguria, and the Cottian Alps. And, as a king sends ministers into his provinces, the Pope sent deacons and sub-deacons (*rectores patrimonii*), officials who united the attributes of spiritual with those of temporal overseers, or government councillors. The accounts of these officials were severely scrutinised, for Gregory possessed too strict a sense of honour to permit the ecclesiastical treasury to be polluted by questionable gains.

The many letters which he addressed to these rectors of patrimonies give an insight into the condition of the Roman peasant, such as it remained for several centuries. The property of the Church was cultivated by *coloni,* men bound to the soil, who paid a tax in money or in kind. It was usually named *pensio,* and collected by *conductores* or farmers of revenue. These officials frequently extorted half the gains of the coloni, and while they arbitrarily raised the measure of corn, at times compelled the peasants to increase the "modius" from the legitimate 16 sextarii, or 24 Roman pounds, to 25 sextarii, and out of 20 bushels of grain to surrender one. Gregory taxed these oppressions, fixing the modius decisively at 18 sextarii, and decreeing that out of 35 bushels one only was to be given up. These regulations affected Sicily, still the granary of Rome, from which regularly twice in the year, in spring and autumn, a fleet of corn sailed to Portus to supply the storehouses of the city. Were supplies lost at sea, the loss fell upon the poor coloni, amongst whom the compensation was divided; and Gregory warned the rectors not to delay the voyage beyond the favourable season, otherwise the loss would be ascribed to them. The economical regulations were exemplary. A register was kept for each colonus, called *Libellus securitatis.* This register stated the price paid, and to it the colonus could appeal. Had a failure of harvest or other misfortune befallen him, he might reckon on the equity of the Pope to accord him a new inventory of cows, sheep, and swine. S. Peter's estates in Sicily prospered, and many salutary improvements were instituted. The great Pope proved himself an excellent landlord, and, when sitting his horse in a procession, might have boasted that his palfrey was provided by the same ancient Trinacria, the renowned horses of which had once been the theme of Pindar's song. We cherish some doubts, however, as to whether Pindar would have considered the descendant race of apostolic steeds worthy of an ode. "Thou hast sent me," Gregory once wrote to the sub-deacon, Peter, "a miserable horse and five good asses. The horse I cannot ride, because he is wretched, nor mount the asses, because they are asses."

16. GIBBON'S VIEW OF BYZANTINE HISTORY [1]

The history of the Byzantine Empire, as that history is commonly understood, begins with the time when Constantine the Great in the early part of the fourth century moved the capital of his empire from Rome to Byzantium, which he renamed Constantinople, on the shores of the Bosphorus, and lasts until the capture of the city by the Turks in 1453. From one point of view the so-called Byzantine Empire was a continuation of the old Roman Empire and some writers have therefore called it the Eastern Roman Empire or the Later Roman Empire. But it should be remembered that Byzantine civilization is fundamentally Greek rather than Roman and that it was affected as well by oriental, early Christian and even barbarian influences.

Edward Gibbon considered that the history of the Byzantine Empire was dull, dreary and of little importance. This was the view commonly held in Gibbon's time.

I have now deduced from Trajan to Constantine, from Constantine to Heraclius, the regular series for the Roman emperors; and faithfully exposed the prosperous and adverse fortunes of their reigns. Five centuries of the decline and fall of the empire have already elapsed; but a period of more than eight hundred years still separates me from the term of my labors, the taking of Constantinople by the Turks. Should I persevere in the same course, should I observe the same measure, a prolix and slender thread would be spun through many a volume, nor would the patient reader find an adequate reward of instruction or amusement. At every step, as we sink deeper in the decline and fall of the Eastern empire, the annals of each

[1] Edward Gibbon, *The History of the Decline and Fall of the Roman Empire.* With notes by Dean Milman, M. Guizot and Dr. William Smith, 6 vols. New York, Harper and Brothers (no date), vol. V, pp. 13–15.

succeeding reign would impose a more ungrateful and melancholy task. These annals must continue to repeat a tedious and uniform tale of weakness and misery; the natural connection of causes and events would be broken by frequent and hasty transitions, and a minute accumulation of circumstances must destroy the light and effect of those general pictures which compose the use and ornament of a remote history. From the time of Heraclius, the Byzantine theatre is contracted and darkened: the line of empire which had been defined by the laws of Justinian and the arms of Belisarius, recedes on all sides from our view; the Roman name, the proper subject of our inquiries, is reduced to a narrow corner of Europe, to the lonely suburbs of Constantinople; and the fate of the Greek empire has been compared to that of the Rhine, which loses itself in the sands, before its waters can mingle with the ocean. The scale of dominion is diminished to our view by the distance of time and place; nor is the loss of external splendor compensated by the nobler gifts of virtue and genius. In the last moments of her decay, Constantinople was doubtless more opulent and populous than Athens at her most flourishing aera, when a scanty sum of six thousand talents, or twelve hundred thousand pounds sterling, was possessed by twenty-one thousand male citizens of an adult age. But each of these citizens was a freeman who dared to assert the liberty of his thoughts, words, and actions, whose person and property were guarded by equal law; and who exercised his independent vote in the government of the republic. Their numbers seem to be multiplied by the strong and various discriminations of character; under the shield of freedom, on the wings of emulation and vanity, each Athenian aspired to the level of the national dignity; from this commanding eminence, some chosen spirits soared beyond the reach of a vulgar eye; and the chances of superior merit in a great and populous kingdom, as they are proved by experience, would excuse the computation of imaginary millions. The territories of Athens, Sparta, and their allies, do not exceed a moderate province of France or England; but after the trophies of Salamis and Platea, they expand in our fancy to the gigantic size of Asia, which had been trampled under the feet of the victorious Greeks. But the subjects of the Byzantine empire, who assume and dishonor the names both of Greeks and Romans, present a dead uniformity of abject vices, which are neither softened by the weakness of humanity, nor animated by the vigor of memorable crimes. The freemen of antiquity might repeat with generous enthusiasm the sentence of Homer, "that on the first day of his servitude, the captive is deprived of one-half of his manly virtue." But the poet had only seen the effects of civil or domestic slavery, nor could he foretell that the second moiety of manhood must be annihilated by the spiritual despotism which shackles not only the actions, but even the thoughts, of the prostrate votary. By this double yoke, the Greeks were oppressed under the successors of Heraclius; the tyrant, a law of eternal justice, was degraded by the vices of his subjects; and on the throne, in the camp, in the schools, we search, perhaps with fruitless diligence, the names and characters that may deserve to be rescued from oblivion. Nor are the defects of the subject compensated by the skill and variety of the painters. Of a space of eight hundred years, the four first centuries are overspread with a cloud interrupted by some faint and broken rays of historic light: in the lives of the emperors, from Maurice to Alexius, Basil the Macedonian has alone been the theme of a separate work; and the absence, or loss, or imperfection of contemporary evidence, must be poorly supplied by the doubtful authority of more recent compilers. The four last centuries are exempt from the reproach of penury; and with the Comnenian family, the historic muse of Constantinople again revives, but her apparel is gaudy, her motions are without elegance or grace. A succession of priests, or courtiers, treads in each other's footsteps in the same path of servitude and superstition: their views are narrow, their judgment is feeble or corrupt: and we close the volume of copious barrenness, still ignorant of the causes of events, the characters of the actors, and the manners of the times, which they celebrate or deplore. The observation which has been applied to a man, may be extended to a whole people, that the energy of the sword is communicated to the pen; and it will be found by experience, that the tone of history will rise or fall with the spirit of the age.

17. THE BYZANTINE EMPIRE AND ITS SIGNIFICANCE[1]

Frederic Harrison, historian and thinker of the Victorian era, held quite a different view of the thousand years and more of Byzantine history from that of Gibbon. In a lecture given at Cambridge University in 1900 he brings out clearly and forcefully the achievements of Byzantine civilization, a civilization which he holds to have been unfairly neglected and unduly depreciated by earlier historians.

In reading this selection, however, the student will do well to bear in mind the following comment of one of America's ablest historical scholars, Henry Osborn Taylor:

"Find what interest one may in medieval Byzantium,—and it is full of instruction,—still it is a tale of what had reached its zenith, of what was past its best strength, a tale of decadence postponed with skill and energy, and yet only postponed."

[1] Frederic Harrison, *Byzantine History in the Early Middle Ages*. The Rede Lecture, delivered in the Senate House, Cambridge, June 12, 1900. London, Macmillan and Co., 1900; reprinted in F. Harrison, *Among my Books*, London, Macmillan and Co., 1912, pp. 180–212. By permission of The Macmillan Company, publishers.

In one of the most suggestive of his essays, Professor Freeman calls the Roman Empire on the Bosporus "the surest witness to the unity of history." And Professor Bury, whose great work has done so much to develop that truth, insists that the old Roman Empire did not cease to exist until the year 1453, when Mohammed the Conqueror stormed Constantinople. The line of Roman emperors, he says, "continued in unbroken succession from Octavius Augustus to Constantine Palaeologus." Since George Finlay, nearly fifty years ago, first urged this truth on public attention, all competent historians have recognised the continuity of the civilisation which Constantine seated on the Golden Horn; and they have done justice to its many services to the West as well as to the East. But the nature of that continuity, the extent of these services, are still but dimly understood by the general public. Prejudice, bigotry, and rhetoric have done much to warp the popular conception of one of the chief keys to general history. In spite of all that scholars have said, the old sophism lingers on that the empire and civilisation of Rome ended with Romulus Augustulus in 476, until, in a sense, it was revived by the great Charles; that, in the meanwhile, a vicious and decaying parody of the Empire eked out its contemptible life on the Bosporus.

Such was the language of the popular writers of the last century, and Gibbon himself did something to encourage this view. When in his 48th chapter, he talked of Byzantine annals as "a tedious and uniform tale of weakness and misery," and saw that he still had more than eight centuries of the history of the world to compress into his last two volumes, we suspect that the great master of description was beginning to feel exhausted by his gigantic task. In any case, his undervaluing Byzantine history as a whole is the main philosophical weakness of his magnificent work of art. The phrases of Voltaire, Lebeau, and of papal controversialists still linger in the public mind; and in the meantime there exists no adequate history in English of the whole course of the Roman Empire on the Bosporus. This still forms the great *lacuna* in our historical literature.

Modern historians continually warn their readers to cast off the obsolete fallacy that a gulf of so-called dark ages separates ancient from modern history; that ancient history closes with the settlement of the Goths in Rome, whilst modern history mysteriously emerges somewhere in the ninth or tenth century. We all know now that, when the northern races settled in Western Europe, they assimilated much that they inherited from Rome. In truth, the Roman Empire, transplanted on to the Bosporus, maintained for many centuries an unbroken sequence of imperial life; retaining, transforming, and in part even developing, the administrative system, the law, the literature, the arts of war, the industry, the commerce, which had once been concentrated by the Caesars in Italy. After all the researches of

Finlay, Freeman, Bryce, Hodgkin, Bury, Fisher, Oman, Dill, to say nothing of a crowd of French, German, Italian and Russian specialists, we must regard these facts as amongst the truisms of general history.

The continuity of government and civilisation in the Empire of New Rome was far more real than it was in Western Europe. New Rome never suffered such abrupt breaks, dislocations, such changes of local seat, of titular and official form, of language, race, law, and manners, as marked the re-settlement of Western Europe. For eleven centuries Constantinople remained the continuous seat of an imperial Christian government, during nine centuries of which its administrative sequence was hardly broken. For nine centuries, until the piratical raid of the Crusaders, Constantinople preserved Christendom, industry, the machinery of government, and civilisation from successive torrents of barbarians. For seven centuries it protected Europe from the premature invasions of the Crescent; giving very much in the meantime to the East, receiving very much from the East, and acting as the intellectual and industrial clearing-house between Europe and Asia. For at least five centuries, from the age of Justinian, it was the nurse of the arts, of manufacture, commerce, and literature, to Western Europe, where all these were still in the making. And it was the direct and immediate source of civilisation, whether secular or religious, to the whole of Eastern Europe, from the Baltic to the Ionian Sea.

In picturesque and impressive incidents, in memorable events and dominant characters, in martial achievement and in heroic endurance, perhaps even in sociologic lessons, Byzantine history from the first Constantine to the last is as rich as the contemporary history either of the West or of the East. It would be a paradox to compare the great Charles, or the great Otto, or our own blameless Alfred, with even the best of the Byzantine rulers of their age, or to place such men as Gregory the Great, or Popes Silvester or Hildebrand, below even the best of the Partriarchs of the Holy Wisdom. Nor have the Orthodox Church or the Eastern Romans such claims on the gratitude of mankind as are due to the Church Catholic and the Teutonic heroes who founded modern Europe. But the three centuries of Byzantine history from the rise of the Isaurian dynasty in 717 down to the last of the Basilian emperors in 1028, will be found as well worthy of study as the same three centuries in Western Europe, *i.e.* from the age of Charles Martel to that of Henry the Saint.

During those three centuries at least, the eighth, ninth, and tenth, the Emperors of New Rome ruled over a settled State which, if not as powerful in arms, was far more rich in various resources, more cultured, more truly modern, than any in Western Europe. I am not about to attempt, in the short space at my disposal, even a brief sketch of these three centuries of crowded story. I purpose only to touch on some of the special features of its civilisation and culture, which, for the three centuries so often called the darkest ages of Europe, made Constantinople the wonder and envy of the world. Byzantine history has its epochs of ebb and flow, of decay, convulsion, anarchy, and recovery, as had the empire at Old Rome. This Roman Empire was the most continuous institution in Europe, next after the Catholic Church; and, like the Church, it had the same marvellous recuperative energy. It is true that it had none of the latent power of growth which Frank, Lombard, Burgundian, and Saxon possessed. It was from first to last a conservative, tenacious, and more or less stationary force. But it kept alive the principles of order, stability, and continuity, in things material and in things intellectual, when all around it, on the east and on the west, was racked with the throes of new birth or tossed in a weltering chaos. Byzantine story is stained red with blood, is black with vice, is disfigured with accumulated waste and horror—but what story of the eighth, ninth, and tenth centuries is not so disfigured and stained? And even the atrocities of Constantinople may be matched in the history of the Papacy in these very ages, and in the intrigues and conspiracies which raged around the thrones of Frank, Lombard, Burgundian, and Goth.

Strangely enough, the inner life of this Byzantine history has yet to be opened to the English reader. For these three centuries that I am treating, Finlay has given us about 400 pages; and Finlay, alas, is no longer abreast of modern authorities, and was writing, let us remember, the history of Greece. Mr. Bury's two volumes stop short as yet with Irene at the end of the eighth century, and Dr. Hodgkin has drawn rein at the same date. For the period I am treating, we have but a hundred pages or so in Mr. Bury's second volume, and the mordant epigrams of Gibbon are about of equal bulk. For the law, the literature, the economics, the administration, the ceremonial, the art, the trade, the manners, the theology of this epoch we have to depend on a mass of foreign monographs,—French, German, Greek, and now Russian and American,—on Rambaud, Schlumberger, Labarte, Bayet, Zachariae, Krumbacher, Heimbach, Krause, Neander, Salzenberg, Huebsch, Kondakov, De Vogüé, Bordier, Texier, Hergenröther, Heyd, Fr. Michel, Silvestre, Didron, Mortreuil, Duchesne, Paspates, Buzantios, Van Millingen, Frothingham. So far as I know, we had not, in 1900, a single English study on the special developments of civilisation on the Bosporus from the fourth to the twelfth century. Here are a score of monographs open to the research of English historians.

Current misconceptions of Byzantine history mainly arise from inattention to the enormous period it covers, and to the wide differences which mark the various epochs and dynasties. The whole period from the first Constantine to the last is about equal to the period from Romulus to Theodosius. The Crusaders' raid, in 1204, utterly ruined Constantinople, and from that time till the capture by the Turks it was a feeble wreck. Even at the date of the First Crusade, about a century earlier, the Empire had been broken by the campaign of Manzikert; so that the lively pictures of the First Crusade by Scott and Gibbon present us with the State in an age of decadence. The epoch when Byzantine was in the van of civilization, civil, military and intellectual, stretches from the reign of Justinian (527) to the death of Constantine VIII (1028), a period of exactly five centuries —more than the whole period of the Roman Republic.

During those five centuries there were a series of alternate periods of splendour, decline, revival, expansion, and final dissolution. The rulers differ from each other as widely as Trajan differs from Nero or Honorius; the times differ as widely as the age of Augustus differs from the ages of Cato or of Theodoric. There were ages of marvellous recovery under Justinian, again under Heraclius, again under Leo the Isaurian, then under Basil of Macedon, next under Nicephorus Phocas, and lastly under Basil II, the slayer of the Bulgarians. There were ages of decay and confusion under the successors of Heraclius, and under those of Irene, and again those of Constantine VIII. But the period to which I desire to fix attention is that from the rise of the Isaurian dynasty (717) to the death of Basil II (1025), rather more than three centuries. During the eighth, ninth, and tenth centuries the Roman Empire on the Bosporus was far the most stable and cultured power in the world, and on its existence hung the future of civilisation.

Its power was due to this—that for some five centuries of the early Middle Ages which form the transition from polytheism to feudalism, the main inheritance of civilisation, practical and intellectual, was kept in continuous and undisturbed vitality in the empire centred round the Propontis—that during all this epoch, elsewhere one of continual subdivision and confusion, the southern and eastern coast of Italy, Greece and its islands, Thrace, Macedonia, and Asia Minor as far as the Upper Euphrates, were practically safe and peaceful. This great tract, then the most populous, industrious, and civilised of the world, was able to give itself to wealth, art, and thought, whilst East and West were swept with wars of barbarous invaders. The administration of the Empire, its military and civil organisation, remained continuous and effective in the same seat, under the same law, language, and religion, during the whole period; and the official system worked under all changes of dynasty as a single organic machine. It was thus able to accumulate enormous resources of money and material, and to equip and discipline great regular armies from the martial races of its complex realm, such as were wholly beyond the means of the transitory and ever shifting kingdoms in the rest of Europe and Asia.

Western Europe, no doubt, bore within its bosom the seeds of a far greater world to come, a more virile youth, greater heroes and chiefs. But wealth, organisation, knowledge, for the time were safeguarded behind the walls of Byzantium—to speak roughly, from the age of Justinian to that of the Crusades. Not only did the empire of New Rome possess the wealth, industry, and knowledge, but it had almost exclusive control of Mediterranean commerce, undisputed supremacy of the seas, paramount financial power, and the monopoly of all the more refined manufactures and arts. In the middle of the tenth century, the contrast between the kingdom of Otto the Great and the empire of Constantine Porphyrogenitus was as great as that between Russia under Peter the Great and France in the days of the Orleans Regency.

From the seventh to the thirteenth century Constantinople was far the largest, wealthiest, most splendid city in Europe. It was in every sense a new Rome. And, if it were at all inferior as a whole to what its mother was in the palmy age of Trajan and Hadrian, it far surpassed the old Rome in its exquisite situation, in its mighty fortifications, and in the beauty of its central palace and church. A long succession of poets and topographers have recounted the glories of the great city—its churches, palaces, baths, forum, hippodrome, columns, porticoes, statues, theatres, hospitals, reservoirs, aqueducts, monasteries, and cemeteries. All accounts of early travellers from the West relate with wonder the splendour and wealth of the imperial city. "These riches and buildings were equalled nowhere in the world," says the Jew Benjamin of Tudela in the twelfth century. "Over all the land there are burghs, castles, and country towns, the one upon the other without interval," says the Saga of King Sigurd, fifty years earlier. The Crusaders, who despised the Greeks of the now decayed empire, were awed at the sight of their city; and as the pirates of the Fifth Crusade sailed up the Propontis they began to wonder at their own temerity in attacking so vast a fortress.

The dominant note of all observers who reached Constantinople from the North or the West, at least down to the eleventh century, even when they most despised the effeminacy and servility of its Greek inhabitants, was this: they felt themselves in presence of a civilisation more complex and organised than any extant. It was akin to the awe felt by Goths and Franks when they first fell under the spell of Rome. At the close of the sixth century, as Dr. Hodgkin notes of Childebert's fourth invasion of Italy, "Mighty were a few courteous words from the great Roman Emperor to the barbarian king"—the king whom Maurice the "Imperator semper Augustus" condescends to address as "vir gloriosus." And this idea that New Rome was the centre of the civilised world, that Western sovereigns were not their equals, lasted down to the age of Charles. When the Caroline Empire was decaying and convulsed, the same idea took fresh force. And the sense that the Byzantine world had a fullness and a culture which they had not, persisted until the Crusades effectually broke the spell.

This sentiment was based on two very real facts. The first was that New Rome prolonged no little of the tradition, civil and military organisation, wealth, art, and literature, of the older Rome, indeed far more than remained west of the Adriatic. The second, the more important, and the only one on which I now desire to enlarge, was that, in many essentials of civilisation, it was more modern than the nascent nations of the West. Throughout the early centuries of the Middle Ages—we may say from the age of Justinian to that of Hildebrand—the empire on the Bosporus perfected an administrative service, a hierarchy of dignities and offices, a monetary and fiscal system, a code of diplomatic formulas, a scientific body of civil law, an imperial fleet, engines of war, fortifications, and resources of maritime mobilisation, such as were not to be seen in Western kingdoms till the close of the Middle Ages, and which were gradually adopted or imitated in the West. At a time when Charles, or Capet, or Otto were welding into order their rude peoples, the traveller who reached the Bosporus found most of the institutions and habits of life such as we associate with the great cities of much later epochs. He would find a regular city police, organised bodies of municipal workmen, public parks, hospitals, orphanages, schools of law, science, and medicine, theatrical and spectacular amusements, immense factories, sumptuous palaces, and a life which recalls the Cinque Cento in Italy.

It is quite true that this imperial administration was despotic, that much of the art was lifeless and all the literature jejune; that cruelty, vice, corruption, and superstition were flagrant and constant, just as the European Renascence had cruelty, vice and corruption, at the very heart of its culture. The older historians are too fond of comparing the Leos and Constantines with the Scipios and the Antonines, instead of comparing them with the Lombard, Frank, or Bulgarian chiefs of their own times. And we are all too much given to judge the Byzantines of the eighth, ninth, and tenth centuries by the moral standards of our own age; to denounce their pompous ceremonials, their servile etiquette, their frigid compositions, and their savage executions. We forget that for many centuries Western chiefs vied with each other in copying and parading the external paraphernalia of the Roman emperors in their Byzantine ceremonial: their crowns, sceptres, coins, titles, palaces, international usages, golden bulls, pragmatic sanctions, and court officialdom. There is hardly a single symbol or form of office dear to the monarchies and aristocracies of Europe of which the original model was not elaborated in the Sacred Palace beside the Golden Horn. And most of these symbols and offices are still amongst the most venerable insignia to-day at the State functions of Tsar, Kaiser, Pope and King.

The cohesive force of the Byzantine monarchy resided in its elaborate administration, civil and military. It formed a colossal bureaucracy centred round the sacred person of Sovereign Lord of so many races, such diverse provinces, such populous towns, united by nothing but one supreme tie of allegiance. No doubt it was semi-Oriental, it was absolutist, it was oppressive, it was theocratic. But for some seven centuries it held together a vast and thriving empire, and for four centuries more it kept in being the image and memory of empire. And with all its evils and tyranny, it was closely copied by every bureaucratic absolutism in modern Europe. And even to-day the *chinovnik* of Russia, the *Beamten* of Prussia, and the *administration* of France trace their offices and even their titles to the types of the Byzantine official hierarchy.

Much more is this true of ceremonial, titles, and places of dignity. We may say that the entire nomenclature of monarchic courts and honours is derived direct from Byzantine originals, ever since Clovis was proud to call himself *Consul* and *Augustus,* and to receive a diadem from Anastasius, and ever since Charles accepted the style of Emperor and Augustus, pacific, crowned of God in the Basilica of St. Peter on Christmas Day, 800; when the Roman people shouted "Life and Victory," just as the Byzantines used to do. When in the tenth century our Edward the elder was styled *Rex invictissimus* and Athelstan called himself *Basileus of the English,* they simply borrowed the Greek formulas of supreme rank. We are amused and bewildered, as we read Constantine the seventh on the *Ceremonies of the Court,* by the endless succession of officials, obeisances, compliments, gesticulations, and robings which he so solemnly describes: with his great chamberlain, his high steward, his chief butler, his privy seal, his gold stick, his master of the horse, lords and ladies in waiting, right honourables, ushers, grooms, and gentlemen of the guard. But we usually forget that the Bourbons, the Hapsburgs, Hohenzollerns, and Romanoffs have maintained these very forms and dignities for centuries. . . .

And it would be quite wrong to assume that the organisation of the Empire was a rigid and unchanging system. On the contrary, it steadily developed and was recast according to the necessities of the case. In the main, these necessities were the shrinkage of the boundaries, the loss of rich provinces, and, above all, the pressure of Oriental invaders together with the growth of the western Kingdoms and empire. Nor was there anything casual or arbitrary in these changes. The process of Orientation and of Autocracy which Aurelian and Diocletian had begun in the third century had been developed into a system by Constantine when he planted the

Empire on the Bosporus and founded an administrative and social hierarchy in the fourth century. Justinian in the sixth century introduced changes which gave the empire a more military and more centralised form to meet the enemies by which it was surrounded. Heraclius and his dynasty in the seventh century carried this process still further under the tremendous strain to which their rule was exposed. They instituted the system of *Themes,* military governorships under a general having plenary authority both in peace and war; and the system of *Themes* was developed, in the eighth and ninth century, until in the tenth they are classified by Constantine Porphyrogenitus, who mentions about thirty. During the whole period, from the seventh to the eleventh centuries inclusive, the organisation was continually developed or varied, not violently or improvidently, but to meet the needs of the time. There is reason to believe these developments to have been systematic, continuous, and judicious. If we compare them with the convulsions, anarchy, racial and political revolutions which shook Western Europe during the same epoch, we cannot deny that the tyrannies and formalities of the Byzantine Court were compatible with high aptitude for Imperial government, order, and defence. Alone amongst the nations of the world, the Empire maintained a systematic finance and exchequer, a pure standard coinage, and a regular commercial marine.

For the historian, the point of interest in this Byzantine administration is that, with all its crimes and pomposities, it was systematic and continuous. It never suffered the administrative and financial chaos which afflicted the West in the fifth century, or in the ninth century after the decay of the Carlings, and so on down to the revival of the Holy Roman Empire by Otto the Great. It is difficult to overrate the ultimate importance of the acceptance by Charles of the title of Emperor, or of its revival by Otto; and history has taken a new life since the modern school has worked out all that these meant to the West. But we must be careful not to fall into the opposite pitfall, as if the Roman Empire had been translated back again to the West, as some clerical enthusiasts pretended, as if the Empire of Charles was a continuous and growing organism from the time of Charles down to Rudolph of Hapsburg, or as if the coronation of Charles or of Otto at Rome broke the continuity of Empire at the Bosporus, or even greatly diminished its authority and prestige. On the contrary, these Western ceremonies affected it only for a season, and from time to time, and affected its temper more than its power.

The Western Empire, in spite of the strong men who at times wielded its sceptre, and whatever the fitful burst of force it displayed, was long before it quite recognised its own dignity and might; it was very vaguely and variously understood at first by its composite parts; and for the earlier centuries was a loose, troubled, and migratory symbol of rank rather than a fixed and recognised system of government. All this time the Emperors in the vermilion buskins were regularly crowned in the Holy Wisdom; they all worshipped there, and all lived and ruled under its shadow. Their palaces by the Bosporus maintained, under every dynasty and through every century, the same vast bureaucratic machine, and organised from the same centre the same armies and fleets; they supported the same churches, libraries, monasteries, schools, and spectacles, without the break of a day, however much Muslim invaders plundered or occupied their Asiatic provinces, and although the rulers of Franks or Saxons defied their authority or borrowed their titles. The Empire of Franks and Teutons was not a systematic government and had no local seat. That of the Greeks, as they were called, had all the characters of a fixed capital and of a continuous State system.

There is nothing in all history more astonishing and more worthy of study than the continual rallies of this Roman Empire. There is an alternate ebb and flow in the extent and power of the Empire most fascinating to observe. The wonderful revival under Justinian, and again that under Heraclius in the sixth and seventh centuries, are familiar enough even to the general reader, as well as the troubles which supervened under their respective successors. The more splendid and more permanent rally under the Isaurian dynasty and again under the Basilian dynasty, the whole period from 717 for three centuries, to the last of the Basilian Emperors, in 1028, is less familiar to English readers, and yet is rich with incidents as well as lessons. The anarchy which followed the fall of the miserable tyrant Justinian II seemed certain to ruin the whole Empire. From this fate it was saved by the Isaurian (or Syrian), Leo III and his descendants and successors; and again order and empire were saved by Basil I of Macedon and his descendants, who ruled for 160 years. The onward sweep of the conquering Muslims had roused the whole Empire to defend its existence. And all through the eighth, ninth, and tenth centuries it found a succession of statesmen and warriors from Asia Minor and Thrace whose policy and exploits at least equal any recorded in the same age either in the East or the West. And it is to be noted that these two glorious periods of the Byzantine power coincided with the great revival of the Franks under Pippin and his dynasty, and that of the Saxons under Henry the Fowler and the dynasty of the Ottos.

Nothing could have saved the Empire but its superiority in war—at least in defence. And this superiority it possessed from the sixth to the eleventh centuries. It was a strange error of the older historians, into which Gibbon himself fell, that the Byzantine armies were wanting in courage, discipline, and organisation. On the contrary, during all the early Middle Ages they were the only really scientific army in the world. They revolutionised the art of war, both in theory and practice, and in some points brought it to a stage which was only reached in quite modern times, as for instance in mobilisation and in providing ambulance corps. They quite recast the old Roman methods and armies, whilst retaining the discipline, spirit, and thoroughness of Rome. The great changes were four-fold: (1) they made it as of old a native army of Roman subjects, not of foreign allies or mercenaries; (2) they made its main force cavalry, in lieu of infantry; (3) they changed the weapons to bow and lance instead of sword and javelin—and greatly developed body armour; (4) they substituted a composite and flexible army-corps for the old legion. Men of all races were enlisted, save Greeks and Latins. The main strength came from the races of the highlands of Anatolia and Armenia—the races which defended Plevna.

When, towards the close of the fourth century, the battle of Adrianople rang the knell of Roman infantry, the Byzantine warriors organised an army of mounted bowmen. . . . The cataphracti, or mail-clad horsemen, armed with bow, broadsword, and lance, who formed nearly half the Byzantine armies, were immensely superior both in mobility, in range, and in force to any troops of old Rome, and they were more than a match for any similar troopers that Asia or Europe could put into the field. From the sixth to the tenth centuries we have still extant scientific treatises on the art of war under the names of Maurice, Leo, and Nicephorus. When to this we take into account the massive system of fortification developed at Constantinople, the various forms of Greek fire, their engines to project combustible liquids, and one form that seems the basis of gunpowder, and last of all the command of the sea, and a powerful service of transports and ships of war, we need not doubt Mr. Oman's conclusion that the Byzantine Empire had the most efficient forces then extant, nor need we wonder how it was that for eight centuries it kept at bay such a host of dangerous foes.

The sea-power of the Empire came later, for the control of the Mediterranean was not challenged until the Saracens took to the sea. But from the seventh to the eleventh centuries (and mainly in the ninth and tenth) the Empire developed a powerful marine of war galleys, cruisers, and transports. The war galleys or *dromonds,* with two banks of oars, carried 300 men each, the cruisers 100, and many of them were fitted with fighting-towers and machines for hurling explosives and liquid combustibles. Hand-grenades, and apparently guns whence gunpowder shot forth fire-balls but not bullets, were their armament. When Nicephorus Phocas recovered Crete from the Saracens, we are told that his expedition numbered 3300 ships of war and transports, and carried infantry, bowmen, and cavalry, a siege-train, and engines, in all amounting to 40,000 or 50,000 men. Nothing in the tenth century could rival such a sea-power. He might fairly boast as Emperor to the envoy of Otto that he could lay any coast town of Italy in ashes. Such was the maritime ascendancy of Byzantium, until it passed in the eleventh century to the Italian republics.

The most signal evidence of the superior civilisation of Byzantium down to the tenth century is found in the fact that alone of all states it maintained a continuous, scientific, and even progressive system of law. Whilst the *Corpus Juris* died down in the West under the successive invasions of the Northern nations, at least so far as governments and official study was concerned, it continued under the Emperors in the East to be the law of the State, to be expounded in translations, commentaries, and handbooks, to be regularly taught in schools of law, and still more to be developed in a Christian and modern sense. It was the brilliant proof of Savigny that Roman law was never utterly extinct in Europe, and then rediscovered in the twelfth century. As he showed, it lingered on without official recognition among Latin subject races in a casual way, until what Savigny himself calls the Revival of the Civil Law at Bologna in the twelfth century. But for official and practical purposes, the *Corpus Juris* of Justinian was superseded for six centuries by the various laws of the Teutonic conquerors These laws, whatever their interest, were rude prescriptions to serve the time, without order, method, or permanence, the sure evidence of a low civilisation. . . .

Now, there was no revival of Roman Law in Byzantium, because there it never was extinct. Justinian's later legislation was promulgated in Greek, and his *Corpus Juris* was at once translated, summarised, and abridged in the East. Although schools of law existed in Constantinople and elsewhere, the seventh century, in its disasters and confusion, let the civil law fall to a low ebb. But the Isaurian dynasty, in the age of the Frank King Pippin, made efforts to restore and to develop the law. The *Ecloga* of Leo III and Constantine V was promulgated to revise the law of persons in a Christian sense. It was part of the attempt of the Iconoclasts to form a moral reform in a Puritan spirit. This was followed by three special codes—(1) A maritime code, of the Rhodian law, as to loss at sea and commercial risks; (2) a military code or law martial; (3) a rural code to regulate the police of country populations. And a register of births for males was instituted throughout the Empire at the same time.

In the ninth century the Basilian dynasty issued a new legislation which, whilst professing to restore the *Corpus Juris* of Justinian, practically accepted much of the moral reforms of the Isaurians. . . . The great work of the Basilian dynasty was the *Basilica,* in sixty books, of Basil I and Leo VI, the Philosopher, about 890, an epoch that Mr. Bryce justly calls "the nadir of order and civilisation" in the West, at the time when the Carolines ended with Charles the Fat and Lewis the Child. The *Basilica,* which filled six quarto volumes, stood on a par with the *Corpus Juris* of Justinian. It was a systematic attempt to compile a complete code of law, based on the Roman law, but largely reforming it from the influences of Christianity, humanity, and the advancing habits of a new society.

We thus have in Greek a new *Corpus Juris,* a long series of institutions, amendments, text-books, scholiasts, and glosses, down to the foundation at Constantinople of a new school of law by Constantine Monomachus in the middle of the eleventh century, so that the continuity of civil law from Tribonian to Theophilus the Younger is complete. . . . These Greek translations and comments are of great value in determining the texts of the Latin originals. The *Basilica,* indeed, was as permanent as the *Corpus Juris,* and has formed the basis of civil law to the Christian communities of the East, as it is to this day of the Greeks. Nor is it worthy of attention only for its continuity and its permanence. It is a real advance on the old law of Rome from a Christian and modern sense. The *Basilica* opens with a fine proem, which is an admirable and just criticism of the *Corpus Juris.* "Justinian," says Basil, "had four codes. We combined the whole law in one. We omit and amend as we go on, and have collected the whole in sixty books." The influence of Christianity and its effect on personal law was feeble enough in the code of Justinian. The Isaurian and Basilian laws are deeply marked by the great change. They proclaim the principle and work it out to its conclusions—that "there is no half measure between marriage and celibacy." Concubinage disappears and immoral unions become penal. The marriage of slaves is gradually recognised, and the public evidence of marriage is steadily defined. The law of divorce is put very much on the basis of our existing conditions. The wife is gradually raised to equality of rights. She becomes the guardian of her children; women can legally adopt; there can be no tutelage of minors during the life of *either* parent. The property of husband and wife is placed under just conditions, the *patria potestas* is abolished in the old Roman sense, and the succession on death of either spouse is subject to new regulations. The cumbrous number of witnesses to a testament is reduced; the old formal distinctions between personal and real property are abolished, and a scheme of liquidated damages is introduced. There is no feudal system of any kind. There is a systematic effort to . . . give the cultivator "fixity of tenure."

Here, then, we have proof that the grand scheme of Roman law, which was officially ignored and forgotten in the whole West for six centuries, was continuously studied, taught and developed by Byzantines without a single interruption, until it was moulded by Christian morality and modern sentiment to approach the form in which the civil law is now in use in Europe. No higher evidence could be found to show that civilisation, morality, and learning were carried on for those troubled times in the

Greek world with a vigour and a continuity that have no counterpart in Latin and Teutonic Europe. Strangely enough, this striking fact was ignored till lately by civilians, and is still ignored by our English jurists. The learning on the Graeco-Roman law between Justinian and the school of Bologna is entirely confined to foreign scholars; and I have not noticed anything but brief incidental notices of their labours in the works of any English lawyer. It is a virgin soil that lies open to the plough of any inquiring student of law.

Turn to the history of Art. Here, again, it must be said that from the fifth to the eleventh century the Byzantine and Eastern world preserved the traditions, and led the development of art in all its modes. We are now free of the ancient fallacy that Art was drowned beneath the waves of the Teutonic invaders, until many centuries later it slowly came to life in Italy and then north of the Alps. The truth is that the noblest and most essential of the arts—that of building—some of the minor arts of decoration and ornament, and the art of music, down to the invention of Guido of Arezzo in the eleventh century, lived on and made new departures, whilst most of the arts of form died down under the combined forces of barbarian convulsions and religious asceticism. And it was Byzantium which was the centre of the new architecture and the new decoration, whilst it kept alive such seeds of the arts of form as could be saved through the rudeness and the fanaticism of the early Middle Ages. To the age of Justinian we owe one of the greatest steps ever taken by man in the art of building. The great Church of the Holy Wisdom exerted over architecture a wider influence than can be positively claimed for any single edifice in the history of the arts. We trace enormous ramifications of its example in the whole East and the whole of the West, at Ravenna, Kief, Venice, Aachen, Palermo, Thessalonica, Cairo, Syria, Persia, and Delhi. And with all the enthusiasm we must feel for the Parthenon and the Pantheon, for Amiens and Chartres, I must profess my personal conviction that the interior of Agia Sophia is the grandest in the world, and certainly that one which offers the soundest basis for the architecture of the future.

The great impulse given to all subsequent building by Anthemius and Isodorus lay in the perfect combination of the dome on the grandest scale with massive tiers of arches rising from colossal columns—the union of unrivalled engineering skill with exquisite ornament, the whole being a masterpiece of subtlety, sublimity, harmony, and reserve. It is true that the Pantheon, which we now know to be of the age of Hadrian, not of Augustus, and the vast *caldaria* of the Thermae, had given the earliest type of the true dome. It is true that the wonderful artifice of crowning the column with the arch in lieu of architrave was invented some centuries earlier. But the union of dome, on the grandest scale and in infinite variety, with arched ranges of columns in rows and in tiers—this was the unique triumph of Byzantine art, and nothing in the history of building has borne a fruit so rich. Ravenna, Torcello, St. Mark's, and Monreale are copies of Byzantine churches. Aachen, as Freeman recognises, is a direct copy of Ravenna, from whence Charles obtained ornaments for his palace chapel. And on both sides of the Rhine were constant copies from the city of the great Charles. It is quite true that French, Rhenish, Russian, Moorish, and Saracen architects developed, and in their façades, towers, and exteriors, much improved on the Byzantine type, which, except in Italy, was not directly copied. But the type, the original conception, was in all cases derived from the Bosporus.

Without entering on the vexed problem of the mode and extent of the direct imitation of Byzantine architecture either in the East or the West, we must conclude, if we carefully examine the buildings in Greece and the Levant, in Armenia and Syria, and on the shores of Italy, that the Bosporus became the *nidus* of a building art which had a profound influence on Asia and Europe from the sixth to the twelfth centuries. And when justice is done to its constructive science, to its versatility, and at the same time to its severe taste and dignity, this Byzantine type is one of the most masculine and generative forms of art ever produced by human genius. The Holy Wisdom is twice the age of the Gothic cathedrals, and it will long outlive them. In beauty of material it far surpasses them, and if it has been outvied in mass by the mighty temples of the Renascence, it far exceeds these in richness, in subtlety, and in refinement.

The people who evolved a noble and creative type of architecture could not be dead to art. But even in the arts of form we rate the Byzantines too low. From the sixth to the eleventh century Western Europe drew from Byzantium its type of ornament in every kind. This was often indirectly and perhaps unconsciously done, and usually with great modifications. But all careful study of the mosaics, the metal work, the ivories, the embroideries, the carvings, the coins, the paintings, and the manuscripts of these ages establishes the priority and the originality of the Byzantine arts of decoration. It is undoubted that the art of mosaic ornament had its source there. Mosaic, with its Greek name, was introduced into the ancient world from the East by Greece. But the exquisite art of wall decoration by glass mosaic which we are now reviving was a strictly Byzantine art, and from the fifth to the twelfth century was carried into Europe by the direct assistance of the Byzantine school. The rigid conservatism of the Church, and the gradual decline of taste, stereotyped and at last destroyed the art; but there still exist in Constantinople and in Greece glass mosaic figures as grand as anything in the decorative art of any age.

In the end superstition and immobility more or less stifled the growth of all the minor arts at Byzantium, as confusion and barbarism submerged them in the West. What remnants remained between the age of Justinian and the age of the Normans were nursed beside the Bosporus. The art of carving ivory certainly survived, and in the plaques and caskets which are spared we can trace from time to time a skill which, if it have wholly degenerated from Graeco-Roman art, was superior to any we can discover in the West till the rise of the Pisan school. The noble Angel of our own museum, the Veroli casket of South Kensington, and some plaques, diptychs, oliphants, vases, and book-covers, remain to prove that all through these early times Byzantine decoration dominated in Europe, and occasionally could produce a piece which seemed to anticipate good Gothic and Renascence work.

It is the same in the art of illuminating manuscripts. Painting, no doubt, declined more rapidly than any other art under the combined forces of barbarism and the gospel. But from the fifth to the eleventh century the paintings in Greek manuscripts are far superior to those of Western Europe. The Irish and Caroline schools developed a style of fine calligraphy and ingenious borders and initials. But their figures are curiously inferior to those of the Byzantine painters, who evidently kept their borderings subdued so as not to interfere with their figures. Conservatism and superstition smothered and eventually killed the art of painting, as it did the art of sculpture, in the East. But there are a few rare manuscripts in Venice, the Vatican, and the French Bibliothèque Nationale—all certainly executed for Basil I, Nicephorus, and Basil II in the ninth and tenth centuries—which in drawing, even of the nude, in composition, in expression, in grandeur of colour and effect, are not equalled until we reach the fourteenth century in Europe. The Vatican, the Venice, and the Paris examples, in my opinion, have never been surpassed.

The manufacture of silks and embroidered satins was almost a Greek monopoly all through the Middle Ages. Mediaeval literature is full of the splendid silks of Constantinople, of the robes and exquisite brocades which kings and princes were eager to obtain. We hear of the robe of a Greek senator which had 600 figures picturing the entire life of Christ. Costly stuffs and utensils bore Greek names and lettering down to the middle of the fifteenth century. *Samite* is Greek for six-threaded stuff. . . . And some exquisite fragments of embroidered robes of Greek work are preserved in the Vatican and many Northern museums and sacristies. The diadems, sceptres, thrones, robes, coins, and jewels of the early Mediaeval princes were all Greek in type, and usually Byzantine in origin. So that Mr. Frothingham, in the *American Journal of Archaeology* (1894), does not hesitate to write: "The debt to Byzantium is undoubtedly immense; the difficulty consists in ascertaining what amount of originality can properly be claimed for the

Western arts, industries, and institutions during the early Middle Ages."

We err also if we have nothing but contempt for the Byzantine intellectual movement in the early Middle Ages. It is disparaged for two reasons—first, that we do not take account of the only period when it was invaluable, from the eighth to the eleventh centuries; and, secondly, because the Greek in which it was expressed falls off so cruelly from the classical tongue we love. But review the priceless services of this semi-barbarous literature when literature was dormant in the West. How much poetry, philosophy, or science was there in Western Europe between Gregory the Great and Lanfranc? A few ballads, annals, and homilies of merit, but quite limited to their narrow localities. For the preservation of the language, literature, philosophy, and science of Greece mankind were dependent on the Roman Empire in the East, until the Saracens and Persians received and transmitted the inheritance.

From the time of Proclus in the fifth century, there had never been wanting a succession of students of the philosophers of Greece; and it is certain that for some centuries the books and the tradition of Plato and Aristotle were preserved to the world in the schools of Alexandria, Athens, and then of Byzantium. Of the study and development of the civil law we have already spoken. And the same succession was maintained in physical science. Both geometry and astronomy were kept alive, though not advanced. The immortal architects of the *Holy Wisdom* were scientific mathematicians, and wrote works on Mechanics. The mathematician Leo, in the middle of the ninth century, lectured on Geometry in the Church of the Forty Martyrs at Constantinople, and he wrote an essay on Euclid, when there was little demand for science in the West, in the age of Lewis the Pious and the descendants of Egbert. In the tenth century we have an essay dealing with a treatise of Hero on practical geometry. And Michael Psellus in the eleventh century, the "Prince of Philosophers," wrote, amongst other things, on mathematics and astronomy. From the fourth to the eleventh century we have a regular series of writers on medicine, and systematic treatises on the healing art.

On other physical sciences—Zoology, Botany, Mineralogy, and Geography—a series of Greek writers and treatises are recorded which partly survive in text or in summaries. I need hardly add that I do not pretend to have studied these works, nor do I suppose that they are worth study, or of any present value whatever. I am relying on the learned historian of Byzantine literature, Krumbacher, who has devoted 1200 pages of close print to these middle Greek authors, and on other biographical and literary histories. The point of interest to the historian is not the absolute value of these forgotten books. It is the fact that down to the age of the Crusades a real, even if feeble, sequence of thinkers was maintained in the Eastern

Empire to keep alive the thought and knowledge of the ancient world whilst the Western nations were submerged in revolution and struggles of life or death. Our tendency is to confine to too special and definite an era the influence of Greek on European thought, if we limit it to what is called the Renascence after the capture of Constantinople by the Turks. In truth, from the fifth century to the fifteenth there was a gradual Renascence, or rather an infiltration of ideas, knowledge, and art, from the Grecised Empire into Western Europe. It was never quite inactive, and was fitful and irregular, but in a real way continuous. Its effect was concealed and misrepresented by national antipathies, commercial rivalries, and the bitter jealousies of the two Empires and the two Churches. The main occasions of this infiltration from East to West were undoubtedly—first, the Iconoclast persecutions, then the Crusades, and finally the capture of the City by Mohammed the Conqueror. The movement, which we call the Renascence, may have been the more important of the three, but we must not ignore the real effect of the other two, nor the constant influence of a more advanced and more settled civilisation upon a civilisation which was passing out of barbarism through convulsions into order and life.

The peculiar, indispensable service of Byzantine literature was the preservation of the language, philology, and archaeology of Greece. It is impossible to see how our knowledge of ancient literature or civilisation could have been recovered if Constantinople had not nursed through the early Middle Ages the vast accumulations of Greek learning in the schools of Alexandria, Athens, and Asia Minor; if Photius, Suidas, Eustathius, Tzetzes, and the Scholiasts had not poured out their lexicons, anecdotes, and commentaries; if the *Corpus Scriptorum historiae Byzantinae* had never been compiled; if indefatigable copyists had not toiled in multiplying the texts of ancient Greece. Pedantic, dull, blundering as they are too often, they are indispensable. We pick precious truths and knowledge out of their garrulities and stupidities, for they preserve what otherwise would have been lost for ever. It is no paradox that their very merit to us is that they were never either original or brilliant. Their genius, indeed, would have been our loss. Dunces and pedants as they were, they servilely repeated the words of the immortals. Had they not done so, the immortals would have died long ago.

Of the vast product of the theology of the East it is impossible here to speak. As in the West, and even more than in the West, the intellect of the age was absorbed in spiritual problems and divine mysteries. The amount of its intellectual energy and its moral enthusiasm was as great in the East as in the West; and if the general result is so inferior, the reason is to be found not in less subtlety or industry in the Greek-speaking divines, but rather in the lower social conditions and the rigid absolutism under which they worked. From the first, the Greek Church was half Oriental, profoundly mystical and metaphysical. But we must never depreciate that Orthodox Church which had its Chrysostom, its Cyril and Methodius, the Patriarch Photius, and Gregory of Nazianzus, with crowds of preachers, martyrs, and saints; which, in any case, was the elder brother, guide, and teacher for ages of the Church Catholic; which avoided some of the worst errors, most furious conflicts, the grossest scandals of the Papacy; and which brought within its fold those vast peoples of Eastern Europe which the Roman communion failed to reach.

The Greek Church, which never attained the centralisation of the Church of Rome, was spared some of those sources of despotism and corruption which ultimately tore the Western Church in twain. And, if it never became so potent a spiritual force as was Rome at its highest, in the Greek Church permanent conflict with the Empire and struggles for temporal dominion were unknown. The Greek Church, however, had its own desperate convulsions in the long and fierce battle between Iconoclasts and Iconodules. It would be a fatal error to undervalue this great and significant schism as if it were a mere affair of the use of images in worship. Iconoclasm was one of the great religious movements in the world's history—akin to Arianism, to the Albigensian heresies of the thirteenth century, akin to Mahometanism, akin to Lutheranism, akin to some forms of Puritanism, though quite distinct from all of these. It was evidently a bold and enthusiastic effort of Asiatic Christians to free the European Christians of the common Empire from the fetichism, idol-worship, and monkery in which their life was being stifled.

The Isaurian chiefs had the support of the great magnates of Asia Minor, of the mountaineers of Anatolia, and the bulk of the hardy veterans of the camp. Their zeal to force on a superstitious populace and on swarms of endowed orders of ecclesiastics a moral and spiritual reformation towards a simpler and more abstract Theism—to purge Christianity, in fact, of its grosser anthropomorphism—this is one of the most interesting problems in all history. And all the more that it was a moral and spiritual reform attempted, not by poor zealots from the depths of the popular conscience, but by absolute sovereigns and unflinching governments, which united something of the creed of the Waldenses to the cruel passions of Simon de Montfort. The movement showed how ready was the Asiatic portion of the Empire to accept some form of Islam; and we can well conceive how it came that Leo III was called ". . . imbued with the temperament of an Arab." The whole story has been shamelessly perverted by religious bigotry, and we know little of Iconoclasm, except in the satires of their enemies the Iconodules. One of the greatest rulers of the Empire has been stamped with a disgusting nickname, and it is difficult now to discover what is the truth about the entire dynasty and movement. Mr. Bury has given us some admirable chapters on this remarkable reformation of faith and manners. But we need a full history of a very obscure and obstinate conflict which for a century and a half shook the Empire to its foundations, severed the Orthodox Church from the Church Catholic, and yet greatly stimulated the intercourse of ideas and arts between the East and the West.

In pleading for a more systematic study of Byzantine history and civilisation in the early Middle Ages, I am far from pretending that it can enter into rivalry with that of Western Europe. I do not doubt that it was a lower type; that neither in State nor in Church, neither in policy nor in arms, in morals, in literature, or in art, did it in the sum equal or even approach the Catholic Feudalism of the West. And assuredly, as the West from the time of Charles and Otto onwards rose into modern life, Eastern Christendom sank slowly down into decay and ruin. My point is simply that this Byzantine history and civilisation have been unduly depreciated and unfairly neglected. And this is especially true of English scholars, who have done little indeed of late in a field wherein foreign scholars have done much. It is a field where much remains to be done in order to redress the prejudices and the ignorance of ages, multiplied from of old by clerical bigotry, race insolence, and the unscrupulous avarice of trade. Hardly any other field of history has been so widely distorted and so ignorantly disparaged.

Let me also add that it is for a quite limited period in the thousand years of Byzantine history that I find its peculiar importance. The Justinian and Heraclian periods have brilliant episodes and some great men. But the truly fertile period of Byzantine history, in its contrast with the reaction upon the West, lies in the period from the rise of the Isaurian to the close of the Basilian dynasty—roughly speaking, for the eighth, ninth, tenth, and first half of the eleventh centuries. . . . When the Basilian dynasty ended, great changes were setting in, both in the East and the West. The rise of the Seljuks and of the Normans, the growth of Italian commerce, the decay of the Eastern Empire, the struggles of the Papacy and the Western Empire, and finally the Crusades, introduce a new World. It is the point at which Byzantine history loses all its special value for the problems of historical continuity and comparison. And yet it is the point at which a new colour and piquancy is too often given to Byzantine annals.

In the eighth, ninth, and tenth centuries we may trace a civilisation around the Bosporus which, with all its evils and the seeds of disease within it, was in one sense far older than any other in Europe, in another sense, was far more modern; which preserved things of priceless value to the human race; which finally disproved the fallacy that there had ever been any prolonged break in human evolution; which was the mother and the model of secular churches and mighty kingdoms in Eastern Europe, churches and kingdoms which are still not willing to allow any superiority to the West, either in the region of State organisation or of spiritual faith.

18. THE YOUTH OF MOHAMMED[1]

Among the scenes from the life of Mohammed there are some that have been very ably described by Sir William Muir, who with great diligence perused original sources. This description of the youth of the Arab prophet explains the development of his mind and character, the contact with his father and brothers, and his early acquaintance with Khadija.

The youth of Mohammad passed away without any other incidents of interest. At one period he was employed, like other lads, in tending the sheep and goats of Mecca upon the neighbouring hills and valleys. He used when at Medina to refer to this employment and to say that it comported with his prophetic office, even as it did with that of Moses and David. On one occasion, as some people passed him carrying a load of *Arāḳ* berries, the Prophet said to his companions: "Pick me out the blackest of them, for they are sweet;—even such was I wont to gather when I fed the flocks of Mecca at Ajyād. Verily there hath been no prophet raised up, who performed not the work of a Shepherd." The hire received for this duty would contribute towards the support of his needy uncle, Abu Tālib, and the occupation itself was congenial with his thoughtful and meditative character. While he watched the flocks, his attention would be riveted by the signs of an unseen Power spread all around him: the twinkling stars and bright constellations gliding through the dark blue sky silently along, would be charged to him with a special message; the loneliness of the desert would arm with a deeper conviction that speech which day everywhere utters unto day; while the still small voice, never unheard by the attentive listener, would swell into grander and more imperious tones when the tempest swept with its forked lightning and far-rolling thunder along the vast solitudes of the mountains about Mecca. Thus, we may presume, was cherished a deep and earnest faith in the Deity as an ever-present, all-directing Agent;—a faith which in after days the Prophet was wont to enforce from the memories, no doubt, of these days, by eloquent and heart-stirring appeals to the sublime operations of Nature and the beneficent adaptations of an ever-present Providence.

Our authorities all agree in ascribing to the youth of Mohammad a modesty of deportment and purity of manners rare among the people of

[1] Sir William Muir, *The Life of Mohammad from the Original Sources,* new and revised edition by T. H. Weir, Edinburgh, John Grant, 1923, pp. 18–21, 22–27.

Mecca. His virtue is said to have been miraculously preserved. "I was engaged one night" (so he himself relates) "feeding the flocks in company with a lad of Koreish. And I said to him, if thou wilt look after my flock, I will go into Mecca and divert myself there, even as youths are wont by night to divert themselves." But no sooner had he reached the precincts of the city, than a marriage feast engaged his attention, and he fell asleep. On another night, entering the town with the same intentions, he was arrested by heavenly strains of music, and, sitting down, slept till morning. Thus he escaped temptation. "And after this," said Mohammad, "I no more sought after vice; even until I had attained unto the prophetic office." Making every allowance for the fond reverence which favoured the currency of such stories, it is quite in keeping with the character of Mohammad that he should have shrunk from the coarse and licentious practices of his youthful friends. Endowed with a refined mind and delicate taste, reserved and meditative, he lived much within himself, and the ponderings of his heart no doubt supplied occupation for leisure hours spent by others of a lower stamp in rude sports and profligacy. The fair character and honourable bearing of the unobtrusive youth won the approbation of his fellow-citizens; and he received the title, by common consent, of *AL-AMIN,* "the Faithful."

Thus respected and honoured, Mohammad lived a quiet and retired life in the family of Abu Tālib, who (as we have seen) was prevented by limited means from occupying any prominent position in the society of Mecca. At last, finding his family increase faster than the ability to provide for them, Abu Tālib bethought him of setting his nephew, now of mature age, to earn a livelihood for himself. Mohammad was never covetous of wealth, or at any period of his career energetic in the pursuit of riches for their own sake. If left to himself, he would probably have preferred the quiet and repose of his present life to the bustle and cares of a mercantile journey. He would not spontaneously have contemplated such an expedition. But when the proposal was made, his generous soul at once felt the necessity of doing all that was possible to relieve his uncle, and he cheerfully responded to the call. The story is as follows:—When his nephew was now five-and-twenty years of age, Abu Tālib addressed him in these words: "I am, as thou knowest, a man of small substance; and truly the times deal hardly with me. Now here is a caravan of thine own tribe about to start for Syria, and Khadīja, daughter of Khuweilid, needeth men of our tribe to send forth with her merchandise. If thou wert to offer thyself, she would readily accept thy services." Mohammad replied: "Be it so as thou hast said." Then Abu Tālib went to Khadīja, and inquired whether she wished to hire his nephew, but he added: "We hear that thou hast engaged such an one for two camels, and we should not be content that my nephew's hire were less than four." The matron discreetly answered: "Hadst thou asked this thing for one of a distant or alien tribe, I would have granted it; how much rather now that thou askest it for a near relative and friend!" So the matter was settled, and Mohammad prepared for the journey. When the caravan was about to set out, his uncle commended him to the men of the company. Meisara, servant of Khadija, likewise travelled along with Mohammad in charge of her property. The caravan took the usual route to Syria, the same which Mohammad had traversed with his uncle thirteen years before. In due time they reached Bosra, on the road to Damascus, about sixty miles to the east of the Jordan. The transactions of that busy mart, where the practised merchants of Syria sought to overreach the simple Arabs, were ill suited to the tastes and habits of Mohammad; yet his natural sagacity and shrewdness carried him prosperously through the undertaking. He returned from the barter with a balance more than usually in his favour. . . .

When Mohammad had disposed of the merchandise and, according to her command, purchased for his mistress such things as she had need of, he retraced his steps in company with the caravan to his native valley. The mildness of his manners and kind attention had won the heart of Meisara, and, as they drew near to Mecca, the grateful servant persuaded Mohammad to go in advance of the rest, and bear to his mistress first tidings of the successful traffic. Khadīja, surrounded by her maidens, was sitting upon the upper storey of her house, on the watch for the earliest glimpse of the caravan, when a camel was seen rapidly to advance from the expected quarter, and as it approached she perceived that Mohammad was the rider. He entered, recounted the prosperous issue of the adventure, and enumerated the various goods which agreeably to her commission he had purchased for her. She was delighted at all she heard; but there was a charm in the dark and pensive eye, in the noble features, and the graceful form of her assiduous agent as he stood before her, which pleased her even more than her good fortune. The comely widow was now forty years of age, she had been twice married, and had borne two sons and a daughter. Yet she cast a fond eye upon the thoughtful youth of five-and-twenty; nor, when he departed, could she dismiss him from her thoughts.

Khadīja was a Koreishite lady, distinguished by fortune as well as by birth. Her father, Khuweilid, was the grandson of Asad, and Asad was the grandson of Kosai. Khuweilid commanded in the Sacrilegious War a considerable section of Koreish, and so did his nephew 'Othmān. Her substance, whether inherited, or acquired through her former marriages, was very considerable; and by means of hired agents she had increased it largely in mercantile speculation. To the blessing of affluence, she added the more important endowments of discretion, virtue, and an affectionate heart; and, though now mellowed by a more than middle age, she retained a fair and attractive countenance. The chief men of Koreish were not insensible to these charms, and many sought her in marriage; but choosing rather to live on in dignified and independent widowhood, she had rejected all their offers. The tender emotions, however, excited by the visit of Mohammad overpowered her resolution. Meisara continued to sound in her not unwilling ears the praises of his fellow-traveller. At last her love became irresistible, and she resolved in a discreet and cautious way to make known her passion to its object. A sister (according to other accounts, a servant) was the agent deputed to sound his views. "What is it, O Mohammad," said she, adroitly referring to the unusual circumstance of his being unmarried at so mature an age,—"what is it that hindereth thee from marriage?" "I have nothing," replied he, "in my hands wherewithal I might marry." "But if haply that difficulty were removed, and thou wert invited to espouse a beautiful and wealthy lady of noble birth, who would place thee in affluence, wouldest thou not desire to have her?" "And who," said Mohammad, startled at the novel thought, "might that be?" "It is Khadīja." "But how can I attain unto her?" "Let that be my care," returned the female. The mind of Mohammad was at once made up, and he answered, "I am ready." The female departed and told Khadīja.

No sooner was she apprised of his willingness to marry her, than Khadīja despatched a messenger to Mohammad or his uncle, appointing a time when they should meet. Meanwhile, as she dreaded the refusal of her father, she provided for him a feast; and when he had well drunk and was merry, she slaughtered for the company a cow, and casting over her father perfume of saffron or ambergris, dressed him in marriage raiment. While thus under the effects of wine, the old man united his daughter to Mohammad in the presence of his uncle Hamza. But having recovered his senses, he began to look around with wonder, and inquire what meant these symptoms of a nuptial feast, the slaughtered cow, the perfumes and the marriage garment. So soon as he was made aware of what had happened—for they told him "The nuptial dress was put upon thee by Mohammad thy son-in-law"—he fell into a violent passion, and declared that he would never consent to give away to that poor youth a daughter courted by the great men of Koreish. The friends of Mohammad replied indignantly that the alliance had not originated in their wish, but was the act of no other than his own daughter. Weapons were drawn, and blood might have been shed, when the old man became pacified, and at last was reconciled.

Notwithstanding its stormy and inauspicious opening, the connubial state proved, both to Mohammad and Khadīja, one of unusual tranquillity and happiness. Upon him the marriage conferred a faithful and affectionate companion, and, in spite of her age, a not unfruitful wife. Khadīja, on her part, fully appreciated the noble genius and commanding mind of Mohammad, which his reserved and contemplative habit, while it veiled from others, could not conceal from her. She conducted as before the duties of her establishment, and left him to enjoy his leisure hours, undisturbed and free from care. Her house was thenceforward his home, and her bosom the safe receptacle of those doubts and longings after spiritual light which now began to agitate his soul.

Within the next ten or twelve years, Khadīja bore to Mohammad two sons and four daughters. The firstborn was named Al-Kāsim; and after him, according to Arabian custom, Mohammad received the title of ABU'L-KASIM, "Father of Al-Kāsim." This son died at the age of two years. Meanwhile, his eldest daughter Zeinab was born; and after her, at intervals of one or two years, three other daughters, Rokeiya, Fātima, and Um Kulthūm. Last of all was born his second son, who died in infancy. Selma, maid of Safīya, Mohammad's aunt, officiated as midwife on these occasions. Khadīja sacrificed at the birth of each boy two kids, and one at the birth of every girl. Her children she nursed herself. Many years after, Mohammad used to look back to this period of his life with fond remembrance. Indeed so much did he dwell upon the mutual love of Khadīja and himself, that the envious 'Ā'isha declared herself more jealous of this rival whom she had never seen, than of all the other wives who contested with her the affection of the Prophet.

No description of Mohammad at this period has been attempted by traditionists. But from the copious accounts of his person in later life, an approximate outline may be traced of his appearance in the prime of manhood. Slightly above the middle size, his figure though spare was handsome and commanding; the chest broad and open; the bones and framework large, and the joints well knit together. His neck was long and finely moulded. His head, unusually large, gave space for a broad and noble brow. The hair, thick, jet black, and slightly curling, fell down over his ears. The eyebrows were arched and joined. The countenance thin, but ruddy. His large eyes, intensely black and piercing, received additional lustre from eyelashes long and dark. The nose was high and slightly acquiline, but fine, and at the end attenuated. The teeth were far apart. A long black bushy beard, reaching to the breast, added manliness and presence. His expression was pensive and contemplative. The face beamed with intelligence, though something of the sensuous might also be discerned. The skin was clear and soft; the only hair that met the eye was a fine thin line which ran down from the neck towards the navel. His broad back leaned slightly forward as he walked; and his step was hasty, yet sharp and decided, like that of one rapidly descending a declivity.

There was something unsettled in his bloodshot eye, which refused to rest upon its object. When he turned towards you, it was never partially, but with the whole body. Taciturn and reserved, he was yet in company distinguished by a graceful urbanity. His words were pregnant and laconic; but when it pleased him to unbend, his speech was often humorous and sometimes pungent. At such seasons he entered with zest into the diversion of the moment, and now and then would laugh immoderately. But in general he listened to the conversation rather than joined in it.

He was the subject of strong passions, but they were so controlled by reason and discretion, that they rarely appeared upon the surface. When much excited, the vein between his eyebrows would mantle, and violently swell across his ample forehead; yet he was cautious and circumspect, and in action kept ever aloof from danger. Generous and considerate towards his friends, he knew, by well-timed favour and attention, how to gain over even the disaffected and rivet them to his service. His enemies, so long as they continued their opposition, were regarded by him with a vindictive and unrelenting hatred; yet he rarely pursued a foe after he had tendered timely submission. His commanding mien inspired the stranger with an undefined and indescribable awe; but on closer intimacy, apprehension and fear gave place to confidence and love.

Behind his quiet retiring exterior lay hid a high resolve, a singleness of purpose, a strength and fixedness of will, a sublime determination, destined to achieve the marvellous work of bowing towards himself the heart of all Arabia as the heart of one man. Khadīja was the first to perceive the noble and commanding qualities of her husband, and with a childlike confidence surrendered to him her soul, her will, and faith.

19. THE HEGIRA [1]

One of the latest biographies of Mohammed or Mahomet is a sketch by a French writer, Émile Dermenghem. In The Life of Mahomet *this author has made an attempt to reproduce as nearly as possible the original sources which tell of the contact between the Arab prophet and his immediate followers. The conversations translated here may not repeat exactly every word spoken, but they seem very nearly true. Furthermore, there is in this remarkable book an atmosphere which greatly helps the western reader to*

[1] Émile Dermenghem, *The Life of Mahomet*, translated by Arabella Yorke, London, George Routledge and Sons, 1930, pp. 141–143, 144–147, 148, 150, 150–153.

understand the environment in which Mahomet labored. The chapter on the Hegira is particularly instructive and interesting, partly because this event, the so-called Hegira, was the most important in the life of Mahomet and in the history of Mohammedanism.

On the desert plain of 'Aqaba of Mina at the foot of a forbidding mountain the pilgrims of Yathrib performed the thousand-year-old magic rite of throwing stones against a small column; then, night having come on, they went into their tents and slept. The victims had been sacrificed and the pilgrimage was over.

Not all of them, however, really slept. Just before midnight seventy-five of them arose noiselessly and went towards the plain of 'Aqaba, seating themselves on the rocks to wait in silence. It was a solemn and decisive moment. Doubtless, these men did not realize that this midnight gathering marked a turning point in the history of the world; yet they did realize the gravity of their act. These were the Mussulmans of Yathrib converted by Mus'ab ben 'Omair and a secret meeting with the Prophet had been arranged.

The year before (621) in the same spot and under similar conditions Mahomet had met twelve pilgrims from Yathrib who took an oath, in their own names and in those of their absent wives, to associate no other creature with God, not to steal, not to commit adultery, not to kill their children even though they found themselves too poor to nourish them, not to slander, and to obey the Prophet in all things just.

These Arabs of Yathrib, accustomed to the monotheistic idea through association with their Jewish allies, now wondered whether this extraordinary man was not the Prophet so often spoken of by the children of Israel, whose coming was to announce the end of the world. In that case, it were better to adhere to him from the first. Some of them, however, hoped that his coming to Yathrib would bring peace to the city, long torn by a ruinous civil war between the rival tribes of the Aws and the Khazraj.

These circumstances shaped the destiny of Mahomet. For more than ten years he had preached in vain to his fellow-townsmen. After having sacrificed his comfort, his fortune and his peace of mind, Mahomet reached middle age without any dream of retiring in peace and tranquillity; on the contrary, he was ready to make new sacrifices. Spurred on by unexpected support, he began to think of exiling himself and so embark on the great adventure. The people of Yathrib would give him, perhaps, the support he had failed to find either amongst his own people or those of Taïf.

It was midnight. Several men draped in white climbed the slope—Mahomet and the Mussulmans of Mecca. Mahomet addressed a pathetic speech to the converts of Yathrib and recited from the Koran. He implored them to worship openly the true God and to follow him, God's Prophet, through both good and evil fortune, to give to the faithful of Mecca the same protection they would afford to their own wives and children. . . .

He stretched his hand towards them and they all swore faith unto him. El Barra' was the first to touch his hand; when all of them, including two women, had done the same, El 'Abbas ben 'Obada said to Mahomet:—

"In the name of Him who sent you to us with the Truth, tomorrow, if you wish it, we will attack the idolaters of Mina!"

"I have not received such an order from God," replied Mahomet. "Return in peace."

It was at this taking of the oath for the second time at 'Aqaba, known as "the men's oath" (the oath of the previous year was known as "the women's oath"), that the principle of the holy war was proposed for the first time. Until then, God had not permitted his Prophet to draw the sword; for the Koran contained only exhortations of patience. During thirteen years Mahomet and his followers had answered persecution by gentleness and forgiveness. Henceforth, the Mussulmans were permitted to render blow for blow, but only when the specific order came from on high.

As the gathering was dispersing, the conspirators heard a mysterious, threatening voice coming from behind the rocks of Mina. This strange cry in the night troubled them greatly, but Mahomet (they say) declared it to be the voice of the demon, from whom they had nothing to fear, telling them to enter their tents and sleep peacefully. Could the mysterious voice have been a spy sent by the Qoraishites?

Mahomet ordered his followers to go to Yathrib in small groups. About a hundred men and women thus exiled themselves and the prophet remained with 'Ali and Abu Bakr although the latter also wanted to go to Yathrib.

"Do not be impatient," said Mahomet. "Wait for me, for I, too, soon hope to be authorized (by God) to emigrate."

"Really! You expect that?" exclaimed Abu Bakr in great joy. "I would give my father and my mother to redeem you!"

Abu Bakr therefore made arrangements to take flight at the same time as his friend; and held in readiness two swift she-camels that had been fed for four months on the leaves of the *samora*.

Mahomet came to his house every evening, but one day he arrived at noon.

"Something serious has happened," Abu Bakr said to himself.

"Make everyone leave who is under your roof," Mahomet whispered.

"Only my two daughters, 'Aïsha and Asma, are here."

"Very well, I have just received the authorization to leave."

"Then I shall accompany you, O Messenger of God!"

"You may accompany me."

All had been carefully prepared. Had the Chorashites known of Mahomet's attempt to leave, they might have killed him. The story goes that 'Ali lay in Mahomet's bed wrapped in the Prophet's green cloak, well-known to everyone. The Prophet then went to Abu Bakr's house and they fled together. For three days and three nights they hid in a cave on Mt. Thawr, three miles from Mecca to the southwest, on the other side from the road to Yathrib.

The time was past for patiently bearing persecution, for turning the other cheek. Islam must either conquer or die. Other prophets had come and had performed miracles but the people had put them to death or held them in derision. Mahomet performed no miracles; neither did he intend to allow himself to be put to death. He had tried gentle persuasion, he had borne every manner of persecution, he had been spared nothing. Now, the last one, he must fly with Abu Bakr, hiding under his cloak the flickering flame of the new faith. Other prophets had come with miracles and holy words. Now Mahomet had come with the sword.

A new life had begun for him. Hereafter he must be a general and the chief of a state. Without ceasing to be an inspired prophet declaiming the suras, he must be a political leader. Perhaps at times he looked back on the past with longing. Perhaps in the midst of harsh realities that destroyed his dream, in the midst of the ebb and flow of earthly matters, he longed for the days spent in the exaltation of solitary meditation in the cave on Mt. Hira, the days when he preached in secret to Khadīja, 'Ali and Zaid, the days when he cried aloud in the Ka'ba that there was but one living God.

And so, too, perhaps in the midst of the voluptuous pleasures of the harem amongst his nine wives, some selected for love and others for political reasons, he longed for the pure joys of his fireside with the gentle Khadīja. A new life indeed. . . .

At this moment he was taking away with him the germ of salvation rejected by his fellow-citizens, the seed which later must be preserved beneath a dome of steel; for paradise lies in the shadow of the sword. With his faith, he fled from the midnight treachery of his countrymen. The pale moon lengthened their two shadows on the sand. Could they escape the pursuit of an entire city, the pursuit of those Arabs so skilful in detecting traces? They hid in the cave. . . .

The days passed anxiously. The two men drank fresh milk and heated what remained on the rocks to keep it from turning. The Qoraishites searched the entire countryside. Mahomet, rigid as a stretched bow, prayed; quicker than the flight of an arrow his prayer mounted to the one Being without whom no creature can exist, without whom the mountains would collapse, the stars crumble into dust, the light of the sun go out, and all souls perish. . . .

Finally the pursuers departed. The two listeners heard their cries to each other and the footsteps of their horses as they turned homewards.

"Glory to God!" cried Mahomet. "God is indeed greatest!" . . .

Mahomet and Abu Bakr mounted and set off, accompanied by the guide and 'Amir on foot. Wishing to avoid the chief route, they went diagonally in a northerly direction, along the borders of the Red Sea. They travelled all that night and part of the next morning without stopping. In order to encourage the camels, the guide sang to them in a monotonous chant tuned to the rhythm of their footsteps.

When the heat became intense and the route was completely deserted, they stopped at the foot of a great rock casting a cool shadow on a small patch of ground never reached by the sun. Abu Bakr spread a fur upon which his friend, worn out by fatigue and thirst, might rest. A shepherd with several sheep came to repose in the shade. Abu Bakr asked him to milk one of his ewes, bidding him remove all hairs and dust from the udder. Then pouring some water from his leather bottle into the milk to cool it, he offered the bowl to the Prophet.

"Is it not time to set forth again?" asked Mahomet.

"Yes, the sun is beginning to go down."

The Qoraishites, however, had offered a reward of a hundred camels to anyone who would bring back Mahomet, dead or alive. All the neighbouring tribes were warned. Soraqa ben Malik, a Bedouin of the Madbah tribe, resolved to gain the reward. One of his tribesman pointed out some dark shapes going in the direction of the coast.

"These must be So-and-So and So-and-So gone in search of straying camels," he said, wishing secretly to take advantage of the knowledge, and he remained several minutes in the group to divert their attention; but going home, he sent a servant to post a horse behind a sand dune and slipped out of the rear end of his tent, armed from head to foot.

Soon he almost caught up with the Prophet and his companions. He could hear the Prophet reciting from the Koran. The fugitives were unarmed. Abu Bakr, turning his head, realized that he would soon be at their side, and manifested his uneasiness to the Prophet. But a strange fear suddenly came over Soraqa; his horse slipped, or stumbled against a stone. Mahomet, seeing his distress, addressed him in eloquent words, and the Bedouin, who was in an awkward position and also greatly impressed, begged the four men to spare him and to intercede with heaven in his favour.

Then he turned homewards and covered up the flight of the Prophet by saying to those he met on the way:

"I am taking charge of the pursuit on this side. You go the other way."

Being a canny Bedouin, however, he had asked Mahomet to make a mark on his quiver in testimony of their meeting. Years later, after Islam had triumphed, he made good use of this.

The fugitives continued their path towards Yathrib. They crossed the dunes, where the vegetation had begun to dry up under the summer sun, the hills, of a muddy yellow or a dull blue, were dotted with little trees, whose leaves were eaten in times of scarcity; they then passed a volcanic region where the desert takes on a tragic aspect with its plains of black lava and its mountains of old craters spotted with blue basalt, rose porphyry and silvery soapstone. The farther north they went, the more scarce water became. Little springs surrounded by palm-trees, open wells of yellowish water along the trail or natural cisterns in the hollows of the rocks were all that could be found. The region was inhabited by nomads with a few permanent inhabitants living in miserable villages of mud houses covered with tiles of lava.

After seven days of travel, they approached Yathrib. Already they had came upon the great *kasbas* of the tribes living in the suburbs and they could hear the doves cooing to each other in the towers. The fugitives were beyond all danger. The Banu Sahm tribe, headed by its Sheikh, Boraïda, came forth to meet the Prophet. Ez Zubaïr, Asma's husband, was at the head of a caravan coming from Syria which had crossed them on their route. He had furnished them with new white garments.

At last, on a Monday, the 12th Rabi', they reached Quba, two miles from Yathrib, where they were joined by 'Ali, who arrived in a pitiful state, having made the trip on foot, travelling by night and hiding by day. Quba was a village on a fertile hillside, covered with gardens and vineyards, date, fig, orange and pomegranate trees. The Prophet stayed there four days and laid the foundations of what was perhaps the first mosque. On Friday after having delivered a long sermon and his first public prayer, Mahomet made a triumphant entry into Yathrib, now Medina, as we have already related.

Several days later, the faithful Zaid, 'Aïsha and Asma, the two daughters of Abu Bakr, and the family of the Prophet, arrived. Thus all the Moslems of Mecca, excepting some slaves, some of lukewarm faith, and a few renegades "unfaithful to their own souls," had left their native country. They were called the Emigrants, *Mohajirûn*. The inhabitants of Medina were known as the Aids of the Prophet, the *Ansar*. All were his Companions, *Sahaba*.

Such was the celebrated emigration, the Hegira, from which the Caliph 'Omar dated the Moslem era.

20. *MOHAMMED AS A PROPHET*[1]

In the preceding selection we have seen how the Hegira took place. We are now prepared to take up the story after this flight by Mohammed and his followers to the city which is now called Medina. Mohammed as a prophet has been described by Thomas Carlyle in a lecture devoted entirely to this subject. A part of this lecture is reproduced here.

In the thirteenth year of his mission, finding his enemies all banded against him, forty sworn men, one out of every tribe waiting to take his life, and no continuance possible at Mecca for him any longer, Mahomet fled to the place then called Yathreb, where he had gained some adherents; the place they now call Medina, or "*Medinat al Nabim,* the City of the Prophet," from that circumstance. It lay some 200 miles off, through rocks and deserts; not without great difficulty, in such mood as we may fancy, he escaped thither, and found welcome. The whole East dates its era from this Flight, *Hegira,* as they name it: the Year 1 of this Hegira is 622 of our Era, the fifty-third of Mahomet's life. He was now becoming an old man; his friends sinking round him one by one; his path desolate, encompassed with danger: unless he could find hope in his own heart, the outward face of things was but hopeless for him. It is so with all men in the like case. Hitherto Mahomet had professed to publish his Religion by the way of preaching and persuasion alone. But now, driven foully out of his native country, since unjust men had not only given no ear to his earnest Heaven's message, the deep cry of his heart, but would not even let him live if he kept speaking it—the wild Son of the Desert resolved to defend himself, like a man and Arab. If the Koreish will have it so, they shall have it. Tidings, felt to be of infinite moment to them and all men, they would not listen to these; would trample them down by sheer violence, steel and murder: well, let steel try it, then! Ten years more this Mahomet had; all of fighting, of breathless, impetuous toil and struggle; with what result we know.

Much has been said of Mahomet's propagating his Religion by the sword. It is no doubt far nobler what we have to boast of the Christian Religion, that it propagated itself peaceably in the way of preaching and conviction. Yet withal, if we take this for an argument of the truth or falsehood of a religion, there is a radical mistake in it. The sword indeed: but where will you get your sword! Every new opinion, at its starting, is precisely in a *minority of one*. In one man's head alone, there it dwells as yet. One

[1] Thomas Carlyle, *Heroes and Hero Worship,* Lecture II: "The Hero as Prophet. Mahomet: Islam." Published separately by Maynard, Merrill and Co., New York, 1882, pp. 28–33.

man alone of the whole world believes it; there is one man against all men. That *he* take a sword, and try to propagate with that, will do little for him. You must first get your sword! On the whole, a thing will propagate itself as it can. We do not find, of the Christian Religion either, that it always disdained the sword, when once it had got one. Charlemagne's conversion of the Saxons was not by preaching. I care little about the sword: I will allow a thing to struggle for itself in this world, with any sword or tongue or implement it has, or can lay hold of. We will let it preach, and pamphleteer, and fight, and to the uttermost bestir itself, and do, beak and claws, whatsoever is in it; very sure that it will, in the long run, conquer nothing that does not deserve to be conquered. What is better than itself, it cannot put away, but only what is worse. In this great Duel, Nature herself is umpire, and can do no wrong: the thing which is deepest-rooted in Nature, what we call *truest,* that thing, and not the other, will be found growing at last.

It was during these wild warfarings and strugglings, especially after the Flight to Mecca, that Mahomet dictated at intervals his Sacred Book, which they name *Koran,* or *Reading,* "Thing to be read." This is the Work, he and his disciples made so much of, asking all the world, Is not that a miracle? The Mahometans regard their Koran with a reverence which few Christians pay even to their Bible. It is admitted everywhere as the standard of all law and all practice; the thing to be gone upon in speculation and life; the message sent direct out of Heaven, which this Earth has to conform to, and walk by; the thing to be read. Their Judges decide by it; all Moslems are bound to study it, seek in it for the light of their life. They have mosques where it is all read daily; thirty relays of priests take it up in succession, get through the whole each day. There, for twelve hundred years, has the voice of this Book, at all moments, kept sounding through the ears and the hearts of so many men. We hear of Mahometan Doctors that had read it seventy thousand times!

Very curious: if one sought for "discrepancies of national taste," here surely were the most eminent instance of that! We also can read the Koran; our Translation of it, by Sale, is known to be a very fair one. I must say, it is as toilsome reading as I ever undertook. A wearisome confused jumble, crude, incondite; endless iterations, longwindedness, entanglement; most crude, incondite;—insupportable stupidity, in short! Nothing but a sense of duty could carry any European through the Koran. We read in it, as we might in the State-Paper Office, unreadable masses of lumber, that perhaps we may get some glimpses of a remarkable man. It is true we have it under disadvantages: the Arabs see more method in it than we. Mahomet's followers found the Koran lying all in fractions, as it had been written down at first promulgation; much of it, they say, on the shoulder-blades of mutton, flung pellmell into a chest: and they published it, without any discoverable order as to time or otherwise;—merely trying, as would seem, and this not very strictly, to put the longest chapters first. The real beginning of it, in that way, lies almost at the end: for the earliest portions were the shortest. Read in its historical sequence it perhaps would not be so bad. Much of it too, they say, is rhythmic; a kind of wild, chaunting song, in the original. This may be a great point; much perhaps has been lost in the Translation here. Yet with every allowance, one feels it difficult to see how any mortal ever could consider this Koran as a Book written in Heaven, too good for the Earth; as a well-written book, or indeed as a book at all; and not a bewildered rhapsody; written, so far as writing goes, as badly as almost any book ever was! So much for national discrepancies, and the standard of taste.

Yet I should say, it was not unintelligible how the Arabs might so love it. When once you get this confused coil of a Koran fairly off your hands, and have it behind you at a distance, the essential type of it begins to disclose itself; and in this there is a merit quite other than the literary one. If a book come from the heart, it will contrive to reach other hearts; all art and authorcraft are of small amount to that. One would say the primary character of the Koran is this of its *genuineness,* of its being a *bona-fide* book. Prideaux, I know, and others have represented it as a mere bundle of juggleries; chapter after chapter got up to excuse and varnish the author's successive sins, forward his ambitions and quackeries: but really it is time to dismiss all that. I do not assert Mahomet's continual sincerity: who is continually sincere? But I confess I can make nothing of the critic, in these times, who would accuse him of deceit *prepense,* of conscious deceit generally, or perhaps at all;—still more, of living in a mere element of conscious deceit, and writing this Koran as a forger and juggler would have done! Every candid eye, I think, will read the Koran far otherwise than so. It is the confused ferment of a great rude human soul; rude, untutored, that cannot even read; but fervent, earnest, struggling vehemently to utter itself in words. With a kind of breathless intensity he strives to utter himself; the thoughts crowd on him pellmell; for very multitude of things to say he can get nothing said. The meaning that is in him shapes itself into no form of composition, is stated in no sequence, method, or coherence;—they are not *shaped* at all, these thoughts of his; flung out unshaped, as they struggle and tumble there, in their chaotic inarticulate state. We said "stupid": yet natural stupidity is by no means the character of Mahomet's Book; it is natural uncultivation rather. The man has not studied speaking; in the haste and pressure of continual fighting, has not time to mature himself into fit speech. The panting, breathless haste and vehemence of a man struggling in the thick of battle for life and salvation;

this is the mood he is in! A headlong haste; for very magnitude of meaning he cannot get himself articulated into words. The successive utterances of a soul in that mood, colored by various vicissitudes of three-and-twenty years; now well uttered, now worse: this is the Koran.

21. THE KORAN [1]

The Koran, like the Bible, is a book which by many people is said to be "revealed" or "inspired." The contents of the Koran, according to the Mohammedans, were revealed to Mohammed and written down by his immediate followers, to whom he is supposed to have related them. Generally speaking the Koran is much inferior to the Bible, both in contents and literary value. The earlier chapters in the Koran are certainly not very interesting, nor are they very instructive or inspiring. An excellent analysis of the whole work has been given by an English scholar, George Sale, which he published as an introduction to his translation of the Koran. We have selected from this translation the fifty-sixth chapter.

Chapter LVI

The Inevitable

In the Name of the Most Merciful God.

When the inevitable day of judgment shall suddenly come, no soul shall charge the prediction of its coming with falsehood: it will abase some, and exalt others. When the earth shall be shaken with a violent shock; and the mountains shall be dashed in pieces, and shall become as dust scattered abroad; and ye shall be separated into three distinct classes: the companions of the right hand; (how happy shall the companions of the right hand be!) and the companions of the left hand: (how miserable shall the companions of the left hand be!) and those who have preceded others in the faith shall precede them to paradise. These are they who shall approach near unto God: they shall dwell in gardens of delight: (There shall be many of the former religions; and few of the last.) Reposing on couches adorned with gold and precious stones; sitting opposite to one another thereon. Youths which shall continue in their bloom for ever, shall go round about to attend them, with goblets, and beakers, and a cup of flowing wine: their heads shall not ache by drinking the same, neither shall their reason be disturbed: and with fruits of the sorts which they shall choose, and the flesh of birds

[1] Translated into English immediately from the Arabic by George Sale. Philadelphia, J. B. Lippincott and Co., 1871, pp. 435–438.

of the kind which they shall desire. And there shall accompany them fair damsels having large black eyes; resembling pearls hidden in their shells: as a reward for that which they shall have wrought. They shall not hear therein any vain discourse, or any charge of sin; but only the salutation, Peace! Peace! And the companions of the right hand (how happy shall the companions of the right hand be!) shall have their abode among lote trees free from thorns, and trees of mauz loaded regularly with their produce from top to bottom; under an extended shade, near a flowing water, and amidst fruits in abundance, which shall not fail, nor shall be forbidden to be gathered: and they shall repose themselves on lofty beds. Verily we have created the damsels of paradise by a peculiar creation: and we have made them virgins, beloved by their husbands, of equal age with them; for the delight of the companions of the right hand. There shall be many of the former religions, and many of the latter. And the companions of the left hand (how miserable shall the companions of the left hand be!) shall dwell amidst burning winds, and scalding water, under the shade of a black smoke, neither cool nor agreeable. For they enjoyed the pleasures of life before this, while on earth; and obstinately persisted in a heinous wickedness: and they said, After we shall have died, and become dust and bones, shall we surely be raised to life? Shall our forefathers also be raised with us? Say, verily both the first and the last shall surely be gathered together to judgment, at the prefixed time of a known day. Then ye, O men, who have erred, and denied the resurrection as a falsehood, shall surely eat of the fruit of the tree of al Zakkum, and shall fill your bellies therewith: and ye shall drink thereon boiling water; and ye shall drink as a thirsty camel drinketh. This shall be their entertainment on the day of judgment. We have created you: will ye not therefore believe that we can raise you from the dead? What think ye? The seed which ye emit, do ye create the same, or are we the creators thereof? We have decreed death unto you all: and we shall not be prevented. We are able to substitute others like unto you in your stead, and to produce you again in the condition or form which ye know not. Ye know the original production by creation; will ye not therefore consider that we are able to produce you by resuscitation? What think ye? The grain which ye sow, do ye cause the same to spring forth, or do we cause it to spring forth? If we pleased, verily we could render the same dry and fruitless, so that ye would not cease to wonder, saying verily we have contracted debts for seed and labour, but we are not permitted to reap the fruit thereof. What think ye? The water which ye drink, do ye send down the same from the clouds, or are we the senders thereof? If we pleased, we could render the same brackish: will ye not therefore give thanks? What think ye? The fire which ye strike, do ye produce the tree whence ye obtain the same, or are we the producers thereof? We have ordained the same for an admonition, and an advantage to those who travel through the deserts. Wherefore praise the name of thy Lord, the great God. Moreover I swear by the setting of the stars; (and it is surely a great oath, if ye knew it;) that this is the excellent Koran, the original whereof is written in the preserved book: none shall touch the same, except those who are clean. It is a revelation from the Lord of all creatures. Will ye, therefore, despise this new revelation? And do ye make this return for your food which ye receive from God, that ye deny yourselves to be obliged to him for the same? When the soul of a dying person cometh up to his throat, and ye at the same time are looking on; (and we are nigher unto him than ye, but ye see not his true condition;) would ye not, if ye are not to be rewarded for your actions hereafter, cause the same to return into the body, if ye speak the truth? . . . Whether he be of the companions of the right hand, he shall be saluted with the salutation, Peace be unto thee! by the companions of the right hand, his brethren: or whether he be of those who have rejected the true faith, and gone astray, his entertainment shall consist of boiling water, and the burning of hell fire. Verily this is a certain truth. Wherefore praise the name of thy Lord, the great God.

22. *ARABIC CIVILIZATION IN SPAIN*[1]

John William Draper (1811–1882), an Englishman who migrated to America, became professor of chemistry in the University of the City of New York (now New York University) and later president of the medical school of the same institution. He distinguished himself both as a scientist and a historian. His chief work, from which an extract is here given, was his History of the Intellectual Development of Europe, *first published in 1863. "It remains today," according to the Dictionary of American Biography, "after sixty-seven years, a work of prime importance."*

Renouncing the orthodox beliefs of his youth Dr. Draper became critical of historical Christianity. On the other hand he came to admire the achievements of the medieval Arabs. So he paints a glowing picture, perhaps too glowing, of Arabic civilization in Spain at a time when the civilization of Christian Europe was about at its lowest ebb.

A pressure upon the Italian system had meantime been arising in the West. It was due to the presence of the Arabs in Spain. It is necessary, therefore, to relate the circumstances of their invasion and conquest of that

[1] J. W. Draper, *History of the Intellectual Development of Europe,* Fifth Edition. New York, Harper and Brothers, 1872, pp. 345; 347–356.

country, and to compare their social and intellectual condition with the contemporary state of Christendom.

From the barbarism of the native people of Europe, who could scarcely be said to have emerged from the savage state, unclean in person, benighted in mind, inhabiting huts in which it was a mark of wealth if there were bulrushes on the floor and straw mats against the wall; miserably fed on beans, vetches, roots, and even the bark of trees; clad in garments of untanned skin, or at the best of leather—perennial in durability, but not conducive to personal purity—a state in which the pomp of royalty was sufficiently and satisfactorily manifested in the equipage of the sovereign, an ox-cart, drawn by not less than two yokes of cattle, quickened in their movements by the goads of pedestrian serfs, whose legs were wrapped in wisps of straw; from a people, devout believers in all the wild fictions of shrine-miracles and preposterous relics; from the degradation of a base theology, and from the disputes of ambitious ecclesiastics for power, it is pleasant to turn to the south-west corner of the continent, where, under auspices of a very different kind, the irradiations of light were to break forth. The crescent in the West was soon to pass eastward to its full. . . .

Scarcely had the Arabs become firmly settled in Spain when they commenced a brilliant career. Adopting what had now become the established policy of the Commanders of the Faithful in Asia, the Emirs of Cordova distinguished themselves as patrons of learning, and set an example of refinement strongly contrasting with the condition of the native European princes. Cordova, under their administration, at its highest point of prosperity, boasted of more than two hundred thousand houses, and more than a million of inhabitants. After sunset, a man might walk through it in a straight line for ten miles by the light of the public lamps. Seven hundred years after this time there was not so much as one public lamp in London. Its streets were solidly paved. In Paris, centuries subsequently, whoever stepped over his threshold on a rainy day stepped up to his ankles in mud. Other cities, as Granada, Seville, Toledo, considered themselves rivals of Cordova. The palaces of the khalifs were magnificently decorated. Those sovereigns might well look down with supercilious contempt on the dwellings of the rulers of Germany, France, and England, which were scarcely better than stables—chimneyless, windowless, and with a hole in the roof for the smoke to escape, like the wigwams of certain Indians. The Spanish Mohammedans had brought with them all the luxuries and prodigalities of Asia. Their residences stood forth against the clear sky, or were embosomed in woods. They had polished marble balconies, overhanging orange-gardens; courts with cascades of water; shady retreats provocative of slumber in the heat of the day; retiring-rooms vaulted with stained glass, speckled with gold, over which streams of water were made to gush; the floors and walls were of exquisite mosaic. Here, a fountain of quicksilver shot up in a glistening spray, the glittering particles falling with a tranquil sound like fairy bells; there, apartments into which cool air was drawn from the flower-gardens, in summer, by means of ventilating towers, and in winter through earthen pipes, or caleducts, imbedded in the walls—the hypocaust, in the vaults below, breathing forth volumes of warm and perfumed air through these hidden passages. The walls were not covered with wainscot, but adorned with arabesques, and paintings of agricultural scenes and views of Paradise. From the ceilings, corniced with fretted gold, great chandeliers hung, one of which, it is said, was so large that it contained 1084 lamps. Clusters of frail marble columns surprised the beholder with the vast weights they bore. In the boudoirs of the sultanas they were sometimes of verd antique, and incrusted with lapis lazuli. The furniture was of sandal and citron wood, inlaid with mother-of-pearl, ivory, silver, or relieved with gold and precious malachite. In orderly confusion were arranged vases of rock crystal, Chinese porcelains, and tables of exquisite mosaic. The winter apartments were hung with rich tapestry; the floors were covered with embroidered Persian carpets. Pillows and couches, of elegant forms, were scattered about the rooms, perfumed with frankincense. It was the intention of the Saracen architect, by excluding the view of the external landscape, to concentrate attention on his work; and since the representation of the human form was religiously forbidden, and that source of decoration denied, his imagination ran riot with the complicated arabesques he introduced, and sought every opportunity of replacing the prohibited works of art by the trophies and rarities of the garden. For this reason, the Arabs never produced artists; religion turned them from the beautiful, and made them soldiers, philosophers, and men of affairs. Splendid flowers and rare exotics ornamented the courtyards and even the inner chambers. Great care was taken to make due provision for the cleanliness, occupation, and amusement of the inmates. Through pipes of metal, water, both warm and cold, to suit the season of the year, ran into baths of marble; in niches, where the current of air could be artificially directed, hung dripping alcarazzas. There were whispering-galleries for the amusement of the women; labyrinths and marble play-courts for the children; for the master himself, grand libraries. The Khalif Alhakem's was so large that the catalogue alone filled forty volumes. He had also apartments for the transcribing, binding, and ornamenting of books. A taste for caligraphy and the possession of splendidly illuminated manuscripts seems to have anticipated in the khalifs, both of Asia and Spain, the taste for statuary and paintings among the later popes of Rome.

Such were the palace and gardens of Zehra, in which Abderrahman III honoured his favourite sultana. The edifice had 1200 columns of Greek,

Italian, Spanish, and African marble. Its hall of audience was incrusted with gold and pearls. Through the long corridors of its seraglio black eunuchs silently glided. The ladies of the harem, both wives and concubines, were the most beautiful that could be found. To that establishment alone 6300 persons were attached. The body-guard of the sovereign was composed of 12,000 horsemen, whose cimeters and belts were studded with gold. This was that Abderrahman who, after a glorious reign of fifty years, sat down to count the number of days of unalloyed happiness he had experienced, and could only enumerate fourteen. "Oh man!" exclaimed the plaintive khalif, "put not thy trust in this present world."

No nation has ever excelled the Spanish Arabs in the beauty and costliness of their pleasure-gardens. To them we owe the introduction of very many of our most valuable cultivated fruits, such as the peach. Retaining the love of their ancestors for the cooling effect of water in a hot climate, they spared no pains in the superfluity of fountains, hydraulic works, and artificial lakes in which fish were raised for the table. Into such a lake, attached to the palace of Cordova, many loaves were cast each day to feed the fish. There were also menageries of foreign animals; aviaries of rare birds; manufactories in which skilled workmen, obtained from foreign countries, displayed their art in textures of silk, cotton, linen, and all the miracles of the loom; in jewelry and filigree-work, with which they ministered to the female pride of the sultanas and concubines. Under the shade of cypresses cascades disappeared; among flowering shrubs there were winding walks, bowers of roses, seats cut out of the rock, and crypt-like grottoes hewn in the living stone. Nowhere was ornamental gardening better understood; for not only did the artist try to please the eye as it wandered over the pleasant gradation of vegetable color and form—he also boasted his success in the gratification of the sense of smell by the studied succession of perfumes from beds of flowers.

To these Saracens we are indebted for many of our personal comforts. Religiously cleanly, it was not possible for them to clothe themselves according to the fashion of the natives of Europe, in a garment unchanged till it dropped to pieces of itself, a loathsome mass of vermin, stench, and rags. No Arab who had been a minister of state, or the associate or antagonist of a sovereign, would have offered such a spectacle as the corpse of Thomas à Becket when his haircloth shirt was removed. They taught us the use of the often-changed and often-washed under-garment of linen or cotton, which still passes among ladies under its old Arabic name. But to cleanliness they were not unwilling to add ornament. Especially among women of the higher classes was the love of finery a passion. Their outer garments were often of silk, embroidered and decorated with gems and woven gold. So fond were the Moorish women of gay colors and the lustre of chrysolites, hyacinths, emeralds, and sapphires, that it was quaintly said that the interior of any public building in which they were permitted to appear looked like a flower-meadow in the spring besprinkled with rain.

In the midst of all this luxury, which cannot be regarded by the historians with disdain, since in the end it produced a most important result in the south of France, the Spanish khalifs, emulating the example of their Asiatic compeers, and in this strongly contrasting with the popes of Rome, were not only the patrons, but the personal cultivators of all the branches of human learning. One of them was himself the author of a work on polite literature in not less than fifty volumes; another wrote a treatise on algebra. When Zaryab the musician came from the East to Spain, the Khalif Abderrahman rode forth to meet him in honor. The College of Music in Cordova was sustained by ample government patronage, and produced many illustrious professors.

The Arabs never translated into their own tongue the great Greek poets, though they so sedulously collected and translated the Greek philosophers. Their religious sentiments and sedate character caused them to abominate the lewdness of our classical mythology, and to denounce indignantly any connexion between the licentious, impure Olympian Jove and the Most High God as an insufferable and unpardonable blasphemy. Haroun Alraschid had gratified his curiosity by causing Homer to be translated into Syriac, but he did not adventure on rendering the great epics into Arabic. Notwithstanding this aversion to our graceful but not unobjectionable ancient poetry, among them originated the Tensons, or poetic disputations, carried afterward to perfection among the Troubadours; from them, also, the Provençals learned to employ jongleurs. Across the Pyrenees, literary, philosophical, and military adventurers were perpetually passing; and thus the luxury, the taste, and above all, the chivalrous gallantry and elegant courtesies of Moorish society found their way from Granada and Cordova to Provence and Languedoc. The French, and German, and English nobles imbibed the Arab admiration for the horse; they learned to pride themselves on skilful riding. Hunting and falconry became their fashionable pastimes; they tried to emulate that Arab skill which had produced the celebrated breed of Andalusian horses. It was a scene of grandeur and gallantry; the pastimes were tilts and tournaments. The refined society of Cordova prided itself in its politeness. A gay contagion spread from the beautiful Moorish miscreants to their sisters beyond the mountains; the south of France was full of the witcheries of female fascinations, and of dancing to the lute and mandolin. Even in Italy and Sicily the love-song became the favorite composition; and out of these genial but not orthodox beginnings the polite literature of modern Europe arose. The pleasant epidemic spread by degrees along every hillside and valley. In monasteries, voices that had vowed celibacy might be heard caroling stanzas of which St. Jerome would hardly have approved; there was many a juicy abbot, who could troll forth in jocund strains, like those of the merry sinners of Malaga and Xeres, the charms of women and wine, though one was forbidden to the Moslem and one to the monk. The sedate greybeards of Cordova had already applied to the supreme judge to have the songs of the Spanish Jew, Abraham Ibn Sahal, prohibited; for there was not a youth, nor woman nor child in the city who could not repeat them by heart. Their immoral tendency was a public scandal. The light gaiety of Spain was reflected in the coarser habits of the northern countries. . . .

Even as early as the tenth century, persons having a taste for learning and for elegant amenities found their way into Spain from all adjoining countries; a practice in subsequent years still more indulged in, when it became illustrated by the brilliant success of Gerbert, who, as we have seen, passed from the infidel University of Cordova to the papacy of Rome.

The khalifs of the West carried out the precepts of Ali, the fourth successor of Mohammed, in the patronage of literature. They established libraries in all their chief towns; it is said that not fewer than seventy were in existence. To every mosque was attached a public school, in which the children of the poor were taught to read and write, and instructed in the precepts of the Koran. For those in easier circumstances there were academies, usually arranged in twenty-five or thirty apartments, each calculated for accommodating four students; the academy being presided over by a rector. In Cordova, Granada, and other great cities, there were universities frequently under the superintendence of Jews; the Mohammedan maxim being that the real learning of a man is of more public importance than any particular religious opinions he may entertain. In this they followed the example of the Asiatic khalif, Haroun Alraschid, who actually conferred the superintendence of his schools on John Masué, a Nestorian Christian. The Mohammedan liberality was in striking contrast with the intolerance of Europe. Indeed, it may be doubted whether at this time any European nation is sufficiently advanced to follow such an example. In the universities some of the professors of polite literature gave lectures on Arabic classical works; others taught rhetoric or composition, or mathematics, or astronomy, or other sciences. From these institutions many of the practices observed in our colleges were derived. They held Commencements, at which poems were read and orations delivered in presence of the public. They had also, in addition to these schools of general learning, professional ones, particularly for medicine.

With a pride perhaps not altogether inexcusable, the Arabians boasted of their language as being the most perfect spoken by man. Mohammed himself, when challenged to produce a miracle in proof of the authenticity of his mission, uniformly pointed to the composition of the Koran, its unapproachable excellence vindicating its inspiration. The orthodox Moslems—the Moslems are those who are submissively resigned to the Divine will—are wont to assert that every page of that book is indeed a conspicuous miracle. It is not then surprising that, in the Arabian schools, great attention was paid to the study of language, and that so many celebrated grammarians were produced. By these scholars, dictionaries, similar to those now in use, were composed; their copiousness is indicated by the circumstance that one of them consisted of sixty volumes, the definition of each word being illustrated or sustained by quotations from Arab authors of acknowleged repute. They had also lexicons of Greek, Latin, Hebrew; and cyclopedias such as the Historical Dictionary of Sciences of Mohammed Ibn Abdallah, of Granada. In their highest civilization and luxury they did not forget the amusements of their forefathers—listening to the tale-teller, who never failed to obtain an audience in the midst of Arab tents. Around the evening fires in Spain the wandering literati exercised their wonderful powers of Oriental invention, edifying the eager listeners by such narrations as those that have descended to us in the Arabian Nights' Entertainments. The more sober and higher efforts of the educated were, of course, directed to pulpit eloquence, in conformity with the example of all the great Oriental khalifs, and sanctified by the practice of the Prophet himself. Their poetical productions embraced all the modern minor forms—satires, odes, elegies, etc.; but they never produced any work in the higher walks of poesy, no epic, no tragedy. Perhaps this was due to their false fashion of valuing the mechanical execution of a work. They were the authors and introducers of rhyme; and such was the luxuriance and abundance of their language, that, in some of their longest poems, the same rhyme is said to have been used alternately from the beginning to the end. Where such mechanical triumphs were popularly prized, it may be supposed that the conception and spirit would be indifferent. Even among the Spanish women there were not a few who, like Velada, Ayesha, Labana, Algasania, achieved reputation in these compositions; and some of them were daughters of khalifs. And this is the more interesting to us, since it was from the Provençal poetry, the direct descendant of these efforts, that European literature arose. Sonnets and romances at last displaced the grimly-orthodox productions of the wearisome and ignorant fathers of the Church.

If fiction was prized among the Spanish Arabs, history was held in not less esteem. Every khalif had his own historian. The instincts of the race are perpetually peeping out; not only were there historians of the Commanders of the Faithful, but also of celebrated horses and illustrious camels. In connexion with history, statistics were cultivated; this having been, it may be said, a necessary study, from the first enforced on the Saracen officers in their assessment of tribute on conquered misbelievers, and subsequently continued as an object of taste. It was, doubtless, a similar necessity, arising from their position, that stamped such a remarkably practical aspect on the science of the Arabs generally. Many of their learned men were travellers and voyagers, constantly moving about for the acquisition or diffusion of knowledge, their acquirements being a passport to them wherever they went, and a sufficient introduction to any of the African or Asiatic courts. They were thus continually brought in contact with men of affairs, soldiers of fortune, statesmen, and became imbued with much of their practical spirit; and hence the singularly romantic character which the biographies of many of these men display, wonderful turns of prosperity, violent deaths. The scope of their literary labors offers a subject well worthy of meditation; it contrasts with the contemporary ignorance of Europe. Some wrote on chronology; some on numismatics; some, now that military eloquence had become objectless, wrote on pulpit oratory; some on agriculture and its allied branches, as the art of irrigation. Not one of the purely mathematical, or mixed, or practical sciences was omitted. Out of a list too long for detailed quotation, I may recall a few names. Assamh, who wrote on topography and statistics, a brave soldier, who was killed in the invasion of France, A. D. 720; Avicenna, the great physician and philosopher, who died A. D. 1037; Averroes, of Cordova, the chief commentator on Aristotle, A. D. 1198. It was his intention to unite the doctrines of Aristotle with those of the Koran. To him is imputed the discovery of spots upon the sun. The leading idea of his philosophy was the numerical unity of the souls of mankind, though parted among millions of living individuals. He died at Morocco. Abu Othman wrote on zoology; Alberuni, on gems—he had travelled to India to procure information; Rhazes, Al Abbas, and Al Beithar, on botany—the latter had been in all parts of the world for the purpose of obtaining specimens. Ebn Zoar, better known as Avenzoar, may be looked upon as the authority in Moorish pharmacy. Pharmacopoeias were published by the schools, improvements on the old ones of the Nestorians: to them may be traced the introduction of many Arabic words, such as sirup, julep, elixir, still used among our apothecaries. A competent scholar might furnish not only an interesting, but valuable book, founded on the remaining relics of the Arab vocabulary; for, in whatever direction we may look, we meet, in the various pursuits of peace and war, of letters and of science, Saracenic vestiges. Our dictionaries tell us that such is the origin of admiral, alchemy, alcohol, algebra, chemise, cotton, and hundreds of other words. The Saracens commenced the application of chemistry, both to the theory and practice of medicine in the explanation of the functions of the human body and in the cure of its diseases. Nor was their surgery behind their medicine. Albucasis, of Cordova, shrinks not from the performance of the most formidable operations in his own and in the obstetrical art; the actual cautery and the knife are used without hesitation. He has left us ample descriptions of the surgical instruments then employed; and from him we learn that, in operations on females in which considerations of delicacy intervened, the services of properly instructed women were secured. How different was all this from the state of things in Europe: the Christian peasant, fever-stricken or overtaken by accident, hied to the nearest saint-shrine and expected a miracle; the Spanish Moor relied on the prescription or lancet of his physician, or the bandage and knife of his surgeon.

In mathematics the Arabians acknowledged their indebtedness to two sources, Greek and Indian, but they greatly improved upon both. The Asiatic khalifs had made exertions to procure translations of Euclid, Apollonius, Archimedes, and other Greek geometers. Almaimon, in a letter to the Emperor Theophilus, expressed his desire to visit Constantinople if his public duties would have permitted. He requests of him to allow Leo the mathematician to come to Bagdad to impart to him a portion of his learning, pledging his word that he would restore him quickly and safely again. "Do not," says the high-minded khalif, "let diversity of religion or of country cause you to refuse my request. Do what friendship would concede to a friend. In return, I offer you a hundred weight of gold, a perpetual alliance and peace." True to the instincts of his race and the traditions of his city, the Byzantine sourly and insolently refused the request, saying that "the learning which had illustrated the Roman name should never be imparted to a barbarian."

From the Hindus the Arabs learned arithmetic, especially that valuable invention termed by us the Arabic numerals, but honourably ascribed by them to its proper source, under the designation of "Indian numerals." They also entitled their treatises on the subject "Systems of Indian Arithmetic." This admirable notation by nine digits and cipher occasioned a complete revolution in arithmetical computations. As in the case of so many other things, the Arab impress is upon it; our word cipher, and its derivatives, ciphering, etc., recall the Arabic word tsaphara or ciphra, the name for the o, and meaning that which is blank or void. Mohammed Ben Musa, said to be the earliest of the Saracen authors on algebra, and who made the great improvement of substituting sines for chords in trigonometry, wrote also on this Indian system. He lived at the end of the ninth century; before the end of the tenth it was in common use among the African and Spanish mathematicians. Ebn Junis, A.D. 1008, used it in his astronomical works. From Spain it passed into Italy, its singular advantage in commercial computation causing it to be eagerly adopted in the great trading cities. We still use the word algorithm in reference to calculations. The study of algebra was intently cultivated among the Arabs, who gave it the name it bears. Ben Musa, just referred to, was the inventor of the common method of solving quadratic equations. In the application of mathematics to astronomy and physics they had been long distinguished. . . .

Almaimon had also ascertained the size of the earth from the measurements of a degree on the shore of the Red Sea—an operation implying true ideas of its form, and in singular contrast with the doctrine of Constantinople and Rome. While the latter was asserting, in all its absurdity, the flatness of the earth, the Spanish Moors were teaching geography in their common schools from globes. In Africa, there was still preserved, with almost religious reverence, in the library at Cairo, one of brass, reputed to have belonged to the great astronomer Ptolemy. Al Idrisi made one of silver for Roger II, of Sicily; and Gerbert used one which he had brought from Cordova in the school he established at Rheims. It cost a struggle of several centuries, illustrated by some martyrdoms, before the dictum of Lactantius and Augustine could be overthrown. Among problems of interest that were solved may be mentioned the determination of the length of the year by Albategnius and Thebit Ben Corrah; and increased accuracy was given to the correction of astronomical observations by Alhazen's great discovery of atmospheric refraction. Among the astronomers, some composed tables; some wrote on the measure of time; some on the improvement of clocks, for which purpose they were the first to apply the pendulum; some on instruments, as the astrolabe. The introduction of astronomy into Christian Europe has been attributed to the translation of the works of Mohammed Fargani. In Europe, also, the Arabs were the first to build observatories; the Giralda, or tower of Seville, was erected under the superintendence of Geber, the mathematician, A. D. 1196, for that purpose. Its fate was not a little characteristic. After the expulsion of the Moors it was turned into a belfry, the Spaniards not knowing what else to do with it.

23. *REFLECTION OF AN ARABIAN PHILOSOPHER*[1]

The following excerpt from Dr. Draper's History of the Intellectual Development of Europe *brings out the mental struggles of an Arabian philosopher seeking the nature of reality and shows what conclusion the sage finally reached.*

Before showing how the Arabian intellect pressed upon Rome, and the convulsive struggles of desperation which Rome made to resist it, I must

[1] J. W. Draper, *History of the Intellectual Development of Europe*. Fifth Edition. New York. Harper and Brothers, 1872, pp. 362–364.

for a moment consider the former under another point of view, and speak of Saracen philosophy. And here Algazzali shall be my guide. He was born A. D. 1058.

Let us hear him speak for himself. He is relating his attempt to detach himself from the opinions which he had imbibed in his childhood: "I said to myself, 'My aim is simply to know the truth of things; consequently, it is indispensable for me to ascertain what is knowledge.' Now it was evident to me that certain knowledge must be that which explains the object to be known in such a manner that no doubt can remain, so that in future all error and conjecture respecting it must be impossible. Not only would the understanding then need no efforts to be convinced of certitude, but security against error is in such close connection with knowledge, that, even were an apparent proof of falsehood to be brought forward, it would cause no doubt, because no suspicion of error would be possible. Thus, when I have acknowledged ten to be more than three, if any one were to say, 'On the contrary, three is more than ten, and, to prove the truth of my assertion, I will change this rod into a serpent,' and if he were to change it, my conviction of his error would remain unshaken. His manoeuvre would only produce in me admiration for his ability. I should not doubt my own knowledge.

"Then was I convinced that knowledge which I did not possess in this manner, and respecting which I had not this certainty, could inspire me with neither confidence nor assurance; and no knowledge without assurance deserves the name of knowledge.

"Having examined the state of my own knowledge, I found it divested of all that could be said to have these qualities, unless perceptions of the senses and irrefragable principles were to be considered such. I then said to myself, 'Now, having fallen into this despair, the only hope of acquiring incontestable convictions is by the perceptions of the senses and by necessary truths.' Their evidence seemed to me to be indubitable. I began, however, to examine the objects of sensation and speculation, to see if they possibly could admit of doubt. Then doubts crowded upon me in such numbers that my incertitude became complete. Whence results the confidence I have in sensible things? The strongest of all our senses is sight; and yet, looking at a shadow, and perceiving it to be fixed and immovable, we judge it to be deprived of movement; nevertheless, experience teaches us that, when we return to the same place an hour after, the shadow is displaced, for it does not vanish suddenly, but gradually, little by little, so as never to be at rest. If we look at the stars, they seem to be as small as money-pieces; but mathematical proofs convince us that they are larger than the earth. These and other things are judged by the senses, but rejected by reason as false. I abandoned the senses, therefore, having seen all my confidence in their truth shaken.

"'Perhaps,' said I, 'there is no assurance but in the notions of reason, that is to say, first principles, as that ten is more than three; the same thing can not have been created and yet have existed from all eternity; to exist and not to exist at the same time is impossible.'

"Upon this the senses replied, 'What assurance have you that your confidence in reason is not of the same nature as your confidence in us? When you relied on us, reason stepped in and gave us the lie; had not reason been there, you would have continued to rely on us. Well, may there not exist some other judge superior to reason, who, if he appeared, would refute the judgments of reason in the same way that reason refuted us?. The non-appearance of such a judge is no proof of his non-existence.'

"I strove in vain to answer the objection, and my difficulties increased when I came to reflect on sleep. I said to myself, 'During sleep you give to visions a reality and consistence, and you have no suspicion of their untruth. On awakening, you are made aware that they were nothing but visions. What assurance have you that all you feel and know when you are awake does actually exist? It is all true as respects your condition at that moment; but it is nevertheless possible that another condition should present itself which should be to your awakened state that which to your awakened state is now to you sleep; so that, as respects this higher condition, your waking is but sleep.'"

It would not be possible to find in any European work a clearer statement of the skepticism to which philosophy leads us than what is thus given us by this Arabian. Indeed, it is not possible to put the argument in a more effective way. His perspicuity is in singular contrast with the obscurity of many metaphysical writers.

"Reflecting on my situation, I found myself bound to this world by a thousand ties, temptations assailing me on all sides. I then examined my actions. The best were those relating to instruction and education, and even there I saw myself given up to unimportant sciences, all useless in another world. Reflecting on the aim of my teaching, I found it was not pure in the sight of the Lord. I saw that all my efforts were directed toward the acquisition of glory to myself. Having, therefore, distributed my wealth, I left Bagdad and retired into Syria, where I remained two years in solitary struggle with my soul, combating my passions, and exercising myself in the purification of my heart and in preparation for the other world."

This is a very beautiful picture of the mental struggles and the actions of a truthful and earnest man. In all this the Christian philosopher can sympathize with the devout Mohammedan. After all, they are not very far apart. Algazzali is not the only one to whom such thoughts have occurred, but he has found words to tell his experience better than any other man. And what is the conclusion at which he arrives? The life of man, he says, is marked by three stages: "the first, or infantile stage, is that of pure sensation; the second, which begins at the age of seven, is that of understanding; the third is that of reason, by means of which the intellect perceives the necessary, the possible, the absolute, and all those higher objects which transcend the understanding. But after this there is a fourth stage, when another eye is opened, by which man perceives things hidden from others—perceives all that will be—perceives the things that escape the perceptions of reason, as the objects of reason escape the understanding, and as the objects of the understanding escape the sensitive faculty. This is prophetism." Algazzali thus finds a philosophical basis for the rule of life, and reconciles religion and philosophy.

24. *THE HISTORY OF THE FRANKS, BY GREGORY OF TOURS. EXTRACTS* [1]

Gregory of Tours was born in central Gaul in the year 538. He spent nearly his whole life in the same region, chiefly at Tours, hence his name, Gregory of Tours. Both his father and mother belonged to the privileged classes, and according to him he was related to all the bishops of Tours throughout its history, with the exception of only five. It was natural for him, therefore, to enter the service of the Church. Nor was it difficult for him to become a bishop himself. In this capacity he wrote his History of the Franks, *a work of great historical importance, although dressed in clumsy and inaccurate Latin. We are indebted to the author for the very intimate picture he gives of social life among the Franks in the sixth century.*

The first of the extracts from his work reproduced below tells of the religious fervor of the celebrated Salvian, who, as we have seen before, left an important description of Roman civilization in the sixth century. Many modern readers will be struck by the simple faith and what might be called credulity of this bishop and of the author himself.

In the next chapter we read about civil war among the Franks, while the following selections describe the habits of some of the important Frankish kings and of their followers. It will be seen that the Franks of the sixth and seventh centuries were still in many respects barbarians.

[1] *History of the Franks by Gregory Bishop of Tours,* Selections translated by Ernest Brehaut, New York, Columbia University Press, 1916, pp. 169–172; 189–190; 191–192; 231; 235.

Book VII

Chapter 1. Death of the Holy Bishop Salvius [1]

Though it is my desire to continue the history which the previous books have left untold, still affection requires me first to tell somewhat concerning the death of the blessed Salvius, who, as is well known, died in this year. As he himself was wont to relate he continued for a long time in the secular garb and with secular judges devoted himself to worldly cases, but yet he never entangled himself in the passions in which the mind of the young is usually involved. And finally when the odor of the divine breath had touched his inward parts, he left the warfare of the world and sought a monastery, and being even then devoted to godliness he understood that it was better to be poor with the fear of God than to pursue the gains of the perishing world. In this monastery he continued a long time under the rule established by the fathers. And when he had reached a more mature strength both of understanding and of life, the abbot who was over this monastery died and he took up the task of feeding the flock; and whereas he should have shown himself more commonly among his brethren for their correction, after he had attained this honor he was more retiring; and so he sought for himself a more secluded cell; now in the former, as he himself told, he had changed the skin of his body more than nine times, from scourging himself with too great determination. Then after receiving the office, while he devoted himself to prayer and reading, contented with this abstinence, he kept considering whether it was better for him to be hidden among the monks or to take the name of abbot among the people. Why say more? He said farewell to his brethren and they to him, and was immured. While thus immured he continued in all abstinence more than before; and in his love of charity he sought when any strangers came to bestow his prayers on them and administer the grace of the blessed bread abundantly, which brought sound health to many who were infirm. And once he lay panting on his bed worn out by a high fever, and behold his cell was suddenly brightened by a great light and quivered. And he lifted his hands to heaven and breathed out his spirit while giving thanks. With mingled cries of mourning the monks and his mother took the dead man's body out [of the cell], washed and clothed it and placed it on a bier and spent the night in weeping and singing psalms. In the morning while preparations for the funeral went on the body began to move on the bier. And behold his cheeks regained

[1] Salvius died Sept. 10, 584. Chilperic's death which closes Book VI occurred in 584. On Salvius see p. 8.

color and, as if roused from a deep sleep, he stirred and opened his eyes and lifted his hands and said: "Merciful God, why hast Thou allowed me to return to this gloomy place of life on earth, since Thy mercy in heaven would be better for me than vile life in this world?" His people were wonder-struck and asked what such a prodigy could mean, but he made no answer to their questions. He rose from the bier, feeling no harm from the painful experience he had suffered, and continued for three days without the support of food or drink. On the third day he called the monks and his mother and said: "Listen, dear ones, and understand that what you look upon in this world is nothing, but it is like the prophet Solomon's song, 'All is vanity.' Happy is he who can live in the world so as to deserve to see the glory of God in Heaven." Having said this he began to doubt whether to say more or be silent. When he said no more he was beset by the entreaties of his brethren to tell what he had seen, and he went on: "Four days ago when my cell quivered and you saw me lifeless, I was seized by two angels and carried up to the high heavens, so that I thought I had under my feet not only this filthy world but the sun also, and the moon, the clouds, and the stars. Then I was taken through a door brighter than this light into that dwelling in which all the pavement was like shining gold and silver, a brightness and spaciousness beyond description, and such a multitude of both sexes was there that the length and breadth of the throng could not be seen. A way was made for me through the press by the angels who guided me, and we came to a place which I had already seen from a distance; a cloud hung over it brighter than any light, in which no sun or moon or star could be seen, but excelling all these it gleamed more brightly than the light of nature, and a voice came out of the cloud like a voice of many waters. Then I, a sinner, was humbly greeted by men in priestly and worldly dress who, my guides told me, were martyrs and confessors whom we worship here with the greatest reverence. I stood where I was bidden and a very sweet odor enveloped me so that I was refreshed by this sweetness and up to the present have wanted no food or drink. And I heard a voice saying: 'Let him return to the world since he is necessary to our churches.' It was only the voice that was heard, for it could not be seen who spoke. And I threw myself on the pavement and said with loud weeping: 'Alas, Alas, Lord, why didst Thou show me this if I was to be deprived of it? Behold to-day Thou wilt cast me out from Thy face to return to the sinful world and never to be able to return here again. I beseech Thee, Lord, not to take Thy mercy from me but permit me to stay here and not fall thither and perish.' And the voice which spoke to me said: 'Go in peace, for I am your keeper until I bring you back to this place.' Then I was left alone by my companions and departed weeping by the gate by which I entered and returned here." When he had said this and all present were wonderstruck, God's saint began to weep and say: "Woe is me who have dared to reveal such a mystery. For the pleasant odor which I brought from the holy place, by which I have been supported the last three days without eating or drinking, has gone. My tongue too is covered with grievous sores and swollen so that it seems to fill the whole of my mouth. And I know that it was not well pleasing to my Lord God to make these secrets known. But Thou knowest, Lord, that I did this in simplicity of heart, not in boastfulness. I beg Thee, be kind and do not abandon me, according to Thy promise." After this he said no more and took food and drink. Now as I write this I am afraid that some reader may not believe it, according to what Sallust the historian says: "When you speak of the virtue and fame of good men each calmly believes what he thinks it easy for himself to do; beyond that he considers it falsely invented." For I call all-powerful God to witness that I learned from his own lips all that I have told. A long time after, the blessed man was taken from his cell, chosen bishop, and ordained against his will. And when he was, I think, in his tenth year as bishop, the plague grew worse in Albi, and the greatest part of the people had now died and few of the citizens remained, but the blessed man, like a good shepherd, never consented to leave the place, but he continually urged those who were left to devote themselves to prayer and to keep watch continually and to be engaged always in good works and profitable thought, saying: "Do this so that if God wishes you to go from this world you can enter not into judgment but into rest." And when by God's revelation, as I suppose, he recognized the time of his calling, he made himself a tomb and washed his body and clothed it; and thus always intent upon heaven he breathed out his blessed spirit. He was a man of great holiness and not greedy at all; he never wished to possess gold. If he took it under compulsion he at once paid it out to the poor. In his time when Mummolus the patrician took many captives from that city he followed him and ransomed them all. And the Lord gave him such favor with that people that the very men who took the captives made him concessions in the price and also gave him gifts. And so he restored the captives taken from his country to their former liberty. I have heard many good things about this man, but as I desire to return to the history I have undertaken I pass them over for the most part.

Chapter 2. Fighting between men of Chartres and Orleans

Now when Chilperic had died and had found the death he had long been looking for, the men of Orleans united with those of Blois made an attack on the people of Châteaudun and defeated them, taking them off their guard; they burned their houses and crops and whatever they could not carry away conveniently, and they plundered flocks and herds and carried off all that was not fast. Upon their departure the men of Châteaudun with the rest of the men of Chartres pursued them closely and treated them in the same way as they were treated, leaving nothing in their houses or outside their houses or of their houses. And while they were still abusing one another and raging, and the men of Orleans were ready to fight the men of Chartres, the counts intervened and at a hearing before them peace was made, on condition that on the day when court was to be held the side which had flamed out wrongfully against the other should make payment according to justice. And thus the war was ended.

. . . .

Book VIII

Chapter 1. Visit of the King at Orleans

Now king Gunthram in the twenty-fourth year of his reign started from Chalons and went to the city of Nevers. For he was going to Paris by invitation to receive from the holy font of regeneration Chilperic's son, whom they were already calling Clothar. And he left the territory of Nevers and came to the city of Orleans and at that time appeared much among the citizens. For on receiving invitations he went to their homes and partook of the repasts offered him. He received many gifts from them and bestowed many gifts on them in a very generous way. And when he came to the city of Orleans the day was the festival of the blessed Martin, namely the fourth before the Nones of the fifth month [July 4]. And a huge throng of people came to meet him with standards and banners, singing praises. And here the Syrian language, there that of the Latins, and again that even of the Jews, sounded together strangely in varied praises, saying: "Long live the king; may his reign over the people last unnumbered years." And the Jews who were to be seen taking part in these praises said: "May all the nations honor you and bend the knee and be subject to you." And so it happened that when the king was seated at dinner after mass he said: "Woe to the Jewish tribe, wicked, treacherous, and always living by cunning. Here's what they were after," said he, "when they cried out their flattering praises to-day, that all the nations were to honor me as master. [They wish me] to order their synagogue, long ago torn down by the Christians, to be built at the public cost; but by the Lord's command I will never do it." O King glorious for wonderful wisdom. He so understood the craft of the heretics that they entirely failed to get from him what they were going to propose later. At the dinner the king said to the bishops who were present: "I beg you to give me your blessing to-morrow in my house and bring me salvation by your coming, so that I may be saved when in my humility I receive your words of blessing." When he said this all thanked him, and as dinner was finished we rose.

. . . .

Chapter 3. The Singers and Mummolus' Solver

Meantime when the dinner was now half over the king asked me to request my deacon who had sung the responsory at the mass the day before, to sing. When he had sung he next asked me to request all the bishops who, at my instance, had come prepared, to appoint each a single clerk from his service to sing before the king. And so I made the request at the king's command, and they sang, each to the best of his ability, a psalm before the king. And when the courses were being changed the king said: "All the silver you see belonged to that perjurer Mummolus, but now by the help of God's grace it has been transferred to my ownership. I have already had fifteen of his dishes like the larger one you see yonder melted down, and I have kept only this one and one other of a hundred and seventy pounds. Why [keep] more than enough for daily use? It is too bad, but I have no other son than Childebert, and he has enough treasures which his father left him beside what I had sent to him from the property of this wretch which was found at Avignon. The rest must be given for the necessities of the poor and the churches."

Chapter 4. Praise of King Childebert

"There is only one thing that I ask of you, my lord bishops, namely, to pray God's mercy for my son Childebert. For he is a man of sense and ability so that one so cautious and energetic as he could scarcely be found in many years. And if God would deign to grant him to these Gauls perhaps there would be hope that by him our race, greatly weakened though it is, can rise again. And I have confidence that this will happen through His mercy because the indications at the boy's birth were of this sort. For it was the holy day of Easter and my brother Sigibert was standing in the church and the deacon was walking in procession with the holy book of the Gospels, and a messenger came to the king, and the words of the deacon as he read from the Gospels and of the messenger were the same: 'To thee a son has been born.' And when they both spoke together all the people cried out: 'Glory to all-powerful God.' Moreover he was baptized on the holy day of Pentecost and was made king also on the holy day of the Lord's birth. And so if your prayers attend him, God willing he will be able to rule." So the king spoke and all prayed the Lord in His mercy to keep both kings safe. The king added: "It is true that his mother Brunhilda threatens my life, but I have no misgiving on this account. For the Lord who has saved me from the hands of my enemies will save me from her plots too."

. . . .

Book X

Chapter 3. King Childebert's Army goes into Italy

And Chedinus with thirteen dukes entered Italy on the left and took five strongholds and exacted oaths of fealty. But dysentery affected his army severely—because the air was new to his men and disagreed with them—and many died of it. But when the wind rose and it rained and the air began to freshen a little it brought health in place of sickness. Why more? For about three months they wandered through Italy without accomplishing anything or being able to take vengeance on their enemies, since they were shut up in strongholds, or to capture the king and take vengeance on him, since he was shut up within the walls of Pavia, and then the army sickened as we have said because of the unhealthfulness of the air and grew weak from hunger and prepared to return home after exacting oaths of fidelity and subjecting to the king's rule the people of the country which his father had held before and from which they took captives and other booty. And returning thus they were so starved that they sold their armor and clothing to buy food before they came to their native place. . . .

. . . .

Chapter 10. Killing of Chundo the Chamberlain

In the fifteenth year of king Childebert which is the twenty-ninth of Gunthram, while king Gunthram was hunting in the Vosges forests he found traces of the killing of a buffalo. And when he harshly demanded of the keeper of the forest who had dared to do this in the king's forest, the keeper named Chundo the king's chamberlain. Upon this he ordered Chundo to be arrested and taken to Chalons loaded with chains. And when the two were confronted with each other in the king's presence and Chundo said that he had never presumed to do what he was charged with, the king ordered a trial by battle. Then the chamberlain offered his nephew to engage in the fight in his place and both appeared on the field; the youth hurled his lance at the keeper of the forest and pierced his foot; and he presently fell on his back. The youth then drew the sword which hung from his belt but while he sought to cut his fallen adversary's throat he himself received a dagger thrust in the belly. Both fell dead. Seeing this Chundo started to run to Saint Marcellus's church. But the king shouted to seize him before he touched the sacred threshold and he was caught and tied to a stake and stoned. After this the king was very penitent at having shown himself so headlong in anger as to kill hastily for a trifling guilt a man who was faithful and useful to him.

25. *THE LIFE OF CHARLEMAGNE, BY EGINHARD*[1]

Eginhard was born among the Austrasian Franks, and at a very early age entered the service of Charlemagne at Aachen (Aix-la Chapelle). Here he attended the school of the famous Alcuin. Afterward the king appointed him his private secretary and chaplain. In this capacity Eginhard was always at the king's side, both in peace and war. Furthermore, he was superintendent of public works under Charlemagne, and supervised the building of palaces and bridges. After Charlemagne's death he retired to an abbey, where he died in 844.

Eginhard wrote Charlemagne's biography in Latin. Although his diction left much to be desired, the biography was "the most distinguished piece of history from the sixth to the eighth century; indeed the only one which can be called a history. For it is not a mere chronicle, but a political biography, written by one who was an eye-witness of the events he narrates, and who understood their importance."

1. The Franks in olden times used to choose their Kings from the family of the Merwings, which royal line is considered to have come to an end in the person of Hilderic III, who was deposed from the throne by command of Stephen, the Roman Pontiff, when his long hair was cut off and he was placed in a monastery.

Although the line of the Merwings actually ended with Hilderic, it had nevertheless for some time previously been so utterly wanting in power that it had been able to show no mark of royalty except the empty kingly title. All the resources and power of the Kingdom had passed into the hands of the Prefects of the palace, who were called the "Mayors of the palace," and by them the supreme government was administered. Nothing

[1] *Life of the Emperor Karl the Great,* translated from Eginhard by William Glaister, London, George Bell and Sons, 1877, pp. 26–88. Used by permission.

was left to the King. He had to content himself with his royal title, long hair, and hanging beard. Seated in a chair of state, he used to display an appearance of power by receiving foreign ambassadors on their arrival, and by giving them on their departure, as if on his own authority, those answers which he had been taught or commanded to give.

Thus, except his useless title, and an uncertain allowance for his subsistence, which the Prefect of the palace used to furnish at his pleasure, there was nothing that the King could call his own, unless it were the profits of a single farm, and that a very small one, where was his home, and where he had such servants as were needful to wait on him, and who paid him the scanty deference of a most meagre court.

Whenever he went anywhere he used to travel in a waggon drawn by a yoke of oxen, with a rustic oxherd for charioteer. In this manner he proceeded to the palace, and to the public assemblies of the people held every year for the despatch of the business of the Kingdom, and he returned home again in the same sort of state. The administration of the Kingdom, and every matter which had to be undertaken and carried through, at home and abroad, was managed by the Mayor of the palace.

2. At the time of the deposition of Hilderic the office of Mayor was filled by Pippin, the father of King Karl. The office seemed now to be almost hereditary; for Pippin's father, Karl, had also held it, and with great renown, since he had quelled throughout all Frank-land those usurpers who had tried to assume independent authority. He had also utterly defeated the Saracens, who were at that time attempting to establish themselves in Gaul, in two great battles, the first in Aquitain, near the city of Poictiers, and the second near Narbonne on the river Birra, and had compelled them to retire into Spain.

Karl had himself also been preceded in the Mayorship by his father, Pippin, an honour which was conferred by the people only on those who were distinguished from the commonalty by their noble birth and great wealth.

When Pippin had held for some years this office (nominally as the lieutenant of King Hilderic), which had descended from father and grandfather to himself and his brother Karloman, and had been by them jointly administered with the greatest goodwill, Karloman, we know not why, but probably because he desired a more secluded life, relinquished the arduous government of a temporal Kingdom and betook himself to a private life at Rome. While he was there he became a monk, and put on the dress of the order. Having built a monastery on Mount Soracte, adjoining the Church of S. Sylvester, he there enjoyed for several years the repose he sought for, in company with the brothers of the order who had gone with him. He was, however, obliged to change his place of residence, because many of the Frankish nobility, when making pilgrimages to Rome to fulfil their vows, broke, by their frequent visits to him, that quiet which he most of all desired, since they were unwilling to pass by unnoticed one who had formerly been their King. As constant interruptions of this sort hindered the object of his retirement, he withdrew to the Monastery of S. Benedict on Mount Casino, in the province of Samnium, and there passed the remainder of his life in religious exercises.

3. Pippin, however, who by the authority of the Roman Pontiff, from being the Mayor of the palace, had risen to be the King, governed the Franks solely in his own person for fully fifteen years. He died of dropsy at Paris towards the close of the Aquitanian war, which he had begun against Waifar, the duke of that country, and which was carried on continuously during nine years. He left two sons, Karl and Karloman, who by God's will succeeded to the Kingdom.

The Franks, in a general assembly convened with much solemnity, appointed them both Kings, as soon as they had agreed to the following conditions:—For the purposes of government the whole realm was to be equally divided; Karl was to reign over that part which had belonged to their father Pippin, and Karloman over that portion which had belonged to their uncle Karloman.

When they had both agreed to these terms, each received that portion of the kingdom which had been assigned him. Agreement between the brothers was thus established, though it was only preserved with the greatest difficulty, since many of the friends of Karloman set themselves to work to break the friendship, some even going so far as to have thoughts of plunging the brothers into civil war. But there was more distrust than real danger, as in the end proved to be the case. For when Karloman died, his wife, with his sons and some of his chief nobility, slighted her husband's brother and fled into Italy, and for no reason whatever placed herself and children under the protection of Dedier, King of the Lombards. Karloman died after two years of joint sovereignty, when his brother Karl, with the consent of all the Franks, was made (sole) King.

4. I pass by the birth, infancy, and childhood of Karl, because there is no written record concerning them, nor is any one now known to survive who can speak from personal knowledge. I have therefore thought it foolish to write about them, and have given my attention to relating and explaining those actions, habits, and other portions of his life which are not matters of uncertainty; first narrating his military exploits at home and abroad, then his domestic habits and occupations, then his administration of the kingdom, and lastly, about his death, omitting nothing that is worthy and necessary to be narrated.

5. Karl was engaged in many wars. The first he undertook was the

Aquitanian, because there seemed to be good hope of quickly bringing it to an end. It had been begun by his father, but not finished.

His brother at this time was still living, and his aid was asked. Though King Karl was disappointed of his brother's assistance, he nevertheless pursued the campaign he had undertaken with the greatest vigour; he would not withdraw from what he had begun, nor at all desist from the labour of the work, until by great and long-continued perseverance the most complete termination had been achieved. He obliged Hunold, who, after the death of Waifar, had attempted to seize Aquitain and renew the war which was almost ended, to flee from the country and seek refuge in Gascony. Karl, not being satisfied that he should remain there, crossed the river Garonne, and by his ambassadors ordered Loup, the King of the Gascons, to give up the fugitive, adding that if he did not quickly do so, he would proceed to recover him by force of arms. Loup wisely surrendered Hunold. He also placed himself and the province over which he ruled under the sovereignty of Karl.

6. When the war was finished and affairs settled in Aquitain—his partner in the government being now dead—Karl was induced by the prayer and entreaty of Adrian, Bishop of the city of Rome, to undertake a war against the Lombards.

His father had undertaken such a war before, at the request of Pope Stephen, and had met with much difficulty in the matter, because some of the chief men of the Franks, his councillors, had been much opposed to his wishes, and had gone so far as to declare they would desert the King and return home. War had, however, been made against King Aistulf, and had been quickly finished.

There seemed to be a very similar, or rather the same, cause for war to King Karl as there had been to his father. There was not, however, the same difficulty in carrying it out, nor the same result at its conclusion.

Pippin, for his part, after a few days' siege of Pavia, had compelled Aistulf to give hostages, and to restore the fortified towns and castles which he had taken from the Romans, and also to make oath that he would not attempt the recovery of what he restored. Karl, on the other hand, when he had once begun hostilities, did not hold his hand until Dedier, the King, worn out by a long siege, had surrendered at discretion. Adalgis, his son, on whom were fixed the hopes of the nation, was compelled to quit the kingdom and leave Italy altogether. Karl restored to the Romans all that had been forcibly taken from them, and also crushed Hrudogast, Prefect of the parts about Friuli, who was attempting disturbances; and having brought all Italy under his rule, he made his son Pippin King of the conquered territory. The passage of the Alps into Italy was extremely difficult, and I would have here related how great was the toil of the Franks in overcoming the trackless chain of mountains, with peaks towering to the skies, and sharp and perilous rocks, had it not seemed to me to be my present task to record the character of the King's life rather than the incidents of the wars which he waged.

Suffice it, then, to say that the end of this war was that Italy was conquered, King Dedier carried away into perpetual exile, Adalgis, his son, driven from Italy, and all that had been seized by the Lombard Kings was restored to Adrian, the rector of the Roman Church.

The Lombard war being thus finished, the Saxon war, which seemed for the time to have been neglected, was again renewed. No war undertaken by the Franks was so protracted or so fierce, or so full of toil and hardship, since the Saxons, like most of the nations inhabiting Germany, were naturally brave, and, being addicted to heathenism, were hostile to our religion, and thought it no disgrace to dishonour divine laws or violate human ones.

Causes, too, daily arose which contributed to disturb the peace. The boundaries of their country and ours were in the open almost everywhere contiguous. It was only in a few places that large forests, or ranges of mountains coming between, formed a well-defined and natural boundary line to both countries. On the borders therefore, plundering, burning, and bloodshed never ceased.

The Franks were so enraged at this that they judged it now to be no longer a matter of making reprisals, but so important that it warranted them in undertaking an avowed war against them. War therefore was declared, and was carried on continuously during thirty-three years, with much bitterness on both sides, but with greater loss to the Saxons than to the Franks. It was the bad faith of the Saxons which prevented a more speedy termination. It is hard to say how often they were beaten, and humbly surrendered to the King, promising to obey his orders, giving up at once the hostages he asked, and acknowledging the ambassadors sent to them; how sometimes they were so tamed and compliant as even to promise to give up their idolatry, declaring they wished to embrace Christianity. But ready as they were at times to undertake all these things, they were always far readier to renounce them. It is difficult to state correctly to which failing they were more prone, since it is certainly the fact that, after the war was begun, scarcely a single year passed in which they did not pursue this shifty course.

But the magnanimity of the King, and the unwavering firmness of his disposition, alike in adversity and prosperity, could not be shaken by any faithlessness on their part, nor could they divert him from his purpose by tiring him out.

He never allowed any act of insincerity to be done with impunity; either taking the command in person, or despatching an army under his counts, he took vengeance on their perfidy and exacted from them a commensurate penalty.

He pursued this course until all who continued to resist him were overcome and brought into submission. He then transported ten thousand men, taken from both banks of the Elbe, together with their wives and children, and distributed them here and there, in very small groups, in Gaul and Germany.

It was on the following terms, offered by the King and accepted by the Saxons, that this war which had lasted so many years, was brought to a close. The Saxons were to put away their heathen worship and the religious ceremonies of their fathers; were to accept the articles of the Christian faith and practice; and, being united to the Franks, were to form with them one people.

8. Although the war lasted so long, the King himself did not fight more than two pitched battles against the enemy, one near a hill called Osneng, near Theotmel, and the other on the river Hasa, both in the same month and at a few days' interval.

In these two battles the enemy were so thoroughly broken in spirit, and beaten, that they no more dared to challenge the King, or to oppose him on his march, except in places where they were protected by fortifications. There fell in this war more of the Frankish nobility, and of those who enjoyed the highest honours, than of their compeers among the Saxons, and it was in its thirty-third year before it was finished.

During those years many great wars sprang up against the Franks in different parts, which were, by the skill of the King, so well managed that it was not without reason that men were perplexed whether to admire more the patience with which the King pursued his undertakings, or the good fortune which attended them.

This war was begun two years before the Italian war, and although it was carried on at the same time without any intermission, there was no relaxation anywhere. In both places the campaign was equally carried on without diminution of effort, for, of all contemporary sovereigns, King Karl took the highest rank for his good administration, and was most distinguished for his ability. In all his undertakings and enterprises there was nothing he shrank from because of the toil, and nothing he feared because of the danger; but, skilful in weighing everything at its true value, he was neither yielding in adversity nor deceived by the smiles of fortune in prosperity.

9. It was during the time that the Saxon war was being vigorously and incessantly carried on, garrisons having been placed in all the most suitable places on the borders, that Karl marched into Spain with the best-appointed army possible. Having crossed the Pyrenean mountains, he reduced all the

fortified towns and castles he came to, and was on his march home with his army safe and sound, when, in the very pass of the Pyrenees on his way back, he had a slight experience of Gascon treachery.

The army was moving in column, and its formation was much extended, as the narrowness of the pass required, when the Gascons, who had placed ambuscades on the highest ledges of the mountains—the abundant thick cover of wood making the place most suitable for the disposal of an ambush —rushed down from their vantage ground into the valley below, and threw themselves upon the extreme section of the baggage, and on those who were marching with it for its protection. The Gascons attacked them in a hand-to-hand fight, killed them all to a man, and destroyed the baggage; and being protected by the darkness of the night, which was then coming on, they quickly dispersed in all directions.

In this exploit the Gascons were much favoured by the lightness of their weapons and the nature of the place where the attack was made, while the Franks, impeded by their heavy arms and the unevenness of the ground, were at a great disadvantage. . . .

10. Karl also brought the Britons into subjection. They dwelt on the coast in the extreme west of Gaul. They were not obeying the King's orders, so an expedition was sent against them, and they were compelled to give hostages that they would do as they were commanded.

After this the King led his army in person into Italy, and, passing through Rome, marched on to Capua, a city of Campania, and, pitching his camp there, he threatened to make war upon the Beneventines unless they submitted to him. Aragis, the Duke, avoided this by sending his sons, Rumold and Grimold, with a large sum of money, to meet the King. Aragis asked that his sons might be accepted as hostages, and promised that he and his people would obey the King, but prayed that he himself might be excused from personal attendance.

The King, having more regard for what was for the welfare of the people than for the man's obstinacy, granted his request, accepted the hostages he had sent, and for a large sum of money excused him from personal attendance. Only the younger son of Aragis was detained as a hostage; the elder was sent back to his father. When the ambassadors who had come to deliberate upon, and agree to, the engagements of fidelity to be entered into by Aragis, on behalf of the Beneventines, had been dismissed, the King returned to Rome.

Having passed some days there in reverend visitation of the sacred places of the city, he went back again into Gaul.

11. The next war was one which sprang up unexpectedly with the Bavarians. It only lasted for a short time. It was caused by the arrogance and senselessness of Duke Tassilo. He had married a daughter of King

Dedier, who thought through her husband to avenge the exile of her father. Tassilo, being thus urged on by his wife, made an alliance with the Huns, whose territories joined those of the Bavarians on the East, and aimed not only at independence, but even challenged the King to war. Karl, unable to brook such immoderate insolence, moved forward a large army, composed of forces gathered from all sides and commanded by himself, to the river Lech, determined to obtain satisfaction from the Bavarians. Having pitched his camp on the banks of that river, which divides the Bavarians from the Alemanni, he resolved to send ambassadors to sound the mind of the Duke before he entered their country.

It then seemed that Tassilo did not think that it would be for the advantage of either himself or his people to persist in his course of action; he therefore surrendered himself to the King's clemency, and gave the hostages demanded—among them his son Theodon. In addition to this, he pledged his faith with an oath that he would give no heed to any one who might attempt to persuade him to revolt from the King's authority. It was thus that a war which had seemed likely to be a great one was brought to a speedy termination.

Tassilo, however, being soon after summoned to appear before the King, was not permitted to return; and the province over which he ruled was no longer governed by a Duke, but was entrusted to the charge of Counts.

12. When these affairs had been thus settled, a war was begun against those Slavs whom we are accustomed to call Wiltzi, but who, according to their own pronunciation, are more properly called Welatabi. In this war the Saxons fought as our allies, but their allegiance was rather feigned than real. The cause of the war was thus—the Welatabi could be restrained by no commands from harassing with constant invasions the Abodriti, who had long belonged to the Frankish league.

There is a gulf running in from the Western Ocean, stretching toward the East; its length has not been ascertained, but its breadth nowhere exceeds one hundred miles, and in many places it is much narrower. Several nations dwell around this gulf, such as the Danes and Swedes, whom we call Northmen.

In one expedition under his own command he so crushed and tamed them, that they resolved to submit to the uttermost and to refuse nothing.

13. The greatest of all the wars waged by the King, except the Saxon, was that which now followed, against the Avars or Huns. He set about it with far more ardour and preparation than was bestowed upon any of the others. The King himself only made one expedition into Pannonia—it was that province which the Avar race then inhabited; the others he entrusted to the direction of his son Pippin, and to the prefects of the provinces, and to the counts and lieutenants. Although these commanders used

the greatest exertions, it was not until the eighth year that the war was finished.

How many battles were fought, and how much blood shed, is fully attested by the complete depopulation of Pannonia; even the situation of the royal palace of the Kagan is so obliterated that no trace remains of a human habitation.

In this war the whole nobility of the Avars perished, and the glory of their nation was destroyed. All their riches and treasures, which they had long been accumulating, were carried away, nor can memory recall any war of the Franks in which they have gained greater booty or by which they have been more enriched. Indeed, we may confess that, up to this time, the Franks appeared to be a poor nation; but so much gold and silver was found in the palace, and such a quantity of valuable spoil was taken in the battles, as can scarcely be believed.

The Franks justly spoiled the Huns (Avars) of this booty, for the Huns themselves had no right to it, it being the plunder they had carried off from other nations.

Only two of the chief nobility among the Franks fell in this war—Eric, Duke of Friuli, killed in Liburnia, near Tharsatica, a maritime state, having been cut off by an ambush of the inhabitants; and Gerold, Prefect of the Bavarians, who was killed in Pannonia, while drawing up his men in line of battle just before engaging the Huns. By whom he was killed is uncertain, since he was slain, with two others who accompanied him, while riding up and down the ranks, and encouraging each man individually.

With these exceptions, the war was almost a bloodless one for the Franks, and although it lasted longer than its magnitude seemed to warrant, its result was most successful.

14. When this and the Saxon war had been brought to an end which their tediousness made acceptable, the two wars which afterwards occurred, one against the Bohemians, and the other against the Linonians, were only of short duration, being quickly finished under the direction of Karl the younger.

The last war undertaken was against the Northmen who are called Danes, who, at first as pirates, and afterwards with a larger fleet, were ravaging the coasts of Gaul and Germany. Their King, Godfrey, was puffed up with the delusive hope of making himself master of all Germany, and persisted in regarding Frisia and Saxony as his own provinces. He had already brought the Abodriti under his power and had made them tributary to him.

He even used to boast that he would shortly appear with all his forces at Aachen, where the King's court was held. Foolish as his talk was, there were some who did not altogether discredit him. It was rather thought that he would have attempted something of the kind had not his sudden death prevented him. He was slain by one of his own servants, and thus his own life and the war he had begun were brought to an abrupt conclusion.

15. Such were the wars waged by the most potent prince with the greatest skill and success in different countries during the forty-seven years of his reign. Great and powerful as was the realm of the Franks, which Karl had received from his father Pippin, he nevertheless so splendidly enlarged it by these wars that he almost doubled it.

For previously the Eastern Franks had only inhabited that part of Gaul which lies between the Rhine and the Loire, the ocean and Balearic Sea, and that part of Germany situated between Saxony and the Danube, the Rhine and the Saal, which latter river divides the Thuringi from the Sorabi. The Alemanni and Bavarians also belonged to the Frankish confederation. But Karl, by the wars which have been mentioned, conquered and made tributary, first, Aquitania and Gascony, and the whole range of the Pyrenean mountains, as far as the river Ebro, which, rising in Navarre and flowing through the most fertile lands of Spain, mingles its waters with the Balearic Sea beneath the walls of Tortosa; then the whole of Italy, from Aosta to Lower Calabria, where are the boundaries of the Greeks, and Beneventines, an extent of more than a thousand miles in length; then Saxony, which is indeed no small portion of Germany, and is thought to be twice as wide as the part where the Franks dwell, and equal to it in length; then both Pannonias, and Dacia which lies on the other bank of the Danube; also Istria, Liburnia, and Dalmatia, with the exception of the maritime towns, which for friendship's sake, and on account of a treaty, he allowed the Constantinopolitan Emperor to hold; lastly, all the wild and barbarous nations which inhabit Germany between the Rhine and the Vistula, the ocean and the Danube, who speak a very similar language, but are widely different in manners and dress. Chief among these were the Welatabi, Sorabi, Abodriti, and Baemanni, for with these there was fighting; but the rest, who were more numerous, quietly surrendered.

16. The renown of his Kingdom was also much increased by the friendly alliances he cultivated with different kings and nations. Alfonso, King of Gallicia and Asturias, was so bound to him by the ties of friendship that, when he sent him letters or messengers, he used to command that he should be spoken of as being Karl's man. The Kings of the Scots, too, were by his munificence so devoted to his will, that they ever spoke of him as their Lord, and of themselves as his lieges and servants. Letters are still extant from them to him which show that this sort of relationship existed between them.

Haroun, king of the Persians, who, with the exception of India, ruled over nearly all the East, was held by the King in such hearty friendship, that he valued Karl's esteem above that of all other Kings and princes of the world, and thought that he alone was worthy to be honoured by his regard and munificence. When the officers sent by King Karl with offerings to the most sacred sepulchre and place of the resurrection of our Lord and Saviour came to Haroun and announced the pleasure of their master, he not only gave them permission to do as they desired, but granted that that revered and sacred spot should be considered as belonging to King Karl. When the ambassadors set out on their return, he sent with them his own envoys, who conveyed to the King strange and curious gifts, with garments and spices and other rich products of the East, just as he had sent him a few years before, upon his request, the only elephant he then possessed.

The Constantinopolitan Emperors, Nicephorus, Michael, and Leo, of their own accord, also sought his friendship and alliance, and sent to him several embassies; and since by assuming the Imperial title he had laid himself open to the grave suspicion of wishing to deprive them of Empire, he made with them the most binding treaty possible, that there might be no occasion of offence between them. But the Romans and Greeks always viewed with distrust the power of the Franks; hence arose the Greek proverb, "Have a Frank for a friend but not for a neighbour."

17. Illustrious as the King was in the work of enlarging his Kingdom and in conquering foreign nations, and though so constantly occupied with such affairs, he nevertheless began in several places very many works for the advantage and beautifying of his kingdom. Some of these he was able to finish. Chief among them may be mentioned, as deserving of notice, the Basilica of the Holy Mother of God, built at Aachen, a marvel of workmanship; and the bridge over the Rhine at Mainz, five hundred paces in length, so broad is the river at that place. This bridge, however, was destroyed by fire the year before the King died, nor could it be restored on account of his approaching death, although it was in the King's mind to replace the wooden structure by a bridge of stone.

He also began some magnificent palaces, one not far from Mainz, near the village of Ingelheim, and another at Nymeguen, on the river Waal, which flows past the island of the Batavians on the southern side. He was more especially particular in giving orders to the priests and fathers to see to the restoration of those churches under their care, which in any part of his Kingdom he found had fallen into decay, taking care by his officers that his commands were obeyed. He also constructed a fleet for the war against the Northmen. For this purpose ships were built on the rivers of Gaul and Germany which flow into the North Sea. As the Northmen were making a practice of ravaging the coasts of Gaul and Germany with constant harryings, he posted towers and outlooks in all the harbours, and at the mouths of those rivers which ships could navigate. By these defences he prevented any enemy from being able to pass. He did the same thing in the south, on the coast of the provinces of Narbonne and Septimania, and all along the coast of Italy as far as Rome, for in those parts the Moors had lately taken to piracy. Thus Italy suffered no great damage from the Moors, nor Gaul or Germany from the Northmen, during the reign of Karl, except that Civita Vecchia, a city of Etruria, was betrayed to the Moors, who took it and destroyed it, and in Frisia some islands off the German coast were plundered by the Northmen.

18. Such does it appear was the character of the King, in defending, enlarging, and beautifying his Kingdom, and one must be permitted to admire his mental gifts and his great firmness of purpose in all circumstances, whether of prosperity or adversity.

I will now begin to speak of other matters relating to his private and domestic life. On the death of his father he bore all the jealousy and illwill of his brother, in the division of the Kingdom, with so much patience and forbearance that he astonished everybody, for he would not allow himself even to be provoked to anger by him.

It was by the desire of his mother that he took for his wife, a daughter of Dedier, King of the Lombards; but at the end of a year he divorced her, for what reason is uncertain. He then married Hildegard, a Swabian lady of noble birth, by whom he had three sons, Karl, Pippin, and Ludwig, and three daughters, Hruodrud, Berthrad, and Gisla. He had also three other daughters, Theoderada and Hiltrud by his wife Fastrada, a German of the Eastern Franks, and Ruodhaid by a concubine whose name I do not remember. On the death of Fastrada he married Liudgard, of the Alemanni nation. She bore him no children. After her death he had three concubines, Gersuinda, of the Saxon nation, by whom he had a daughter named Adaltrud; Regina, who bore him Drogo and Hugh; and Adalinda, who had a son named Theoderick. His mother Berthrad lived with him to old age, in great honour, being looked up to by her son with the greatest respect, so that no difference ever arose between them, except with regard to the divorce of the daughter of King Dedier, whom she had persuaded him to marry. She did not die until after the death of Hildegard, having lived to see three grandsons and as many grand-daughters in the house of her son. She was buried by the King with much honour in the church of S. Dionysius, where his father had been laid. He had one sister, Gisela, who was dedicated to a religious life from her earliest years. Like his mother, she was regarded by the King with the greatest affection. She died a few years before him, and was buried in the convent to which she had retired.

19. The King thought so much about the education of his children that he caused both sons and daughters to be early instructed in those liberal studies which attracted his own attention. As soon as his sons were old

enough he caused them to ride on horseback, as was the Frankish custom, and to practise themselves in arms and hunting. He bade his daughters that they should learn wool-spinning and the use of the distaff and spindle, and be taught to employ themselves industriously in every virtuous occupation, that they might not be enervated by idleness.

Of this large family, two sons and one daughter died before him—Karl, the eldest, and Pippin, whom he had made King of Italy, and Hruodrud, his eldest girl, who had been betrothed to Constantine VI, the Emperor of the Greeks. Pippin left surviving one son, Bernhard, and five daughters, Adalhaid, Atula, Guntrada, Berthaid, and Theoderada. The King showed marked tokens of his affection toward them, allowing his grandson to succeed to his father's Kingdom, and bringing up his grand-daughters with his own daughters. He bore the deaths of his sons and daughters with that greatness of soul for which he was distinguished; but his resignation was not greater than his affection, for he mourned for them with tears. So also, when the death of Adrian, the Roman Pontiff, was announced to him, regarding him as his chief friend, he wept for him as if he had lost the son or brother that was dearest to him. For he was most sincere in his friendships, being readily open to form them and most constant in retaining them, cherishing with the most sacred regard those whom he had united to himself in ties of affection.

He was so careful in the bringing up of his sons and daughters that when at home he never dined without them, and they always accompanied him on his journeys, his sons riding by his side, and his daughters following close behind, attended by a train of servants appointed for that purpose. His daughters were very fair, and he loved them passionately. Strange to say, he would never consent to give them in marriage, either to any of his own nation or to foreigners; but he kept them all at home and near his person at all times until his death, for he used to say that he could not deprive himself of their society. . . .

20. He had also by one of his concubines another son, Pippin, whom I have omitted to mention among the others; he had a good countenance, but was deformed by a hunch back. When his father was wintering in Bavaria, being detained there by the war against the Huns, this son Pippin pretended sickness, and formed a conspiracy against the King, together with some of the chief men of the Franks, who had seduced him with the foolish hope of making him King. The plot being discovered and his fellow conspirators punished, Pippin's hair was shorn off, and he was allowed to pass his time in religious exercises in the abbey at Pruhm. To this he readily consented. Another dangerous conspiracy against the King had been set on foot before in Germany. Some of its authors were condemned to the loss of their eyes, others saved their limbs, but all were exiled. None, however,

were put to death, except three, who drew their swords in defence against those sent to take them, and went so far as to kill some of them. These were slain because there was no other way of dealing with them.

It is thought that in both instances the cruelty of Queen Fastrada was the original cause of these conspiracies against the King, and he seems to have departed very far from the usual gentleness and clemency of his natural disposition in permitting the Queen's inhumanity. The King himself during all his life was regarded by all men, both at home and abroad, with such love and affection that he, at least, was never charged by any one with wanton cruelty.

21. He had a great fondness for foreigners, and was so anxious to entertain them that their great numbers became an improper burden, not merely to the palace, but even to the Kingdom. The King, however, in keeping with his generosity, was very little oppressed by any such thoughts, since a reputation for liberality and the reward of renown well compensated such inconveniences.

22. The person of Karl was large and robust, and of commanding stature, though not exceeding good proportions, for it appears that he measured seven feet in height. The top of his head was round, his eyes large and animated, his nose somewhat long, his hair white, and his face bright and pleasant; so that, whether standing or sitting, he showed very great presence and dignity. Although his neck was thick and rather short, and his belly too prominent, still the fair proportions of his limbs concealed these defects. His walk was firm, and the whole carriage of his body was manly. His voice was clear, but not so strong as his frame would have led one to expect. His health was good until the last four years of his life, when he was attacked with frequent fevers, and latterly walked lame on one foot. Even in illness he leaned more on his own judgment than on the advice of physicians, whom he greatly disliked, because they used to recommend him to leave off roasted meats, which he preferred, and to accustom himself to boiled.

He took constant exercise in riding and hunting, which was natural for a Frank, since scarcely any nation can be found to equal them in these pursuits. He also delighted in the natural warm baths, frequently exercising himself by swimming, in which he was very skilful, no one being able to outstrip him. It was on account of the warm baths there that he built the palace of Aachen, living there constantly during the last years of his life and until his death. He not only invited his sons to bathe with him, but also his chief men and friends, and occasionally even a crowd of his attendants and guards, so that at times one hundred men or more would be bathing together.

23. He wore the dress of his native country—that is, the Frankish; on his body a linen shirt and linen drawers; then a tunic with a silver border,

and stockings. He bound his legs with garters and wore shoes on his feet. In the winter he protected his shoulders and chest with a vest made of the skins of otters and sable. He wore a blue cloak, and was always girt with his sword, the hilt and belt being of gold and silver. Sometimes he wore a jewelled sword, but only on great festivals, or when receiving foreign ambassadors. He thoroughly disliked the dress of foreigners, however fine, and he never put it on except at Rome—once at the request of Pope Adrian, and again a second time, to please his successor, Pope Leo. He then wore a long tunic, chlamys, and shoes made after the Roman fashion. On festivals he used to walk in processions clad in a garment woven with gold, and shoes studded with jewels, his cloak fastened with a golden clasp, and wearing a crown of gold set with precious stones. At other times his dress differed little from that of a private person.

24. In his eating and drinking he was temperate; more particularly so in his drinking, since he had the greatest abhorrence of drunkenness in anybody, but more especially in himself and his companions. He was unable to abstain from food for any length of time, and often complained that fasting was injurious to him. He very rarely feasted, only on great festive occasions, when there were very large gatherings. The daily service of his table was only furnished with four dishes, in addition to the roast meat, which the hunters used to bring in on spits, and of which he partook more freely than of any other food.

While he was dining he listened to music or reading. History and the deeds of men of old used to be read. He derived much pleasure from the works of St. Augustine, especially from his book called "Civitas Dei." ("The City of God.") He took very sparingly of wine and other drinks, rarely taking at meals more than two or three draughts. In summer, after the midday repast, he would take some fruit and one draught, and then, throwing aside his clothes and shoes as at night, he would repose for two or three hours. He slept at night so lightly that he would break his rest four or five times, not merely by awaking, but even getting up.

While he was dressing and binding on his sandals, he would receive his friends; and also, if the Count of the palace announced that there was any cause which could only be settled by his decree, the suitors were immediately ordered into his presence, and, as if sitting in court, he heard the case and gave judgment. And this was not the only business that used to be arranged at that time, for orders were then given for whatever had to be done on that day by any officer or servant.

25. He was ready and fluent in speaking, and able to express himself with great clearness. He did not confine himself to his native tongue, but took pains to learn foreign languages, acquiring such knowledge of Latin that he used to repeat his prayers in that language as well as in his own. Greek

he could better understand than pronounce. In speaking he was so voluble that he almost gave one the impression of a chatterer. He was an ardent admirer of the liberal arts, and greatly revered their professors, whom he promoted to high honours. In order to learn grammar, he attended the lectures of the aged Peter of Pisa, a deacon; and for other instruction he chose as his preceptor Albinus, otherwise called Alcuin, also a deacon—a Saxon by race, from Britain, the most learned man of the day, with whom the King spent much time in learning rhetoric and logic, and more especially astronomy. He learned the art of computation, and with deep thought and skill very carefully calculated the courses of the planets.

Karl also tried to write, and used to keep his tablets and writing-book under the pillow of his couch, that when he had leisure he might practise his hand in forming letters; but he made little progress in a task too long deferred, and begun too late in life.

26. The Christian religion, in which he had been brought up from infancy, was held by Karl as most sacred, and he worshipped in it with the greatest piety. For this reason he built at Aachen a most beautiful church, which he enriched with gold and silver, and candle-sticks, and also with lattices and doors of solid brass. When columns and marbles for the building could not be obtained from elsewhere, he had them brought from Rome and Ravenna.

As long as his health permitted, he was most regular in attending the church at matins and evensong, and also during the night, and at the time of the Sacrifice; and he took especial care that all the services of the church should be performed in the most fitting manner possible, frequently cautioning the sacristans not to allow anything improper or unseemly to be brought into, or left in, the building.

He provided for the church an abundance of sacred vessels of gold and silver, and priestly vestments, so that when service was celebrated it was not necessary even for the doorkeepers, who are the lowest order of ecclesiastics, to perform their duties in private dress. He carefully revised the order of reading and singing, being well skilled in both, though he did not read in public, nor sing, except in a low voice and only in the chorus.

27. He was most devoted in providing for the poor, and in charitable gifts, which the Greeks calls almsgiving. In this matter he took thought not only for those of his own country and kingdom, but also for those whom he heard were living in poverty beyond the seas, in Africa, Egypt, and Syria, at Carthage, Alexandria, and Jerusalem, to whom he used to send money in compassion for their wants. It was on this account especially that he courted the friendship of foreign princes, that he might be able to become a solace and comfort to those Christians who were living under their rule.

He held the church of the blessed Peter the Apostle, at Rome, in far higher regard than any other place of sanctity and veneration, and he enriched its treasury with a great quantity of gold, silver, and precious stones.

To the Pope he made many and rich presents; and nothing lay nearer his heart during his whole reign than that the city of Rome should attain to its ancient importance by his zeal and patronage, and that the church of St. Peter should, through him, not only be in safe keeping and protection, but should also by his wealth be ennobled and enriched beyond all other churches. Although he thought so much of this, it was only four times, during the forty-seven years of his reign, that he had leisure to go to Rome for prayer and supplication.

28. The last visit he paid to Rome was not only for the above reasons, but also because the Romans had driven Pope Leo to ask his assistance—for they had grievously ill-treated him; indeed, his eyes had been plucked out and his tongue cut off.

Karl therefore went to Rome, and stayed there the whole winter in order to reform and quiet the Church, which was in a most disturbed state. It was at this time that he received the title of Emperor and Augustus, to which at first he was so averse that he remarked that had he known the intention of the Pope, he would not have entered the Church on that day, great festival though it was.

He bore very quietly the displeasure of the Roman Emperors, who were exceedingly indignant at his assumption of the Imperial title, and overcame their sullenness by his great magnanimity, in which, without doubt, he greatly excelled them, sending them frequently embassies, and styling them his brothers in his letters to them.

29. After he had taken the Imperial title, he turned his attention to the laws of his people, which seemed greatly to need it, since the Franks have two laws, which differ much in many places.

Karl's intention was to add what was wanting in each, to assimilate discrepancies, and to correct what was mischievous and wrongly expressed. In the end, however, he did nothing more than add a few capitularies, and those imperfect ones.

He, however, caused the unwritten laws, of all the nations under his rule, to be tabulated and reduced to writing. He also wrote out and committed to memory the rude and very ancient songs which told of the exploits and wars of the kings of old. He also began a grammar of the speech of his country. He also gave names in the national tongue to the months of the year, for up to this time the Franks had distinguished them partly by Latin and partly by barbarian names. He likewise gave the proper names to the twelve winds, for previously names were known for hardly four. . . .

30. Towards the close of his life, when bowed down by disease and old age, he summoned to him his son Ludwig, the King of Aquitain, who

alone survived of the sons of Hildegard, and in a solemn assembly of the chief men of the whole realm of the Franks, and with their unanimous consent, appointed Ludwig his partner in the whole Kingdom and heir of the Imperial Title. He then placed the royal crown on his head and bade that he be saluted as Emperor and Augustus.

This proposal was received by all who were present with great approbation. It seemed to them as if Heaven inspired the King in advancing the prosperity of the Kingdom, for this arrangement increased his own dignity and struck foreign nations with no slight awe.

The King then dismissed his son into Aquitain, and, although weakened by age, went on his usual hunting expedition in the neighbourhood of the palace at Aachen. In this pursuit he passed the remainder of the autumn, and returned to Aachen early in November. During the winter, in the month of January, he was confined to his bed by a sharp attack of fever. He at once prescribed for himself a lowering diet, which was his usual treatment of fever, thinking that by this means he could throw off the disease, or at least control it; but inflammation of the side, which the Greeks call pleurisy, supervened. He still continued to starve himself, only keeping himself up by occasionally taking liquids; and on the seventh day after he had been confined to his bed he received the Holy Communion, and died soon after, at nine o'clock, on the 28th January, in the seventy-third year of his age and forty-seventh of his reign.

31. His body was reverently washed and tended, and then carried into the church and buried, to the great grief of all his people. There was some doubt at first where was the most proper place for his burial, for during his life he had given no orders on this matter. At last it was agreed by all that he could be buried in no more fitting place than in the church which he had built at his own cost at Aachen, out of love to God and our Lord Christ, and to the honour of the ever blessed Virgin, His Mother. So he was buried there on the same day that he died. Above his tomb was erected a gilded monument, with his effigy and title upon it. His dignity was thus described—

UNDER THIS TOMB IS PLACED THE BODY OF KARL, THE GREAT AND ORTHODOX EMPEROR, WHO GLORIOUSLY ENLARGED THE REALM OF THE FRANKS, AND SUCCESSFULLY REIGNED DURING FORTY-SEVEN YEARS. HE DIED IN THE SEVENTY-THIRD YEAR OF HIS AGE,

JANY. XXVIII., ANNO DOMINI DCCCXIIII.

INDITION VII.

26. *THE SARACENS IN ITALY AND SICILY*[1]

In the time of Charlemagne the Duchy of Benevento which comprised most of southern Italy, stretching from the "heel" and "toe" of the boot-shaped peninsula nearly as far north as Rome, was in the hands of the Lombards. Charlemagne was never able really to conquer it, though he claimed its homage and though he had wrested the control of northern Italy from his Lombard enemies. The island of Sicily, together with the southernmost parts of Italy, was under the rule of the Byzantine Empire. Shortly after Charlemagne's death, however, the Saracens, comprising in this case chiefly the Arabs who had conquered northern Africa and the native Berbers of that region, whom the Arabs had subjected and converted to Islam, began the conquest of Sicily, which after many years of fighting they succeeded in bringing fully under their sway. The city of Palermo, captured in 831, became their capital and in course of time came to rival Cordova and Cairo in prosperity and culture.

Before they had completed the conquest of Sicily the Saracens turned to Italy, overrunning the Duchy of Benevento and making raids in other parts of the peninsula. In 846 they even attacked the suburbs of Rome itself. Gradually, however, the Christians succeeded in dislodging them from one stronghold after another and finally drove them from the peninsula in the early part of the tenth century. They lasted in Sicily until after the middle of the eleventh century when their power gave way to Norman rule. Long after Mohammedan control ended, however, Sicily retained a strong impress of Saracen civilization.

In the following selection a brief but vivid account is given of the Mohammedan conquests in Sicily and Italy.

The Lombard duchy of Benevento stood firm as ever under two noble chiefs, Arechis and Grimbald; these assumed the crown and sceptre, together with the title of prince. It is no slight boast, that they were the only rulers in Christendom able to withstand the German, the new Emperor of the West, though he was aided by the Popes. All that he could do after seven years of warfare was to take Chieti, and to exact a yearly tribute. "With the help of God I will ever be free," was the declaration of his Lombard enemy. Yet it may be doubted whether this stout resistance was of any real advantage to Italy. A broad line, thanks to Arechis and his son, was drawn between the

[1] T. L. Kington-Oliphant, *History of Frederick the Second, Emperor of the Romans,* 2 vols., London, Macmillan and Company, 1862. Vol. I, pp. 4–12. By permission of The Macmillan Company, publishers.

North and South; Rome, lying between the two powers, was fully aware of the advantages she derived from this disunion of the peninsula; and many centuries rolled away before Italy could be anything more than a geographical name.

The bones of Charlemagne had scarcely been laid in the earth, before a new event of European interest took place. Sicily had long smarted under the incursions of Moslem pirates. The female captives, torn from her shores, had given the name of Sikilliat to a mansion near the Caliph's abode. The images of gold and silver, once the boast of Sicilian shrines, had been carried off and sold through Moslem agency to the idolaters in Hindostan, though the more orthodox of the Saracens had felt a pang of remorse at this traffic in the works of Satan. But in the year 827, the systematic conquest of the island was undertaken; it had escaped the yoke for a century and a half, mainly on account of the constant civil wars among the African Moslems. Two parties had been warring with each other in Sicily for six years; the weaker side, headed by Euphemius, called in the aid of the unbelievers. The city of Kairewan, which had taken the place of destroyed Carthage as the mistress of Africa, sent forth a small army of Arabs and Berbers, besides warriors from Spain and distant Khorassan. The invaders, led by Ased, a renowned lawyer, landed at Mazara, routed the Greek host, and were soon encamped in the old stone quarries of Syracuse. Repulsed from the capital, they withdrew into the West of Sicily, and were reinforced from Spain; Palermo fell into their hands after a year's siege, and became their main stronghold. Hence they went forth, year after year, to ravage the Christian cities, and to bear off thousands of captives. It was a great day for Islam when the hitherto impregnable Castro Giovanni, the famous Enna, was stormed; the savage conquerors gave all the glory to Allah, and sent to the Caliph many of the patrician ladies, forming a part of the enormous booty taken. This city, in the centre of the island, had baffled the Africans for thirty years. The Greek Emperors and Empresses were too much occupied with the abolition and restoration of images to pay earnest attention to Syracuse; the Venetians were chased home up the Adriatic; the Neapolitans made a base league with the infidels, and caused the fall of Messina; Rome owed her safety to the heroism of her Pope, Leo IV; but the city of Bari was placed under the rule of Bagdad for a short time by an adventurous Sultan. The Saracens now proceeded to elect a Wali for the Great Land, by which Italy was meant, while Sicily was governed by a Sahib.

There was always much disunion among the Moslem conquerors, and the Greek power in the island thus gained a long respite. The Berbers, mostly given to industry, held the country between Mazara and Girgenti; while the Arabs, the superior race, were established to the North, between Trapani and Palermo. These last furnished the lawyers, governors, and captains of

Sicily; from them was recruited the *Giund,* an hereditary class of armed nobility, paid by Christian money. The *gezia* was a poll tax levied upon all who were not Moslem, in consideration of which the tributaries were allowed to enjoy their own religion. The Sicilian Christians were forbidden to carry arms, to mount horses, to build high mansions, to drink while in public, or to celebrate pompous funeral rites. They were forced to wear a peculiar dress, to rise up to a true believer, and to abstain from building new churches and cloisters. Moslem women were not to be annoyed by the presence of Christian females at the baths, and Moslem ears were not to be scandalized by the sound of the reading of the Gospel or the ringing of bells. But Christian slaves, thanks to the merciful laws of Mohammed, were better off in Sicily than in Italy or France; any one of them might take a short cut to freedom by professing Islam. The three vales, into which the island is divided, were under very different institutions; that of Mazara was full of slaves, that of Noto was held by Christians in a state of vassalage, while the Val Demone abounded in independent or tributary commonwealths. The vast estates of the Roman epoch were now happily subdivided into many small farms, paying rent to the Moslem landlords, who had dispossessed the former owners. The mild policy of the conquerors is plain from the few martyrdoms recorded; the most renowned Sicilian saint of the time is John of Rachetta, called the modern Elias, whose adventures in Africa recall the history of Joseph.

In 877, Giafar led on the Moslem once more to the siege of the Christian capital. They battered and undermined for months the defences of Ortygia, and had the credit of inventing the mangonels and petriers, the chief trust of mediaeval engineers. The days of Hamilcar and Gelon seemed to have returned; the Africans of the West were once more beleaguering the Greeks in the noble old city, which had now little help to expect from the East. The soldiers who should have relieved it (the siege lasted almost a year) were kept at Constantinople to build a church. Still the Maronites, Tarsites, and Peloponnesians stood at bay in the breach for twenty days and nights, though reduced to eat the corpses of the slain and the grass that was growing on the walls. But a sudden assault of the besiegers carried the town, and an awful massacre followed. The brave governor and seventy nobles were afterwards butchered in cold blood with stones, clubs, and lances; one hero, who during the siege had often been heard to curse the Prophet's name, was torn asunder, while the Moslem mangled his corpse with their teeth. Never did a Christian city yield so large a booty. Two months were spent in pulling down the walls and churches; the prisoners were then dragged across the island to Palermo, which henceforth took the place of Syracuse, just as Cairo and Kairewan had supplanted older foundations. The captive clergy were shut up in foul prisons along with negroes and Jews for seven years, after escaping the perils of a religious dispute with the Wali, though a cry for the blood of the polytheists was uttered by a fanatical Imaum.

Ibrahim Ibn Ahmed, at whose command the siege of Syracuse had been undertaken, was a man of great genius, but was guilty of wholesale barbarities in Africa. He suppressed the revolt of the Sicilian Moslem, putting to death the leaders of both Arabs and Berbers, whom he played off against each other; Palermo was sacked by his African soldiery in the year 900 with horrible cruelty. Having received orders from Bagdad to resign his power in Africa, he came to wage the holy war in Sicily, which he had hitherto governed from afar. He completed the conquest of the island, a work of eighty years, by the storm of Taoromina; the citizens, who had all jeered at the reproofs of the modern Elias, were ruthlessly butchered. The victor now assailed the mainland; his son had already seized and depopulated Reggio. "I will take care of Italy," cried Ibrahim, "I will do what I please with the dwellers therein; expect me at Rome, and then will come the turn of Constantinople." But Italy was saved; this new Alaric died under the walls of Cosenza, and Naples was relieved from her agony of fear at his approach. The Tenth century is chiefly taken up with the struggles of the Sicilian Emirs to shake off the yoke of Kairewan. These struggles were at first fruitless; the rising dynasty of the Fatimites made its power felt in the island; Palermo was sacked over and over again, to chastise its rebellions, and one of the satraps sent from Africa made it his boast that he had slaughtered more than half a million of his fellow-Moslem. A strict account was exacted from the corsairs of their Italian booty; the Fatimite ruler complained that his generals ate the camel themselves and brought him only the ears. But in 948, a famous warrior, Hassan the Kelbite, landed in Sicily, who made the Emirate hereditary in his house for a hundred years. His descendants claimed the title of Malek or King, named their own viziers, and waged a successful war against the hosts of Armenians, Russians and Paulician heretics, poured into the lost provinces by the reviving Empire of the East. Palermo flourished in spite of its rebellions and the consequent massacres; Cordova and Bagdad were its only rivals. It boasted of a mosque, once a Christian church, said to contain the bones of Aristotle; this stood in the street still called the Cassaro from the Old Alcazar. There were five hundred mosques in the city, and nine gates; many mills were turned by the neighbouring streams, while the sugar-cane and papyrus grew not far from the walls. Ibn Haukal, a contemporary of St. Dunstan who visited Palermo, complains of the citizens as more prone to vice than to virtue, besides being very filthy in their habits in spite of the numerous baths; they could hardly be brought to keep the Ramazan or to fast at all; they would sit idly, young and old, at the city gates, like monks begging; it was plain that there was a good deal of Greek blood in these sleek professors of Islam.

The later Kelbites degenerated from their fathers, who had so manfully faced the assaults of both the Eastern and Western Caesars. The Moslem nobility began to die out, and lingered only in the Christian part of the island. The persecuted followers of Ali fled to Sicily for refuge, and civil wars were soon raging; each chief seized on all the towns he could, while the central authority was at an end. The hopes of the vassals were rising. Pisa had already begun that career of conquest in Sardinia and Sicily, which may be read in rude Latin verse engraved on the west front of her noble cathedral. More formidable foes were even nearer at hand, at whose approach the native Christians took courage. A few Sicilian monasteries had survived all through the dreary seven generations of Mohammedan oppression; religion in that country has invariably allied itself with patriotism. The hermits of Sicily went forth to proclaim her wrongs throughout Europe. St. Nilus, the statesman and prophet of Rossano, clad in sackcloth which he changed only once a year, was honoured by Emperors and Popes. St. Vitalis lived on Mount Etna, St. Philaret at Traina; while the Syracusan Simeon astonished the Germans by making the top of the old Roman gate at Trèves his perpetual abode. The deliverance of his country was nigh; and while welcoming a people back into the Christian fold, we need not regret the hundred and twenty Moslem, who made a name for themselves in grammar, philology, law, medicine, theology, and poetry, while basking in the smiles of the Palermitan court.

Sicily had been undergoing for more than two centuries the sharp discipline of the Saracen scymitar; her sister provinces of the mainland had been almost equally harassed by three different masters, the champions of three different rituals. Not many years after Charlemagne's death the great duchy of Benevento, which had once included almost the whole of Southern Italy, fell to pieces. Its work was done; it had stayed the progress of Charlemagne. The Greeks were now able to retake most of their lost provinces: while the degenerated Lombard princes of Benevento, Salerno, and Capua found their only safety in feudal dependence upon the German sovereigns. The Saracens were called in by the contending parties; these unbelievers established themselves on Monte Gargano, the renowned sanctuary of St. Michael, but their great encampment was on the banks of the Garigliano. They swept the country, carrying off all the horses, arms, and young women; Monte Cassino was now for the second time destroyed. After their inroads had been pushed as far inland as Narni, they were exterminated in 916 by a combination of Greeks and Lombards, aided by the Pope and King Berengar. The oppressive exactions of the Eastern Greeks were still more systematic; they made slaves of those of their brother Christians who had submitted to the Saracens; the only way of saving the Calabrian peasants from their masters expectant, the foreign soldiery, was first to embark the troops on board ship, and then to set free the crowd of captives remaining on the shore. The Byzantine Empire was now being revived by the energy of Nicephorus Phocas, John Zimisces, and the Slayer of Bulgarians; who built Troja, Melfi, and Firenzuola, and established at Bari their Catapan, a magistrate with absolute powers, whence the Capitanata takes its name.

27. *FRANCE IN THE NINTH AND TENTH CENTURIES*[1]

The author of the following selection gives a graphic description of the desolation and disorder in France that came with the decline and break-up of Charlemagne's once mighty Empire. Chaotic conditions such as these paved the way for the full development of the feudal system.

The night of the ninth century. . . . What is its course? Dimly the records give a glimpse of a people scattered and without guidance. The Barbarians have broken through the ramparts. The Saracen invasions have spread in successive waves over the South. The Hungarians swarm over the Eastern provinces. "These strangers," writes Richer, "gave themselves over to the most cruel outrages; they sacked town and village, and laid waste the fields. They burned down the churches and then departed with a crowd of captives, and no one said them nay."

The realm they have burnt, wasted, and spoilt,
Great numbers they carry off captive bound,
Little children and women of high birth,
Noblemen too with blows they drive off on foot.
(Ogier the Dane, v. 401.)

The Normans from the north penetrate by way of the rivers to the very centre of France, "skimming over the ocean like pirates." Chartres, in the heart of the realm, was wont to take pride in its name, "the city of stone," *urbs lapidum*. The Normans appear, and Chartres is sacked.

William le Breton boasts the antiquity and wealth of the town of Autun; but the Barbarians have scattered these riches and its site is overgrown with weeds.

"The country is laid waste as far as the Loire," says the chronicler of Amboise, "so completely that where once were prosperous towns, wild animals now roam. The plain where once the harvests ripened now knows only

[1] Fr. Funck-Brentano, *The Middle Ages*. Translated from the French by Elizabeth O'Neill, M.A. G. P. Putnam's Sons, New York, 1926, pp. 1–3.

'The thistle and the sharp-thorned briar.' "
(Virgil, Bucolics, v. 39.)

And Paris? "What shall I say of her?" writes Adrevald. "That town once resplendent in her wealth and glory, famed for her fertile lands, is now but a heap of ashes."

In the course of the ninth and tenth centuries all the towns of France were destroyed. Can one imagine the slaughter and plunder concentrated in such a statement?

In the little country villages the houses crumble to dust, the walls of the churches are full of cracks, their roofs gape wide, the tabernacles are overgrown with weeds while ivy clings to their capitals. The house of God has become a den where foxes burrow and birds of prey have their nests, where one may see the lidless eyes of the owl shine unblinking through spiders' webs.

Powerless to resist the invaders, many men-at-arms join them. They plunder together, and as there is no longer any supreme authority, private quarrels, of man against man, family against family, of district against district, break out, are multiplied, and never-ending. "And three men cannot meet two without putting them to death." "The statutes of the sacred canons and the capitularies of our ancestors have become void," writes Carloman in his palace of Verneuil (March 884). Private wars become common. "In the absence of a central authority," says Hariulf, "the stronger break out into violence." "Men destroy one another like the fishes of the sea" (Council of Trosly).

There was nothing but attacks, rescues, captures, and reprisals, which one can picture from the story, told by Richer, of a leader who was conducting his army over the land from which the enemy drew his supplies. He ravaged it with such fury that "he did not leave even her cabin to a poor old woman in her second childhood."

There is no longer any trade, only unceasing terror. Fearfully men put up buildings of wood only. Architecture is no more.

In the time of Charles the Great, and under his great military power, it would have been possible to discern a society in dissolution. And how much more was the disorder to manifest itself afterwards. At the end of the tenth century was there any remnant, ever so small, of the social, political, and economic conditions established in Gaul by the Romans, or even introduced after their time in rough fashion by the Barbarians?

Everything is changed. The monk Paul, who lived in the eleventh century, speaks of a collection of charters, the most ancient of which dated from the ninth century: "What changes! The rolls preserved in the archives of our abbey show that the peasants of that time lived under customs which those of today know no longer; even the words which they used are not those of the present day." And further on: "I have found the names of places, persons, and things changed since that time to such a degree that not only have they disappeared, but it is no longer possible to identify them; far from having preserved them, men do not even know them" (Cartulary of Saint-Père).

The peasant has abandoned his ravaged fields to avoid the violence of anarchy. The people have gone to cower in the depths of the forests or in inaccessible regions, or have taken refuge in the high mountains.

The ties which united the inhabitants of the country have been burst asunder; customary and legal usage have broken down. Society has no longer any governance.

28. *ORIGINS OF FEUDALISM* [1]

The feudal system, of course, is far from easy to understand. The student approaching the problem for the first time, however, will probably find his difficulties considerably lessened if he reads with care the following selection by the late Professor George Burton Adams of Yale University. It would be difficult to find a clearer explanation of the origins of the feudal system than that made by this well-known historian. Students should read it critically, however, and compare it with other more recent explanations of feudal origins, for some of Professor Adams' findings are now called in question.

Out of the fragments of the Carolingian empire the modern nations were finally to arise. But there was in the meantime, as we have seen, a considerable period, after the fall of the old government, before any real national governments, at all corresponding to the modern idea, came into existence. This is the period when the feudal system was the prevailing form of political organization.

In any detailed history of civilization it would be necessary to give much space to the feudal system, both because of the large field which it occupies in the middle ages, and also because it is one of the most influential of medieval institutions, the source of legal principles and social ideas, which are, even now, by no means obsolete.

The question of the origin of the feudal system is one of the most difficult in all institutional history, for one reason, because it took its rise in ages which have left us very scanty historical material, and for another, because it originated in the domain of extra-legal and private operations, and under

[1] George B. Adams, *Civilization during the Middle Ages.* New York, Charles Scribner's Sons, 1907, pp. 194–213; 216–217. Copyright, 1894, by Charles Scribner's Sons. By permission of the publishers.

the influence of forces which leave but slight traces of their working. Every important point in this history has been the subject of long and violent controversy, and is so still, though to a less extent. It may be said that opinion is now practically united upon the main points, and that present differences concern minor points of detail, or the amount of emphasis which shall be placed upon certain facts.

Before entering upon the details of the origin of the feudal system, there is one general consideration which has an important bearing upon the study which should be made clear. It is necessary here, and in all institutional history, to distinguish very carefully between two sets of causes or antecedents. First, there is the general cause, or the prevailing condition of things in the society of the time, which renders a new institution necessary; and, second, there is the old institution, on which the prevailing cause seizes, and which it transforms into a new one. Both these are always present. No institution ever starts into life wholly new. Every new institution has its foundation far in the past in some earlier one. The prevailing necessity transforms it into a new institution, but the character of the new creation is as much conditioned by the character of the old as it is by the new necessity which it is made to meet. The sneer which is sometimes heard against that sort of investigation which seeks the foundations of a new institution in those which have preceded it, as merely antiquarian, is proof only of a very narrow conception of history.

The application of this to the present case becomes clear enough when the problem before us is specifically stated. It is not to account for the rise of feudal forms in general, but to account for that peculiar feudal system, which arose in western Europe in the middle ages. It is undoubtedly true that institutions have existed in Japan, and in Central Africa, and in various Mohammedan states, almost everywhere, indeed, which are justly called feudal. It is true that under certain political conditions human nature turns, naturally as it would seem, to forms of government which are feudal. And it is necessary to take these political and social conditions into account in our study of the problem more fully than has been done, perhaps, by some merely institutional historians. They are among the most essential causes at work. But when taken alone they merely account for the rise of feudal forms in general. They give us no reason for the fact that in institutional details these various feudal systems differ from one another in essential particulars. To explain this fact we must turn to the earlier institutional foundation on which the social forces built.

By "the feudal system," when used without qualification, we always mean the system of medieval western Europe, and in accounting for its origin we have two sets of facts to consider—the condition of society which gave such forms an opportunity to develop, and the earlier institutions which were transformed by these social conditions into the historical feudal system, and which determined the form assumed by many of the special features of that system.

This historical feudal system came into existence in the eighth and ninth centuries, owing to the political disorders of the time, and the inability of the central government—even of so strong a government as Charlemagne's—to do its necessary work without some such help. It is itself a crude and barbarous form of government in which the political organization is based on the tenure of land; that is, the public duties and obligations which ordinarily the citizen owes to the state, are turned into private and personal services which he owes to his lord in return for land which he has received from him. The state no longer depends upon its citizens, as citizens, for the fulfilment of public duties, but it depends upon a certain few to perform specified duties, which they owe as vassals of the king, and these in turn depend upon their vassals for services, which will enable them to meet their own obligations toward the king.

There are always present in this historical feudal system two elements very closely united together, but which are really distinct, and which must be kept apart from one another in mind if we are to understand the origin of the system. One of these relates wholly to land and the tenure by which it is held. This land element is the "benefice" or "fief." The other is the personal relation, the bond of mutual fidelity and protection which binds together the grades in the feudal hierarchy. This personal element is the relation of lord and vassal. In the ideal feudal system these two are always united, the vassal always receives a fief, the fief is always held by a vassal. In practice they were sometimes separated, and in some countries such a separation was recognized by the feudal law.

There are, then, these two specific questions concerning the origin of the feudal system: How did these two institutions, vassalage and the benefice, come into existence and become united; and how did public duties, for example military service, get attached to them, and become changed in this way into private services which one paid as a form of land rent?

When we come to trace the origin of these two institutions we find that we are carried back to the time of political insecurity when the Roman empire was falling to pieces, just before and at the moment of the German invasions. Then began the conditions which called these institutions into existence, and which, continuing in the main unchanged through the whole period, transformed them into the perfected feudal system.

As the real power which the Roman emperor had at his command declined, his ability to protect the citizens and preserve order in the outlying provinces became less and less. The peace and security which Rome had formerly established could no longer be maintained, and the provinces fell a prey to various disorders. Usurping emperors, peasants in insurrection, revolted troops, bands of invading Germans, marauders of all sorts appeared everywhere, and the state could not hold them in check.

But the individual must obtain protection at some price. If he owns land, he will need protection in order to cultivate it and enjoy the returns; if he has no land, he will still need protection for his life and his means of livelihood. If he cannot get it from the state, he must seek it where he can find it. In such political conditions there always arises a class of men strong enough from wealth or position or abilities to give some degree of protection to weaker men. The weaker men take refuge with the stronger and increase their power, which thus grows into a little semi-detached fragment of the state, and the germ of the feudal system has come into existence.

In the later Roman empire, under the influence of these conditions, two practices arose which we need to notice. One of them related to land, the other to persons owning no land. In the case of the first the small landowner, long at an economic disadvantage, and now, in the midst of the crowding evils of the time, threatened with total destruction, gave up his land to some large landowner near him, whose position was strong enough to command or compel respect from vagrant enemies, and received it back from him to cultivate, no longer as owner, but as a tenant at will.

As the form of tenure in such cases a peculiar kind of lease, which had been known to the Roman law as the *precarium,* received a very great extension in practice. Under this form the owner granted the use of a piece of property to another, without rent and with no period of time specified, but revocable at the will of the owner. This was the kind of tenure by which the small landholder held and cultivated the land which he had been obliged to surrender to some strong man for fear of losing it entirely. He lost the ownership of it; he held it only so long as his lord might please, but his actual condition was much improved. In the growing scarcity of laborers he was not likely to be disturbed in his tenure, and he had now an armed force which could be depended on to keep off all marauders not actually armies, and he had a right to take refuge in his lord's fortress on some not distant hilltop when a more serious invasion threatened.

The other practice was adopted to meet the case of the freeman who owned no land, and it gave rise to an institution closely resembling the clientel which Cæsar describes as prevailing in Gaul at the time of his conquest, and not unlike the earlier Roman institution of patron and client. The dependent is often called a client in the language of the time, and the institution itself the *patrocinium*.

In a case of this sort the poor freeman goes to the rich and strong man who can afford him protection, and explaining that he can no longer care for or support himself, begs to be taken under his protection and furnished with shelter and support. The rich man grants the petition, adds the client to his household, and expects from him, in return, such services as a freeman may perform. There seem to have been no specified services, nor peculiar duty of fidelity in this arrangement, but its obligations were probably clearly enough defined in the customary law which all understood.

In this way many local magnates of the age of the invasion collected about them considerable forces, composed also partly of armed slaves and serfs, and so added greatly to their own power, and furnished the locality with some degree of security. In some instances, both in the East and in the West, we know that such private forces amounted to respectable armies and served to protect extensive territories, or even to turn the march of an invading tribe.

It is important to notice that, in the case of the freeman entering into either of these relations, the personal one or the one relating to land, there was no loss of political status or personal freedom. The dependent, under the new arrangement, remained, in either relation, exactly what he had been before, both in reference to his duties to the government and his personal rights.

It was of course true, as the history of the Roman tax system makes evident, that the rich man might be so strong in his district that he could refuse to meet his obligations toward the government, and set the local officers at defiance, and so be able to protect from the burdens of the state the poorer men who became his clients and dependents. This was no doubt one reason for the rapid extension of these practices. But if he did this, it was an illegal usurpation, not a recognized change in the status or duties of his dependents. That such results did follow is clear enough from the attitude of the state toward these practices, which it pronounced illegal and forbade under the heaviest penalties. But it was powerless to interfere, and even the death penalty had no effect to check them. Indeed, if the state had been strong enough to stop them, it would have been strong enough to have preserved such general security that no necessity for such customs would ever have arisen.

The results, as seen at the time of the invasions, have many features in common with the later feudal system, and it is right, in the sense mentioned at the beginning of the chapter, to speak of them as feudal, but they are still very far from being the historical feudal system.

In the first place, the characteristic feature of the later feudalism was lacking. These two practices remained entirely distinct from one another. They were not yet united into a single institution. The personal relation, or clientage, did not imply at all the reception of land, and holding land by the *precarium* tenure involved no obligation of service.

In the second place, there was no common organization, either expressed or implied, as there was in the completed feudal system, between the various local powers which had been formed. They were merely private and wholly separate fragments into which the state had fallen. In other words, there was not enough connection between them, taken alone, to have preserved the state, as a state, through a period of political chaos, but they would have produced a thousand little local states wholly independent and sovereign.

In the third place, the state regarded these institutions not merely as unconstitutional and improper for itself, but also as illegal and improper for private citizens. The local potentate might actually have usurped, as we know he did, many of the functions of the state, judicial as well as military, and have excluded practically the state from his whole territory and taken its place himself, but this was a usurpation and strictly forbidden by the laws. In the later feudal system the similar practices are not merely recognized by the government as legal, but they are even, in some cases, enjoined as duties, and become, practically at least, the very constitution of the state, so that in many cases the sovereignty exercised by the feudal baron over his territory was the only sovereignty exercised by the state.

The Franks, when they entered Gaul, found these customs prevailing there, as in all the provinces of the empire. They dealt with them, as they did with many Roman institutions which they found, they allowed them to continue in use and they adopted them themselves. It was under the conditions which prevailed in the Frankish kingdom, and by means of the legal expedients adopted by the Frankish kings, that these primitive beginnings were developed into the feudal system of Europe.

The conquest was indeed a most serious crisis in the history of feudalism. Had they been disposed to do so, the Frankish kings would doubtless have found it easier than the Roman emperors had done, to crush out these institutions, still in a formative condition, and to establish a centralization, if not more complete in theory, certainly more so in fact. The government which they did found had many of the features of an absolutism incompatible with the continued growth of these institutions. If they had destroyed them, and entirely prevented their further growth, their government would have escaped its most dangerous enemy of the future—the one to which it was finally compelled to surrender. But the more simple political mind of the Frank could not perceive this danger so clearly as the Roman did, and another fact was an even more decisive influence against any change. The Franks themselves had institutions and practices which were so similar to those of the Romans that it was the most natural thing imaginable for them to adopt these, and to regard them at once, as they had never before been regarded, as perfectly legal, because the corresponding German institutions were. The German customs and the Roman customs ran rapidly together into a common practice, and the German variations from the Roman added very essential elements of their own to the common product, so that the feudal system presents one of the clearest cases that we have of the union of the German and the Roman factors together to form the new institution.

The most striking of these German institutions was the *comitatus*, which we have briefly described in the chapter on the German invasions. The old theory of its relation to the origin of feudalism is now abandoned, but its place has been taken by a clear recognition of the very important contribution which it made to the final result. It was an institution corresponding very closely to the Roman client system which we have described above. It was a purely personal relationship of mutual protection, service, and support, between a chief and certain men, usually young men of the tribe, voluntarily entered into on both sides. But it had certain distinctive features of its own, which are lacking in the Roman institution, but characteristic of the later feudalism. It was not regarded by the Germans as a mere business transaction of give and take, but was looked upon as conferring especial honor on lord and man alike. It was entered upon by a special ceremonial, and sanctioned by a solemn oath, and the bond of personal fidelity established by it was considered to be of the most sacred and binding character. All these ideas and customs passed from the *comitatus* into the feudal system.

The Roman practices in this matter, which the Franks found in Gaul, seemed to them, therefore, very natural and proper, and they adopted them at once, and it seems evident, as the Franks became settled upon the land and the members of the original royal *comitatus* came to have private interests and landed possessions which made it difficult for them to fulfil the duties of the old relation, or to be used for its purposes, that their place was taken by persons who had entered into a personal relation to the king, corresponding, both in motive and in form, rather to the Roman *patrocinium* than to the German *comitatus*. So that the institution which survived in the new state was the Roman rather than the German, which must necessarily have disappeared in the decidedly changed conditions of the national life, but it was the Roman essentially modified by ideas and usages from the German.

It was some little time after the conquest, so far as the documents allow us to judge, before the word *vassus* began to be employed for the man in this personal relation. Originally applied to servants not free, it came into gradual use for the free clients, and acquired a distinctly honorable meaning in somewhat the same way as the English word knight.

In reference to the land relationship, which we have described, it has been conclusively shown lately, in opposition to earlier theories, that the German kings, following native German ideas, did probably from the beginning make donations of land, which carried only a limited right of ownership, and which fell back in certain contingencies to the donor. Such practices would make it easy for the Franks to understand and adopt the Roman practice of the *precarium,* and it appears to have been so adopted, quite extensively, by German private landowners who found themselves in a similar position to the Roman, and to have been continued also as before, by Roman subjects of the Frankish state. But still, to all appearances, it was not adopted in any really important way by the kings, until the beginning of the Carolingian period, and the chief agent in carrying over the *precariœ,* as the word came to be written, from the Roman to the German state, seems to have been the church.

The church appears to have used this tenure very extensively under the empire, both as a means of increasing its territories—the donor retaining the use of his grant for life—and also as a convenient way of bestowing upon persons, whose support or favor it desired to secure, lands which it could not alienate. It seems to have introduced a small rent-charge, as a sign of ownership, and to have tended to limit such grants to a specified time, commonly five years, or the life-time of the recipient. These practices it continued in very frequent use under the Frankish kingdom.

Through the Merovingian period of Frankish history, therefore, these institutions remained in very much the same shape in which they were under the empire, except that they were not now regarded as illegal. It is in the Carolingian period that they took the next great steps in their development—the steps that were essentially necessary to the formation of the historical feudal system. They then became united as the two sides of a single institution, and they were adopted by the government as a means of securing the performance of their public duties by the subjects of the state. The simplest example of this process is the transformation of the citizen army into a feudal army, and this gives us also, in its main features, the history of the joining together of the benefice and vassalage.

Originally neither of these primitive Roman institutions had, as it would seem, any especially military character. And this is, with an insignificant modification, as true of the Merovingian as of the Roman period. In such troubled times, however, as those which brought these institutions into use, military service would certainly be one of the most frequent services needed from the dependent, and apparently some of them at least were constantly employed as an armed force, but there was, during the earlier period, no necessary connection of this military service with these relationships either of person or of land. The first beginnings of this connection were made at the opening of the Carolingian age under Charles Martel; the completion of it—the establishment of military service as the almost indispensable rule in feudalism—was hardly accomplished before the period ends.

The occasion which led to the beginning of this change was the Arabian attack on Gaul, and the necessity of forming a cavalry force to meet it. Originally the Franks had fought on foot. But the Arabs were on horseback, and their sudden raids, which continued in south Gaul long after the battle of Tours, could not be properly met, and the defeated enemy properly pursued without the use of horse. But this was putting a heavy burden of expense on the citizen, who armed and supported himself, and who was already severely oppressed by the conditions of the service. The state must aid him to bear it. This it could do only by grants of land.

The first Carolingian princes had, however, but scanty resources in this direction. The royal domains had been exhausted under the Merovingian kings. Their own house possessions, though very extensive, would not go far toward meeting the needs of a family, gradually usurping the royal power, and so in need of means to purchase faithful support. They lay, besides, in Austrasia, at a distance from the country which was in especial need of defence. There was in the case but one resource open—the extensive lands of the church, amounting, in some parts of the kingdom, to one-third of the territory.

It had long been the custom for the state to make use of church lands, a bit here and there, to meet some special need; but now, in the face of this great necessity, there was, seemingly, a more extensive confiscation, for which Charles Martel secured an evil place in the memory of the church. It was not, however, a confiscation in form, and his successors succeeded in making a definite arrangement with the church, regulating and sanctioning, in a limited way, this use of church lands.

The *precariæ* furnished a convenient tenure for the purpose. By it the ownership of the church was, in form, preserved by the payment of a small fee, while the use of the land passed to the appointee of the king. These grants became technically known in the church records as *precariæ verbo regis,* grants at the royal command.

As the object was to maintain a cavalry force, the prince bestowed these grants of land upon his vassals who were bound to him by a personal bond of especial fidelity and service, and who were to be enabled, by the additional income secured them by the grant, to furnish mounted soldiers to the army. They divided the land among their own vassals in the same way, and at this time the word "benefice" came into gradual use for the land granted.

In this way the first steps were taken toward uniting these two institutions into a single one, and toward introducing the special obligation of military service as a condition on which the land was held. But it must not be understood that the process was by any means completed as yet. It was a very slow and a very gradual change, extending throughout the whole Carolingian period.

The efforts which were made by Charlemagne to reform, or rather to enforce, the military system of the kingdom, had a very important influence in the same direction. With the growth in size of the Frankish empire, requiring campaigns at such great distances and almost constantly, their original military system of unpaid service from all the freemen, which was common to all the German tribes, had come to be a serious burden upon the Franks. Indeed, the poorer citizens, who could no longer bear it, were striving to escape from it in every possible way, and the armies threatened to disappear. This danger Charlemagne tried to overcome by a series of enactments. He allowed several of the poorer freemen to unite in arming and maintaining one of their number in the army. He directed that vassals of private individuals must perform military service as the vassals of the king did, thus trying to hold to their duty those who had sought to escape from it by such an arrangement. He also ordained that the lord should be held responsible for the equipment and appearance in the field of his vassals, or should pay the fine for their failure to appear. Finally, when these proved of no avail, he issued an ordinance which apparently brought a great principle of human nature to his aid by allowing the vassals to come into the field under the command of their lords instead of with the general levy of the country under the count. The natural desire of the lord for influence and consideration would make him wish to appear at the head of as large and fine a body of vassals as possible, and the expedient seems to have proved successful enough to be adopted regularly in the generations following. But the result of it was to make the army more and more completely a feudal army, and though it seems certain that the freemen, who remained throughout the whole feudal period holders of land and free laborers in considerable numbers outside the feudal system, were never excused from military duty, and were summoned occasionally to actual service, still the state in the main depended no longer upon citizens for its army, but upon vassals who served as a duty growing out of their holding of land.

In this way one important duty of the citizen, that of defending the community, was transformed from a public obligation into a matter of private contract, and became one of the ordinary conditions upon which lands were held.

A like transformation took place during this same time in regard to other functions of the state—the judicial, for example—which also passed into the hands of private individuals and became attached to the land. In this way the great fiefs came to possess what the French feudal law called "justice"—*jurisdictio*—that is, full sovereignty, so that the state was practically excluded from all contact with any persons residing within the limits of the fief. The process by which this transformation was accomplished, in respect to the other functions of the state, is by no means so clear as it is in the case of the military. In the instance, for example, of the judicial power of the state, there is probably no subject connected with the origin of the feudal system which is still the subject of so much controversy, and on which so many varying views are still maintained, as upon the way in which this power passed into private hands.

The process was undoubtedly largely aided by the "immunities." These were grants of privilege to churches or to private individuals, by virtue of which the ordinary officers of the state were forbidden all entry upon the specified domain, and the owner took the place of the officers in reference to the state. This did not at once remove these estates from the control of the government. The landowner became independent of the ordinary officers, but not of the state, whose officer he became for his own land, though often possessing, instead of the state, the entire judicial revenue, but it did undoubtedly favor the development of private jurisdiction and virtual independence, and probably in many cases fully accounts for the sovereignty of the fief. The government, which found it so difficult during this time to control its own officers and to keep the functions of the state in operation by their means, would often find it entirely impossible to prevent the great landowner who had received a grant of immunity from throwing off all dependence upon the government and setting up a state of his own.

In the case of many fiefs, however, no immunity existed, and the process must have been a different one. Our knowledge of the actual process is so slight that almost every one of the various theories which have been advanced to explain it has some reasonable foundation, but the one which seems probable for the majority of cases is that of Beaudouin, who maintains that it was, in reality, a usurpation.

The holder of the fief was locally strong. He could and did maintain some real degree of order and security. It was by virtue of this fact that his power had been developed and continued to be obeyed. In theory the state was absolute. It was supposed to control almost every detail of life. And this theory of the power of the state continued to exist and to be recognized in the days of the most complete feudalism. But actually the state could do nothing. Its real power was at the opposite extreme from its theoretical. The great difficulty of intercommunication rendered it impossible for the state to bring its power into direct contact with all parts of the country. It had no strong and organized body of officers on whom it could depend. Every officer, military or administrative, was a local magnate doing his best to throw off the control of the state, and using his official position to aid him in this purpose. There was no strong feeling of unity among the people which it could call to its aid. There were no common feelings or ideas or interests which bound the dweller at the mouth of the Loire to the dweller at the mouth of the Seine. Patriotism and a common national feeling were wanting. Everything was local and personal. Even in the church was this the case in the tenth century, Europe at large hardly knowing who was pope in Rome, and the common organization almost falling to pieces, while in Rome itself the papacy sank to its lowest point of degradation, a prey to local faction and made to serve local interests. If this were true of the church, much more was it true of the state, which had no such general organization and no such basis of common feelings. The sovereign of the moment had only such an amount of power as he might derive from lands directly in his hands, that is, from his own local fief. The great advantage which the first Capetians had over their Carolingian rivals was, as we have seen, that they had a very strong local power of this sort, while the Carolingians had really none; but even this power which the first Capetians had was not enough to enable them to exercise the functions of a real government within the other large fiefs. Certainly there was no such power in the hands of the later Carolingians. These functions, which the government was powerless to exercise, fell naturally into the hands of the local magnate and were exercised by him.

Sometimes it was a real usurpation, the baron assuming and continuing offices which the state should have discharged. More often, no doubt, it was a transformation of duties which the state had once lodged in his hands, as an immunity, perhaps, or in making him its own administrative officer, duke or count, a transformation of such a sort that the baron no longer performed these, as a representative of the state, but by virtue of his own property right, and the persons living within his domain, fulfilled these duties, no longer as obligations due to the state, but as personal duties due to their immediate lord.

. . . .

We have endeavored to present in this sketch, as fully as possible in the space at our command, the rise of the feudal system. Comparatively insignificant practices, of private and illegal origin, which had arisen in the later Roman empire, and which were continued in the early Frankish kingdom, had been developed, under the pressure of public need, into a great political organization extending over the whole West, and virtually supplanting the national government. The public need which had made this development necessary was the need of security and protection. Men had been obliged to take refuge in the feudal castle, because the power of the state had broken down. This break-down of the state, its failure to discharge its ordinary functions, was not so much due to a lack of personal ability on the part of the king, as to the circumstances of the time, and to the inability of the ruling race as a whole to rise above them. The difficulty of intercommunication, the break-down of the old military and judicial organization, partly on account of this difficulty, thus depriving the state of its two hands, the lack of general ideas and common feelings and interests, seen for example in the scanty commerce of the time, the almost total absence, in a word, of all the sources from which every government must draw its life and strength, this general condition of society was the controlling force which created the feudal system. The Germans, in succeeding to the empire of Rome, had inherited a task which was as yet too great for the most of them, Merovingian and Carolingian alike. Only by a long process of experience and education were they to succeed in understanding its problems and mastering its difficulties. This is only saying in a new form what we have before said in other connections, that the coming in of the Germans must of necessity have been followed by a temporary decline of civilization. This was just as true of government and political order as of everything else, and the feudal system is merely, in politics, what the miracle lives and scholasticism are in literature and science.

29. *THE ENGLISH MANOR IN THE THIRTEENTH CENTURY* [1]

For more than twenty years Rowland E. Prothero, later Lord Ernle, as chief agent of the Duke of Bedford, looked after the vast agricultural interests of that nobleman. Earlier in life he had graduated from Oxford with honors in the classics and modern history. Thus he was exceptionally well fitted as a practical agriculturist and as a student of history to write on English Farming, Past and Present.

Lord Ernle's discussion of the medieval manor and manorial economy in England is closely packed with relevant information.

On a manorial estate, at the beginning of the thirteenth century, only the church, the manor-house, and perhaps the mill, rose out conspicuously. There were no detached, isolated farm-houses; but the remaining buildings of the village, grouped together in a sort of street, were the homes of the peasantry, who occupied and cultivated the greater part of the land. At some little distance from the village stood the manor hall or grange, with its outbuildings, garden, and fishpond, surrounded by clay-built walls with thatched tops. The style and extent of the buildings depended on whether the house was the permanent or occasional residence of the lord; they also varied with the importance of the manor, and the wealth of its owner. The house itself was built either of timber and clay, or of stone, for brickmaking was still a

[1] The Right Honorable Lord Ernle (Rowland E. Prothero), *English Farming, Past and Present.* London and New York, Longmans, Green, and Company, 1912, pp. 4–28.

forgotten art. It often consisted of a single hall, plastered inside, open to the roof, and earth-floored, which served as court of justice, diningroom, and bedchamber. At one end of the central room was a stable; at the other a chamber, kitchen, or larder. Below one part of the ground floor was a cellar; above another part was, perhaps, a "solar," or parlour, approached by an outside staircase. If the manor was sufficiently important, there were probably added a detached building for the farm servants, and a chamber for the bailiff. The outbuildings consisted of bake-house, stables, dairy, cattle and poultry houses, granary, and dove-cote. Some of the oldest specimens of domestic architecture are granaries, like Hazelton or Calcot in Gloucestershire, or the dove-cotes which still in country districts mark the former sites of manor-houses. Repairs of the walls and buildings of the manor-house were among the labour services of the tenantry, who dug, tempered, and daubed the clay, cut and carted the timber, and gathered the straw or reeds for thatching. Where technical skill was needed they were aided by craftsmen, who either held land in reward for their special services, or, on the smaller manors, were hired for the occasion.

Tufts of trees, conspicuous in the hedgeless expanse of arable land by which they were surrounded, marked the sites of villages, as they still do in the high table-land of the Pays de Caux. Under their shelter clustered the homes of the peasantry, clay-walled, open-roofed, earth-floored, chimneyless sheds, covered in with straw or reeds or heather, and consisting of a single room. Here, divided by a hurdle or wattle partition, lived, not only the human inhabitants, but their cows, pigs, and poultry. Close by were the tofts and crofts of the open-field farmers, each with its miniature hay-rick and straw-stack; and the cottages and curtilages of the cottagers, "fencèd al aboute with stikkes." Here were the scanty gardens in which grew the vegetables, few but essential to the health of a population which lived almost entirely on salted meat and fish often half-cured and half-putrid. These homesteads were in early times the only property held by members of the township in exclusive separate occupation. They were also, at first, the only permanent enclosures on the commonable land. But, as agriculture advanced, pasture paddocks ("gerstuns" or "garstons") for rearing stock, calves, or fattening beasts, or for the working oxen, which could not endure his "warke to labour all daye, and then to be put to the commons or before the herdsman," were enclosed in the immediate neighbourhood of the village. In these enclosures, or "happy garstons" as they were called at Aston Boges, were held the village merrymakings, the rush-bearings, the May games, the summerings at St. John's Eve, the public breakfasts, and the distribution of bread and ale in Rogation week.

The land comprised in a thirteenth century manor was generally divided into four main portions, and, speaking generally, was cultivated on cooperative principles; the demesne or "board" land, reserved for the lord's personal use, surrounding the manor-house, and forming the smaller portion of the whole; the free land occupied by freemen holding by military service, or by some form of fixed rent in money or in kind; the unfree land, occupied by various classes of bondmen, holding by produce-rents and labour services which varied with the custom of the manor; the common pastures and untilled wastes on which the tenants of the manor and the occupiers of certain cottages, in virtue of their holdings, fed their live-stock. This right of pasture must be clearly distinguished from those rights which, at certain seasons of the year, were exercised by the associated partners over the cultivated arable and meadow lands of the village farm. Thus the lord's demesne, using the word in its narrower sense, might be kept in hand, or let on lease to free or unfree tenants, or thrown into the village farm, or dealt with as to portions in each of these three ways. But whether the land was treated as a compact whole, like a modern home farm, or whether the landlord, as a shareholder in the village association, allowed it to be cut up into strips and intermixed with other holdings, the demesne was mainly cultivated by the labour services of the unfree peasantry. The rest of the land of the manor, forming the larger portion of the cultivated area, was farmed by village partners, whose rent chiefly consisted in the labour, more or less definite in amount, which they were obliged to perform on the lord's demesne.

In this method of cultivating a manorial estate there are many contrasts with the modern system. The three-fold division of the agricultural interests into landlord, tenant farmer, and wage-earning labourer was practically unknown. Landowner and tenant-labourer owned, occupied, and cultivated the soil, and the gradual relaxation of the labourer's tenure of the land, and the interposition of the tenant farmer between the two existing classes, sum up the early social history of English farming. In the thirteenth century, muscles were more essential to the prosperity of the landlord than money rents. The cultivators of the soil grew their produce, not for sale, but for their own consumption. Each manor or village was isolated and self-sufficing. Only in the neighbouring towns was there any market for the produce of the farm. Few manufactured articles were bought. Salt, tar, iron (bought in four-pound bars), mill-stones, steel for tipping the edges of implements, canvas for the sails of the wind-mill, cloths for use in the dairy, in the malthouse, or in the grange, together with the dresses of the inhabitants of the hall, and a few vessels of brass, copper, or earthenware, satisfied the simple needs of the rural population. Hands were therefore more required than money on manorial estates. If the manor was well stocked with labour, the land paid; when the stock of labour shrank, the profits dwindled. It was in order to retain a sufficient supply of labour on the land that bondmen were restrained from leaving the manor to assume the tonsure of the clerk or the flat cap of the apprentice, to become soldiers or to work outside the manor. Even their marriages were carefully controlled by licences It was, again, in order to exact and supervise the due performance of labour services that the lord of the manor maintained his large official staff—his seneschal, if he owned several manors, his steward, his bailiff, and the various foremen of the labourers, such as the reeve, the hayward, the head-reaper, and the granger. But with the thirteenth century begins the practice of keeping estate accounts, in which the amount and cash values of the labour services are entered. Thus the uncertainty of villein-tenure was modified, and the means were prepared for commuting obligations to work into their money equivalents. Already the causes were operating which hastened the process, and changed agriculture from a self-sufficing industry into a commercial system of farming for profit. Population was increasing; trade was growing; urban classes, divorced from rural pursuits, were forming; means of communication were improving; money taxes took the place of personal services; the standard of living rose; coin was needed, not only to meet the demands of the government, but to buy the luxuries of more civilised life.

The obligations of the peasantry to cultivate the demesne varied, not only with local customs, but with the seasons. Their most important services were the autumnal, Lenten, and summer ploughings on the three fields, into which the arable land of the demesne was generally divided. The crops grown were, as winter seeds, wheat and rye, and, as spring seeds, oats, barley, beans, peas, or vetches. In smaller quantities, flax, hemp, and saffron were locally raised in separate plots. Roots, clover and artificial grasses were still unknown. Rotations of crops, as they are now understood, were therefore impossible. The soil was rested by fallowing the one-half, or the one-third, of the arable land required by the two or the three course system. Red rivet, or a lost white variety, was then recommended for wheat-sowing on light land, red or white pollard for heavy soils, "gray" wheat for clays. But on the tenants' land, rye was the chief grain crop. It is the hardiest, grows on the poorest soils, makes the toughest straw. Rye was then the bread-stuff of the English peasantry, as it still is in Northern Europe. The flour of wheat and rye were often mixed together, and bread made in this form was called "maslin." It retained its moisture longer than pure wheaten bread, and, as Fynes Moryson says in his *Itinerary* (1617), was used by labourers because it "abode longer in the stomach and was not so soon digested with their labour." Wheat and rye were sometimes sown together. But as rye was slower to ripen, the better practice was to sow it alone and earlier, lest, as Tusser (1557) writes, "rye tarry wheat, till it sheds as it stands." The mixed cultivation was, however, recommended as a cure for mildew, and for this reason prevailed in Yorkshire in 1797. Barley was the drink-corn, as rye was the bread-corn, of the Middle Ages. It was of two kinds. The head with two rows of grain seems to have been used exclusively for brewing; the coarser four-rowed head, known as "drage," was used partly for brewing, partly for feeding pigs and poultry. Barley and oats were often sown together. In the North, oats were extensively cultivated; but they were grey-awned, thin, and poor. In the Midlands and South of England they were comparatively rare on tenants' land.

The fallows were three times ploughed in preparation for wheat and rye. The seed began to be sown after Lammas Day (August 12), and at latest was completed by Hallowmas (November 1). For oats, beans, and peas, the land was ploughed and the seed sown between the Feast of Purification (February 2) and Easter. Oats were said to be best sown in "the dust of March." "On St. Valentine's Day cast beans in clay. But on St. Chad sowe good or bad." That is to say, the time for sowing beans was between February 14 and March 2. Barley came last. The land was ploughed and sown between Hoke-tide (the third Tuesday after Easter) and Pentecost. The ploughings were performed, and the teams supplied and driven, partly by the servants of the demesne, partly by the tenants. Sometimes ploughmen seem to have been hired. The harrowings were similarly provided for, and the harrow, often a hawthorn tree, weighted on its upper side with logs, was supplied from the lord's waste. Here also harrowers seem to have been sometimes specially hired. In this case they possibly provided their own home-constructed implements with sharp points or teeth like the modern type of harrow. When the fallows were first broken up, as was then the practice, in March, or when the land was prepared for barley, the ground was often so hard that the clods had to be subsequently broken. For this purpose the ploughman, holding the principal hale of the plough in his left hand, carried in his right a "clotting beetle," or "maul," such as that which is depicted in the Cotton MSS. A "Dover-court beetle" was a necessary tool in the days of Tusser; and Plot, whose *Natural History of Oxfordshire* appeared in the seventeenth century, recommends its use after the land was harrowed.

The amount of wheat, rye, beans, and peas usually sown to the acre was only two bushels; and of oats and, strangely enough, of barley, four bushels. The yield of wheat rarely exceeded five-fold, or ten bushels to the acre; that of the leguminous crops ranged from three- to six-fold, or from six to twelve bushels to the acre; that of oats and barley varied from three- to four-fold, or from twelve to sixteen bushels to the acre. Considerable care was exercised in the choice and changes of the seed-corn, which was often one of the produce-rents of the tenants. On the Berkeley Estates (1321) the seed was changed every second or third year; the upland corn being sown in the vale, and vice versa. Wheat rarely followed a spring grain crop. If it did, it may be supposed that it received the greater part of the manure mixed with earth, which the tenants carted from the demesne yard, and spread on the manor farm. From the point of view of manuring the land, the right of folding was a valuable privilege. Tenants, unless they purchased a licence to fold their sheep on the land they occupied, were often obliged to feed and fold their flocks on the lord's land for fallow or in his own fold. Sometimes the herbage of the lord's land for fallow was sold to a sheep-master to be depastured on the land. Lime was used on heavy clays, or to destroy moss. The value of marl in improving the texture of sandy soils and some kinds of clays was appreciated. On the Berkeley Estates it was first used in the fortieth year of Henry III. But the cost was excessive. "Marl," says Fitzherbert, "is an excellent manure, and . . . exceeding chargeable." Sea sand was used near the coast; soot and even street refuse were employed on home farms. Drainage, except in the form of ridging the surface of wet soils, was rarely practised. Sometimes, as Palladius recommends (Book VI. st. 6), shallow trenches filled with gravel, stones, or hollow alder stems, and turfed over, were cut, and, on the manors belonging to the Collegiate body of St. Paul's Cathedral, it was one of the labour services to clean out the ditches. But the science of deep drainage made little progress before the nineteenth century. Beans were often dibbed; but all other seed was sown broadcast. The actual labour of sowing was probably performed by the lord's bailiff, or the hayward, with his own hand, as, at the beginning of the last century, all seed was sown by the farmer himself. The hoeing and the weeding of the crops were among the labour services of the tenants. In cleaning land the maxim was ancient;

"Who weeds in May
Throws all away."

and the crops were generally weeded in June or the first few days of July. Walter of Henley (thirteenth century) gives St. John's Day (June 24) as the earliest date for cleaning the land. "If," he says, "you cut thistles fifteen days or eight before St. John's Day, for each one will come two or three." On a Suffolk manor, in the fourteenth century, sixty "sarclers," or weeders, were employed in one day, armed, if the weather was dry, with a hook or forked stick, and, in wet weather, with nippers.

The meadows of the demesne were mown, and the hay made, carted, and put on the manorial ricks, by the labour services of the tenants. They also reaped, bound, gathered, loaded, carted, and stacked the corn crops in the lord's grange. They also threshed the corn, and winnowing fell to the dairywoman, or "Daye." If any corn was sent for sale to the markets, it was carried there by the labour services of the tenants, in their carts drawn by their teams. Harvestings in the Middle Ages were picturesque scenes of bustle and of merriment among the thousands to whom they meant the return of plenty. On 250 acres at Hawstead in Suffolk, towards the close of the fourteenth century, were grown wheat, oats, barley, peas, and "bolymong," a mixture of tares and oats. The grain crops were cut and housed in two days. On the first day appeared thirty tenants to perform their "bedrepes," and 244 reapers; on the second day, the thirty tenants and 239 reapers, pitchers, and stackers. Many of this assembly were the smaller peasantry on the manor; the rest were the lord's farm servants, together with wandering bands of "cockers" or harvesters, who had already begun to travel the country at harvest time. A cook, brewer, and baker were hired to supply dinner at nine and supper at five. Reapers were organised in bands, or "setts," of five. The anonymous author of *Hosebonderie* (thirteenth century) calculates that each band could reap and bind two acres a day. Barley and oats, as well as peas and beans, were generally mown; rye and wheat were reaped. . . .

The most important crops of the farm were the corn crops of wheat, rye, and barley, which were raised for human food and drink. Their consumption, especially if the lord of the manor lived on the estate, was enormous. Domestic households were considerable, and often only the bailiff was paid money wages. Rations were also allowed to tenants when performing many of their services. Though the manual and team work of the tenants provided most of the labour of the farm, the lord also employed a large permanent staff of agricultural servants, most of whom were occupied in the care of live-stock. Such were the horseman or waggoner, oxherd or ploughman, cowherd, shepherd, swineherd, warrener, and keepers of hawks and dogs, whose wages were mostly paid in kind. There were, besides, other servants in husbandry, hired for special occasions, whose food and drink formed a large portion of their payment. The granary was, therefore, rarely so full that any surplus remained for sale. For such ready-money as he needed, the lord looked mainly to the produce of his live-stock. For their consumption were grown the remaining crops—the hay, beans, peas, and oats; though oats were not only used for human food, but in some districts were brewed into inferior beer.

Horse-farms appear in some estate accounts; but they probably supplied the "great horse" used for military purposes. On an ordinary farm the horses used for farm-work were mostly homebred, and were divided into cart-horses, and—under the names of stotts, "affers," or "avers"—plough-horses. Colts, not needed to keep up the supply, were sold. Plough-teams were seldom made up of horses only; if horses were used at all, they were mixed with oxen. But, as a rule, oxen were preferred to horses. Though horses worked more quickly, when the ploughman allowed them to do so,—they pulled less steadily, and sudden strains severely tested the primitive plough-gear. On hard ground they did less work, and only when the land was stony had they any advantage. Economical reasons further explain the preference for oxen. From St. Luke's Day (October 18) to April, both horses and oxen were kept in the stalls. During these twenty-five weeks neither could graze, and Walter of Henley calculates that the winter-keep of a horse cost four times that of an ox. Horses needed more attendance; they required to be rubbed, curried, and dressed. Oxen were less liable to sickness than horses. The harness of the ox, mainly home-made from materials supplied on the estate, was cheaper to provide and repair. Shod only on the forefeet, the shoeing of the ox cost less than that of the horse. When either horse or ox was past work, the profit of the one lay in his hide; of the other, not only in his hide, but the larder: the ox was "mannes meat when dead, while the horse is carrion." Great care was taken both of horses and of oxen. In *Seneschaucie* (thirteenth century) the duties both of the waggoner and oxherd are carefully defined; each was expected to sleep every night with his charges.

Cattle were seldom fattened even for the tables of the rich; oxen were valued for their power of draught: cows for their milk. It may, indeed, be said that fresh butcher's meat was rarely eaten, and that, if it was, it was almost universally grass-fed. No winterkeep or feeding stuff was available; not even carrots or parsnips were known. The commons, generally unstinted, carried as much stock as could keep skin and bone together in the winter, and the lord could not only turn out on them his own sheep and cattle, but licence strangers for money payments to do the same. Even if the commons were stinted, the margin was too bare to mean abundance. The best pastures were either in the lord's own hands, and were saved by him at the expense of the commons, or were let out to individuals in separate occupations. Even among these superior feeding-grounds, there were few enclosures which would fatten a bullock. At the wane of the summer, the cattle had the aftermath of the hay meadows, and the stubble and haulm of the arable lands. During this season they were at their best. They only survived the winter months in a state of semi-starvation on hay, straw, and tree-loppings. It was, therefore, the practice at the end of June to draft the aged cows, worn-out oxen, and toothless sheep, or "crones," prepare them as far as possible for the butcher, slaughter them in the autumn, and either eat them fresh or throw them into the powdering tub to be salted for winter consumption. "For Easter at Martinmas (November 11) hange up a biefe" is the advice of Tusser.

The dairy produce was a greater source of money revenue, though the home consumption of cheese must have been very large. But the management was necessarily controlled, like the management of the stock, by the winter scarcity. The yield of a cow during the twenty-four weeks from the middle of April to Michaelmas was estimated at four-fifths of her total annual yield. Six to ten ewes gave as much milk as one cow; but the best practice was to cease milking ewes at Lammas Day (August 12). Cheese-making formed an important part of the dairywoman's duties, and the purchase of the cloths and utensils used in its manufacture are a serious item in estate accounts. Cheese seems generally to have been made of skim-milk, though superior varieties were doubtless found on the lord's table. Most of the butter made in the summer months was either sold, or salted and preserved in pots and barrels for winter use. The butter-milk was either drunk, made into curds, or more rarely used to fatten pigs. The curds were eaten with wine or ale; the whey, under the name of "whig," made a cool and wholesome summer drink. During the winter months, milk fetched three times its summer price, and was generally sold. For this, among other reasons, calves were timed to fall before autumn. In the scarce months of winter, the price obtained for milk during eight weeks was supposed to be worth more than a calf. Small open-field farmers must usually have sold their calves as soon as possible. The same practice prevailed on the demesne. The total number of live-stock, including horses but not including sheep, sold from the manor of Forncett in thirteen years, between 1272 and 1306, was 152. Out of this total 99 were calves. The cows of the demesne were under the care of a cowherd, who was required to sleep every night with his charges in the sheds.

Sheep were the sheet anchor of farming. But it was not for their mutton, or for their milk, or even for their skins, that they were chiefly valued. Already the mediaeval agriculturist took his seat on the wool-sack. As a marketable commodity, both at home and abroad, English long wool always commanded a price. It was less perishable than corn, and more easily transported even on the worst of roads. To the Flemish weavers it was indispensable, for Spanish wool could not be used alone, and the supply from Saxony was not as yet developed. The washing and shearing of sheep were among the labour services of the tenantry. Certain districts, especially Shropshire, Leominster, and the Cotswolds, were from very early times famous for the excellence of their wool. So far as its quality depended on breed rather than on soil, some care, as evidenced by the higher prices paid for rams, was taken to improve the flocks. From Martinmas to Easter sheep were kept in houses, or in moveable folds of wooden hurdles, thatched at the sides and tops. During these months they were fed on coarse hay or peas-haulm, mixed with wheaten or oaten straw. For the rest of the year they browsed on the land for fallows, in woodland pastures, or on the sheep commons. But in the autumn they were not allowed to go on the ground, till the sun had purified the land from the "gelly or matty rime," which was supposed to engender scab. So also they were driven from the damp, low-lying grounds lest they should eat the white water-snails which our ancestors suspected of breeding the rot. These two diseases made sheep-farming, in spite of its profits, a risky venture. The scab does not seem to have attacked sheep before the latter end of the thirteenth century; but, from that time forward, the tar-box was essential to every shepherd. The rot is carefully treated by Walter of Henley, if he is the real author of the passage interpolated in the Bodleian manuscript of his work. The writer discusses the symptoms of the disease. White veins under the eyelids, wool that can be easily pulled away from the ribs, a skin that will not redden when rubbed, are signs of unsoundness. Another sign is when the November hoar-frost melts rapidly on the fleece, for the animal is then suffering from an unnatural heat. The losses of the flockmasters from the "murrain," to use the generic term for diseases employed by mediaeval writers, were so severe as to create another danger. The minute instructions against fraud given to the official staff show that shepherds not infrequently produced the skin, and explained the disappearance of the carcase by death from disease. "Let no sheep," says the author of *Seneschaucie,* "be flayn before it be seen and known for what fault it died." The value of the flock made the shepherd one of the most important of farm servants. He was required to be a patient man, "not overhasty," never to be absent without leave at "fairs, markets, wrestling-matches, wakes, or in the tavern," and always to sleep in the fold together with his dog. Later writers insist on the value of lameness in the shepherd, as a lame man was unlikely to overdrive his sheep.

Swine were the almost universal live-stock of rich and poor. As consumers of refuse and scavengers of the village, they would, on sanitary grounds, have repaid their keepers. But mediaeval pigs profited their owners much, and cost them little. It was a Gloucestershire saying:

"A swine doth sooner than a cowe
Bring an ox to the plough."

In other words, a pig was more profitable than a cow. For the greater part of the year pigs were expected to pick up their own living. When the wastes and woodlands of a manor were extensive, they were, except during three months of the year, self-supporting. They developed the qualities necessary for taking care of themselves. The ordinary pigs of the Middle Ages were long, flat-sided, coarse-boned, lop-eared, omnivorous animals, whose agility was more valuable than their early maturity. Growth and flesh were the work of time: so also were thickened skin, developed muscles, and increased weight of bone. The styes were often built in the woods, whence the pigs were only brought to feed on the arable land after the crops were cleared, or, at times of exceptional frost, to subsist on the leavings of the threshing-floor. During most months of the year they ranged the woods for roots, wild pears, wild plums, crab apples, sloes, haws, beech-mast, and acorns. Only when the sows were farrowing, or when animals were being prepared for the rich man's table, were they specially fed. Pigs were fatted on inferior corn, especially coarse barley, peas, beans, skim- and butter-milk, or brewers' grains which were readily obtainable when nearly every household brewed its own barley beer. The amount consumed varied with the purpose intended to be served. The boar was fatted for the feast on ten times the grain bestowed in finishing ordinary animals for conversion into salted pork or smoke-dried bacon. Walter of Henley implies that some attention was given to breed, as he recommends the use of well-bred boars. But the only quality on which he insists is that the animal should be able to dig, or, in other words, support itself. Modern ideas of purchasing corn for fattening purposes, or of converting into pork or bacon farm-produce for which no ready market was available, scarcely entered into the heads of mediaeval farmers. On the contrary, they tell us that if pigs were entirely dependent on the crops of the arable land, they could not be kept at a profit, when the wages of the swineherd, the cost of the grain consumed, and the damage done to growing crops had been taken into account. Some trade was, however, carried on in stores. This is proved by the records of Forncett manor (*A Norfolk Manor,* 1086–1565), which show that, in years when no pigs were kept, stores were bought and fatted for the larder.

The poultry yard was under the care of the dairywoman, who sometimes seems to have had the poultry to farm at so much a head. Ducks are not mentioned in any of the mediaeval treatises on farming, though they appear in the Berkeley accounts in 1321: guineafowl and turkeys were unknown. But the number of geese and fowls, and, on important estates, of peacocks and swans, was large, and it was swollen by the produce-rents which were often paid in poultry and eggs. The author of *Hosebonderie* gives minute instructions as to the produce for which the dairywoman ought to account. "Each goose ought to have five goslings a year": each hen was to answer for 115 eggs and seven chickens, "three of which ought to be made capons, and, if there be too many hen chickens, let them be changed for cocks while they are young, so that each hen may answer for three capons and four hens a year. And for five geese you must have one gander, and for five hens one cock." Besides the poultry yard, the dove-cote or pigeon-house was a source of profit to the lord and of loss to the tenant. Prodigious numbers of pigeons were kept; not only were they eaten, but their dung was prized as the most valuable of all manures. The privilege of keeping a pigeon-house was confined to manorial lords and jealously guarded, and every manor had its dove-cote. The story of the French Revolution shows how bitterly the peasants resented the plunder of their hard-earned crops by the lord's pigeons.

Doubtless many a British peasant in mediaeval times was stirred to the same hostility by the same nuisance.

To the produce of the crops and the live-stock of the demesne must be added game, rabbits from the "conygarth" or warren, cider from the apples, oil from the nuts, honey and wax from the bee-hives, and sometimes grapes from the vineyards. Bee-keeping was an important feature of agricultural industry. The ancient proverb says: "He that hath sheep, swine, and bees, sleep he, wake he, he may thrive." Honey, besides being the only sugar, was invaluable in the still-room, and in the arts of the apothecary, physician, and "chirurgeon." It was an ingredient in mead and metheglyn. It was used in embalming, in medicines, and in such decoctions as mulse water, oenomel, honey water, rodomel, or quintessence. Wax was not only necessary for the candles of the wealthy, but, like honey, was largely used in mediaeval medicine. Mixed with violets, it was a salve: it was also one of the ingredients of "playsters, oyntementes, suppositories, and such like." In some districts of England, vineyards formed part of the equipment of manors; one was made by Lord Berkeley towards the close of the reign of Edward III, and his biographer suggests that he learned the "husbandry . . . whilst hee was prisoner in ffrance or a Traveller in Spaine." Few great monasteries were without vineyards, which are mentioned thirty-eight times in Domesday Book. It is not necessary to explain the disappearance of the vine by a change of climate. Wine was then often sweetened with honey and flavoured with blackberries and spices. Unless it came from abroad, it was rarely drunk in its pure state. It would, therefore, be unsafe to found any theory of climatic change upon the production of a liquid which, in its natural state, may frequently have resembled vinegar.

Besides the produce of the live-stock and crops of his demesne, the lord of the manor had other sources of revenue. There were the fixed money or produce rents for their land paid by free tenants and bondmen, and the money payments which were sometimes accepted in lieu of labour services. Sales of timber and underwood, of turf, of herbage, licences to fold on the tenant's land, or licences to turn pigs into the lord's woods for beechmast or acorns, brought in varying sums of money. The mill at which the tenants ground their corn was his property. Whether the miller was his servant, or farmed the receipts, a considerable proportion of the tolls went into the landlord's purse, though the cost of repairs and upkeep diminished the net profits. On some manors the oven in which the bread was baked was also the property of the lord of the manor. The fees and fines levied and settled by the manorial courts in the course of a year were surprisingly large; besides their administrative work, they were at once the guardians and the interpreters of the customs of the manor. The range of business administered in these courts, to which the tenants, both free and bond, were summoned as jurors, therefore embraced the domestic and financial affairs of the manor. Here were paid the fees for permission to reside outside the manor, to send children to school, to enter minor orders, to apprentice a son to a trade, or to marry a daughter. Here too were imposed the fines for slovenly work at harvest, for selling cattle without the lord's leave, for appropriating commons and wastes, for moving a neighbor's landmark, for neglecting to repair a cottage, for failing to discharge labour dues. Here too were fixed the contributions of the tenantry in money or labour towards the maintenance of the by-roads within the manor, and the fines for neglect of the duty to keep their surfaces in repair, to provide for their proper drainage, and to remove obstructions. Here also crime was punished; offenders against life or property, as well as poachers, were mulcted; wrangling scolds and tavern-hunters were presented; idlers were deprived of their holdings, and, as a last resort, expelled from the manor. Here too were fixed and levied the necessary contributions for the repair of the stocks, the pillory, the ducking-stool, and the pound. Here the miller would be fined for mixing rubbish with his flour, the baker for selling short weight, the brewer who adulterated his beer, the ale-wife and the tavern-keeper who used false measures or mixed the drink they sold with peony seed, salt or garlick, the carrier for failing to deliver goods, the householder who harboured a stranger without a licence. Here also were received and entered fees of tenants for admission to their holdings, and the payment of fines by sons who succeeded their fathers. Here, finally, on the sworn evidence of a body of jurors chosen from the tenants, were drawn up the surveys of the manor which recorded the exact condition of the estate—the total acreage of the demesne, and of each of the arable fields, of the meadows, the several pastures and the pasturage, and their annual values; the state of the woods and the coppices, how much could be cut, and what they were worth yearly; the acreage of the commons and the stock which they would carry; the number of the live-stock of various kinds; the holdings of the free tenants, and their rents or services; the holdings of the villeins, bordars, and cottagers, their services and money equivalents; the profits of fisheries, mills, and incidental manorial rights; the number of tenants who had finally commuted their services for fixed payments in cash, or those who, at the discretion of the lord, either rendered labour services or paid the money values, and of those who still discharged their personal obligations by actual work.

The remainder of the cultivated land of the manor was occupied by tenants who paid rents in the form of military or labour services, or money, or produce. Their farm practices, crops, and live-stock were the same as those of the demesne, though their difficulties in combating winter scarcity were greater. Free tenants, whose tenure was military service, or who had commuted the personal obligations for quit-rents, may sometimes have held land, like modern farmers, in their exclusive occupations for individual cultivation. . . .

The varieties of tenure were great. So also were the varieties of social condition, and of the obligations by which the grades of those social conditions were governed. The distinctions between freemen and bondmen and between freehold and bond tenure had been, in the eye of the law, broad and deep. But custom had gradually intervened, and, with endless variety of practice, mitigated the severity of legal theory. At law the bondman's position was subject to the lord's caprice. Unlike the freeman, he was tied to the manor; he could not leave it without licence from the lord, and payment of a fine. His services were uncertain in amount, and could be increased at the lord's pleasure. He paid a fine to marry his daughter, to send his son to school, to make him a priest or an apprentice. His lands and his goods and chattels might be seized by his lord, and when he died, his holding was given to whom the lord willed: his heir bought a licence to inherit even his moveables, and paid a fine when he was admitted to his father's tenancy. In the thirteenth century, some at least of these conditions had been modified. The bondman's services had become fixed; he could buy and sell, hold property, and dispose of his possessions by will. In theory he might still be at the mercy of the lord's will: but custom had so regulated the exercise of that will that it could no longer be capricious.

Speaking broadly, the mass of the occupiers of land were, in the eye of the law, unfree—bondmen who rented the shares in the land which they cultivated for themselves by labour services on the lord's demesne. It was the amount and certainty of their services which determined the rank of the unfree. Sometimes the service was for the autumn only, or for autumn and spring work, whether on specified days or at particular periods; sometimes of team work, sometimes of manual labour, sometimes of both; sometimes of week-work throughout the year, and either of one, two or three days in each week. All their spare time was spent on their own holdings. Of this semi-servile class the villeins formed the aristocracy. The villein was neither a servant in husbandry nor a labourer for wages. He occupied land, and, like Chaucer's ploughman, had "catel" of his own. He was a partner in the village association, holding land of various amounts. In theory the size of his holding was based on the number of oxen which, in discharge of his share of the joint liability, he could contribute to the manorial plough-team. A "hide" of land, which Professor Maitland considers to have been "the land of a household," was treated as the area which a team of eight oxen could plough in a working year. Its extent may have varied. But, if the size was 120 acres, then each hide consisted of four portions of 30 acres, called "virgates," or 8 portions of 15 acres, called "bovates." Thus the eighth part of the hide, or "bovate," was the land of one ox; the fourth part of the hide, or "virgate," was the land of two oxen; and the whole hide was the land of the complete team of eight oxen. It was on this basis that the tenemental land, in theory, and sometimes in practice, was divided. The typical holding of the villein was regulated by his capacity to furnish one or two oxen to the team. In other words, it was the "virgate" or "yardland" of 30 acres, though one-ox holdings or "bovates" of 15 acres, and even half-ox holdings, were frequent.

Villeins of the higher grade were generally distinguished from inferior orders of the semi-servile classes of the peasantry by the size of their holdings in the village farm, by the certainty of their agricultural services on the demesne, and by the obligation to do team-work rather than manual labour. The smaller the holding, the vaguer the labour obligations, the more manual the work,—the lower was the grade of the villein. Besides the villeins there were other orders of bondmen—such as the rural handicrafts men—men who were specially provided with land, and the bordars and cottars, who rented particular cottages and garden ground, which often carried with them from two to five acres of arable land, together with common rights. The two latter classes, besides their obligatory manual services, probably eked out their subsistence either as hired labourers on the demesne or by supplying the labour for which their wealthier neighbours were responsible. At the bottom of the social ladder were the serfs, to whom strict law assigned no rights, though there were many varieties in their grades and position. Their chief badge of serfdom was the indeterminate character of their services—the obligation to labour in the manner, at the time, and for the wage, if any, which the lord directed. But the serf might occupy land, own cattle, and labour for himself. Thus, out of these various classes, free and unfree, sprang small landowners, tenant farmers, copyholders, and wage-earning labourers.

Round the village, or "town," in which were gathered the homesteads of the inhabitants, lay the open arable fields, which were cultivated in common by the associated partners. Here were grown the crops which Shakespeare enumerates. These were the lands "of Ceres":

> "—thy rich leas
> "Of wheat, rye, barley, vetches, oats, and peas."

Here, at harvest time, the yellow of the corn crops alternated with the dark and light greens of beans or peas and the brown of the bare fallows. This cultivated area, which included the driest and soundest of the land, was hedgeless, open, and unenclosed, divided by turf-grown balks into fields—two, three, or, rarely, four in number. If the former, one field lay fallow, while the other was under tillage for corn, or beans, or peas. This dual system still prevailed near Gloucester in the nineteenth century, and existed at Stogursey in Somersetshire in 1879. But from the Norman Conquest onward the three-field system was the most prevalent. Down to the middle of the reign of George III the arable land received the unvarying triennial succession of wheat or rye, of spring crops such as barley, oats, beans, or peas, and of fallow. During these seven centuries a more scientific rotation was in some districts adopted. Thus at Aston Boges, in Oxfordshire, a fourth course was interposed. But, speaking generally, open-field husbandry rather retrograded than advanced, as the discipline of manorial officials relaxed.

Each of the three arable fields was subdivided into a number of shots, furlongs, or flats, separated from one another by unploughed bush-grown turk balks, varying in width from two to sixteen feet. These flats were in turn cut up into parallel acre, half-acre, or quarter-acre, strips coinciding with arrangement of a ploughed field into ridges and furrows. If the strips were acre strips they were a furlong in length (220 yards) and 4 rods (22 yards) in breadth. Ploughmen still measure the acre in the same way as the open-field strip. Theoretically each flat was square, with sides of 40 poles, containing 10 acres; in practice every variety of shape and admeasurement was found. But, though the pole from which the acre was raised varied from the 13½ feet of Hampshire to the 24 feet of Cheshire, two sides of the flats always ran parallel. Thus each of the three arable fields resembled several sheets of paper, cut into various shapes, stitched together like patchwork, and ruled with margins and lines. The separate sheets are the flats; the margins are the headlands running down the flats at right angles to, and across the ends of, the parallel strips which are represented by the spaces between the lines. The lines themselves are the "balks" of unploughed turf, by which the strips were divided from each other. The strips appear under different names. For instance, in Scotland and Northumberland they were called "rigs"; in Lincolnshire "selions"; in Nottinghamshire "lands"; in Dorsetshire "lawns"; in North Wales "loons"; in Westmoreland "dales," and their occupiers "dalesmen"; in Cambridgeshire "balks"; in Somersetshire "raps"; in Sussex "pauls"; elsewhere in southern counties "stitches." When the strips were stunted by encountering some obstacle, such as a road or river, they were called "butts." Stray odd corners which did not fit in with the parallel arrangement of the flats were "crustae," that is, pieces broken off, "pightels," "gores," "fothers," and "pykes," because, as Fitzherbert explains, they were "often brode in the one ende and a sharpe pyke in the other ende."

The arable fields were fenced against the live-stock from seed-time to harvest, and the intermixed strips were cultivated for the separate use of individuals, subject to the compulsory rotation by which each of the three fields was cropped. On Lammas Day separate uses ended, and common rights recommenced; hence fields occupied in this manner were, and are, called Lammas Lands or "half-year lands." After harvest the hayward removed the fences, and the live-stock of the community wandered over the fields before the common herdsman, shepherd, or swineherd. The herdsman, in the reign of Henry VIII, received 8d. a year for every head of cattle entrusted to his care, and the swineherd 4d. for every head of swine. When sheep were folded on the cultivated land, each farmer provided, during the winter months, his own fold and fodder for his flock. Richard Hooker, while he held the country living of Drayton Beauchamp in Buckinghamshire, was found by two of his former pupils, "like humble and innocent Abel, tending his small allotment of sheep in a common field." That no occupier might find all his land fallow in the same year, every one had strips in each of the three arable fields. If the holding of the open-field farmer consisted of thirty acres, there would thus be ten acres in each field. In other words, he would have ten acres under wheat and rye, ten acres under spring crops, and ten acres fallow. The same care was taken to make the divisions equal in agricultural value, so that each man might have his fair proportion of the best and worst land. To divide equally the good and bad, well and ill situated soil, the bundle of strips allotted in each of the three fields did not lie together, but was intermixed and scattered.

In the lowest part of the land—if possible along a stream—lay the "ings," "carrs," "leazes," or meadows, annually cut up into lots or doles, and put up for hay. These doles were fenced off to be mown for a separate use of individuals either from Candlemas (February 2), or, more usually, from St. Gregory's Day (March 12) to Midsummer Day; from July to February, or later, they were open, common pasturage. Sometimes the plots, which varied in size from a half-acre downwards, went with the arable holdings, so that the same man annually received the same portion of meadow. Sometimes the plots were balloted for every year. Each lot was distinguished by a name, such as the cross, crane's foot, or peel, *i.e.* baker's shovel, which will often explain puzzling field-names. Corresponding marks were thrown into a hat or bag and drawn by a boy. This balloting continued up to the last century in Somersetshire, and still continues at Yarnton in Oxfordshire. After the hay had been cut and carried, the meadows reverted to common occupation, and were grazed indiscriminately by the live-stock of the village, till they were again fenced off, allotted, and put up for hay.

On the outskirts of the fields nearest to the village lay one or more "hams" or stinted pastures, in which a regulated number of live-stock might graze, and therefore supplying superior feed. Brandersham, Smithsham, Wontnersham, Herdsham, Constable's Field, Dog Whipper's Land, Barber's Furlong, Tinker's Field, Sexton's Mead, suggest that sometimes special allotments were made to those who practised trades of such general utility as the stockbrander, the blacksmith, the mole-catcher, the cowherd, the constable, the barber, the tinker, and the sexton. The dog-whipper's usefulness is less obvious; but possibly he was employed to prevent the live-stock from being harried by dogs. Even the spiritual wants of the village were sometimes supplied in the same way. Parson's Close and Parson's Acre are not uncommon. It is significant that no schoolmasters seem to have been provided for by allotments of land.

Besides the open arable fields, the meadows, and the stinted hams, there were the common pastures, fringed by the untilled wastes which were left in their native wildness. These wastes provided fern and heather for litter, bedding, or thatching; small wood for hurdles; tree-loppings for winter browse of live-stock; furze and turves for fuel; larger timber for fencing, implements, and building; mast, acorns, and other food for the swine. Most of these smaller rights were made the subject of fixed annual payments to the manorial lord; but the right of cutting fuel was generally attached to the occupation, not only of arable land, but of cottages. The most important part of these lands were the common pastures, which were often the only grass that arable farmers could command for their live-stock. They therefore formed an integral and essential part of the village farm. No rights were exercised upon them by the general public. On the contrary, the commons were most jealously guarded by the privileged commoners against the intrusion or encroachments of strangers. The agistment of strange cattle or sheep was strictly prohibited: commoners who turned out more stock than their proper share were "presented" at the manorial courts and fined; cottages erected on the commons were condemned to be pulled down; the area within which swine might feed was carefully limited, and the swine were to be ringed. Those who enjoyed the grazing rights were the occupiers of arable land, whose powers of turning out stock were, in theory, proportioned to the size of their arable holdings, and the occupiers of certain cottages, which commanded higher rents in consequence of the privilege. It was on these commons that the cattle and sheep of the village were fed. Every morning the cattle were collected, probably by the sound of a horn, and driven to the commons by the village herdsman along drift ways, which were enclosed on either side by moveable or permanent fences to keep the animals from straying on to the arable land. In the evening they were driven back, each animal returning to its own shelter, as the herd passed up the village street. Similarly, the sheep were driven by the village shepherd to the commons by day, and folded at night on the wheat fallows. Sheep were the manure carriers, and were prized as much for their folding quality as for their fleeces. In some districts they were kept almost entirely for their agricultural value to the arable land. Until the winter they were penned in the common fold on the fallows or the stubbles. After the fallows had been ploughed, and before the crops on the other fields were cleared, they had only the commons. During winter each commoner was obliged to find hay for his sheep and his own fold, the common shepherd penning and folding them so as gradually to cover the whole area.

The open-field system, thus briefly sketched with its arable, meadow, and permanent pasture land, prevailed at some time or other throughout England, except perhaps in the south-west. The following description of the crofters' holdings in Skye in 1750 might have been written, with but few alterations, of half the cultivated area of England in the eighteenth century: "A certain number of tacksmen formed a copartnery and held a tract of land, or township, for which they paid tribute to the chief, and each member was jointly and severally responsible. The grazing was in common. All the arable land was divided into ridges, assigned annually by lot among the partners. Each might have a dozen or more of these small ridges, and no two contiguous except by accident; the object being to give each partner a portion of the better and inferior land. The copartner appears to have had cotters under him, for whose work he paid." The prevalence of the system may still be traced with more or less distinctness in rural England. The counties in which it was most firmly established are counties of villages, not of scattered farmsteads and hamlets. Turf balks and lynches record the time when "every rood of ground maintained its man." Irregular and regular fences, narrow lanes and wide highways, crooked and straight roads, respectively suggest the piecemeal or the wholesale enclosure of common fields. The waving ridges on thousands of acres of ancient pasture still represent the swerve of the cumbrous village plough with its team of eight oxen. The age of the hedgerow timber sometimes tells the date of the change. The pages appropriated to hedges by agricultural writers of the eighteenth century indicate the era of the abolition of open fields, and the minuteness of their instructions proves that the art of making hedges was still in its infancy. The scattered lands or ordinary farms, compared with the compact "court," "hall," or "manor" farm, recall the fact that the lord's demesne was once the only permanent enclosure. The crowding together of the rural population in villages betrays the agrarian partnership, as detached farmsteads and isolated labourers' dwellings indicate the system by which it has been supplanted.

30. THIRTEENTH CENTURY AGRICULTURE[1]

Walter of Henley, who appears to have been a knight and later to have become a friar, was at one time the bailiff or overseer of an English manor

[1] *Walter of Henley's Husbandry, together with an Anonymous Husbandry, Seneschaucie and Robert Grosseteste's Rules.* Translated and edited by Elizabeth Lamond. London and New York, Longmans, Green and Company, 1890, pp. 3, 5, 7, 9, 11, 13, 15.

in the thirteenth century, responsible directly to the lord of the manor for the management of his estate. From his experience as a practical agriculturist Walter gives advice on such matters as how to get the best results from the labor of oxen and horses, how to supervise farm workers effectively, how to plough efficiently, etc.

Advice to the Lord of the Manor

This is the treatise on husbandry that a good man once made, whose name was Sir Walter of Henley; and this he made to teach those who have lands and tenements and may not know how to keep all the points of husbandry, as the tillage of land and the keeping of cattle, from which great wealth may come to those who will hear this teaching and then do as is found written herein.

The father having fallen into old age said to his son, Dear son, live prudently towards God and the world. With regard to God, think often of the passion and death that Jesus Christ suffered for us, and love Him above all things and fear Him and lay hold of and keep His commandments; with regard to the world, think of the wheel of fortune, how man mounts little by little to wealth, and when he is at the top of the wheel, then by mishap he falls little by little to poverty, and then into wretchedness. Wherefore, I pray you, order your life according as your lands are valued yearly by the extent, and nothing beyond that. If you can approve your lands by tillage or cattle or other means beyond the extent, put the surplus in reserve, for if corn fail, or cattle die, or fire befall you, or other mishap, then what you have saved will help you. If you spend in a year the value of your lands and the profit, and one of these chances befall you, you have no recovery except by borrowing, and he who borrows from another robs himself; or by making bargains, as some who make themselves merchants, buying at twenty shillings and selling at ten. It is said in the proverb, "Who provides for the future enjoys himself in the present." You see some who have lands and tenements and know not how to live. Why? I will tell you. Because they live without rule and forethought and spend and waste more than their lands are worth yearly, and when they have wasted their goods can only live from hand to mouth and are in want, and can make no bargain that shall be for their good. The English proverb says, "He that stretches farther than his whittle will reach, in the straw his feet he must stretch." Dear son, be prudent in your doings and be on your guard against the world, which is so wicked and deceitful.

Have nothing from anyone wrongfully, nor seek occasion towards anyone to have his goods, for it is said in the English proverb, "One year or two, wrong will on hand go, and ever at an end, wrong will wend." If anyone comes into your court, let him be amerced by his peers; if your conscience tells you that they have amerced him too highly do you lessen it, so that you be not reproved here or before God. Acquaint yourself with true men and have the love of your neighbours, for it is said in the French proverb, "Who has a good neighbour has a good morrow." Keep your mouth prudently, that you be not justly reproved. . . .

Survey your lands and tenements by true and sworn men. First survey your courts, gardens, dove-houses, curtilages, what they are worth yearly beyond the valuation; and then how many acres are in the demesne, and how much is in each cultura, and what they should be worth yearly; and how many acres of pasture, and what they are worth yearly; and all other several pastures, and what they are worth yearly; and wood, what you can sell without loss and destruction, and what it is worth yearly beyond the return; and free tenants, how much each holds and by what service; and customary tenants, how much each holds and by what services, and let customs be put in money. And of all other definite things put what they are worth yearly. And by the surveyors inquire with how much of each sort of corn you can sow an acre of land, and how much cattle you can have on each manor. By the extent you should be able to know how much your lands are worth yearly, by which you can order your living, as I have said before. Further, if your bailiffs or provosts say in their account that so many quarters have been sown on so many acres, go to the extent, and perhaps you shall find fewer acres than they have told you and more quarters sown than was necessary. For you have at the end of the extent the quantity of each kind of corn with which one shall sow an acre of land. Further, if it is necessary to put out more money or less for ploughs, you shall be confirmed by the extent. How? I will tell you. If your lands are divided in three, one part for winter seed, the other part for spring seed, and the third part fallow, then is a ploughland nine score acres. And if your lands are divided in two, as in many places, the one half sown with winter seed and spring seed, the other half sown fallow, then shall a ploughland be eight score acres. Go to the extent and see how many acres you have in the demesne, and there you should be confirmed.

Some men will tell you that a plough cannot work eight score or nine score acres yearly, but I will show you that it can. You know well that a furlong ought to be forty perches long and four wide, and the king's perch is sixteen feet and a half; then an acre is sixty-six feet in width. Now in ploughing go thirty-six times round to make the ridge narrower, and when the acre is ploughed then you have made seventy-two furlongs, which are six leagues, for be it known that twelve furlongs are a league. And the horse or ox must be very poor that cannot from the morning go easily in pace three leagues in length from his starting-place and return by three o'clock. And I will show you by another reason that it can do as much. You know that there are in the year fifty-two weeks. Now take away eight weeks for holy days and other hindrances, then are there forty-four working weeks left. And in all that time the plough shall only have to plough for fallow or for spring or winter sowing three roods and a half daily, and for second fallowing an acre. Now see if a plough were properly kept and followed, if it could not do as much daily. And if you have land on which you can have cattle, take pains to stock it as the land requires. And know for truth if you are duly stocked, and your cattle well guarded and managed, it shall yield three times the land by the extent. If free tenants or customary tenants deny services or customs you will see the definite amount in the extent.

If you must choose a bailiff or servant, do not choose them for kindred or liking, or other reasons, if they are not of good reputation, and let them be true and prudent and know about cattle and tillage. Have no provosts or messers except from your own men, if you have them, and that by election of your tenants, for if they do wrong you shall have recovery from them.

At the beginning of fallowing and second fallowing and of sowing let the bailiff, and the messer, or the provost, be all the time with the ploughmen, to see that they do their work well and thoroughly, and at the end of the day see how much they have done, and for so much shall they answer each day after unless they can show a sure hindrance. And because customary servants neglect their work it is necessary to guard against their fraud; further, it is necessary that they are overseen often; and besides the bailiff must oversee all, that they all work well, and if they do not well let them be reproved.

With a team of oxen with two horses you draw quicker than with a team all horses, if the ground is not so stony that oxen cannot help themselves with their feet. Why? I will tell you: the horse costs more than the ox. Besides a plough of oxen will go as far in a year as a plough of horses, because the malice of ploughmen will not allow the plough (of horses) to go beyond their pace, no more than the plough of oxen. Further, in very hard ground, where the plough of horses will stop, the plough of oxen will pass. And will you see how the horse costs more than the ox? I will tell you. It is usual and right that plough beasts should be in the stall between the feast of St. Luke and the feast of the Holy Cross in May, five-and-twenty weeks, and if the horse is to be in a condition to do his daily work, it is necessary that he should have every night at the least the sixth part of a bushel of oats, price one halfpenny, and at the least twelve pennyworth of grass in summer. And each week more or less a penny in shoeing, if he must be shod on all four feet. The sum is twelve shillings and fivepence in the year, without fodder and chaff.

And if the ox is to be in a condition to do his work, then it is necessary that he should have at least three sheaves and a half of oats in the week, price one penny, and ten sheaves of oats should yield a bushel of oats in measure; and in summer twelve pennyworth of grass: the sum three shillings, one penny, without fodder and chaff. And when the horse is old and worn out then there is nothing but the skin; and when the ox is old with ten pennyworth of grass he shall be fit for the larder, or will sell for as much as he cost. April is a good time for fallowing, if the earth breaks up after the plough; and for second fallowing after St. John's Day, when the dust rises behind the plough; and for ploughing for seed when the earth is firm and not too cracked. But he who has much to do cannot wait for all the good seasons. And when you fallow, if you find good earth deep down, then plough a square ridge, to let the good land rest, but do not cut off the bad land; and plough cleanly, so that none remains covered or uncovered. At second fallowing do not go too deep, but so that you can just destroy the thistles, for if the earth is ploughed too deep at second fallowing, and the earth is full of water, then when one must plough for sowing the plough shall reach no sure ground, but goes floundering, as in mud. And if the plough can go two fingerlengths deeper than at second fallowing, then the plough will find sure ground, and clear and free it from mud, and make fine and good ploughing.

At sowing do not plough large furrows, but little and well laid together, that the seed may fall evenly; if you plough a large furrow to be quick you will do harm. How? I will tell you. When the ground is sown, then the harrow will come and pull the corn into the hollow which is between the two ridges, and the large ridge shall be uncovered, that no corn can grow there. And will you see this? When the corn is above ground go to the end of the ridge, and you will see that I tell you truly. And if the land must be sown below the ridge see that it is ploughed with small furrows, and the earth raised as much as you are able. And see that the ridge which is between the two furrows is narrow. And let the earth which lies like a crest in the furrow under the left foot after the plough be overturned, and then shall the furrow be narrow enough. . . .

31. RETURNS EXPECTED FROM THE SOIL[1]

How little the soil yielded in medieval times as compared with these days of scientific agriculture may be seen from Walter of Henley's estimate of returns that might reasonably be expected from arable land in his day.

[1] *Walter of Henley's Husbandry, together with an Anonymous Husbandry, Seneschaucie and Robert Grosseteste's Rules.* Translated and edited by Elizabeth Lamond. London and New York, Longmans, Green and Co., 1890, pp. 71–73. Reprinted by permission of the Royal Historical Society, London, copyright owners.

As to the issue of the grange, one must see how much there is sown of each corn and how much it yields for issue by right and common return; barley ought to yield to the eighth grain, that is to say, a quarter sown should yield eight quarters; rye should yield to the seventh grain, and beans and peas to the sixth. And dredge of barley and oats, if equally mixed, to the sixth, but if there is more barley than oats, less. And also the mixtelyn of wheat and rye, if it is equally mixed it should yield to the sixth, and if there is more wheat than rye, less. And wheat ought by right to yield to the fifth grain and oats to the fourth, but because lands do not yield so well one year as another, nor poor land as the good, and besides it may happen that the winter sowing takes well and the spring sowing fails, and sometimes the spring sowing takes well and the winter sowing fails, and because, if the land does not yield more than was sown, then the lord loses, and if it yield less he who renders account pays it himself. And so one cannot be sure of the yield above mentioned and not because many people take it so by the grain. And he who does not wish it so, let him put a true man in whom he trusts over the threshing. And it is well that he who is over the threshing should tally the product of each mow of the grange by itself to see how many quarters each mow yields by itself. And if there be a stack outside, let it be measured by rod and by foot, the breadth, length, and height, when it is about to be threshed, and tally each stack by itself, and then it will be possible to know the yield and issue of each mow outside as well as of each stack within the grange; but let the stacks be each year of the same size in breadth and length and height. And if he wish to sell his corn in gross, he will know better how much each stack is worth according to the price of corn. And although he sell the corn in gross, it is well to tally it and see the issue of each mow and of each stack, as the more often he proves it the more sure he will be of the yield, because corn does not yield equally each year. Take care that he who is over the threshing, if he thresh any old corn among the new, that he thresh and tally the old quite by itself; and let the provost answer in his roll for the sale of the corn quite by itself, to see the issue of each year, if it yields its seed. And if you make malt, he must always answer you, for nine quarters, a tenth at the least; and this is a little yield, but it is fixed thus because corn can be made to sprout too much to make a good return for profit, whereby the malt is worth much less and will yield less ale.

32. TRACES OF THE MEDIEVAL MANORIAL SYSTEM IN PREWAR AUSTRIA-HUNGARY[1]

In a book dealing primarily with Slavic immigrants in the United States Miss Emily Balch has taken occasion to discuss agricultural conditions in the former Austro-Hungarian Empire, the land from which many of these immigrants came. Many of those who read the following selection from Miss Balch's book will be surprised to learn how many distinctive characteristics of the medieval agricultural system persisted practically down to our own time in a not unenlightened part of Europe. They will perceive, too, some of the reasons why that system stood in the way of agricultural progress.

While it is true that each Slavic national group, each Slavic territory, must be studied separately to be understood, there are certain features which occur in all, and which in spite of some repetition, may to advantage be discussed in a preliminary way in their general bearings.

One of the most important general facts about our Slavic immigrants is that apart from the early Bohemian movement they for the most part represent the peasant class. There is, I think, much misunderstanding in America as to what this means. A peasant seems to be understood as a synonym for a member of the lowest possible social class; a being devoid of all claims to respect who takes a great step up when he becomes a factory employe. Such views rest on a serious misconception. The peasant is a landholder, more nearly comparable to the American farmer than to any other class among us, and at home is far from being at the bottom of the social ladder. The old peasant life, the substratum of all European history, is known to us as Americans only through literature, history and travel, for America has never had a peasantry, and in England, from which we derive, agriculture has been carried on for centuries, not by peasant proprietors, but by landless laborers. Yet the system which still largely subsists in Austria and Hungary was one universal throughout feudal Europe, passing away in some countries earlier, in others later. In Austria, up to 1848, mediaeval conditions were comparatively little changed. Actual serfdom, in the sense of absence of all personal rights, had indeed disappeared in the fifteenth century. But up to 1848 the legal ownership of land was still all vested in the lords or landed class; the peasants had only so-called *unterdominium* in their holdings, which were of two main classes, those which were inherited and those held for life only.

The peasant holding involved very definite duties and rights. In return

[1] Emily G. Balch, *Our Slavic Fellow Citizens.* New York, Charities Publication Committee, 1910, pp. 37–44. By permission of the Russell Sage Foundation, publishers.

for his land the peasant had to do a certain amount of work for his lord, and these labor dues (Bohemian, *robota*) were often very oppressive. At certain seasons, as Christmas or Easter, he had to pay special dues in kind, such as poultry or eggs. Besides all this, the lord still retained many of the old privileges, such as hunting rights and the monopoly of milling, brewing and of selling drinks. The peasant could not sell or mortgage his land except on certain conditions nor without permission, and he could not throw up the land at will, nor withdraw from it without supplying a responsible substitute,—his son, for instance. Above all, he could not divide it. On the other hand, he had carefully defined privileges as to the use of wood, pasturage, and so on.

The regular peasant holding differed in size according to locality. In general, it comprised probably 50 or 60 yokes of arable land (35 to 42 acres). Below the "full peasant" were poorer classes, the half peasant and the quarter peasant with correspondingly smaller holdings; and below these, lower classes still,—cottiers, laborers and so on. In the time of Maria Theresa the man with an eighth of a peasant holding counted as a cottier merely.

In 1848 serfdom, in the sense in which it still existed, was abolished in Austria, and also in Hungary where the conditions had been similar to those in Austria. The peasant became a free peasant proprietor, repaying gradually to the state the redemption money which the state had advanced to the landlords. The payment was practically completed in Austria by 1872.

In many parts of Austria it was not till the sixties that the peasant was given the right to subdivide his land. In 1867–1869 the right was made general, except for the Tyrol and in certain excepted cases. This liberty has produced very different results in different provinces. In the German Alpine territory custom has, in general, preserved the size of the holdings, and in many cases a prosperous and substantial peasantry has maintained itself. In other districts, on the contrary, where it has not been the custom to leave the land to one heir, but to divide it equally among the children, extreme subdivision has resulted in increasing indebtedness, frequent foreclosures and general impoverishment.

While it is nearly two generations since the old agrarian system, resting on an unfree peasant class, was legally abolished, its results are by no means a thing of the past. In a Hungarian village which I visited there was an old man who still remembered being beaten as a boy by the lord's steward for some trivial fault in connection with the feudal field work. One even hears of the old feudal dues being paid by ignorant peasants in out-of-the-way spots just as in our South unpaid labor was for some time given by negroes who did not know that they were free. In some places in Hungary there are still actually unfree tenants called Zeliary, who are kept bound to the soil by a sort of peonage system. They are under a debt for their land which they are never allowed to work off, so that they are not at liberty to leave the place and try to do better elsewhere. Consequently the landlord is at liberty to make his own terms. The hideous poverty resulting in one such village is something which I can never forget.

Shocking as such conditions of acute misery are they are less serious than the hampering effects of certain widespread remnants of the mediaeval system. The holding of a peasant in Austria, as in mediaeval England, was not one compact area like an American farm; instead it consisted of a number of scattered strips. If a man held 30 acres, he had perhaps 60 half-acre strips, not contiguous, but lying interwoven with those of other as designated shares of great open fields. The different holdings being thus interlocked, all had to follow the same plan of farming and sow and harvest at the same date and, what is involved in this, raise practically the same crops. . . .

This subdivision of the land, with all its consequences, survives in much of Austria and Hungary today, and makes it almost impossible to break away from the antiquated "three-field" system of agriculture which, in the absence of sufficient fertilizer or scientific rotation of crops, kept one-third of the soil fallow each year, one-third in autumn-sown crops and one-third in spring-sown.

Among the Slovaks one can see now Langland's "fair field full of folk," and for the same reason. I have counted thirty men ploughing at the same time, each working his share of the same big unbroken field,—open, for each man's share is marked, not by hedge fence or wall, but only by a furrow some thirty centimeters (or about a foot) wide, which must not be planted. It is said, and I believe the case has actually occurred, that the strips are sometimes so narrow that a man must walk on his neighbor's land to lead the ploughhorse on his own. You may follow such a strip with the eye, over hollow and swell, till it disappears over the last ridge in sight. When land is divided, for instance among sons, each strip is generally split lengthwise to insure equality. Otherwise one might get the sunny slope and the rich hollow, another the cold slope and a poor bit of sandy soil. Thus the strips get ever narrower. This system is wasteful in every way. First, it is wasteful of land. Where the holdings are in strips only seven meters wide, the boundary furrows take up nearly a tenth of the land. Moreover, the strips being straight, if a field happens not to be rectangular, awkward corners are left which must be laboriously worked by hand. It is wasteful of time, for a man has to travel all over the crazy-quilt of the township to work his many scattered bits of land.

This system though thoroughly superannuated, is hard to change. The process of "commassation," by which all the land is thrown together and redivided in equivalent lump lots is hard to carry out fairly, and impossible to carry out to the satisfaction of all concerned. Simpler, though less adequate, is a readjustment which forms lots of more reasonable shapes, and relocates them so that their owners have access to their pieces freely, instead of having to get at them across their neighbors' lots, and so only under severe restrictions, as is necessarily the case with the intermixed strip holdings.

A peasant is thus something quite distinct from anything that we know in America. On the one hand, he is a link in a chain of family inheritance and tradition that may run back for centuries, with a name, a reputation, and a posterity. On the other hand, he is confessedly and consciously an inferior. It is part of his world that there should be a God in heaven, and masters on the earth.

When the peasant's holding became his own property, a large part of the land in the village probably remained in the hands of the lord. The typical village has one considerable gentleman's estate and a number of small properties. So the peasant takes off his cap to those dressed like gentlefolk, known or unknown. He bears himself toward them with an inherited respect. At the same time there is a sense of profound and hardly bridgeable difference between himself and gentlemen, a feeling which may be friendly, but is sometimes colored by distrust or intense antagonism.

On the other hand, if the peasant has his superiors, he also has recognized inferiors, and in many places three classes of them. First is the cottager or cottier, (German *Häusler,* Bohemian *chalupnik*), the man who, with a house and bit of field, has yet no pretensions to getting his living off his land. Cottagers may eke out their living with trades, as shoemakers or smiths or weavers, for example, or they may hire themselves to work for other landowners in their free time. In a satire of the Bohemian writer Havlíček's he is describing how, in an interregnum in heaven, everything nevertheless went on in the old way:

> All the rivers still were wet,
> The stones they still were hard,
> And the cottagers' wives complained
> That peasants are (too) proud.

Secondly, there are the day laborers, who often live in cottages belonging to their employer, and may be paid partly in cash, partly in kind.

Thirdly, there are the "farm servants" not servants in the American sense, but rather what we should call "farm hands." These are both men and girls, and are generally hired by the year, and boarded by their employer. You will often find peasants living so wretchedly that we should consider them on the brink of misery, who yet are worlds above their servants housed more like animals than people. On the other hand, in a well-to-do Moravian village there were often comfortable one or two-room homes in the back part of the main house, where married farm servants kept house in privacy and comfort.

In his circumstances the peasant may be not only prosperous but rich,—very rich, even, if one takes his way of living and aspirations into account. But he is more likely to be hard pressed with work, with care, perhaps with debt. His roof may leak, his meal chest show the bottom, his crop be sold to the usurer before it is sown,—he is still a property owner, a tax payer, a permanent constituent of an old social order, known to and knowing all his associates, and enjoying a respect nicely adjusted to his acres and family.

His son's marriage, his daughter's dowry, the pensioning of his superannuated parents, the paying off the portions of his brothers and sisters, all are questions of property consideration; one might almost say that they have a dynastic character.

The peasant is an entirely different type from the workingman. He has not the workingman's quickness, nor all that he has gained in intelligence and self-reliance through competition, frequent change of place, and the trituration of city and factory life. On the other hand, he has the conservatism, the solidity, the shrewdness, the self-respect that go with property, independence, and an assured social position. He is likely to be hard and niggardly; this is perhaps the ugliest side. He and his are likely to be in some degree coarse, with the coarseness of those that have to deal with nature not mainly as the source of aesthetic emotions but of a good litter of pigs and a proper production of manure.

33. MONASTICISM IN THE EAST [1]

Monasticism is a very ancient institution. Long before there were Benedictines and Augustinians, monastic orders were flourishing in Egypt, Asia Minor, and other regions in the Near East. Although in the history of Europe the religious orders in the West played a far more important rôle than the others, it is necessary for a proper understanding of the former to study those organizations that preceded them in the East. The following account presents the story of the earlier Christian brotherhoods.

At the heart of monasticism is the vision of an ideal life. The true monk desires to get away from the temptation and distraction of the world, that he may dwell with God.

[1] G. Hodges, *The Early Church.* Boston and New York, Houghton Mifflin Company, 1915, pp. 150–167. Used by permission of, and by arrangement with Houghton Mifflin Company.

The belief that such a life could thus be realized was based on arguments derived from psychology and from philosophy.

The psychological reason for monasticism was drawn from the fact that the body affects the soul. Let us shut out all disquieting sounds and disturbing voices, and continue in silence, that we may have a composed spirit. Let us build a wall between us and the pride of the eye, that we may not see the splendor of the world nor be exposed to its solicitations. Especially, let us live in such a state that we may be free to discipline the body, to bring it into bondage that our soul may be at liberty, to minimize it for the magnifying of our spirit. It was discovered by primitive man that fasting induces a certain psychological condition, wherein, the body being abandoned and forgotten, the soul sees visions and hears voices, and attains the beatitude of ecstasy. It was found that protracted abstinence produced a gradual intoxication of the soul. It became one of the unsuspected luxuries of the saints.

The philosophical reason for monasticism was drawn from the theory that the body corrupts the soul. Matter being essentially evil, and the body being the source of all sin, our proper procedure is to make the body weak. Only by ascetic practices may we attain the victory of the spirit. . . .

The tendency toward monasticism, psychological and philosophical, was assisted by the hardness and the badness of the world.

It was a hard world out of which men fled to save their lives. Some abandoned it on account of the cost of living. The burden of expense was made uncommonly heavy in the fourth century by a new method of financial administration in the empire. The patrician class, including many very rich men, was exempt from taxation. The slave class could not be taxed. Accordingly, all the responsibility for maintaining the government was put upon the plebeians, the men of business, merchants and manufacturers. They were compelled to serve in the curia of their town, and in that capacity had to pay the assessed taxes out of their own pockets. Thus they were at first impoverished and then ruined, and finally taxed out of existence. Some of them fled from the world. They sought the simple life of the monastery. . . .

The world was not only hard but bad, and men went out of it to save their souls. One day, in Egypt, about the beginning of the last quarter of the third century (there is no definite record of either date or place) a young man named Antony, hearing in church the word of the Lord, "If thou wouldst be perfect, go, sell that thou hast, and give to the poor, and thou shalt have treasure in heaven: and come, follow me," obeyed. The three hundred acres which he had inherited from his father he divided among his neighbors, and betook himself to the desert. There he won those victories over divers temptations which Athanasius made famous in the book which he wrote about him. He was the first known pioneer of Christian monasticism. . . .

Antony was a hermit rather than a monk. Finding a deserted fort on the bank of the Nile, opposite the Fayum, he made its walls a barrier between him and all mankind. He came not out, nor saw the face of man, for twenty years. But in the meantime others of like mind, fugitives like himself from the hardness and the badness of the world, had gathered about him. They had built their huts around his fort like the tents of a besieging army. They felt that to be near to him, even though they could not see him, was to be near to God in whose presence he lived. Thus the name "monk" (*monos*), which at first had meant one who lives alone, came to mean one who indeed lives alone but in company with many others also living alone in the same neighborhood. Antony found himself surrounded by a multitude of solitaries. At last he came out, in response to their calls, and taught them the rules which he had adopted for himself.

The next step was taken, a few years later, by Pachomius. In southern Egypt, near Dendera, he organized the monks among whom he lived into a community. Under his leadership their huts were arranged in rows, and the lane (*laura*) between them gave the name "laura" to this first monastery. He suggested a habit, a tunic of white sheepskin with a hood. Their prescribed food was bread and water, with a little fruit and vegetables, once a day. Pachomius appointed hours for prayer. Common meals and common prayers necessitated a refectory and a chapel. The life of the community was made more normal and healthful by the undertaking of regulated work: the brothers tilled the ground, and made mats and baskets which were sold for their support. Pachomius founded nine such monasteries for men and one for women, all under the same rule, and the number of these communities increased rapidly.

Thus beside the informal, partially regulated, Antonian monasticism of northern Egypt, grew this Pachomian monasticism of southern Egypt, in which the principle of solitude was displaced, in great measure, by the principle of brotherhood. The banks of the Nile and the adjacent deserts were populated by these devotees.

In the middle of the fourth century, at a time when there were no communities of monks outside of Egypt, two young men at the University of Athens determined to take up the monastic life. One was named Basil, the other was named Gregory.

Cappadocia, the district from which these two men came, had an unsavory reputation in the contemporary world. Cappadocia, Caria and Crete were called "the three bad K's" (*tria kappa kakista*). Men who had their residence in more favored regions liked to tell how a viper bit a Cappadocian, and the viper died. It was a forlorn land, they said, buried under snow in winter, and inhabited by timid and treacherous people. . . .

Basil's grandfather and grandmother had suffered in the Diocletian persecution, and for seven years had lived in the wild woods of Pontus. His father, a man of wealth, was a famous teacher of rhetoric; his mother was celebrated for her beauty. Of their nine children,—four sons and five daughters,—three sons and three daughters were canonized as saints. The son who did not become a saint was a lawyer, and attained eminence as a judge; nothing is known of the unsainted daughters. Basil was at first taught at home by his father, and then sent to school in the Cappadocian Caesarea. There he met Gregory.

Gregory's father was a bishop, whose diocese consisted of his own little town. He had once belonged to an obscure sect in which Christianity was mingled with Persian and Hebrew elements; fire was revered as the symbol of God, and the Sabbath was rigorously kept. There were many such bishops, each in his village church, like the early Congregational ministers of New England. And there were many such sects, little experiments in Christian ecclecticism. Gregory's mother, however, was a person of such strictness of devotion, and so remote from any idea of compromise, that she would not even look at a pagan temple when she passed it in the street. She took him to church, from the days of his earliest childhood, and dedicated him to the ministry. She did not, however, have him baptized: that was not yet the rule. Presently he was sent to study in Caesarea.

The two friends went up to the University of Athens: first Gregory, then Basil. Years after, when Gregory preached the sermon at the funeral of Basil, he recalled their student days together, and told how he protected Basil from the customary initiation of freshman. It was a rough ceremony which ended with the subjection of the novice to an involuntary bath. "I kept him from being hazed at college," said Gregory, "when he was a freshman."

Students gathered in great numbers, and from long distances, in the University of Athens. One of the contemporaries of Gregory and Basil was Julian, afterwards emperor and called the "Apostate." They studied rhetoric and philosophy: rhetoric meaning Greek literature,—the poets, tragedies and historians; philosophy meaning logic, ethics and physics.

Basil and Gregory were interested not only in rhetoric and in philosophy, but in religion. "Two ways were known to us, the first of greater value, the second of smaller consequence: the one leading to our sacred buildings and the teachers there, the other to secular instructors." They agreed that they would seek the monastic life together. Their studies ended, Gregory went home to help his father in his little diocese of Nazianzus; Basil undertook a journey to the East, partly for the joy of strange sights in strange lands, partly for the purpose of learning what manner of life the monks were living by the Nile.

In the course of his travels Basil visited the Antonian and the Pachomian communities. To his practical, administrative mind the life of brotherhood looked better than the life of solitude. This he resolved to practise. He returned to Cappadocia, full of enthusiasm, eager to recite the lessons he had learned, and called on Gregory to join him. After some debate as to the best place for a monastic retreat,—Basil preferring Annesi and Gregory preferring Tiberina,—they decided on Annesi. . . .

There they settled, where the summer verified the glowing praise of Basil, and the winter confirmed the laments of Gregory. No doubt, they encountered hardship: that is what they sought. Happily for their health, Basil's mother was living just across the river, and saw to it that the young monks did not starve. They said their prayers, and read the works of Origen from which they made a series of selections which they afterward published. They went without food and without sleep, to their hearts' content. Other like-minded persons joined them. The ascetic spirit was in the common air of Cappadocia and Pontus. Already there were hermits, living as Antony had begun to live; and many others, keeping rules of strictness in their own homes. When a man like Basil, of wealth and high social station, a graduate of the University of Athens, betook himself to a glen beside a river, there were many to follow him. The conditions which had surrounded Antony and Pachomius surrounded him. And Basil and Gregory, like their predecessors in Egypt, were moved to make for themselves and their pious neighbors a rule of life.

Letters of Basil, and two series of Rules, preserve for us his ideals of the monastic manner of living.

In one letter, the second in a collection of more than three hundred, he discusses the matter in detail. We must strive, he says, after a quiet mind. He who lives in the world is exposed to perpetual distraction; he is anxious about his wife and children, worried by the care of his house and the oversight of his servants, distressed by misfortunes in trade and quarrels with his neighbors. Every day darkens the soul. The only escape is by the way of solitude. Let there be, then, such a place as ours, separate from intercourse with men, that the tenor of our exercises be not interrupted from without.

The day begins with prayers and hymns; thus we betake ourselves to our labors, seasoned with devotion. The study of the Bible is our instruction in our duty. This, too, is very important—to know how to converse, to be measured in speaking and hearing, to keep the middle tone of voice. As to dress, a tunic with a girdle is sufficient, avoiding bright colors and soft materials. Shoes should be cheap but serviceable. Beyond this, we pay no heed to our appearance. Indeed, garments not over clean and hair not smoothly brushed indicate a humble and submissive spirit. So, too, as to food: for a man in good health bread will suffice, and water will quench thirst; some vegetables may be added. Before and after eating, let grace be said. Let there be one fixed hour for taking food, that of all the twenty-four this alone may be spent upon the body. Let sleep be broken in upon by prayer and meditation. . . .

Basil's "Longer and Shorter Rules," so called, are in the form of conferences or instructions. They appear to have been written by Basil with the help of Gregory for the communities which assembled around their retreat in Pontus.

They enjoin withdrawal from the world, and renunciation of all private property, though this is not enforced with thoroughgoing strictness. Hours are appointed for daily prayer: on waking from sleep, in the midst of the morning, at noonday, in the midst of the afternoon, at the close of the day, on retiring to rest, at midnight, and before the dawn,—eight times. Watching and fasting are so regulated as to restrain excessive austerity; life is to be plain and simple, without needless distress. During meals a book is read, "and the brethren are to think more of what they hear than of what they eat." Bread and fish are appropriate, remembering the miracle in the wilderness. "To fast or watch more than the rest is self-will and vain-glory."

The Rules prescribe work as an essential part of life. Basil suggests the quiet trades, and such as do not minister to luxury,—weaving, shoe-making, carpentering, especially agriculture. The better educated among the brethren are to find their work in study, especially the study of the Bible; they are also to teach the young, who may be sent by their parents to the monastery school. The brethren are to engage in works of charity, ministering to the poor and caring for the sick, but in all cases for the sake of the soul rather than for the relief of the body.

Over the community is a superior, who assigns the tasks, and who is to be obeyed so long as his commands are not contrary to God's commandments. Other officers have their appropriate responsibilities. Confessions are to be made to the senior brethren, especially to those who are skilled in such ministration; the confessor exercises his office not because of appointment, but because of natural ability. Basil prefers many small communities, such as can have one lamp and one fire, as contrasted with the vast fraternities of Egypt. These communities he would have federated, with regular conferences of their superiors. Some communities will be of men, others of women,—the women making and mending the men's clothes; the men helping the women with their accounts, and administering the sacraments.

These Basilian Rules, which determined the ideals and the modes of life of monasticism not only in Asia Minor but throughout the Eastern Church, and determine them to this day, improved upon the Antonian and the Pachomian Rules in their emphasis upon social duty. The disciples of Antony, in spite of their residence in a community, were at heart hermits; and although the monasteries of Pachomius brought the brethren nearer together, still the solitary life was regarded as more acceptable with God. But Basil organized a brotherhood. The monastic life, as he saw it, was to be lived in common. The dormitory, the refectory, the chapel, the work of the monastery farm, kept the monks together. Basil related them not only to each other, but to the outside world. He came to see that the best place for a monastery is not in the midst of a wilderness, but in the neighborhood of a city, where the school and the hospital of the cloister are accessible to the people.

Out of the serenity of this monastic life, Basil and Gregory were called into the active service of the church. Gregory went to help his father, the bishop of Nazianzus; Basil went to help the aged bishop of Caesarea. In so doing they set an example which is still followed in the Eastern Church. In Greece, in Russia, to this day, the bishop is chosen from the monastery. It seemed at first to relate the church to the world. Out of the discipline of seclusion, in the strength of holy meditation, came the bishop, as the Master descended from the Hill of the Transfiguration to enter into social service in the plain. But the eventual result was to incapacitate the church for influential work. The bishops came from the monasteries ignorant of the world about them, speaking a language and living a life of their own. Before the fourth century was ended, the Eastern Church had retired from that control of public affairs into which the Western Church was triumphantly entering.

34. EXTRACTS FROM THE RULE OF ST. BENEDICT [1]

Benedict of Nursia, a well-born Italian who lived in the latter part of the fifth century and the first half of the sixth, becoming disgusted with the worldly and dissipated life at Rome where he had gone to be educated, went off to a little place called Subiaco to live in a cave as a hermit. In course of time disciples gathered about him and with some of these he went to Monte Cassino, about half-way between Rome and Naples. Here he established a monastery from which developed the order of Benedictine monks. For the governance of his followers he worked out a rule which became the most famous and influential of all the monastic regulations the western world has known.

[1] The Rule of St. Benedict. Translated into English. A Pax Book (Manuals of the Inner Life Series). London, Society for Promoting Christian Knowledge, 1931, pp. 1–2; 5–6; 8–9; 10–12; 13–14; 19; 21–23; 44–46; 53–54; 58–62; 70–72; 76–77. Used by permission.

Idleness, Benedict held, was the enemy of the soul. So he ordered that each brother should devote a certain number of hours a day to manual labor and to reading. Authorities differ in their estimates of the amount of time to be given to each. The time to be devoted to manual labor averaged perhaps five to seven hours a day, to reading perhaps two hours. In any case the provisions relating to these two matters exercised a remarkable influence on medieval monasticism and hence on medieval civilization.

Here Beginneth the Prologue To a Rule For Monasteries

Hearken continually within thine heart, O son, giving attentive ear to the precepts of thy master. Understand with willing mind and effectually fulfil thy holy father's admonition; that thou mayest return, by the labour of obedience, to Him from Whom, by the idleness of disobedience, thou hadst withdrawn. To this end I now address a word of exhortation to thee, whosoever thou art, who, renouncing thine own will and taking up the bright and all-conquering weapons of obedience, dost enter upon the service of thy true king, Christ the Lord.

In the first place, then, when thou dost begin any good thing that is to be done, with most insistent prayer beg that it may be carried through by Him to its conclusion; so that He Who already deigns to count us among the number of His children may not at any time be made aggrieved by evil acts on our part. For in such wise is obedience due to Him, on every occasion, by reason of the good He works in us; so that not only may He never, as an irate father, disinherit us His children, but also may never, as a dread-inspiring master made angry by our misdeeds, deliver us over to perpetual punishment as most wicked slaves who would not follow Him to glory.

. . . .

We have therefore to establish a school of the Lord's service, in the institution of which we hope we are going to establish nothing harsh, nothing burdensome. But if, prompted by the desire to attain to equity, anything be set forth somewhat strictly for the correction of vice or the preservation of charity, do not therefore in fear and terror flee back from the way of salvation of which the beginning cannot but be a narrow entrance. For it is by progressing in the life of conversion and faith that, with heart enlarged and in ineffable sweetness of love, one runs in the way of God's commandments, so that never deserting His discipleship but persevering until death in His doctrine within the monastery, we may partake by patience in the suffering of Christ and become worthy inheritors of His kingdom. Amen.

. . . .

What Kind of Man an Abbot Ought to Be

An abbot who is worthy to preside over a monastery ought always to remember what he is called and to justify his title by his deeds. For he is deemed in the monastery the representative of Christ, since it is by His title he is addressed, for the Apostle says: "Ye have received the Spirit of adoption of sons in which it is we cry out Abba, Father." And so an abbot ought not to teach, establish, or order anything contrary to the spirit of the Lord's revealed will, but let his commandments and teaching, as being the leaven of divine justice, sprinkle the minds of the disciples.

. . . .

Let him show no favouritism in the monastery. Let not one be loved more than another, unless it be one whom he has found to excel in good deeds and obedience. Let not one of gentle birth be placed higher than one who was recently a serf, unless there be some other and reasonable cause. Let it be so however if it shall have seemed good to the abbot on just grounds; and so let him do concerning the place of anyone whomsoever; but otherwise let them keep their own places; for whether bondmen or freemen we are all one in Christ and under the one Lord bear equal rank of subjection, for there is no acceptation of persons with God. In His sight we are differentiated one from the other in respect to this only, namely, if we be found humble and to excel others in good deeds. Therefore let him have an equal love towards all; let one and the same discipline be meted out to all according to their merits.

For in his teaching the abbot ought always to keep to that apostolic formula in which it is said; "Convince, entreat, rebuke"; that is to say, mingling according to circumstances gentleness with severity, let him show the sternness of a master, the affection of a father; that is to say, he ought to convince the undisciplined and restless almost harshly; but to entreat the obedient, the meek and the patient, that they progress still better. But the negligent and the haughty we admonish him to rebuke and correct. And let him not close his eyes to the sins of those who do amiss, but almost as soon as they begin to appear let him cut them off at the roots and master them, mindful of the judgment against Eli the priest in Silo. The more dignified and the intellectually minded let him correct by word at their first and second admonition; but the froward, the hard, the proud and the disobedient let him coerce at the very first offence by the stripes of corporal punishment, knowing it is written: "A fool is not corrected by words";

and again: "Strike thy son with the rod and thou wilt free his soul from death."

. . . .

Concerning the Calling of the Brethren to Council

As often as any special business has to be transacted in the monastery, let the abbot convoke the whole community and himself state what is the matter in hand. And having listened to the counsel of the brethren, let him settle the matter in his own mind and do what seems to him most expedient. And we have thus said that all are to be called to council because it is often to a junior that the Lord reveals what is best. But let the brethren so give counsel with all subjection and humility that they presume not with any forwardness to defend what shall have seemed good to them; but rather let the decision depend upon the abbot's discretion, so that he shall decide what is best, that they all may yield ready obedience; but just as it behoves the disciples to be obedient to the master, so also it becomes him to arrange all things prudently and justly.

. . . .

Concerning Obedience

The first degree of humility is obedience without delay. This is becoming to those who value nothing as more dear to them than Christ, on account of the holy servitude they have professed, whether through fear of hell or on account of the glory of life eternal. As soon as any order has been given by a superior, as being the same as if the order were divinely given, they can brook no delay in carrying it out. Concerning these the Lord says: "As the ear heard, he obeyed Me." And again He says to teachers: "He who hears you, hears Me."

Therefore such as these, at once relinquishing what they are doing, desert their own will and quickly freeing their hands by leaving unfinished what they were about, proceed with the foot of ready obedience to carry out the order given.

. . . .

Concerning Silence

Let us do what the prophet says: "I said, I will watch my ways, that I transgress not with my tongue. I set a watch upon my mouth. I became dumb and humbled and silent from good." Here the prophet shows, if one ought sometimes to abstain from speaking good for the sake of keeping silence, how much more ought one to be deterred from evil words on account of the penalty of sin. Wherefore even though it is always for good and holy converse that tends to edification, let but rare leave to talk be granted to fully trained disciples, on account of the importance of silence; because it is written: "In much speaking thou wilt not escape sin." And elsewhere: "Death and life are in the power of the tongue." For to speak and to teach becomes the master, to be silent and to listen beseems the disciple. And so if anything has to be asked of the superior let it be asked with all humility and with reverent subjection.

But all manner of buffoonery and idle, mirth-provoking words we adjudge should be perpetually restrained in every place; and for such discourse we permit not the disciple to open his mouth.

. . . .

Concerning Humility

Brethren, the sacred Scriptures cry out to us and say: "Every one who exalts himself will be humbled, and every one who humbles himself will be exalted."

In saying this it reveals that all exalting is a form of pride, against which the prophet shows that he is on his guard by saying: "Lord, my heart is not exalted nor mine eyes unlifted; and I have not concerned myself with great things nor with wonderful things above my reach." But why? "If I have not been of humble mind, but exalted my soul, then as if a weaned child upon his mother's breast, such let my soul's retribution be." Whence, brethren, if we wish to attain the highest point of humility and if we wish quickly to reach that heavenly exaltation which is attained through humility in this present life, we must by what we do to attain it set up that ladder which appeared in Jacob's dream and by which angels were shown to be both descending and ascending; for without doubt we are not to understand that descending and ascending but as descending by exaltation and ascending by humility.

. . . .

How the Monks are to Sleep

Let them sleep singly in separate beds. Let them receive bedding suitable to their manner of life, at the discretion of the abbot. If it can be done, let all sleep in one room; but if their number does not allow of this, let them repose by tens or twenties with their seniors who have charge of them. Let a candle burn continually in the dormitory until morning; Let them sleep clothed and girded with girdles or cords, but let them not have knives at their sides while they sleep, lest by chance while dreaming they wound a sleeper; and let them be monks always ready; and upon the signal being given let them rise without delay and hasten one after the other, yet with all gravity and decorum, to be ready in good time for the Work of God. Let not the younger brethren have their beds by themselves, but among those of the seniors; and let them be allowed gently to encourage one another as they rise for the Work of God, because some may feel drowsy and listless.

. . . .

Concerning Excommunication for Offences

If any brother be found to be contumacious or disobedient or proud or murmuring or in any other way out of harmony with the holy rule and despising the precepts of his seniors, let such an one be admonished, in accordance with our Lord's precept, once and again privately by his seniors. If he amend not, let him be publicly rebuked before all. But if even so he be not amended let him be subjected to excommunication, if he understand the nature of that penalty; but if he be obdurate, let him undergo corporal punishment.

. . . .

What the Measure of Excommunication Should Be

The degree of excommunication or punishment should be meted out according to the measure of the fault; and let the abbot adjudicate as to the comparative gravity of faults. If now any brother be found at fault in lesser degree let him merely be excluded from the common table: and for one excluded from the common table this shall be the rule: that in the oratory he does not intone psalm or antiphon, nor read a lesson, until satisfaction be made; and that he have his meal alone and after the brethren have had theirs, so that, for example, if the brethren eat at noon, that brother eat at three o'clock; if the brethren at three o'clock, he at six, until he obtain pardon by making due satisfaction.

. . . .

Concerning Graver Faults

But that brother who is found guilty of a grave fault, let him be excluded from the table and likewise from the oratory. Let not any of the brethren consort with him nor talk to him. When at the work assigned him let him be alone, continuing in penitence and sorrow, having in mind that terrible denunciation of the Apostle who says: "A man of such a kind as is this handed over to Satan for the destruction of the flesh, that his spirit may be saved in the day of the Lord." And by himself let him partake of his food, in quantity and at the hour that the abbot may see to be suitable for him; and neither let him be blessed by anyone who happens to be passing him, nor yet the food that is given to him.

. . . .

Concerning Those Who Without the Orders of the Abbot Consort With the Excommunicate

If any brother shall have presumed to consort with an excommunicated brother without the abbot's orders, in any way whatsoever, or to talk to him, or to send a message to him, let him incur the like punishment of excommunication.

. . . .

Whether Monks Ought to Have Anything of Their Own

Very specially is this vice of private ownership to be cut off from the monastery by the roots; and let not anyone presume to give or accept anything without the abbot's orders, nor to have anything as his own, not anything whatsoever, neither book, nor writing-tablet, nor pen; no, nothing at all, since indeed it is not allowed them to keep either body or will in their own power, but to look to receive everything necessary from their monastic father; and let not any be allowed to have what the abbot has not either given or permitted. And let all things be common to all, as it is written: "Neither did any one of them say or presume that anything was his own." But if anyone shall have been caught indulging in this most baneful vice, let him be admonished once and again; if then he shall not have amended, let him be subjected to correction.

. . . .

Concerning the Weekly Reader

Reading ought not to be wanting to the brethren when they eat at table; and let not anyone presume to read there because he happens to have casually picked up the book, but let one who is to read for the whole week enter upon his office on the Lord's day: and when he enters upon his office let him, after the Mass and Communion, beg of all prayers for himself that God avert from him the spirit of pride: and let this versicle be said in the oratory thrice by all, he himself however beginning it: "Thou shalt open my lips, O Lord; and my mouth shall shew forth Thy praise"; and so having received his blessing let him enter upon his office of reading; and let complete silence be kept so that the whispering of none be heard there, nor the voice of any but of him only who is reading; and let the brethren who are eating and drinking pass each other such things as they require so that no one may have to ask for anything; but if it should be necessary, it were better to make request by means of some sound-signal rather than by word of mouth; and let not anyone presume to ask any question there whether about the reading or otherwise, that occasion be not given for talking, unless by chance the superior wish to say anything briefly for the purpose of edification.

And let the brother who is weekly reader receive a "mixtum" before he begins to read, both because of the Holy Communion and also lest by chance it be too great strain upon him to keep his fast; and afterwards let him take his meal with the weekly kitcheners and the servitor. And let not all the brethren read or sing in order, but only those who may edify their hearers.

. . . .

Concerning the Quantity of Foods

We believe that for the daily refection in all the months of the year, alike when it is at the sixth hour of the day as when it is at the ninth, two cooked dishes will avail, in consideration of the weakness of different individuals, that he who perchance cannot eat of one may be sufficiently catered for by the other; so for all the brethren let two cooked dishes suffice; and if there be fruit in addition or young vegetables let there be added a third dish also. Of bread let one pound by weight suffice, whether there be but one meal, or both dinner and supper, though if they are going to sup let a third part from that same pound be kept back by the cellarer and served when they sup. But if by chance any hard work shall have been done, it shall be within the discretion and power of the abbot to make some addition, if it be expedient, so long as all surfeiting be avoided and he take care that indigestion never overcome the monks; for nothing is so adverse to any Christian as surfeiting, as says our Lord: "See to it that your hearts be not weighed down with surfeiting." And let not the same quantity be served to boys of tender age, but less than to their elders, moderation being observed in all cases. And let all abstain from the eating of the flesh of quadrupeds, although excepting from this rule the weak and the sick.

. . . .

Concerning the Quantity of Drink

Everyone has his own proper gift from God, one after this manner and another after that; and so it is with some misgiving we appoint the measure of other men's living: however, duly considering the weak we believe that half a pint of wine per head per day suffices; but let those to whom God gives the power of endurance of abstinence know that they shall have their due reward. But if the necessities of the place, or the work, or the heat of the summer should call for more, let it stand within the discretion of the superior to grant more, he taking all care that neither surfeiting or drunkenness creep in. Although we read that wine is by no means for monks, yet because in our time monks cannot be persuaded to see this, at all events let us agree as to this, that we will not drink to satiety, but somewhat sparingly; because: "Wine makes even the wise to fall away." But where the necessities of the place make it clear that not even the above mentioned measure can be found necessary, but less by far, or even none at all, let those who live there bless God and not murmur; for this especially is what we are admonishing, that they be free from murmuring.

. . . .

Concerning the Daily Manual Work

Idleness is inimical to the soul; and therefore the brethren ought to be occupied, at fixed seasons, with manual work and again at fixed seasons with spiritual reading; and so we think the hours for each should be arranged on this plan: that is to say that from Easter to the first of October they go out in the morning from Prime and work at whatever has to be done until nearly the fourth hour: and from the fourth hour have time for reading until about the sixth hour. And when they rise from the table after the sixth hour let them rest upon their beds in complete silence; or if by chance anyone should wish to read, let him so read that he may not disturb anyone else. Let None be said in good time, about the middle of the eighth hour, and then again let them work at whatever has to be done, until Vespers. And let them not be distressed if poverty or the needs of the place should require that they busy themselves about gathering in the crops with their own hands; for then are they truly monks, when they live by the work of their own hands, as did our fathers and the apostles. Let everything be done in moderation however on account of the faint-hearted.

And from the first of October until the beginning of Lent let them have reading time until the end of the second hour; and at the second hour let Terce be said and then all go to work until None at whatever is assigned them. But as soon as the first signal for None is made, let each and all break off from their work and be ready by the time the second signal has sounded. And after dinner let them have time for their studies and for learning the psalms. But in Lent let them have time for their studies from morning until the end of the third hour; and let them go to work at whatever is assigned them until the end of the tenth hour. In Lent moreover let them each have a book from the library and read it straight through: and these books are to be given out at the beginning of Lent. And above all let one or two seniors be deputed to go round the monastery and keep observation during reading hours lest by chance any brother be found morose and idle, or chatting instead of intent upon his reading; and therefore be not only useless to himself but also a distraction to others. And if, which be far from us, such an one be found, let him be corrected once and yet again; and if then he be not amended let him be subjected to correction according to rule in such wise that others be put in fear. And let not brother associate with brother at times not appointed for that purpose.

Further on the Lord's day let all have time for reading, except those who have been deputed for various duties; but if there shall be anyone so uninterested or so inert that through lack of will-power or of ability he can neither study nor read let there be some work assigned him that he may not be idle. To weak and delicate brethren let there be assigned such suitable occupation and duties that they be neither overcome of idleness nor so oppressed by exhaustion through work that they be driven to flight. Their weakness is to be taken into consideration by the abbot.

. . . .

Of How Guests Are to Be Received

Let all guests that happen to come be received as Christ, because He is going to say: "A Guest was I and ye received Me." And let suitable honour be shewn to them all, especially to those of the household of the faith and to strangers. When therefore a guest shall have been announced, let him be met by the superior or by the brethren, with all due courtesy; and let them at once betake themselves to prayer together and so let them associate together in peace, because the kiss of peace may not be offered first, but only when preceded by prayer, so as to avoid the snares of Satan: and in the salutation itself let all humility be manifest. Whenever guests arrive or depart, let Christ be adored in them—for Him indeed we receive in them—by bowing of the head or by full prostration. And when the guests have been received let them be taken to pray and then let the superior, or whomsoever he shall have appointed, sit with them. Let the divine law be read in the presence of a guest, that he may be edified; and after this let all courtesy be shewn him. For hospitality's sake the superior may break his fast, unless by chance it be a fast-day of obligation, the which cannot be violated: but let the brethren continue their custom of fasting. Let the abbot serve water for the guests' hands; and let both the abbot and also the whole community wash all the guests' feet: and the washing finished let them say this versicle: "We have received Thy mercy, O God, in the midst of Thy temple." And above all let care be scrupulously shewn in receiving the poor and strangers; for in them specially is Christ received. For the fear that the rich inspire itself secures deference for them.

35. SERVICES OF THE BENEDICTINE MONKS TO SOCIETY [1]

The abuses that developed in the medieval Church have been so emphasized, especially by Protestant historians and by historians unconsciously influenced by the Protestant tradition, that it is easy to forget how much good the clergy did. It seems worth while, therefore, to call attention to some of the services rendered to society by the monks of the Benedictine order. The little account here given, however, can convey but a faint impression of the importance of the many kinds of useful work in which the medieval clergy engaged.

In the course of four centuries the institution of Benedict had accomplished its work in the history of civilization and had now fallen into decay. Its mission had consisted in helping to form the new Christian society. In the midst of barbarian nations Benedictine monks had represented in their communities an orderly, if one-sided society, whose form was that of a family under the guidance of a father, and united by principles of authority and love. The laws of civic life had perished; but the Benedictines had written a new code of civil law, and the rule of Benedict was the most ancient law book of the Middle Ages. Thus the seeds of a society of brotherly love were sown in the midst of barbarism. While the world was reduced to a smoking cinderheap, these societies led peaceable, industrious and holy lives. They displayed a realm of moral ideals to the rude nations around, a realm where temporal wants were unknown, and where obedience and humility flourished. With Apostolic zeal they converted the heathen. Under their guidance the gospel aided the sword of Charles in the conquest of new provinces, and in extending the confines of the Church. Their convents were the refuges of misfortune and guilt, and at the same time the honoured colonies of learning, the only schools left to the impoverished human race, the asylum where the last remains of classic culture found shelter. Their dreams or ideals were lost to sight in the furthest distance of heaven. Nevertheless they sowed and reaped and gathered the fruits of the earth into spacious granaries. Since they themselves possessed estates, and laboured in the field according to the practical rule of Benedict, they became founders

[1] Ferdinand Gregorovius, *History of the City of Rome in the Middle Ages*. Translated from the Fourth German edition by Annie Hamilton. 8 Vols. London, George Bell and Sons, 1894, Vol. III, pp. 307–308. Used by permission.

of cities and colonies, and numberless tracts of land owed their cultivation, inhabitants and prosperity to Benedictine energy. The order accomplished a great work of civilization by the social principle of Christian love, by schools, by agriculture, by the foundation of towns, by a thousand peaceful means in the midst of rude, opposing forces, and by the association of secular elements with the Church. The glorious mission which the institution of Benedict thus achieved secures it a foremost place in the annals of mankind. In spite of the many reformations which followed in after times, in spite of the new and in part famous orders which arose, no society ever attained either the Christian virtues or the social importance of Benedict's foundation, for all obeyed some special impulse, were at the service of the Church, and were the outcome of some tendency of the time.

36. HENRY CHARLES LEA DEPICTS THE STRUGGLE BETWEEN POPE NICHOLAS I AND EMPEROR LOTHAIR FOR TEMPORAL AND SPIRITUAL SUPREMACY [1]

The ninth century was a period of disorder in western Europe. Charlemagne was succeeded in 814 by his son Louis the Pious, who because of his religious fervor received the surname from the leading bishops in his empire. As a ruler, however, he was practically a failure, and almost at the outbreak of his reign the Northmen began to attack and plunder the wealthiest parts of the Frankish Empire. His three sons did not improve matters when in 843 they divided the empire among them, the center from Italy across the Alps and along the Rhine to the North Sea going to the eldest son, named Lothair. The latter also received the imperial title. Emperor Lothair in turn was followed by three sons. In 844 he gave Italy to his son Louis, who in 850 became emperor, while in 855 another son, called Lothair II, received the lower Rhine region. Lothair II soon encountered serious difficulties. In the first place, his kingdom was coveted by two uncles, who ruled respectively France and Germany. In the second place, he became involved in a divorce suit and as a result aroused the enmity of Pope Nicholas I (858–870). This pope appeared upon the scene at a critical time, and he found at his disposal tremendous opportunities of enhancing the prestige of the Church. It was about him that Henry Charles Lea wrote, "The man was not wanting to the opportunity."

The man was not wanting to the opportunity. The circumstances which I have briefly sketched had placed in the hands of the church weapons of

[1] Henry C. Lea, *Studies in Church History*. Philadelphia, Henry C. Lea's Son and Co., 1883, pp. 168–176. By permission of Lea & Febiger, pubishers, and Arthur H. Lea, copyright owner.

vast and indefinite power. The times were ripe for their employment, for the necessities of the age demanded an intellectual tyranny to coerce and counterbalance the countless blind and aimless despotisms of individual chieftains, who were rapidly crushing out what little mental life was left in Europe. The arm to wield these weapons was found when Nicholas I ascended the pontifical throne. To the service of the cause he brought a dauntless spirit, an unconquerable will, an unbending energy, a prudent daring, and a knowledge of the men and the tendencies with which he had to deal, that enabled him to establish as absolute rights the principles which had previously been more or less speculative. The history of the Divorce of Teutberga, which marks an era in ecclesiastical annals, is a fair illustration of the manner in which he reduced to practice the theories of the False Decretals, and laid the foundation of that papal omnipotence which was to overshadow Christendom.

On the retirement of the emperor Lothair, his son of the same name succeeded to that portion of his dominions which took from him the appellation of Lotharingia, modernized into Lorraine, and extending from Switzerland to the mouths of the Rhine. Married in 856 to Teutberga, the uncontrolled licentiousness of the young king led him within the next year to abandon her for a succession of concubines, one of whom, Waldrada, with whom he had had relations previous to his marriage, succeeded in permanently captivating his fickle passions and weak understanding. The favorite resolved to share her paramour's crown, and Lothair, ready to secure her smiles at any cost, entered eagerly into a disgusting conspiracy. A charge of the foulest incest was brought against the unhappy queen, who, by means which can readily be guessed, was forced to a confession. Condemned to perpetual penance in a convent by the Lotharingian prelates at the synod of Metz, she succeeded in escaping to France, where she was duly protected by Charles le Chauve, with the true Carlovingian desire of nursing trouble for his nephew. Meanwhile Lothair caused another synod to be assembled at Aix-la-Chapelle, where, on stating his piteous case, deprived of his wife and unable to restrain his passions, the charitable bishops, after due deliberation, declared that a woman stained with the crimes confessed by Teutberga was not canonically a wife, and that he was at liberty to marry. His nuptials with Waldrada were immediately celebrated, and Gunthair, Archbishop of Cologne, the instigator and manager of the plot, received his appropriate reward in the dishonor of a niece, whose promised elevation to the throne had been the prize held out for his co-operation. Lothair, in his pollution, might forget the world, but the world did not forget him. His uncle, Charles le Chauve, hankering after the fertile plains of Austrasia, began to hint that his nephew had forfeited all claim to human society, and Teutberga's powerful family urged her to appeal to the central arbiter at Rome. The occasion was one in which the common feelings of mankind would excuse any stretch of avenging prerogative, and Nicholas seized it with vigorous joy. The comparison is instructive between his alacrity and the prudent reticence of Adrian in the previous century. A moralist would find it difficult to draw the line between the connubial irregularities of Charlemagne and those of Lothair; but Hermengarda found no puissant pope to force her inconstant husband into the paths of dissimulation, or to justify wrong by cruelty. When Charlemagne grew tired of a wife, he simply put her aside, nor would Adrian or Leo have thanked the meddling fool who counselled interference. But times had changed since then, and other principles had gained supremacy. According to Isidor, the holy Calixtus I had decreed that an unjust decision, rendered under the pressure of kings or potentates, was void—an axiom which, however morally true, carried with it the dangerous corollary that, if it meant anything, there must be some one to decide upon the injustice of the sentence. If a king had procured it, the only arbiter to revise it was the pope, to whom a canon of Ingilram's had specially attributed the power of abrogating at will the proceedings of any local synod.

As supreme judge of all questions, Nicholas accordingly addressed himself to the work. To his first legates Lothair simply responded that he had only complied with the decrees of the national synod; and the legates, heavily bribed, advised him to dispatch to Rome Gunthair, with his tool Thietgaud, Archbishop of Treves, who could readily make all things right with the Holy Father. The legates, on their return, had to seek safety in flight from the indignation of Nicholas; but the two archbishops, in the self-confidence of craft and stupidity, appeared before a synod called for the purpose, and presented the acts of the synods of Metz and Aix, in the full expectation of their authoritative confirmation. The deliberation was short; the two archbishops were recalled to hear sentence of deposition from their sees, and degradation from the priesthood; the synod of Metz was stigmatized as "tanquam adulteris faventem, prostibulum"; and a sentence of excommunication was suspended over the heads of all the Lotharingian prelates, to be removed only by prompt retraction of their acts, and individual application to the pope. The proceeding was somewhat violent, as it amounted to condemnation in the absence of the accused, with no array of witnesses and evidence such as the canons required, even the acts of the Lotharingian synods not having been acknowledged by the archbishops without equivocation. Gunthair, breathing furious revenge, and Thietgaud, stupefied by the blow, betook themselves at once to the Emperor Louis, Lothair's brother. He listened to their story, and eager to avenge his brother, and to suppress the rising insubordination of the pontiff, he marched directly on Rome. The fasts and prayers of Nicholas availed little against the reckless soldiery of Louis; a massacre ensued, and the pope, escaping in a boat across the Tiber, lay hidden for two days, without meat or drink, in the cathedral of St. Peter. A sudden fever, however, opportunely laid hold of the emperor, and there were not wanting counsellors who attributed it to the sacrilege which he had committed. Louis, therefore, sent for Nicholas, made his peace, and withdrew, commanding the archbishops to return home and consider themselves degraded. Thietgaud, a fool rather than a knave, submitted without further resistance; but Gunthair addressed an epistle to his brother bishops, exhorting them to repel the encroachments of the papacy, which was aspiring to the domination of the world, and retorting on the pope his sentence of excommunication. This document his brother Hilduin, an ecclesiastic, laid on the tomb of St. Peter, after forcing an entrance with arms, and killing one of the guards. On their return home, Thietgaud abstained from officiating, but Gunthair, still threatening vengeance, took possession of his diocese, until the frightened Lotharingian bishops induced Lothair to depose him, while they individually and humbly made their peace with Rome, by submitting to all the requisitions of the pontiff. Another legate, Arsenius, was sent with instructions to enforce the threatened excommunication of Lothair, if he persisted in iniquity, and with letters to Charles le Chauve and Louis le Germanique, denouncing the conduct of their nephew with an acerbity till then unknown in the intercourse between popes and kings. Lothair felt himself unable to face the storm which he had aroused. He professed himself in all things an obedient son of the church, he put away Waldrada, who promised to seek absolution in Rome, and he took back the unfortunate Teutberga, under menace of eternal punishment in the name of God and St. Peter. Then suddenly all was again confusion, as untamed human passions struggled against the unaccustomed bonds. Waldrada escaped from the custody of Arsenius and returned to her infatuated lover, while the queen was subjected to every kind of humiliation and oppression. But Nicholas was equal to the strife which he had provoked, and on which he had staked the future of the papacy, and, indeed, of Christian civilization. Waldrada he excommunicated. Charles le Chauve, with whom Teutberga had again taken refuge, he encouraged with a laudatory epistle, mingled with threats concerning a rumored arrangement by which an abandonment of her cause was to be purchased by a cession of territory; and, in spite of the interference of the Emperor Louis, he caused another synod to confirm the degradation of the delinquent archbishops. Teutberga herself, worn out by seven years of persecution, petitioned the pontiff for peace, and begged to be separated from Lothair, that she might end her days in quiet; but the victory was not yet gained, and Nicholas scornfully refused her request. An endeavor of Lothair to settle the question by appeal to the wager of battle was rejected with indignation, and for the third time he ordered the timid prelates of Lotharingia to enforce the sentence of excommunication pronounced against the aspiring concubine. Commands were addressed to Louis le Germanique to join in the pressure on Lothair, and to desist from his intercession in behalf of the deposed archbishops, while the prelates of Germany received a sharp reproof for joining in the appeal.

The opposition of monarch and prelate was at last broken down, and Waldrada was forced to Rome; but before his triumph was complete Nicholas died, leaving to his successor Adrian II the legacy of this quarrel, and the widening schism of the Greek church, which he had rashly provoked. Lothair, hoping to find the new pope more considerate of the regal dignity, intimated a desire to visit Rome in person, to justify his course, and to be reconciled to the church. Less imperious than his predecessor, Adrian welcomed the apparently repentant sinner. The excommunication of Waldrada was removed on condition of absolute separation from her lover; and, that Lothair's journey might be impeded by no pretext, epistles were addressed to Charles and Louis, commanding them not to trouble Lotharingia during the pious absence of its king. An honorable reception awaited Lothair. He was admitted to communion on the oath, which no one believed, that he had obeyed the commands of Nicholas as though they had been those of Heaven, and had abstained from all intercourse with Waldrada. The victory of the pope was as complete as the abasement of the king. The sacrament was administered as an ordeal, in which the courtiers of Lothair were associated as accomplices in his guilt, and both parties separated, equally satisfied with the result. A still further triumph, however, was reserved for the church by one of those mysterious occurrences which account for the belief, then universally prevalent, of special interpositions of Providence. Lothair was scarce fairly started on his return home, when his progress was arrested at Piacenza by an epidemic which broke out among his followers; and there, after a short illness, died the miserable young king and his partners in guilt. Of course, the effect was prodigious. Divine justice had completely vindicated the acts of Nicholas and Adrian; and God himself had condescended to execute the sentence of the church on the hardened adulterer, who had sought to shield himself by sacrilegious perjury from the punishment due to his offences.

The papacy had thus triumphed over both church and state, and Heaven had sanctioned the immense extension of prerogative. The principle was asserted and maintained, that an appeal to the ecclesiastical jurisdiction barred all subsequent reclamation to the ordinary tribunals—a doctrine capable of infinite applications and illimitable results. By deposing and degrading Gunthair and Thietgaud, without a preliminary trial at home, without an accuser, and without the ordinary judicial formalities, Nicholas erected himself into a judge of first and last resort, without responsibility and without appeal—the sole arbiter of destiny for the highest dignitaries of the hierarchy. By annulling the acts of the Lotharingian synods, and forcing their members not only to submit to this, but humbly to apologize for the iniquity of their decrees, he established a complete ascendency over the provincial prelacy, and vindicated the supremacy of the Holy See as the only irrefragable authority in the church. Nor was the victory over the secular power less complete. When Lothair appeared before the papal legates to answer the appeal of Teutberga, he acknowledged the jurisdiction of popes over monarchs; and however he might subsequently dissemble, he never afterwards dared to deny it, each step only serving to confirm that jurisdiction in its most absolute sense. And when Adrian threatened the kings of France and Germany, and ordered them not to interfere with Lotharingia during the absence of their nephew, he placed himself at the head of Christendom, as the self-constituted sovereign of sovereigns. The moral effect was not less decisive. An unarmed priest, unable to protect his palace or his person from the brute force of his enemy, Nicholas, under the guardianship of Heaven, walked without swerving along the path which he had marked out, over the prostrate necks of kings and prelates, clothed only in the mysterious attributes of his station, and invoking the Most High in the name of truth and justice. What wonder that the populations should revere him as the Vicegerent of Christ, as the incarnate representative of God, and that the most extravagant pretensions ascribed to him by Ingilram or Isidor were regarded as his legitimate and imprescriptible prerogatives?

It will be observed throughout this affair, that the weapon relied upon to enforce obedience was the deprivation of communion, involving, in the case of ecclesiastics, degradation from their benefices, and in that of laymen, exclusion from the Christian church. It was in this that the power to bind and to loose found its readiest practical expression, and the control which the church thus acquired over the life of man in this world and his salvation in the next, opened out before it a career of boundless supremacy which will be considered in a subsequent essay.

Yet it must not be supposed that the vast powers thus successfully asserted by Nicholas and Adrian descended in an unbroken line from them to Innocent III. Society was still too rude, and its anarchic elements too tumultuous, to submit without many struggles to the absolute despotism of influences purely spiritual and moral. Its protest against subjection took many and various forms, and the vices and weaknesses of the clergy seemed at times to postpone indefinitely the ultimate triumph. The tenth century was yet to see the darkest period in papal annals, infamously illustrated by Marozia and John XII, when the Holy Father was the puppet of any savage noble who could control the miserable population of Rome. Whatever wrongs Italy may have suffered from the Tedeschi, the world yet owes to them that Teutonic power rescued the papacy from this degradation, and placed it in hands less incompetent to discharge the weighty trust. Blindly working for the present, the Saxon and Franconian Emperors little thought that they were elevating an influence destined to undermine their own, or that the doctrines of Isidor, in the mouth of a priest, would break the power of an iron Kaiser, the warrior of sixty battles.

37. LETTERS OF GREGORY VII AND HENRY IV [1]

It was one of the chief aims of the great reforming Pope, Gregory VII, to prevent the appointment of bishops and abbots by lay rulers. Therefore a synod over which the Pope presided, meeting at Rome, declared lay investiture illegal; for by lay investiture secular rulers had virtually controlled the appointment of many of the higher clergy. The Pope then sent the decree, together with a letter of admonition to the King of the Germans, later Emperor of the Holy Roman Empire. The decree has been lost but the letter has come down to us.

The moment of the letter's arrival was inauspicious. Henry had just won a victory over the Saxons which greatly increased his power in Germany and so was little disposed to brook reproof. In fiery anger he sent a letter to the Pope, defying him and declaring him deposed.

The two letters are here quoted in translation.

Letter of Gregory VII to Henry IV, Dec. 1075

Bishop Gregory, servant of the servants of God, to King Henry, greeting and apostolic benediction:—that is, if he be obedient to the apostolic chair as beseems a Christian king. Considering and carefully weighing with what strict judgment we shall have to render account for the ministry entrusted to us by St. Peter, chief of the apostles, it is with hesitation that we have sent unto thee the apostolic benediction. For thou art said knowingly to exercise fellowship with those excommunicated by a judgment of this apostolic chair, and by sentence of a synod. If this be true, thou dost know thyself that thou may'st receive the favour neither of the divine nor of the apostolic benediction unless—those who have been excommunicated being separated from thee, and compelled to do penance—thou do first, with condign repentance and satisfaction, seek absolution and indulgence for

[1] Ernest F. Henderson, *Select Historical Documents of the Middle Ages*. London, George Bell and Sons, 1896, pp. 367–373. Used by permission.

thy transgression. Therefore we counsel thy Highness that, if thou dost feel thyself guilty in this matter, thou do seek the advice of some canonical bishop with speedy confession. Who, with our permission enjoining on thee a proper penance for this fault, shall absolve thee and shall endeavour by letter to intimate to us truly, with thy consent, the measure of thy penitence.

For the rest it seems strange enough to us that, although thou dost transmit to us so many and such devoted letters; and although thy Highness dost show such humility through the words of thy legates—calling thyself the son of holy mother church and of ourselves, subject in the faith, one in love, foremost in devotion;—although, finally, thou dost commend thyself with all the devotion of sweetness and reverence: thou dost, however, at heart and in deeds most stubborn, show thyself contrary to the canonical and apostolic decrees in those things which the religion of the church enjoins as the chief ones. For, not to mention other things, in the affair of Milan the actual outcome of the matter shows plainly how thou didst carry out—and with what intent thou didst make them—the promises made to us through thy mother and through our confrères the bishops whom we sent to thee. And now, indeed, inflicting wound upon wound, contrary to the establishments of the apostolic chair, thou hast given the churches of Fermo and Spoleto—if indeed a church could be given or granted by a man—to certain persons not even known to us. On whom, unless they are previously well known and proven, it is not lawful even regularly to perform the laying on of hands.

Since thou dost confess thyself a son of the church it would have beseemed thy royal dignity to look more respectfully upon the master of the church,—that is, St. Peter, the chief of the apostles. To whom, if thou art of the Lord's sheep, thou wast given over by the Lord's voice and authority to be fed; Christ Himself saying: "Peter, feed my sheep." And again: "To thee are given over the keys of the kingdom of Heaven, and whatsoever thou shalt bind upon earth shall be bound also in Heaven; and whatsoever thou shalt loose upon earth shall be loosed also in Heaven." Inasmuch as in his seat and apostolic ministration we, however sinful and unworthy, do act as the representative of his power: surely he himself has received whatever, through writing or in bare words, thou has sent to us. And at the very time when we are either perusing the letters or listening to the voices of those who speak, he himself is discerning, with subtile inspection, in what spirit the instructions were issued. Wherefore thy Highness should have seen to it that no discrepancy of good will should have been found towards the apostolic chair in thy words and messages. And, in those things through which the Christian faith and the state of the church chiefly progress towards eternal salvation, thou should'st not have denied the reverence due, not to us, but to God Almighty—disregarding the fact that the Lord saw fit to say to the apostles and their successors: "Who hears you, hears me; and who scorns you, scorns me." For we know that he who does not refuse to show faithful obedience to God, does not scorn to observe our commands—even as if he had heard them from the lips of the apostle himself—and the things which, following the decrees of the holy fathers, we may have said. For if, out of reverence for the chair of Moses, the Lord ordered the apostles to observe whatever the scribes and Pharisees sitting above them should say: it is not to be doubted but that the apostolic and evangelic teaching, the seat and foundation of which is Christ, should be received—and observed—by the faithful with all veneration from the lips of those who have been chosen for the service of preaching.

In this year, indeed,—a synod being assembled around the apostolic chair, over which the heavenly dispensation willed that we should preside; at which, moreover, some of thy faithful subjects were present: seeing that the good order of the Christian religion has now for some time been falling away, and that the chief and proper methods of gaining souls had long fallen into abeyance and, the devil persuading, been trampled under foot, we, struck by the danger and the clearly approaching ruin of the Lord's flock, reverted to the decrees and to the teachings of the holy fathers—decreeing nothing new, nothing of our own invention. We did decree, however, that, error being abandoned, the first and only rule of ecclesiastical discipline was again to be followed, and the well-worn way of the saints to be re-sought. Nor indeed do we know of any other entrance to salvation and eternal life which lies open to the sheep of Christ and their shepherds, save the one which, as we have learned in the gospel and in every page of the divine Scriptures, was shown by Him who said: "I am the door, he who entereth through me shall be saved and shall find pasture," was preached by the apostles and followed by the holy fathers. This decree, moreover, which some, preferring human to divine honours, do call an unbearable weight and immense burden—we, however, by a more suitable name, as a necessary truth and light for regaining salvation—we did judge should be devoutly received and observed, not only by thee and by those of thy kingdom, but by all the princes and peoples of the world who confess and cherish Christ. Although we much desired, and it would have most beseemed thee, that, as thou dost surpass others in glory, honour and valour, so thou should'st be superior in thy devotion to Christ. Nevertheless, lest these things should seem beyond measure burdensome or wrong to thee, we did send word to thee through thy faithful servants that the changing of an evil custom should not alarm thee; that thou should'st send to us wise and religious men from the land, who, if they could, by any reasoning, demonstrate or prove in what, saving the honour of the Eternal King and without danger to our souls, we might moderate the decree as passed by the holy fathers, we would yield to their counsels. In which matter, indeed, even though thou had'st not been so amicably admonished by us, it would nevertheless have been but right that, before thou did'st violate apostolic decrees, thou should'st, by negotiation, make demands from us in cases where we oppressed thee or stood in the way of thy prerogatives. But of how much worth thou did'st consider either our commands or the observance of justice, is shown by those things which were afterwards done and brought about by thee.

But since, inasmuch as the still long-suffering patience of God invites thee to amend thy ways, we have hopes that, thy perception being increased, thy heart and mind can be bent to the obedience of the mandates of God: we warn thee with paternal love, that, recognizing over thee the dominion of Christ, thou do reflect how dangerous it is to prefer thine own honour to His; and that thou do not impede, by thy present detraction from it, the liberty of the church which He considered worthy to join to Himself as His spouse in celestial union; but that thou do begin, with faithful devotion, to lend it the aid of thy valour, in order that it may best increase to the honour of God Almighty and of St. Peter; by whom also thy glory may deserve to be increased. All of which, in return for the victory recently conferred upon thee over thy enemies, thou should'st recognize to be now most clearly due from thee to them; so that, when they reward thee with noteworthy prosperity, they may see thee the more devout for the benefits granted. And, in order that the fear of God, in whose hand and power is every kingdom and empire, may remain fixed in thy heart more deeply than our admonition, bear in mind what happened to Saul after the victory which, by the prophet's order, he enjoyed; and how he was chidden by God when he boasted of his victory, not carrying out the commands of that same prophet; but what favour followed David for the merit of humility amid the distinctions of valour.

Finally, as to the things which we have seen and noted in thy letter we keep silent; nor will we give thee a sure reply until thy legates, Rapoto, Aldepreth and Udescalc, and those whom we sent with them shall return to us and more fully reveal thy will to us in those matters which we entrusted to them to treat of with thee.

Given at Rome on the 6th day before the Ides of January, in the 14th indiction.

Henry IV's Answer to Gregory VII, Jan. 24, 1076

Henry, king not through usurpation but through the holy ordination of God, to Hildebrand, at present not pope but false monk. Such greeting as this hast thou merited through thy disturbances, inasmuch as there is no grade in the church which thou hast omitted to make a partaker not of honour but of confusion, not of benediction but of malediction. For, to mention few and especial cases out of many, not only hast thou not feared to lay hands upon the rulers of the holy church, the anointed of the Lord—the archbishops, namely, bishops and priests—but thou hast trodden them under foot like slaves ignorant of what their master is doing. Thou hast won favour from the common herd by crushing them; thou hast looked upon all of them as knowing nothing, upon thy sole self, moreover, as knowing all things. This knowledge, however, thou hast used not for edification but for destruction; so that with reason we believe that St. Gregory, whose name thou hast usurped for thyself, was prophesying concerning thee when he said: "The pride of him who is in power increases the more, the greater the number of those subject to him; and he thinks that he himself can do more than all." And we, indeed, have endured all this, being eager to guard the honour of the apostolic see; thou, however, hast understood our humility to be fear, and hast not, accordingly, shunned to rise up against the royal power conferred upon us by God, daring to threaten to divest us of it. As if we had received our kingdom from thee! As if the kingdom and the empire were in thine and not in God's hand! And this although our Lord Jesus Christ did call us to the kingdom, did not, however, call thee to the priesthood. For thou hast ascended by the following steps. By wiles, namely, which the profession of monk abhors, thou hast achieved money; by money, favour; by the sword, the throne of peace. And from the throne of peace thou hast disturbed peace, inasmuch as thou hast armed subjects against those in authority over them; inasmuch as thou, who wert not called, hast taught that our bishops called of God are to be despised; inasmuch as thou hast usurped for laymen the ministry over their priests, allowing them to depose or condemn those whom they themselves had received as teachers from the hand of God through the laying on of hands of the bishops. On me also who, although unworthy to be among the anointed, have nevertheless been anointed to the kingdom, thou hast lain thy hand; me who—as the tradition of the holy Fathers teaches, declaring that I am not to be deposed for any crime unless, which God forbid, I should have strayed from the faith—am subject to the judgment of God alone. For the wisdom of the holy fathers committed even Julian the apostate not to themselves, but to God alone, to be judged and to be deposed. For himself the true pope, Peter, also exclaims: "Fear God, honour the king." But thou who dost not fear God, dost dishonour in me his appointed one. Wherefore St. Paul, when he has not spared an angel of Heaven if he shall have preached otherwise, has not excepted thee also who dost teach otherwise upon earth. For he says: "If any one, either I or an angel from Heaven, should preach a gospel other than that which has been preached to you, he shall be damned." Thou, therefore, damned by this curse and by the judgment of all our bishops and by our own, descend and relinquish the apostolic chair which thou hast usurped. Let another ascend the throne of St. Peter, who shall not practice violence under the cloak of religion, but shall teach the sound doctrine of St. Peter. I Henry, king by the grace of God, do say unto thee, altogether with all our bishops: Descend, descend, to be damned throughout the ages.

38. CANOSSA: LAMBERT OF HERSFELD'S ACCOUNT[1]

The selection from the medieval chronicler, Lambert of Hersfeld, here given is one of a number of extracts on the Canossa episode presented by Professors Duncalf and Krey in their Parallel Source Problems in Medieval History. *Their purpose is not merely to introduce students to the sources on which our knowledge of certain parts of medieval history is based but also to enable them to compare the various accounts, note discrepancies and try to determine from narratives often conflicting what really happened. Here only one extract is given. Students who wish to compare it with other accounts of the same episode are referred to the* Parallel Source Problems *itself.*

The selection from Lambert is here preceded by a brief introduction to the chronicler and his work taken from the Parallel Source Problems.

[*Introduction by Professors Duncalf and Krey*]

With literary historians the account by the monk Lambert of Hersfeld has long been the favorite description of Henry at Canossa. Even more scholarly historians have been fascinated by his dramatic and well-written description of those events, and only in comparatively recent years has Lambert been subjected to that incisive criticism from which his style and plausibility had so long kept him immune. He was not an eye-witness to the events which he here describes. His monastery had, it is true, sheltered Henry during some of his earlier struggles, and had also suffered his wrath. The people at Hersfeld followed the career of the king with more than ordinary interest. The monastery was so situated that many travelers of note stopped there, and the important communications of both king and pope were frequently made known to them. Thus, when one of their most scholarly monks began his account of the struggles of king Henry he found an abundance of material from which to construct his account. He wrote his work in the form of annals, beginning with Adam, and closing just before the election

[1] Frederic Duncalf and August Krey, *Parallel Source Problems in Medieval History.* New York, Harper and Brothers, 1912, pp. 34–35; 42–56. Used by permission of publisher and authors.

of Rudolph at Foresheim in the spring of 1077. The whole narrative presumes to be an impartial statement of events, and was so regarded for a long time. A careful reading, however, will reveal not only a wealth of information, but also an exercise of imagination unusual for his time. In addition students of Latin may detect some passages which bear more than an accidental resemblance to ancient writings, in which he was remarkably well read. Nevertheless, this account has much value.

Lamberti Annales (*the Annals of Lambert*)

When Worms had been surrendered and the bishop was assured a most peaceful position the Saxons and Swabians returned home proudly happy. They had sent legates to the pope to insure his presence on the day set for calming the storms of civil war throughout Gaul.[1] The king, for his part, realized that his safety depended upon his obtaining absolution from the anathema before the year was up. Furthermore, for reasons of his own, he did not regard it as very safe to air his case before the pope in the presence of such hostile accusers. Under the circumstances, therefore, he came to the conclusion that it would be best to meet the pope in Italy just as he was setting out for Gaul. There he would try to gain absolution from the anathema in any way that he could. Once this was obtained, his other difficulties must be easily dispelled. No religious scruples would then interfere with his holding a meeting with the princes and obtaining the counsel and loyalty of his friends against his enemies. Leaving Spires accordingly a few days before Christmas, he began the journey with his wife and young son. No German of any prominence, only one man of inferior rank, accompanied him on this journey out of the kingdom. In need of provisions for so long a journey he besought aid of many whom he had helped in his happier days. Only a few, grateful either for past favors or compassionate for his present condition, afforded him any assistance. To this state of calamity and misfortune had he suddenly fallen from the very height of rank and affluence. There were at the same time other excommunicates who were hurrying to Rome with a most ardent desire to obtain absolution; but either from fear of the princes or, even more, of the pope, they would not let the king join them.

The winter this year was consistently violent and inclement. The Rhine, ice-bound, remained passable for pedestrians from the Festival of St. Martin (November 11) almost to the Calends of April. The vines in most places withered up, their roots snapped off by the cold. King Henry, on his way to Italy, celebrated Christmas in Burgundy at a place called Besançon. He was received here magnificently enough, considering his condition at the time,

[1] For Germany.

and was entertained by his maternal uncle, count William, who had very large and prosperous holdings there. His reason for veering from the right road off into Burgundy was that he ascertained that all the roads and approaches into Italy, commonly called passes, had been closed with guards by the dukes Rudolph, Welf, and Berthold for the very purpose of preventing his passage. After a proper observance of Christmas he set out from there and came to a place called Cinis. Here he met his mother-in-law and her son, Amadeus, a man of eminent authority, extensive possessions, and very honorable reputation in these parts. At his approach they received him with honor. Nevertheless, they refused to grant him an escort through their territory unless he paid them the five adjacent Italian bishoprics as the price of the journey. This the counselors of the king regarded as excessive and intolerable. But, since it was absolutely necessary for him to procure passage in any way that he could, and since they were unaffected by any ties of relationship or compassion for his misfortune, it was reluctantly arranged, after much negotiation, that they were to receive a certain province of Burgundy that was rich in all things as the price of his passage. Thus did the indignation of the Lord turn from him persons bound to him not only by oath and many benefices, but actual friends and relatives. . . His trouble in getting permission to cross was followed by another difficulty. The winter was very bitter and the mountains through which the passage lay, stretching far and wide with peaks reared up almost to the clouds, were encumbered with masses of snow and ice. Passage by horse or footman over that slippery and precipitous descent was impossible without great danger. But the anniversary of the day on which the king had been excommunicated was threateningly near and would permit no delay in the journey. He knew that, unless he were absolved from the anathema by this day, it was decreed by a general sentence of the princes that his cause be forever lost and his kingdom gone without hope of restitution. Accordingly he procured some of the natives, who were familiar with the country and accustomed to the rugged summit of the Alps, to go ahead and in every way possible mitigate the difficulties of the trip for his party. Under their guidance they reached the crest of the range with some difficulty, but the descent, precipitous and, as has been said, slippery with glacial ice, defied any farther advance. The men, however, were ready to brave all danger by strength. Now crawling on hands and feet, now leaning on the shoulders of their guides, staggering over the slippery places, falling sometimes, sliding more, and at a serious risk of their lives, they managed at last to reach the level land. The queen and the women in attendance on her were placed on the skins of oxen and dragged along by the guides in charge of the party. Of the horses, some were placed on certain contrivances, while the others were dragged along with their feet tied together. Many of them died while they were being dragged along, more sickened, while but few passed through the danger whole and unaffected.

When the rumor spread through Italy that the king was coming, that he had overcome the dangers of the mountains and was established within the confines of Italy, all the bishops and counts of the region crowded to him and received him with the greatest honor and magnificence as befitted a king. Within a few days he was surrounded by an innumerable host. For there were those who from the very beginning of his reign had desired this advent. Italy was constantly infested with wars, party strife, robberies, and assaults of various kinds on individuals. This and every other invasion upon the law and the rights of the many by the presumptuous few they expected him to correct with the royal censure. Then, too, it had been noised about that he was hastening in great anger to depose the pope. This also pleased many, for it would afford them the opportunity of obtaining fitting vengeance upon him who had so long suspended them from ecclesiastical communion.

Meantime, the pope was on his way to Germany. The princes who had met at Oppenheim had sent letters to him urging him to meet them at Augsburg on the day of the Purification of Saint Mary (February 2) to discuss the case of the king. Accordingly, in spite of the dissuasion of the Roman nobles who feared the uncertain outcome of the affair, he hastened his departure as much as he could in order to be there on the appointed day. His escort was furnished by the countess Matilda. . . . When he had started he learned unexpectedly that the king was already in Italy. At the urgence of Matilda, therefore, he retired into a certain highly fortified place called Canossa, to wait there until he had more carefully ascertained the purpose of the king's coming. He wished to know whether the king came to ask for pardon, or whether he was wrathfully seeking to avenge the excommunication by force.

King Henry, however, had a conference with the countess Matilda, and sent her to the pope, laden with prayers and promises. With her he sent also his mother-in-law, his son, likewise the margrave Azzo, the abbot of Cluny, as well as some of the princes of Italy who need not be mentioned. They begged the pope to absolve him from the excommunication and not rashly to place faith in the accusations of the German princes who were moved rather by the passion of spite than by the love of justice. When the pope heard this message he said that it was unfitting and quite contrary to ecclesiastical law to air the case of a defendant in the absence of the accusers. Nay, more, he told them that if the king were confident of his innocence he should lay aside every scruple of fear and trustfully present himself at Augsburg on the day on which the princes had decided to come together. There, when the charges of both sides had been heard, he would receive most righteous justice on every point, without prejudice or favor, according to ecclesiastical law. To this they answered that the king would never in the world evade a trial which he knew would be a most unassailable vindication and recommendation of his equity and innocence. But, they urged, the anniversary of the day on which the king had been excommunicated was drawing near, and the princes of the kingdom who had held aloof thus far pending the outcome of this affair were growing impatient. If he were not absolved before that day, according to Palatine law, he would be held unworthy of royal dignity and undeserving of any further hearing to prove his innocence. For this reason, they said, he seeks absolution so resolutely, and is ready to offer any form of satisfaction which the pope may demand in order only to be absolved from the anathema and to receive the grace of ecclesiastical communion. As for the charges which his accusers bring against him, he will be ready to make full answer, as if nothing had been done by this agreement, when and wherever the pope may ordain. Then, according to the pope's sentence, he will be ready to receive his kingdom again if he refute the charges, or resign with equanimity if his case is lost.

For a long time the pope refused to consider it, for he feared that the king was inconstant and of a disposition easily influenced by his immediate attendants. Overcome at last by the importunities of these zealous advocates as well as by the weight of their opinions, he said, "If he is truly penitent, let him give to our power his crown and other insignia of his kingdom as an evidence of truth and as an act of penance: and, after being so obstinate, let him profess himself unworthy of the kingdom." The envoys considered this too harsh, and they urged him strongly to temper his sentence and not utterly destroy a reed, already shattered, by the severity of his decision. Upon this exhortation he very reluctantly agreed that the king might come in person and, if he performed true penance for his admitted errors, the sin which he had committed by inflicting contumely upon the apostolic chair he might now expiate by obedience to it.

He came as he was ordered; the castle being inclosed by a triple wall, he himself was admitted within the inclosure of the second wall, while his attendants were left outside. There, his royal regalia laid aside and without any evidence of royalty or display of pomp, he stood as a humble penitent with bare feet from morning to night seeking the sentence of the pope. This he did on the next day, and again on the third. On the fourth he was finally admitted to the papal presence, and after much discussion on both sides he was at last absolved from excommunication on the following conditions. First, that at the time and place which the pope should designate, he should appear before the German princes assembled in general council and should answer the charges preferred against him. There, with the pope as judge, if so it seemed to expedite matters, he should accept his decision, retain his kingdom if he refuted the charges, or give it up with equanimity if the charges were proven and he was held unworthy of the throne according to ecclesiastical law. Second, that whether he retained or lost his kingdom, he should seek vengeance on no one for this trouble. Third, that up to the day when, after proper discussion, his case had been ended, he should wear no ornaments of royal elegance, no insignia of royal dignity; he should not by his own right do anything in the administration as he was wont to do; decide nothing which ought rightly to be considered; and, finally, he should levy no royal or public taxes except for the sustenance of himself and his immediate servants. Fourth, that all who had pledged loyalty to him by oath should meantime in the presence of God and men remain free and unhindered by the bonds of this oath and the obligations of loyalty. Fifth, that he should forever dismiss from intimacy with himself Robert, bishop of Babenberg, Oudalric of Cosheim, and others by whose counsel he had betrayed himself and his state. Sixth, that if the charges were refuted and he retained his kingdom, he should always be obedient to the Roman pontiff and comply with his decrees, and in accord with him stand forth as the worldly powerful co-operator in the correction of the abuses against the laws of the church which had by a pernicious custom grown up in the kingdom. Last, that if he falsely agreed to any of these conditions the absolution which he had so earnestly sought would be endangered; nay, more, he would be considered as already convicted and confessed. He should then seek no further audience to prove his innocence, and the princes of the kingdom, thereby freed from all religious scruples in regard to their oath, would create another king upon whom they could agree. These conditions the king accepted gratefully and promised with the most sacred assertions possible that he would observe all of them. And it was not a case of an acceptance of faith by one making rash promises, for the abbot of Cluny, though his monastic religion kept him from taking oath, interposed his faith before the eyes of the All-seeing God, while the bishop of Zeitz, the bishop of Vercelli, the margrave Azzo, and the other princes at the gathering confirmed by oath, over sacred relics, that the king would do as he had promised and would be led from his word neither by any temporary straits nor by a change in succeeding events.

When the excommunication was thus absolved the pope celebrated the solemn mass. When the sacred offering was ready he called the king and the rest of the people to the altar. Extending the body of the Lord with his hand, he said, "I have for some time received letters from you and your adherents in which you claim that I occupy the papal chair through the heresy of simony and that my life is spotted with various other crimes before as well as after I had received the episcopate, which, according to the canons, would have prevented all access to the sacred orders. This I could refute by the testimony of many suitable witnesses, both of those who are intimately acquainted with my career from the very beginning, as well as of those who are responsible for my elevation to the episcopacy. Yet, lest I seem to rely too much on human rather than on divine witness and in order to bring the whole scandal to short account before all, behold this body of the Lord which I am about to take. May it be for me this day the test of my innocence. May the Omnipotent God by His judgment either clear me of the crime charged against me if I am innocent or strike me with a sudden death if I am guilty." With these and other terrible words he prayed the Lord to be most just judge of his case and asserter of his innocence, and then he took part of the sacred wafer and consumed it. This he did freely while the people acclaimed aloud their praises to God and offered thanks for his innocence. Then, commanding silence, he turned to the king and said: "Do therefore, my son, if it pleases you, what you have just seen me do. The princes of Germany have for days confused our ears with their accusations. They heap a great multitude of crimes upon you for which they think that you should not only be suspended from all administration of public affairs, but from ecclesiastical communion also, and even from any intercourse in secular life whatever for all time. They are especially anxious to fix a day and place and have an audience accorded them for the discussion of the charges which they bring against you. And you know best that human judgments often vacillate, and that falsity is sometimes more persuasive than truth. An untruth adorned with ornaments of words, with suavity, and by the genius and fluency of eloquent men, receives a more welcome hearing than the truth ungraced with eloquence which is often despised. Since, therefore, I wish you good counsel, all the more since you have in your calamities sought the patronage of the apostolic chair as a suppliant, so do as I admonish. If you know that you are innocent and that your reputation has been assailed with false charges by your enemies in a spirit of calumny, take the remainder of this sacred wafer and thus free, in a moment, the Church from the scandal of God and yourself from the uncertainty of a long dispute. Then your innocence will be proved by God's witness, every mouth turned against you in scandal will be stopped, and, with me as your advocate and the most vehement maintainor of your innocence, the princes will be reconciled to you, the kingdom restored, and the storms of civil war, with which it has been so long harassed, allayed." The king, astonished at this unexpected situation, became very much embarrassed, looked around for excuses, and, drawing away from the multitude, he discussed with his friends how he might evade such an awful test, which was a matter of difficulty. When he had recovered his spirits he talked to the pope of the absence of the princes who had kept faith with him in his trouble; that without the accord of the accusers the effect of such a test would be destroyed, and that the incredulous would question a satisfaction rendered in the presence of the few here assembled. Therefore, he earnestly besought the pope to defer the whole matter to a general council where, while the accusers were gathered together and the accusations and the persons of the accusers were discussed according to the ecclesiastical law as the princes of the realm had proposed, he might refute the charges. With great dignity the pope granted his petition, and when the solemn mass was ended he invited the king to dinner. And when this was ended and he had instructed him carefully as to what he must observe, the pope dismissed him with kindness and in peace to the men who had so long remained outside the walls. Furthermore, he sent out the bishop of Zeitz, Eppo, before him to absolve from their excommunication those who had incurred it by indifferently associating with the excommunicate before his absolution, kindly warning them not to occasion any stain upon the communion just newly received.

39. *RESULTS OF THE INVESTITURE CONFLICT IN GERMANY* [1]

The aftermath of the Investiture Conflict has usually received little attention in the textbooks. These books emphasize the Concordat of Worms, it is true, in accordance with whose provisions the German kings surrendered the claim to invest bishops and abbots with ring and staff; and they show that in practice the Concordat signified in Germany the persistence of a certain amount of influence on the part of the monarch over ecclesiastical elections, while in Italy and the kingdom of Burgundy or Arles the clergy chose their own bishops and abbots. But of further results they generally have little to say.

Professor James Westfall Thompson, however, points out that as a result of the Investiture Conflict both the German bishops and the German feudal nobility made substantial gains in power at the expense of the monarch.

On September 8, 1122, a council met at Worms. The Concordat of Worms in 1122 distinguished between the spiritual and the temporal functions of bishops and abbots and instituted a double investiture, the Emperor investing the new incumbent with the fiefs and secular authority of the office, the Pope or his legate with the spiritual title and authority. The loaf was divided, apparently into equal portions. But the pope had the difference between a half loaf and no bread.

[1] J. W. Thompson, *Feudal Germany*. Chicago, The University of Chicago Press, 1928, pp. 157–159, 160, 161–162, 162–163, 163–164. Used by permission.

Yet the Concordat of Worms really settled nothing permanently, for the papacy soon claimed that the terms of the Concordat were only applicable to the rule of Henry V and that the church was not so bound to his successors. Neither Pope nor Emperor, as the future was to show, nor the German bishops, were satisfied with the halfway nature of the arrangement. At most it was only an armistice. It glossed the question; it did not determine it. The most that it proved was the temporary exhaustion of both combatants. It was too irrepressible a conflict to be settled by any half-measures. The real winner was the German episcopate, who in the preliminaries in 1121 had declared that they would make the right of imperial investiture their own. They kept their word only too well. For they made the claim for secular investiture not only the emperor's, but their own. The real Prinz-Bischof of Germany dates from this time. The episcopal lands became less church domains than fiefs. It is not long before we find the bishops boldly alluding to their episcopal lands as *terra nostra.*

The Concordat of Worms did not terminate the struggle between the Empire and the Holy See; it did not mark the ruination of the Holy Roman Empire; it did not destroy the Ottonian-Salian monarchy. Its terms were made neither by the German King nor the Pope, but by the German feudal princes. The German feudality were the arbitrators between Henry V and Calixtus II. The German clergy still remained dependent upon the Emperor. The crown still retained the right of eminent domain over church property, the right of proprietorship remained, and the bond which bound the clerical feudality to the crown as supreme proprietor was guaranteed in the article of the pact; the bishops were compelled to swear fidelity and to do homage; the heavy financial exactions long laid upon their lands were continued; the resources of the Staufer kings in the twelfth century were chiefly derived from the property of the Church.

The famous clause requiring the *presentia regis* for valid election and that requiring investiture before consecration, saved not only the honor, but the authority of the king. He could block the candidacy of a bishop who was displeasing to him. The great purposes for which Gregory VII had struggled were unfulfilled at Worms. Calixtus II renounced the pretensions of his predecessor.

What loss of power the German king suffered in 1122 redounded, not to the profit of the papacy, but to that of the German princes, whose influence henceforth was vital in episcopal elections. Hadrian IV recognized that the Concordat of Worms was merely a suspension of hostilities, not a victory for the Holy See, when he renewed the conflict under Frederick Barbarossa. . . .

The application of the Concordat of Worms varied in time and place according to the interest of politics and the obstacles or the support which it met. Lothar II was conciliatory; Frederick I, the opposite. The consequence was that conflicts over the election of bishops tended to throw a large amount of control into the hands of the canons, who often succeeded in eliminating outside influences in the choice, both imperial and papal. The Council of the Lateran in 1139 encouraged this practice as a means to extrude the secular factor in episcopal elections and the Lateran Council in 1215 made it general, saving always the confirmation of choice by the papacy. . . .

Under Frederick I the German church was the right arm of his power, the most effective instrument of his policy. The bishops were finally and permanently englobed in the German feudal system. Frederick I, when the bishops of Oldenburg and Halberstadt refused to do military service for him in Italy (1155), promptly seized their manors and annexed them to the fisc. . . . As to nominations to ecclesiastical dignities, while an appearance of election was pretended, actually Frederick I claimed the right to designate incumbents to vacant church offices; his control of ecclesiastical offices was complete and decisive.

As the result of his defeat by the Lombard communes at Legnano in 1176 Frederick I was compelled to renounce his grandiose purpose of establishing a powerful monarchy in North Italy at the Peace of Venice. But his power in Germany still remained undiminished. The fall of Henry the Lion in 1181 (whose alleged "treason" at Legnano is impossible of occurrence since the lay princes of Germany were not obliged to participate in Italian expeditions) and the brilliant diet of Mainz in 1184 are striking evidence of the abiding power of Frederick I. . . .

But the final victory of the Holy See over the Empire in the time of Innocent III was more owing to the civil conflict then raging in Germany than to the natural power of the papacy. With the fall of Henry the Lion in 1181 and the passing of the old duchies of the high feudal age, the ancient sectionalism which had often made the dukes protagonists of regional aspirations and sentiments passed away also. In its stead grew up the rank weed of feudal particularism, something ignoble and vicious, and unpossessed of those virtues of local pride and patriotism which, with all its faults, had been attached to the motives and the policy of the ancient duchies, now mutilated or destroyed. The ambitious and selfish feudal princes of Germany, lay and clerical, ruined the autonomy of the once glorious kingdom, and in so doing wrecked the Empire too. But the victory was not unto the Pope. The Fürsten demanded the right of investiture in their own territories. As princes the German bishops were as free of papal control in the thirteenth century as their predecessors had been in the eleventh and twelfth. The mastery of the emperors over the German church was destroyed, but the mastery of the papacy was not established in its room.

Certainly not the state nor yet the church was the ultimate winner in the great controversy. The real winners were the feudalized bishops and abbots and the German feudality. The princes, bishops and warlike abbots of Germany, with their worldly ways, their hard faces, their political interests, lords of church lands which were actually huge ecclesiastical fiefs, and the German feudality were the real victors in the war. The sources upon this subject are rich, varied, and unanimous. In the bitter warfare of the partisans both sides had pillaged wantonly. Probably there was not a bishopric or monastery in all Germany which was not despoiled at least once. . . .

40. *FREDERICK BARBAROSSA* [1]

The struggle between Empire and Papacy, of which the Investiture Conflict was one great phase, burst into flames again in the strife between the Emperor Frederick Barbarossa on the one hand and the Lombard towns and Papacy on the other. In his Holy Roman Empire *James Bryce, later Lord Bryce, at one time ambassador to the United States and author of* The American Commonwealth, *gives a clear and vivid account of this strife and shows us something of its significance.*

The reign of Frederick the First, whom the Italians surnamed Barbarossa, is the most brilliant in the annals of the Empire. Its territory had been wider under Charles, its strength perhaps greater under Henry the Third, but it never appeared in such pervading vivid activity, never shone with such lustre of chivalry, as under the prince whom his countrymen have taken to be one of their national heroes, and who is still, as the half-mythic type of Teutonic character, honoured by picture and statue, in song and in legend, through the breadth of the German lands. The reverential fondness of his annalists and the whole tenour of his life go far to justify this admiration, and dispose us to believe that nobler motives were joined with personal ambition in urging him to assert so haughtily and carry out so harshly those imperial rights in which he had unbounded confidence. Under his guidance the Transalpine power made its greatest effort to subdue the two antagonists which then threatened and were fated in the end to destroy it—the Papacy and the spirit of municipal independence in Italy.

Even before Gregory VII's time it might have been predicted that two such potentates as the Emperor and the Pope, closely bound together, yet each with pretensions wide and undefined, must ere long come into collision. The boldness of that great pontiff in enforcing, the unflinching firmness of

[1] James Bryce, *The Holy Roman Empire*. New York, The Macmillan Company, New edition, enlarged and revised throughout, 1926, pp. 167–181. By permission of The Macmillan Company, publishers.

his successors in maintaining, the supremacy of clerical authority, inspired their supporters with a zeal and courage which more than compensated the advantages of the Emperor in defending rights he had long enjoyed. On both sides the hatred was soon very bitter. But even had men's passions permitted a reconciliation, it would have been found difficult to bring into harmony adverse principles, theoretically irresistible, yet mutually destructive. As the spiritual power, in itself purer, since exercised over the soul and directed to the highest of all ends, eternal felicity, was entitled to the obedience of all, laymen as well as clergy; so the spiritual person, to whom, according to the view then universally accepted, there had been imparted by ordination a mysterious sanctity, could not without sin be subject to the lay magistrate, be installed by him in office, be judged in his court, and render to him any compulsory service. Yet it was no less true that civil government was indispensable to the peace and advancement of society; and while it continued to subsist, another jurisdiction could not be suffered to paralyze its workings, nor one-half of the people be altogether removed from its control. Thus the Emperor and the Pope were forced into hostility as champions of opposite systems, however fully each might admit the strength of his adversary's position, however bitterly he might bewail the violence of his own partisans. There had also arisen other causes of quarrel, less respectable but not less dangerous. The pontiff demanded and the monarch refused the lands which the Countess Matilda of Tuscany had bequeathed to the Holy See; Frederick claiming them as feudal suzerain, the Pope eager by their means to carry out those schemes of temporal dominion which Constantine's donation sanctioned, and Lothar's apparent renunciation of the sovereignty of Rome had done much to encourage. As feudal superior of the Norman kings of Naples and Sicily, as protector of the towns and barons of North Italy who feared the German yoke, the successor of Peter wore already the air of an independent potentate.

No man was less likely than Frederick to submit to these encroachments. He was a sort of imperialist Hildebrand, strenuously proclaiming the immediate dependence of his office on God's gift, and holding it every whit as sacred as his rival's. On his first journey to Rome he refused to hold the Pope's stirrup, as Lothar had done, till Pope Hadrian the Fourth's threat that he would withhold the crown enforced compliance. Complaints arising not long after on some other ground, the Pope exhorted Frederick by letter to show himself worthy of the kindness of his mother the Roman Church, who had given him the imperial crown, and would confer on him, if dutiful, benefits still greater. This word benefits—*beneficia*—understood in its usual legal sense of "fief," and taken in connection with the picture set up at Rome to commemorate Lothar's homage, provoked angry shouts from the nobles assembled in Diet at Besançon in Burgundy; and when the legate (afterwards Pope Alexander III) answered, "From whom, then, if not from our Lord the Pope, does your king hold the Empire?" his life was scarcely safe from their fury. On this occasion Frederick's vigour and the remonstrances of the Transalpine prelates obliged Hadrian to explain away the obnoxious word, and remove the picture. Soon after the quarrel was renewed by other causes, and came to center itself round the Pope's demand that Rome should be left entirely to his government. Frederick, in reply, appeals to the civil law, and closes with the words, "Since by the ordination of God I both am called and am Emperor of the Romans, in nothing but name shall I appear to be ruler if the control of the Roman city be wrested from my hands." That such a claim should need assertion marks the change since Henry III; how much more that it could not be enforced. Hadrian's tone rises into defiance; he mingles the threat of excommunication with references to the time when the Germans did not yet possess the Empire. "What were the Franks till Pope Zacharias welcomed Pipin? What is the Teutonic king now till consecrated at Rome by holy hands? The chair of Peter has given and can withdraw its gifts."

The disputed papal election that followed Hadrian's death produced a second and more momentous conflict. Frederick, as head of Christendom, proposed to summon the bishops of Europe to a general council, over which he should preside, like Justinian or Heraclius. Quoting the favourite text of the two swords, "On earth," he continues, "God has placed no more than two powers: above there is but one God, so here one Pope and one Emperor. Divine Providence has specially appointed the Roman Empire as a remedy against continued schism." The plan failed; and Frederick adopted the candidate whom his own faction had chosen, while the rival claimant, Alexander III, appealed, with a confidence which the issue justified, to the support of sound churchmen throughout Europe. The keen and long doubtful strife of twenty years that followed, while apparently a dispute between rival Popes, was in substance an effort by the secular monarch to recover his command of the priesthood; not less truly so than that contemporaneous conflict of the English Henry II and St. Thomas of Canterbury, with which it was involved. Unfrequently supported, not all Alexander's genius and resolution could have saved him: with the aid of the Lombard cities, whose league he had counselled and hallowed, and of the fevers of Rome, by which the conquering German host was suddenly annihilated, he won a triumph the more signal that it was over a prince so wise and so pious as Frederick. At Venice, which, inaccessible by her position, maintained a sedulous neutrality, claiming to be independent of the Empire, yet seldom led into war by sympathy with the Popes, the two powers whose strife had roused all Europe were induced to meet by the mediation of the doge Sebastian Ziani. Three slabs of red marble in the porch of St. Mark's point out the spot where Frederick knelt in sudden awe, and the Pope with tears of joy raised him, and gave the kiss of peace. A later legend, to which poetry and painting have given an undeserved currency, tells how the pontiff set his foot on the neck of the prostrate king, with the words, "The young lion and the dragon shalt thou trample under feet." It needed not this exaggeration to enhance the significance of that scene, even more full of meaning for the future than it was solemn and affecting to the Venetian crowd that thronged the church and the piazza. For it was the renunciation by the mightiest prince of his time of the project to which his life had been devoted; it was the abandonment by the secular power of a contest in which it had twice been vanquished, and which it could not renew under more favourable conditions.

Authority maintained so long against the successor of Peter would be far from indulgent to rebellious subjects. For it was in this light that the Lombard cities appeared to a monarch bent on reviving all the rights his predecessors had enjoyed: nay, all that the law of ancient Rome gave her absolute ruler. It would be wrong to speak of a rediscovery of the civil law. That system had never perished from Gaul and Italy, had been the groundwork of some codes or bodies of customs and the substance, modified only by the changes in society, of many others. The Church excepted, no agent did so much to keep alive the memory of Roman institutions. The twelfth century now beheld the study cultivated with a surprising increase of knowledge and ardour, expended chiefly upon the extracts from the classical jurists contained in the Digest of the Emperor Justinian. First in Italy and the schools of the South, then in Paris and Oxford, they were expounded, commented on, extolled as the perfection of human wisdom, the sole, true and eternal law. Vast as has been the labour and thought expended from that time to this in the elucidation of the civil law, it is hardly too much to say that in acuteness, in subtlety, in all the branches of the legal science and art which can subsist without help from historical knowledge and the methods of historical criticism, these so-called Glossatores have been seldom equalled and never surpassed by their successors. The teachers of the canon law, who had not as yet become the rivals of the civilian, and were accustomed to recur to his books where their own were silent, spread through Europe the fame and influence of the Roman jurisprudence; while its own professors were led both by their feeling and their interest to give to all its maxims the greatest weight and the fullest application. Men just emerging from barbarism, with minds unaccustomed to create and blindly submissive to authority, viewed written texts with an awe to us incomprehensible. All that the most submissive jurists of Rome had ever ascribed to their monarchs was directly transferred to the Cæsarean majesty who inherited their name. He was "Lord of the world," absolute master of the lives and property of all his subjects, that is, of all men; the sole fountain of legislation, the embodiment of right and justice. These doctrines, which the great Bolognese jurists, Bulgarus, Martinus, Hugolinus and others who surrounded Frederick, taught and applied, as matter of course, to a Teutonic, a feudal king, were by the rest of the world not denied, were accepted in fervent faith by his German and Italian partisans. "To the Emperor belongs the protection of the whole world," says bishop Otto of Freysing. "The Emperor is a living law upon earth." To Frederick, at the diet of Roncaglia, the archbishop of Milan speaks for the assembled magnates of Lombardy: "Do and ordain whatsoever thou wilt, thy will is law; as it is written, 'Quicquid principi placuit legis habet vigorem, cum populus ei et in eum omne suum imperium et potestatem concesserit.'" The Hohenstaufen himself was not slow to accept these magnificent ascriptions of dignity, and though modestly professing his wish to govern according to law rather than override the law, was doubtless roused by them to a more confident assertion of a prerogative so hallowed by age and by what seemed a divine ordinance.

That assertion was most loudly called for in Italy. The Emperors might appear to consider it a conquered country without privileges to be respected, for they did not summon its princes to the German diets, and overawed its own assemblies at Pavia or Roncaglia by the Transalpine host that followed them. Its crown, too, was theirs whenever they crossed the Alps to claim it, while the elections on the banks of the Rhine might be adorned but could not be influenced by the presence of barons from the southern kingdom. In practice, however, the imperial power stood lower in Italy than in Germany, for it had been from the first intermittent, depending on the personal vigour and present armed support of each invader. The theoretic sovereignty of the Emperor-king was nowise disputed: in the cities toll and tax were of right his: he could issue edicts at the Diet, and require the tenants in chief to appear with their vassals. But the revival of a control scarcely exercised since Henry IV's time was felt as an intolerable hardship by the great Lombard cities, proud of riches and population equal to that of the duchies of Germany or the kingdoms of the North, and accustomed for more than a century to a turbulent independence. For republican institutions and popular freedom Frederick had little sympathy. At Rome the people, stirred by the fervour of Arnold of Brescia, had renewed, but with larger ideas the attempt of Crescentius. The city had thrown off the yoke of its bishop, and a commonwealth under consuls and senate professed to emulate the spirit while it renewed the forms of the primitive republic. Its leaders had written to Conrad III, asking him to help them to restore the Empire to its position under Constantine and Justinian; but the German, warned by St. Bernard, had preferred the friendship of the Pope. Filled with a vain conceit of their own importance, they repeated their offers to Frederick when he sought the crown from Hadrian the Fourth. A deputation, after dwelling in high flown language on the dignity of the Roman people, and their kindness in bestowing the sceptre on him, a Swabian and a stranger, proceeded to demand a largess ere he should enter the city. Frederick's anger did not hear them to the end: "Is this your Roman wisdom? Who are ye that usurp the name of Roman dignities? Your honours and your authority are yours no longer; with us are consuls, senate, soldiers. It was not you who chose us to be rulers, but Charles and Otto that rescued you from the Greek and the Lombard, and conquered by their own might the imperial crown. That Frankish might is still the same: wrench, if you can, the club from Hercules. It is not for the people to give laws to the prince, but to obey his command." This was Frederick's version of the "Translation of the Empire."

He who had been so stern to his own capital was not likely to deal more gently with the rebels of Milan and Tortona. In the contest by which Frederick is chiefly known to modern Italy, he is commonly painted as the foreign tyrant, the forerunner of the Austrian oppressor, crushing under the hoofs of his cavalry the home of freedom and industry. Such a view is unjust to a great man and his cause. To the despot liberty is always license; yet Frederick was the enforcer of admitted claims; the aggressions of Milan threatened her neighbours; the refusal, where no actual oppression was alleged, to admit his officers and allow his regalian rights, seemed a wanton breach of oaths and engagements, treason against God no less than himself. Nevertheless our sympathy must go with the cities, in whose victory we recognize the triumph of freedom and civilization. Their resistance was at first probably a mere aversion to unused control, and to the enforcement of imposts less offensive in former days than now, and by long dereliction apparently obsolete. Republican principles were not avowed, nor were sentiments of Italian nationality appealed to. But the progress of the conflict developed new motives and feelings, and gave the cities clearer notions of what they fought for. As the Emperor's antagonist, the Pope was their natural ally: he blessed their arms, and called on the barons of Romagna and Tuscany for aid; he made "The Church" ere long their watchword, and helped them to conclude that league of mutual support by means whereof the party of the Italian Guelfs was formed. Another cry, too, began to be heard; hardly less inspiriting than the last, a cry that had been silent for thirteen centuries, the cry of freedom and municipal self-government—freedom little understood and terribly abused, self-government which the cities who claimed it for themselves refused to their subject allies, yet both of them, through their divine power of stimulating effort and quickening sympathy, as much nobler than the harsh and sterile system of a feudal monarchy as the citizen of republican Athens had risen above the slavish Asiatic or the brutal Macedonian. Nor was the fact that Italians were resisting a Transalpine invader without its effect. There was as yet no distinct national feeling, for half Lombardy, towns as well as rural nobles, fought under Frederick; but events made the cause of liberty always more clearly the cause of patriotism, and increased that fear and hate of the Tedescan for which Italy has had such bitter justification.

The Emperor was for a time successful: Tortona was taken, Milan razed to the ground, her name apparently extinguished. Greater obstacles had been overcome, and a fuller authority was for the moment exercised than in the days of Otto the Great or Henry the Third. The glories of the first Frankish conqueror were triumphantly recalled, and Frederick was compared by his admirers to the hero whose canonization he had procured and whom he strove in all things to imitate. "He was esteemed," says one, "second only to Charles in piety and justice." "We ordain this," says a decree: "Ut ad Caroli imitationem ius ecclesiarum statum reipublicæ incolumem et legum integritatem per totum imperium nostrum servaremus." But the hold the name of Charles had on the minds of the people, and the way in which he had become, so to speak, an eponym of Empire, has better witnesses than grave documents. A rhyming poet sings:

> "Quanta sit potentia vel laus Friderici
> Cum sit patens omnibus, non est opus dici;
> Qui rebelles lancea fodiens ultrici
> Repræsentat Karolum dextera victrici."

The Diet at Roncaglia was a chorus of gratulations over the re-establishment of order by the destruction of the dens of unruly burghers.

This fair sky was soon clouded. From her quenchless ashes uprose Milan; Cremona, forswearing old jealousies, helped to rebuild what she had destroyed, and the confederates, committed to what seemed an all but hopeless strife, clung faithfully together till on the field of Legnano the Empire's banner went down before the carroccio of the free city. Times were changed since Aistulf and Desiderius trembled at the distant tramp of the Frankish hosts. A new nation was arising, slowly reared through suffering into strength, now at last by heroic deeds conscious of itself. The power of Charles had overleaped boundaries of nature and language that were too strong for his successor, and that grew henceforth ever firmer, till they made the Empire itself a delusive name. Frederick, though harsh in war, and now baulked of his most cherished hopes, could honestly accept a state of things it was beyond his power to change: he signed cheerfully and kept dutifully the peace of Constance, which left him little but a titular supremacy over the Lombard towns.

At home no Emperor since Henry III had been so much respected and so generally prosperous. Uniting in his person the Saxon and Swabian families, he healed on the northern side of the Alps the long feud of Welf and Waiblingen: his prelates were faithful to him, even against Rome: no turbulent rebel disturbed the public peace. Germany was proud of a hero who maintained her dignity so well abroad, and he crowned a glorious life with a happy death, leading the van of Christian chivalry against the Musulman. Frederick, the greatest of the Crusaders, as St. Louis is the best, is among the noblest types of mediæval character in many of its shadows, in all its lights.

Legal in form, though in practice sometimes admitting the exercise of an almost absolute authority, the government of Germany was, like that of other feudal kingdoms, restrained chiefly by the difficulty of coercing refractory vassals. All depended on the monarch's character, and one so vigourous and popular as Frederick could generally lead the majority with him and overawe the rest. A false impression of the real strength of his prerogative might be formed from the readiness with which he was obeyed. For this was largely due to the tact which was happily united with his firmness. He repaired the finances of the kingdom, controlled the dukes, introduced a more splendid ceremonial, endeavoured to exalt the central power by multiplying the nobles of the second rank, afterwards the "college of princes," and by trying to substitute the civil law and Lombard feudal code for the old Teutonic customs, different in every province. If not successful in this project, he fared better with another. Since Henry the Fowler's day towns had been growing up through Southern and Western Germany, especially where rivers offered facilities for trade. Cologne, Treves, Mentz, Worms, Speyer, Nürnberg, Ulm, Regensburg, Augsburg, were already considerable cities, not afraid to beard their lord or their bishop, and promising before long to counterbalance the power of the territorial oligarchy. Policy or instinct led Frederick to attach them to the throne, enfranchising many, granting, with municipal institutions, an independent jurisdiction, conferring various exemptions and privileges; while receiving in turn their good-will and loyal aid, in money always, in men when need came. His immediate successors trod in his steps, and thus there arose in the state a third order, the firmest bulwark, had it been rightly used, of imperial authority; an order whose members, the Free Cities, were through many ages the centres of German intellect and freedom, the only haven from the storms of civil war, the surest hope of future peace and union. In them national congresses used, in the dark days after 1815, to meet: from them aspiring spirits strove to diffuse those ideas of Germanic unity and free self-government, which they had done much to keep alive. Out of so many flourishing commonwealths, four only were spared by foreign conquerors and faithless princes till the day came which made them again the members of a great and truly German state. To the primitive order of freemen, scarcely existing out of the towns, except in Swabia and Switzerland, Frederick further commended himself by allowing them to be admitted to knighthood, by restraining the license of the nobles, by imposing a public peace, by making justice in every way more accessible and impartial. To the southwest of the green plain that girdles in the rock of Salzburg, the gigantic mass of the Untersberg frowns over the road which winds up a long defile to the glen and lake of Berchtesgaden. There, far up among its limestone crags, in a spot scarcely accessible to human foot, the peasants of the valley point out to the traveler the black mouth of a cavern, and tell him that within Barbarossa lies amid his knights in an enchanted sleep, waiting the hour when the ravens shall cease to hover round the peak, and the pear-tree blossom in the valley, to descend with his Crusaders and bring back to Germany the golden age of peace and strength and unity. Often in the evil days that followed the fall of Frederick's house, often when tyranny seemed unendurable and anarchy endless, men thought on that cavern, and sighed for the day when the long sleep of the just Emperor should be broken, and his shield be hung aloft again as of old in the camp's midst, a sign of help to the poor and the oppressed.

41. *AN ELEVENTH CENTURY PILGRIMAGE TO THE HOLY LAND*[1]

Before the time of the Crusades there were many Christian pilgrimages to the Holy Land, the pilgrims being often led to undertake the arduous journey as penance for their sins. As Professor Dana Munro points out (The Middle Ages, *pp. 242–243*)*, it is known that in the eighth century there were at least 6 such pilgrimages, in the ninth century 12, in the tenth 16, and in the eleventh 117. Obviously these pilgrimages helped pave the way for the crusades.*

In the autumn of 1064 an exceptionally large expedition of pilgrims set forth from Germany under the leadership of some German bishops. In a scholarly essay based on original sources Professor Einar Joranson of the University of Chicago narrates the adventures of these pilgrims. Extracts from this essay are presented in the following selection.

From indirect evidence we learn that the preparations for the journey, particularly in the case of the bishops, had been elaborate. Not only were the prelates provided with many comforts which pilgrims as a rule disdained; but also they planned by an ostentatious display of wealth and magnificence

[1] Einar Joranson, *The Great German Pilgrimage of 1064–1065*. In *The Crusades and Other Historical Essays,* Presented to Dana C. Munro by his Former Students. New York, F. S. Crofts and Co., 1928, pp. 14–43 (condensed). By permission of author and publisher.

to impress their importance and dignity upon the minds of the peoples through whose lands their journey would lead. At the halting places their quarters were hung with dorsals and draperies; and the salvers and table vessels used at their sumptuous repasts were of gold and silver. Money was brought in plentiful supply by the wealthy; and the general equipment probably included large stores of victuals. That the baggage was conveyed by horses and mules, is certain; but it cannot be established that any of the participants were mounted. The hitherto prevailing opinion that some or all were furnished with arms, is contradicted by the sources and must be abandoned; we have evidence, direct as well as indirect, which conclusively proves that our pilgrims were *unarmed*. Since from the outset they appear to have formed one large body, it may be supposed that a time and point of ultimate departure had been agreed upon in advance; and we shall perhaps not err in assuming that the designated place of concentration was either Ratisbon or Passau.

Archbishop Siegfried, though he preceded the other prelates in rank, cannot be regarded as the real director of the enterprise. All the important sources testify that the dominant personality on the journey was Bishop Gunther of Bamberg. Gunther was of high birth and very affluent. By contemporaries who probably had personal acquaintance with him, he is described as a man of imposing stature and striking comeliness; though younger than his fellow-bishops, he so far surpassed them in mental and moral qualities and in intellectual accomplishments, that after he was dead he seemed to have been the "ornament and pillar of the entire realm." Such was his perfection in manifold virtues, continues the Annalist of Nieder-Altaich, that in his own time he had been rarely if ever excelled, and it was almost unbelievable that posterity would behold his equal. On the pilgrimage to Jersusalem this alleged superman became, chiefly no doubt by reason of his admirable physique, the cynosure of vulgar curiosity; around the places where he was lodged the inquisitive would gather in great throngs, much to the annoyance of the other bishops who, in order to terminate the nuisance, would often compel Gunther to go out and make public exhibition of his person.

Toward the middle of November, 1064, the pilgrims set forth from Germany. The passage through Hungary probably offered no serious difficulty, although Bishop Gunther later complained that the Magyars had proved faithless in service. But in Bulgaria, after the Morava River had been crossed, dangers from thieves and robbers became frequent. These troubles Lambert of Hersfeld attributes, obviously not without reason, to the lordly style in which the bishops traveled. He severely censures the pompous parade of episcopal wealth as a piece of temerity which might have subverted the whole enterprise had not divine mercy intervened. The barbarians, says

Lambert, came in troops from the towns and the fields to behold these illustrious men, whose foreign apparel and gorgeous equipment they regarded at first with curiosity and then with cupidity. We may believe that the barbarians thus affected included the Bulgars; for Gunther accuses that people of being stealthy pilferers. But a far worse enemy was encountered in the Uzes, who had recently penetrated into Bulgaria, Macedonia, and Thrace; before the unrestrained fury of these terrible nomads the pilgrims fled. Yet by the exercise of prudence and caution they were able at last to reach the city of Constantinople.

While Gunther intimates that he found the Constantinopolitans puffed up with Greek and imperial hauteur, the Annalist of Nieder-Altaich assures us that the pilgrims conducted themselves in a manner so estimable that the arrogant Byzantines greatly marveled at them. Upon Gunther they gazed as upon a great spectacle, refusing, however, to believe that he was a bishop; he was taken to be the king of the Romans who had assumed the disguise of a bishop because he could not otherwise have gone through those realms (the Saracen dominions are probably meant) to the Holy Sepulchre. After a sojourn of several days in the Byzantine capital our pilgrims moved on into Asia Minor, which then, it should be remembered, was still included within the boundaries of the eastern empire. Gunther's letter indicates that they suffered on this stage of the journey at the hands of the "Romanites . . . who raged with a ferocity exceeding that of all other humans and even animals." Yet, distressed though they were, our travelers ceased not to pursue their goal . . . (*and so passed from Byzantine into Saracen territory*).

. . . .

Continuing, not without sundry troubles and anxieties, on the journey southward the pilgrims reached Caesarea on Maundy Thursday, which in the year 1065 fell on March 24. The religious rites proper to the day were celebrated, and congratulations were exchanged in the belief that all perils had now been evaded; for it was computed that from Caesarea to Jerusalem was not more than a two days' journey. But on the morrow, *i.e.* Good Friday, March 25, between six-thirty and eight o'clock in the morning, just as they had passed beyond the village of Kafar Sallām (Capharsala) and were one day's journey or a little more from the city of Ramlah, suddenly they encountered a horde of Arabs. The news, swiftly broadcast, of the arrival of very distinguished men, had caused the Arabs to flock together from every direction, in large numbers and under arms, for the purpose of securing booty.

Probably these Bedouins did not expect to obtain what they desired without a struggle, and in order to secure treasure they were perhaps ready to resort to any extreme, yet it can hardly be doubted that they would have permitted the pilgrims to pass if the latter had promptly offered to surrender all their possessions. There is no evidence that any such offer was made. Lambert of Hersfeld tells us, however, that most of the pilgrims, mindful that they had solemnly dedicated their safety to God, refrained on religious grounds from using force and corporeal arms in self-defense. These non-resistants, it appears, were the first to be attacked. The Bedouins, obviously but mistakenly anticipating resistance, fell upon them "as famished wolves leap upon long-desired prey," massacring the foremost, prostrating and wounding the others, and utterly despoiling all of whatever they possessed. Among the wounded ones Lambert reckons Bishop William of Utrecht who, his arm almost crippled by blows, was left naked and half dead. But the Bedouins, once in possession of the booty, evidently paid no further attention to these harmless victims of their fury; those still alive (including Bishop William?) were permitted, and were able despite the maltreatment they had suffered, to proceed to Ramlah, a distance of at least one day's journey.

Meanwhile the other pilgrims, probably a rather large minority, had apparently become persuaded that the pious quest of the Holy Sepulchre did not, in a case of necessity, preclude forcible defense of life and property; and since this group included at least three of the wealthy prelates with their following, men who undoubtedly were anxious to preserve the treasure they had brought, it may be presumed that the decision to fight was largely due to their influence. Though these pilgrims like the non-resistants were unarmed, that fact did not discourage them; for they had observed that the locality through which they were then traveling, abounded in stones. Availing themselves of these, they hurled them at the Arabs in an attempt to impede their assaults. But with the enemy pressing incessantly forward, the pilgrims were at great disadvantage and soon found it necessary to seek shelter. Yielding ground little by little, they moved toward Kafar Sallām, the village which had been passed earlier in the morning and which now was not far distant. The retreat, perhaps not too orderly when it began, became in the end a precipitate flight, attended, we are told, by casualties so numerous and so miserable as to beggar description. The Annalist of Nieder-Altaich states that Bishop William of Utrecht was among those killed or wounded during this retreat; whereas Lambert, whose account is more detailed, includes William, as we have seen, among the non-resistants who had submitted to abuse and robbery at the first attack. In any case it is clear that William did not return with his fellow-bishops to Kafar Sallām.

Formerly a thriving village, Kafar Sallām at the time of which we are speaking was in all likelihood a deserted place. The pilgrims found here an unoccupied structure variously referred to as a *castellum* or an *atrium*. Apparently the *atrium* had a court, for it was inclosed by a wall with a gated entrance. The Annalist of Nieder-Altaich speaks of two stone towers, one of which may perhaps be identical with a certain *domus* which Lambert locates in the centre of the *atrium*. The *domus,* Lambert goes on to explain, had a rather lofty upper story (*cenaculum*) prepared, purposely as it were, to stand a siege; but the wall inclosing the *atrium* was so poor and weak that even without the application of force it might easily have crumbled of age alone.

With a not inconsiderable, though quite miscellaneous, body of followers Bishops Siegfried, Gunther, and Otto proceeded to occupy the *atrium* and its two towers. The ecclesiastics took possession of that tower which Lambert designates as the *domus*. In its upper story the bishops of Mainz and Bamberg with their clergy established themselves, leaving the lower story for the bishop of Ratisbon and the remaining clergy. At first it was hoped that the beasts of burden might also be brought within the walls. But the gateway proved too narrow to admit them, encumbered as they were with bulks of baggage; and by reason of the enemy's imminence, it was impossible to unload the carriers; consequently, horses and mules together with the effects and supplies they bore were lost. Yet the occupants of the *atrium* had by no means been utterly impoverished; they still retained not only their money and treasure—which, to judge from the magnitude of the efforts made respectively to gain and to retain possession of them, must have been very considerable—but also, it would seem, a goodly portion of ecclesiastical paraphernalia. They were, however, if we may trust our sources, totally devoid of victuals. Undaunted in their plight, our pilgrims closed the gates of the *atrium* and made ready to continue resistance; while the Arabs, after they had apportioned among themselves the captured horses, mules, and baggage, lost no time in resuming the attack with a vengeance.

The lay pilgrims, scurrying busily to and fro, tried bravely to keep the enemy at a distance and to defend the wall. Though at first they had to fight with whatever came to hand, chiefly stones and sticks, they were not long restricted to such primitive weapons. For on the one hand the Arabs, angered by resistance on the part of men they had supposed defenseless, surged vigorously forward and hurled a great cloud of missiles (javelins?) into the camp; on the other, the pilgrims, by pressing in upon the attacking enemy, frequently were able to wrench out of the hands of the Bedouins their shields and swords. As a result, the pilgrims became to some extent provided with regular arms and began to feel capable of more than mere defense of the wall; occasionally they dared sally forth from the gate, to engage their opponents in hand-to-hand combat. These sorties, which according to Lambert were uniformly successful and which probably proved somewhat costly to the Arabs, seem to have determined the latter to abandon their disorderly assaults and to proceed to a close investment of the *atrium;* by means of hunger and exhaustion, they would compel those to surrender whom it had proved impossible to subdue by force of arms.

The Arabs, whose hordes may have been swelled by late comers, by this time numbered according to the (possibly exaggerated) Christian estimate, something like twelve thousand men. In any case, they were sufficiently numerous to be able to relieve each other in carrying on the operations, and so to avoid giving respite to the beleaguered pilgrims. That these, lacking all the necessaries of life, would long bear up under the ceaseless labor of fighting, was not expected. In fact the struggle, which had begun on the morning of Good Friday, March 25, continued for at least forty-eight hours without intermission. The Arabs, it is said, gnashed their teeth like infuriated wolves who, with their prey in the gullet, are prevented from gulping it down; while the Christians, suffering though they were from hunger, thirst, and vigils, yet after the fashion of men facing death, forgot their present distress in an ardent effort to preserve their lives—and, we may add with Marianus Scottus, their money. Indeed, since the latter undoubtedly was the real bone of contention, it may be held that the lives of the pilgrims were endangered chiefly or perhaps only because they declined to give up their money.

After several days of fighting the besieged Christians resolved to treat with their enemies.

Resorting promptly to negotiation, the pilgrims, says Lambert, through an interpreter requested the privilege of (a conditional) surrender. Marianus Scottus tells us that they offered to give up all their money, save what was needed for victuals on the homeward journey. Whether a definite reply was given to this request, is uncertain; but we know that the Arabs agreed to a cessation of hostilities and that the leader, escorted by several sheiks, afterward proceeded to the *atrium*—ostensibly, adds the Annalist of Nieder-Altaich, to ascertain how much the Christians were willing to pay for their lives and the privilege of departure. Obviously the fact that the negotiations were to be concluded in the *atrium* was a great advantage for the pilgrims; and the subsequent events indicate that their leaders had from the outset clearly perceived this advantage and were fully prepared to exploit it. Probably the wealthy Gunther and his more or less opulent associates, in despite of the offer to surrender, had not yet given up all hope of saving their treasure.

Though the armistice was declared at approximately the third hour (ca. 8:00 A.M.) of Easter Day, the leader of the Arabs did not arrive in the *atrium* until about the ninth hour (ca. 2:00 P.M.). In the meantime he took measures to prevent a promiscuous dispersal of the anticipated booty. When he had learned that the pilgrims were ready to surrender, he sped at full gallop to his front ranks and discreetly moved the remainder of his forces back to a point from which the multitude would be unable to press its way into the stronghold. Then followed the selection of sixteen or seventeen distinguished sheiks who were to accompany their leader to the place of negotiation.

Armed with swords the sheiks entered the *atrium,* at whose opened gate the leader posted his son with a guard, to bar entrance to others; for there was danger that some Bedouin, greedy of plunder, might disobey orders and try to rush in after the sheiks. The manner in which the pilgrims managed their visitors clearly shows that they were acting in accordance with a skillfully devised plan. All the sheiks were not permitted to ascend to the upper story of the house or tower which contained the bishops. Nine had to remain in the lower story, where Bishop Otto of Ratisbon and his companions were lodged. The other seven together with the leader must climb a ladder to reach the *cenaculum.* Here they were greeted by a spectacle evidently calculated to impress upon them the high dignity of the persons with whom they were to deal. In the hall, which had been decked with the seemingly indispensable dorsals, draperies, etc., and which was filled with many knights, the sheiks found seated in state the "glorious" bishops of Mainz and Bamberg. In the latter, *i.e.* Gunther, the Arab leader promptly and correctly recognized the real director of the pilgrim hostilities. According to Lambert, Gunther began to plead with the Bedouin that having taken all the pilgrims had down to the last farthing, he permit them to go away empty-handed. This statement may or may not be true: but that Gunther now or at any other moment was ready to surrender his treasure, seems highly improbable. On the contrary, the sequel will show not only that Gunther himself had determined to apply *Faustrecht* to the solution of his problem, but that he and his companions had fully matured a plan whereby the sheiks would become the means of saving their treasure.

Gunther's alleged request, Lambert goes on to indicate, met no favor. The savage Bedouin, at once elated by apparent victory and irate over the not inconsiderable losses he had suffered during the recent fighting, was in no mood to entertain petitions however humble; he as conqueror would impose his terms on the vanquished. The attitude and intentions of the barbarian were made clear, we may believe, not only in words but also by a symbolical act which, with some variations, is described by each one of our three chief informants. Unrolling the linen turban, which in Arabic fashion was wound about his head, the sheik made of it a noose which he flung round the neck of the still seated Gunther. As he did this (perhaps before, or directly afterward), the Bedouin uttered something in Arabic indicating that by the capture of Gunther he held all the pilgrims in his power, that he would take all they had, and that he would hang Gunther and as many others as he chose. Marianus Scottus adds a threat to the effect that Gunther would be subjected to vampirism; and according to the (probably exaggerated) statement of Lambert, all the pilgrims were to be made victims of both vampirism and cannibalism.

Whatever he may have said, it is clear that by his insolence the sheik played into the hands of his enemy. Bishop Gunther quickly perceived in the ignominious treatment he had received, not only personal insult but profanation of a priest of Christ. No sooner had he learned from an interpreter the full meaning of the Bedouin's words, than he leaped forward from his seat and thrust his fist into the face of his would-be captor "with such force that by the single blow he hurled him in consternation headlong to the floor." Nay, more. Improving on the previous symbolism of his opponent, Gunther pressed his foot down upon the neck of the prostrate Bedouin and urged his comrades to action. The effect of this piece of episcopal daring was nothing short of electrical. So promptly came response to the bishop's summons, with such correctness and precision were his orders executed, that one cannot but conclude that every move had been planned in advance.

Acting upon directions from Gunther, clergymen and laymen alike fell upon the sheiks in the *cenaculum,* stripped them of swords and clothing, and bound them so tightly with their hands against their backs, that in most cases blood issued forth as the finger nails penetrated into the skin. After the sheiks in the lower story had been similarly fettered, all the laymen, vociferously summoning the "Creator of all things" to their aid, eagerly resumed arms, manned the wall again, and drove off the Bedouins who under the leader's son had been left to guard the entrance to the *atrium.* So completely, according to Lambert, had the unexpected success revived the strength and spirits of the previously outworn and discouraged pilgrims, that the Arabs, unable to conceive of any other reason for the new turn in the situation, concluded that their sheiks had been put to death. Infuriated, the members of the horde closed ranks and prepared by storm to force their way into the *atrium.* Bishop Gunther, however, had both anticipated this as an eventual danger and in good season taken measures which would effectively neutralize it. The naked and fettered sheiks had been exposed at that point on the wall where the hostile attack was expected to be most violent and the shower of missiles thickest: above each one stood an improvised executioner holding unsheathed in his hand the sword of the sheik, and ready if necessary to dispatch him. As the Bedouins charged forward they were warned by the interpreter in the service of the pilgrims that the sheiks would be decapitated if they did not desist from attack, a warning which was reinforced by imploring cries for consideration and mercy directed to the Bedouins by the sheiks themselves.

These supplications were effective at least with the sons and friends of the sheiks, who promptly did what they could with voice and gesture to stem the onslaught of their fellows. But on the question as to whether the lives of the sheiks were worth more than the booty, the members of the horde divided and presently fell to fighting, thus providing the pilgrims with a respite from hostilities—hostilities which, as the event proved, were not to be resumed.

Soon afterward, and probably before the close of Easter Sunday, there came to the *atrium* a messenger who brought the comforting news that a large Saracen force was on its way to liberate the besieged. The messenger had been dispatched from Ramlah by those pilgrims whose religious scruples against fighting had on the preceding Friday caused them to submit without resistance to attack and spoliation. Upon their arrival at Ramlah, the Saracen seat of government for the surrounding region, they had recited their woeful experiences to the governor and begged him to go to the relief and deliverance of their fighting brethren at Kafar Sallām. The emir, Mohammedan though he was, readily acceded to this request; for he reflected, says the Annalist of Nieder-Altaich, that if the pilgrims perished in such miserable slaughter no one would afterward come through that land for the sake of prayer, and in consequence he and his people would suffer serious loss. When the intelligence brought by the messenger was surreptitiously communicated to the Bedouins, these immediately abandoned all thought of continuing the siege and, departing each in his own direction, swiftly vanished from sight. Also, amidst the commotion and confusion which ensued in the *atrium,* it became possible for one of the captive sheiks, aided by a Saracen whom the pilgrims had employed as their guide, to effect his escape. So great was the resentment over this, that the pilgrims could hardly refrain from laying hands on the culprit through whose compliance the thing had happened.

At about the ninth hour (ca. 2:00 P.M.) of the following day, *i.e.* Monday, March 28, the expected governor arrived with a considerable army. Though he was pacifically received in the *atrium,* many of the pilgrims were at first inclined to doubt that one 'pagan" would undertake to prevent another from persecuting the Christians. Would Satan cast out Satan? From these anxieties they were soon relieved by the emir, who ordered the captives to be brought before him. After he had inspected the sheiks and listened to a detailed account of what had taken place, the emir is (by Lambert) said to have expressed gratitude to the pilgrims for the splendid service they had rendered in capturing these men; for they were most bitter enemies of the government, they had for many years infested the dominions of the caliph with assiduous devastations, and in battle they had often crushed large contingents endeavoring to subdue them. The sheiks were committed to guards instructed to preserve them alive for the "king of the Babylonians," *i.e.* Mustansir, the reigning though hardly ruling caliph of Cairo.

Having received a consideration of five hundred golden *bezants,* the emir escorted his protégés to Ramlah, where he and the townsmen forced them against their will to remain two weeks. But they were at length dismissed by the emir who, in order to eliminate further peril at the hands of robbers, arranged to have them conducted to Jerusalem by a guard of light-armed youths. Amid tears of joy and prayers of thankgiving the Holy City was finally entered on April 12; thirteen days were spent here, days marked by many devotions. With vows fulfilled the pilgrims departed rejoicing, and still under escort, toward Ramlah. Probably they had not even yet completely exhausted their treasure, for it is said that the Bedouins, multiplied in numbers and grieving because their booty had escaped them, lay in ambush at all the approaches to the highways. Fully aware of this danger, the pilgrims determined to avoid the land route through Palestine and to seek transportation by sea. Such was furnished by certain merchants whose identity cannot be definitely established. Having advanced the passage money, our pilgrims with the rise of a favorable wind boarded ship, probably at Jaffa, and after a prosperous sail landed safely on the eighth day in the port of Laodicea. Here they tarried for some days before setting out on the journey through "Licia" and Asia Minor.

Meeting frequently with great difficulties and often fatigued, no doubt, by the labor of travel on foot, they wended their weary steps homeward. There was gladness when after having trudged over roads that appeared interminable they reached at length the confines of Hungary and the banks of the Danube. But hardly had the pilgrims crossed the Danube when the joy of approaching the fatherland was dimmed. On the river bank Gunther fell on his knees to thank God that he had arrived thus far; for now he was certain that if death should overtake him before the journey's end, faithful hands would bear his body to Bamberg. Seriously ill, the bishop could proceed no farther than Oedenburg, where after having made confession to his three fellow-bishops and many other clergymen, and having received the sacrament, he died on July 23.

The great pilgrimage had ended with the premature death of its resourceful, valiant, and now widely mourned hero. Gunther, however, was but one of the many whose lives had been lost in this adventure. For "out of seven thousand, not two thousand returned"; and these came back "measurably attenuated in material resources."

The eleventh century has often been regarded as a period of transition from the peaceful pilgrimages of the early middle ages to the military expeditions of the crusading era; and scholars have sought to trace the transition process along two supposedly well-marked lines of development: (1) pilgrimages of the old type—*i.e.* unimportant journeyings of single individuals or of a few persons traveling together—while they had by no means ceased, were gradually being supplemented by enterprises of fairly large proportions, numbering hundreds and even thousands of participants; (2) because of the rise of new conditions along the routes leading to Jerusalem, these troops of pilgrims began to travel under arms and were prepared to defend themselves against possible attacks. Let it be admitted that the point first mentioned is fully validated by the testimony cited in its support. As much cannot be said for the second contention. Decisive evidence has never been adduced to prove that pilgrims, prior to the crusades, had begun to arm for defense. Establishment of the fact that the greatest pilgrimage of the eleventh century was made up exclusively of unarmed men, inevitably raises the question whether any pilgrimage in the pre-crusading period really was an expedition under arms. The need for detailed investigation of this larger problem is sharply signalized by the results of the present study.

We have seen that many of our pilgrims when attacked, refused for religious reasons to defend themselves; that these non-resistants were emulating the ancient pilgrim ideal, is clear. But it is also apparent that with the others this ideal was losing, if it had not already lost, its hold; pilgrims though they were, Gunther and his followers did not hesitate to fight when in their judgment it seemed advisable or necessary. But the fact that they had fought to save worldly treasure was so utterly out of harmony with the prevailing concept of the pilgrim that but a single chronicler had the courage even to suggest it. Carefully dissembling or ignoring this spiritually discomforting bit of history, all the other chroniclers who describe or mention the hostilities at Kafar Sallām are at pains to justify the pilgrims for having fought at all. These phenomena are not without interest; for do they not announce the advent of a new concept, one thoroughly familiar to the crusading epoch, that of the warrior pilgrim?

There is yet another consideration. The recent statement that "the origin of the Holy Wars was (in no small degree) due to the expansion of the Seljūq Empire," may perhaps not be an exaggeration; but to say that "as long as the Arabs held Jerusalem the Christian pilgrims from Europe could pass unmolested," is to ignore or impugn well established facts. That the pilgrims did *not* pass unmolested in the third quarter of the eleventh century, is proved by the enterprise above described and, apparently, by other evidence. The truth is that maltreatment of pilgrims in Palestine antedated, by many years, the Seljūq occupation of that land. Whether, as is usually assumed, the hardships were increased as a result of the establishment of Turkish domination, is a matter which, though questionable, cannot here be determined. In any case the fact remains that the outrages suffered by

Bishop Gunther and his companions at the hands of the Bedouins, constitute the most flagrant instance on record of the persecution of occidental Palestine pilgrims prior to the crusades. Perhaps such persecution did not of itself generate the crusading idea; but that it became one of several pretexts for the crusades and was employed, even in the Clermont address of Pope Urban II, as argument in justification of a military offensive against Islam, can hardly be doubted.

42. *THE FIRST CRUSADE: EXTRACTS FROM A CHRONICLE*[1]

One of the best sources for the history of the First Crusade is the Historia Hierosolymitana *of Fulcher of Chartres. Fulcher was a priest who himself went on the crusade and in October, 1097, became the chaplain of one of the leaders, Baldwin of Flanders. His account of the great movement is comparatively unbiassed.*

In the first of the two following selections is given a part of Fulcher's version of the famous speech of Pope Urban II at Clermont in southern France, appealing to Christians to take the cross and go forth to fight the infidel. This speech has been called "the most effective oration recorded in history." For other accounts of it the reader is referred to Professor Krey's excellent work on The First Crusade, *from which these two selections have been taken.*

In the second extract Fulcher tells how Baldwin of Flanders left the main army and went to Edessa, of which he became the ruler. Later, on the death of his brother, Godfrey of Bouillon, Baldwin became "King of Jerusalem."

I. The Summons to the Crusade

In all parts of Europe peace, goodness, faith, were boldly trampled under foot, within the church and without, by the high, as well as by the low. It was necessary both that an end be put to these evils, and that, in accordance with the plan suggested by Pope Urban, they turn against the pagans the strength formerly used in prosecuting battles among themselves. . . .

He saw, moreover, the faith of Christendom greatly degraded by all, by the clergy as well as by the laity, and peace totally disregarded; for the princes of the land were incessantly engaged in armed strife, now these, now

[1] August C. Krey, *The First Crusade. The Accounts of Eye-witnesses and Participants.* Princeton, N. J., Princeton University Press, 1921. (Translations by Professor Krey.) Used by permission.
I. The Summons to the Crusade. Fulcher of Chartres. (Krey, pp. 26; 29–30; 40–41.)
II. Baldwin takes Edessa. Fulcher of Chartres. (Krey, pp. 121–123.)

those, quarrelling among themselves. He saw the goods of the land stolen from the owners; and many, who were unjustly taken captive and most barbarously cast into foul prisons, he saw ransomed for excessive sums, or tormented there by the three evils, starvation, thirst, and cold, or allowed to perish by unseen death. He also saw holy places violated, monasteries and villas destroyed by fire, and not a little human suffering, both the divine and the human being held in derision.

When he heard, too, that interior parts of Romania were held oppressed by the Turks, and that Christians were subjected to destructive and savage attacks, he was moved by compassionate pity; and prompted by the love of God, he crossed the Alps and came into Gaul. He there called a council at Clermont in Auvergne, which council had been fittingly proclaimed by envoys in all directions. It is estimated that there were three hundred and ten bishops and abbots who bore the crozier. When they were assembled on the day appointed for the council, Urban, in an eloquent address full of sweetness, made known the object of the meeting. With the plaintive voice of the afflicted Church he bewailed in a long discourse the great disturbances which, as has been mentioned above, agitated the world where faith had been undermined. Then, as a supplicant, he exhorted all to resume the fullness of their faith, and in good earnest to try diligently to withstand the deceits of the devil, and to raise to its pristine honor the status of Holy Church, now most unmercifully crippled by the wicked.

. . . .

But the Pope added at once that another trouble, not less, but still more grievous than that already spoken of, and even the very worst, was besetting Christianity from another part of the world. He said: "Since, O sons of God, you have promised the Lord to maintain peace more earnestly than heretofore in your midst, and faithfully to sustain the rights of Holy Church, there still remains for you, who are newly aroused by this divine correction, a very necessary work, in which you can show the strength of your good will by a certain further duty, God's concern and your own. For you must hasten to carry aid to your brethren dwelling in the East, who need your help, which they have often asked. For the Turks, a Persian people, have attacked them, as many of you already know, and have advanced as far into the Roman territory, as that part of the Mediterranean which is called the Arm of St. George; and, by seizing more and more of the lands of the Christians, they have already often conquered them in battle, have killed and captured many, have destroyed the churches, and have devastated the kingdom of God. If you allow them to continue much longer, they will subjugate God's faithful yet more widely.

"Wherefore, I exhort with earnest prayer—not I, but God—that, as heralds of Christ, you urge men by frequent exhortation, men of all ranks, knights as well as foot-soldiers, rich as well as poor, to hasten to exterminate this vile race from the lands of your brethren, and to aid the Christians in time. I speak to those present; I proclaim it to the absent; moreover, Christ commands it. And if those who set out thither should lose their lives on the way by land, or in crossing the sea, or in fighting the pagans, their sins shall be remitted. This I grant to all who go, through the power vested in me by God. Oh, what a disgrace, if a race so despised, base, and the instrument of demons, should so overcome a people endowed with faith in the all-powerful God, and resplendent with the name of Christ! Oh, what reproaches will be charged against you by the Lord Himself if you have not helped those who are counted, like yourselves, of the Christian faith! Let those who have been accustomed to make private war against the faithful carry on to a successful issue a war against infidels, which ought to have been begun ere now. Let those who for a long time have been robbers now become soldiers of Christ. Let those who once fought against brothers and relatives now fight against barbarians, as they ought. Let those who have been hirelings at low wages now labor for an eternal reward. Let those who have been wearing themselves out to the detriment of body and soul now labor for a double glory. On the one hand will be the sad and poor, on the other the joyous and wealthy; here the enemies of the Lord; there His friends. Let no obstacle stand in the way of those who are going, but, after their affairs are settled and expense money is collected, when the winter has ended and spring has come, let them zealously undertake the journey under the guidance of the Lord."

. . . .

After this speech, those present were very enthusiastic in the cause, and many, thinking that nothing could be more laudable than such an undertaking, at once offered to go and diligently exhort the absent. Among these was the Bishop of Puy, Adhemar by name, who later acting as the Pope's vicegerent prudently and wisely led the whole army of God and vigorously inspired them to accomplish the undertaking. So, when those things which have been mentioned were determined upon in the council and unanimously approved of, and after the papal blessing was given, they withdrew to their homes to make known to those who were not present at the council what had been done. When these tidings were proclaimed throughout the provinces, they agreed under oath that the peace which was called the Truce should be kept mutually by all. Finally, then, many persons of every class vowed, after confession, that they were going with a pure intent whither they were ordered to go.

Oh, how fitting and how pleasing to us all to see those crosses, beautiful, whether of silk, or of woven gold, or of any kind of cloth, which these pilgrims, by order of Pope Urban, sewed on the shoulders of their mantles, or cassocks, or tunics, once they had made the vow to go. It was indeed proper that soldiers of God who prepared to fight for His honor should be signed and fortified by this fitting emblem of victory; and, since they thus marked themselves with this symbol under the acknowledgment of faith, finally they very truly obtained the Cross of which they carried the symbol. They adopted the sign that they might follow the reality of the sign.

It is evident that a good intention brings about the achievement of a good work, and that good work earns the soul's salvation. For if it is good to intend well, it is still better to accomplish a good work which has been planned. Therefore, the best thing one can do is to provide for the salvation of his soul by a worthy action. Let each one then plan good deeds, which by still more worthy action he will fulfil, so that he shall at length receive the never ending reward which he has earned. So Urban, a man prudent and revered, conceived a work by which the whole universe prospered. For he restored peace and re-established the rights of the church in their pristine condition. And with a lively determination he also made an effort to drive out the pagans from the Christian lands. Therefore, since he endeavored in every way to glorify everything which was God's, almost all voluntarily submitted themselves to his paternal direction.

II. Baldwin Takes Edessa

But when we had traversed a day's journey from there and were now not more than three days from Syrian Antioch, I, Fulcher, withdrew from the main army with Count Baldwin, brother of Duke Godfrey, and turned towards the region of the province which is to the left.

Baldwin was indeed a very fine knight, who sometime before had left the army. With his men he had very boldly taken the city called Tarsus of Cilicia from Tancred, who, with the consent of the Turks, had already sent his men into the city. Leaving guards in it, Baldwin returned to the army. So, trusting in God and in his own strength, he collected a few soldiers and set out towards the Euphrates; and he there took many towns both by force and by strategy. Among those which he captured was a very rich one called Turbezel. The Armenians who dwelt there gave it up peacefully to him; and many others became subject to him.

Since his fame had circulated far and wide, the prince of the city of Edessa sent a delegation to him. Edessa was a most celebrated city and most fruitful in the products of the earth. This city is in Syrian Mesopotamia, about twenty miles beyond the above mentioned Euphrates, and about a hundred or a few more miles from Antioch. Baldwin was asked by the Duke to go there, and to agree that they should be mutual friends as long as they both should live, that they should be like father and son. And if by chance the Duke of Edessa himself should die, Baldwin should immediately come into possession of all his land, just as if he were his own son. Since he had no son or daughter, and since he was unable to defend himself against the Turks, this Greek wished himself and his land to be defended by this Baldwin, for he had heard that both he and his soldiers were most brave fighters.

As soon as Baldwin had heard this offer, and had been persuaded of its truth by the oath of the deputies from Edessa, he set out with his little army of about eighty knights and crossed the Euphrates. After we had crossed this river, we went on very hastily all night, and, very much afraid, we passed between the Saracen forts, leaving them on either side of us. When the Turks in the fortified town of Samosata had heard this, they set ambush for us along the way by which they thought we would go. But the following night a certain Armenian most hospitably entertained us in his castle and warned us to guard ourselves from the ambush of the enemy. Wherefore, for two days we remained concealed in this place. But the Turks, wearied by such delay, on the third day, rushed down in a sudden onslaught from their place of hiding and, with flags flying, ran before the stronghold in which we were; and the booty which they found there in the pastures they seized before our eyes. We went out against them; but because we were too few, we were unable to contend with them. They shot arrows, but wounded none of us. However, they left in camp one of their men killed with a lance. His horse was kept by the one who unhorsed him. Then the pagans left, but we stayed there. The following day we resumed our journey and passed in front of the Armenian forts. When they heard that we were going to defend them from the Turks, under whose yoke they had for so long been oppressed, it was wonderful to see how they advanced to meet us, humbly and for the love of God. They carried crosses and banners, and they kissed our robes and our feet.

(February 20, 1098.) At length we reached Edessa where the aforesaid Duke of the city and his wife, together with the citizens, gladly received us; and what had been promised by Baldwin they fulfilled at once. After we had delayed there for fifteen days, the citizens wickedly plotted to kill their prince because they hated him, and to set up Baldwin as ruler over the land in his place. This was suggested; and it was done. Baldwin and his men were much grieved that they were not able to obtain mercy for him. As soon as Baldwin had accepted as a gift from the citizens the principality of this man who had been wickedly murdered, he began a war against the

Turks who were in the country. Often he conquered, either killing or taking them prisoners. However, it happened, also, that many of our men were killed by the Turks.

I, Fulcher of Chartres, was chaplain for the same Baldwin. . . .

43. CHRISTIANS AND MOHAMMEDANS IN THE HOLY LAND[1]

It is natural to take it for granted that Christians and Mohammedans, whenever they came in contact with each other, were always at odds and usually engaged in conflict. Professor Dana C. Munro of Princeton University, however, distinguished historian and authority on the Crusades, shows that in the Holy Land Christians and Mohammedans were often on excellent terms, worked and played games together, went hunting together and sometimes even intermarried.

The term crusade, when pronounced, arouses in our minds the thought of a holy war. We picture the crusaders as devout warriors, full of fanaticism, waging incessant strife against the infidels. The latter we think of as equally fanatical, engaged in a Jihad, a holy war of extermination, against the Christians. These ideas are derived originally from the works of the contemporary chroniclers, both Frankish and Mohammedan. The crusaders who wrote the chronicles were usually members of the clergy and were interested chiefly in depicting the victories and defeats of the soldiers of the cross. They represented the kings as indefatigable warriors. They regarded the slaughter of the Mussulmans as a pious duty. The Moslem chroniclers foster the same idea, for, in speaking of the Franks, they repeat constantly, "May Allah curse them!" Thus has been formed the belief in the fanaticism of both Christians and infidels, which we find reflected in the pages of Wilken, Michaud, and most of the earlier writers on the crusades.

But when we extend our study to the laws of the Kingdom of Jerusalem, to the legal documents which were the result of their daily activity, to the coins which were struck by the Christian and Muslim princes, to the accounts of the travelers who visited the Holy Land while under the Frankish rule, to the books written by the Armenian and Greek contemporaries, we obtain an entirely different picture. We find but slight indications of a fanatical spirit on either side. We see the Christians and infidels in constant and friendly intercourse. We learn that each respected the other, that each

[1] Dana C. Munro, *Christian and Infidel in the Holy Land,* in *The International Monthly,* vol. IV (July–December, 1901), pp. 690–692, 693–694, 696–698, 701–702, 703–704, 726–728, 728–730, 732–733, 740–741. Used by permission.

was ready to learn and to copy such customs as seemed advantageous, and, finally, that they trusted one another.

On re-reading the chronicles, with this additional knowledge and with greater care, the second view is confirmed. Military achievements, it is true, form the main substance of the narrative, but whole years are passed over without a comment, because the author found no congenial material to record. And although he wrote mainly of warfare, frequently it was a strife not against the infidel, but against the co-religionist. Furthermore, in many instances Christian and Mussulman fought side by side against either Christians or Mussulmans, as the interests of the moment determined. Involuntary expressions of admiration for the enemy occur frequently, especially in the Arabic historians. Gradually the impression is formed that their constantly recurring "May Allah curse them!" is merely a stylistic phrase, and has but little meaning. Müller was right when he wrote, "The whole of the Christians, as of the Mohammedans, were really in earnest only twice; the former in 1099, the latter in 1187. On the first occasion, the Franks took Jerusalem from the Mohammedans; on the second, the Mohammedans recaptured it from the Franks; and with this the history of the religious wars, properly speaking, was ended."

We are apt also to mistake the motives of the Christians. In discussing the causes of the crusades, almost all historians, until recently, have laid the main stress upon the religious characteristics of the age. We have been taught that the men in the West, especially at the beginning of the movement, were inspired by a feeling of fanaticism, by a spirit of asceticism, which led hundreds of thousands to offer themselves eagerly for service in the cause of Christ. Undoubtedly, religious enthusiasm was one of the causes. No great movement in the Middle Ages can be fully explained without an understanding of the part which religion played in the lives of the people. But, lately, specialists have felt that this explanation was inadequate. There has been a more or less conscious tendency to return to the standpoint of Heeren, who explained the crusades as primarily a colonizing movement. He argued that they were very similar to the migrations of the Normans which resulted in building up colonies and states in Southern Italy. Kugler stated the case even more strongly. His words were, "Among specialists in medieval history, it is an accepted fact that the crusades were to a great extent the result of economic causes, and that they belong to the general history of colonization."

This point of view receives additional confirmation when we study the preliminaries of the first crusades. Pope Urban II, in his speech at the Council of Clermont, used every argument which he thought would attract men to undertake a crusade. In particular, according to Robert the Monk, he dwelt upon the advantages to be secured by the conquest of Jerusalem.

"This land which you inhabit," he said, "is too small for your large population; it does not abound in wealth; and it furnishes scarcely food enough for its cultivators. . . . The land [*i.e.* the Holy Land] is fruitful above all others, like another paradise of delights." It is to be noted that Urban took it for granted that the Holy Land would be held by the conquerors.

. . . .

The regulations which were made upon entering the enemy's country show the purpose of the chiefs. Each one was to possess any city in which he was the first to plant his banner. As Raymond of Agiles complained, "Each one wished only the greatest possible advantage for himself and thought not at all of the common good." Baldwin and Tancred, as soon as they reached Cilicia, endeavored to make conquests for their own profit. When the former was offered the opportunity of ruling in Edessa, he abandoned promptly all farther participation in the expedition against Jerusalem. On the death of his wife, he married almost immediately an Armenian princess, in order to make his position as ruler of Edessa more secure. The progress of the main army was impeded constantly by the quarrels which arose concerning the ownership of individual cities which had been conquered. After the capture of Antioch, for instance, farther advance was delayed for a long time by the quarrels which arose about the possession of this and other cities. In fact, the leaders showed such an evident desire to neglect the conquest of Jerusalem, in order to obtain possession in the more wealthy Syria, that the common people rebelled and forced the nobles to continue the march. Before Jerusalem was conquered the leaders attempted to decide to whom it should be given.

After the great victory over the Egyptians near Ascalon, in 1099, the city itself was lost to the Christians, because Count Raymond was determined he would have it or else no one should. Duke Godfrey demanded it as a part of his possessions. In consequence of their strife, Ascalon, which had been on the point of surrendering, was not captured. A little later, the mutual hostility of Raymond and Godfrey had the same result in the case of Arsuf, which Raymond had almost succeeded in capturing. In the following years, whenever any one secured a foothold anywhere, he attempted immediately to extend his possessions. Aid was obtained from the Genoese and Venetians by grants of quarters in cities to be captured in the future. Repeatedly, lands not yet conquered were given to the Church. Baldwin in the early years of his reign styled himself "King of Asia and Babylon," a title which is indicative of a purpose to make further conquests.

In the pursuance of this policy of conquest, the coast cities were captured, much of the interior country was covered with the castles of the crusaders, and the natives were reduced to subjection. Then the most important problem which confronted the Franks was the maintenance of their rule over an alien, mixed population far more numerous than themselves, which was separated from them by the barriers of religion, language, and customs. To any one who has been accustomed to think of men in the Middle Ages as narrow, intolerant, and bigoted, their conduct is very instructive. They realized that if they wished to be successful, they must secure the good will of the natives. They were intent mainly on extending their colonies and increasing their commerce. They were forced by their position to depend, to a great extent, upon the services of the natives, Christian and infidel; and, consequently, in spite of the objections of the fanatical, most of the leaders endeavored to conciliate the inhabitants of all races and creeds.

. . . .

The inhabitants whom they found in the Holy Land were of various races and creeds. The largest element in the population was composed of the Syrians,—Christians who spoke Arabic and used the Greek liturgy, but who were nominally subject to the Roman Church. They were for the most part agricultural laborers or artisans. Closely connected with the Syrians were the Maronites, who were renowned for their skill as archers, and who formed one of the most useful portions of the Frankish infantry. The Jacobites and Nestorians appear to have been the most civilized of the native Christians. They had excellent schools and were well-versed in the knowledge then common in the Orient. The Armenians were especially numerous in the North and were renowned for their bravery. They had welcomed the crusaders, "who," as Matthew of Edessa wrote, "came to break the chains of the Christians, to free from the yoke of the infidels the holy city of Jerusalem, and to tear from the hands of the Mussulmans the consecrated tomb which received a God." They joined eagerly in fighting the Mussulmans and were the most important allies of the Franks. The Greeks or Griffons formed a considerable part of the population, especially in the North. Finally there were a few Georgians or Iberians.

Of the non-Christian natives the Arabs and Turks were the most prominent. The civilization of the former was far superior to that of the Franks. The Turks were not very numerous. They had but recently obtained possession of the land and were for the most part soldiers; they were of little or no importance for cultivating the land or in commerce. Besides the orthodox Mohammedan there were Druses, Nosairis, or Ansarians, Bathenians, or Ismaelians, and Bedouins.

Of Jews and Samaritans, Benjamin of Tudela, who was in the Holy Land about 1165, enumerated 2,500 or more in the account of his travels, and it is probable that he was speaking only of the heads of the families. They were employed mainly in dyeing and glass-making.

The Europeans in the Holy Land were styled collectively Franks, but under this designation were included Frenchmen, Normans, Italians, Lothringians, and Provençals, not to mention the other nations which were less numerously represented. In the early decades of the twelfth century, the men from the North,—the Lothringians at Jerusalem, the Normans at Antioch,—were the most numerous, and under their leadership the conquests were made. Later the Provençals and Italians became the dominant party; they were more interested in trade, and did not care to make any conquests which would not be profitable. The Southern nations mixed more readily with the native populations, and, as their offspring, we find a large number of half-breeds, the so-called Pullani.

From this brief enumeration the great diversity of peoples and creeds is evident. This very diversity caused all to become less narrow-minded, more tolerant. Furthermore, when differences arose between the representatives of two nations, the Germans and Frenchmen, for example, each party sought allies on all sides, regardless of race or creed. In this way national differences were becoming constantly less important; a cosmopolitan feeling, if we may be allowed to use a much abused phrase, arose. As is indicated by the existence of the class of Pullani, the Franks became intimately associated with the native Christians; and we have already spoken of the aid furnished by the Maronites, Armenians, and Turcopoles in warfare. But it was not merely with the Christian natives that they were associated; they entered into fully as close an intimacy with the Saracens.

. . . .

But the intercourse was not wholly, or even generally, of a hostile character. The Franks were brought into constant and friendly relations with the Muslims in the pursuits of peace. All of their lands had to be cultivated by the native farmers, and many of these were Mohammedans. Frequently, the Christian lord was surrounded almost exclusively by the Muslim population. As the latter understood farming much better than the Franks, the crusaders soon learned to depend upon them. Through the commerce the Christians and infidels were brought into close connection. The Genoese, Pisans, Venetians, and others had taken part in the crusade chiefly for the purpose of advancing their trade. All of the Franks were compelled to depend upon the Mohammedans for some of the necessities of life. Syria had enjoyed a very extensive commerce before the crusades, and many of the cities carried on a very considerable caravan trade. Consequently, friendly relations were established, from the very beginnings, with the most important Moslem centres of commerce. In 1099, almost as soon as Jerusalem had been conquered, a firm peace was established with Ascalon, which controlled the commerce between

Egypt and Syria, and with Damascus, which was important for the overland caravan trade.

The necessity of protection for individuals when traveling also led to much friendly intercourse. It was a common practice for a leader on either side to request a safe conduct from his adversary for any one who wished to travel either for business or for pleasure. This was seldom violated. Ousâma's autobiography furnishes several instances of such safe conducts and of the ease with which they were granted. Ousâma obtained one from Baldwin III when he wished his wives and children to travel through the Christian territories. In this instance, Ousâma charged Baldwin with having caused the wreckage of the vessel on which his family had taken passage, in order to obtain the booty; but he stated, also, that Baldwin at once sent on his wives and children in safety and gave to them five hundred pieces of gold for their journey. On another occasion, a Christian knight visited Ousâma's father, simply out of curiosity, in order to see the man who had struck a memorable blow. Tancred, indefatigable warrior as he was, exchanged safe conducts with his foes, and made use of their hospitality for his followers.

The Franks frequently found it necessary to seek the aid of the natives in the arts and industries. Their houses were built after Oriental models. Their palaces and churches were decorated by the Greek and Arab artists. The dyeing and glass-making, as has been already noted, were in the hands of the Jews. In their dress they copied the Oriental forms, because they found them better suited to the country. At their feasts and festivals the Muslim dancing girls were in great demand, in spite of the opposition of the Church.

. . . .

The superior knowledge of medicine and of the natural sciences possessed by the Arabs caused some of the Franks to distrust them greatly. The crusaders frequently attributed any sudden death to poison. They believed, as in the account quoted from Jacques de Vitry, that the Arabs had the ability to administer poison that did not effect the system at first, but that would work after a given time, which might be a week, a month, or a year. The death of Godfrey, of Tancred, and of other knights was imputed by some to poison administered by the infidel. Ousâma ridicules a Frank who tried to collect the value of a horse from the Arab of whom he had bought it more than a year before, because the horse had suddenly died. The Frank thought it must have been poisoned before the sale had been made.

. . . .

In their amusements Christians and infidels mingled very readily. During the truces, the two frequently engaged in jousts and proved one another's skill in horsemanship, in the use of the lance, in the wielding of the sword, and in the hurling of the spear. All, even the knights of the religious orders, entered with zest into these friendly rivalries. Both Christian and infidel were extremely fond of hunting and falconry. A long section in the Assizes is devoted to the laws concerning the latter subject. Ousâma, in his autobiography, devoted many pages to accounts of hunting experiences and to the art of falconry. The crusading leaders took their hunting dogs and falcons with them as a matter of course when they set out on the holy war. As the close proximity of the enemy exposed both parties to constant attack, hunting agreements were made by which each might hunt in security on disputed territory. Gifts of dogs and hawks were interchanged, and friendships were sometimes formed because of the mutual interest in breeding hunting animals.

Children on either side were often given as hostages and thus obtained a knowledge of both civilizations. Sometimes they were sent to the castle of a noble who professed the opposite faith, simply to be educated, just as the sons of knights in the West were sent to serve as pages. Ousâma told of such an offer made to him by one of his Christian friends, who said: "Oh, my brother! I am going home and I should like, with your consent, to take your son with me (the boy was then fourteen years old). He will see our knights, he will then learn wisdom and chivalry. When he comes back, he will be an intelligent man." Ousâma was much hurt at the implied slur upon his own countrymen, but courteously veiled his resentment, and alleged as a reason for his refusal, that the boy's grandmother was too fond of him to part with him. The Frank then desisted from his request, saying that he had no desire to cause sorrow to the grandmother.

As shown by the letter of Fulk of Chartres, quoted later, intermarriages between the members of the two religious faiths were not unknown. In addition, Christian women taken as slaves by the Muslims frequently became the mothers of future warriors, who were generally well disposed towards the Christians. The Franks, with natural egotism, thought that Nur ed-din derived his ability and valor from a Christian mother. Many romantic tales concerning the fortunes of Christian maidens and their children were current in the crusading States, and were interwoven into the popular songs of the day.

Another means of bringing about intercommunication between Christian and infidel was the possession of common places of worship. Jerusalem, as is well known, was a holy city to both. The Muslims made pilgrimages to the so-called Temple, which they believed to be the place from which Mohammed had started on his famous night-journey. They had learned from their Christian neighbors to honor certain images. One statue of the Virgin in a small village near Damascus was reverenced by both Moslem and Christian, who visited it in order to be healed of their diseases. In Egypt the fig-tree which had offered its fruit to the Virgin, and the spring in which she had washed the clothes of the infant Jesus were honored by the followers of both religions.

These associations and the points of similarity between the two religions caused many a debate. As the Mohammedans were often more learned and better skilled in dialectics than their Christian opponents, the latter sometimes found themselves silenced, if not convinced. Not frequently Christians became renegades and passed over to the Moslem faith, especially in times of disaster and danger, when it seemed as if Islam had proved itself the superior and, consequently, the true religion. Less frequently the reverse happened. But after the victory at Ascalon, in 1099, some of the Mohammedans adopted the faith of the conquerors, and there were converts on many other occasions. At the siege of Acre, in the third crusade, when the inhabitants feared that the city might be taken at any moment, many begged for baptism. . . .

In the laws we find the Syrians . . . the ones best treated and most highly regarded by the legislators. It was important to the Franks to win the favor of a class of inhabitants who were devoted to agriculture and commerce, and who were very numerous. According to the few statistics given by William of Tyre and Raymond of Agiles, there were 100,000 Syrians in Lebanon and the district about Tripolis alone. From the history of Jerusalem proper a few examples will serve as illustrations. Godfrey was renowned for governing equally well Syrians, Greeks, and Franks. Baldwin I summoned native Christians to repeople Jerusalem, and granted important commercial privileges in the city to Syrians, Armenians, Greeks, and even Saracens. The Syrians were especially favored by the Franks at all times. They were protected in the ownership of property, they were admitted to all the rights which the citizens possessed, they were allowed to maintain their own courts, and in the Frankish courts they were allowed to testify against the Franks.

This same regard for the feelings of the natives is shown very clearly in the coins struck by the Christian princes. Baldwin I at Edessa, that is, in 1099 or 1100, coined money representing himself with a cross in his hand and a Greek emblem, "Baldwin, servant of the cross." All of the Frankish rulers in the North used Greek legends. This was a device to make their money circulate more readily among the natives, who were accustomed to use the Greek language. Tancred went one step farther when he was prince of Antioch. He not only used a Greek legend, but was represented as wearing a turban. One of his coins is very interesting. One side Christ is represented with a nimbus, on the reverse the legend in Greek is "the Grand Emir Tancred." In the Kingdom of Jerusalem the Venetians soon obtained the privilege of minting the money, on condition of paying a tax of fifteen percent to the King. The coins which they struck were the so-called "besans saracénats," that is, the Saracenic besants. These had Arabic inscriptions, usually a text from the Koran, and were an almost exact imitation of the common Arabic coins. In fact, in all the European collections of coins they were for a long time classed as Mohammedan coins. It was formerly one of the great problems in numismatics to explain the non-existence of any coins of the Latin Kingdom of Jerusalem. Many coins struck by Christians in the Holy Land are still erroneously supposed to be Arab coins. In the thirteenth century, some Christians were wounded in their conscience by the minting of such coins with the Muslim religious texts. Pope Innocent IV forbade it under penalty of excommunication. Saint Louis forced a modification, so that a Christian legend replaced the Muslim text, and a minute cross was inserted in an inconspicuous place. But the Arab letters were still retained for the legend, in order not to shock the feelings of the natives with whom they wished to carry on commerce.

. . . .

The travelers among the Mohammedans had to pay what the Arabs considered a very moderate toll on entering the Christian territories. But this was not levied upon merchants, because they paid on their wares. In the period just before the capture of Jerusalem, in 1187, the most important merchant in Syria was an Arab who had his agents in all of the Christian cities. Almost all of the great industries remained in the hands of the Syrians or Jews, while the Mediterranean commerce was in the hands of the Italians and Provençals. This again caused very intimate relations between the Christians, infidels, and Jews. How close the relations were and how early they were formed is shown by the enthusiastic words of Fulk of Chartres, who took part in this first crusade, and afterwards became a native of the Holy Land. "We men of the West have become Orientals. He who was a Roman or a Frank is now a Galilean or Palestinian. He who was from Rheims or Chartres is now a Tyrian or Antiochian. We have already forgotten the places of our birth; to most they are either unknown or unheeded. Some possess already their own houses and servants as if they had inherited them from ancestors; others have already married, and not, indeed, a woman of their own country, but a Syrian or an Armenian, sometimes even a baptized Saracen." Continuing, he says that they had acquired property so that the poor man had grown wealthy and the landless knight had become the lord of a city. The different languages were used in common by invaders and natives, and each trusted the other. He who had been a foreigner was now a native. Daily their relatives and parents were deserting all their former possessions and were following them to the Holy Land. Why should any one who had met with such good fortune in the East return to the West? God wished to make them all wealthy.

An equal toleration was shown in matters of religion. In the Church of the Holy Sepulchre, the Greek priests, although they were regarded as heretics, were allowed to officiate in the services with the Latin priests. The biblical lessons were read and explained first in Latin and then in Greek. In the Norman principality of Antioch a similar policy was followed. The Greek patriarch was allowed to retain his position, and only after his death was a Latin patriarch elected. A Jacobite patriarch, although he was a heretic, was ordained by the Latin bishops. Throughout the possessions of the Franks, the Mohammedans were allowed to have mosques in Christian cities and to worship publicly.

From another source, some of the Syrians and men of other nations, especially the Jews, gained great advantage. Each Italian colony of merchants in the Frankish cities formed a Commune whose territory and members were inviolable and independent. Each administered its own affairs and used its own laws. Because of the advantages which could be gained by the employment of the natives, the consuls, who were the heads of the Communes, admitted some of them to a participation in its privileges. In this way they escaped much of the taxation and were judged by their own laws.

. . . .

In conclusion, it is necessary to indicate briefly the causes of the check given in 1187, and of the final destruction of the promising Christian colonies. The great and ever present obstacle which prevented the success of the crusaders as colonists, and a cordial association between the two peoples, was the fanaticism of the war-party among the Franks, and especially of the newcomers. For there were always two parties in the Latin Kingdom; one wished to wage incessant war against the infidel, the other desired to maintain peace with the Mussulmans and to live on terms of friendship with the natives. The latter was generally more powerful, as has been indicated above, but at any time it was possible that some rash act of an adventurer might precipitate a general war. Such was the fatal attack upon the Saracen caravan made by Reginald of Châtillon, which aroused Saladin to vengeance, which caused the capture of Jerusalem, which led to the third crusade.

For a few years both crusaders and Mussulmans were thoroughly aroused. Cruel and bloody deeds, such as the slaughter of Muslim captives at Acre, embittered the minds of the contestants. But even these had little or no lasting effect. After the departure of Richard the Lion-Hearted from the Holy Land, and after the death of Saladin, religious enthusiasm died out on both sides and the position of the Christians improved. The latter gradually regained many of their former possessions. Cordial relations were reëstablished. It seemed probable that the Frankish colonies would again prosper and that the fusion of the various races would continue. By the diplomatic crusade of Frederick II, the holy city itself was restored to the Christians, and the Mohammedans were closely associated with them in many mutual interests. In spite of the opposition which his conduct aroused on the part of the patriarch and clergy, most of the Franks acquiesced in his arrangements, because they realized that friendly relations with the Muslim princes were essential to their prosperity.

But, in 1244, one of the great inundations of a barbarous race from the interior of Asia swept over Palestine and Syria. Everywhere it wrought ruin and destruction. For a time, the Franks were able to hold the walled cities, especially those on the seacoast, but gradually their position became untenable, and they were compelled to withdraw from the Holy Land. After an existence of nearly two centuries the last of the Frankish colonies was destroyed.

44. *SIZE AND OWNERSHIP OF GENOESE SHIPS IN THE TWELFTH AND THIRTEENTH CENTURIES*[1]

Historians are more cautious than they used to be about attributing too much to the influence of the Crusades. A careful historian would not now assert, for example, that the remarkable development of the Mediterranean trade of the Italian cities in the twelfth and thirteenth centuries was due entirely to the Crusades. The Italian cities had a flourishing commerce with the Mohammedans of Spain, Egypt and Tunis, regions in which no Crusades, in the commonly accepted sense of the term, were conducted. Nevertheless it may be asserted without fear of contradiction that the Crusades stimulated considerably the trade of the Italian cities and among other things influenced an increase in the size of sea-going vessels, since ships had to be made larger to provide adequately for the transportation of men, horses and provisions to the Holy Land.

Historical scholarship is under a debt of gratitude to Professor Eugene Byrne, who through painstaking study of manuscript sources has shed much light on the twelfth and thirteenth century commerce of Genoa, one of the most flourishing of the Italian coast cities of that time.

The size and capacity of the thirteenth century ships are surprisingly large. The dimensions of the ships built in Genoa for St. Louis, or if already on the

[1] Eugene H. Byrne, *Genoese Shipping in the Twelfth and Thirteenth Centuries.* Cambridge, Mass., The Mediaeval Academy of America, 1930, pp. 9-21. Used by permission.

water and leased or sold to him, fall somewhat short of those of the largest Venetian ship offered to the king, which had a length over-all of 110 feet, and a maximum beam of 41 feet, according to Jal's reckoning. The largest Genoese ship, the "Paradisus," he reckons at slightly over 83 feet. One of the largest vessels built in Genoa for St. Louis carried four ship's boats (three being the usual number) of which the greatest was equipped with fifty-two oars. The largest of these vessels were equipped for the carriage of one hundred horses in addition to crusaders and their attendants, with a door at the stern for entrance. Such vessels accommodated at least a thousand passengers when engaged in an ordinary voyage. The suspicion with which modern historians, with some justification, regard round numbers given by mediaeval writers may in this instance be brushed aside. I have found a Genoese document of the year 1248, in which one of the owners of a ship, the "Oliva," states explicitly that he has already sold eleven hundred places (*plazas*) on that vessel presently bound for Syria. That the "Oliva" was not of extraordinary size is shown by the fact that she carried seventy-five mariners in addition to officers and servants, whereas some Genoese ships of the period required as many as a hundred. It should be observed that of a thousand or more passengers the great majority would be pilgrims and for each pilgrim the space considered sufficient was very small. In Marseilles it was fixed by law, and Genoese vessels would naturally be forced to meet the custom of the rival port. When engaged in a trading voyage such crowded conditions would not be tolerated by the merchants nor would the requirements of merchants' cargoes permit such numbers on board. In view of these figures one may read with some tolerance the statements that Richard the Lion-Hearted on his crusade met with Saracen ships carrying fifteen hundred men. Unfortunately no figures giving size and capacity of twelfth century Genoese ships have survived, but conditions in the years of the third crusade may have justified the construction of some vessels as large as those in use in the thirteenth century.

It is more difficult to reckon the cargo capacity of those vessels when devoted to trade alone. Naturally the contracts with St. Louis for transports fail to state the burden. Moreover in the many contracts in the Genoese archives between groups of merchants and the owners of a ship chartered for a trading voyage, the merchants do not always contract for the entire cargo space but only for the major portion thereof, leaving the owners free to use or sell the balance to other merchants. However, we fortunately have a contract covering the cargo of one of the largest and most famous of the Genoese merchant vessels of the mid-thirteenth century, sailing year after year to the East, the "Paradisus Magnus," said to have been the flag ship of St. Louis. In 1251 she was about to sail for Tunis and thence, if the merchants chose, to Syria, manned by one hundred mariners. The merchants agreed that for the voyage from Tunis to Genoa, if they decided not to go to Syria, they would give the owners a cargo of 8000 *cantaria,* equivalent to 600 tons, dead cargo weight. This figure probably represents the maximum burden of Genoese ships in this period. It is greater than the estimate of the maximum burden of Venetian ships for this period given by Sombart as 480 tons, and let it be observed, offers an interesting comparison with the known burden of Spanish, Dutch and English merchant vessels engaged in the transoceanic trade of the sixteenth century, listed by the same authority as 600 to 800 tons. It should be noted, however, that such a cargo might not have been carried on the longer, more hazardous voyage to the Levant, since the contract above mentioned specified that if the vessel went to Syria the cargo carried must conform to the law of Genoa; perhaps the cargo of ships sailing from Genoa to the Levant was already regulated and limited by Genoese law, as we know from the laws themselves was the case in the next century. Yet it is apparent that the maximum size and capacity of mediaeval ships was considerably larger than has hitherto been supposed.

. . . .

Proprietary interest in shipping underwent an interesting transformation in this period as a result on the one hand of the increase in the size and cost of the ships, on the other hand of the enlarged opportunity for profit from investments in trading vessels. In that period after the middle of the twelfth century when the sources enable us first to observe the details of commercial operations, the relatively small ships then in use were owned either by individuals alone or in simple partnership with a few others, and were operated in person by one or more of the owners. With few exceptions the ship-owners were not men of high commercial or financial position, and did not participate to any appreciable extent in the overseas trade, but devoted their efforts to the sailing and management of the ships as a source of profit. In other words, they were not merchants, except incidentally, but shippers; skipper and ship-owner were in the main identical, and distinct from the merchant class in their prime activities. This is the case without exception in the ownership of the smaller vessels engaged in trade with nearby regions. In the ownership of the larger ships engaged in trade across the sea either to North Africa or to the East, there are few exceptions; one finds a few merchants of note owning and operating their own bottoms,—Solomon of Salerno the rich Jew, a Vento, a Picamiglio, a Castagna, a Streiaporco, Bisaccia, among scores of men owning and operating ships but otherwise cutting no figure in trade. In these same years, the first and second decades of the second half of the twelfth century, the situation with respect to ownership begins to change: one notes the first traces of fractional ownership soon to be characteristic of all Genoese shipping. In 1156 the owner of a ship trading to Palermo contracts loans of two merchants and offers each as security, *quarterium unum navis mee.* About the same time Solomon of Salerno and Marchio Castagna, on the eve of the latter's departure for Spain, made a formal statement of the property of their partnership which was to be actively renewed after Marchio's return, consisting chiefly of dye-wood, pepper, plumes, and bezants; but Marchio stated "that of the revenue of a quarter of the ship which he and Amico Vacca took to Alexandria, a fifth is in the aforesaid common account of him and Solomon. And so for the collection of all these and of the rest of the revenue he has appointed Solomon in his place . . . in confessing that another fifth of the revenue of that quarter is Guglielmo Pietro Nanfi's . . . to whom he has transferred it." There is here illustrated the division of ownership into convenient fourths, then for purposes of alienation by sale or otherwise into fractions of a fourth, leading shortly to ownership expressed in terms of very small fractions of a ship. The operation of the ship is carried on by one or more of the several owners; skipper and owner are soon no longer distinct from the merchant who, eager for gain, readily acquires partnership in a vessel engaged in trade. The next step is logical and follows quickly in the period of high commercial prosperity opening with the last years of the twelfth century and continuing through most of the thirteenth,—the systematic organization of the ownership of vessels into shares, called *loca* in Genoa.

This system of ownership by shares, arising from the growing demand for shipping necessary for the rapidly expanding commerce, met that demand advantageously. The risk of loss, the *risicum,* an ever present factor in the minds of the investors and particularly potent in the molding of mediaeval commercial institutions, was divided among many investors who were at the same time enabled to participate in the possible profits of several ships with proportionately smaller risk of loss and greater surety of profit. While heavy investors in trade, including the entire merchant class, were thus enabled to participate in the profits of shipping, lesser individuals, men, women and minors also found here an encouragement for the investment of their money across the seas, all with relative safety in view of the divided risk. Ownership by *loca* characterized the entire field of Genoese shipping until about the middle of the thirteenth century, when the accumulation of vast fortunes by families and individuals and the increasing security of overseas trade made it no longer so imperative; it then partially gave way to a different type of ownership to be discussed later. For more than half a century, however, the system of *loca* in its various aspects presents an interesting picture of investments.

Loca in ships of all sizes and types were owned, bought and sold, pledged, hypothecated, given in *accomendatio* as freely in Genoa as merchandise of any sort. Men and women from all ranks in society owned shares; members of a family pooled their resources and those of minor wards to purchase shares, individuals sometimes owning a mere fraction of a *locum*. *Loca* were regarded as particularly good security for one of the favorite forms of investment across the sea, the sea loan (*foenas nauticum*) which permitted a high interest, 20 percent. to 50 percent. in view of the risk, and which was repaid only if the ship arrived safely at the prescribed destination. In the trade with the Levant, for example, the loans on shares in the first half of the thirteenth century were as important as any form of investment therein. In the hands of merchants they offered a ready means of raising money by loan to purchase goods in Genoa before departure or abroad in a trading port. Investors who remained at home were able to participate in the profits of foreign trade at high potential rate with a minimum risk of loss, and without effort. The effect as a stimulus to trade and to shipping is incalculable, but must have been very great.

The number of *loca* in a single ship is often given by an owner when selling or pledging his own share, and varies from sixteen to seventy. Search for a document showing the disposition of shares at the time of construction of a vessel has been fruitless, but enough evidence exists to prove that the number of *loca* in a ship was the same as the number of mariners required to man the vessel of a certain type. A lawsuit, involving the ownership of shares in a vessel sold in Syria, occurred in Genoa in 1224. In the mass of testimony from owners, ex-consuls in Syria, and common seamen, one of the latter who had been employed on the ship, was asked how he knew there were twenty-six *loca* in the ship. He replied "that he had heard it said on the said ship and he saw there twenty-six mariners and that for each *locum* there was one mariner and well he knew that Guglielmo de Rampono had two *loca* in said ship because he himself had heard this said by Guglielmo and by the scribe of the ship and that the same Guglielmo fed two mariners on said ship at his table, namely him and another and I heard it said by the scribe of the ship that Guglielmo alone was to carry us as expenses for two *loca*." In another instance I find a receipt for 89 bezants given "for the expenses and wages of two mariners which fell upon me to pay for two shares which I hold in the ship." It is evident that the shares were equivalent in number to the mariners aboard, were registered by the scribe of the ship . . . in his record wherein he charged the expenses of operating the vessel per *locum* in order that the profits might be reckoned and paid per *locum* to the share-holders on completion of the voyage. In fact this may have been required by law; in Barcelona the builders of a ship in partnership were required, on beginning construction, to specify how many shares the vessel would have, and such may have been the law or the custom in Genoa. It would be simple enough to arrange for subscriptions of investments in *loca* from the very beginning in that case. The close connection between share-holders and mariners appears also in one of the few fragments of Genoese sea-law of the thirteenth century. The law provides that if some shares in a ship are sold (abroad?) and some are retained by their original owners, the mariners who pertain to the latter, must remain on the ship and perform the services contracted. Those mariners who pertain to the shares sold must serve the owners of those shares on another ship if they acquire an interest therein, unless released from their contract or unless their food is withheld. If the shareholders do not buy shares in another ship the mariners must remain with the vessel on which they sailed, and may be required to do so by the sellers of shares unless the purchasers were Saracens. On the other hand, if the mariners have been hired and are being fed in common by the owners as a group, division of the mariners in case of sale of shares must be made by lot according to the shares in the ship. The mariners were paid for a certain term or for a certain voyage. It is evident that frequently the share-holders were active participants in the voyage as merchants; if not, they placed their shares in the hands of others who were going on the voyage, one of whom might act as *patronus* in command of the voyage. Owners of several shares are found entrusting two *loca* to one merchant, one *locum* to another, while merchants about to depart on a voyage assemble under their direction many shares to be administered by them for a portion of the profits, usually one fourth, in *accomendatio,* as they would assemble money for investment in trade. In fact in the thirteenth century shares in ships were handled as freely as any other form of personal property, and with the same elastic treatment as capital. They were regularly pledged as security for loans with which to put the ship in commission, to pay mariners' wages, to purchase goods for export, or to meet other obligations in Genoa before departure. Shares in a ship when bought and sold or given in *accomendatio* vary in value according to the state of her equipment at the time. One finds shares in a certain ship sold, for example, at £12 *sol.* 10 each but shares in the same vessel given in *accomendatio* after the ship has been provisioned and manned with a crew are valued at £70. By the middle of the century the Genoese banks were owners of *loca* which they entrusted to agents exactly as individual investors were accustomed to do, to be sold, leased, or operated for profit on freight as opportunity offered. I have one example of the owners of the shares in a ship entrusting them all to the mate (*nauclerius*) employed by them to manage the vessel in which he owned shares; one fourth of the profits were to be his *pro naucleria,* but if they leased the vessel to others, and the mate found employment on another ship, he agreed to place the salary (*naucleriam*) received therefrom to the credit of their ship, the profits of which would be apportioned to the share-holders, of whom he was one.

After the middle of the thirteenth century I find few references to *loca.*

By that time the accumulation of capital in the hands of individual investors, of family combinations, of fairly permanent associations in trade, and of organized banking houses, had increased to such an extent that it was possible for smaller groups of men safely to build, own, and operate their vessels profitably without division into many *loca*. In 1246 and again in 1268 Genoese ship-building received a remarkable stimulus from the requirements of St. Louis for his crusades. On both occasions the royal agents entered into contracts with Genoese ship-owners, and with the commune itself, for the sale and lease of scores of ships to the French king. Many of the leading families in Genoa, many groups of prominent merchants, pooled their capital in vast amounts to build new ships, to recondition vessels already on the water, in order to supply the royal demands. For the king's first expedition, two Genoese of wide experience in maritime operations, Ugo Lercario and Jacopo di Levanto, on being appointed admirals to the king, formed a *societas* for two years duration for the combination of all their resources on the basis of equal division of the profits. They entered into many agreements with owners of ships in Genoa, for the sale or lease of vessels to the French authorities at the best prices obtainable with an occasional allowance of 50 marks to be used at their discretion by way of bribe. From the documents it is impossible to discover whether all the many new vessels constructed were owned by a wide number of holders of *loca,* or by a relatively small group of individuals. When scores of individuals agree each to build a ship of fifty mariners to be leased to the king at £4000 *tur.* each, and when a group of three men agrees to build twelve *taridae,* each with two masts, one hundred and fifty oars, stalls for twenty horses, requiring twenty mariners as a crew, one is inclined to believe that the current practice of ownership in *loca* may have been generally resorted to on the occasion of St. Louis's first crusade, and that in most cases the men forming contracts with the royal agents offered shares for subscription or purchase. On the occasion of St. Louis's second expedition however, the Genoese ship-builders shrewdly required a cash payment, amounting usually to more than half, when the contract was drawn, with a promise that the balance would be paid within a specified time, eight to forty-five days, after delivery of the vessel at Toulon or Aigues Mortes. With such amounts in hand it is probable that small groups of capitalists formed associations to finance the construction and equipment of the vessels. The stimulus given Genoese ship-building by St Louis was very great, his specifications down to the smallest details of equipment, even to carpenter's tools and kitchen utensils, were explicit. The effect on shipping and all allied industries is incalculable; the need for materials, especially masts, was so great that the Genoese stipulated that they be allowed to fetch timber from the royal forests in France free of tolls. In this activity in ship-building the system of ownership by *loca* appears to give way gradually to ownership by small groups of wealthy capitalists whose resources were increasing enormously in the second half of the century.

So pervasive had been the system of *loca* in what was one of the most important fields of capitalistic endeavor, and so familiar was it to every class of Genoese society for more than half a century that one is tempted to conclude that it may have exercised a significant influence upon financial operations of a different and wider type of cooperation, such as the *maone* of Ceuta and of Chios, which in turn were preliminary steps toward the creation of that triumph of Genoese finance, the Bank of St George.

45. *THE TOWNS AND THEIR STRUGGLE FOR EMANCIPATION* [1]

The origin of the medieval towns is a subject on which no one can speak with much assurance, because it is very difficult and often impossible to tell how certain towns emerged from the mists of an unknown past. Two French historians have, however, added much to our knowledge of cities in the ninth and tenth centuries. They have also shed new light on the manner in which a large number of towns freed themselves from the control of nobles, bishops, kings, dukes, and counts. Although in the following narrative they have naturally devoted themselves largely to the cities of medieval France, they have by no means ignored the towns of neighboring countries.

The history of the towns and of urban civilization during the first centuries of the middle ages is little known; indeed it would be truer to say that it is almost entirely unknown. The meager documents which these times have left us touch only the greater political events, the history of kings and of the more prominent characters; as to the fate of the people, the anonymous masses, they give us but rare and vague ideas. Nevertheless, though explicit statements are lacking, we may see in part what was the lot of the urban groups and of the individuals who composed them.

The Roman Empire bequeathed to the middle ages a goodly number of towns. Of these the most important by reason of population, wealth, and rank, were the cities. There were about one hundred and twelve such towns in ancient Gaul. Other towns, called *castra,* were simply fortified places. The cities, which for a long time had enjoyed a considerable degree of freedom, possessed municipal institutions; but this régime, under oppressive action of

[1] A. Giry and A. Réville, *Emancipation of the Medieval Towns.* Translated and edited by Frank Greene Bates and Paul Emerson Titsworth (*Historical Miscellany* Edited by E. W. Dow). New York, Henry Holt and Co., 1907, pp. 1–6, 8, 9–12, 16–17, 18–19, 28–29, 31–33. Used by permission.

the fisc and of an overwhelming centralization, was in full disintegration as early as the fourth century, even before the invasions had precipitated the fall of the Empire. In the anarchy which followed the arrival of the Barbarians, nothing remained standing of all this structure, for no one was interested in preserving it. The Roman municipal régime expired.

What, then, became of the cities? In most of them a certain personage soon distinguished himself among the inhabitants and gained over them an undisputed preëminence: this was the bishop. He was no longer simply the first priest of his town, he was its lord. As early as the end of the seventh century, perhaps before, Tours was under the rule of its bishop. Thus it was that most of the old Roman cities became, in the middle ages, episcopal seigniories. This was the case with Amiens, Laon, Beauvais, and many others.

All, however, did not have the same fate. Some, in consequence of wars, or of partitions, passed into the hands of lay princes. Angers belonged to the court of Anjou, Bordeaux to the duke of Aquitaine; Orleans and Paris were directly under the king. Elsewhere, beside the old city where the bishop ruled, there sprang up a new town, the bourg, which was under another lord, lay or ecclesiastical: thus at Marseilles the city was under the bishop, and the town under the viscount. In the same way the bourg was distinguished from the city at Arles, Narbonne, Toulouse, and Tours. Other places again, pillaged, ruined, and depopulated, lost their rank as towns and were reduced to simple villages, or were even blotted out. London, after the English invasions, was a heap of ruins, and the courses of the old Roman roads which intersected it were so completely obscured that the new streets, marked out in the same directions when the town was reviving in the middle ages, no longer coincided with them. . . .

Such are the vague ideas which we possess concerning the political changes in the Roman towns at the beginning of the middle ages: with so much the more reason do we know nothing of the history of the small towns, of the simple fortified bourgs, which were built in great numbers at the end of the Empire. All must have come to constitute seigniories, but we do not know how this transformation took place.

We might expect then to find at the dawn of the eleventh century only a small number of towns, shattered and fallen remnants of the ancient cities and bourgs surviving in a new age. But while these lived on obscurely down to the time when they were to reappear in public life, there were groups of more recent origin which had sprung up on all sides. The numerous domains into which the land had been divided under Roman domination met various fates. Although most of these domains were sparsely settled and became later simple rural parishes, others attracted immigrants who grouped themselves in large numbers under the shadow of the seigniorial castle or abbey; and on their sites future towns formed slowly. Such domains, nameless in the sixth century, had become important centers in the eleventh. Examples are numerous. In the southern provinces, Montpellier and Montauban; in the northern, Bruges, Ghent, Lille; in the central, Blois, Châteaudun, and Etampes grew up around castles. More numerous still, especially in the north, were the towns which owed their origin to the protection of an abbey. Such were Saint-Denis, Saint-Omer, Saint-Valery, Remiremont, Münster, Weissenburg, Redon, Condom, Aurillac, and many others.

It is uncertain at just what time and under what circumstances the movement of concentration was brought about; but it is probable that a variety of causes called it forth. The assurance of finding under the protection of certain seigniors a paternal government, security, impartial justice, and other similar guaranties, must certainly have attracted to their domains a host of peasants in search of better conditions, and this explains perhaps the fortune of many small ecclesiastical bourgs. "There is good living under the cross," runs an old saying. Elsewhere it was a clever expedient of the lords, like the establishing of a market, which brought strangers upon their lands, and instead of a simple castle there soon appeared a town. Such is the history of Cateau-Cambrésis. Among the most important of these causes, however were the Norman invasions, which, for a century, laid waste the country, ruined the peasants, and drove them within fortified walls. The most interesting example of this cause is the origin of Saint-Omer. In the ninth century, as a simple abbey under the protection of Saint Bertin, it was devastated twice in succession, in 860 and 878, together with the region which surrounded it. Taught by experience, the monks surrounded their monastery by walls, so that when the Normans returned the third time in 891, the abbey was in position to resist them. This domain was settled so rapidly that by the tenth century the former monastery had become a town.

To-day, of more than five hundred French towns hardly eighty date back to the Gallo-Roman period; the others are for the most part fortified villages. The generic name which is given them is simply the Latin word *villa,* which means rural domain.

Care should be taken not to overestimate the importance of the urban communities during the first centuries of the middle ages. They were more numerous than important, and it is probable that they were neither very populous nor very rich. In a backward state of civilization it is impossible for towns to develop. A large city can live only by the exchange of its products for those things which it does not produce but which are brought to it. Without commerce there can be no large cities. Now, in that obscure age which extends from the fifth to the tenth century, all commerce was reduced to an indispensable minimum, except during an ephemeral renaissance in the time of Charlemagne. Only the shores of the Mediterranean continued to be frequented by merchants, and the relations between Provence, Italy, Greece, and the Orient were never entirely broken. In consequence, the cities of that privileged region preserved, it seems, a commercial class and a certain degree of prosperity. Everywhere else commerce was nearly annihilated, because there was neither the security nor the centers of exchange which it needed. Each domain lived upon itself, was almost self-sufficient; made the iron, wood, and woolen articles it needed, as well as produced its own wheat. The towns probably did the same; they were rural bourgs, and the inhabitants were peasants who worked on the surrounding land. Besides, custom did not aid in their development. Kings, nobles, Gallo-Roman and Germanic proprietors preferred to live in the country; the towns were no longer the theater of great events.

It is difficult to form a clear picture of the urban groups at that time and of the people that composed them. The new small towns huddled around the castles, abbeys, and churches. The old cities, once spacious, razed their former suburbs and restricted their limits so as to have less area to defend, as at Paris, Bordeaux, Evreux, Poitiers, and Sens. Roman monuments are discovered to-day outside the enclosures which these towns made for themselves at the time of the invasions. All towns, whenever possible, encircled themselves with ramparts, with embattled walls surrounded by moats, and armed their counterscarps with traps, abatis, and palisades. Inside the city the population, although not numerous, must have lived crowded together, as the architecture of the houses shows. The Roman dwelling was spread out in a comfortable way, with large inner court, the atrium, and was generally low. Now the atrium was given up, filled in, and the roof rose high over a series of stories, which perhaps already were built so as to overhang, to gain still more room. As for monuments, the only ones which adorned the towns were those which the Romans had left. And sometimes even these were appropriated to strange uses, like the temple of Vesuna at Perigueux, which was changed into a tower for purposes of defense, or like the circus of Nîmes, which sheltered a part of the inhabitants and formed a veritable "quarter." Sometimes, too, these monuments were destroyed that the materials might be used for other constructions, especially for fortifications.

Between the church and the seigniorial dwelling, which was usually built to one side upon a precipitous hill or upon an artificial mound, the townsman passed his monotonous life, happy when a private war or an incursion for pillage did not bring upon his house or upon him the horrors of assault. Of political rights, he had none. The lord or his officers ruled the inhabitants as masters, imposed dues upon them, arrested, and judged them. The civil condition of the inhabitants must also have grown harder. It seems, indeed, that the number of freemen had noticeably diminished in the towns as well as in the country. Perhaps the cities of the south, thanks to their privileged situation, may have escaped in part this social decline; but this decline was general in the north, where only those preserved their independence who made it their business to bear arms in the following of a seignior and to live at the expense of others.

Thus from the sixth to the tenth century, townsmen did not count in society. Bishop Adalberon, in a famous poem to King Robert, considered around him only two classes: churchmen and nobles, beneath whom, but very far beneath, were the commons who worked. . . .

There came a day when the towns demanded of their lords guaranties against the arbitrary exploitation of which they were victims; when certain of them demanded and obtained a relative autonomy; when those serfs and commons that bishop Adalberon looked down upon with scorn, treated with their masters upon an equal footing. This movement of emancipation of the towns, which extended throughout western Europe from the end of the tenth century to the thirteenth, has received the name of the communal revolution. . . .

The real cause of the emancipation of the towns . . . lay in the economic and social transformation which was taking place from the tenth to the twelfth century, in the revival of labor and of production in all its forms, which was then stirring Europe. From the end of the tenth century, the feudal world was in process of organization; in the midst of the universal parceling, a relative degree of order prevailed; there was no longer the anarchy of former times, and each lord endeavored to organize and exploit his fief for his best interests: new markets were opened; relations were established between town and town. Traffickers multiplied and ventured far from the walls which protected them; men began again to exchange commodities: local commerce was reëstablished. At the same time, the society which had been languishing in the villages and bourgs contracted the taste for travel and adventure, for pilgrimages even to the Holy Land; the world grew larger; the horizon of men's minds broadened; relations were opened between the north and the south, between the occident and the orient; commerce on a large scale was revived. The result upon the towns was immediately felt. Necessarily poor and weak when there was no commerce, they now grew in wealth and population. The inhabitants soon became able to resist their lords. The best proof in support of this explanation is that the path of emanicipation followed exactly the great commercial currents of the time. The first towns were the cities of Italy; then came the towns of the Rhine,—that great highway of commerce which united northern Europe with the Mediterranean,—and the principal places of Flanders, Hainault, and Picardy, that is to say, the principal commercial centers of the middle ages. And it was the merchants who directed the communal revolution in each town: their associations were the cradles of the communes and often their place of meeting, their gild-hall, the cloth-hall as at Beauvais, Ypres, and Arras, was the first town hall.

But, it will be asked, how could the townspeople everywhere be organized against their lords? How could they be grouped thus in opposition to the powers over them? The reason is that everywhere the towns were suffering from the same evils. The preambles of the charters of the communes give most eloquent testimony on the subject. Louis VII confirmed the commune of Mantes "because of the excessive oppression under which the poor were groaning." The counts of Ponthieu assured liberties to the towns of Abbeville and Doullens, "to free them from the wrongs and exactions which the townspeople continued to suffer at the hands of the lords of the land." The evils which these documents signalize were without doubt of long standing; they must have called forth complaints for a long time. But when there came to be in each urban community a merchant aristocracy, wealthy, bold, and capable of consecrating its resources to the work of common emancipation, complaints led to acts, and the revolution began.

This revolution developed very early upon the shores of the Mediterranean, in Italy and in Provence. Here the old cities had never ceased to have trade relations with the Orient; their traffic, although reduced by the universal disorganization into which Europe fell at the beginning of the middle ages, does not seem to have suffered complete interruption. Even the more recent towns attracted to themselves a portion—often considerable—of this commerce. Not only did Venice, Genoa, and Amalfi send their galleys into the Byzantine Empire, but Arles, a city of less importance, sustained with Greece relations regular enough to be mentioned as early as 921. In the eleventh and twelfth centuries, when the passion for pilgrimages and crusades spread abroad, this commerce greatly increased, not only with Constantinople but especially with the Infidel. Thus the urban communities of the south were early richer and more populous than elsewhere. In them was formed an opulent burghal class, experienced in business, capable of resisting the lords, and even of triumphing over them.

This was so much more the case because these towns, different from the northern bourgs, were inhabited not simply by common people. The small nobles also lived in them. . . . Again, the southern lords, who were more civilized, more broad-minded, and more far-sighted, took an interest, not only in war and in the crusades but also in the commerce which was enriching them while it enriched their subjects. They understood more quickly, perhaps, the advantage which there was for them in freeing the working classes, who should be more prosperous according as they were more independent, and they did not show toward the efforts of the communities the savage and obstinate hostility that was seen elsewhere.

Finally, the sovereigns were far away. The king of France was not likely to interfere in favor of a vassal, such as the count of Toulouse, who might be threatened by the ambitious designs of his lesser subjects. The German emperor never appeared in Provence, and made into Italy only rapid and infrequent expeditions. In short, the most diverse circumstances united to render the emancipation of the Mediterranean towns prompt, easy, and complete.

Like that of the Italian cities, and for the same reason, the emancipation of the communities of Provence, though somewhat later, was precocious. If the Italian cities obtained full liberty as early as the eleventh century, those of southern France were only beginning their transformation at that time, and this work of emancipation, less favored by circumstances, was prolonged until the year 1200 and later. It is very difficult to fix with greater precision the time when the towns of southern France succeeded in escaping from the seigniorial despotism. One must not think that they did not enjoy any independence until they were in possession of a communal charter and of a clearly organized municipal administration; these did not come until later. The oldest charters of enfranchisement granted them date from the twelfth century and do not antedate the charters of liberties given the towns of the north. Many even were not issued before the first years of the thirteenth century. But at that time these communities had long enjoyed, in fact if not in law, incontestable privileges, and some of these must have had a very remote origin. . . .

The emancipation of the towns of central and northern France, of Germany, and of England, followed closely the emancipation of the Mediterranean cities. The first manifestations were in Flanders, on the banks of the Rhine, and in the French provinces of the northeast. As early as 957 the inhabitants of Cambrai, taking advantage of the absence of their bishop, banded together and had the audacity to shut the gates of the town in his face when he returned. In 967 the abbey of Saint Arnulf of Metz granted a charter of liberties to the bourg of Morville-sur-Seille, and some years later, in 984, it granted another to the domain of Broc. In 1003 the emperor, Henry II, recognized privileges for the bourg of Cateau-Cambrésis. Nevertheless these were rare and premature cases, and more than half a century passed before other attempts came to light. Then, however, they multiplied. Saint-Quentin conquered its title of commune before 1077, and Beauvais before 1099; Arras became independent in the course of the eleventh century; Noyon emancipated itself about 1108; Valenciennes in 1114; Amiens between 1113 and 1117; Corbie about the year 1120; Soissons about 1126; Bruges, Lille, and Saint-Omer about 1127; and Ghent and Liège a few years after. This was the heroic age of the communal revolution. From this time on the movement was accentuated; the budding desire for independence spread from town to town. The freed cities became models; their successes emboldened others. The wave reached its height in the twelfth century and in the first half of the thirteenth; then it slowly receded. It had done its work in two hundred years. The cities had obtained satisfaction. The map of feudal Europe was dotted from north to south and from east to west with independent or privileged communities. The public mind was penetrated by a new idea, that of the free town; the political vocabulary was enriched by a new word, commune.

This work of emancipation was not carried out without great difficulties. The urban communities were less populous, less rich, and less strong in the north than upon the shores of the Mediterranean. Besides, the seigniorial class was so powerful in the north that the people there seemed incapable of making way against it. Finally, the king of France, the king of England, and the German emperor were near at hand, and it seemed certain that they would sustain their vassals energetically. . . .

Like the feudal lords and for the same reasons, the French kings, in principle, refused independence to the towns of their domain. Louis VII suppressed with severity a seditious attempt at Orleans. But upon the lands of their vassals, where they intervened as suzerains, they did not have the same reasons for declaring and enforcing their opinion. Here their policy, which was not inspired by any fixed principle, lacked clearness and continuity. Tradition formerly attributed to Louis VI the honor of having "freed the communes." Such, however, was not the case. While he confirmed a number of charters granted by the lords, on the other hand he did not hesitate to aid by his own forces barons who were struggling against rebellious communities: the bishop of Noyon, and the abbots of Saint-Riquier and Corbie. In the same year, 1112, he protected the commune of Amiens and destroyed that of Laon. Very sensitive to the attractions of gain, he sometimes offered independence to towns, but, money in hand, he was ready to turn against them, if later he found it to his advantage. Upon the square of Laon, over which the bishop and the people were disputing, his support was literally bid off at auction. His successor, Louis VII, apparently saw more clearly that communes upon the lands of vassals whom he feared were natural allies of the crown in the camp of the enemy, and that it was to his interest to aid in their development. If he protected the rights of the archbishops of Rheims and of Sens, of the bishops of Beauvais, Châlons-sur-Marne, Soissons, of the abbots of Tournus and of Corbie, on the other hand he multiplied the concessions of charters and sustained the emancipated towns against the hostility of the lords. Philip Augustus, accentuating this policy, confirmed charters granted by others, and he even freed a number of communities in the district which he united to the crown, and even in the domain. But he made them pay for his support, and he imposed upon them his protection, giving out liberties with one hand while with the other he extended royal supremacy. This systematic benevolence was tardy, for the communal revolution was by that date drawing to a close. So it may be said, in résumé, that in the beginning the towns met a universal resistance, which in some cases was never done away with but in others was weakened or transformed at the bidding of interest. . . .

In this common work of enfranchisement the lot of the towns of the Empire was peculiar. Instead of conquering their liberties all at once by force or by some adroit maneuver, and of extending them little by little by taking advantage of every favorable circumstance, as the other communities did, they were obliged to pass through two clearly separated stages to attain independence. In the twelfth century, like all the other urban agglomerations, they strove to free themselves. But the emperor, upon whom they were directly dependent after he had raised them to the rank of tenants-in-chief, held them under his powerful hand and consented to grant them only civil liberties. Each time that they desired autonomy and independence they met with his refusal. In 1161, Barbarossa subjugated the burghers of Treves, who had conspired against their archbishop. In 1163, learning that the people of Mainz had killed their lord, he hastened thither, sacked the city, and razed the ramparts. Thus in the twelfth century the towns gained only the most essential liberties: guaranties against the arbitrary power of their lords; never political independence. In the middle of the thirteenth century, however, the Swabian dynasty died out and feudal Germany enjoyed a prolonged interregnum. The towns, which now had only local sovereigns to oppose them, pressed their claims, and after a struggle in which success and failure were mingled, many of them triumphed. Metz, which had been enjoying certain liberties since the twelfth century, then attained full independence. Strassburg obtained a municipal administration distinct from the episcopal administration. Besançon organized a commune and in 1290 had its emancipation sanctioned by the new emperor, Rudolph. The second stage was passed a hundred years after the first, and it was then that the famous free towns of the Empire were constituted.

Thus all Europe presented the same spectacle from the eleventh to the thirteenth century. The urban communities, before so humble and so profoundly silent that we know almost nothing of them, were developing, were raising their voices, and were all tending toward the same end, emancipation. Everywhere, in spite of diversities of place, time, circumstances, obstacles, or aids, they reached their goal or approached it more or less closely. It was a universal current which carried all with it. . . .

As they had attained their emancipation by the most diverse ways, the towns of the middle ages were not likely to have any uniform constitution, and their independence, like their organization, varied greatly from one center to another. One commune was almost autonomous, while another had only the appearance of liberty. In some cases the source of authority resided in a general assembly of the inhabitants, in others the power was in the hands of an oligarchy formed of a few families who reserved for themselves the magistracies and the municipal offices. Thus it is impossible to characterize the situation in these towns comprehensively and precisely. And on the other hand, between the localities which were most independent and those which remained under the immediate surveillance of royal or seigniorial officials, there were so many intermediate types, . . . the transitions from one to another were so imperceptible, that it is no less difficult to find categories into which they can be grouped for systematic study. They formed a continuous hierarchy without breaks, or without periods of arrested development. Nevertheless historians are accustomed to rank them in two distinct classes: communes and towns of burgessy. Under the name of communes they designate those centers which had acquired from their lord a certain degree of political independence. In the towns of burgessy, on the contrary, the inhabitants had gained civil liberties only, guaranties against the administrative, fiscal, judicial, and military despotism of the master; they had not conquered the right to govern themselves. This division is purely arbitrary. It does not date from the middle ages and in practice it would be difficult, if not impossible, to distinguish clearly the least free of the communes from the most independent of the towns of burgessy. With this reservation we shall make use of it, because it is used and is perhaps as good as any.

Whether extended or restricted, the rights of the commune were almost always set forth in a written indenture, a contract which was entered into between the commune and the lord, a fundamental agreement which could be referred to in case of new difficulties or of disputes, and which served at the same time as a certificate of birth and as a deed of constitution. This was the communal charter. It is true that certain places, like Abbeville, are cited where emancipation was not at first sanctioned upon parchment, but these are exceptions to the rule.

Although these charters were zealously guarded in coffers, the keys of which were in possession of the municipal authorities alone, they have rarely been preserved to us in their original form; usually they are known only by more recent confirmations. They differed remarkably from each other. That of Corbie comprised only seven articles; that of Molliens-Vidame, a little place in Picardy, contained sixty. The length of the act was not in proportion to the importance of the place. They were drawn up ordinarily in the form of a seigniorial, but sometimes in an impersonal, style. The clauses were usually an enumeration without order, often ambiguous, and at times contradictory. As a rule they aimed principally to guarantee the existence of the communal bond, to regulate the relation of the commune to its suzerain, especially in the matter of justice and of imposts, and to determine the rights and privileges of the burgesses. These liberties, as they were called, concerned the limitation of the taille, taxes, corvées, tolls, banalities, chevauchée, and war, and the exercise and extent of seigniorial justice. The charters rarely described the whole municipal constitution. Generally they mentioned only the innovations and illuminated the doubtful points, while they passed in silence established usages which were not subjects of dispute. Hence the incoherence, vagueness, and incompleteness apparent in these charters.

46. *A TWELFTH CENTURY COMMUNAL REVOLT*[1]

Early in the twelfth century there lived in an abbey between Laon and St. Quentin, about seventy-five miles northeast of Paris, the Abbot Guibert of Nogent-sous-Coucy. A keen observer he was, being interested not only in religious matters but following closely the practices of laymen in town and country. His abbey was located but a short distance from Laon, where in 1115 a revolt broke out against the bishop and the nobles. The latter had long extorted in the form of taxes and contributions a very large share of the money earned by the burghers in the city. This practice had at first resulted only in suppressed discontent, but finally the enraged people could stand it no longer and rose against the hated bishop. Their revolt was described by the abbot just mentioned.

Now after some time when he [the Bishop of Laon] had set out for England to extract money from the English king, whom he had served, and who had formerly been his friend, the Archdeacons Walter and Guy, with the nobles of the city, devised the following plan: Of old time such ill-fate had settled upon that city that neither God nor any lord was feared therein, but according to each man's power and lust the state was involved in rapine and murder. For to begin with the source of the plague, whenever it happened that the king came there, he who ought to have exacted respect for himself with royal severity, was himself first shamefully fined on his own property. When his horses were led to the water morning or evening, his grooms were beaten and the horses carried off. It was known that the very clergy were held in such contempt, that neither their persons nor their goods were spared, as it is written, "Like as the people, so the priest." But what shall I say about the baser people? No one of the countrymen came

[1] *The Autobiography of Guibert, Abbot of Nogent-sous-Coucy.* Translated by C. C. Swinton Bland. (Broadway Translations. Medieval Section Edited by G. G. Coulton), London, George Routledge and Sons, New York, E. P. Dutton and Co., 1925, pp. 152–165, 167–169, 178. Used by permission.

into the city, no one except under the safest conduct approached it, who was not thrown into prison and held to ransom, or was not, as opportunity served, drawn without cause into a lawsuit.

As an example let me adduce one practice, which occurring amongst barbarians or Scythians, men having no code of laws, would be regarded as most iniquitous. When on the Saturday the country populace from different parts came there to buy and sell, the townfolk carried round as for sale, beans, barley or any kind of corn in cup and platter or other kind of measure in the market-place, and when they had offered them for sale to the countrymen seeking such things, the latter having settled the price promised to buy. "Follow me," said the seller, "to my house that you may there see the rest of the corn which I am selling you, and when you have seen it, may take it away." He followed, but when he came to the bin, the honest seller, having raised and held up the lid, would say, "Bend your head and shoulders over the bin, that you may see that the bulk does not differ from the sample which I shewed you in the market-place." And when the buyer getting up on the pediment of the bin leaned his belly over it, the worthy seller standing behind lifted up his feet and pushed the unwary man into the bin, and having put the lid down on him as he fell, kept him in safe prison until he ransomed himself. Such and like things were done in the city. No one was safe going out at night. There remained for him nothing but plunder, capture or murder.

The clergy with the archdeacons considering this, and the nobles catching at pretexts for exacting money from the people, offer them through agents the choice of making composition by paying a sum to cover them. Now Commune is a new and bad name of an arrangement for all the poorest classes to pay their usual due of servitude to their lords once only in the year, and to make good any breach of the laws they have committed by the payment fixed by law, and to be entirely free from all other exactions usually imposed on serfs. The people seizing on this opportunity for freeing themselves gathered huge sums of money to fill the gaping mouths of so many greedy men. And they, pleased with the shower poured upon them, took oaths binding themselves in the matter.

A pledge of mutual aid had been thus exchanged by the clergy and nobles with the people, when the Bishop returned with much wealth from England and being moved to anger against those responsible for this innovation, for a long time kept away from the city. But a quarrel full of honour and glory began between him and Walter, the Archdeacon, his accomplice. The Archdeacon made very unbecoming remarks about his Bishop on the subject of the death of Gerard. Whether the Bishop had any talk on the matter with others I know not, but this I do know, that he complained to me about him saying, "Lord Abbot, if it should so happen that Walter should start any charges against me at any council, would you take it without offence? Is it not he, who at the time when you left your fellow-monks and went to Ely, openly flattered you, but secretly raised dissensions against you, publicly taking your side, but privately stirring me up against you?" With such speeches did he try to win me to oppose that dangerous man, conscious of the weight of his charges, fearful and suspicious of universal condemnation.

Saying therefore that he was moved with relentless wrath against those who had taken that oath and the principals in the transaction, in the end his loud-sounding words were suddenly quieted by the offer of a great heap of silver and gold. Therefore he swore that he would maintain the rights of the Commune according to the terms duly drawn up at Noyon and Saint-Quintin. The King too was induced by a bribe from the people to confirm the same by oath. O my God, who could say how many disputes arose when the gifts of the people were accepted, how many after oath had been sworn to reverse what they had agreed to, whilst they sought to bring back the serfs who had been freed from the oppression of their yoke, to their former state. At least there was implacable hate by the Bishop and nobles against the citizens, and whereas he has not the power to crush the freedom of the French, after the fashion of Normandy and England, the pastor is weak and forgetful of his sacred calling through his insatiable greed. Whenever one of the people entered a court of law, where he was dependent not on the justice of God, but on his ability to please his judges, if I may say so, he was drained of his substance to the last penny.

Hence because the taking of gifts is wont to be attended by the subversion of all justice, the coiners of the currency, knowing that if they did wrong in their office, they could save themselves by money bribes, corrupted the coinage with so much base metal that through this very many were reduced to poverty. For as they made coins of the cheapest bronze, which in a moment by certain dishonest arts they made brighter than silver, (shame on them!) fond men were deceived, and giving up their goods of great or little value, got in exchange nothing but dross. And the patient suffering of this by the Lord Bishop was well rewarded, and thus not only within the province of Laon but in all directions the ruin of many was hastened. And when he was deservedly powerless to uphold the value of his own currency wickedly debased by himself, he instituted pence of Amiens, also most debased, to be current in the city for some time; but when he could by no means keep that up, he struck an impression of his own time, on which he had stamped a pastoral staff to represent himself. This was received with such laughter and scorn, that it had less value than the debased coinage.

Meantime since, on the issue of each of these new coins, proclamation was made that no one should criticise the wretched impression, there ensued frequent occasion for accusing the people of speaking evil of the Bishop's ordinances, and hence exaction of all sorts of heavy fines could be carried out. Moreover a certain monk of the very worst reputation in every respect, named Theodorus of Thorn, of which place he was a native, brought very large quantities of silver from Flanders. Bringing all this down to the false standard of the Laon mint, he scattered it all over the surrounding province. By appealing to the greed of the rich with his hateful presents and bringing in lies, perjury and want, he robbed his country of truth, justice and wealth. No act of an enemy, no plunderings, no burnings have hurt the province more ever since the Roman walls contained the ancient mint of the city.

But since "Impiety long hidden does violence at times to the show of honour artfully drawn over it, and things evident cannot be concealed; as bright light pierces through glass, so does it through the countenance," that which he did to Gerard hiding his hand in it, he did to another Gerard some time afterwards and gave manifest proof of his cruelty. It was an older Gerard, perhaps a foreman over the countrymen who belonged to him; and because he was more attached to Thomas, reputed son of Enguerrand, of whom we have spoken before, the most wicked man we have known in this generation, the Bishop regarded him as a general enemy. Seizing him therefore and thrusting him into prison in the palace, he had his eyes put out at night by the hands of his negro servant. By this deed he brought open shame upon himself and the old story of what he had done to the first Gerard, was renewed, both clergy and people being aware that the canon of Toledo, if I am not mistaken, forbade the infliction of death or the passing of a sentence of death or mutilation by bishops, priests and clergy and the very rumour of such acts raised the anger of the King. Perhaps too, it reached the ears of the Apostolic see; at least I know the Pope suspended him from his office, and I believe, for no other reason. But to make matters worse, during his suspension he dedicated a church. Therefore he goes to Rome and by persuasive words the Pope's anger is assuaged, and he is sent back to us with his authority restored. And so, God seeing that pastors and flock were by act and will partners in wickedness, could no longer restrain his judgment and at last permitted the malice that had been conceived to break out into open rage, which in its headlong mad career was through the vengeance of God shattered by a dreadful fall.

Having therefore summoned the nobles and certain of the clergy on the last day of Lent in the holy days of Passion of our Lord, he determined to urge the annulment of the Commune, to which he had sworn, and had by bribes induced the King to swear, and the day before the Passover, that is to say, on the day of the Lord's Supper, he summoned the King to this pious duty and instructed the King and all his people to break their oaths, in which snare he had first placed his own neck, on the day, that is, on which his predecessor, Ascelin, had betrayed his King as aforesaid. For on that day, when he should have performed that most glorious of all a prelate's duties, the consecration of the oil and the absolution of the people from their sins, he was not even seen to enter the church. He was intriguing with the King's courtiers for the annulment of the Commune and for the restoration by the King of the laws of the city to their former state. But the citizens fearing their overthrow, promised four hundred (perhaps more) pounds to the King and his courtiers. In reply the Bishop begged the nobles to go with him to interview the King. They promised on their part seven hundred pounds, and King Louis, son of Philip, of conspicuous person and a mighty warrior, hating sloth in business, of dauntless courage in adversity, and in other respects a good man, in this was not very just that he gave ear and attention too much to worthless persons debased by greed. And this redounded to his own great loss and blame and the ruin of many, which it is certain took place here and elsewhere.

The King's craving for money being turned therefore, as I said, to feed upon the larger promise, through his consent the oaths of the Bishop and the nobles became void without any regard for honour or the sacred season. That night because of the outbreak of disorder caused by his most unjust blow, although the King had a lodging elsewhere, he was afraid to sleep outside the Bishop's palace. Very early in the morning the King departed and the Bishop assured the nobles they need have no fear about the agreement to pay so much money, knowing that he himself would pay whatever they had promised. "And," said he, "if I do not perform my promise, hand me over to the king's prison for ransom."

The compact of the Commune being broken, such rage, such amazement seized the citizens that all the officials abandoned their duties and the stalls of the craftsmen and cobblers were closed and nothing was exposed for sale by the innkeepers and hucksters, who expected to have nothing left when the lords began plundering. For at once the property of all was calculated by the Bishop and nobles, and whatever any man was known to have given to arrange the Commune, so much was demanded of him to procure its annulment. These events took place on the day of the Passover, which is called the preparation, and on the holy Sabbath when their minds were being prepared to receive the body and blood of the Lord, they were made ready for murders only here, for perjury there. Why say more? All the efforts of the prelate and nobles in these days were reserved for fleecing their inferiors. But those inferiors were no longer moved by mere anger, but goaded into a murderous lust for the death of the Bishop and his accomplices and bound themselves by oath to effect their purpose. Now they say that four hundred took the oath. Such a mob could not be secret and when it came to the ears of Anselm towards evening of the holy Sabbath, he sent word to the Bishop, as he was retiring to rest, not to go out to the early morning service, knowing that if he did he must certainly be killed. But he, infatuated with excessive pride said, "Fie, surely I shall not perish at the hands of such." Yet notwithstanding his scornful words, he did not dare to rise for matins or to enter the church. The next day, as he followed the clergy in procession, he ordered his household people and all the soldiers coming behind him to carry short swords under their garments. In this procession, when a little disorder, as is likely in a crowd, began to rise, one of the citizens coming out of the crypt and thinking the time had come for the murder, to which they were sworn, began to cry out in a loud voice as a signal, "Commune, Commune!" over and over again. And because it was a feast day, this was easily stopped, yet it brought suspicion on the other party. And so, when the service of the mass was over, the Bishop summoned a great number of countrymen from the episcopal manors and manned the towers of the church and gave orders that his palace should be guarded, although he was almost as much hated by them, as they knew that the piles of money, which he had promised the King, must be drained from their own purses.

Now on the second day after Easter it is the custom for the clergy to assemble at St. Vincent's. Since therefore the conspirators had been anticipated the day before, they had decided to act on this day, and would have done so, if they had seen that all the nobles were with the Bishop. For they had found one of the nobles in the suburb, a harmless man, who had recently married a young cousin of mine, a woman of modest character. But they were unwilling to attack him fearing to put others on their guard. Having therefore reached the third day of Easter and feeling more secure the Bishop allows those men to depart, whom he had put in the towers and palace to protect him. On the fourth day I went to him, because I had been plundered of my supply of corn and of some legs of pork, called bacon, through his disorders. When interviewed by me and requested to relieve the city of these great disturbances, he replied, "What do ye think they can do by their riots? If John, my moor, were to take by the nose the most powerful man amongst them, he would not dare so much as to grunt. For just now I have compelled them to renounce what they call their Commune for so long as I live." I spoke, and then seeing the man overcome with pride, I refrained from saying more. Yet before I left the city, by reason of his instability we quarrelled with mutual recriminations. But although he was warned by many of the imminent peril, he took no notice of any one.

The next day, that is, the fifth in Easter week, after midday, as he was engaged in business with Archdeacon Walter about the getting of money, behold there arose a disorderly noise throughout the city, men shouting "Commune!" and again through the middle of the chapel of the Blessed Mary through that door by which the murderers of Gerard had come and gone, there citizens now entered the Bishop's court with swords, battle-axes, bows and hatchets, and carrying clubs and spears, a very great company. As soon as this sudden attack was discovered, the nobles rallied from all sides to the Bishop, having sworn to give him aid against such an onset, if it should occur. In this rally Guinimon, the chatelain, an aged nobleman of handsome presence and guiltless character, armed only with shield and spear, ran out through the church and as he entered the Bishop's hall, was the first to fall, struck on the back of the head with a battle-axe by a certain Rainbert, who was his fellow-citizen. Immediately afterwards Regnier, of whom I spoke before as married to my cousin, hurrying to enter the palace, was struck from behind with a spear when trying to enter by mounting on the pulpitum of the Bishop's chapel, and there falling headlong was at once consumed by the fire of the palace from his waist downwards. Ado, the Vidame, quarrelsome, but brave, separated from the rest and able to do little by himself among so many, as he was striving to reach the Bishop's palace, encountered the full force of the attack, but with spear and sword made such a stand that in a moment he struck down two of those who came on. Then mounting the dining-table in the hall, wounded now in the knees and other parts of the body and at last only supporting himself on his knees, whilst striking at his assailants all round him, he kept them off for a long time, until, becoming exhausted, he was struck through the body with a lance and after a little was reduced to ashes by the fire in that house.

Next the outrageous mob attacking the Bishop and howling before the walls of his palace, he with some who were succouring him fought them off by hurling of stones and shooting of arrows. For he now, as at all times, shewed great spirit as a fighter; but because he had wrongly and in vain taken up another sword, by the sword he perished. Therefore being unable to stand against the reckless assaults of the people, he put on the clothes of one of his servants and flying to the vaults of the church hid himself in a cask, shut up in which with the head fastened on by a faithful follower he thought himself safely hidden. And as they ran hither and thither demanding where, not the Bishop, but the hangdog, was, they seized one of his pages, but through his faithfulness could not get what they wanted. Laying hands on another, they learn from the traitor's nod where to look for him. Entering the vaults therefore, and searching everywhere, at last they found him in the following manner.

There was a pestilent fellow, a bondman of the church of the Blessed Vincent, but for a long time an official and overseer of Enguerrand of Coucy, who being set over the collection of tolls paid for crossing the bridge called Soord, sometimes watched until there were only a few travellers passing, and having robbed them of all their property, in order that they might make no complaint against him, threw them into the river with a weight round their necks. How often he had done this, God only knows. The number of the thefts and robberies being more than any one could count, the unchecked wickedness of his heart, and one as might say, was displayed also in the truculence of his looks. This man having incurred the displeasure of Enguerrand, went over wholly to the party of the Commune in Laon. He who had spared neither monk nor clerk nor stranger, in fact no sex, was last of all to be the slayer of a bishop. He the leader and instigator of this attack searched most diligently for the Bishop, whom he hated more bitterly than the rest.

And so, as they sought for him in every vessel, this fellow halted in front of that cask, where the man was hiding, and having broken in the head, asked again and again who was there. And he, hardly able to move his frozen lips under his blows, said "A prisoner." Now the Bishop was wont in mockery to call him Isengrin, I suppose, because of his wolfish look, for so some people call wolves. The wretch, therefore, says to the Bishop, "Is this my Lord Isengrin stored away?" Renulf therefore, sinner though he was, yet the Lord's anointed, was dragged forth from the cask by the hair, beaten with many blows and brought out into the open air in the narrow lane of the clergy's cloister before the house of the chaplain Godfrey. And as he piteously implored them, ready to take oath that he would henceforth cease to be their Bishop, that he would leave the country, and as they with hardened hearts jeered at him, one named Bernard and surnamed de Brueys, lifting his battle-axe brutally dashed out the brains of that sacred, though sinner's, head, and he slipping between the hands of those who held him, was dead before he reached the ground stricken by another thwart blow under the eye-sockets and across the middle of the nose. There brought to his end, his legs were cut off and many another wound inflicted. But Thibaut seeing the ring on the finger of the erstwhile prelate and not being able to draw it off, cut off the dead man's finger and took it. And so stripped to his skin he was thrown into a corner in front of his chaplain's house. My God, who shall recount the mocking words that were thrown at him by passers-by, as he lay there, and with what clods and stones and dirt his corpse was covered? But before I go on to other matters, I must say that a certain act did much to bring about his end. Two days, I think, before his death there was a meeting of the chief of his clergy, because he had recently told the King when staying in the city, that the clergy were not to be considered, because they were almost all of them born king's serfs. When confronted with his words, he denied them, speaking after this manner, "May the Holy Communion, which I have just received at that altar"—stretching out his right hand towards it—"turn to my ruin, and I call down the sword of the Holy Spirit on my soul, if I spoke such words to the King about you." When they heard this, some were utterly confounded and swore (by the Sacrament) that they heard him out of his own mouth tell the King that. Manifestly the instability of his character and his false tongue brought on him his ruin. . . .

The tale of how the wives of the nobles behaved at such a crisis, is a pleasant one. The wife of Ado, the Vidame, seeing her husband, when the rising began, joining the Bishop's party, and believing it meant instant death, began to beg his pardon for any wrong she had done him, clinging closely to him for some time with cries of sorrow and giving him her last kisses as she said, "Why, do you leave me to the swords of the townspeople?" He grasped the woman's right hand and holding his lance told his steward (who happened to be amongst the first of the traitors) to carry his shield behind him. He not only did not carry his shield behind, but reviling him cut him down. No longer then did he acknowledge him whose servant he was and on whom he was waiting a little while before at dinner. His wife, therefore, passing safely through the mobs was concealed in the house of a certain doorkeeper of the Bishop, but when she saw the assault and the firing of the building, she turned to fly just where chance took her. And having fallen in the way of some of the women of the town, she was seized by them, beaten with their fists and stripped of the costly clothes she was wearing and was scarcely able to reach St. Vincent's clad in nun's habit.

But my cousin, when her husband left her, not troubling about the house and furniture and only keeping a cloak for herself, with manlike agility climbed the wall which surrounded the garden and jumped down from it. Then taking refuge in the hovel of some poor woman and perceiving after a little the flames increasing, she rushed to the door which the old woman had barred, broke the bar with a stone, and wrapping herself in the habit and veil, which she had obtained from a kinswoman, in the belief that she could be kept safe among the nuns, and then seeing the fire burning hotly there, turned back on her tracks and fled to a house farther off until the next day; then being sought for by her kinsfolk she appeared and thereupon the anguish she had felt through the fear of death was changed to more violent grief for her husband.

Some others, that is the wife and daughters of the castellan Guinimar with many more hid themselves in mean places. But Walter the Archdeacon, being with the Bishop and seeing the hall besieged, because he knew he had always added oil to the flames, leapt out through the window of the house into the gardens of the prelate and from the wall which surrounded it, into the vineyards, then by unfrequented ways with his head covered, betook himself to the Castle of Mons Acutus. But when the citizens could not find him anywhere, they said in jest that through fear of them he was keeping close to the sewers. The wife, too, of Roger, the lord of Mons Acutus, named Armengard, being that day in the city, as her husband was castellan of the abbey after Gerard, with the wife of Ralph, the serving man of the nuns, I believe, and in the garb of a nun reached St. Vincent's by way of the valley of Bibracina. But the six-years-old son of that Ralph was carried out by some one under a cloak to save him, and was met by a hanger-on, who looked to see what was under the cloak and thereupon cut his throat, as he lay in the other's arms.

And so through the vineyards lying between two spurs of the mountain the fugitive clergy and women passed that day and night, men having no fear of the woman's dress, nor women of the men's. . . .

These events took place in the year 1115 of the Incarnation of our Lord, on the sixth day of Easter and the 30th of April.

47. *VARIOUS KINDS OF GILDS*[1]

Since much misunderstanding has been caused in this country by superficial accounts of the gild system and by numerous misleading definitions of the word "gild," or "guild," it is very fortunate that a definitive treatment of the subject has been presented by Professor A. P. Usher. This author explains at some length how the term "gild" originated and how it became misunderstood by many writers.

The interest of modern readers in the craft gilds of the middle ages has created special associations between the general term "gild" and this particular form of gild. A number of writers, including Professor W. J. Ashley, have given added currency to such a specialization of meaning by using the phrase "gild system" to describe the form of industrial organization which is more precisely described as the craft or handicraft system. This laxity of usage has been peculiarly unfortunate because it adds to the obscurities and complexities of a subject that is beset with the difficulties that come from ambiguities of terminology and misleading connotations. The word "gild" or "guild," is derived from not less than three roots, and possesses, therefore, even at the outset, a wide range of meanings, some of which have no significant relation to each other. The first of these roots was used in the sense of payment, compensation, offering, sacrifice, worship, idol. The second root expressed the notion of combined or collective action, a meeting. The third root was associated with the idea of a banquet. The

[1] A. P. Usher, *An Introduction to the Industrial History of England*. Boston, Houghton Mifflin Company, 1919, pp. 165–167, 167–170, 170–172, 173–179. Used by permission of, and by arrangement with Houghton Mifflin Company.

word was thus not clearly specialized in the meaning of an association and might refer with obvious propriety to a number of different kinds of societies.

The disposition of the earlier Teutonic writers to trace all gilds to a common Teutonic origin was not unnatural, but one cannot help feeling that this unduly literal scholarship added gratuitous difficulties to the problems connected with these different types of association. Three distinct types of society might be described as gilds: associations for charitable and religious purposes; associations for commercial or social purposes; and associations designed to share with the municipal authority the supervision of fellow-craftsmen. In England and in Germany these associations were all called gilds, though there were usually elements in the name of the society that would be sufficient to indicate the general purpose of the association. Religious associations were usually placed under the patronage of some saint, or connected with the celebration of some religious festival. Gilds of Corpus Christi, of the Holy Trinity, of the Blessed Virgin, were to be found in many towns. Some of these religious titles appear in connection with associations that were not exclusively religious in character. . . .

All writers have recognized that these three types are somewhat distinct, but many have insisted that the growth of these different forms of association is dominated by some common principle. This thesis was given wide currency by Professor Brentano's essay on the "Origin and Development of Gilds," and later writers in dealing with English problems have found it difficult to emancipate themselves from the influences of the misleading suggestions of the old Anglo-Saxon term. The French terminology is different, and French writers have maintained more explicit distinctions among these various forms of association. The religious association is designated by a special term both in Latin and in French (*fraternitas*-confrérie). The merchant gild for some reason as yet unexplained has left little trace in the history of French commerce. A derivative from the root "gild" appears in French terminology in this connection. The craft gild is designated by the term "métier," the general term for craft. It is therefore necessary to distinguish in French between the organized and unorganized crafts, and thus we have the "métier libre"—a mere group of unorganized craftsmen distinguished from the "métier juré," the chartered craft whose members swear to observe the statutes of the organization. The confrérie, or religious fraternity, plays about the same rôle in France as the religious "gild" in England.

There may have been significant differences in the development of the gild merchant in France, but we can at least affirm that such associations existed. The craft gilds in France and in England also exhibit differences of form. The most notable differences in the history of gilds in the two countries is that in France these forms appear more clearly to be different kinds of associations. The members of these societies were drawn from a single class, and in many cases the same people belonged to two societies or gilds; the different forms thus exerted curious reciprocal influences upon each other, as they were all a part of the daily life of a fairly definite group. The close relations of the different forms of gild to each other cannot be effectively studied, however, unless the larger differences of form and purpose are carefully distinguished. . . .

The fact that a single term was applied to a variety of organizations in the middle ages can hardly be taken as evidence of a common purpose, and it happens that there is fairly definite evidence that there was no clear fraternal element in the craft gild of the pure type. In the course of development in England the religious and industrial organizations of craftsmen frequently became one society rather than two parallel organizations of the same persons. To that extent a fraternal element crept into the craft organizations, but it would be an exaggeration to suppose that the craft gild was in general a kind of fraternity. Both on the Continent and in England the religious society and the administrative organization of the craft were distinct; they were different organizations of essentially the same group of men. Although the modern trade union is not comparable to the craft gild, the relation between workingmen's benefit societies and the trade union is substantially similar to the relation that existed between the religious fraternity and the craft gild. These various kinds of gilds are not merely variations from a common type, but essentially different organizations, owing their origin to widely different circumstances and having notably different functions and purposes.

Scattered evidence of religious organizations begins to appear in the Saxon period, but no considerable mass of evidence about such bodies is available until the late fourteenth century. In 1389 the King ordered an inquiry into the property and regulations of these gilds. Each gild was thus required to make some statement of its purposes and of the property in its possession. A large number of the replies of the gilds are still extant. These documents comprise the primary source of knowledge of such gilds. Many of the gilds had doubtless been in existence a long time, but it is seldom possible to trace their history into the remote past. We cannot even be certain that the religious gild of that period was substantially similar to the earlier organizations to which references exist. It would seem, however, that certain purposes were present in all such associations.

The gilds were formed primarily to insure the celebration of masses for the souls of deceased members. This general purpose naturally included the funeral ceremonies, and in some cases an appropriate funeral was guaranteed to members. In order to assure the saying of the masses, the gild was usually endowed with property whose revenue was applied to the payment of gild chaplains. Because this property was really devoted to religious purposes it became a matter of real concern to discover the amount of gild property. The inquiry of 1389 was inspired by royal jealousy of ecclesiastical endowments, and soon afterward the general statute of mortmain was declared to be applicable to gild property. The growth of the religious gilds was thus restricted, and at the time of the Reformation these gilds were technically dissolved, though they were in many instances able to reorganize under new names with new characters.

Although the celebration of religious services was the general and primary function, the activities of the gilds were not confined to such things. Schools were frequently maintained by the gilds and one of the colleges at Cambridge was endowed by the gild of Saint Mary and Corpus Christi. Relief was usually given to brothers or sisters who were in distress through sickness or poverty.

These religious fraternities were usually composed of a number of people worshiping in the same church. In many cases a number of members of a single craft might be prominent in the gild, for the craftsmen were usually grouped in one or more districts of the town and would thus naturally worship at the same church. But even in these cases the craft was not really the basis of the organization. Persons not of the craft would be included, and women were more freely admitted to these gilds than to the craft associations. Nor should one suppose that these gilds were composed exclusively of artisans. The rolls of the gilds of Saint Mary and Corpus Christi at Cambridge contain many names that have no occupational designation with them; the proper inference from such silence is of course uncertain, but it is not unlikely that such persons would have been merchants or persons whose income was derived from land.

There is no certain basis of information as to the usual number of members, but lists of founders or charter members are in most cases short, seldom more than ten or a dozen names. . . .

Once established the gild was likely to grow to considerable proportions.

These gilds elected their own officers, usually a warden and alderman, at times a clerk, or treasurer, and a summoner. These officials were presumed to exercise the necessary administrative functions and in addition to adjust disputes among the members of the gild. New rules and regulations were made in the general meetings of the gild as a whole. These business meetings should be distinguished from the general assemblies of the members at funerals or church services, and likewise from the feasts held each year. At all these occasions, however, the members of most London gilds and of various gilds in other towns appeared in a distinctive costume or livery. This costume was made at the direction of the wardens and paid for by members at cost. If complete it consisted of both hood and gown, but sometimes the hood was allowed to suffice.

There is reference at times to the secrets of the gilds, and there are many indications that the authorities at all times distrusted these religious organizations, fearing apparently that other purposes were concealed beneath these professions of religious zeal and charitable intentions. In the early times, too, the Church distrusted them. In the fourteenth century the religious gilds of London, locally known as the parish gilds, seem to have had covert political significance. But of these matters there is no proof.

The gild merchant presents a most complex array of problems: there are certain elements of kinship with the religious gilds; some powers were exercised that were later the peculiar privilege of the craft gilds; and some of the general concerns of the town were administered by the gild merchant with a measure of autonomy difficult of comprehension to modern minds. The gild merchant was frequently dedicated to some patron saint, or associated with some church festival, and the pious observances of the simple religious gilds were maintained. The fraternal elements are also conspicuous. Sick members were frequently cared for; members who fell into poverty were given a small stipend, and if a member were imprisoned the officers of the gild were in many cases required to procure his deliverance if possible. These features of the gild merchant owed their origin to the circumstances that led to the rise of the religious gilds.

The relation to the craft gilds is a matter of greater importance. It would seem that the gild merchant exercised a general supervision over the crafts, substantially similar to the supervision that was later exercised separately by the individual crafts. The very important inspection of all manufactured goods sold was in the early period exercised by the general gild merchant. Bad workmanship was punished. Rules were laid down with reference to the exercise of various crafts. It would seem, therefore, that the craft gilds were in a sense subsidiary organizations, designed to discharge more completely and adequately powers which required a detailed knowledge of the craft not readily acquired by outsiders. In some instances this splitting-off of the larger crafts from the general gild merchant can be traced in detail. Weavers or other craftsmen would meet surreptitiously in the gild rooms to make rules for themselves, thus assuming to act with the authority of the entire gild. But although there are instances of this sort, it would seem that in general the crafts received their grants of authority directly from the municipality or from the King. The process of specialization of function within the gild merchant, if it actually occurred, was obscured by this reference to the ultimate administrative authorities. For the most part, the relationship between the gild merchant and the craft gild in England was not very close.

The craft organizations have been presumed by some to represent some measure of opposition between the wealthy merchants and the less well-to-do artisans. In some of the German cities there were serious class conflicts between these groups, and the craft gilds rose to power on the ruins of the older institution. In England there is little evidence of any general struggle between the artisans and the merchants, and it is hardly likely that the formation of the craft gilds was merely due to specialization of functions within the larger association. . . .

The gild merchant was an important but subsidiary part of the administrative machinery of the borough. It was subordinated to the town magistrates, but enjoyed a greater degree of autonomy than any modern department of municipal government. The general administration of the borough was in the hands of the borough assembly. This assembly elected both administrative and judicial officers, who thus executed both civil and criminal law. The gild merchant was charged with the regulation of trade, the supervision of the crafts, and with certain judicial or quasi-judicial functions with reference to commercial matters, primarily disputes among members of the gild.

The essential privilege of the gild was the monopoly of trade within the town. In the letter of the law this monopoly was absolute and its enforcement would seem to suggest the policy of municipal selfishness which is the basis of the old idea of a "town economy." The monopoly of trade was, however, less restrictive in fact than would appear on the surface of the regulations. The clause, "so that no one who is not of the gild may trade in the said town, except with the consent of the burgesses," seems categorical: the actual significance of the monopoly was in fact qualified by the admission of non-residents to the privileges of the gild, and by the extension of privileges of wholesale trading to non-members upon the payment of certain duties. The actual rigidity of the gild monopoly thus turns entirely upon the proportion of resident to non-resident members, a subject upon which we are not well informed. In Dublin, between 1225 and 1250 about one half the free citizens were non-residents, so far as may be judged from the place names that follow the names of the citizens, and in the list of one hundred and ninety-one persons admitted to the gild merchant of Dublin in 1226, ninety-six were non-residents. The records of Leicester reveal a large non-resident membership in the gild merchant, and there is no reason to believe that these towns were exceptional. Unfortunately we have few lists of members of the gild merchant, and little work has been done on the lists we have. Still it is clear that we must not assume membership to be confined to residents.

The resident population of a town was not identical with either the municipal corporation or the gild merchant. Neither of these bodies were local bodies in the sense that we would naturally suppose from our modern conceptions of citizenship and towns. Persons living in the vicinity and persons living in privileged jurisdictions within the town were freely admitted to membership in the gild merchant, though they were usually excluded from citizenship. The necessities of trade made it essential to adopt a relatively broad policy, and the differences between the body of citizens and the body of members of the gild merchant amounted to an enfranchisement of commerce. Members of religious houses were by necessity excluded from citizenship even if the order was physically situate in the town, but these monastic houses were important commercially both by reason of the quantities of wool at their disposal and by reason of their purchase of raw materials and manufactures. The country gentry, too, might well find it convenient to possess trading privileges in the neighboring town. Merchants with definite trading interests in a small group of towns would find it specially advantageous to be members of the gild merchant in each of the towns in which they had commercial concerns. The gild merchant was thus an extension of facilities for trading rather than a restrictive feature; it supplemented the markets and the fairs.

There were restrictions upon the complete freedom of trade. Casual merchants could not come to a town when no fair was in progress and sell their wares in competition with the merchants who were regularly doing business in the place. Many incidents can be found of determined opposition to such sporadic trading by aliens or foreigners. The payment of dues required of non-members is also a matter that requires some care in interpretation. The dues were in most instances seignorial or royal dues from which the gild as a whole had secured exemption by paying an annual sum into the royal treasury. This sum was doubtless smaller than a sum representing an exact capitalization of the dues chargeable. By paying a lump sum the gild members reduced the fiscal burden and escaped many exactions to which they would otherwise have been subject, but there was some justice in requiring non-members to pay dues, inasmuch as they did not contribute to the general payment to the royal treasury.

It will be evident that the extent and nature of the commercial monopoly exercised by the gild merchant can easily be misunderstood. Generalization is hazardous, whether with reference to particular towns or to particular periods. These strictures upon the theory of exclusiveness are not designed to be generalizations, but merely indications of the dangers of interpreting literally these various terms which have in all cases taken on new meanings in our modern life. The gild had a monopoly of trade, but it was in fact an inclusive monopoly. Both town and gild have left record of a policy of the closed door; but it is easy to forget that pains were taken to get everybody inside before the door was closed.

The right to participate in the bargains of fellow-gildsmen is indicative of the inclusive character of the gild monopoly. The ordinances of the gild merchant at Southampton provide "that a gildsman shall have a share in all the merchandise which another gildsman buys, if he is on the spot where the merchandise is bought." At Berwick even those who were not present at the transaction were allowed to share, provided that they paid the buyer twelve pence for profit. "This privilege," says Lipson, "was intended to foster equality, and protect the poor from falling into the hands of the few. It embodied the principle that every burgess should have a share in the trade sufficient for the maintenance of himself and his family." The gild at times engaged in joint purchases. In a number of towns the trade in specified articles was restricted to the officers of the gild in their official capacity. The profits were turned into a common purse. Aliens were at times required to make tender of their entire cargo to the gild as a whole. . . .

The organization of the gild merchant was similar to that of most gilds. The primary source of authority was the general assembly of all the members. For administrative purposes an alderman and assistants were elected. There were from two to four assistants designated by names that varied in the different towns: stewards, *échevins,* and wardens were the terms most used. There were at times subordinate officials: farthingmen, levelookers, gildans, heyners, tasters, cup-bearers, ushers, doorkeepers, a dean, clerks, a treasurer a marshal, sergeants, collectors, bailiffs, and provosts. The functions of these minor officials are not wholly certain. The meetings were called "gilds," or "morning talks." They were held annually, semi-annually, or quarterly, for the purpose of admitting new members, inflicting penalties for failure to observe the statutes, or making new ordinances. Both at these regular meetings and on special occasions there was much eating and drinking: "drinkings with spiced cake bread and sundry wines, the cups serving merrily about the house."

The study of the conditions at Paris at the close of the thirteenth century was designed to suggest that the essential feature of a craft gild was the right to elect wardens to exercise the "view" of the craft. The craft gild, according to this interpretation, is to be conceived as a body of craftsmen possessed of some measure of autonomous power. The organization would become a definite part of the municipal administration, exercising powers that would otherwise be within the province of the municipality. This conception is in general applicable to English conditions, but there are subordinate forms of gilds which might easily be a source of confusion.

Associations of craftsmen are found which are not craft gilds in any technical sense, notably religious gilds composed primarily of members of a single craft. Religious gilds can usually be distinguished from true craft gilds by their more inclusive membership and their fraternal and spiritual purposes. More serious confusion can arise with reference to organizations of craftsmen that received charters from the King. Grants of privilege from the King were not uncommon in the early period, and after the Reformation they become particularly important. It may seem pedantic to distinguish these two types of grant of power, but it will be evident that the King could grant privileges that could not be secured from a municipality. A town could grant the "view" of the craft in that town, the King could grant the "view" of the craft in the kingdom as a whole. Royal grants frequently carried exemptions from supervision by the municipal authorities. Such grants were usually made to alien craftsmen settling in England, and in such cases the grant included two distinct sets of privileges. The King alone could grant authority to hold property in a corporate capacity, so that the craft gild could not become an endowed corporation without a royal grant. After the Reformation this power became particularly desirable and many of the crafts sought royal charters and paid good prices for them. The history of organizations of craftsmen in England is thus complex to a degree, and many of these forms cannot be adequately described as gilds; in the later period the term "company" was usually applied.

Apart from the royal charters granted to groups of aliens, which begin to appear in the fourteenth century, there are instances of a significant exercise of the royal prerogative in behalf of native artisans. The history of London affords the clearest evidence of the character and purport of these early grants, though these cases are not unique by any means. The Bakers, the Fishmongers, and the Weavers of London obtained privileges from the King, so that they formed definite jurisdictions before the founding of the municipality in 1191. All three of these groups of artisans stood outside the municipal constitution. Closely associated with these groups of artisans were similar bodies that are designated as the "adulterine" gilds. They seem to have been organized after the same general manner, though they had no royal grant of privilege, or at least no recognized grant. These organizations, particularly in London, exerted a profound influence upon the municipal institutions that took form soon afterward.

There were thus three distinct types of craft organization designated casually as gilds: religious gilds of craftsmen; autonomous crafts, possessed of no general political or jurisdictional privileges; craft organizations chartered by the King having perhaps the right to hold property, the right to supervise the craft throughout a considerable area, and possibly the right to hold court independently of the municipal authority. The presence of these variant forms makes it essential to form some judgment of the purposes and importance of each, and for this reason the suggestions to be derived from comparisons with French conditions would seem to be of special importance.

The autonomous craft gild charged by the municipality with the supervision of the craft in that town was typical in the sense that such an organization tended to become established in the crafts that were sufficiently large to make such organization practicable. In the smaller towns, and with reference to the less important crafts, such organizations emerge at a late period, but with the exception of colonies of aliens such organizations tended to become the basis of the administrative control of industry. When royal incorporation of native craftsmen became common in the sixteenth century, the purposes of the organization were altered in a number of respects so that the frequent designation of these later associations as "companies" indicates a change in character as well as a change in name.

48. CRAFT GILD ORDINANCES[1]

In many medieval towns the master workmen organized themselves in fraternities, commonly known as craft gilds. For the regulation of their affairs the craftsmen frequently drew up ordinances which were often submitted to the town authorities for their approval. A number of these sets of ordinances are published in H. T. Riley's Memorials of London and London Life, *a valuable collection of source material for the history of London in later medieval and early modern times.*

The London Hatters, 1347

In the first place,—that six men of the most lawful and most befitting of the said trade shall be assigned and sworn to rule and watch the trade, in such manner as other trades of the said City are ruled and watched by their Wardens.

Also,—that no one shall make or sell any manner of hats within the franchise of the City aforesaid, if he be not free of the same City; on pain of forfeiting to the Chamber the hats which he shall have made and offered for sale.

Also,—that no one shall be made apprentice in the said trade for less a term than seven years, and that, without fraud or collusion. And he who shall receive any apprentice in any other manner, shall lose his freedom, until he shall have bought it back again.

Also,—that no one of the said trade shall take any apprentice, if he be not himself a freeman of the said City.

Also,—that the Wardens of the said trade shall make their searchers for all manner of hats that are for sale within the said franchise, so often as need shall be. And that the aforesaid Wardens shall have power to take all manner of hats that they shall find defective and not befitting, and to bring

[1] H. T. Riley, *Memorials of London and London Life in the XIIIth, XIVth and XVth Centuries.* London, Longmans, Green and Company. *Articles of the London Hatters,* 1347, pp. 239–240. By permission of the Guildhall Library, London.

them before the Mayor and Aldermen of London, that so the defaults which shall be found may be punished by their award.

Also,—whereas some workmen in the said trade have made hats that are not befitting, in deceit of the common people, from which great scandal, shame, and loss have often arisen to the good folks of the said trade, they pray that no workman in the said trade shall do any work by night touching the same, but only in clear daylight; that so, the aforesaid Wardens may openly inspect their work. And he who shall do otherwise, and shall be convicted thereof before the Mayor and Aldermen, shall pay to the Chamber of the Guildhall, the first time 40d., the second time half a mark, and the third time he shall lose his freedom.

Also,—that no one of the said trade shall be admitted to be free of the City, or to work in the said trade, or to sell any manner of hats within the said franchise, if he be not attested by the aforesaid Wardens as being a good and lawful person, and as a proper workman.

Also,—that no one of the said trade shall receive the apprentice or serving-man of another, until he has fully completed his term, or his master has given him a proper dismissal; on pain of paying, for every time, to the said Chamber half a mark, down to the fourth time, when he shall lose his freedom, until he shall have bought it back again.

Also,—that no one of the said trade shall receive the serving-man of another to work, so long as he is in debt to his master; but he is to remain in the service of his master, until he shall have made satisfaction for the debt which he owes him. And he who shall receive such serving-man otherwise, shall pay to the said chamber for every time 40d; but only down to the fourth time, when he shall lose his freedom, until he shall have bought it back again.

Also,—whereas foreign folks of diverse Countries do bring to the said City divers manners of hats to sell, and carry them about the streets, as well before the houses of freemen of the said trade, as elsewhere; and thereby bar them of their dealings and of their sale, so that the freemen of the said trade in the City are greatly impoverished thereby; it is agreed that no strange person bringing hats to the City for sale, shall sell them by retail, but only in gross, and that, to the freemen of the City; on pain of losing the same.

49. THE HANSEATIC LEAGUE [1]

Perhaps the most interesting and the most famous league of cities in medieval times was the Hansa League, usually called Hanse League or Hanseatic

[1] Helen Zimmern, *The Hansa Towns*. New York, G. P. Putnam's Sons, 1891, pp. 82–104. Courtesy of G. P. Putnam's Sons, publishers.

League in English and American textbooks. It reached its greatest power in the fourteenth century, to which period the following selection is devoted.

Our League had attained its maturity. As we have seen from its origin and as we shall see until its decadence, security and extension of commerce was its one aim and solicitude. The Hanseatics were at all times desirous to extend their markets abroad, to obtain, if possible, the monopoly of trade, and it must be admitted that they succeeded admirably in achieving the end they had in view. When we look back and consider the disorganized state of the empire and the slight support they received from their nominal liege lord, it seems strange that they did not take this occasion to constitute themselves also into a political union, forming independent states after the pattern of the Italian commercial republics. In general, the towns in pursuing their policy took as little real notice of the authority of the emperor, as the emperor of the interests and doings of the towns.

Even our shrewd Hansa merchants, it would seem, were afraid outwardly to present a bold front to their rulers, though secretly they defied them and circumvented their laws. The very existence of the federation was illegal, and in direct contravention to one of the chief clauses of the Golden Bull, which forbade all associations and unions within the empire. It is no doubt on this account that the Hansa, like the Venetian Republic, kept its organization so secret. Even in its own day people were but vaguely informed as to the working of its government, and as to the number and extent of its dominions.

The very natural question arises now that our League is mature, How many cities did it count in its federation? but it cannot be answered with precision. Nay, this question can receive no final reply in any period of the Hansa's history. The towns that joined did not always do so permanently, or were not able to maintain their place, and to fulfil their duties. Often, too, they proved restive and were "unhansed," and it was no easy or inexpensive matter to be readmitted. The ban of the Hansa was more potent than that of pope or emperor. A town that fell under it lost its commerce at one blow. Thus, for example, Bremen, headstrong and stiff-necked, anxious to play an undue part in the Hansa League, saw itself shut out in 1356, because one of its burghers had traded with Flanders at a time when such trading was forbidden. The municipality, called upon to punish him, took his part, with the result that for thirty years the town was "unhansed," thirty miserable years, during which "the city was impoverished, grass grew in its streets, and hunger and desolation took up their abode in its midst," so writes a contemporary eyewitness. Reinstated at last, Bremen had to take up heavy responsibilities in atonement for its misdeeds.

On another occasion Brunswick fell into the hands of discontented artizans, who headed a revolt of several towns against the League. A fulminating decree was issued by the Hansa with the same results as in the case of Bremen. Misery and hunger in this case also proved persuasive, and, at last, after six years, this proscribed town was readmitted. It had to send deputies to Lübeck, who craved pardon in the most abject terms, and who had to accept the most humiliating conditions. Besides questions of internal management, the Brunswickers undertook to build a votive chapel in the town in memory of their bad behaviour, and to send pilgrims to Rome who should crave the Papal pardon for the murders of councillors committed by the rioters. Two burgomasters of Brunswick, and eight of the chief citizens walked humbly in procession, bare-headed, bare-footed, carrying candles in their hands from the church of our Lady at Lübeck, to the town hall, where in the great council chamber of the League, before an enormous crowd, they had publicly upon their knees to confess their repentance for what unruly passion had caused them to do, and to implore their confederates to pardon them for the love of God, and the honour of the Virgin Mary.

More and more did Lübeck come to take the leading place among the cities. Her laws ruled at the Hansa diets. They were reckoned the wisest ever framed by an autonomous community, and are still quoted with respect. The right to use Lübeck law was as eagerly craved by distant cities as the Greek colonies craved the holy fire from native altars. No wonder Lubeck's merchants loved to quote the proud couplet:

"Was willst begehren mehr,
Als die alte Lübsche Ehr?"
("What more will you desire than the old Lübeck honour?")

Aeneas Sylvius Piccolomini, afterwards Pope Pius II, when travelling through Europe as Chancellor of the Emperor Frederick III, visited Lübeck, and writes of it as the town which surpasses all others in the wealth and magnificence of its buildings and churches. The same praise is echoed a little later by a rare guest, the Metropolitan of Moscow, who passed through Lübeck on his way to Florence, to be present at the great church council held there by Eugene IV. Aeneas also visited Danzig, and says it was so well equipped for land and sea warfare, that it could call under arms at least 50,000 men.

The prominence of the cities varied greatly. Circumstances which at one time might be to their advantage, might at another time prove adverse. Thus Wisby, after its sacking by Waldemar, was the victim of an accidental fire, which destroyed all that the Dane had spared. In consequence it fell at once from its position of importance, and its very site, once the source of its strength, became the cause of its downfall, for it proved a most convenient station to pirates. Where the merchant had safely halted, he was now in peril of life and goods.

To the question put at various times to the Hansa's ambassadors "which are the Hansa's cities?" evasive replies were given, either "those towns that fought the Hansa's battles"; or a few were enumerated, and the list closed with a colossal etcetera, etcetera. For they were not easily caught napping, these worthy burghers, and had ever in view "the interests of the common German merchants," which they feared might be endangered by too much publicity. Still, they had become a power that could not be hid and seeing how well they realized this in most respects, it is the more curious that they did not avail themselves of their chance of attaining political autonomy. The more curious too, because, as a rule, the Hanseatics, like the modern Italians, knew so well how to draw profit out of all the dissensions and disorders that agitated Europe.

It was indeed a vast dominion that stood under the sway of the Hansa. In the course of less than a hundred years there had arisen on the Baltic coast, within the area of two hundred and fifty miles, no fewer than fourteen cities of first-class importance, not to name those that already existed there. Thus the merchants held in their possession the mouths of all the great Baltic rivers, on all of which they founded harbours and depots. Germany in that epoch evinced a power of colonization which in its successes recalls the most brilliant moments of the extension of Greek life in the Mediterranean. In more modern times only the North American soil has exercised an attraction similar to that of the Baltic coasts, and has shown an equal power of upraising cities within a brief space of time. Many of the towns boasted a far larger population than they have at this day. Thus Lübeck in the fourteenth century counted eighty thousand inhabitants, as against forty-eight thousand in 1870.

An interesting contemporary opinion on our merchants is extant from the pen of a learned and travelled Italian, Marino Sanudo, a pious Venetian, who set forth early in the fourteenth century with a mission to stir up the Christian world, and organize a new Crusade, for Askelon, the last stronghold of the Romish Church, had fallen into the hands of the unbelievers. His first purpose was to gauge the fighting power of the various European maritime states, for it was a fleet rather than an army that was required. In his journeyings he ventured as far north as the Baltic, and thus reports in his letter to Pope John XXII:

"In Alemannia live many peoples that could prove most useful to us. . . . I have seen with my own eyes that these coasts of Alemannia are quite similar to the Venetian. The inhabitants, strong of limb and practised in arms, are mostly warriors; others well skilled in dyke-making; besides, they are rich, and what is yet more commendable, they show a warm zeal for the affairs of the Holy Land."

After enumerating other advantages to be gained from these allies, he is however obliged to draw his Holiness' attention to a serious drawback on their part, namely, "that the Germans are enormous eaters, which arouses anxiety in respect to supplies when the fleet shall find itself in the hot regions."

A love for feasting meets us repeatedly in the old chronicle reports on the German merchants, and shows that in those days there also held good what Hawthorne has more recently expressed, that the Germans need to refresh exhausted nature twice as often as any other peoples. Then, as now, they were an upright, thorough, massive race, not made of too fine a clay and wanting rather on the aesthetic side; a want sure to strike the more finely strung senses of an Italian.

It is certain that the fourteenth century was in many respects the epoch when the Hansa cities flourished most actively. Neither before nor after did they have so many sided an importance for the whole life of the German nation. It was a stirring period in the history of the European continent; when the Minnesingers gave place to the Mastersingers; when learning, hitherto stored up jealously in the monasteries and the libraries of the princes, had found its way out among burghers and laymen; when protectors of art and science were more often simple merchant princes than noble-born beggars. In a word, it was an epoch when the middle class sprang into full being, and took its due and proper place as a link between the nobility and the common people.

Towards bringing about this state of things the Hansa had greatly contributed. If it failed to emancipate itself entirely from the empire, it was yet ever keenly desirous of emancipating itself from its petty suzerains. Thus the burghers of Lübeck, Cologne, Goslar, and other cities were early forbidden to hold posts under the lord of the domain, no matter how lucrative such posts might be. Wismar, engaged on one occasion in a dispute with the Dominican monks concerning the repair of the town walls, and obliged to cede to these ecclesiastics because the lord of the land was favourable to the Church, carefully recorded the occasion in its "town book," "in order," as it wrote, "that it might remember the circumstance on some future and more favourable occasion." "To pay them out" is implied though not expressed in the phrase.

With the same insistence and energy the towns made good their claims when it was requisite to protect the burgher in his commerce, this source of life to all the cities. Formerly, it is true, the German merchants had appeared in the foreign markets as "the men of the emperor," but now the emperors had no longer might wherewith to back their right, and more efficient protection was called for. This each found in his own city. Hundreds and thousands of treaties and letters of freedom attest to the fact that the towns recognized their duties towards their citizens and practised them most strenuously. Sometimes these were written out in the name of a princeling, whose signature it was always possible to buy for hard cash; but as time went on the towns gradually took an entirely independent stand, so that from France to the Russian districts of Smolensk the whole continent was over-spread with a network of diplomatic and commercial contracts eagerly supported and extended by the towns.

The first thing sought for from the territorial lords, was protection for person and property from the gang of banditti who dwelt in every castle under the leadership of some titled robber; then protection against the cruel rights of wreckage and salvage, which declared all such goods the property of the territorial lord; further, release from imprisonment for debts and other misdemeanours incurred within the jurisdiction of the city and to be dealt with by itself alone; assistance in obtaining payment of foreign debts; freedom from the so-called "judgments of God" in the form of torture, walking on red-hot irons, &c.; regulation and diminution of local taxes and tolls on the lading or unlading of vessels, the weighing of merchandise; permission to fell wood to repair ships; in a word, one and all of the necessary permits to render more easy and profitable the intercourse between towns and nations.

In each foreign country the Hanseatics had always their permanent settlement, known as the *Kontor,* and for these they had early obtained a species of autonomy that permitted them to exercise jurisdiction according to their native laws over their own country people. Defaulters were judged by Hanseatic rules, and the "common merchant" found a help and support against the foreigners among whom he for the moment resided and with whom he traded.

The shrewd towns knew well how to estimate the value of such foreign settlements, and it is noteworthy that they never accorded reciprocal rights. In vain foreigners pleaded permission to found similar settlements in the Hansa's dominions; the towns always skilfully declined such requests. Thus in Cologne foreign merchants were not allowed to reside longer than six weeks at a stretch, and this only three times in the year; therefore only eighteen weeks in all. Similar and even more restrictive regulations prevailed in the other cities.

It is curious to note that, until the end of the thirteenth century, it was chiefly the inland towns who were the great traders, but when they needed for their trade the highway of the ocean, gradually the maritime ports had taken the place of importance. One of the chief lines of sea traffic was that between Bruges in Flanders and Northern Russia. On this route hundreds of ships sailed annually, all owned by the "Easterlings," as the Baltic merchants were called to distinguish them from the inland traders. It was not until the fifteenth century that we find Dutchmen, Zealanders, and Frisians striving to come into serious competition with the Hansa.

A decree that no German merchant might go into partnership with a Russian, Fleming, or Englishman, no doubt aided greatly this exclusive possession of the Baltic Sea. In Russia waterways led them as far as Smolensk; and, later on, they penetrated even further inland, by utilizing the roads that had been made by the German knights whose seat of might was Pomerania and Livonia. The Marienburg, the chief house of the Order, proved a welcome halting station for the merchant travellers, where they found safety and shelter. Furs were largely obtained from the inner districts of Russia. "They are plentiful as dung there," writes the pious chronicler, Adam of Bremen; adding, "for our damnation, as I believe, for *per fas et nefas* we strive as hard to come into the possession of a marten skin as if it were everlasting salvation." According to him, it was from this cause and from Russia "that the deadly sin of luxurious pride" had overspread the West.

Wax, that played so large a part in mediaeval religious rites, and was required in great abundance, was furnished by the "honey-trees" of the virgin Russian forests. Leather, skins, tallow, and all species of fat, were also among the chief products of Russia and the exports of the Hansa. In return, they imported into that empire the produce of the looms of Germany, England, and Flanders, the fine Flemish cloths, the coarser English and German. Silk, too, and linen were valued goods. Important also were all manner of worked metal objects, and such wares as town industries manufacture. Beer, too, was a valued and most profitable article of commerce. This drink was brewed in superior excellence in Northern Germany, the hops being grown on the spot. Contemporary writers tell how outside all the northern cities hop gardens flourished. This beer was never wanting at any carouse in the whole stretch of land from Flanders to Finland; a heavy, heady beverage, which would now be deemed unpalatable and indigestible. Some specimens are preserved to this day in the Danzig *Topenbier* and the Brunswick *Mumme*. To this thirst for ale Hamburg largely owes its prosperity. For many long years it was the greatest beer-making town of the North, boasting in the fourteenth century no less than five hundred breweries.

From Sweden the Hanseatics fetched copper and iron; in many cases they had acquired the sole possession of the mines. Scandinavia also furnished skins, as well as the various forest products of wood, potash, pitch, and tar. From Blekingen, as at this day, the merchants brought granite, and from Gothland and Bornholm limestone, both stones being required for those building purposes for which the native material of brick did not suffice. Already the Baltic supplied the Netherlands with grain.

The Hansa carried in return to Sweden, Finland, and Russia the requirements of daily life, since these countries possessed neither manufactures nor skilled labour. Down to the altar shrines and the psalters of the Church the merchants brought the evidences of civilized workmanship to these lands. The very furs they had taken thence were returned to their northern homes; of course manipulated and worked up. Even the English, more advanced in handicraft, submitted to the same *regime*. It used to be said on the European continent in those days: "We buy the fox skins from the English for a groat, and re-sell them the foxes tails for a guilder." With England indeed the Hansa's intercourse was most active, as we shall show more in detail later on.

Danzig owes almost all its splendour to the English trade. This city dealt largely in Austrian and Hungarian products, which were distributed from out its harbour. English crossbowmen received all the wood for their bows from Austria by way of Danzig. They were made from the yew tree, which was considered especially adapted to this end.

What the German merchant obtained as produce from Russia, Scandinavia, and other parts of Europe, not to mention the special productions of his own towns, he distributed either at home or in the world-famed markets of Bruges and London, for the Hansa was then the only intermediary between East and West. For more than three hundred years Bruges maintained its place as the central market for the whole of Europe this side the Alps. Here could be met traders from all parts; the Lombard bankers and money-changers, the Florentine, Spanish, Portuguese, French, Basque, English, Scotch, North and South Germans. It was from Bruges that the Baltic merchant supplied his home and Northern Germany with the products of the East, which the South German had brought from Venice and over the Alpine passes along the Rhine. In Bruges he could buy the fruits of the Mediterranean, the silks of Florence, the oils of Provence, the wines of Spain and Italy. These meetings of merchants were wont to take place at stated times, intercourse being thus made surer and easier. This custom laid the foundation for those annual fairs for the exchange of wares, of which one yet survives in Germany in little diminished importance, namely, the great fair of Leipzig, where all the German publishers meet to exchange the intellectual productions of the year.

Another source of wealth to the cities arose from the circumstance that they not only supplied the requirements of the mass, but were also the purveyors to the princes and the aristocracy. We find in their books that these frequently owed them heavy sums for furs, Flanders cloth, and choice wines. They were also most often their bankers, for the towns and, above all, Lübeck, the centre of cash transactions, were held desirable places for money investments. Even in the distant districts of Sweden people knew no better mode of investing capital than to confide it to Lübeck merchants.

Of course the conditions of trade were vastly different from those of today. Above all, the merchants had to act more in person. Posts did not exist, orders and contracts, therefore, could rarely be made by letter, for it mostly required a special messenger to carry these. It was hence almost the rule that the merchant accompanied his wares "over sea and sand," as the phrase went. For the sake of greater security, and in order also to diminish expenses, many would club together to charter a ship. It was usual to interest the captains in the sales of the wares, it being held advisable that every one on board should have an advantage in bringing the goods safe to land and in their profitable disposal. This custom arose from the dangers that lurked from robbers, while insurance of goods in transit was yet unknown. By interesting captain and crew pecuniarily they were less likely to throw the goods overboard in a storm, or to allow pirates quietly to board and rob the vessels; both matters of common occurrence.

If it was dangerous to travel by water, it was yet far worse to travel by land. Not to mention that there were few roads, that the mud often lay piled wheel high, so that the strongest horses could not pull the carts; the presence of robbers was a constant cause of fear on the road. Many of these were, as we know, the lordlings of the land in disguise, and hence they naturally turned a deaf ear to the repeated petitions of the merchants to keep the highways in better order. Added to this, each lord had the right to demand toll for the passing of his dominions and the toll stations were often very close together. Thus, for example, within a space of fifteen miles from Hamburg the merchant encountered no less than nine. Fortunately the tables of tolls in those days were not too complicated. They were generally paid by waggon, or ship load, regardless of contents.

The Middle Ages were ignorant of protective taxes. These impediments to the useful exchange of international produce were reserved for the invention and practice of our more enlightened centuries. It is characteristic that the oath which played so great a part in all mediaeval transactions, social and political, was also employed to settle the toll dues of the traveller. A crucifix was held before him; on this he swore that he was not defrauding, that the weight of his wares, as stated by him, was accurate, and herewith the transaction was completed. It was, however, necessary to be most careful not to diverge from the toll roads. If a merchant was found on a bye-road his goods were confiscated and he himself imprisoned. On this account, too, companionship was sought after, the leadership of some one familiar with the ground, and hence merchants and merchandize generally moved in caravans.

It is worthy of note that all the trade of that time was strictly legitimate, and what is known as real merchant's business. Speculation hardly existed. Commission and agency dues were not wholly unknown, but happily there was not existent that pernicious scourge of modern trade, the time bargains, which permit merchandize to be sold a dozen times over before it actually exists. It was honest, true trade, which only sold what it could show. Therefore, it could uphold and practise the axiom, "ware for ware, or for cash." In certain districts, for example Russia, barter was more common than money payments. Credit was absolutely forbidden in certain towns and in certain branches of trade. If credit was allowed the borrower had to find a surety, and to go surety was a grave matter, of which the consequences might easily prove disastrous, entailing loss of property and often of personal freedom.

Payments were usually made in coined money, but bar silver was also employed, especially in Russia, and bills of exchange were not quite unknown. The bills were payable as a rule either at Lübeck or Bruges. Silver was the chief currency, but in the fourteenth century Lübeck was permitted to coin gold. It made guilders after the pattern of the Florentine ducats. The gold to coin them with was bought at Bruges. We must remember that money had a far higher value in those days than in ours, and that if we want to arrive at a just comparison with our own times, we must multiply the sums by seventy or seventy-five. The most common form of reckoning was the Flemish, *i.e.*, one pound, equal to twenty shillings at twelve groats each; in a word, exactly the reckoning that has survived in England to this day. The pound of money was originally a weight. The best money was that of Lübeck, and, above all, the English contracted to be paid in pounds of the "Easterlings," their generic name for the Baltic merchant. As a survival and abbreviation of this phrase we in England say pound sterling to this day. A bad light upon the morality and conditions of the period is thrown by the fact that the petty kings, seeing that their coins were often refused and mistrusted, did not hesitate to coin and give currency to false money bearing the imprint of the League. We come across frequent bitter and often useless complaints on this subject.

50. THE "DONATUS," FROM 500 TO 1500 THE LEADING TEXTBOOK OF GRAMMAR[1]

Introduction by Wayland Johnson Chase

The most widely used textbook of Latin grammar in Western Europe during the whole of the medieval period is a rather small volume, called the Donatus. *As is explained below, it was composed in the fifth century, and enjoyed such a high reputation that even after the spread of humanism and the publication of new and better textbooks, it continued to be employed into the sixteenth century.*

Learning and education, throughout the Middle Ages, survived because of the fostering care taken by the Christian church. Originating in the days of the Roman Empire, this church had recruited its membership from people of many and diverse races, bound together by the might of Rome's power and the universal use of the Latin language. From this universality of Latin it had resulted that for centuries before the Roman Empire came to an end Latin had been both the spoken tongue of all churchmen, whether in the British Isles or on the Continent, and the literary language in which church records and church doctrines were written. Far into the period which followed the overthrow of Rome's power Latin continued to be the language of both speech and writing among ecclesiasts, and also the literary tool of scholarship and officialdom. Indeed, it is safe to assert that until about the twelfth century there was practically no writing done in Western Europe except in Latin. In those Middle Ages the church-fostered education existed not for priests alone, for from the ranks of those trained in church schools were drawn ministers of state, secretaries of feudal nobles, diplomatists, lawyers, and physicians, architects, and musicians. The bailiff of the manor and the merchant required Latin for their accounts, and the town clerk, for their minutes. Today we have the Latin books in which Columbus studied navigation and geography, and it was in Latin that the captains of his day and later studied military tactics. Indeed, proceedings in law were recorded in Latin in England as late as 1730. The common use of it among all educated men made and kept it, throughout the Middle Ages and far into modern times, a truly international speech. This gave to authors like Erasmus a public comprising the whole civilized world, and rendered scholars cosmo-

[1] *The Ars Minor of Donatus,* translated from the Latin by Wayland Johnson Chase, Madison, Wisconsin, University of Wisconsin Press, 1926; pp. 3–5, 29.

politan in a sense almost inconceivable to the student of today. Moreover, the Latin-speaking world was not merely that of the Romanic and Germanic peoples of Europe. This speech of Caesar and Cicero, before the Middle Ages passed, had penetrated far into Slavic lands; into Iceland and Greenland and perhaps to the shores of North America; and it became widespread in Southeastern Europe and Western Asia when, because of the crusading expeditions, there had come to be a Latin Kingdom of Jerusalem and a Latin Empire of Constantinople.

In this widely extending area, knowledge of Latin, therefore, was indispensable. So the schools everywhere were Latin schools and learning to read was learning Latin, and the study of grammar of this tongue was the recognized route to mastery of the power to read, speak, and write.

By far the most commonly used grammar between 400 A. D. and 1500 was an elementary textbook which, in its long career, appeared under many titles, the most usual of which was *Donati De Partibus Orationis Ars Minor,* translatable into the *Lesser Study of Donatus about the Parts of Speech.* As will appear, this title came to be commonly contracted to *Ars Minor,* or to *Donatus, Donat,* or *Donet.*

The author was a teacher of rhetoric in Rome around 350 A. D., and perhaps bore the additional name of Aelius, which, however, appears not to have been attached to his name in any of the early manuscripts of his grammars. Our slight knowledge of him as teacher is derived principally from a passing reference or two to him made by a renowned pupil of his, Jerome, the Church Father and translator of the Bible into the Vulgate. He, quoting Terence's "Every good thing has been said before," wrote, "My master, Donatus, used to say, 'Perish those who have said our good things before us.' "

Besides his work on grammar, this Donatus was the author of commentaries on Terence and Virgil. His full grammatical treatise comprised two sections, of which the *Ars Minor* is the first. The other, about five times its size, was commonly known as the *Ars Maior,* its full title being *Donati Grammatici Urbis Romae Ars Grammatica.* It treats of these topics: the voice, letters, syllables, metrical feet, accents, punctuation marks, the parts of speech, defects and excellences of language, poetical license in forms and in syntax, and figures of rhetoric, and contains many citations from the classical writers, especially Virgil. By the sixth century this had a specially formidable rival in the grammatical treatise of Priscian, who lived in Constantinople around 515. Donatus' elementary treatise, however, the *Ars Minor,* was unequaled by any of its many rivals, and for more than a thousand years was the staff most leaned upon by beginners in Latin study, not only in Europe, but also in the Latin states erected by the crusaders in Asia.

Ars Minor of Donatus Concerning the Parts of Speech

How many parts of speech are there? Eight. What? Noun, pronoun, verb, adverb, participle, conjunction, preposition, interjection.

Concerning the Noun

What is a noun? A part of speech which signifies with the case a person or a thing specifically or generally. How many attributes has a noun? Six. What? Quality, comparison, gender, number, form, case. In what does the quality of nouns consist? It is two-fold, for either it is the name of one and is called proper, or it is the name of many and is called common. How many degrees of comparison are there? Three. What? Positive, as learned; comparative, as more learned; superlative, as most learned. What nouns are compared? Only commun nouns signifying quality or quantity. . . .

51. THE AUTOBIOGRAPHY OF PETER ABELARD[1]

Peter Abelard was born in Brittany about the year 1079, the son of a nobleman. He received an excellent education, and after having refuted the famous William of Champeaux in Paris he established himself there as a lecturer in philosophy, attracting large crowds of auditors. At the age of thirty-six he met a girl called Heloise, whose uncle requested him to give her instruction. She was fifteen then, "her face not unfair," as he himself testified, and before long teacher and pupil fell in love with each other. A long tragedy followed when the uncle discovered what had happened. Heloise entered a convent and Abelard became a monk, but their love lived on, as may be gathered from their letters. The first of these letters differs from all the others, as it is in the nature of an autobiography and addressed by Abelard to a friend, wherefore in some editions of Abelard's letters it is omitted. The title is, A History of the Calamities of Abelard. *Approximately one-half of this interesting composition has been reproduced below, translated from the Latin by C. K. Scott Moncrieff.*

Chapter I. Of the birthplace of Peter Abelard *and of his parentage.*

I then was born in a certain town which, situated at the entering into Brittany, distant from the city of Nantes about eight miles, I believe, in an

[1] *The Letters of Abelard and Heloise,* translated from the Latin by C. K. Scott Moncrieff. New York, Alfred A. Knopf, 1926, pp. 3–24. By permission of and special arrangement with Alfred A. Knopf, Inc., authorized publishers.

easterly direction, is properly known as Palatium. As by the nature of the soil or of my blood I am light of heart, so also I grew up with an aptitude for the study of letters. A father, moreover, I had who was to no small extent imbued with letters before he girded on himself the soldier's belt. Whence, at a later time, he was seized with so great a love of letters that whatever sons he had he was disposed to instruct in letters rather than in arms. And so it befell us. I too, being the first-born, in so far as I was dearer to him than the rest, so much the more diligently did he care for my education. And I, when I advanced farther and had more facility in the study of letters, so much the more ardently did I adhere to it, and with such love of that study was I consumed that, abandoning the pomp of military glory with the inheritance and the privileges of a first-born son to my brother, I finally relinquished the court of Mars that I might be educated in the lap of Minerva. And inasmuch as I preferred the equipment of dialectic to all the teachings of philosophy, I exchanged those weapons for these and to the trophies of war preferred the conflicts of discussion. Thereafter, perambulating divers provinces in search of discussion, wherever I had heard the study of this art to flourish, I became an emulator of the Peripatetics.

Chapter II. Of the persecution of him by his master William. *Of his mastership at Melun, at Corbeil and in Paris. Of his retirement from the city of Paris to Melun, his return to Mont Sainte-Genevieve and to his own country.*

I came at length to Paris, where this study had long been greatly flourishing, to *William* styled "of Champeau," my preceptor, a man at that time pre-eminent, rightly and by common repute, in this teaching: with whom I stayed for a while, welcomed by him at first but afterwards a grave burden to him, since I endeavoured to refute certain of his opinions and often ventured to reason with him, and at times shewed myself his superior in debate. Which things indeed those who among our fellow-scholars were esteemed the foremost suffered with all the more indignation in that I was junior to them in age and in length of study. Hence arose the beginnings of my calamities which have continued up to the present time, and the more widely my fame extended, the more the envy of others was kindled against me. At length it came to pass that, presuming upon my talents beyond the capacity of my years, I aspired, boy as I was, to the mastership of a school, and found myself a place in which to practise, namely Melun, at that time a town of note and a royal abode. My master afore-named suspected this plan and, seeking to remove my school as far as possible from his own, secretly employed all the means in his power to contrive that before I left his school he might take from me mine and the place that I had selected. But inasmuch as among the powerful in the land he numbered several there who were jealous of him, relying upon their help I succeeded in obtaining my desire and won the support of many for myself by the manifest display of his envy. And from this beginning of my school, so much did my name in the art of dialectic begin to be magnified that not only the repute of my fellow-scholars but that of the master himself began to decline and was gradually extinguished. Hence it came about that, presuming more largely upon myself, I made haste to transfer my school to the town of Corbeil, which is nearer to the city of Paris, so that there opportunity might furnish more frequent contests of disputation. Not long afterwards, however, being stricken with an infirmity by the immoderate burden of my studies, I was obliged to return home, and for some years, being banished, so to speak, from France, I was sought out more ardently by those to whom the teaching of dialectic appealed.

But a few years having gone by, when for some time I had recovered from my infirmity, that teacher of mine, *William,* Archdeacon of Paris, laying aside his former habit transferred himself to the order of the regular clergy, with the intention, as was said, that being thought to be more religious he might be promoted to a higher grade in the prelacy, as shortly happened, he being made Bishop of Chalons. Nor did this change of habit call him away either from the city of Paris or from his wonted study of philosophy; but in that same monastery to which for religion's sake he had repaired, he at once opened public classes in his accustomed manner. Then I returning to him that from his lips I might learn rhetoric, among the other efforts of our disputations, contrived, by the clearest chain of argument, to make him alter, nay shatter, his former opinion with regard to universals. For he had been of this opinion touching the community of universals, that he maintained a thing as a whole to be essentially the same in each of its individuals, among which, foresooth, there was no difference in essence but only variety in the multitude of their accidents. He now so corrected this opinion that thereafter he proclaimed the thing to be the same not essentially, but indiscriminately. And inasmuch as this has always been the main question among dialecticians concerning universals so much so that even *Porphyry* in his Isagoga, when he treats of universals, does not presume to define it, saying: "For this is a most weighty business," after he had corrected and then perforce abandoned his opinion, into such neglect did his instruction fall that he was scarcely admitted to be a teacher of dialectic at all; as if in this opinion about universals consisted the sum total of that art. Hence did my teaching acquire so great strength and authority that they who formerly adhered most vehemently to our said master and attacked my doctrine most strongly now flocked to my school, and he who had succeeded to our master's chair in the school of Paris offered me his own place, that there among the rest he might submit himself to my teaching where formerly his master and mine had flourished.

And so after a few days, I reigning there in the study of dialectic, with what envy our master began to consume away, with what rage to boil, is not easily expressed. Nor long sustaining the heat of the affliction that had seized him, he cunningly attempted to remove me once again. And because in my conduct there was nothing whereon he could openly act, he laboured to remove the school from him who had yielded up his chair to me (charging him with the vilest accusations), and to substitute a certain other, one of my jealous rivals, in his place. Then I, returning to Melun, established my school there as before; and the more openly his jealousy pursued me, the more widely it enlarged my authority, according to the words of the poet:

> Envy seeketh the heights, the winds blow on the mountain-tops.

Not long after this, when it came to his knowledge that well-nigh all his disciples were in the utmost hesitation as to his religion, and were murmuring vehemently as to his conversion, in that evidently he had not retired from the city, he transferred himself and his conventicle of brethren, with his school, to a certain village at some distance from the city. And immediately I returned from Melun to Paris, hoping that thenceforth I should have peace from him. But seeing that, as I have said, he had caused my place there to be filled by one of my rivals, outside the city on the Mount of Saint Genevieve I pitched the camp of our school, as though to beleaguer him who had occupied my place. Hearing which, our master straightway returning unashamed to the city, brought back such pupils as he might still have, and the conventicle of brethren to their former monastery, as though to deliver his soldier, whom he had abandoned, from our siege. In truth, whereas he intended to advantage him, he greatly harmed him. He, forsooth, had until then retained sundry disciples, principally for the lectures on *Priscian* in which he was considered to excel. But after the master arrived he lost them one and all, and so was compelled to cease from the tenour of his school. And not long after this, as though despairing for the future of any worldly fame, he too was converted to the monastic life. Now after the return of our master to the city, the conflicts of discussion which our scholars waged as well with him as with his disciples, and the results which fortune in these wars gave to my people, nay to myself in them, thou thyself hast long known as matters of fact. But this saying of *Ajax* I may with more modesty than he repeat and more boldly utter:

> Shouldst thou demand the issue of this fight,
> I was not vanquished by mine enemy.

As to which, were I silent, the facts themselves speak and its outcome indicates the whole matter. But while these things were happening my dearest mother *Lucy* obliged me to return home. Who, to wit, after the conversion of *Berenger,* my father, to the monastic profession, was preparing to do likewise. Which being accomplished, I returned to France, principally that I might learn divinity, when our afore-mentioned master *William* attained to the Bishopric of Chalons. In this study, moreover, his own master, *Anselm* of Laon, was of great and long-established authority.

Chapter III. How he came to Laon to the master Anselm.

I came therefore to this old man, who owed his name rather to long familiarity than to his intelligence or his memory. To whom if any came knocking upon his door in uncertainty as to some question, he departed more uncertain still. Indeed, he was admirable in the eyes of his hearers, but of no account in the sight of questioners. His fluency of words was admirable but in sense they were contemptible and devoid of reason. When he kindled a fire he filled his house with smoke, rather than lighted it with the blaze. His tree, in full life, was conspicuous from afar to all beholders, but by those who stood near and diligently examined the same it was found to be barren. To this tree therefore when I had come that I might gather fruit from it, I understood that it was the fig-tree which the Lord cursed, or that old oak to which *Lucan* compares *Pompey,* saying:

> There stands the shadow of a mighty name,
> Like to a tall oak in a fruitful field.

Having discovered this, not for many days did I lie idle in his shadow. But as I gradually began to come to his lectures more rarely, certain among the more forward of his disciples took it amiss, as though I were shewing contempt for so great a master. Thereafter him also secretly exciting against me with vile suggestions, they made me offensive in his sight. But it fell upon a day that after certain controversies of opinion we scholars were disporting ourselves. When, after a certain one had inquired of me with menacing intent what I thought as to the reading of the Holy Scriptures, I, who had as yet studied nothing save physics only, replied that it was indeed most salutary, the study of this lore in which the salvation of the soul is revealed, but that I marvelled greatly that, to them who were literate men, the Scriptures themselves or the glosses upon them should not be sufficient, so that they should require no other instruction. Many of those present, laughing at me, asked whether I was able and presumed to approach this task. I replied that I was ready to try it if they wished. Then, shouting together and laughing all the more: "Certainly," they said, "we agree. Let some one find, therefore, and bring to us here an expositor of some little read Scripture, and let us put what you promise to the proof."

And they all agreed upon the most obscure prophecy of *Ezekiel*. And so, taking up the expositor, I at once invited them to attend my lecture on the morrow, who, pouring counsels into my unwilling ears, said that in so weighty a matter there was nothing to be gained by haste, but that seeing my inexperience I must give longer thought to the examination and strengthening of my exposition. But I indignantly replied that it was not my custom to advance by practice but rather by intelligence; and added that either I abandoned the contest altogether or they, abiding by my judgment, must come to my lecture without delay. And my first lecture indeed few attended, since that to all it seemed ridiculous that I, who hitherto had been almost wholly unacquainted with Holy Writ, should so hastily approach it. To all, however, who did attend, that lecture was so pleasing that they extolled it with singular commendation, and compelled me to furnish further glosses in the style of my first lecture. Which becoming known, those who had not been present began to flock eagerly to my second lecture and my third, and all alike were solicitous at the start of each to take down in writing the glosses which I had begun on the first day.

Chapter IV. Of the persecution of him by his master Anselm.

Wherefore the old man aforesaid, being stirred by vehement envy, and having already been stimulated against me by the persuasion of divers persons, as I have before recounted, began no less to persecute me over the Holy Scriptures than our *William* had aforetime done over philosophy. Now there were at the time in this old man's school two who appeared to predominate over the rest, namely *Alberic* of Rheims and *Lotulph,* a Lombard: who, the more they presumed upon themselves, were the more kindled against me. And so, his mind greatly perturbed by their suggestions, as later it came to light, this old man boldly forbade me to continue further the work of interpretation which I had begun in his place of teaching. Advancing this pretext forsooth, that if perchance I were to write anything in error in my work, being still untrained in that study, it might be imputed to him. This coming to the ears of the scholars, they were moved with the utmost indignation against so manifest a calumny of envy, the like of which had never befallen any man yet. Which, the more manifest it was, the more honourable was it to me, and so by persecution my fame increased.

Chapter V. How, having returned to Paris, he completed the interpretations which he had begun to deliver at Laon.

So, after a few days, returning to Paris, the schools that had long before been intended for me and offered to me, from which I had at first been driven out, I held for some years in quiet, and there at the opening of my course I strove to complete those interpretations of *Ezekiel* which I had begun at Laon. Which indeed were so acceptable to their readers that they believed me to be no less adept in the Holy Scriptures than they had seen me to be in philosophy. Whence in both kinds of study our school vehemently multiplying, what pecuniary gain and what reputation it brought me cannot have failed to reach your ears. But inasmuch as prosperity ever puffs up fools, and worldly tranquillity enervates the vigour of the mind, and easily loosens it by carnal allurements, when now I esteemed myself as reigning alone in the world as a philosopher, nor was afraid of any further disturbance, I began to give rein to my lust, who hitherto had lived in the greatest continence. And the farther I advanced in philosophy or in the Holy Scriptures, the farther I receded by the impurity of my life from philosophers and divines. For it is well known that philosophers, not to say divines, that is to say men intent on the exhortations of Holy Scripture, have excelled principally by the grace of continence. When, therefore, I was labouring wholly in pride and lechery, the remedy for either malady was by divine grace conferred on me, albeit unwilling; and first for lechery, then for pride. For lechery, indeed, by depriving me of those parts with which I practised it; but for the pride which was born in me from my surpassing knowledge of letters, as is said by the Apostle: "Knowledge puffeth up"—by humiliating me by the burning of that book in which most I gloried. The story of both which things I wish you now to learn more accurately from a statement of the facts than by common hearsay, in the order in which they befell me. Since, therefore, I ever abhorred the uncleanness of harlots, and was withheld from the society of noble women by the assiduity of my studies, nor had ever held much conversation with those of the common sort, lewd fortune, as the saying is, caressing me, found a more convenient opportunity whereby she might the more easily dash me down from the pinnacle of this sublimity; so that in my overweening pride, and unmindful of the grace I had received, divine pity might recall me humbled to itself.

Chapter VI. How having fallen in love with Heloise *he was thereby wounded as well in body as in mind.*

Now there was in this city of Paris a certain young maiden by the name of *Heloise,* the niece of a certain Canon who was called *Fulbert,* who, so great was his love for her, was all the more diligent in his zeal to instruct her, so far as was in his power, in the knowledge of letters. Who, while in face she was not inferior to other women, in the abundance of her learning was supreme. For inasmuch as this advantage, namely literary knowledge, is rare in women, so much the more did it commend the girl and had won her the greatest renown throughout the realm. Seeing in her, therefore, all those things which are wont to attract lovers, I thought it suitable to join her with myself in love, and believed that I could effect this most easily. For such renown had I then, and so excelled in grace of youth and form, that I feared no refusal from whatever woman I might deem worthy of my love. All the more easily did I believe that this girl would consent to me in that I knew her both to possess and to delight in the knowledge of letters; even in absence it would be possible for us to reach one another's presence by written intermediaries, and to express many things more boldly in writing than in speech, and so ever to indulge in pleasing discussions.

So, being wholly inflamed with love for this girl, I sought an opportunity whereby I might make her familiar with me in intimate and daily conversation, and so the more easily lead her to consent. With which object in view, I came to terms with the aforesaid uncle of the girl, certain of his friends intervening, that he should take me into his house, which was hard by our school, at whatever price he might ask. Putting forward this pretext, that the management of our household gravely hindered my studies, and that the expense of it was too great a burden on me. Now he was avaricious, and most solicitous with regard to his niece that she should ever progress in the study of letters. For which two reasons I easily secured his consent and obtained what I desired, he being all agape for my money, and believing that his niece would gain something from my teaching. Whereupon earnestly beseeching me, he acceded to my wishes farther than I might presume to hope and served the purpose of my love: committing her wholly to my mastership, that as often as I returned from my school, whether by day or by night, I might devote my leisure to her instruction, and, if I found her idle, vehemently chastise her. In which matter, while marvelling greatly at his simplicity, I was no less stupefied within myself than if he had entrusted a tender lamb to a ravening wolf. For in giving her to me, not only to be taught but to be vehemently chastised, what else was he doing than giving every licence to my desires and providing an opportunity whereby, even if I did not wish, if I could not move her by blandishments I might the more easily bend her by threats and blows. But there were two things which kept him most of all from base suspicions, namely his love for his niece and the fame of my continence in the past.

What more need I say? First in one house we are united, then in one mind. So, under the pretext of discipline, we abandoned ourselves utterly to love, and those secret retreats which love demands, the study of our texts afforded us. And so, our books lying open before us, more words of love rose to our lips than of literature, kisses were more frequent than speech. Oftener went our hands to each other's bosom than to the pages; love turned our eyes more frequently to itself than it directed them to the study of the texts.

That we might be the less suspected, blows were given at times, by love, not by anger, affection, not indignation, which surpassed all ointments in their sweetness. What more shall I say? No stage of love was omitted by us in our cupidity, and, if love could elaborate anything new, that we took in addition. The less experienced we were in these joys, the more ardently we persisted in them and the less satiety did they bring us. And the more this pleasure occupied me the less leisure could I find for my philosophy and to attend to my school. Most tedious was it for me to go to the school or to stay there; laborious likewise when I was keeping nightly vigils of love and daily of study. Which also so negligently and tepidly I now performed that I produced nothing from my mind but everything from memory; nor was I anything now save a reciter of things learned in the past, and if I found time to compose a few verses, they were amorous, and not secret hymns of philosophy. Of which songs the greater part are to this day, as thou knowest, repeated and sung in many parts, principally by those to whom a like manner of life appeals.

What was the sorrow, what the complaints, what the lamentations of my scholars when they became aware of this preoccupation, nay perturbation of my mind, it is not easy even to imagine. For few could fail to perceive a thing so manifest, and none, I believe, did fail save he to whose shame it principally reflected, namely the girl's uncle himself. Who indeed, when divers persons had at divers times suggested this to him, had been unable to believe it, both, as I have said above, on account of his unbounded affection for his niece and on account also of the well known continence of my previous life. For not readily do we suspect baseness in those whom we most love. Nor into vehement love can the base taint of suspicion find a way. Whence cometh the saying of Saint *Jerome* in his Epistle to *Sabinian* (the eight-and-fortieth): "We are always the last to learn of the evils of our own house, and remain ignorant of the vices of our children and wives when they are a song among the neighbours. But what one is the last to know one does at any rate come to know in time, and what all have learned it is not easy to keep hidden from one." And thus, several months having elapsed, it befell us also. Oh, what was the uncle's grief at this discovery!

What was the grief of the lovers themselves at their parting! What blushing and confusion for me! With what contrition for the girl's affliction was I afflicted! What floods of sorrow had she to bear at my shame! Neither complained of what had befallen himself, but each the other's misfortune. But this separation of our bodies was the greatest possible coupling of our minds, the denial of its satisfaction inflamed our love still further, the shame we had undergone made us more shameless, and the less we felt our shame the more expedient our action appeared. And so there occurred in us what the poets relate of Mars and Venus when they were taken. Not long after this, the girl found that she had conceived, and with the greatest exultation wrote to me on the matter at once, consulting me as to what I should decide to do; and so on a certain night, her uncle being absent, as we had planned together I took her by stealth from her uncle's house and carried her to my own country without delay. Where, in my sister's house, she stayed until such time as she was delivered of a man child whom she named *Astrolabe*.

Her uncle, however, after her flight, being almost driven mad, with what grief he boiled, with what shame he was overwhelmed no one who had not beheld him could imagine. How he should act towards me, what snares he should lay for me he knew not. If he were to kill me, or to injure my body in any way, he feared greatly lest his beloved niece might be made to pay the penalty in my country. To seize my person and coerce me anywhere against my will was of no avail, seeing that I was constantly on my guard in this respect, because I had no doubt that he would speedily assault me if it were worth his while or if he dared. At length I, in some compassion for his exceeding anxiety and vehemently accusing myself of the fraud which my love had committed, as though of the basest treachery, went to supplicate the man, promising him also such further amends as he himself should prescribe. Nor, I asserted, did it appear remarkable to any who had experienced the force of love and retained a memory of the ruin to which even the greatest men, from the very beginning of the human race, had been brought down by women. And, that I might conciliate him beyond all that he could hope, I offered him the satisfaction of joining her whom I had corrupted to myself in marriage, provided that this were done in secret lest I incurred any detriment to my reputation. He assented, and with his own word and kiss, as well as with those of his household, sealed the concord that I had required of him, the more easily to betray me.

Chapter VII. The afore-mentioned girl's dissuasion of him from marriage. He takes her, however, to wife.

Straightway I, returning to my country, brought back my mistress that I might make her my wife. She, however, did not at all approve this action, nay utterly deprecated it for two reasons, namely the danger as well as the disgrace to myself. She vowed that he could never be placated by any satisfaction in the matter, as the event proved. She asked me, also, what glory she was like to have from me when she made me inglorious and equally humiliated herself and me. What a penalty this world would be entitled to exact from her if she took from it so bright a lantern, what maledictions, what prejudice to the Church, what tears of philosophers would follow such a marriage. How indecorous, how lamentable it would be were I to dedicate myself, whom nature had created for all mankind, to a single woman, and subject myself to so base a condition. She vehemently detested this marriage, because it was in every respect a shame and a burden to me. She set before me at the same time my own disgrace and the difficulties of matrimony which the Apostle exhorts us to avoid when he says: "Art thou loosed from a wife? Seek not a wife. But and if thou marry, thou hast not sinned; and if a virgin marry, she hath not sinned. Nevertheless such shall have trouble in the flesh: but I spare you." And again: "But I would have you without carefulness."

But if I accepted neither the counsel of the Apostle nor the exhortations of the Saints as to the heavy yoke of marriage, at least, she said, I should hearken to the philosophers, and pay regard to what things were written by them or concerning them on this matter. Which in great measure the Saints also diligently do for our censure. As in that passage of Saint *Jerome* in his First Book against *Jovinian,* where he recalls that *Theophrastus,* after diligently expounding in great detail the intolerable annoyances of marriage, and its perpetual disquietudes, shewed by the clearest reasoning that a wise man ought not to take a wife, where he himself also ends these reasonings of philosophic exhortation with the following conclusion: "What Christian does not *Theophrastus* confound, arguing thus?" In the same book, she went on, *"Cicero,"* saith *Jerome,* "being asked by *Hircius* that after the repudiation of *Terentia* he would marry his sister, absolutely refused to do so, saying that he could not give his attention at the same time to a wife and to philosophy. He does not say, 'give attention,' but he adds what is tantamount that he does not wish to do anything which can be reckoned equal with the study of philosophy." But, to say no more of this obstacle to philosophic study, consider the state itself of honourable conversation. For what concord is there between pupils and serving-maids, desks and cradles, books or tablets and distaves, styles or pens and spindles? Who, either, intent upon sacred or philosophic meditations can endure the wailing of children, the lullabies of the nurses soothing them, the tumultuous mob of the household, male as well as female? Who, moreover, will have strength to tolerate the foul and incessant squalor of babes? The rich, you will say, can, whose palaces or ample abodes contain retreats, of which their opulence does not feel the cost nor is it tormented by daily worries. But the condition of philosophers is not, I say, as that of the rich, nor do those who seek wealth or involve themselves in secular cares devote themselves to divine or philosophic duties. Wherefore also the eminent philosophers of yore, utterly despising the world, not so much leaving the age as flying from it, forbade themselves all kinds of pleasure, that they might rest in the embrace of their philosophy alone. One of whom, and the greatest, *Seneca,* instructing *Lucilius,* saith (in his three-and-seventh epistle): "When thou mayest be idle is no time for philosophy, we must neglect all else that we may devote ourselves to this for which no time is long enough." It matters little whether one omit or be intermittent in the study of philosophy; for where it is interrupted it does not remain. We must resist other occupations, and not extend them but put them away. What now among us they endure who rightly are called monks, those endured also from desire for philosophy who stood out among the Gentiles as noble philosophers.

For among every people, Gentile as well as Jewish or Christian, some men have always stood out by faith or by the respectability of their morals, taking pre-eminence over the rest, and segregating themselves from the people by some singularity of continence or abstinence. Among the Jews, indeed, in ancient times, the Nazarites, who consecrated themselves to the Lord according to the Law, or the Sons of the Prophets, followers of *Elias* or *Eliseus,* of whom (as witnesseth Saint *Jerome,* in his fourth and thirteenth epistles) we read in the Old Testament as monks. More recently, also, those three sects of philosophy which *Josephus* distinguishes in the Eighteenth Book of Antiquities, some Pharisees, others Sadducees and others Essenes. But among us, the monks, who imitate either the common life of the Apostles or that earlier and solitary life of *John.* And among the Gentiles, as has been said, the philosophers. For the name Wisdom or Philosophy they applied not so much to the perception of learning as to strictness of life, as we learn from the derivation of the word itself, and also from the testimony of the Saints. Of which is that passage of Saint *Augustine* in the eighth book, Of the City of God, where he distinguishes the races of philosophers: "The Italian race had as their founder *Pythagoras* the Samian, from whom the very name Philosophy is said to have been derived. For whereas before him they were called wise who appeared to outshine the rest by some manner of praiseworthy living, he being asked what was his profession replied that he was a philosopher, that is a student or lover of wisdom, for to profess oneself wise seemed to him the height of arrogance." So in the passage where it is said: "who appeared to outshine the rest by some manner of praiseworthy living," it is clearly shewn that the wise men of the Gentiles, that is to say the philosophers, were so named rather in praise of their lives than of their learning. How soberly, though, and continently these lived it is not for me now to shew by examples, lest I seem to be offering instruction to Minerva herself. If, however, laymen and Gentiles lived thus, bound by no profession of religion, how does it behove thee, who art a clerk and a canon, to act, that thou prefer not base pleasures to thy sacred duties, that this Charybdis swallow thee not quick, that thou immerse not thyself shamelessly and irrevocably in these obscenities? Nay, if thou care not for the prerogative of the clerk, do thou at least defend the dignity of the philospher. If the reverence due to God be contemned, at least let the love of honour temper thy shamelessness. Remember that *Socrates* was wedded, and with how sordid a case he first purged that stain on philosophy, that thereafter other men might by his example be made more prudent. Which is not overlooked by *Jerome,* writing of the said *Socrates* in his first against *Jovinian:* "Once upon a time, when he had withstood the endless invective poured upon him by *Xanthippe* from an upper storey, being drenched with unclean water he made no more answer than, as he wiped his head: 'I knew that rain must follow all that thunder.' " Finally she observed both how dangerous it would be for me to bring her back, and how much dearer it would be to her, and more honourable to me, to be called mistress than wife, that affection alone might hold me, not any force of the nuptial bond fasten me to her; and that we ourselves, being parted for a time, would find the joy of meeting all the keener, the rarer our meetings were.

With these and similar arguments seeking to persuade or dissuade me, since she could not bend my obstinacy, nor bear to offend me, sighing vehemently and weeping, she brought her exhortation to an end in this manner. One thing, she said, remains to the last, that after the ruin of us both our suffering may be no less than the love before it. Nor in this speech, as the whole world was to know, was the spirit of prophecy lacking. And so, commending our infant son to my sister, we returned privily to Paris, and a few days later, having kept secret vigils of prayer by night in a certain church, there at the point of dawn, in the presence of her uncle and divers of our own and his friends, we were plighted together by the nuptial benediction.

Presently we withdrew privily apart, nor did we see each other afterwards save seldom and by stealth, concealing as far as possible what we had done. Her uncle, however, and his servants, seeking a solace for their ignominy began to divulge the marriage that had been celebrated, and to break the promise they had given me on that head. But she began to anathematise to the contrary, and to swear that their story was altogether false. Whereby he being vehemently moved began to visit her with frequent contumely.

On learning of this I removed her to a certain Abbey of nuns near Paris, which is called Argenteuil, where she herself as a young girl had been bred up and schooled. The garments also of religion, which befitted the monastic profession, except the veil, I had fashioned for her and put them on her. Hearing which, the uncle and his kinsmen and associates were of the opinion that I had played a trick on them, and had taken an easy way to rid myself of *Heloise,* making her a nun. Whereat vehemently indignant, and conspiring together against me, on a certain night while I slumbered and slept in an inner room of my lodging, having corrupted a servant of mine with money, they punished me with a most cruel and shameful vengeance. . . .

Chapter VIII. Of the injury to his body. He becomes a monk in the Monastery of Saint Denis: Heloise *a nun at Argenteuil.*

But day coming the whole town congregating round about me, with what amazement they were transfixed, with what an outcry they lamented, with what clamour they wearied me, with what tribulations disturbed me it would be difficult, nay impossible to relate. The clergy principally, and most of all my scholars tormented me with intolerable lamentations and wailings, so that I was hurt far more by their compassion than by the passion of my wound, felt more occasion to blush than to bleed, and was troubled rather by modesty than by pain. It occurred to my mind with what glory I had but recently shone, how easily and in a moment this had been brought low, nay, utterly extinguished. . . .

Plunged in so wretched a contrition, it was the confusion of shame, I confess, rather than the devotion of conversion that drove me to the retirement of a monastic cloister. She, moreover, had already at my command willingly taken the veil and entered a convent. And so both the two of us at one time put on the sacred habit, I in the Abbey of Saint Denis and she in the Convent of Argenteuil aforesaid. Who indeed, I remember, when divers in compassion of her tried vainly to deter so young a woman from the yoke of the monastic rule, as from an intolerable burden, breaking out, as best she could amid her tears and sobs, into that famous complaint of *Cornelia,* answered:

> Great husband, undeserving of my bed!
> What right had I to bow so lofty a head?
> Why, impious female, did I marry thee,
> To cause thy hurt? Accept the penalty
> That of my own free will I'll undergo . . .

And with these words she hastened to the altar and straightway, before the Bishop, took the blessed veil from the altar and publicly bound herself to the monastic profession.

Meanwhile I had scarcely recovered from my injury when the clergy, pouring in upon me, began to make incessant demands both of our Abbot and of myself, that what hitherto I had done from eagerness for wealth or praise I should study now to do for the love of God, considering that the talent which had been entrusted to me by God would be demanded of me by Him with usury, and that I who hitherto had aimed principally at the rich should henceforth devote myself to the education of the poor. And to this end chiefly, I should know that the hand of the Lord had touched me, namely that being naturally set free from carnal snares and withdrawn from the turmoil of secular life, I might devote myself to the study of letters Nor should I become a philosopher of the world so much as of God.

Now this Abbey of ours to which I had repaired was entirely abandoned to the secular life, and that of the lewdest. Whereof the Abbot himself exceeded the rest of us no more in rank than in the dissoluteness and notorious infamy of his life. Their intolerable filthiness I frequently and vehemently, now in private now publicly attacking, made myself burdensome and odious beyond measure to them all. And so, greatly rejoicing at the daily importunities of my pupils, they sought an opportunity whereby they might remove me from their midst. And so my pupils long continuing to insist, and importuning the Abbot also, and the brethren intervening, I withdrew to a certain cell, to devote myself as of old to my school. Thereto indeed so great a multitude of scholars poured in that neither was the place sufficient for their lodging nor the soil for their sustenance. There, as more became my profession, giving my attention principally to the Holy Scriptures, I did not altogether lay aside the teaching of the secular arts in which I was more fully versed, and which they demanded most of me; but made of them, as it were, a hook wherewith I might draw them, enticed by the philosophic savour, to the study of the true philosophy, as (the Ecclesiastical History reminds us) was the custom of the greatest of the Christian philosophers, *Origen*. Inasmuch, therefore, as the Lord appeared to have conferred on me no less of His grace in the Holy Scriptures than in profane letters, our school began to multiply exceedingly in both classes, and all the rest to be greatly attenuated. Whereby I aroused the envy and hatred of the other masters against myself. Who detracting me in every way possible, two of them in particular were always objecting to me in my absence that it was evidently contrary to the profession of a monk to be detained by the study of secular books, and that, without myself having had a master, I had presumed to aspire to a mastership in the Holy Scripture, seeking evidently thus to interdict me from every exercise of scholastic teaching, where to they incessantly incited Bishops, Archbishops, Abbots and whatever persons bearing a name in religion they might approach.

52. *ABELARD'S BOOK OF CONTRADICTIONS, ENTITLED "SIC ET NON," OR "YES AND NO"* [1]

This celebrated work has great historical significance, because it proves that early in the twelfth century there were already scholars in France who dared to question the opinions of the authorities in the Church. Abelard

[1] The original is given in *Patrologia Latina,* ed. by J. P. Migne, vol. CLXXVIII, Paris, 1885, col. 1339–1610.

actually proceeded to show that these authorities disagreed on numerous important articles of faith. His book, "Sic et Non," contains one hundred and fifty-eight propositions, or questions. Under each title the pronouncements of different scholars are given. Their statements are conflicting, but Abelard did not express his own judgment, leaving his readers to decide for themselves who was right. A number of these titles follow below, preceded by an excerpt from the Prologue. In addition, proposition no. 156[1] *is presented here in extenso, as an illustration of his method.*

Prologue

I wish to collect various sayings of the Fathers which occur to my memory and which, because of the apparent contradiction in them present a problem. They impel young readers to exert themselves most eagerly in the search for the truth, and render their minds more acute by means of the inquiry. This investigation is in fact the first key to wisdom, that is to say, assiduous or frequent inquiry, which is very strongly advocated by that most far-sighted of all philosophers, Aristotle, when he says in exhorting the studious, "Perhaps it is difficult to express oneself with confidence on such matters, unless these have often been discussed. To entertain doubt concerning some of them is not without advantage." For it is through doubting that we arrive at inquiry, and through inquiry we perceive the truth, according to the Truth Himself. "Seek," He says, "and ye shall find, knock and it shall be opened unto you" [Matthew VII]. And, in order to instruct us by His own example, He chose to be found at the age of twelve interrogating the doctors, sitting in their midst, showing us the appearance of a pupil asking questions, rather than that of a master who teaches, although there is in Him the complete and perfect wisdom of God.

Inasmuch as some words of the Scriptures have been quoted, it follows that the greater is the authority commanded by the Scriptures, the more these words induce one to search for the truth. Hence I have compiled in this volume sayings of the saints, observing the decree of Pope Gelasius concerning the authentic books, having included nothing from apocryphal books. . . . Here follow the propositions collected from these books which seem to contradict each other. Because of this contradiction this compilation of propositions is called *Sic et Non* (*Yes and No*).

I. That faith is based on reason, and the opposite.

II. That faith is of things not seen, and the opposite.

[1] The translation of this proposition is based on that found in Arthur O. Norton, *Readings in the History of Education. Mediaeval Universities.* Cambridge, Mass., Harvard University Press, 1909, pp. 21–24. By permission.

III. That knowledge is not of things not seen but faith is, and the opposite.
IV. That one must believe in God only, and the opposite.
V. That God is not single, and the opposite.
VI. That God is threefold, and the opposite.
XI. That the Divine Persons mutually differ, and the opposite.
XII. That in the Trinity each is one with the other, and the opposite.
XIII. That God the Father is the cause of the Son, and the opposite.
XIV. That the Son is without beginning, and the opposite.
XXVII. That Divine Providence is the cause of things happening, and the opposite.
XXVIII. That nothing happens by chance, and the opposite.
XXXII. That all things are possible to God, and the opposite.
XXXIII. That God does not have a free will, and the opposite.
XXXVIII. That God knows all things, and the opposite.
XXXIX. That the works of men are nothing, and the opposite.
XLVII. That before the creation of man the angel [of darkness] fell, and the opposite.
XLIX. That all classes of celestial spirits are generally called angels, and the opposite.
LI. That the first parents were created mortal, and the opposite.
LIV. That man's first sin did not begin through the persuasion of the devil, and the opposite.
LV. That Eve only, and not Adam, was beguiled, and the opposite.
LVI. That by sinning man lost free will, and the opposite.
LXXVII. That the Jews or the devils knew Christ before His passion, and opposite.
LXXXIV. That Christ, in descending into hell freed all, and the opposite.
LXXXIX. That a creature is to be worshiped, and the opposite.
XCIII. That Peter and Paul and all the apostles are equal, and the opposite.
CVI. That without baptism with water nobody can be saved, and the opposite.
CVII. That baptism wipes out all sins, original as well as one's own, and the opposite.
CXIII. That baptism without the sacrament of the altar suffices, and the opposite.
CXVI. That the sins of the fathers are visited upon the children, and the opposite.
CXXII. That everybody should be allowed to marry, and the opposite.
CXXIX. That it is permitted to marry more than once, and the opposite.

CXXX. That there can be no human sexual intercourse without sin, and the opposite.
CXXXVI. That the love of one's neighbor applies to every man, and the opposite.
CXLII. That saintly works do not justify a man, and the opposite.
CLI. That without confession sins cannot be forgiven, and the opposite.
CLIII. That one should not pray for all, and the opposite.
CLV. That a man may kill himself for some reasons, and the opposite.
CLVI. That it is permitted to kill men, and the opposite.

CLVI.

That it is permitted to kill men, and the opposite thesis.

Jerome on Isaiah, Bk. V. He who cuts the throat of a man of blood, is not a man of blood.

Idem, On the Epistle to the Galatians: He who smites the wicked because they are wicked and whose reason for the murder is that he may slay the base, is a servant of the Lord.

Idem, on Jeremiah: For the punishment of homicides, impious persons and poisoners is not bloodshed, but serving the law.

Cyprian, in the Ninth Kind of Abuse: The King ought to restrain theft, punish deeds of adultery, cause the wicked to perish from off the face of the earth, refuse to allow parricides and perjurers to live.

Augustine: Although it is manslaughter to slaughter a man, a person may sometimes be slain without sin. For both a soldier in the case of an enemy and a judge or his official in the case of a criminal, and the man from whose hand, perhaps without his will or knowledge, a weapon has flown, do not seem to me to sin, but merely to kill a man.

Likewise: The soldier is ordered by law to kill the enemy, and if he shall prove to have refrained from such slaughter, he pays the penalty at the hands of his commander. Shall we not go so far as to call these laws unjust or rather no laws at all? For that which was not just does not seem to me to be a law.

Idem, on Exodus ch. xxvii: The Israelites committed no theft in spoiling the Egyptians, but rendered a service to God at his bidding, just as when the servant of a judge kills a man whom the law hath ordered to be killed; certainly if he does it of his own volition he is a homicide, even though he knows that the man whom he executes ought to be executed by the judge.

Idem, on Leviticus ch. lxxv: When a man is justly put to death, the law puts him to death, not thou.

Idem, Bk. I of the "City of God": Thou shalt not kill, except in the case of those whose death God orders, or else when a law hath been passed to suit the needs of the time and express command hath been laid upon a person. But he does not kill who owes service to the person who gives him his orders, for he is as it were a mere sword for the person who employs his assistance.

Likewise: When a soldier, in obedience to the power under which he is legitimately placed, kills a man, by no law of the state is he accused of murder; nay if he has not done it, he is accused of desertion and insubordination. But if he had acted under his own initiative and of his own will, he would have incurred the charge of shedding human blood. And so he is punished if he does not do when ordered that for which he would receive punishment if he did it without orders.

Idem, to Publicola: Counsel concerning the slaying of men pleaseth me not, that none may be slain by them, unless perhaps a man is a soldier or in a public office, so that he does the deed not in his own behalf, but for others and for the state, accepting power legitimately conferred, if it is consonant with the task imposed on him.

Likewise: It has been said: let us not resist the evil man, let not the vengeance delight us which feeds the mind on others' ill, let us not neglect the reproofs of men.

Idem, to Marcella: If that earthly commonwealth of thine keep to the teachings of Christ, even wars will not be waged without goodwill, for with pitying heart even wars if possible will be waged by the good, so that the lusts of desire may be subdued and those faults destroyed which ought under just rule to be either rooted out or chastised. For if Christian training condemned all wars, this should rather be the advice given in the gospel for their safety to the soldiers who ask for it, namely to throw aside their arms and retire altogether from the field. But this is the word spoken to them: Do violence to no man, neither accuse any falsely; and be content with your wages.

He warns them that the wages that belong to them should satisfy them, but he by no means forbids them to take the field.

Idem, to his comrade Boniface: "I will give thee and thine a useful counsel: Take arms in thy hands; let prayer strike the ears of the creator; because in battle the heavens are opened, God looks forth and awards the victory to the side he sees to be the righteous one."

Idem: The wars to be waged we undertake either at the command of God or under some lawful rule. Else John when the soldiers to be baptized came to him saying, "And what shall we do?" would make answer to them: "Cast aside your arms, leave the service; smite no man; ruin no man."

But because he knew that they did these things because they were in the service, that they were not slayers of men, but servants of the law; and not avengers of their own injuries, but guardians of the public safety, his answer to them was: "Do violence to no man," etc.

Isidore, Etymologiae, Bk. XVIII, ch. iii: A righteous war is one waged according to orders, to recover property or drive back the enemy.

Pope Nicholas to the questions of the Bulgarians: If there is no urgent need, not only in Lent but at all times, men should abstain from battles. If however there is an unavoidable and urgent occasion, and it is not Lent, beyond all doubt preparations for wars should be sparingly made in one's own defence or in that of one's country or the laws of one's fathers: lest forsooth this word be said: A man if he has an attack to make, does not carefully take counsel beforehand for his own safety and that of others, nor does he guard against injury to holy religion.

53. *LECTURING IN THE MEDIEVAL UNIVERSITIES*[1]

There are numerous statutes on the mode of lecturing. At Bologna, and doubtless elsewhere, professors seem to have experienced the difficulty, not unknown to modern teachers, of getting through the entire course within the prescribed time. The students, who regulated the conduct of their teachers, made stringent rules to prevent this, and punished violations of them by fines large enough to make professors take due caution:

We have decreed also that all Doctors actually lecturing must read the glosses immediately after reading the chapter or the law, unless the continuity of the chapters or of the laws requires otherwise, taking the burden in this matter on their own consciences in accordance with the oath they have taken. Nor, with regard to those things that are not to be read, must they yield to the clamor of the scholars. Furthermore we decree that Doctors, lecturing ordinarily or extraordinarily, must come to the sections assigned *de novo,* according to the regulations below. And we decree, as to the close observance by them of the passages, that any Doctor, in his ordinary lecturing in Canon or Civil Law, must deposit, fifteen days before the Feast of Saint Michael, twenty-five Bologna pounds with one of the treasurers whom the rectors have appointed; which treasurer shall promise to give said money to the rectors, or the general beadle in their name, all at once or in separate amounts, as he shall be required by them or by him.

The form, moreover, to be observed by the Doctors as to the sections is this: Let the division of the book into sections (*puncta*) be determined,

[1] The introduction and the following selection are taken from *Readings in the History of Education: Mediaeval Universities* by Arthur O. Norton. Cambridge, Mass., Harvard University Press, 1909, pp. 112–114. By permission.

and then let him be notified. (And if any Doctor fails to reach any section on the specified date he shall be fined five pounds, and for a third and each succeeding violation of the rule, ten pounds.) And if the twenty-five pounds are exhausted, he must deposit in said place a second twenty-five pounds; and the second deposit must be made within eight days from the time when the first was exhausted. . . .

We decree also that no Doctor shall hereafter exceed one section in one lecture. And if the contrary be done by any one he shall be charged with perjury and punished to the extent of three pounds, to be taken from the money deposited for the purpose; and as often as the violation occurs, so often shall the penalty be inflicted, so long as the statute is in force; and the Rector also must exact it.

We add that at the end of a section the Doctors must announce to the scholars at what section they are to begin afterwards, and they shall be obliged to follow that section which they have begun, even to the end of the section. But if by chance, after due weight is given to the glosses or text, it seems useful to transfer a part of the lecture to another section, he shall be obliged in his preceding lecture to announce that to the scholars, so that those who wish may make provision before-hand; under penalty of five Bologna shillings for each occasion for the Doctor who does to the contrary.

We order this statute to be published in each school at the beginning of the term. . . .

Since topics not read by the Doctors are completely neglected and consequently are not known to the scholars, we have decreed that no Doctor shall omit from his sections any chapter, decretal, law, or paragraph. If he does this he shall be obliged to read it within the following section. We have also decreed that no decretal or decree or law or difficult paragraph shall be reserved to be read at the end of the lecture if, through such reservation, promptness of exit at the sound of the appointed bell is likely to be prevented.

54. *A MEDIEVAL DISSERTATION* [1]

Author's reasons for undertaking the discussion.

Let it be known to you all that, whilst I was in Mantua, a certain Question arose, which, often argued according to appearance rather than to truth remained undetermined. Wherefore, since from boyhood I have ever been nurtured in love of truth, I could not bear to leave the Question I have spoken of undiscussed: rather I wished to demonstrate the truth concerning

[1] Arthur O. Norton, *Readings*, pp. 116–120.

it, and likewise, hating untruth as well as loving truth, to refute contrary arguments. And lest the spleen of many, who, when the objects of their envy are absent, are wont to fabricate lies, should behind my back transform well-spoken words, I further wished in these pages, traced by my own fingers, to set down the conclusion I had reached and to sketch out, with my pen, the form of the whole controversy.

THE QUESTION: IS WATER, OR THE SURFACE OF THE SEA, ANYWHERE HIGHER THAN THE EARTH, OR HABITABLE DRY LAND?

Affirmative Argument: Five affirmative arguments generally accepted.
Reason 1. Geometrical Proof: Earth and Water are spheres with different centers; the center of the Earth's sphere is the center of the universe; consequently the surface of the Water is above that of the Earth.
Reason 2. Ethical Proof: Water is a nobler element than Earth; hence it deserves a nobler, or higher, place in the scheme of the universe.
Reason 3. Experimental Proof: based on sailors seeing the land disappear under their horizon when at sea.
Reason 4. Economical Proof: The supply of Water, namely, the sea, must be higher than the Earth; otherwise, as Water flows downward, it could not reach, as it does, the fountains, lakes, etc.
Reason 5. Astronomical Proof: Since Water follows the moon's course, its sphere must be excentric, like the moon's excentric orbit; and consequently in places be higher than the sphere of the Earth.

Negative Argument: These reasons unfounded.
I. Refutation by Observation.

Water flows down to the sea from the land; hence the sea cannot be higher than the land.
II. Refutation by Reasoning:

A. Water cannot be higher than the dry land.

Proof: Water could only be higher than the Earth,
1. If it were excentric, or
2. If it were concentric, but had some excrescence.

But since
x. Water naturally moves downwards,
and
y. Water is naturally a fluid body:

1. Cannot be true, for three impossibilities would follow:
a. Water would move upwards as well as downwards;
b. Water and Earth would move downwards in different directions;
c. Gravity would be taught ambiguously of the two bodies.

Proof of these impossibilities by a diagram.

2. Cannot be true, for
   a. The Water of the excrescence would be diffused, and consequently the excrescence could not exist:
   b. It is unnecessary, and what is unnecessary is contrary to the will of God and Nature.

B. All land is higher than the sea.

Proof: It has been shown that Water is of one level, and concentric with the Earth:

Therefore, since the shores are higher than the edges of the sea, and since the shores are the lowest portions of the land,

It follows that all the land is higher than the sea.

C. Objections to the foregoing reasoning, and their refutation.

1. *Possible affirmative argument:* Earth is the heaviest body hence it is drawn down to its own center, and lies beneath the lighter body, Water.
2. *Objection to this argument:* Earth is the heaviest body only by comparison with others; for Earth is itself of different weights.
3. *Refutation of this objection:* On the contrary, Earth is a simple body, and as such subject to be drawn equally in every part.
4. *Answer to the refutation, with minor objections and their refutation.*

Since the objection is in itself sound, and Earth by its own Particular Nature, due to the stubbornness of matter, would be lower than the sea; and since Universal Nature requires that the Earth project somewhere, in order that its object, the mixture of the elements, may be fulfilled:

It follows that there must be some final and efficient cause, whereby this projection may be accomplished.

a. The final cause has been seen to be the purpose of Universal Nature.

b. The efficient cause cannot be (i) the Earth, (ii) the Water, (iii) the Air or Fire, (iv) the heaven of the Moon, (v) the Planets, nor (vi) the Primum Mobile:

Therefore it must be ascribed to the heaven of the Fixed Stars (for this has variety in efficiency, as is seen in the various constellations), and in particular to those Stars of the Northern Hemisphere which overhang the dry land.

(x) *First objection:* Why is the projecting continent then, not circular, since the motion of these stars is circular?

Answer: Because the material did not suffice for so great an elevation.

(y) *Second objection:* Why is this elevation in this particular place?

Answer: Because God whose ways are inscrutable, willed it so. We should therefore desist from examining too closely the reasons, which we can never hope to fathom.

D. *Refutation of the original arguments:*

Reason 1. Invalid because Earth and Water are spheres with the same center.

Reason 2. Invalid because of the external influence of Universal Nature, counteracting the internal influence of Particular Nature.

Reason 3. Invalid because it is sphericity of the sea and not the lowness of the land which interferes with one's view at sea.

Reason 4. Invalid because Water does not flow to the tops of mountains, but ascends thither in the form of vapors.

Reason 5. Invalid because Water imitating the moon in one respect, need not imitate it in all.

55. *EDUCATIONAL VALUE AND INFLUENCE OF THE MEDIEVAL UNIVERSITY* [1]

In the following selection the leading English authority on the medieval universities sums up the merits and defects, as he sees them, of a medieval university education.

What was the real value of the education which the medieval University imparted? That is quite a different question of course from the question of the intrinsic importance of the scholastic Theology and Philosophy, or again of medieval Jurisprudence and Medicine, in the history of thought; just as the intrinsic value of Greek Literature and Philosophy to the world is quite a distinct problem from the educational value of an ordinary classical education to the average boy. It is true that the problems are not unconnected, and it may sometimes be a melancholy necessity that to enable one man to study a subject with effect a dozen should be doomed to study it without profit. But for the present it is the education value of the medieval University system that is in question.

To the modern student, no doubt, the defects of a medieval education lie upon the surface. The external defects of the University organization have already been incidentally noticed. In the older University system of northern Europe there is the want of selection and consequent incompetency of the teachers, and the excessive youth of the students in Arts. In the higher Faculties too we have encountered the constant effort on the part of the

[1] Hastings Rashdall, *The Universities of Europe in the Middle Ages,* 2 vols., Oxford, at the Clarendon Press, 1895. Vol. II, part ii., pp. 703–712. Used by permission.

Doctors to evade the obligation of teaching without surrendering its emoluments, while the real teaching devolved upon half-trained Bachelors. It is, indeed, in the Student-Universities that the chairs would appear to have been most competently filled and their duties most efficiently discharged; in medieval times students were more anxious to learn than teachers were to teach. In the earlier period again there was an utter want of discipline among students who ought to have been treated as mere schoolboys. The want was partially corrected by the growth of the College system, but the improvement in this respect was balanced by the decay and degradation in the higher intellectual life of the Universities. The Englishman, accustomed to divide all human intellects by the broad line which separates the "passman" from the "honourman," will further notice a want of classification in the system. The *Organon* and the *de Anima* must probably have been above the heads of a very large proportion of the mere schoolboys who were set down to them. It is perhaps to this cause (the want of funds was another) that we must attribute the very small proportion of students who ever attained even the B.A. degree, in spite of the mildness of medieval Examiners. There is considerable reason to believe that in the Middle Ages a larger proportion than at the present day of the nominal students derived exceedingly little benefit from their University education.

"Oxoniam multi veniunt, redeunt quoque stulti."

In the earlier part of our period this must have been peculiarly the case, when so little exertion on the part of the student himself was required. A man was allowed year after year to sit through lectures of which he might not understand one word; later on this defect was partly remedied by the multiplication of "exercises" in College and Hall.

For the fairly competent student the main defects of a medieval education may be summed up by saying that it was at once too dogmatic and too disputatious. Of the superstitious adherence to Aristotle or other prescribed authority sufficient illustrations have already been given. It is of course a direct outcome of the intellectual vice of the age—a vice of which the human mind was by no means cured by the Renaissance or the Reformation. It lasted longest where it was most out of place. In the middle of the seventeenth century a Doctor of Medicine was compelled by the English College of Physicians to retract a proposition which he had advanced in opposition to the authority of Aristotle under threat of imprisonment. It may seem a contradiction to allege that this education by authority was at the same time too controversial. Yet the readiness with which the student was encouraged to dispute the thesis of a prescribed opponent, and the readiness with which he would swear to teach only the system of a prescribed authority, were but opposite sides of the same fundamental defect—the same fatal indifference to facts, the facts of external nature, the facts of history, and the facts of life. Books were put in the place of things. This is a defect which was certainly not removed by the mere substitution of Classics for Philosophy. If in medieval times words were often allowed to usurp the place of things, they were not allowed to usurp the place of thought. For a moment no doubt the human mind was brought into real and living contact with a new world of thought and action, of imagination and art, of literature and history, by the "New Learning"; but ere long Classical education in turn became almost as arid and scholastic—as remote from fruitful contact with realities—as the education of the Middle Ages. The history of education is indeed a somewhat melancholy record of misdirected energy, stupid routine, and narrow one-sidedness. It seems to be only at rare moments in the history of the human mind that an enthusiasm for knowledge and a many-sided interest in the things of the intellect stirs the dull waters of educational commonplace. What was a revelation to one generation becomes an unintelligent routine to the next. Considered as mere intellectual training, it may be doubted whether the superiority of a Classical education, as it was understood at the beginning of this century,[1] to that of the medieval Schools was quite so great as is commonly supposed. If in the Scholastic age the human mind did not advance, even Macaulay admits that it did at least mark time. The study of Aristotle and the Schoolmen must have been a better training in subtlety and precision of thought than the exclusive study of a few poets and orators. However defective its methods of achieving that end, the Scholastic education at least aimed at getting to the bottom of things, although Renan (who gives it this praise) has also pointed out the supreme defect of Scholasticism when he says that its method was incapable of expressing "nuances," while truth lies in the "nuances." But as a practical training in readiness and facility of expression the habit of disputation may have been quite as valuable an exercise as the practice of construing and composition, though the dialect acquired was different enough.

It is surprising how little the intellectual superiority of the eighteenth century over the fourteenth impressed itself upon the course of ordinary School and University education, especially in this country. That on the whole a good eighteenth-century education was healthier, more stimulating, and more rational than a good fourteenth-century education need not be denied; but our intellectual advance since the medieval period had less to do with the improvement in the substance or the method of education than the academic world complacently imagined. It was in the main what he picked up out of School and Lecture-room that differentiated the educated man of the eighteenth century from the educated man of the fourteenth.

But, because it is easy enough to pick holes in the education of the past,

[1] *i.e.* the nineteenth century (Ed.).

it must not for one moment be supposed that the education either of the scholastic or of the ultra-classical period was of little value. Up to a certain point—and this is the one consolation to the educational historian—the value of education is independent either of the intrinsic value or of the practical usefulness of what is taught. The intelligent modern artisan educated at a Board-school [1] or the half-educated man of the world possesses at the present day a great deal more true and useful knowledge than a medieval Doctor of Divinity. But it can on no account be admitted that this puts the uneducated man of modern times on a level with the educated man of the Middle Ages. And the educated man—the man who has spent many of his maturer years in subtle and laborious intellectual work—will generally show his superiority to the uneducated man even in the most severely practical affairs of life when once the former comes seriously to apply himself to them. It was emphatically so in the Middle Ages. Kings and princes found their statesmen and men of business in the Universities—most often, no doubt, among those trained in the practical Science of Law, but not invariably so. Talleyrand is said to have asserted that Theologians made the best diplomats. It was not the wont of the practical men of the Middle Ages to disparage academic training. The rapid multiplication of Universities during the fourteenth and fifteenth centuries was largely due to a direct demand for highly educated lawyers and administrators. In a sense the academic discipline of the Middle Ages was too practical. It trained pure intellect, encouraged habits of laborious subtlety, heroic industry, and intense application, while it left uncultivated the imagination, the taste, the sense of beauty—in a word, all the amenities and refinements of the civilized intellect. It taught men to think and to work rather than to enjoy. Most of what we understand by "culture," much of what Aristotle understood by the "noble use of leisure," was unappreciated by the medieval intellect. On the speculative side the Universities were (as has been said) "the school of the modern spirit": they taught men to reason and to speculate, to doubt and to inquire, to find a pleasure in the things of the intellect both for their own sake and for the sake of their applications to life. They dispelled for ever the obscurantism of the Dark Ages. From a more practical point of view their greatest service to mankind was simply this, that they placed the administration of human affairs—in short, the government of the world—in the hands of educated men. The actual rulers—the Kings or the aristocrats—might often be as uneducated or more uneducated than modern democracies, but they had to rule through the instrumentality of a highly educated class.

In criticizing medieval culture and education, attention is sometimes too much confined to the Scholastic Philosophy and Theology. The Scholastic Philosophy and Theology do, indeed, represent the highest intellectual de-

[1] An English common school (Ed.).

velopment of the period. But they do not represent the most widely diffused or the most practically influential of medieval studies. Law was the leading Faculty in by far the greater number of medieval Universities: for a very large proportion of University students the study of Arts, in so far as they pursued it at all, took the place of a modern school rather than of a modern University. From a broad political and social point of view one of the most important results of the Universities was the creation, or at least the enormously increased power and importance, of the lawyer-class. Great as are the evils which society still owes to lawyers, the lawyer-class has always been a civilizing agency. Their power represents at least the triumph of reason and education over caprice and brute force. Lawyers have moderated or regulated despotism even when they have proved its most willing tools: just as in modern democratic communities their prominence must be looked upon as an important conservative check upon democracy.

Over the greater part of Europe the influence of the Universities meant more than this. It brought with it the increasing modification of legal and political institutions by the Roman Law, whether directly or through the Canon Law, whether by avowed adoption or by gradual and unconscious infiltration and imitation. This too was a civilizing agency, though here again an increase of civilization had often to be bought by a decline of rude, barbaric liberty. Our own country is here the exception which proves the rule. Our own Universities are differentiated from those of the rest of the world by the small extent to which they have been, or still are, places of professional education. How far the different course which the development of our institutions has taken as compared with those of the Continent, and the large measure of Germanic liberty which they retained, are due to the absence of Civilian influence, is an inquiry which has perhaps been too much neglected by our constitutional historians. It must not be supposed, indeed, that even in England the influence of the Universities upon our institutions has been small. To say nothing of the considerable infiltration of the Roman through the Canon Law into English Law and still more into English Equity, the Common Law escaped the modifications which nearly every legal system in Europe underwent at the hands of University-bred lawyers only by the creation of a rival Legal Science, and even of a virtual University of English Law in London, which would hardly have been possible but for the example supplied by the Roman Law and its academic Professors. . . .

It is more directly relative to our subject to examine what have been the effects of the medieval Universities upon our modern educational system. The genius of the Middle Age showed itself above all in the creation of institutions. The institutions of the Middle Age are greater—they may prove more imperishable—even than its Cathedrals. The University is a distinctly medieval institution. By that is implied not merely that in the most altered and the most modern of the Schools so called there are customs, offices, titles, for the explanation of which we must go back to the history of the thirteenth century with its Guild movement, its Cathedral Schools, and especially its great struggle between the Chancellor of Paris and the Society of Masters. The very idea of the institution is essentially medieval, and it is curious to observe how largely that idea still dominates our modern schemes of education. Persons to whom the term "medieval" is synonymous with "ideal," and those with whom it is a term of abuse, agree in the assumption that Universities must exist. And yet they did not exist in the most highly cultivated societies of the ancient world. It is entirely misleading to apply the name to the Schools of ancient Athens or Alexandria. If higher education is to exist, there must obviously be teachers to impart it, and it is likely that particular places will become famous for particular studies. But it is not necessary that the teachers should be united into a corporate body enjoying more or less privilege and autonomy. It is not necessary that the teachers of different subjects should teach in the same place and be united in a single institution—still less that an attempt should be made to make the teaching body representative of the whole cycle of human knowledge. It is not necessary that studies should be grouped into particular Faculties, and students required to confine themselves more or less exclusively to one. It is not necessary that a definite line of study should be marked out by authority, that a definite period of years should be assigned to a student's course, or that at the end of that period he should be subjected to examination and receive, with more or less formality and ceremony, a title of honour. All this we owe to the Middle Ages. Similar needs might no doubt in course of time have independently evolved somewhat similar institutions in a somewhat different form. But, in the form in which we have them, teaching corporations, courses of study, examinations, degrees, are a direct inheritance from the Middle Ages: and it would not be difficult to show that these inherited institutions carry with them not a few assumptions in educational theory and method which might have appeared questionable enough to an ancient thinker. However much the modern mind may in certain directions be reverting to the ideas and spirit of the old world, education, like so much else in the modern world, will always exhibit a vast and incalculable difference from the education of ancient Greece or ancient Rome just because the Middle Ages have intervened.

How much is lost and how much gained by the educational machinery which the Middle Ages have created for us would be a difficult inquiry. That something is lost is evident. Something of the life and spontaneity of old-world culture certainly seems to be gone for ever. Universities have often had the effect of prolonging and stereotyping ideas and modes of thought for a century or more after the rest of the world has given them up. It is surprising how slowly an intellectual revolution affects the course of ordinary education. But educational traditions are marvellously tenacious, quite apart from institutional machinery such as that of the Universities: and education itself must always be, from the necessities of the case, a tradition. In all machinery there is some loss, and yet it is only by means of machinery that culture can be permanently kept alive and widely diffused. The machinery by which this process is carried on among ourselves is as distinctly a medieval creation as representative government or trial by jury. And it is a piece of institutional machinery which has outlived almost every other element in the education which it was originally intended to impart.

56. *HIGH SCHOLASTICISM AND ITS THEOLOGY* [1]

One of the most difficult and least understood problems in medieval history is scholasticism and medieval theology in general. Professor W. Walker, who was for many years professor of ecclesiastical history in Yale University, attempted to analyze for American students the thoughts of the greatest philosophers and theologians produced in the Christian countries of Europe in the period from 1050 to 1350.

The recovery of the whole of Aristotle, the rise of the universities, and the devotion of the mendicant orders to learning, ushered in a new period of Scholasticism in the thirteenth century, and marked the highest intellectual achievement of the Middle Ages. The movement toward this "modern theology," as it was called, was not without much opposition, especially from traditionalists and adherents to the Augustinian Neo-Platonic development. Aristotle met much hostility. A series of great thinkers, all from the mendicant orders, made his victory secure. Yet even they, while relying primarily on Aristotle, made much use of Plato as reflected in Augustine and the Pseudo-Dionysius.

To Alexander of Hales (?–1245), an Englishman and ultimately a Franciscan, who taught in Paris, was due the treatment of theology in the light of the whole of Aristotle. Yet to him the Scripture is the only final truth. With this new period of Scholasticism a broader range of intellectual interest is apparent than in the earlier, though the old problem between realism and nominalism continued its pre-eminence. Alexander was a moderate realist. Universals exist *ante rem* in the mind of God, *in re* in the things themselves, and *post rem* in our understanding. In this he was followed by Albertus Magnus and Aquinas.

[1] Williston Walker, *History of the Christian Church.* New York, Charles Scribner's Sons, 1924, pp. 269–277. Used by permission of Charles Scribner's Sons.

Albertus Magnus (1206?–1280), a German and a Dominican, studied in Padua, and taught in many places in Germany, but principally in Cologne. He served as provincial prior for his order, and was, for a few years, bishop of Regensburg. The most learned man of his age, his knowledge of science was really remarkable. His acquaintance not merely with Aristotle, but with the comments of Arabian scholars, was profounder than that of Alexander of Hales. He was, however, a great compiler and commentator rather than an original theological genius. That which he taught was brought to far clearer expression by his pupil, Thomas Aquinas.

Thomas Aquinas (1225?–1274) was a son of Landulf, count of Aquino, a small town about half-way between Rome and Naples. Connected with the German imperial house of Hohenstaufen and with that of Tancred, the Norman Crusader, it was against the wishes of his parents that Thomas entered the Dominican order in 1243. His spiritual superiors were aware of his promise, and sent him to Cologne to study under Albertus Magnus, who soon took his pupil to Paris. On receiving the degree of bachelor of divinity, Thomas returned to Cologne in 1248, and now taught as subordinate to Albertus Magnus. These were years of rapid intellectual growth. Entrance into the Paris faculty was long refused him on account of jealousy of the mendicant orders, but in 1257 he was given full standing there. From 1261 for some years he taught in Italy, then once more in Paris, and finally, from 1272, in Naples. He died, on his way to the Council of Lyons, in 1274. In these crowded years of teaching Thomas was constantly consulted on important civil and ecclesiastical questions, and was active in preaching; yet his pen was busy with results as voluminous as they were important. His great *Summa Theologiae* was begun about 1265, and not fully completed at his death. Personally he was a simple, deeply religious, prayerful man. Intellectually his work was marked by a clarity, a logical consistency, and a breadth of presentation that places him among the few great teachers of the church. In the Roman communion his influence has never ceased. By declaration of Pope Leo XIII (1878–1903), in 1879, his work is the basis of present theological instruction.

Closely associated with Aquinas in friendship and for a time in teaching activities in the University of Paris, was John Fidanza (1221–1274), generally known as Bonaventura. Born in Bagnorea, in the States of the Church, he entered the Franciscan order in 1238, rising to become its "general" in 1257. A year before his death he was made a cardinal. Famed as a teacher in Paris, he was even more distinguished for his administration of the Franciscan order and for his high character. Much less an Aristotelian than Aquinas, he was especially influenced by the Neo-Platonic teachings of Augustine and Pseudo-Dionysius. He was essentially a mystic. By meditation and prayer one may rise into that union with God which brings the highest knowledge of divine truth. Yet, though a mystic, Bonaventura was a theologian of dialectic ability whose work, more conservative and less original than that of Aquinas, nevertheless commanded high respect.

According to Aquinas, in whom Scholasticism attained its noblest development, the aim of all theological investigation is to give knowledge of God and of man's origin and destiny. Such knowledge comes in part by reason—natural theology—but the attainments of reason are inadequate. They must be augmented by revelation. That revelation is contained in the Scriptures, which are the only final authority; but they are to be understood in the light of the interpretations of the councils and the Fathers—in a word, as comprehended by the church. The truths of revelation cannot be attained by reason, but they are not contrary to reason, and reason can show the inadequacy of objections to them. Aquinas is thus far from sharing Anselm's conviction that all truths of Christianity are philosophically demonstrable; but he holds that there can be no contradiction between philosophy and theology, since both are from God.

In treating of God Aquinas combined Aristotelian and Neo-Platonic conceptions. He is the first cause. He is pure activity. He is also the most real and perfect of existences. He is the absolute substance, the source and end of all things. As perfect goodness, God does always that which He sees to be right. Regarding the Trinity and the person of Christ, Aquinas stood essentially on the basis of Augustine and the Chalcedonian formula.

God needs nothing, and therefore the creation of the world was an expression of the divine love which He bestows on the existences He thus called into being. God's providence extends to all events, and is manifested in the predestination of some to everlasting life, and in leaving others to the consequences of sin in eternal condemnation. Aquinas's position is largely determinist. Man has, indeed, in a certain sense, freedom. His will acts; but that does not preclude the determining or permissive providence of God. The divine permission of evil results in the higher good of the whole. Though sin is no less sinful, its existence permits the development of many virtues which go to make strength of character in those who resist.

Aquinas abandoned the ancient distinction between "soul" and "spirit." The soul of man is a unit, possessing intellect and will. It is immaterial. Man's highest good is the vision and enjoyment of God. As originally created man had, in addition to his natural powers, a super-added gift which enabled him to seek that highest good and practise the three Christian virtues—faith, hope, and love. This Adam lost by sin, which also corrupted his natural powers, so that his state became not merely a lack of original righteousness, but a positive turning toward lower aims. Sin is, therefore, more than merely negative. In this fallen state it was impossible for Adam to please God, and this corruption was transmitted to all his posterity. Man still has the power to attain the four natural virtues, prudence, justice, courage, and self-control; but these, though bringing a certain measure of temporal honor and happiness, are not sufficient to enable their possessor to attain the vision of God.

Man's restoration is possible only through the free and unmerited grace of God, by which man's nature is changed, his sins forgiven, and power to practise the three Christian virtues infused. No act of his can win this grace. While God could conceivably have forgiven man's sins and granted grace without the sacrifice of Christ—here Aquinas differed from Anselm—the work of Christ was the wisest and most efficient method God could choose, and man's whole redemption is based on it. That work involved satisfaction for man's sin, and Christ won a merit which deserves a reward. It also moves men to love. Aquinas thus developed and combined views presented by Anselm and Abelard. Christ's satisfaction superabounds man's sin, and the reward which Christ cannot personally receive, since as God He needs nothing, comes to the advantage of His human brethren. Christ does for men what they cannot do for themselves.

Once redeemed, however, the good works that God's grace now enables man to do deserve and receive a reward. Man now has power to fulfil not only the precepts but the counsels of the Gospel. He can do works of supererogation, of which the chief would be the faithful fulfilment of the monastic life. He can not merely fit himself for heaven; he can add his mite to the treasury of the superabundant merits of Christ and the saints. Yet all this is made possible only by the grace of God. Aquinas thus finds full room for the two dominating conceptions of mediaeval piety—grace and merit.

Grace does not come to men indiscriminately. It has its definite channels and these are the sacraments, and the sacraments alone. Here Scholasticism attained far greater clearness of definition than had previously existed. The ancient feeling that all sacred actions were sacraments was still alive in the twelfth century, but Hugo of St. Victor and Abelard clearly placed five in a more conspicuously sacramental category than others, and Peter Lombard defined the sacraments as seven. Whether this reckoning was original with him is still an unsolved problem; nor was it at once universally accepted. The influence of his *Sentences* ultimately won the day. As enumerated by Peter Lombard, the sacraments are baptism, confirmation, the Lord's Supper, penance, extreme unction, ordination, and matrimony. All were instituted by Christ, directly or through the Apostles, and all convey grace from Christ the head to the members of His mystical body, the church. Without them there is no true union with Christ.

Every sacrament consists of two elements which are defined in Aristotelian terms of form and matter—a material portion (water, bread, and wine, etc.); and a formula conveying its sacred use ("I baptize thee," etc.). The administrant must have the intention of doing what Christ and the church appointed, and the recipient must have, at least in the case of those of years of discretion, a sincere desire to receive the benefit of the sacrament. These conditions fulfilled, the sacrament conveys grace by the fact of its reception—that is *ex opere operato*. Of this grace God is the principal cause; the sacrament itself is the instrumental cause. It is the means by which the virtue of Christ's passion is conveyed to His members.

By baptism the recipient is regenerated, and original and previous personal sins are pardoned, though the tendency to sin is not obliterated. Man is now given the grace, if he will use it, to resist sin, and the lost power to attain the Christian virtues. Infant baptism had become the universal practice, but in the time of Aquinas immersion was still the more prevalent form, and had his approval.

The sole recognized theory regarding Christ's presence in the Supper was that which had been taught by Paschasius Radbertus and Lanfranc, and had been known since the first half of the twelfth century as transubstantiation. It had been given full dogmatic authority by the Fourth Lateran Council in 1215. Aquinas but added clearness of definition. At the words of consecration by the priest the miracle is wrought by the power of God, so that while the "accidents" (shape, taste, and the like) remain unaltered, the "substance" is transformed into the very body and blood of Christ.

Aquinas also accepted and developed the view that the whole body and blood of Christ is present in either element. It was far from original with him, but had grown with the increasing custom of the laity to partake of the bread only. A withdrawal of the cup instigated by the clergy did not take place. The abandonment of the cup was rather a layman's practice due to fear of dishonoring the sacrament by misuse of the wine. Such anxiety had manifested itself as early as the seventh century in the adoption of the Greek custom of dipping the bread in the wine—a practice repeatedly disapproved by ecclesiastical authority, but supported by lay sentiment. By the twelfth century the laity were avoiding the use of the wine altogether, apparently first of all in England. By the time of Aquinas lay communion in the bread alone had become prevalent. Similar considerations led to the general abandonment by the Western Church, in the twelfth and thirteenth centuries of the practice of infant communion, which had been universal, and which continues in the Greek Church to the present.

Mediaeval piety and worship reach their highest point in the Lord's Supper. It is the continuation of the incarnation, the repetition of the passion, the source of spiritual upbuilding to the recipient, the evidence of his union with Christ, and a sacrifice well pleasing to God, inclining Him to be gracious to those in need on earth and in purgatory.

Penance, though not reckoned a sacrament of equal dignity with baptism or the Lord's Supper, was really of great, if not prime, importance in mediaeval practice. Mediaeval thought regarding the personal religious life centred about the two conceptions of grace and merit. Baptism effected the forgiveness of previous sins; but for those after baptism penance was necessary. The Latin mind has always been inclined to view sin and righteousness in terms of definite acts rather than as states, and therefore to look upon man's relations to God under the aspects of debt and credit—though holding that the only basis of credit is the effect of God's grace. These tendencies were never more marked than in the scholastic period. They represented widespread popular views which the schoolmen explained theologically, rather than originated.

According to Aquinas, penance involves four elements, contrition, confession, satisfaction, and absolution. Contrition is sincere sorrow for the offense against God and a determination not to repeat it. Yet Aquinas holds that, as all sacraments convey grace, a penance begun in "attrition," that is, in fear of punishment, may by infused grace become a real contrition.

Private confession to the priest had made gradual progress since its advocacy by the old British missionaries. Abelard and Peter Lombard were of opinion that a true contrition was followed by divine forgiveness, even without priestly confession, though they thought such confession desirable. The Fourth Lateran Council, in 1215, required confession to the priest at least once a year of all laymen of age of discretion. Such confession thereby became church law. Alexander of Hales argued its necessity, and Aquinas gave it more logical exposition. It must be made to the priest as the physician of the soul, and include all "deadly" sins—the catalogue of which was now much larger than in the early church.

Though God forgives the eternal punishment of the penitent, certain temporal penalties remain as a consequence of sin. This distinction was clearly made by Abelard and became the current property of the schoolmen. These temporal penalties satisfy the sinner's offense against God so far as it is in his power to do so. They also enable him to avoid sin in the future. They are the "fruits of repentance." It is the business of the priest to impose these satisfactions, which, if not adequate in this life, will be completed in purgatory.

On evidence thus of sorrow for sin, confession, and a willingness to give satisfaction, the priest, as God's minister or agent, pronounces absolution. Here, then, was the great control of the priesthood over the laity till the Reformation, and in the Roman Church to the present. Without priestly pardon no one guilty after baptism of a "deadly" sin has assurance of salvation.

A great modification of these satisfactions was, however, rapidly growing in the century and a half before Aquinas. A remission of a portion or of all of these "temporal" penalties could be obtained. Such remission was called an "indulgence." Bishops had long exercised the right to abridge satisfactions in cases where circumstances indicated unusual contrition. Great services to the church were held to deserve such consideration. Peter Damiani (1007?–1072) regarded gifts of land for a monastery or a church as affording such occasions. These did not constitute the full indulgence system, however. That seems to have originated in southern France, and the earliest, though not undisputed, instance is about the year 1016. Their first conspicuous employment was by a French Pope, Urban II (1088–1099), who promised full indulgence to all who engaged in the First Crusade, though Pope Alexander II had given similar privileges on a smaller scale for battle against the Saracens in Spain about 1063. Once begun, the system spread with great rapidity. Not only Popes but bishops gave indulgences, and on constantly easier terms. Pilgrimages to sacred places or at special times, contributions to a good work, such as building a church or even a bridge or a road, were deemed deserving of such reward. The financial possibilities of the system were soon perceived and exploited. Since "temporal" penalties included those of purgatory, the value of an indulgence was enormous, though undefined, and the tendency to substitute it for a real penance was one to which human nature readily responded.

Such was the practice to which Aquinas now gave the classic interpretation. Following Alexander of Hales, he taught that the superabundant merits of Christ and of the saints form a treasury of good works from which a portion may be transferred by the authority of the church, acting through its officers, to the needy sinner. It can, indeed, avail only for those who are really contrite, but for such it removes, in whole or in part, the "temporal" penalties here and in purgatory. Indulgences were never a license to commit sin. They were an amelioration of penalties justly due to sins already committed and regretted. But, however interpreted, there can be no doubt as to the moral harmfulness of the system, or that it grew worse till the Reformation, of which it was an immediately inducing cause.

At their deaths, according to Aquinas, the wicked pass immediately to hell, which is endless, and from which there is no release. Those who have made full use of the grace offered in the church go at once to heaven. The mass of Christians who have but imperfectly availed themselves of the means of grace must undergo a longer or shorter purification in purgatory.

The church is one, whether in heaven, on earth, or in purgatory. When one member suffers, all suffer; when one does well, all share in his good work. On this unity of the church Aquinas bases prayers to the saints and for those in purgatory. The visible church requires a visible head. To be subject to the Roman Pontiff is necessary for salvation. To the Pope, also, belongs the right to issue new definitions of faith, and Aquinas implies the doctrine of papal infallibility.

It was Aquinas's good fortune that his philosophy and his theology alike found a hearty disciple in the greatest of mediaeval poets, Dante Alighieri (1265–1321), whose *Divina Commedia* moves, in these respects, almost wholly in Aquinas's realm of thought.

. . . .

57. *BYZANTINE ART* [1]

Byzantine art, like Byzantine history, has often been severely criticized. "The fate of Byzantine art, as Schnaase has suggested," says Franz von Weber in his History of Medieval Art, *"may be compared to that of Tithonos, beloved by Eos, to whom the gods, at her request, had granted immortality, but not eternal youth, and who was thus condemned to drag out a long existence of the most wretched decrepitude." "Still," he adds, "all was not utterly bad."*

The author of the following selection, however, holds that certain forms of Byzantine art have been distinctly under-rated and finds in them much to awaken admiration and arouse enthusiasm.

It is barely a generation since John Addington Symonds estimated the importance of Byzantine art in the following trenchant sentence: "The so-called Romanesque and Byzantine styles were but the dotage of a second childhood fumbling with the methods and materials of an irrecoverable past." That, indeed, was all he had to say on the subject. Dismissing its effete inspiration with winged words and a distant roll of drums, he went on to consider the beauties of the Renaissance. And what he said has been said again and again by hundreds of honest folk.

I always knew that he was wrong; but life is short, and to explain to the deliberately unreceptive or to the devotedly prejudiced is all so much good time wasted. I have spent it instead scouring the museums of Europe for those precious relics of Byzantine art which he never troubled to look for; I have been to the great citadel itself, Byzantium the golden, and patiently searched for its hundred churches, content with a miraculously saved mosaic here or a lovely carved capital there. And I have

[1] Stanley Casson, *The Lost Millennium*. The *Atlantic Monthly*, December, 1931 (Vol. 148, No. 6), pp. 795–801 (condensed). Used by permission of the *Atlantic Monthly* and the author.

been privileged to be the first infidel to excavate the soil of Stamboul itself, under the very shadow of St. Sophia, to find what I could of the broken fragments of those glowing centuries of Byzantine splendor. And it is all a heart-rending job. For the very thought that a thousand years of art have left hardly enough behind them to fill one museum is grim testimony to the destructive power of that barbarous virility which replaced the ancient stronghold of Constantinople with the warring states of Western Europe.

But when one has found the actualities of Byzantine art, the marvels of those fragile and intimate churches of Byzantium, the austere grace of her paintings, and the incredible delicacy of her jewelry, one is fortified against the vandal criticism of an Italomaniac. But—and this is the mistake that so many of the now more vocal defenders of Byzantine art make—defense is not here to be based on offense. To reinstate Byzantine art as the princess among the great periods that she deserves to be, one need take no other style of art into consideration. The claims of Byzantium are not made more strong by a denigration of Italy, of Persia, or of Islam. That is but to revive the disputes of old religions, to treat art as politics, to prostitute the compelling loveliness of a forgotten world. We can for once take the taste of our mediæval ancestors as our guide; for they, illumined by their own achievements in Gothic or Romanesque or even early Renaissance, still searched and searched again for those priceless gems of Byzantine art which might come their way as imperial gifts, as Crusaders' loot, or as genuine purchase.

Such relics as these have now been brought together from the museums and the cathedrals of Europe into an exhibition of Byzantine art just opened in Paris—the very first of its kind. Without the predatory taste for the Byzantine which the western Barbarians of the Middle Ages possessed in so marked a quality, I doubt if this exhibition would ever have been held. For, as one of its organizers has rightly said: "Our ancestors never missed an opportunity of acquiring an example of Byzantine art; and we can see that they were not mistaken in their choice." *Hommage aux barbares.*

Seeing this exhibition as I have just done, I am fortified anew. For here, now that they are all brought together, the exquisite jewels of Byzantine taste recapture for a passing second the warmth and splendor of the most luxurious and exquisite period of history the world as ever seen. An hour in these quiet rooms in Paris, where so much is collected, and all the sour wit of Gibbon is sweetened. Here is no Decline and Fall; here is the very birth and flowering of a new and gracious and intimate art such as the world has never seen. Indeed, comparisons cannot be made. Byzantine art seems almost to have sprung fully armed from the head of Zeus. For it is Greek in its reserve, Greek in its decision, and Greek in its delicacy; and yet it owes no sort or kind of debt to Greek art at all. It is the Greek spirit working in a new way. It is—or at least Byzantine art of the tenth century is—a completely new contribution to that never-ceasing creative spirit which we call the art of this, that, or the other period.

What struck me here, as indeed it has always struck me in the contemplation of any masterpiece of Byzantine art, though never so forcibly before, is that the Byzantine artist is a master of whatever branch of art he adopts. He, like his ancient Greek progenitor, made into a work of art whatever he handled, so that the distinction into "arts and crafts" becomes meaningless. . . .

Abolish this distinction of arts and crafts and the artist can be active wherever he wishes. And at Byzantium that is exactly what he did. Nothing was too small or too large for him. The same man could carve the lovely marble Madonna relief, eight feet high, that was found a few years ago below the old Palace of the Sultans at Stamboul, and with equal joy a small ivory box a few inches square. The painter of pictures could turn his hand to a small mosaic icon half a foot in length. The sculptor could cut gems and the architect make an inlaid pavement. . . .

Seeing so much Byzantine art gathered in one place, I have gained certain impressions that I have never been able to arrive at before. For seeing the art of a thousand years piecemeal is an exercise in disjunctive absorption that only a fine synthetic brain can master. And I regret that I have a brain that is neither fine nor synthesizing.

I was struck first by the intimacy of Byzantine art. Just as its small and colored churches would warm the heart of the frostiest of worshipers, so its jewels and paintings and silks and ivories demand an instant attention from the most casual and convey an impression of immediate beauty to the most reserved mind. Like all great art, it needs no explanation: it arrives. But to one prepossessed by theories or prejudices it will fail to convey anything. Approach it simply and its answer will be simple.

Firstly its colors. The Byzantines were a subtle folk. They avoided the primary colors like the plague and they avoided subtle nuances as much. They were masters of *selection*. And they selected color in everything. In gems they were austere in their choice. Not a ruby or an emerald or a diamond will you see. They chose above all pale liquid blues—sapphirines and aquamarines. They seem to have had a passion for that strange sea blue that the ancient Greeks strove so often to describe. I have never seen any Byzantine jewel made of carnelian, or of amber, or of topaz. I think they thought such colors slightly vulgar, fit only for barbarians. But both in this exhibition and in all the museums and collections I have ever seen, two stones and two only are predominant—the sea-blue sapphirine and dark green bloodstone, spotted with red. Here and there deep lapis lazuli or amethyst is used, but not often.

These same colors appear again and again in their paintings and mosaics. There is one painting in this exhibition of the Christ on the Cross, sent from

Athens. Below the Cross is Mary mourning. Her tall, strange figure, as far removed from the manner of Italian art as Rubens from Cimabue, is of one color only, a dark and enraptured sea blue. And the rest of the picture is painted on a gold ground, glittering and vivid. The figure of Mary is the figure of Sorrow herself, unmoving, remote, inhuman. There is no appeal here, in the sense that emotion rushes to one's mind; this is the very transcendence of grief. Byzantine art is often called intellectual and inhuman, but here it seems far more human than emotional art in that its meaning cuts straight through the heavings of emotion and conveys the very Platonic Idea itself. *Surréalisme* if you will—immediate contact with the artist's mind. And all this is achieved by a strange color and a strange form. Art critics may rage, but it is formalism blending with realism.

Perhaps in Byzantine silks and tissues the blend of form and color is even more amazing. Think of a silk on which are lions and stags, odd and heraldic, and the only colors dark royal blue, turquoise, and two shades of cream. Or another in orange, tomato red, and white; or a third in blue, black, and purple—all alike in great lozenge designs with griffins and elephants and lions. Together these superb silks bring the court of Byzantium before my eyes—that court which lives in the pages of Anna Comnena or in the dry manual *De Cerimoniis* of Constantine Porphyrogenitus.

Next, what impressed me most was the calm impersonality of Byzantine art in the sense that the personality of the maker himself is imperceptible. You can tell the difference between the good and the brilliant, between the able and the slick, between the firm hand and the weak. But there is no nonsense about detecting the sensitivity of the artist. All one can detect is his immense preoccupation with his task, his utter devotion to what he has to do, and his absolute integrity in doing it. Here is no artist who wants to convey his own character and ideas to you. Instead, he is the essential Greek, aiming at what all artists of genius always aim at—a complete satisfaction of their artistic intentions, no more. So worked the archaic Greeks, with never a thought for glory or recognition. That is why they hardly ever signed their works in archaic Greece and why the Byzantines never signed their work at all. You may search for signatures and all the fun that such things provide for the art critic, and at Byzantium you will search in vain. Romans signed their statues and their gems frequently enough. Romanesque and Gothic Frenchmen and Germans signed their statues as often as they could—Byzantines never. Byzantine artists spoke, in all probability, of the "glory of God," but I doubt if it worried them much! They carved or painted or wove because they loved to do so and because it was their proper profession. . . .

One can just detect the alternations of season, as it were, in the march of artistic production in Byzantium. In the fourth century you can see Roman art suddenly fade and die, to be replaced by a superb formalism, derived, I think, from those strange Syrian folk whose work we see at Palmyra; then for a century all was cold again and nothing stirred. With the building of St. Sophia came a second blaze of skill and genius, to be extinguished almost at once by the fearful assaults of external enemies and the withering blight of Iconoclasm. But the sun rose once more in the eighth and ninth centuries, and by the tenth Byzantine art touched heights of splendor that were never surpassed. The eleventh century and the twelfth saw the Empire a paradise for art and a blaze of wealth that poured in from all four quarters of the earth. Then, in 1204, came the Crusaders and the envious Italians from Venice, with that archbrigand Enrico Dandolo. The Empire crashed, and her gold and jewels and paintings were scattered and burned and sold and bartered to every corner of Barbary—all in the name of Christ and the Holy Land, to which the Crusaders had forgotten to go. A century of darkness followed, with a series of French emperors as incompetent as they were illiterate. They passed, and Greeks again held their city, but it was impoverished and empty, ready only to fall a little later to the gathering vultures. But, in that brief renaissance, art grew and flourished anew, and Byzantine art of the fourteenth and fifteenth centuries is again a sunlit and vivid thing.

Vitality, then, is as strong as integrity with the Byzantine artist. He lives again and again, and his work is never the same. The commonest charge against Byzantine art is that it is repetitive, dull, and traditional, in the sense that there is no creation. To this there can be only one answer—that Byzantine art is perpetual creation, that it is variation within defined limits, and this is the severest test to which an art or an artist can ever be put. That was the secret of Greek art in ancient times. The endless repetition of Apollos and Aphrodites and the rest seems but dull repetition; and yet the greatness of art, as Polyclitus said, its most difficult stage for the artist, was when you came to the point of variation. That which made your Apollo differ from the Apollo of someone else was what decided whether you or he was the great artist. So with the Byzantines. Here are the Virgins, the Pantocrators, the Crucifixions, and the Saints, and in more secular art the great heraldic beasts and the intricate patterns, but the point wherein one saint or griffin differed from another was the point at which one artist could be identified as great and another as merely good.

Sometimes I read that Byzantine art is but a *macédoine* of various Oriental and some Occidental elements, a rehash of oddments garnered by a decadent and weary folk from the various lands of Asia and Europe into which their conquering arms had penetrated. This exhibition at Paris has taught me how far worse than a half truth this creed is, for it suggests the utter artistic sterility of the Byzantines.

Like all great art, Byzantine art drew inspiration from all sources. After all, early Greek art was a blend of Hittite, Assyrian, and Egyptian influences. But there is all the difference in the world between a blend which is a mere aggregation of elements and a blend which is a transformation into something new with a vitality of its own. Those who think that the accusation of being a "blend" is derogative have the minds of grocers. They are thinking in terms of tea and tobacco. Byzantine art, like all great art, borrowed and blended and then moulded it all anew into a fresh creation. And behind the blending, though this is a point that critics mostly forget, was the mind that made the selection. To choose aright you have to have impeccable taste and wise judgment, and those are two precious qualities that make for great art. The swift draftsmanship of the Sassanian artist had the same appeal to the Byzantines that it has for us. The bright liveliness of the Hellenistic painter charmed Byzantine eyes—though it did not control their hands. Syrian austerity, and the ancient hieratic styles of the mighty monuments of Asia, Hittite and other, that still stood above ground, captured their fancy. Thus in their new synthesis we find austerity, freshness of color, and swift delineation faithfully renewed. The sweeping lines of a mosaic apse, the simple fall of drapery on a marble relief or an ivory box, and the massive strength of Byzantine sculptured animals show what were their inspiration. Yet there is no single work of art from Byzantium that one could for a single moment mistake for Sassanian, for Hittite, or for Hellenistic. . . .

Byzantine art satisfies more than most forms of art because it is at once simple, intimate, and unreal. It reflects nothing, interprets nothing, and suggests nothing that is not more or less explicit. My emotional reactions to it are, simply enough, the satisfaction of emotions rather than their awaking. Byzantine art gives rather than takes. That is why I went away so profoundly refreshed. For an art that requires a whole system of responses from the observer is a troublesome art. It presupposes an educated public, and, in consequence, is simply the old snobbery all over again. And worse, it breeds art critics who act as midwives to the ignorant. As soon as art has reached the stage where it needs all this paraphernalia and all these high priests, it may as well shut up shop and produce merely for the delectation of artists. Byzantine art does nothing of the kind. It is understandable at once by the simple-minded peasant and by the emperor's retinue. . . .

The standard of all Byzantine art before the fall of Constantinople in 1453 is astonishingly high. They had the finger skill of the Chinese and the Japanese and a capacity of design worthy only of the ancient Greeks. What a blend that can be their art will show you. Imagine an onyx plate (which I have just seen in Paris) in the centre of which is a gold circular cloisonné plaque. That plaque is not more than an inch and a quarter in diameter, and yet the scene depicted on it is the "Last Supper." Just think what intricate work went to its making, for the designing of every one of the figures at the table in a thin strip of gold, the hollows filled with different-colored enamels! No one but an Oriental could do it to-day. And yet the same artists could carve the great figures of emperors in purple porphyry which have survived the destruction of the Imperial City. The same men made the colored marble revetments which enclose the entire interior of St. Sophia or St. Mark's at Venice. It is this refusal to despise small-scale work which marks the Byzantine as a true artist, devoid of pride. For the true artist sees art in whatever he handles. Such were the Greeks of ancient times and the Greeks of mediæval times.

To-day we are more inclined than we used to be to give Byzantine art its due place in the history of art. But this reinstatement has produced the inevitable exaggeration. Defenders of Byzantine art are often as ridiculous as its opponents. Those who cannot decide between the two should go to the fountainhead itself and examine dispassionately the quiet genius of Byzantine art, which seems to derive an added calm from the fact that it was generated in a turbulent and violent world.

58. *GOTHIC ARCHITECTURE* [1]

In the following selection Ralph Adams Cram, celebrated architect and author, comments on Gothic architecture of which he is an ardent admirer.

I need not remind you of the original significance of the word "Gothic"—how it was given in scorn by the self-sufficient amateurs of the Renaissance to the art they had inherited but could neither appreciate nor rival. To them the word and the work meant anything barbarous and illiterate, and illuminating as this is on the point of their own intelligence, it is, I think, hardly so discreditable as is that effort, of which I have already spoken, on the part of modern commentators to reduce one of the most inspired and inspiring arts to the terms of a few structural formulae. Gothic architecture and Gothic art were an impulse and a tendency: as the Greeks took the simplest conceivable architectural norm and developed it to final perfection, so the mediaeval builders took the most complicated problem and tried to develop it to that point of perfection which they saw in some beatific vision, and which was actually beyond the power of man to attain.

Of course they failed; but they left, not a perfected thing subject neither to change nor to improvement, but a stimulating force ever inciting men to

[1] Ralph Adams Cram, Thomas Hastings and Claude Bragdon, *Six Lectures on Architecture.* The Scammon Lectures for 1915, published for the Art Institute of Chicago by the University of Chicago Press, Chicago, Illinois, pp. 6–10; 45–51. (This selection is by Ralph Adams Cram.) Reprinted by permission of the University of Chicago Press.

take up the work they left unfinished, and high-heartedly to strive once more to achieve the unattainable.

To this extent it was a greater art than had been known before; for its aim was higher, its goal more clearly revealed, and this goal was that which lies at the very root of art itself, viz., the symbolical expression of otherwise inexpressible ideas, *i.e.*, those which by their very nature are so high that they transcend all ordinary and direct modes of human expression. Consciously or unconsciously, mediaeval art was at bottom sacramental, and this explains, in a way, its immortality, its constantly recurring appeal, as it explains the same immortality and appeal by sacramental religion and sacramental philosophy—as of St. Bernard and St. Thomas Aquinas and Hugh of St. Victor—for it is only such art, such philosophy, such religion, that will permanently endure, since these alone are in eternal conformity with life, which also is essentially and unchangeably sacramental.

Between mediaeval civilization and mediaeval art the connection was so close as to amount to practical identity. Rheims, Freiburg, Canterbury, are simply the Middle Ages made visible and translated into the terms of an enduring and dynamic influence. All the joy of life, the vivid vitality, the humor, romance, and mysticism, the simplicity and naïveté of that opulent age find outlet through the wrought stone and wood, glass, and metal that assembled under eager hands and at the impulse of ardent brains to create that plexus of all the arts, a mediaeval cathedral. We may read history without limit and delve in original records for years without acquiring as much sense of the real mediaevalism as we could obtain through a day in Bourges or York or Strasburg—if only there we could find what once was: all the arts assembled together to make a Mass as it was before the shrines and altars and windows were broken, and the bizarre music and tawdry ceremonial of the nineteenth century took the place of the massive Gregorians and the solemn ritual of the fourteenth century. Even now, however, in such a church as Chartres or Seville it is possible to re-create the dead past, as is impossible in schoolroom or study or lecture-hall.

Gothic art is a great unit, and into this enter certain traditional, ethnic, and religious elements that determine, not only its spirit, but its form as well. Under the first heading we have all the classical heritage from Rome and the East through the Latin South of France and the pseudo-Byzantine Carolingians; under the second, the dominating northern blood, which, whether Frank, Norman, or Burgundian, wholly succeeded and dominated the decadent blood of the South; under the third, that all-embracing Catholicism which was the moving and regenerating force, directing, controlling, inspiring, through monastic establishments, military orders and the crusades.

The Romanesque of the eleventh and twelfth centuries in all Europe, the Gothic of the thirteenth, fourteenth, and fifteenth centuries in Flanders,

France, Spain, and England, were the direct expression of the greatest and most beneficent religious reformation ever recorded in Christendom, carrying in its train a civil reformation that redeemed western civilization from the Dark Ages and built up for the first time a great and measurably consistent Christian society. It shows it; for of all art it is at once the most competent and the most inspired, mingled equally of active reason, good sense, brilliant thinking, and a spiritual emphasis, a fine idealism that we may search long in world-annals to equal.

Beginning at the hands of monks of many orders, this art infused the whole Church, being taken up at last by the bishops and focused in the vast and innumerable cathedrals, and so extended through the laity, high and low, until it became an intimate and indispensable attribute of life itself.

. . . .

Architecture . . . is primarily organism; it is also synthesis, that is, it cannot exist without many of the other arts, and when—as in the case of a Gothic cathedral in operation—it combines with itself every other mode of art, then it becomes the greatest art-manifestation possible to fallen man. Chartres or Rheims or Westminster in the fourteenth century during a pontifical mass was undoubtedly the greatest and most comprehensive work of art the mind can conceive or the intelligence bring into being.

This organic quality on which I have laid so much stress, not only because of its essential importance, but also because it is the very quality most lacking today, was determined and assured in the twelfth century. The thirteenth was devoted to perfecting this to the highest possible point and to infusing the result with the spiritual elements of beauty and emotional stimulus. In this the artists of the time were following a natural parallelism with such other commanding artists as Homer, Plato, Shakespeare, Michelangelo, all of whom found their enduring glory, less through original discovery and creation, than through their power of gathering up all the work of their forbears and breathing into it the breath of life.

This great work of organic development may be seen to perfection in the Cathedral of Our Lady of Paris, and it is progressive from east to west. The choir was begun in 1163, the west front completed in 1235, and in these seventy years all the promise of Jumièges was fulfilled in more than abundant measure. From east to west there is a steady growth in certainty of touch, in structural articulation and integrity, and in the development of the sense of pure beauty. The plan is of the simplest—only a parallelogram with one semicircular termination, divided into five aisles, the middle one being twice the width of the others, with all the load concentrated on points distributed with almost the accuracy of an engineer. The interior order—*i.e.,* arcade, triforium, and clerestory—holds still by the somewhat dull mechanism of early Norman work, and the three elements are too nearly alike in vertical height for a result either beautiful or structurally significant. It lacks rhythm and subtlety of composition. The shaft-scheme of such transitional work as Noyon holds here, with cylindrical columns in the arcade supporting multiple shafts above, the vaulting shaft resting directly on the capital of the arcade column—an inorganic device much admired by Gothic theorists of the nineteenth century. On the other hand, the little Lombard round window has blossomed into the "Mystic Rose," which here approaches sublimity, and is used as the central figure of the terminations of nave and transepts. The whole nave is full of trials, experiments, changes, hurriedly adopted and half completed, and the exterior is marked by the same absorbing personality. In the chevet, for example, the mad and unbeautiful flying buttresses are not original; for at first the system was the subsequently standard type—two flights of arches, each properly grounded through pillar or wall-buttress. After a disastrous conflagration, however, some genius with a daring disproportionate to his discretion conceived the idea of covering both aisles with one enormous span. The result never commended itself, however, and is almost unique, but it shows at the same time the nemesis of structural pride that in the end, at Beauvais, was to close the history and the power over beauty of detail that was not mitigated by structural indiscretions; for the design of the buttress pinnacles of these Brobdingnagian arches is perhaps the most beautiful single thing in Gothic architecture. As for the west front, it ever remains the great classical achievement of the Middle Ages, the most superbly conceived work of architecture that has ever issued from the hand of man in any place or at any time. It has no rival in the past, and none is conceivable for the future.

Laon was more or less contemporary with Paris, later if anything; but it is as different as may be. Where Paris is calm, serene, simple, Laon is nervous, complex, almost fantastic. For Paris two vast towers were enough, for Laon seven could hardly suffice. The whole work is tentative, vacillating, romantic, and, it must be confessed, inferior. Only in its conception and composition, however; in detail it is faultless, and one realizes here how, whatever the vagaries of the master-mason, the great body of artificers were always on hand to redeem primary mistakes by their conservative and assured taste and sense of beauty—a condition of things that in a sense marks the length of road we have traveled since then.

With Chartres, Bourges, and Rheims we come to a trinity of masterpieces that group themselves around the crowning years of Catholic civilization and are its sufficient expression and—if this were needed—justification. Chartres dates in the main from 1194, when it was begun anew after a fire that destroyed all but the crypt and the west front, to 1260, when it was consecrated. In plan it is perhaps the noblest of all Gothic churches, while its interior, in point of organism, proportion, relation of parts, articulation, has few rivals. It is, I believe, the most perfect religious interior man has produced, as Paris is the greatest exterior, so far as its façade is concerned.

Bourges was begun in the same year with Chartres and its essential organism then determined, though the west bays of the nave were not completed until the very end of the thirteenth century. Its plan is wholly different from those of Paris, Laon, and Chartres (for there was then no copying of one master-builder by another) and its interior organism is quite original. It has no transepts and therefore no crossing, while its arcade is twice as lofty in proportion as the arcades of its sister-churches. It is the most aspiring and romantic of all and in some respects is the most brilliant in its artistic invention.

Rheims began to rise from its ashes in the year 1211, just when the savage tribes of Prussia began to yield to Christian missionaries—the last of the heathen races of North Europe to accept Christianity for a time—later to overwhelm in the red ruin of shell and flame the great church that in its building marked the moment of their evanescent conversion. The west front, to the base of the upper story of the towers, was finished with the close of the century. In plan, in exterior and interior organism, in detail, and in sculpture, Rheims was the perfected work of the Catholic civilization of the Middle Ages. Every other building shows here and there experiment, uncertainty, an almost nervous reaching out of its creators toward a dim ideal that was yet the one reality. Of this there was nothing in Rheims. It was the work of a master so supreme in his artistry that he laid hold on perfection where his followers struggled toward it. I am not sure that this perfect attainment raised it very far above Chartres or Bourges or Coutances. Final it was, in conception and in every minutest part, but to me there is something in the tremulous daring of Bourges, in the unsatisfied but eager desire of Paris, in the rapt faith and awestruck groping for the hand of God in Chartres, that appeals with a poignancy that in Rheims yields to dumb reverence for final and almost superhuman achievement. After all, man is the creature that *tries,* and in the striving for perfection we do not look for success; we resent it, in a sense, when one approaches it too closely. The great churches of the thirteenth century tried, as man tries, to achieve the unattainable, and in their failure they are sublime. One achieved, or almost achieved—Rheims—and, while we gave it the tribute of awed veneration, our hearts went first to the more human monuments of men, rather than of demigods. Rheims almost achieved the unattainable; its martyrdom has completed what its makers just failed of attaining, and for the future in the hearts of this and every succeeding generation, *in saecula saeculorum,* it will stand first in mind and in heart as the perfect work of man when he wrought in the fear of God.

59. *TROUBADOUR POETRY*[1]

In sunny southern France, especially in that part of it known as Provence, developed the poetry of the troubadours. No one knows just when this type of literature had its beginnings but it would seem to have been in flourishing condition as early as the end of the eleventh century, the time of William, Duke of Aquitaine, the first definitely known troubadour. Sometimes men known as joglars *or* jongleurs *went from place to place reciting the poems written by the troubadours. Sometimes the troubadours themselves wandered, singing their own lays.*

The troubadour sang of romantic love, of chivalrous devotion to women, of court life and of knightly prowess. His was an aristocratic type of literature and made its appeal to the noble classes.

In that form of the troubadour poem known as the "alba," of which the second of the two troubadour poems here given is an example, the lover bemoans the coming of the dawn.

A Poem by Peire Vidal

When the wind is gently blowing
From Provence, I drink the breezes;
All that comes from there so pleases
Me, when I hear men bestowing
Praise on it, I fain would hear
Hundred times as much, for sheer
Joy it is to hear its praises.

Fairer land is no man knowing
Than that land across the seas is
—Where she dwells who my heart's ease is—
'Twixt Vence and the Rhône swift-flowing;
Wherefore 'mid those people dear
I have left my glad heart near
Her who grief to gladness raises.

[1] Barbara Smythe, *Trobador Poets.* Selections from the Poems of Eight Trobadors: translated from the Provençal with Introduction and Notes. London, Chatto and Windus; New York, Duffield and Co., 1911, pp. 160; 183–184. Used by permission of Chatto and Windus, and Oxford University Press, publishers.

Soon can she be overthrowing
Grief, if on one's heart it seizes;
E'en the thought of her appeases
Woe, and he whose praise is glowing
Never to speak false need fear;
Sure it is she has no peer,
None so fair in mirror gazes.

And if wit and art I'm showing,
Then my gratitude for these is
Due to her, for all one sees is
To her inspiration owing;
All that I do well, 'tis clear,
Comes from her alone, the mere
Thought of whom my heart amazes.

. . . .

An Anonymous Alba

Within the orchard, 'neath the mayflowers white,
Two lovers dreamed away the livelong night,
Until the watcher cries the East grows light.
Ah God, ah God, the dawn, how soon it comes!

"Would God the night might never yield to morn,
And that my love might leave me not forlorn,
And that the watcher ne'er might see the dawn.
Ah God, ah God, the dawn, how soon it comes!

"Beloved, when I kiss thee, kiss thou me,
While in the fields the birds make melody;
Let us do this in spite of jealousy.
Ah God, ah God, the dawn, how soon it comes!

"Beloved, let us dream together here,
Within the garden, where the birds sing clear,
Until the watcher warns us day is near.
Ah God, ah God, the dawn, how soon it comes.

"Sweet is the breeze that wafts to me the kiss
Of my fair joyous love, and it is bliss
To drink his sweet breath with my lips like this
Ah God, ah God, the dawn, how soon it comes!"

Gentle the lady is, and courteous too,
And many men her beauty love to view;
Her heart is given to faithful love and true.
Ah God, ah God, the dawn, how soon it comes!

60. *A FRENCH FABLIAU: THE PRIEST WHO HAD A MOTHER IN SPITE OF HIMSELF*[1]

Very different from the romantic songs of the troubadours were the fabliaux. *These have been defined as "laughable stories told in verse." They were written not for nobles and ladies of the aristocracy but for people of low degree, such as merchants and artisans the importance of whom was increasing in the twelfth and thirteenth centuries.*

The fabliaux were "earthy" tales, often ironical and apt to be shockingly coarse. Their authors took delight in making fun of priests and women, as the following example shows.

List, lordings all, for new the tale I tell:
It chanc'd unto a priest I knew right well.
  His aged mother, and a gamesome lass,
With him beneath one roof their days did pass;
The crone, with years bent down, and hunch'd behind,
Show'd in her shape the model of her mind:
The leman had, besure, a pretty face;
Nor fail'd she in the duties of her place;
The crone was busy too, and toil'd amain;
But different deeds a different guerdon gain:
So nothing lack'd the lass; but she might have
Kirtles, and cloaks, and silver girdle brave,
And linings soft of lamb or squirrel's skin:
Forsooth the neighbours made a parlous din;
The matron, ne'ertheless, was choicely fed,
Good pease, good pottage, and the best of bread;

[1] Fabliaux or Tales, Abridged from French Manuscripts of the XIIth and XIIIth Centuries by M. Le Grand (d'Aussy), Selected and Translated into English Verse by the late G. L. Way, Esq., A new Edition, Corrected. 3 vols., London, J. Rodwell, 1815, vol. I, pp. 63–70.

But when she clamour'd to be costlier dress'd,
For here her taste was curious as the best,
Her eloquence might ne'er one whit prevail
Though the priest's ears were deafen'd with the tale.
Hence, loud from morn to evening would she scold,
And every neighbour heard her grievance told,
With calumnies and lies full many a score,
Still as she gadded on from door to door;
Till the whole village 'gan the priest to shun,
And hate him as a hard unnatural son.
  At last, one morn when humour bore the sway,
And, as it chanc'd, it was a summer's day,
He fairly stopp'd the brawl with master-tone,
And bade her take her chattels, and begone.
She not a pace would budge, but— 'Yea!' she cried,
'I go, and bring the bishop by my side;
'Besure thy secret life shall be bewray'd,
'Lewd deeds and dealings with that shameless jade.'—
'Out!'—quoth the priest in choler; 'there's the door—
'Mark well the past, for thou shalt mark no more.'
  Forth far'd the crone, nigh wood; nor slack'd her way
Till prostrate at the bishop's feet she lay;
There rav'd for vengeance, outcast and exil'd,
For vengeance on a base unnatural child,
Who, wanting long time past in reverence meet,
At length had driven her forth into the street
With foul reproach and other nameless ill,
To gratify a strumpet's wanton will.
  With patient ears the prelate heard the crone,
And promis'd her all justice should be done:
And, for his custom'd session was at hand,
Straight to the culprit priest he sent command
There to attend the charges to refute,
And bound the crone to prosecute her suit.
  Now came the day; the priests press on to court,
Two hundred sure, and crowds of meaner sort:
Through the mid-throng the beldam passage made,
And sued full loud for justice undelay'd:
'Peace!' quoth the prelate judge, with look severe;
'Wait thou thy son's approach attendant here;
'If true thy charge, or e'er this court be ended
'His benefice is gone, and he suspended!'

The crone, unskill'd in phrase, now ween'd to see
Her pendent child aloft on gallow-tree,
And felt her inmost bowels yearn amain
For the base bantling she had borne with pain,
And lov'd so dear, and nourish'd at her breast;
And rued her luckless choler unrepress'd
Fain would she flee; but flight may nought prevent
Her son's arrest, and sequent punishment:
This way and that her crafty wit she tries,
And, as a woman rarely lacks device,
So well she sped, that chancing to behold
A chaplain boon, with chin of double fold,
With glossy cheek, just entering at the door,
And a huge mass of cumbrous paunch before,
'Lo here! lo here my bairn!' she 'gan to cry;
'Now, sire, now grant me justice, or I die!'
'Unthankful son!' the prelate straight began
To the strange priest with mute amazement wan,
'Thus dost thou scant thine aged parent there
'To deck thy leman loose with robes of vair?
'Thus shame the church, and bring her wealth to waste
'In harlot revel squander'd and disgrac'd?'—
'Liege lord!' the astonished chaplain cried, 'I know,
'And practis'd once, what sons to mothers owe;
'Many a year since, so may my bones find rest!
'My parent died, and all those duties ceas'd;
'But for that woman there, by day or night
'Till this strange hour she never cross'd my sight!'
'How!' quoth the prelate, kindling as he spoke,
'Thus would'st thou rid thy shoulder from the yoke?
'Thy parent, first ill-treated, then denied,
'And the strong justice of my court defied.
'Hear then—in thee this instant I arrest
'All ministry and function of a priest,
'Unless borne hence with thee this matron wend,
'Hous'd, clad, and cherish'd as thy dearest friend:
'Forth from this hour should she or stranger prove
'That aught thou fail in debt of filial love,
'The law takes course.'—The wrathful prelate ceas'd:
Abash'd full sore retir'd the luckless priest;
In doleful dump he mounts his steed amain
With his foul prize, and homeward turns the rein.

Two miles or more the pair had journey'd on,
When in the road they met the beldam's son;
And, 'Whither bent?' the rueful chaplain cried:
'I to the bishop's court,' the son replied:
'Thee,' quoth the first, 'may like good luck befall!
'I too was summon'd to attend the hall,
'Nor wist I why; and lo, this goodly meed,
'My mother, as it seems, to house and feed.'
The son, who, while the priest his story told,
Eyed the quaint gestures of the beldam old
With nods and winks to keep the secret tight,
Refrain'd from laughter well as mortal might:
'If thou,' quoth he, 'thus early at the court,
'Hast had one mother given thee to support,
'My mind forebodes our worthy prelate's pain
'May gift us tardier travellers with twain.
'What say'st thou, friend? suppose some wight inclin'd
'To take this reverend matron up behind,
'And quit thee of thy charge, and kind entreat;
'What brave reward might recompense the feat?"
'Troth,' quoth the priest, 'to speak without disguise,
'I'm not the man to scant him in his price:
'I'll pay him forty livres by the year,
'Villain or clerk, nor think the bargain dear.'
'Enough, fair brother mine!' returns the son;
'So please the lady here, our deed is done.'
The crone well-pleas'd besure: so, all agreed,
Home son and mother fare on pacing steed;
Each year his plighted dole the chaplain paid,
Nor future plaint to bishop e'er was made.

61. *WANDERING STUDENTS AND THEIR SONGS* [1]

It is rather strange that a book with the attractive title of Wine, Women and Song *by so prolific a writer as J. A. Symonds should be as inaccessible to the average college student as it actually is. Moreover, the booklet is devoted to student life in the Middle Ages and contains some very interesting poems produced by wandering students. Consequently it must appeal to anyone*

[1] J. A. Symonds, *Wine, Women, and Song*. New York and London, G. P. Putnam's Sons, no date, pp. 21–23, 24, 25–27, 54–59, 63–64, 69–74, 91, 175–176. Courtesy of G. P. Putnam's Sons, publishers.

interested in those vagabonds who wandered from one university to another and by their restless habits illustrated the differences between medieval and modern universities. A few of their poems have been reproduced here, together with some of the introductions by Mr. Symonds.

Who were these Wandering Students, so often mentioned, and of whom nothing has been as yet related? As their name implies, they were men, and for the most part young men, travelling from university to university in search of knowledge. Far from their homes, without responsibilities, light of purse and light of heart, careless and pleasure-seeking, they ran a free, disreputable course, frequenting taverns at least as much as lecture-rooms, more capable of pronouncing judgment upon wine or women than upon a problem of divinity or logic. The conditions of medieval learning made it necessary to study different sciences in different parts of Europe; and a fixed habit of unrest, which seems to have pervaded society after the period of the Crusades, encouraged vagabondage in all classes. The extent to which travelling was carried in the Middle Ages for purposes of pilgrimage and commerce, out of pure curiosity or love of knowledge, for the bettering of trade in handicrafts or for self-improvement in the sciences, has only of late years been estimated at a just calculation. "The scholars," wrote a monk of Froidmont in the twelfth century, "are wont to roam around the world and visit all its cities, till much learning makes them mad; for in Paris they seek liberal arts, in Orleans authors, at Salerno gallipots, at Toledo demons, and in no place decent manners."

These pilgrims to the shrines of knowledge formed a class apart. They were distinguished from the secular and religious clergy, inasmuch as they had taken no orders, or only minor orders, held no benefice or cure, and had entered into no conventual community. They were still more sharply distinguished from the laity, whom they scorned as brutes, and with whom they seem to have lived on terms of mutual hostility. One of these vagabond gownsmen would scarcely condescend to drink with a townsman. . . .

It is open to doubt whether the *milites* or soldiers were included with the rustics in that laity, for which the students felt so bitter a contempt. But the tenor of some poems on love, especially the *Dispute of Phyllis and Flora,* shows that the student claimed a certain superiority over the soldier. This antagonism between clerk and rustic was heartily reciprocated. In a song on taverns the student is warned that he may meet with rough treatment from the clodhopper: . . .

The affinities of the Wandering Students were rather with the Church than with laymen of any degree. They piqued themselves upon their title of *Clerici,* and added the epithet of *Vagi.* We shall see in the sequel that they stood in a peculiar relation of dependence upon ecclesiastical society.

According to tendencies prevalent in the Middle Ages, they became a sort of guild, and proclaimed themselves with pride an Order. Nothing is more clearly marked in their poetry than the *esprit de corps,* which animates them with a cordial sense of brotherhood. The same tendencies which prompted their association required that they should have a patron saint. But as the confraternity was anything but religious, this saint, or rather this eponymous hero, had to be a Rabelaisian character. He was called Golias, and his flock received the generic name of Goliardi. Golias was father and master; the Goliardi were his family, his sons, and pupils. *Familia Goliae, Magister Golias, Pueri Goliae, Discipulus Goliae,* are phrases to be culled from the rubrics of their literature.

Much has been conjectured regarding these names and titles. Was Golias a real person? Did he give his own name to the Goliardi; or was he invented after the Goliardi had already acquired their designation? In either case, ought we to connect both words with the Latin *gula,* and so regard the Goliardi as notable gluttons; or with the Provençal *goliar, gualiar, gualiardor,* which carry a significance of deceit? Had Golias anything to do with Goliath of the Bible, the great Philistine, who in the present day would more properly be chosen as the hero of those classes which the students held in horror?

It is not easy to answer these questions. All we know for certain is, that the term Goliardus was in common medieval use, and was employed as a synonym for Wandering Scholar in ecclesiastical documents. . . .

On the Order of Wandering Students
No. 1

At the mandate, Go ye forth,
Through the whole world hurry!
Priests tramp out toward south and north,
Monks and hermits scurry,
Levites smooth the gospel leave,
Bent on ambulation;
Each and all to our sect cleave,
Which is life's salvation.

In this sect of ours 't is writ:
Prove all things in season;
Weigh this life and judge of it
By your riper reason;

'Gainst all evil clerks be you
Steadfast in resistance,
Who refuse large tithe and due
Unto your subsistence.

Marquesses, Bavarians,
Austrians and Saxons,
Noblemen and chiefs of clans
Glorious by your actions!
Listen, comrades all, I pray,
To these new decretals:
Misers they must meet decay,
Niggardly gold-beetles.

We the laws of charity
Found, nor let them crumble;
For into our order we
Take both high and humble;

Rich and poor men we receive,
  In our bosom cherish;
Welcome those the shavelings leave
  At their doors to perish.

We receive the tonsured monk,
  Let him take his pittance;
And the parson with his punk,
  If he craves admittance;
Masters with their bands of boys,
  Priests with high dominion;
But the scholar who enjoys
  Just one coat's our minion!

This our sect doth entertain
  Just men and unjust ones;
Halt, lame, weak of limb or brain,
  Strong men and robust ones;
Those who flourish in their pride,
  Those whom age makes stupid;
Frigid folk and hot folk fried
  In the fires of Cupid.

Tranquil souls and bellicose,
  Peacemaker and foeman;
Czech and Hun, and mixed with those
  German, Slav, and Roman;
Men of middling size and weight,
  Dwarfs and giants mighty;
Men of modest heart and state,
  Vain men, proud and flighty.

Of the Wanderers' order I
  Tell the Legislature—
They whose life, is free and high,
  Gentle too their nature—
They who'd rather scrape a fat
  Dish in gravy swimming,
Than in sooth to marvel at
  Barns with barley brimming.

Now this order, as I ken,
  Is called sect or section,
Since its sectaries are men
  Divers in complexion;
Therefore *hic* and *haec* and *hoc*
  Suit it in declension,
Since so multiform a flock
  Here finds comprehension.

This our order hath decried
  Matins with a warning;
For that certain phantoms glide
  In the early morning,
Whereby pass into man's brain
  Visions of vain folly;
Early risers are insane,
  Racked by melancholy.

This our order doth proscribe
  All the year round matins;
When they've left their beds, our tribe
  In the tap sing latins;
There they call for wine for all,
  Roasted fowl and chicken;
Hazard's threats no hearts appal,
  Though his strokes still thicken.

This our order doth forbid
  Double clothes with loathing:
He whose nakedness is hid
  With one vest hath clothing:
Soon one throws his cloak aside
  At the dice-box' calling;
Next his girdle is untied,
  While the cards are falling.

What I've said of upper clothes
  To the nether reaches;
They who own a shirt, let those
  Think no more of breeches;

If one boasts big boots to use,
  Let him leave his gaiters;
They who this firm law refuse
  Shall be counted traitors.

No one, none shall wander forth
  Fasting from the table;
If thou'rt poor, from south and north
  Beg as thou art able!
Hath it not been often seen
  That one coin brings many,
When a gamester on the green
  Stakes his lucky penny?

No one on the road should walk
  'Gainst the wind—'t is madness;
Nor in poverty shall stalk
  With a face of sadness;
Let him bear him bravely then,
  Hope sustain his spirit;
After heavy trials men
  Better luck inherit!

While throughout the world you rove,
  Thus uphold your banners;
Give these reasons why you prove
  Hearts of men and manners:
"To reprove the reprobate,
Probity approving,
Improbate from approbate
  To remove, I'm moving."

A Wandering Student's Petition
No. 3

I, a wandering scholar lad,
  Born for toil and sadness,
Oftentimes am driven by
  Poverty to madness.

Literature and knowledge I
  Fain would still be earning,
Were it not that want of pelf
  Makes me cease from learning.

These torn clothes that cover me
  Are too thin and rotten;
Oft I have to suffer clod,
  By the warmth forgotten.

Scarce I can attend at church,
  Sing God's praises duly;
Mass and vespers both I miss,
  Though I love them truly.

Oh, thou pride of N——,
  By thy worth I pray thee
Give the suppliant help in need,
  Heaven will sure repay thee.

Take a mind unto thee now
  Like unto St. Martin;
Clothe the pilgrim's nakedness,
  Wish him well at parting.

So may God translate your soul
  Into peace eternal,
And the bliss of saints be yours
  In His realm supernal.

The Confession of Golias
No. 5

Boiling in my spirit's veins
  With fierce indignation,
From my bitterness of soul
  Springs self-revelation:
Framed am I of flimsy stuff,
  Fit for levitation,
Like a thin leaf which the wind
  Scatters from its station.

While it is the wise man's part
  With deliberation
On a rock to base his heart's
  Permanent foundation,
With a running river I
  Find my just equation,
Which beneath the self-same sky
  Hath no habitation.

Carried am I like a ship
  Left without a sailor,
Like a bird that through the air
  Flies where tempests hale her;
Chains and fetters hold me not,
  Naught avails a jailer;
Still I find my fellows out
  Toper, gamester, railer.

To my mind all gravity
  Is a grave subjection;
Sweeter far than honey are
  Jokes and free affection.
All that Venus bids me do,
  Do I with erection,
For she ne'er in heart of man
  Dwelt with dull dejection.

Down the broad road do I run,
  As the way of youth is;
Snare myself in sin, and ne'er
  Think where faith and truth is;
Eager far for pleasure more
  Than soul's health, the sooth is,
For this flesh of mine I care,
  Seek not ruth where ruth is.

Prelate, most discreet of priests,
  Grant me absolution!
Dear's the death whereof I die,
  Sweet my dissolution;
For my heart is wounded by
  Beauty's soft suffusion;
All the girls I come not nigh,
  Mine are in illusion.

'T is most arduous to make
  Nature's self surrender;
Seeing girls, to blush and be
  Purity's defender!
We young men our longings ne'er
  Shall to stern law render,
Or preserve our fancies from
  Bodies smooth and tender.

Who, when into fire he falls,
  Keeps himself from burning?
Who within Pavia's walls
  Fame of chaste is earning?
Venus with her finger calls
  Youths at every turning,
Snares them with her eyes, and thralls
  With her amorous yearning.

If you brought Hippolitus
  To Pavia Sunday,
He'd not be Hippolitus
  On the following Monday;
Venus there keeps holiday
  Every day as one day;
'Mid these towers in no tower dwells
  Venus Verecunda.

In the second place I own
  To the vice of gaming:
Cold indeed outside I seem,
  Yet my soul is flaming:
But when once the dice-box hath
  Stripped me to my shaming,
Make I songs and verses fit
  For the world's acclaiming.

In the third place, I will speak
  Of the tavern's pleasure;
For I never found nor find
  There the least displeasure;
Nor shall find it till I greet
  Angels without measure,
Singing requiems for the souls
  In eternal leisure.

In the public-house to die
  Is my resolution;
Let wine to my lips be nigh
  At life's dissolution:
That will make the angels cry,
  With glad elocution,
"Grant this toper, God on high,
  Grace and absolution!"

With the cup the soul lights up,
  Inspirations flicker;
Nectar lifts the soul on high
  With its heavenly ichor:
To my lips a sounder taste
  Hath the tavern's liquor
Than the wine a village clerk
  Waters for the vicar.

Nature gives to every man
  Some gift serviceable;
Write I never could nor can
  Hungry at the table;
Fasting, any stripling to
  Vanquish me is able;
Hunger, thirst, I liken to
  Death that ends the fable.

Nature gives to every man
  Gifts as she is willing;
I compose my verses when
  Good wine I am swilling.
Wine the best the jolly guest
  Jolly hosts are filling;
From such wine rare fancies fine
  Flow like dews distilling.

Modest Love

No. 15

Summer sweet is coming in;
Now the pleasant days begin;
Phoebus rules the earth at last;
For sad winter's reign is past.

Wounded with the love alone
Of one girl, I make my moan:
Grief pursues me till she bend
Unto me and condescend.

Take thou pity on my plight!
With my heart thy heart unite!
In my love thy own love blending,
Finding thus of life the ending!

Gaudeamus Igitur

No. 60

  Let us live, then, and be glad
While young life's before us!
  After youthful pastime had,
  After old age hard and sad,
Earth will slumber o'er us.

Where are they who in this world,
Ere we kept, were keeping?
Go ye to the gods above;
Go to hell; inquire thereof:
They are not; they're sleeping.

Brief is life, and brevity
Briefly shall be ended:
Death comes like a whirlwind strong,
Bears us with his blast along;
None shall be defended.

Live this university,
Men that learning nourish;
Live each member of the same,
Long live all that bear its name;
Let them ever flourish!

Live the commonwealth also,
And the men that guide it!
Live our town in strength and health,
Founders, patrons, by whose wealth
We are here provided!

Live all girls! A health to you,
Melting maids and beauteous!
Live the wives and women too,
Gentle, loving, tender, true,
Good, industrious, duteous!

Perish cares that pule and pine!
Perish envious blamers!
Die the Devil, thine and mine!
Die the starch-necked Philistine!
Scoffers and defamers!

62. *AUCASSIN AND NICOLETE* [1]

One of the most charming bits of medieval literature that have come down to us is the song-story of Aucassin and Nicolete, the romantic tale of the love

[1] *Aucassin & Nicolete,* done into English by Andrew Lang. London, David Nutt in the Strand, 1896. Reprint, New York, G. E. Stechert and Co., 1928, pp. 3–9; 17–18.

of a young Christian nobleman for a Saracen slave girl. Its author is unknown. It has been conjectured that he was a wandering troubadour. In any case it is evident from the story, particularly from the preference that Aucassin expresses for Hell to Heaven, that the author was far from being dominated by the conventional religious ideas of his time.

The Song-Story of Aucassin and Nicolete

'Tis of Aucassin and Nicolete.

Who would list to the good lay
Gladness of the captive grey?
'Tis how two young lovers met,
Aucassin and Nicolete,
Of the pains the lover bore
And the sorrows he outwore,
For the goodness and the grace,
Of his love, so fair of face.

Sweet the song, the story sweet,
There is no man hearkens it,
No man living 'neath the sun,
So outwearied, so foredone,
Sick and woful, worn and sad,
But is healèd, but is glad
'Tis so sweet.

So say they, speak they, tell they the Tale:

How the Count Bougars de Valence made war on Count Garin de Biaucaire, war so great, and so marvellous, and so mortal that never a day dawned but alway he was there, by the gates and walls, and barriers of the town with a hundred knights, and ten thousand men at arms, horsemen and footmen: so burned he the Count's land, and spoiled his country, and slew his men. Now the Count Garin de Biaucaire was old and frail, and his good days were gone over. No heir had he, neither son nor daughter, save one young man only; such an one as I shall tell you. Aucassin was the name of the damoiseau: fair was he, goodly, and great, and featly fashioned of his body, and limbs. His hair was yellow, in little curls, his eyes blue and laughing, his face beautiful and shapely, his nose high and well set, and so richly seen was he in all things good, that in him was none evil at all. But so suddenly overtaken was he of Love, who is a great master, that he would not, of his will, he dubbed knight, nor take arms, nor follow tourneys, nor do whatsoever him beseemed. Therefore his father and mother said to him;

"Son, go take thine arms, mount thy horse, and hold thy land, and help thy men, for if they see thee among them, more stoutly will they keep in battle their lives, and lands, and thine, and mine."

"Father," said Aucassin, "I marvel that you will be speaking. Never may God give me aught of my desire if I be made knight, or mount my horse, or face stour and battle wherein knights smite and are smitten again, unless thou give me Nicolete, my true love, that I love so well."

"Son," said the father, "this may not be. Let Nicolete go, a slave girl she is, out of a strange land, and the captain of this town bought her of the Saracens, and carried her hither, and hath reared her and let christen the maid, and took her for his daughter in God, and one day will find a young man for her, to win her bread honourably. Herein hast thou naught to make or mend, but if a wife thou wilt have, I will give thee the daughter of a King, or a Count. There is no man so rich in France, but if thou desire his daughter, thou shalt have her."

"Faith! my father," said Aucassin, "tell me where is the place so high in all the world, that Nicolete, my sweet lady and love, would not grace it well? If she were Empress of Constantinople or of Germany, or Queen of France or England, it were little enough for her; so gentle is she and courteous, and debonaire, and compact of all good qualities."

Here singeth one:

Aucassin was of Biaucaire
Of a goodly castle there,
But from Nicolete the fair
None might win his heart away
Though his father, many a day,
And his mother said him nay,
"Ha! fond child, what wouldest thou?
Nicolete is glad enow!
Was from Carthage cast away,
Paynims sold her on a day!
Wouldst thou win a lady fair
Choose a maid of high degree
Such an one is meet for thee."
"Nay of these I have no care,
Nicolete is debonaire,
Her body sweet and the face of her

Take my heart as in a snare,
Loyal love is but her share
That is so sweet."

Then speak they, say they, tell they the Tale:

When the Count Garin de Biaucaire knew that he would avail not to withdraw Aucassin his son from the love of Nicolete, he went to the Captain of the city, who was his man, and spake to him, saying:

"Sir Count; away with Nicolete thy daughter in God; cursed be the land whence she was brought into this country, for by reason of her do I lose Aucassin, that will neither be dubbed knight, nor do aught of the things that fall to him to be done. And wit ye well," he said, "that if I might have her at my will, I would burn her in a fire, and yourself might well be sore adread."

"Sir," said the Captain, "this is grievous to me that he comes and goes and hath speech with her. I had bought the maiden at mine own charges, and nourished her, and baptized, and made her my daughter in God. Yea, I would have given her to a young man that should win her bread honourably. With this had Aucassin thy son naught to make or mend. But, sith it is thy will and thy pleasure, I will send her into that land and that country where never will he see her with his eyes."

"Have a heed to thyself," said the Count Garin, "thence might great evil come on thee."

So parted they each from other. Now the Captain was a right rich man: so had he a rich palace with a garden in face of it; in an upper chamber thereof he let place Nicolete, with one old woman to keep her company, and in that chamber put bread and meat and wine and such things as were needful. Then he let seal the door, that none might come in or go forth, save that there was one window, over against the garden, and strait enough, where through came to them a little air.

Here singeth one:

Nicolete as ye heard tell
Prisoned is within a cell
That is painted wondrously
With colours of a far countrie,
And the window of marble wrought,
There the maiden stood in thought,
With straight brows and yellow hair
Never saw ye fairer fair!

On the wood she gazed below,
And she saw the roses blow,
Heard the birds sing loud and low,
Therefore spoke she wofully:
"Ah me, wherefore do I lie
Here in prison wrongfully:
Aucassin, my love, my knight,
Am I not thy heart's delight,
Thou that lovest me aright!
'Tis for thee that I must dwell
In the vaulted chamber cell,
Hard beset and all alone!
By our Lady Mary's Son
Here no longer will I wonn,
    If I may flee!

Nicolete was in prison, as ye have heard soothly, in the chamber. And the noise and bruit of it went through all the country and all the land, how that Nicolete was lost. Some said she had fled the country, and some that the Count Garin de Biaucaire had let slay her. Whosoever had joy thereof, Aucassin had none, so he went to the Captain of the town and spoke to him, saying:

"Sir Captain, what hast thou made of Nicolete, my sweet lady and love, the thing that best I love in all the world? Hast thou carried her off or ravished her away from me? Know well that if I die of it, the price shall be demanded of thee, and that will be well done, for it shall be even as if thou hadst slain me with thy two hands, for thou hast taken from me the thing that in this world I loved the best."

"Fair Sir," said the Captain, "let these things be. Nicolete is a captive that I did bring from a strange country. Yea, I bought her at my own charges of the Saracens, and I bred her up and baptized her, and made her my daughter in God. And I have cherished her, and one of these days I would have given her a young man, to win her bread honourably. With this hast thou naught to make, but do thou take the daughter of a King or a Count. Nay more, what wouldst thou deem thee to have gained, hadst thou made her thy leman, and taken her to thy bed? Plentiful lack of comfort hadst thou got thereby, for in Hell would thy soul have lain while the world endures, and into Paradise wouldst thou have entered never."

"In Paradise what have I to win? There in I seek not to enter, but only to have Nicolete, my sweet lady that I love so well. For into Paradise go none but such folk as I shall tell thee now: Thither go these same old priests, and halt old men and maimed, who all day and night cower continually before the altars, and in the crypts; and such folk as wear old amices and old clouted frocks, and naked folk and shoeless, and covered with sores, perishing of hunger and thirst, and of cold, and of little ease. These be they that go into Paradise, with them have I naught to make. But into Hell would I fain go; for into Hell fare the goodly clerks, and goodly knights that fall in tourneys and great wars, and stout men at arms, and all men noble. With these would I liefly go. And thither pass the sweet ladies and courteous that have two lovers, or three, and their lords also thereto. Thither goes the gold, and the silver, and cloth of vair, and cloth of gris, and harpers, and makers, and the prince of this world. With these I would gladly go, let me but have with me, Nicolete, my sweetest lady."

"Certes," quoth the Captain, "in vain wilt thou speak thereof, for never shalt thou see her; and if thou hadst word with her, and thy father knew it, he would let burn in a fire both her and me, and thyself might well be sore adread."

"That is even what irketh me," quoth Aucassin. So he went from the Captain sorrowing.

. . . .

Then say they, speak they, tell they the Tale:

Aucassin was cast into prison as ye have heard tell, and Nicolete, of her part, was in the chamber. Now it was summer time, the month of May, when days are warm, and long, and clear, and the night still and serene. Nicolete lay one night on her bed, and saw the moon shine clear through a window, yea, and heard the nightingale sing in the garden, so she minded her of Aucassin her lover whom she loved so well. Then fell she to thoughts of Count Garin de Biaucaire, that hated her to the death; therefore deemed she that there she would no longer abide, for that, if she were told of, and the Count knew whereas she lay, an ill death would he make her die. Now she knew that the old woman slept who held her company. Then she arose, and clad her in a mantle of silk she had by her, very goodly, and took napkins, and sheets of the bed, and knotted one to the other, and made therewith a cord as long as she might, so knitted it to a pillar in the window, and let herself slip down into the garden, then caught up her raiment in both hands, behind and before, and kilted up her kirtle, because of the dew that she saw lying deep on the grass, and so went her way down through the garden.

Her locks were yellow and curled, her eyes blue and smiling, her face featly fashioned, the nose high and fairly set, the lips more red than cherry or rose in time of summer, her teeth white and small; her breasts so firm that they bore up the folds of her bodice as they had been two apples; so slim she was in the waist that your two hands might have clipped her, and the daisy flowers that brake beneath her as she went tip-toe, and that bent above her instep, seemed black against her feet, so white was the maiden. She came to the postern gate, and unbarred it, and went out through the streets of Biaucaire, keeping always on the shadowy side, for the moon was shining right clear, and so wandered she till she came to the tower where her lover lay. The tower was flanked with buttresses, and she cowered under one of them, wrapped in her mantle. Then thrust she her head through a crevice of the tower that was old and worn, and so heard she Aucassin wailing within, and making dole and lament for the sweet lady he loved so well.

63. THE MEDIEVAL CHURCH AT THE HEIGHT OF ITS POWER[1]

In the thirteenth century the medieval Church reached the height of its worldly power. Some of the sources of its tremendous hold on Christendom are discussed by that brilliant student of medieval Church history, the late Henry C. Lea. Mr. Lea points out, further, that gains in power were unfortunately accompanied by the development of certain abuses which tended to undermine the Church's spiritual influence.

As the twelfth century drew to a close, the Church was approaching a crisis in its career. The vicissitudes of a hundred and fifty years, skilfully improved, had rendered it the mistress of Christendom. History records no such triumph of intellect over brute strength as that which, in an age of turmoil and battle, was wrested from the fierce warriors of the time by priests who had no material force at their command, and whose power was based alone on the souls and consciences of men. Over soul and conscience their empire was complete. No Christian could hope for salvation who was not in all things an obedient son of the Church, and who was not ready to take up arms in its defence; and, in a time when faith was a determining factor of conduct, this belief created a spiritual despotism which placed all things within reach of him who could wield it.

This could be accomplished only by a centralized organization such as that which had gradually developed itself within the ranks of the hierarchy. The ancient independence of the episcopate was no more. Step by step the supremacy of the Roman see had been asserted and enforced, until it enjoyed the universal jurisdiction which enabled it to bend to its wishes every

[1] Henry C. Lea, *A History of the Inquisition of the Middle Ages*. New York, The Macmillan Co., 1922, vol. I, pp. 1–8. Used by permission of The Macmillan Company, publishers.

prelate, under the naked alternative of submission or expulsion. The papal mandate, just or unjust, reasonable or unreasonable, was to be received and implicitly obeyed, for there was no appeal from the representative of St. Peter. In a narrower sphere, and subject to the pope, the bishop held an authority which, at least in theory, was equally absolute; while the humbler minister of the altar was the instrument by which the decrees of pope and bishop were enforced among the people; for the destiny of all men lay in the hands which could administer or withhold the sacraments essential to salvation.

Thus intrusted with responsibility for the fate of mankind, it was necessary that the Church should possess the powers and the machinery requisite for the due discharge of a trust so unspeakably important. For the internal regulation of the conscience it had erected the institution of auricular confession, which by this time had become almost the exclusive appanage of the priesthood. When this might fail to keep the believer in the path of righteousness, it could resort to the spiritual courts which had grown up around every episcopal seat, with an undefined jurisdiction capable of almost unlimited extension. Besides supervision over matters of faith and discipline, of marriage, of inheritance, and of usury, which belonged to them by general consent, there were comparatively few questions between man and man which could not be made to include some case of conscience involving the interpellation of spiritual interference, especially when agreements were customarily confirmed with the sanction of the oath; and the cure of souls implied a perpetual inquest over the aberrations, positive or possible, of every member of the flock. It would be difficult to set bounds to the intrusion upon the concerns of every man which was thus rendered possible, or to the influence thence derivable.

Not only did the humblest priest wield a supernatural power which marked him as one elevated above the common level of humanity, but his person and possessions were alike inviolable. No matter what crimes he might commit, secular justice could not take cognizance of them, and secular officials could not arrest him. He was amenable only to the tribunals of his own order, which were debarred from inflicting punishments involving the effusion of blood, and from whose decisions an appeal to the supreme jurisdiction of distant Rome conferred too often virtual immunity. The same privilege protected ecclesiastical property, conferred on the Church by the piety of successive generations, and covering no small portion of the most fertile lands of Europe. Moreover, the seignorial rights attaching to those lands often carried extensive temporal jurisdiction, which gave to their ghostly possessors the power over life and limb enjoyed by feudal lords.

The line of separation between the laity and the clergy was widened and deepened by the enforcement of the canon requiring celibacy on the part of all concerned in the ministry of the altar. Revived about the middle of the eleventh century, and enforced after an obstinate struggle of a hundred years, the compulsory celibacy of the priesthood divided them from the people, preserved intact the vast acquisitions of the Church, and furnished it with an innumerable army whose aspirations and ambitions were necessarily restricted within its circle. The man who entered the service of the Church was no longer a citizen. He owed no allegiance superior to that assumed in his ordination. He was released from the distraction of family cares and the seduction of the family ties. The Church was his country and his home, and its interests were his own. The moral, intellectual, and physical forces which, throughout the laity, were divided between the claims of patriotism, the selfish struggle for advancement, the provision for wife and children, were in the Church consecrated to a common end, in the success of which all might hope to share, while all were assured of the necessities of existence, and were relieved of anxiety as to the future.

The Church, however, offered the only career open to men of all ranks and stations. In the sharply-defined class distinctions of the feudal system advancement was almost impossible to one not born within the charmed circle of gentle blood. In the Church, however much rank and family connections might assist in securing promotion to high place, yet talent and energy could always make themselves felt despite lowliness of birth. Urban II and Adrian IV sprang from the humblest origin; Alexander V had been a beggar-boy; Gregory VII was the son of a carpenter; Benedict XII, of a baker; Nicholas V, of a poor physician; Sixtus IV, of a peasant; Urban IV and John XXII were sons of cobblers, and Benedict XI and Sixtus V of shepherds; in fact, the annals of the hierarchy are full of those who rose from the lowest ranks of society to the most commanding positions. The Church thus constantly recruited its ranks with fresh blood. Free from the curse of hereditary descent, through which crowns and coronets frequently lapsed into weak and incapable hands, it called into its service an indefinite amount of restless vigor for which there was no other sphere of action, and which, when once enlisted, found itself perforce identified irrevocably with the body which it had joined. The character of the priest was indelible; the vows taken at ordination could not be thrown aside; the monk, when once admitted to the cloister, could not abandon his order unless it were to enter another of more rigorous observance. The Church Militant was thus an army encamped on the soil of Christendom, with its outposts everywhere, subject to the most efficient discipline, animated with a common purpose, every soldier panoplied with inviolability and armed with the tremendous weapons which slew the soul. There was little that could not be dared or done by the commander of such a force, whose orders were listened to as oracles of God, from Portugal to Palestine and from Sicily to Iceland. "Princes," says John of Salisbury, "derive their power from the Church, and are servants of the priesthood." "The least of the priestly order is worthier than any king," exclaims Honorius of Autun; "prince and people are subjected to the clergy, which shines superior as the sun to the moon." Innocent III used a more spiritual metaphor when he declared that the priestly power was as superior to the secular as the soul of man was to his body; and he summed up his estimate of his own position by pronouncing himself to be the Vicar of Christ, the Christ of the Lord, the God of Pharaoh, placed midway between God and man, this side of God but beyond man, less than God but greater than man, who judges all, and is judged by none. That he was supreme over all the earth —over pagans and infidels as well as over Christians—was legally proved and universally taught by the mediaeval doctors. Though the power thus vaingloriously asserted was fraught with evil in many ways, yet was it none the less a service to humanity that, in those rude ages, there existed a moral force superior to high descent and martial prowess, which could remind king and noble that they must obey the law of God even when uttered by a peasant's son; as when Urban II, himself a Frenchman of low birth, dared to excommunicate his monarch, Philip I, for his adultery, thus upholding the moral order and enforcing the sanctions of eternal justice at a time when everything seemed permissible to the recklessness of power.

Yet, in achieving this supremacy, much had been of necessity sacrificed. The Christian virtues of humility and charity and self-abnegation had virtually disappeared in the contest which left the spiritual power dominant over the temporal. The affection of the populations was no longer attracted by the graces and loveliness of Christianity; submission was purchased by the promise of salvation, to be acquired by faith and obedience, or was exhorted by the threat of perdition or by the sharper terrors of earthly persecution. If the Church, by sundering itself completely from the laity, had acquired the services of a militia devoted wholly to itself, it had thereby created an antagonism between itself and the people. Practically, the whole body of Christians no longer constituted the Church; that body was divided into two essentially distinct classes, the shepherds and the sheep; and the lambs were often apt to think, not unreasonably, that they were tended only to be shorn. The worldly prizes offered to ambition by an ecclesiastical career drew into the ranks of the Church able men, it is true, but men whose object was worldly ambition rather than spiritual development. The immunities and privileges of the Church and the enlargement of its temporal acquisitions were objects held more at heart than the salvation of souls, and its high places were filled, for the most part, with men in whom worldliness was more conspicuous than the humbler virtues.

This was inevitable in the state of society which existed in the early

Middle Ages. While angels would have been required to exercise becomingly the tremendous powers claimed and acquired by the Church, the methods by which clerical preferment and promotion were secured were such as to favor the unscrupulous rather than the deserving. To understand fully the causes which drove so many thousands in to schism and heresy, leading to wars and persecutions, and the establishment of the Inquisition, it is necessary to cast a glance at the character of the men who represented the Church before the people, and at the use which they made, for good or for evil, of the absolute spiritual despotism which had become established. In wise and devout hands it might elevate incalculably the moral and material standards of European civilization; in the hands of the selfish and depraved it could become the instrument of minute and all-pervading oppression, driving whole nations to despair.

As regards the methods of election to the episcopate there cannot be said at this period to have been any settled and invariable rule. The ancient form of election by the clergy, with the acquiescence of the people of the diocese, was still preserved in theory, but in practice the electoral body consisted of the cathedral canons; while the confirmation required of the king, or semi-independent feudal noble, and of the pope, in a time of unsettled institutions, frequently rendered the election an empty form, in which the royal or papal power might prevail, according to the tendencies of time and place. The constantly increasing appeals to Rome, as to the tribunal of last resort, by disappointed aspirants, under every imaginable pretext, gave to the Holy See a rapidly-growing influence, which, in many cases, amounted almost to the power of appointment; and Innocent II, at the Lateran Council of 1139, applied the feudal system to the Church by declaring that all ecclesiastical dignities were received and held of the popes like fiefs. Whatever rules, however, might be laid down, they could not operate in rendering the elect better than the electors. The stream will not rise above its source, and a corrupt electing or appointing power is not apt to be restrained from the selection of fitting representatives of itself by methods, however ingeniously devised, which have not the inherent ability of self-enforcement. The oath which cardinals were obliged to take on entering a conclave—"I call God to witness that I choose him whom I judge according to God ought to be chosen"—was notoriously inefficacious in securing the election of pontiffs fitted to serve as the vicegérents of God; and so, from the humblest parish priest to the loftiest prelate, all grades of the hierarchy were likely to be filled by worldly, ambitious, self-seeking, and licentious men. The material to be selected from, moreover, was of such a character that even the most exacting friends of the Church had to content themselves when the least worthless was successful. St. Peter Damiani, in asking of Gregory VI the confirmation of a bishop-elect of Fossombrone, admits that he is unfit, and that he ought to undergo penance before undertaking the episcopate, but yet there is nothing better to be done, for in the whole diocese there was not a single ecclesiastic worthy of the office; all were selfishly ambitious, too eager for preferment to think of rendering themselves worthy of it, inflamed with desire for power, but utterly careless as to its duties.

Under these circumstances simony, with all its attendant evils, was almost universal, and those evils made themselves everywhere felt on the character both of electors and elected. In the fruitless war waged by Gregory VII and his successors against this all-pervading vice, the number of bishops assailed is the surest index of the means which had been found successful, and of the men who thus were enabled to represent the apostles. As Innocent III declared, it was a disease of the Church immedicable by either soothing remedies or fire; and Peter Cantor, who died in the odor of sanctity, related with approval the story of a Cardinal Martin, who, on officiating in the Christmas solemnities at the Roman court rejected a gift of twenty pounds sent him by the papal chancellor, for the reason that it was notoriously the product of rapine and simony. It was related as a supreme instance of the virtue of Peter, Cardinal of St. Chrysogono, formerly Bishop of Meaux, that he had, in a single election, refused the dazzling bribe of five hundred marks of silver. Temporal princes were more ready to turn the power of confirmation to profitable account, and few imitated the example of Philip Augustus, who, when the abbacy of St. Denis became vacant, and the provost, the treasurer, and the cellarer of the abbey each sought him secretly, and gave him five hundred livres for the succession, quietly went to the abbey, picked out a simple monk standing in a corner, conferred the dignity on him, and handed him the fifteen hundred livres. The Council of Rouen, in 1050, complains bitterly of the pernicious custom by which ambitious men accumulated, by every possible means, presents wherewith to gain the favor of the prince and his courtiers in order to obtain bishoprics, but it could suggest no remedy. The council was directly concerned only with the Norman dukes, but the contemporary King of France, Henry I, was notorious as a vendor of bishoprics. He had commenced his reign with an edict prohibiting the purchase and sale of preferment under penalty of forfeiture of both purchase-money and benefice, and had boasted that, as God had given him the crown gratis, so he would take nothing for his right of confirmation, reproaching his prelates bitterly for the prevalence of the vice which was eating out the heart of the Church. Yet in time he yielded to the custom, and a single instance will illustrate the working of the system. A certain Helinand, a clerk of low extraction and deficient training, had found favor at the court of Edward the Confessor, where he had ample opportunities of amassing wealth. Happening to be sent on a mission to Henry, he made a bargain by which he purchased the reversion of the first vacant bishopric, which chanced in course of time to be Laon, where he was duly installed. Henry's successor, Philip I, was known as the most venal of men, and from him, by a similar transaction, Helinand purchased, with the money acquired from the revenues of Laon, the primatial see of Reims. Such jobbers in patronage were accustomed to enter into compacts with each other for mutual assistance, and to consult astrologers as to expected vacancies. The manipulation of ecclesiastical preferment was reduced to a system, calling forth the indignant remonstrance of all the better class of churchmen. Instances of these abuses might be multiplied indefinitely, and their influence on the character of the Church cannot easily be overestimated.

64. *POPE INNOCENT III AND KING JOHN OF ENGLAND*[1]

With Innocent III (1198–1216) the Papacy is usually considered to have reached the height of its worldly power. No better evidence of this power is to be found than in the outcome of his struggle with King John of England. An account of the conflict between the two rulers is given in the following selection.

In the sermon preached at the time of his consecration Innocent claimed that, by his position, he was the superior of kings (*excellentis regibus*) and applied to himself the words spoken to the prophet "Lo! I have set thee this day over the nations and over the kingdoms, to pluck up and to break down, and to destroy and to overthrow; to build and to plant." (Jer. 1.10.) In this chapter we shall see how he carried out what he believed to be his divine commission.

In almost every kingdom in Europe Innocent found it necessary, for one cause or another, to interfere. But apart from his interferences there were occasions when kings of their own free will recognized his power. The rulers of Serbia and of Bulgaria applied to him for the right to wear a crown: whilst Pedro of Aragon, noted like so many in that contradictory age, for valour, illicit amours, and attachment to religion, actually surrendered his kingdom to Innocent and received it back as a fief. In Hungary, too, troubles over the succession required Innocent's watchful and effective eye; whilst in distant Armenia he had dealings with the crafty Leo. But perhaps the best idea of Innocent's methods and policy can be obtained by a detailed study of his relations with England during his pontificate.

[1] L. Elliott Binns, *Innocent III*. London, Methuen and Co., Ltd., 1931, pp. 68–81. Used by permission.

Immediately after his accession Innocent received a long letter of complaint from the monks of Christ Church, Canterbury,—ever on the look out to defend their rights against episcopal aggression,—alleging that Hubert Walter, the primate, was building a church at Lambeth with the idea of transferring thither his archiepiscopal seat; and that further, by reason of the many secular offices which he held, his spiritual functions were being neglected. Innocent at once ordered Hubert to demolish the new church. This speedy and peremptory order astounded the archbishop, accustomed as he was to the vacillating and dilatory methods of Innocent's predecessor, and he at once complied with it. To Richard of England the Pope also addressed a letter telling him that he must release Hubert from his office of justiciar and in future refrain from appointing ecclesiastical persons to such posts. The King also complied without delay. Notwithstanding the papal prohibition, however, when John, a few months later, succeeded his brother on the throne of England he immediately made Hubert chancellor. This defiance of the Pope's orders brought with it its own punishment, for Hubert until his death in July 1205, maintained a continual check upon the King's actions.

With Richard Innocent's relations were natural and friendly: one might almost say, in spite of his being the younger man, paternal. Innocent, on his side, was anxious to get Richard to lead a new crusade, ever the Pope's dearest wish; while Richard was anxious that the Pope should support the claims of his nephew, Otto, to the Empire, a thing which on other grounds Innocent was only too willing to do. Richard had also reason for being grateful to the Pope for his insistence that the compensation due from Leopold of Austria, who was now dead, for the unlawful imprisonment of Richard, and Philip Augustus of France entered into a truce for five years, but unfortunately only three months later Richard met his death in an attempt to punish a refractory vassal, and John, who during his brother's lifetime had been plotting with Philip against him, ascended the throne.

Had it been the lot of Richard to have lived in the present era, he would doubtless have been a country gentleman. To his friends he would have been known as "a good sportsman": to his tenants as an absentee landlord (he spent only a few months in England during his reign of ten years): and to his agent as a hard master whose one idea was to get as much from his estates as they would yield. John was an entirely different person. He was mean and petty in everything that he did, and even his sins had no boldness or splendour about them. To isolate one of his qualities is to demean the rest, so evenly were craft and cruelty, weakness and obstinacy, compounded together in his make-up.

From the very first John had trouble with Innocent, for the Pope endeavoured to make him refund the dowry of Berengaria, his brother's widow, as well as pay over a legacy to Otto. With amazing skill John kept putting off Innocent, and it was not till he had become the Pope's vassal that any semblance of justice was done to Berengaria. Otto was more fortunate, for John realized his usefulness in the struggle against Philip of France, and as early as 1207 paid him a large instalment on account of his legacy.

Further difficulties arose over John's repudiation of his wife, Hawisa of Gloucester, and his marriage with Isabella of Angoulême in 1200. Isabella was betrothed to one of John's own vassals, Hugh of Lusignan, Count de la Marche, and this action not only lost John the support of Hawisa's relations, but estranged many of his continental supporters. Hugh himself appealed to John's overlord, Philip Augustus, and as John refused to take notice of the citation to answer the charge against him, Philip began vigorously to press the claims of Arthur of Brittany, the son of John's older brother Geoffry, to the throne of England. In spite of the fact that Philip and John had made a treaty war now followed. Arthur in a rash attempt to seize the person of his grandmother, the famous and redoubtable Eleanor of Aquitaine, fell into the hands of his uncle. He was taken to Falaise, and shortly afterwards, as Roger of Wendover, the chronicler, puts it, "the said Arthur suddenly disappeared." It was an age when inconvenient people had a trick of disappearing—and John's enemies openly accused him of being responsible for his death. The French chronicler, William the Breton, actually says that the King took the boy out in a boat by night, slew him with his own hand, and then, under cover of the darkness, flung his body into the Seine; a graphic and dramatic story, but not a convincing one.

The elimination of Arthur was but a transitory gleam of good fortune for John. Aided by the defection of many of his rival's own vassals, who, like Hugh, had received injury to their honour from their vicious overlord, Philip Augustus quickly overran Normandy. Innocent, in the meantime, at the request of John, had stepped in and tried to restore peace. Philip, however, resented the Pope's interference in a case which clearly came under feudal law, and, smarting no doubt under Innocent's rightful condemnation of his treatment of Ingeborg, informed Innocent that Popes had no business to meddle in the affairs of Kings.

Innocent's method of dealing with this crisis is worthy of close study, and that for two reasons; on the one hand, it is important as giving insight into his methods and principles in general; on the other, as revealing his conception of papal powers and their necessary limits. He is careful to explain to Philip that his intervention was not due to any desire to "disturb or diminish" the legitimate rights of the French king as John's suzerain. But the matter in dispute involved something more than feudal custom. It was also a question of moral law, since a treaty had been broken and one party (John) had appealed to him accusing the other of "sin." As Pope he was the upholder of the moral law (Philip hardly needed reminding of this) and it was his duty to see that it was not disregarded. If Philip was confident in the righteousness of his cause let him submit it to himself, and he as Pope would see that justice was done. Innocent, it will be observed, claims the right to interfere as the upholder of the moral law and as standing for justice, but it will further be observed that this is the sole ground alleged for his intervention. There is no appeal to any political doctrine, nor does the Pope regard himself as having supreme jurisdiction over the secular sphere.

Although John could thus attempt to make use of the Pope when it suited his plans, he shewed little respect for the rights of the Church in his own land; but Innocent was too busy with other matters to interfere until some really vital incident occurred. This as it happened took place in the very next year, for on the death of Hubert Walter on July 13, 1205, grave difficulties arose over the election of a successor.

The right of election actually belonged to the monks of Christ Church, Canterbury, since the Archbishop was their "pastor." But the bishops of the province disputed this on the specious ground that it was not seemly that so small a body should choose one who was to be the head of the whole province. The King, too, had on occasion overruled or ignored their rights and himself chosen an archbishop. On this occasion a number of the younger monks, determined at all costs to exercise their legitimate powers, held a secret meeting on the very night of Hubert's death and elected as his successor, their own sub-prior, Reginald. As this was in the nature of a test case they would have been wiser to have observed the proper rules for a canonical election and certainly to have chosen some more worthy and judicious candidate: for Reginald quickly shewed his unsuitability. In order to lose no time he was immediately despatched, accompanied by four or five of his fellow-monks, to get the Pope's approval, but with strict injunctions to keep the whole matter secret until he arrived in Rome. No sooner, however, was Reginald safely across the channel than he openly announced that he was the archbishop elect,—no doubt the poor man's head had been turned by his elevation—and at once the "fat was in the fire."

The monks who had elected Reginald, through the lack of circumspection in their candidate, were in an exceedingly awkward position. The rest of the chapter were furious, the bishops were furious, and, most significant of all, the King was furious. But John had, as usual, his own methods of coping with the situation. He went down to Canterbury in December, assembled a meeting, at which some of the monks and some of the bishops of the province were present, and made them elect his own candidate, John de Gray, Bishop of Norwich. John then handed over to him the temporalities of the see, and sent off six monks to Innocent to inform him of what had been done, and to ask for his approval. As the bishops had in the meantime sent off at least one representative to the Pope to complain of the violation of their own rights there were three rival deputations at the papal court at the same time.

Some delay at arriving at a decision was naturally inevitable. Each set of monks apparently declared that the candidate of their choice represented the wishes of the whole body: and so for a time there was a deadlock. Innocent commissioned the Bishop of Rochester to make inquiries and at length in December 1206 he gave his judgement. He began by rejecting any claims which the bishops of the province might make to a share in the election. He then declared the two elections already made to be null and void; that of Reginald because it had been made secretly and without the knowledge of the whole body of qualified electors; that of John de Gray because it had been made under compulsion of the King and when the matter had already been referred to himself. He therefore ordered a new election to take place, and since further delay would be harmful and a sufficient number of monks was present in Rome, he decided that it should be held immediately.

The monks sent by John had sworn to elect no one but the King's own candidate. Innocent's first step was, disdainfully, to absolve them from their oaths. He then produced Stephen Langton, who had been a fellow-student of his at Paris, and had him elected. Stephen was an ideal candidate. A cardinal of nine years' standing, a scholar famous throughout Europe, and above all, an Englishman, having been born in Lincolnshire. Innocent at once wrote John telling him of the steps which he had taken and pointing out the obvious suitability of Stephen. He also emphasized his own generosity to the see of Canterbury in releasing "so stout a pillar of the Apostolic See." But John would have none of him; his own "very dear friend" had been rejected; and though Stephen might be an Englishman by birth, he had spent the greater part of his life among the King's enemies in *regno Francorum*. In spite of John's refusal to accept Stephen, Innocent on June 17, 1207, proceeded to consecrate him with his own hands at Viterbo whither he had gone on his triumphal tour of the Patrimony.

John in reply wrote to the Pope threatening "to stop the track by sea against all who would travel to Rome": thus money and clients would be debarred from proceeding to the papal court. He was also so violent in his conduct towards those of the bishops and clergy who took the Pope's side that many of them left the kingdom. Stephen it need hardly be said was not allowed to land in his province. But those who suffered most were the unfortunate monks of Christ Church who out of fear of the Pope had agreed to recognize Stephen; they gained nothing by it, however, and only brought down upon them the King's enmity. This took a characteristic form. He set two knights, men of a resolute and violent character (*milites crudelissimos et humanitatis ignaros* Roger of Wendover terms them) to Canterbury. With drawn swords they rushed into the monastery, and as in the days of Becket, the cloisters rang with the shout of armed men. But the spirit of Becket had departed from Christ Church and the terrified monks, dismayed by the memory of his death rather than inspired by the courage of his resistance, abandoned their charge and fled overseas. In their place monks from the rival convent of St. Augustine were installed.

Such conduct could not be allowed to pass unnoticed. Innocent accordingly sent a mandate to the Bishops of London, Ely and Worcester, empowering them to lay the Kingdom under an interdict unless the King, after a further attempt at persuasion, moderated his conduct. But the efforts of the Pope merely rendered John more furious: he swore "by the teeth of God" that if an interdict were actually placed on his kingdom he would confiscate all ecclesiastical property, expel the clergy, and if he caught any Roman clerks in England or in his other territories he would send them about their business with their eyes plucked out and their noses slit. In March 1208 the interdict was duly laid by the bishops, who at once fled for their lives. The King was as good as his word, he seized all clerical property and that not without violence.

Stephen meanwhile remained quietly at Pontigny, the great Cistercian Abbey at which his famous predecessor, Thomas Becket, had found a refuge. But wiser than Thomas he refrained from any kind of provocative conduct and did his utmost to bring about peace. The Pope himself was working for the same end, but all negotiation was without hope of result owing to the insincerity of John. Then in October 1209 a further step was taken and the King himself formally excommunicated. This had no apparent effect and things drifted on. The country had to suffer the severe discomforts which attended the interdict: the regular services were suspended (though baptism was administered and the the dead buried in silence) and sermons were preached only in the open air. The Cistercians in order to gain the King's favour did not observe the edict, but they gained little good from their action, for if John did not confiscate their goods he laid heavy taxation upon them. In 1211 John professed himself to be anxious to reopen negotiations and Innocent despatched to him as his legates, Pandulf and a Templar named Durand. The legates made some progress and John declared that he was willing to allow the exiled bishops to return to their sees but he would not hear of any compensation being paid to them for the injuries to their property. Innocent then took the final step. In 1212 he declared John deposed from his throne, he proclaimed a crusade against him, and cunningly invited Philip Augustus to put himself at the head of it. Although Philip must have resented the terms in which the invitation was made—he was to lead this crusade in expiation for his sins—he was no doubt rejoiced to have a legitimate pretext for a fresh attack on John's dominions.

John met the threat with his habitual contemptuous scorn. The papal fulminations had not done much harm to his nephew Otto, nor to Philip himself for that matter. To meet the danger of an invasion from France, where Philip was gathering a large army and fleet, he assembled the might of England on Barham Down. They made a brave show and had they been, as Roger puts it, "of one heart and disposition towards the King" he need have feared no invading power. But his subjects were tired of suffering for the sake of one who had forfeited all right to respect, much less to affection. Doubts began suddenly to arise in the mind of John himself; if Philip came over would his barons remain loyal, might not the Church's ban carry weight with them; moreover, a hermit, Peter of Walsefield, had foretold that on Ascension Day John would no longer be king. Like so many irreligious men John was intensely superstitious. He might refuse to communicate at his Coronation Mass, he might commit acts of sacrilege with apparent impunity; but he was scared by the picture of the Final Judgement on the walls of Lincoln cathedral, and when at last death claimed him he ordered his body to be buried in the habit of a monk, hoping thus to escape the penalty of his many sins. At his crisis, with a hated foe about to descend upon his kingdom, and with the prospect of receiving but doubtful support from his justly offended subjects, John by a sudden and unexpected move placed himself beyond the reach of every danger. He made an abject submission to the Pope.

By the terms of this submission John handed over to the Pope his kingdoms of England and Ireland, offering to hold them henceforth as the vassal of the Apostolic See; in addition to the usual payment of Peter's Pence, he promised a tribute of 1000 marks a year.[1] This was indeed an astute move, but none but an utterly shameless and unprincipled man would have been capable of making it. Philip Augustus was completely checked, for Pandulf was at once sent by Innocent ordering him to suspend all his costly preparations. The French king was naturally indignant. But a scapegoat presented itself in the person of Ferrand, Count of Flanders, who had refused to take part in the expedition against John. As he was in secret treaty with him this was not surprising. Philip marched into Flanders and quickly captured Cassel, Ypres, Bruges and Ghent. He also sent a fleet to support the army. This was less successful, being surprised and destroyed at Swinemünde by

[1] This tribute, though not always paid, was never actually repudiated until 1365 when the Popes at Avignon had become the tools of the French kings with whom England was then at war: see Creighton, *History of the Papacy*, I., p. 102.

an English expedition under William Longsword, Earl of Salisbury, and in consequence the French, after having done much damage, were forced to retire.

Stephen, together with the exiled bishops and priests, now crossed over to England and landed at Dover, going on immediately to Winchester for an interview with the King. On July 20, 1213, John, having sworn to behave well in future and to make compensation for his misdeeds of the past, was duly absolved from the sentence of excommunication.

However blameworthy John may appear to have been in his actions no shadow of reproach falls upon Innocent. It is probable that at this stage he had no real conception of the depths of duplicity to which John could descend—though his experiences of John's character should have been enlightening enough. John claimed to be penitent for his misdoings and declared that he was prepared to shew his penitence by carrying out whatever demands were laid upon him. The Pope had no option but to receive him, and having received him to protect him.

65. *THE EMPEROR FREDERICK II* [1]

It has often been said that Emperor Frederick II was the greatest figure of the thirteenth century. An English monk in the monastery of St. Albans probably first styled him "Stupor Mundi," or "The Wonder of the World," and Frederick must have seemed to many of his contemporaries a veritable miracle. An interesting analysis of his personality and character has been presented by Lionel Allshorn.

The monk of St. Albans, in bestowing upon Frederick the title of "the wonder of the world," deems it unnecessary to enlarge upon that title by comment and explanation. We may take it that he is but recording the universal opinion of his age. The magnificent and unparalleled figure of the Roman Emperor had excited in his generation a sentiment of wonder, and whether men marvelled at him with admiration or deprecation, to friend and enemy alike he was a being whose career and personality evoked surpassing interest and profound surprise.

We may conceive easily enough how this sentiment had risen. The sudden change in his fortunes, which in his youth had elevated him from the position of a powerless King to that of the first monarch of Christendom, had no doubt attracted considerable attention; and from henceforth, by vir-

[1] Lionel Allshorn, *Stupor Mundi. The Life and Times of Frederick II, Emperor of the Romans, King of Sicily and Jerusalem, 1194–1250.* London, Martin Secker, 1912, pp. 281–295. Used by permission.

tue of his high office, he could no longer remain in obscurity. But it was the circumstances of his Crusade that first made him the cynosure of all eyes. His abortive embarkation for the Holy Land and the excommunication which had been immediately launched against him formed a dramatic prelude. His subsequent departure in defiance of the ban of the Church and the attack which the enraged Pope had made upon his dominions, offered to Europe the strange spectacle of an Emperor leading a Crusade who was himself the object of a Crusade. The extraordinary success which he had obtained by peaceful means, in spite of the persistent antagonism of the Papal party, had earned him the admiring gratitude of Christendom; while at the same time his friendly intercourse with the Sultan and his broad-minded attitude towards the Infidels had mingled with that admiration an emotion of shocked amazement.

He had returned to his European dominions with his dignity enhanced by the acquisition of the Crown of Jerusalem, and had wrested from the Pope the revocation of the sentence of excommunication. Men had then gradually become informed of his astonishing mental attainments, had learnt of how he could discourse with Jews, Arabians, Frenchmen, Italians and Germans in their own tongues, of how he had mastered the learning of Greece and Rome, of how he could meet on terms of equality, if not superiority, with the greatest scholars of his age in every branch of knowledge. The elegance and magnificence of his Court, its Oriental splendour and its cosmopolitan hospitality, had been noised abroad. His maintenance of a harem, though it would have passed unnoticed had he been merely the King of Sicily, became a glaring defiance of propriety in one who was the chief monarch of Christendom: men whispered in horrified undertones that he was even suspected of indulging in carnal pleasures with Infidel women. He had ignored the prejudices of his day by planting a colony of Saracens in the very heart of his Kingdom and by employing them as his soldiers. He had flouted religious bigotry by allowing Greeks, Jews and Infidels to worship as they pleased. He was even said to have derided the Immaculate Conception, to have placed Christ on a level with Moses and Mahomet, to have become almost a Saracen himself in belief and in manner of life.

His system of government had aroused much the same interest and surprise as would be excited in our own day by the spectacle of a monarch trampling down the established forces of democracy and erecting a despotism upon their ruins. In every other country the royal power was subservient to aristocratic and ecclesiastic privilege. In England the barons had wrested the Great Charter from John, were soon to rise successfully against Henry III. In France the dynasty of Capet had hardly yet begun to assert its supremacy over the forces of feudalism. In the Kingdom of Sicily, however, the nobles and ecclesiastics were stripped of every privilege which conflicted with the royal authority, and a perfectly centralised organisation had been erected in which all power emanated from the King.

Frederick had then entered upon the final stage of that long and bitter struggle with the Papacy which was to endure until his death. This combat between the temporal and the spiritual power, the most vital feature of the history of the Middle Ages, enlisted the passionate interest of the inhabitants of every Christian country: and Frederick, as the object of a peculiarly venomous hatred, as the most redoubtable champion of the temporal cause, had loomed gigantically in the vision of men. His high-handed assertion of the Imperial supremacy in the capture of Gregory's Council had been but an astonishing incident of the struggle: a more lasting marvel lay in his steadfast maintaining of his independence. Where Henry IV had knelt in penitence at Canossa, where Barbarossa had flung himself before the feet of the Pope at Venice, Frederick had never humiliated himself before the Vicar of Christ. John of England had submitted himself and his realm to Innocent III: his successor was too feeble to resist the extortions of the Papal tax-gatherers. The proud Philip Augustus of France had been compelled by the Pope to put away the wife he loved and reinstate a divorced and discarded Queen. There was scarcely a King or Prince in Christendom who had not bowed before the threats of Rome. Frederick alone had resisted to the end, had survived the most furious assaults of Gregory and Innocent, had defied the sentence of deposition and had worn his crowns with scarcely diminished power until the day of his death.

Thus around his name there had gathered a glamour of strangeness and splendour, of genius soaring to perilous questionings of eternal truths, of unbreakable resolution and of unconquerable pride. To his ardent supporters he had become the new Messiah, to his frenzied enemies the Antichrist. To those who stood outside the immediate fury of the strife he was a being beyond the common range of human experience and comprehension. He was the dominating spirit of his age, the supreme centre of interest and wonder, *stupor mundi et immutator mirabilis*.

The historian Freeman has called him "the most gifted of the sons of men; by nature the more than peer of Alexander, of Constantine, and of Charles; in mere genius, in mere accomplishments, the greatest prince who ever wore a crown." So rare an eulogy needs something more than a distinguished source to render it acceptable, but it will bear the scrutiny of scepticism passably well. Certain it is that in his tremendous intellect, in his cultured and enquiring mind, in his broad spirit of toleration, he towered far above his contemporaries: that his system of jurisprudence, his educational and economic regulations, betrayed a singularly enlightened conception of the arts of government. If the more cautious among us may hesitate to endorse the eulogy of Freeman with enthusiasm and conviction, we can at any rate follow him so far as this: we can, nay, we must admit, that in genius Frederick has had no superior among the princes of the world, and that in the potentialities of greatness as a ruler he excelled many who have earned the title of "great." That title would assuredly have been his, had not the enmity of the Papacy prevented him from exercising those potentialities.

"Frederick belongs to no age," continues the same writer; "intellectually he is above his own age, above every age; morally it can hardly be denied that he was below his age; but in nothing was he of his age." If we may accept Freeman's praise of Frederick with some diffidence, we can reject his condemnation with confidence. The vices of the Hohenstaufen Emperor stand out in dark relief against the general enlightenment of his character. His duplicity, cruelty and licentiousness were lamentable enough. But they do not place him morally below his age, for his faults were essentially the faults of his age and of his country.

It was inevitable that Frederick, surrounded from his childhood by intrigues and hostile ambitions, should absorb within himself some of the craft and dissimulation with which he was thus familiarised. He was never the complete Machiavellian, but he was ready enough to employ guile and subterfuge when it seemed profitable.

"Pretend some business," he writes to one of his captains whom he has ordered to obtain possession of a strong castle, "and warily call the Castellan to you: seize on him if you can and keep him till he cause the castle to be surrendered to you." This is a fair example of his duplicity and does not argue in him a high conception of public honour. But it is far removed from dark and damnable treachery, and it can be said in partial extenuation of such methods that no ruler ever prospered in Mediaeval Italy who disdained the wisdom of the serpent.

We need only glance through the pages of any chronicler of Frederick's time to see that in his cruelty he certainly did not exceed the guilt of his contemporaries. We can read, for instance, in Salimbene, of the fate of Alberic de Romano, who, with his wife and family, fell into the hands of his enemies in the year 1260. His six sons, some of them mere children, were hewn into pieces before his eyes and their bleeding limbs thrust into his face. His wife and daughters were stripped from the waist downwards, were paraded through the streets and finally burnt at the stake. After he had witnessed their dying agonies his own flesh was torn with red-hot pincers and his tortured body dragged to death at the tail of a horse. Frederick never descended to such barbarity as this. Nor can he be condemned as below his age when that age had witnessed the atrocities of the Albigensian Crusade, perpetrated with the sanction of the Papacy, hideously sanctified by the pretext of religious zeal. If in his last years, goaded into frequent fits of sinister fury by his implacable enemies, rendered vindictive by treacherous attempts upon his life, Frederick became indiscriminate in his vengeance, his cruelty at any rate was never a lust: he was no Eccelin de Romano to gloat over the suffering of his victims. It was rather an excessive form of severity. We can understand that in an age when such crimes as forgery and theft were punished by execution, a painless death seemed an utterly inadequate penalty for traitors. His cruelty was certainly not greater, either in quantity or quality, than that of his enemies: and on occasions he showed a generous clemency to his defeated foes.

In the matter of sexual morality, the greatest minds have rarely consented to be bound by the code which is accepted by their fellowmen. Frederick was no exception to this rule. Bound by no rigid system of religious belief he was a law unto himself: entirely contemptuous of the conventions of his inferiors—and all men in his sight were the inferior of Caesar—he made no effort to hide from the world the licence which that self-made law permitted him to enjoy. Yet in this vice, as in others, he was not below the standard of his age. The Church itself, which we might expect to represent the highest morality of the time, was besmirched with lewdness from the highest to the lowest of its grades. If the Popes themselves, either through virtue or old age, had renounced the lusts of the flesh, the Papal Court was notorious throughout Europe and polluted every city in which it sojourned. "We found three or four houses of ill fame when we came hither," said the Cardinal Hugh of St. Cher when the Court was leaving Lyons to return to Italy after Frederick's death; "and now, at our departure, we leave the whole city one continuous brothel." Another Cardinal, the warlike Gregory of Montelengo, was reputed to have as many lemans as the Emperor himself. The vow of chastity was openly violated by the parish priests and the abuse of the confessional was widely prevalent. It is significant enough that in the many conditions of peace which were at one time or another demanded from Frederick by the Papacy, he was never commanded to put away his concubines. His supposed intercourse with Infidel women formed one of the charges set forth against him at the Council of Lyons, but his sins with Christian women were ignored. The Church knew too well that in this matter she could not cast the first stone.

He was entirely Oriental in his sexual conduct. He may have been profoundly attached to Bianca Lancia, or to one of his legitimate wives, but their position was only that of the favoured Sultana: they never enjoyed the monopoly of his embraces. He was not a hunter of women: surrounded by a bevy of complaisant beauties who existed solely for his own pleasure, the wives of his subjects were safe from his regards. Yet this Orientalism, though less mischievous than the roving amorousness of a Charles the Second, is less easy to condone. It is sensuality without sentiment, devoid of the glamour of romance; a mere satisfaction of erotic impulse or bodily appetite rather than ardent passion or impetuous desire. It is unforgivable in one of his enlightened mind. We may concede that his morality was not lower than that of his age; but we cannot deny that he transgressed the bounds of that licence which, if we would be tolerant, we must regard as the peculiar privilege of princes.

To the men of his own country these faults in Frederick's character were ordinary enough: they were the sins that might be laid to the charge of any ruler, great or small, in Mediaeval Italy. But there was an offence which, in the eyes of a superstitious age, was far more grievous than these. It is not for lewdness or cruelty or treachery that Dante consigns Frederick to hell, but for unbelief. The poet, Imperialist though he is, cannot ignore the accusation which was made against the Emperor by his enemies, which was confirmed by his own hasty and scornful words. Frederick is an "illustrious hero," his character is "of nobility and righteousness"; but nevertheless, because he doubted the eternal truths, his portion is among the heresiarchs in hell.

How far the popular impression of his scepticism was correct it is, of course, impossible to determine. It is unlikely that he was an atheist, for when he realised that the hand of death was upon him, he said, "The will of God be done." We may believe, however, that a mind of such broad and catholic culture could not but revolt against the narrow dogma of the Church: that mingling in himself the civilisation of both Christendom and Mohammedanism, he viewed the two religions with a certain detachment, and regarded with impatience the claims of either to exclusive infallibility: that to his scientific and enquiring mind any sharply defined doctrine would be unacceptable, especially when it contained so large an element of superstition as the religious belief of his day. Unprovoked by the Papal enmity, he might have veiled his opinions in discreet silence; but harassed beyond measure by an unjust persecution, he was occasionally stung into deriding the religion of which his arch enemy was the earthly head.

To have endorsed these hasty utterances before the world by a public confession of his unorthodoxy would have involved himself and his house in immediate and irretrievable ruin. It was not to be expected that he would gratify the Pope and surrender all for which he had struggled by thus encompassing his own destruction. Such a suicide would have been a black crime in his eyes, a betrayal of his high charge as the guardian of the Imperial heritage, as the champion of mankind against the tyranny of the Popes. He did not hesitate therefore, when publicly charged with the awful sin of heresy, to refute that charge by a vigorous assertion of his implicit faith in the tenets of Christianity. We may even believe that he made this assertion in all good faith, that he considered it incumbent upon him in his public capacity to uphold and maintain a religion which was inextricably mingled with social order and human virtue. Only in the light of this belief can we understand his persecution of heretics, for we may dismiss far from our minds the suspicion of odious hypocrisy which that persecution would otherwise fasten upon his name.

It is always more easy to define the vices of a man than his virtues. The vices of Frederick can be exemplified by material things, his licentiousness by the harem that he maintained for his pleasure, his cruelty by the leaden cope, said to be his own invention, under the weight of which his victims slowly wearied to death. For his great qualities we must look with a wider view, must envisage his whole life. We must note that fine pride which enabled him to resist the allurements of a life of peacefulness and cultured ease, and to end his days in ceaseless warfare and toil. We must regard the all-powerful intellect, the mind freed from the trammels of religious bigotry, the enlightened measures for the prosperity and mental elevation of his people. How far in him the good exceeded the evil, the light triumphed over the darkness, may be gathered from the men who were his friends. The saintly Louis of France found in him more righteousness than in the Vicar of Christ. Hermann von Salza, a man of blameless life and lofty reputation, was his loyal friend and trusty servant as long as he lived. Bernard, the Archbishop of Palermo, against whose name there was no breath of calumny, clung to his side through excommunication and deposition, never denied to him the sacred offices forbidden by the Pope, absolved him on his deathbed and buried him with the full rites of the Church. Even that Pope who summoned in Charles of Anjou to extirpate his house could call him "the noble Frederick" and extol his government of the Kingdom.

But perhaps the most eloquent witness of the admiration he excited in his day lies in the words of one who should have been peculiarly bitter in his condemnation. Salimbene was a Minorite friar, a member of an order which was relentless in its antagonism to the Emperor and which therefore met with the severest repression at his hands. This chronicler speaks first as a friar should speak of one who was under the ban of the Church: "Of faith in God he had none; he was crafty, wily, avaricious, lustful, malicious, wrathful." But having thus enumerated Frederick's vices, he straightway relents, and continues: "And yet a gallant man at times, when he would show his kindness or courtesy; full of solace, jocund, delightful, fertile in devices. He knew to read, write and sing and to make songs and music. He was a comely man and well made, though of middle stature. I have seen him and once I loved him. . . . Moreover he knew how to speak many and varied tongues; and to be brief, if he had been rightly Catholic and had loved God and His Church, he would have had few Emperors his equals in the world."

Yet this Emperor has left little visible impression upon the history of the world. So little indeed that, in England at least, the memory of him has almost vanished from the popular mind: and when the name of Frederick the Second is spoken, it is of his Prussian namesake of a later age that men think, a monarch of far lesser genius and smaller soul. The work that Frederick had been able to accomplish in his Kingdom was utterly destroyed by the invaders who came in answer to the Papal call: the land fell back into darkness and confusion: almost every trace of him was swept away. As for the Empire, there had been little enough work in that wider sphere that he had been allowed to do: the Papacy had seen to that. She knew better than to give him leisure to consolidate the Imperial sway. Frederick maintained the glory of the Empire during his reign by his personal renown: he even extended its territories. But it was diseased at the heart. It rested for its security upon the power of the German throne, and that had been fatally weakened by the long anarchy that had preceded Frederick's accession. He had been unable to remedy that weakness because all his energies had been absorbed in his struggle against the Papacy, and the Popes meanwhile had encouraged the turbulent Princes of Germany in sedition and had finally, by raising a rival Emperor to Frederick, rent Germany in twain. With Frederick's death and the extinction of his house the whole fabric of the Empire collapsed and the policy of the Papacy came to its triumph.

Frederick was thus the last of the great mediaeval Emperors. The Great Interregnum which ensued in Germany after his death lasted for over twenty years. Finally, Rudolf of Hapsburg built from the ruins of the Imperial power a precarious lordship of Germany which he dignified by the name of Empire. But meanwhile Sicily had passed to the House of Anjou; the city states of Northern Italy had secured a complete independence; and Burgundy had turned to France. The Empire of the Hapsburgs was but a shadow of the Empire of the Hohenstaufens.

Frederick has been denied the title of "great," but he has merited the gratitude of mankind. Most of all should Englishmen, who hold themselves to be lovers of those who fight in the cause of liberty, remember his name with reverence and admiration. For Frederick, though an autocrat, was yet a champion of freedom. He strove manfully, and with unwavering courage, against that priestly tyranny which menaced all Europe in his age. Wherever that tyranny has triumphed there have followed evil, oppression, and intolerance, the decay of nations and the abuse of power. England was saved from this, or at least from the danger of this, by Frederick the Second. She suffered grievously enough at the hands of the Popes under her feeble Kings John and Henry III: but if Frederick had not combated the Papal ambitions with all his power, drawn upon himself the full force of the Papal fury, and resisted the might of his enemy to the end, then the lot of England would have been immeasurably worse. If once "the great dragon" had been crushed, then assuredly "the little basilisks" would have been trodden underfoot. But when Frederick had been overcome by death, when his race had been extinguished, and by the time another Pope had arisen of the stamp of Gregory IX and Innocent IV, an Edward I had appeared on the throne of England and a Philip IV on the throne of France. The nations were strong and the opportunity of the Popes had passed.

In his strife with the Papacy, then, lie at once the tragedy and the crown of Frederick's life: the tragedy since, being by nature so wonderfully endowed to govern a realm in peace and glory he was yet denied the expression of his genius; the crown in that he did with his might the thing that his right hand found to do. And if a temple should ever be raised to the memory of those who have struggled for the freedom of man, then Frederick should find a high place in the sanctuary. And upon his image should be engraven the words that he himself uttered: "Let those who shrink from my support have the shame as well as the galling burden of slavery. Before this generation and before the generations to come, I will have the glory of resisting this tyranny."

66. *HERESY IN THE EARLY TWELFTH CENTURY* [1]

Abbot Guibert, who has been mentioned elsewhere (see p. 303), lived in an abbey not far from the city of Soissons in Northern France. He came in contact with some heretics living on a manor near Soissons, and in his autobiography he describes the peculiar views which he alleges were held by these heretics. He also informs us about the way the heretics were treated by the Bishop of Soissons.

But since we have mentioned the heretics whom this abominable man [John, Count of Soissons] loved, a certain man of the country, named Clement, lived with his brother Everard at Bussy, the next manor to Soissons. He, as was commonly reported, was one of the heads of the heresy. About him that foul Count used to say he had found none wiser. But the heresy is not one that openly defends its faith, but condemned to everlasting whispers, spreads secretly. The following is said to be the sum of it.

They acknowledge that the rule of the Son of the Virgin has no reality.

They annul the baptism of young children not yet of an understanding age under godfathers and godmothers.

[1] *The Autobiography of Guibert, Abbot of Nogent-sous-Coucy.* Translated by C. C. Swinton Bland (Broadway Translations. Medieval Section. Ed. by G. G. Coulton). London, George Routledge and Sons, Ltd.; New York, E. P. Dutton and Co., 1925, pp. 205–208. Used by permission.

Moreover, they speak of God's own Word which comes into being by some rigmarole of talk or other.

They so abominate the mystery which is enacted on our altar that they call the mouths of all the priests the mouth of hell.

And if they sometimes receive our sacrament to hide their heresy, they so order their diet as to eat nothing more that day.

They do not separate their cemeteries from other land as being sacred in comparison.

They condemn marriage and propagation by intercourse.

And certainly wherever they are scattered over the Latin world, you may see men living with women without marriage and yet calling them wives, but not keeping to one only, but they are known to lie men with men and women with women.

They abstain from all food which is produced by sexual generation. . . .

A great fire is lighted and a child passed from hand to hand, as they sit in a circle round it, is thrown through the flames until he is dead. Then he is reduced to ashes and the ashes made into bread. To each person a portion is given as a sacrament, and once that has been received, hardly any one gives up that heresy.

If you review the heresies described by Augustine, you will find this like none of them so much as that of the Manichaeans. This which first originated among the more learned classes, reached the country population in a debased form; they priding themselves on keeping up the apostles' manner of life esteem only the reading of their Acts.

Two of these heretics were brought under examination by the very famous Lord Bishop of Soissons, and when they were charged by the Bishop with forming congregations outside the church and were said to be heretics by their neighbours, Clement replied, "Have ye not read, masters, where it is written in the Gospel 'Beati eritis'?" For being illiterate he thought "eritis" meant heretics. He believed also that they were called "heretics" as being without doubt "heritors" of God. When, therefore, they were examined about their belief, they gave most Christian answers, but did not deny their meetings. But as it is the way with such to deny charges and always in secret to draw away the hearts of the dull-witted, they were sentenced to the ordeal of exorcised water. And as it was being got ready, the Bishop asked me to extract from them privately their opinions, and I, proposing to them the subject of infant baptism, they said, "He that believeth and hath been baptised, shall be saved." And when I perceived that a fair saying covered a good deal of wickedness, I asked what they thought of those who are baptised in the faith of others. And they, "In God's name do not expect us to search so deeply." And enumerating the separate heads, "We believe all that you mention." Then remembering that verse to which the Priscillianists formerly agreed, that is, "Do not betray oaths, perjuries, secrets," (August. *On Heresies.*) I said to the Bishop, "Since the witnesses are not present who heard them expressing such opinions, bring them to the ordeal as determined"; for there was a certain lady whose head Clement had turned. There was also a deacon who had heard from the mouth of the man other wicked statements.

And so the Bishop celebrated mass and from his hand they received the sacrament in the following terms: "Let the body and blood of the Lord try you this day." This done, that most pious Bishop and the Archdeacon Peter, a man of great honesty, who had scorned the promises they had made to escape the ordeal, proceeded to the water. The Bishop with many tears recited the litany and then pronounced the exorcism. After that they took oath that they had never believed or taught anything contrary to our faith. Clement being then thrown into the tun floated on the top like a stick. This being seen the whole church was filled with unbounded joy. So great an assembly of both sexes had the fame of this brought together, such as no one present remembered ever to have seen. The other confessed his error, but being impenitent, was thrown into prison with his convicted brother. Two others of the manor of Durmat, proved heretics, had come to look on and were imprisoned with them.

Meanwhile, we went on to the council of Beauvais to consult with the bishops what ought to be done. But in the interval the faithful people fearing weakness on the part of the clergy, ran to the prison, seized them and having lighted a fire under them outside the city, burnt them both to ashes. To prevent the spreading of their cancer, God's people shewed a righteous zeal against them.

67. *THE CHURCH'S ATTITUDE TOWARD HERESY BEFORE THE ESTABLISHMENT OF THE INQUISITION* [1]

The author of the following selection traces the attitude of the Church toward heresy from early Christian times to nearly the middle of the thirteenth century.

The literal and fundamental meaning of the word Heresy is choosing. The heretic is the man who selects certain doctrines, discards others, giving rein to individual preference in the realm of religious belief. Such an attitude is essentially incompatible with the conception that the truth has once and for all been delivered to the saints, that the faith is indivisible and unalter-

[1] A. S. Turberville, *Mediaeval Heresy and the Inquisition.* London, Crosby Lockwood and Son, 1920, pp. 123–139. Used by permission of George Allen & Unwin, Ltd., publishers.

able, to be accepted in its entirety. It is easily understood that eclecticism should be regarded as a danger in the earliest days of a new religion by its adherents. The first proselytes are anxious to define those distinctive features which mark it off from other religions: for all religions have certain elements in common. It was thus in the early stages of Christianity, which shared certain characteristics with such beliefs as Mithraism, Gnosticism, Neoplatonism. The idea of man's need of a mediator with heaven was abroad in the Roman world before the Messiah was proclaimed to it. There thus existed a danger of confusion, that alien shoots of dogma might be grafted upon the pure and original stock of Christianity. The influence of such extraneous sources is apparent in the fourth gospel. Even in the very earliest days when the body of Christian belief consisted of little more than the disciples' recollections of the sayings and actions of their Founder, when the simplest conception of pure and undefiled religion was being taught, even then the faithful were warned to beware of "false prophets," "false teachers" who "privily shall bring in damnable heresies." As the fabric of dogma began to be woven, the note became vehement. St. Paul denounces "false apostles, deceitful workers, transforming themselves into the apostles of Christ." In another place he declares, "But though we, or an angel from heaven, preach any other gospel unto you than that which we have preached unto you, let him be accursed." So far, however, even the idea of what constitutes heresy is vague, and the spirit of tolerance and of brotherliness is strong. The offender is not to be counted as an enemy, but admonished as a brother. The fact is that the flock is so small and the pagan world outside so powerful that internal dissensions cannot be permitted. But the new faith surviving, doctrine becomes more stereotyped, the feeling of later generations more confident. Polycarp finds the heretic to be antichrist, who belongs to the Devil and is the oldest son of Satan, and Tertullian in one passage recommends the employment of compulsion against the heretic.

Such language is not common among the early Fathers. They are themselves members of a society liable to persecution, and they do not preach coercion. Lactantius urges that the only weapon for Christians to use is their reason; they must defend their faith not by violence, but persuasion. The Church in those days had not the opportunity to use force, even if it had wished to: and this fact must be borne in mind in connection with Tertullian's enunciation of the principle of tolerance, when he declares that the selection of his mode of worship is a man's natural right, the exercise of which cannot be either harmful or profitable to his neighbour, and that it is not the part of a religion to compel men to embrace it. In the (only apparent) contradiction between this ruling and the counsel given regarding the treatment of heretics, Tertullian laid down a principle of momentous consequence for the future, namely, that while force should not be applied to the unbeliever, its use is legitimate in the case of the man who has once accepted the faith and erred in it.

With the accession of Constantine, there dawned a new era for the Christian Church. Till then the Roman state had been neutral, when not actively hostile; from this time onwards, with one brief interval, it was an active supporter. The Church became possessed of all the enormous power of the imperial authority. The civil order is definitely Christian, and one of the prime duties of the Emperor, lord of the world, is the protection of the Church. Constantine speedily showed himself anxious to take a leading part in ecclesiastical matters. He had recourse to torture, confiscation of property, exile and possibly the death penalty also in harrying the Donatists.

Donatism was a small thing in comparison with Arianism, which shook the Christian Church to its foundations. When the fathers of Nicaea decided the intricate metaphysical question of "consubstantial," the Emperor proclaimed exile for all who did not accept the Council's decision. Against this determination to root out their enemies, to establish one interpretation of truth by force, the Fathers made no protest, but accepted the intervention of the secular authority on their behalf. There was no thought of the possible consequence of such a pact in the future. The triumph of the orthodox was short-lived. The Arians were victorious later on and in their turn persecuted the Trinitarians. The Christians, said Julian the Apostate, treated each other like wild beasts. The punishments inflicted by one party upon the other included imprisonment, flogging, torture, death. To such a pass had doctrinal differences already brought the adherents of a religion which proclaimed peace and goodwill among men. The tradition of persecution had been thoroughly established. The laws of Theodosius II and Valentinian II enumerate as many as thirty-two different heresies, all punishable, the penalties being such as deprivation of civil rights, exile, corporal punishment and death. But the heresies are carefully differentiated, the severest penalties being reserved for Manichaeism, which had been punished by the Roman state in its pagan, polytheistic and tolerant days, because of its anti-social tendencies. But now orthodox emperors persecuted Arians, Arian emperors persecuted followers of Athanasius, simply because they had taken sides in a theological controversy.

What view did the Church take of the activities of the lay power? Was it actively approving or disapproving, or passively acquiescent? We find some of the Fathers still preaching the old doctrines of tolerance. Athanasius, himself at the time persecuted, declared that persecution was an invention of the Devil. To Chrysostom heretics are as persons diseased, nearly blind, assuredly to be led, not forced. He comments on the parable of the tares, and urges the necessity of being very careful, lest the godly be destroyed together with heretics. Jerome remembers that the Church was founded upon persecutions and martyrdoms and on the whole seems to inculcate lenience in treatment of heretics, though a remark to the effect that Arius, at first only a single spark, not being immediately extinguished, set the whole world on fire, and that corrupted flesh must be cut off, points to a different opinion.

The most significant of the later Fathers is St. Augustine. In his case there is a notable change of front with regard to the treatment of heretics. By temperament he was an advocate of toleration, and at first, like Chrysostom, he appeals to the parable of the tares in justification of tolerance. Heretics should be allowed the opportunity to correct themselves and to repent. They are to be regarded as lost sheep. He is afraid that persecution might lead to those who were in reality heretics becoming hypocritical Catholics. But later on he altered his opinions. He had found that the weapons of persuasion and eloquence were not strong enough to break down the obduracy of his enemies the Donatists. He had been too optimistic. The methods of force employed by the secular power were after all salutary and necessary. "He therefore, who refuses to obey the imperial laws, when made against the truth of God, acquires a great reward; he who refuses to obey, when they are made for support of the divine truth, exposes himself to most grievous punishment." He rejoices, therefore, in a Christianized state. The death penalty he indeed strongly reprobates as contrary to Christian charity, but he approves both banishment and confiscation of property. These later opinions of St. Augustine were largely accepted after him.

An important episode in the history of the Church's attitude to heresy is the execution of the Spanish heretic, Priscillian, by the Emperor Maximus. Priscillian's teachings, akin to Manichaeism, were denounced by several bishops, and it was upon their complaint that the Spaniard was brought before the imperial tyrant. The action of the bishops, who had thus involved themselves in the guilt of blood, wittingly or unwittingly, was severely condemned by St. Ambrose and still more by Martin of Tours, who refused to have any communion with them. This happened in 385. In 447 it seemed that heresy was reviving in Spain, and Pope Leo I expressly commended the act of Maximus. He feared lest, if such damnable error was not crushed, there should be an end to all human and divine law; and if he did not ask for the death sentence, he was quite willing that the Church should acquiesce in the state's severity and reap the advantages resulting from it. Thus to welcome the results of the shedding of blood in cases of heresy, while refusing to accept the responsibility for it, constituted a most dangerous attitude.

For centuries after the days of Leo I heresy almost ceased to be a problem for the Church at all. Western Christendom entered into the gloom of the

Dark Ages, its history the arid record of barbarian invasions and the rivalries of Childerichs and Chilperichs. The human intelligence was dormant: consequently heresy ceased to be a force. When there is no mental activity, no education, no discussion, there may be faith, there can never be heresy. When the darkness lifted a little, heresy once more became a problem. In 1022 thirteen Cathari were burnt by order of, and in the presence of, King Robert II of France. The punishment of heresy by fire was an entire innovation. There was no existing law to sanction it. The stake had been used by Roman emperors to punish parricides, slaves who attempted their masters' lives, and incendiaries, and it still existed as a punishment for sorcerers and witches. The stake may have been used on this occasion because it was an impressive and theatrical death and, a choice being demanded between abjuration and death, it was considered the latter should be specially terrifying. Another execution of Cathari, this time by hanging, took place in 1051 at Goslar in Saxony in the presence of the Emperor Henry III. As in France, so in Germany, the law knew neither the offence nor the punishment. The Emperor was acting simply in the public defence.

It is important to note the part played in the treatment of heretics at this period by the populace. In both the cases just cited the secular prince had in his action the full approval of the people. It is particularly noticed by the chronicles of the first incident that the deed was "regis jussu et universae plebis consensu." And Henry strengthened his position in the absence of any written law by securing the agreement of his subjects. Nothing could be better attested than the crowd's hatred of the heretic in the eleventh and twelfth centuries as far as northern Europe was concerned. In the south it was different. There are several instances of the feeling in the north in the late decades of the eleventh and the early decades of the twelfth century. For example, in 1076 at Cambrai a Catharan who had been condemned by the bishop as a heretic (no sentence pronounced) was seized upon by the bishop's officers and the mob, who placed him in some sort of cabin, which they burned with the prisoner inside it. It is said that the recantation of Roscellinus was due to the threat of death at the hands of the populace. In 1114 certain heretics having been placed provisionally in prison by the Bishop of Strassburg were in the bishop's absence forcibly seized upon by the crowd, who, the chronicler states, feared clerical lenience. They were led out of the town and there burnt alive. A similar event happened in Cologne in 1143; whilst two years later at Liége the clergy only just succeeded in rescuing the crowd's victims from its clutches. Lawless violence against heretics continued to evince itself in France into the following century, there being instances of it in Troyes, Nevers, Besançon, Paris, even at a time when the secular power, under Philip Augustus, was active in bringing heretics to the stake.

What was the attitude of the clergy in this period, during which it seems evident that in northern Europe secular princes and public opinion were united in thinking heresy deserving of death, even by burning? There is the evidence of the mob fearing clerical lenience in one case cited, of the clergy actually intervening against the crowd in another. When the heretics were burnt at Cambrai in 1076 Gregory VII protested and ordered the excommunication of the inhabitants. And there is a very notable protest against the use of force by Wazon, Bishop of Liége (1042–8), who in answer to a query of the Bishop of Châlons as to whether he should yield up heretics to the secular arm or not, referred to the parable of the tares in support of lenience. His successor, Theoduin, on the other hand, is found counselling Henry I of France to mete out punishment to the followers of Berengar of Tours, and about the same time we find the Archbishop of Milan giving some supposed Manichaeans the choice between abjuration and the stake.

The fact that most clearly emerges from the consideration of rather conflicting evidence in this period is the absence of any law regarding heretics. The mob, secular princes and clergy are all acting irregularly, taking measures in self-defence in the absence of written rulings. Generally speaking, it would appear that there is a prevailing idea that heresy merits the extreme penalty. At the same time some attempt was made at various ecclesiastical councils to standardize procedure against heresy.

A Council at Rheims in 1049 spoke only of excommunication as a punishment; one at Toulouse in 1119 did the same, but also called upon the secular arm to render aid. The middle of the twelfth century saw a great revival of both Roman and Canon law and the publication of the Decree of Gratian. The Decree did not put all uncertainty at an end. It certainly laid down a clear ruling regarding the confiscation of property. The heretic, being outside both human and divine law, could not hold property. But regarding the death penalty there could be no plain direction, because on this subject Gratian's authorities were contradictory and remained so despite his efforts to reconcile them. Further efforts at definition were made by ecclesiastical councils during the century. One sitting at Rheims in 1157 demanded banishment and branding for those who simply professed Catharism, for proselytizers perpetual imprisonment; but it seems to hint at the death penalty in the veiled phrase: "carcere perpetuo, nisi gravius aliquid fieri debet visum, recludentur." Another Council at Tours in 1163, presided over by Alexander III, reiterated the demand for incarceration and also ordered the confiscation of goods. The second Council of the Lateran of 1179, lamenting the marked spread of heresy, commended the use of force by the secular arm and proclaimed a two years' indulgence to all who should take up arms against heretics.

The first secular law in the Middle Ages dealing with heresy is English.

In 1166 two Cathari were brought before Henry II at Oxford, whipped and branded with a red key and banished. Shortly afterwards in the same year appeared the clause in the Assize of Clarendon, forbidding the sheltering of heretics on the pain of having one's house destroyed. Other severe secular legislation soon appeared in other countries. In 1194 the Emperor Henry VI ordered the confiscation of the property, and the destruction of the houses, of heretics and inforced fines on communities and individuals who neglected to assist, when they had the opportunity, in the arrest of heretics. The same year Alfonso II of Aragon, aiming at expelling all Manichaeans and Waldenses from his dominions, issued an edict declaring all heretics public enemies and banishing them. The ineffectiveness of this edict is demonstrated by the appearance of a severer one three years later issued by Alfonso's successor, Pedro II, famous as the victor over the Moors at Las Navas de Tolosa, equally notorious for his warlike prowess, his religious zeal, his prodigality and licentiousness. Once again banishment is decreed, but it is added that if any heretics remain in defiance of the edict after a specified date they shall perish at the stake and their effects be confiscated.

Whatever may have been the case earlier, there seems good evidence of the zeal of the clergy against heretics in the latter part of the twelfth century, which saw so much more precision in the declarations of ecclesiastical councils and secular laws on the subject. In 1167 we find the Abbot of Vézelai, when several heretics were before him, appealing to the people to give sentence, and accepting their demand for a death of torture. Some years later at Rheims we find the Archbishop and clergy in agreement with the nobles that two Catharan women should be burnt. Hugh, Bishop of Auxerre (1183–1206), is a busy prosecutor of heretics, causing many to be burnt or exiled. More notable than such isolated instances of clerical activity is the co-operation between Pope and Emperor which led to the important bull entitled *Ad abolendam.* In 1184, Lucius III and Frederick Barbarossa met at Verona, and as the result of their conference this bull was promulgated, which (among other provisions) fixed rules for the prosecution of suspected heretics, the visitation of infected areas and the assistance of all civil authorities. The Emperor for his part placed heretics under the ban of the empire. The decree of Henry VI, already referred to, was plainly based on this action of his predecessor's.

Towards the end of the twelfth century, then, we have clear evidence of secular and ecclesiastical authorities working hand in hand for the suppression of heresy. To the former, heresy seemed equivalent to rebellion; to the latter, equivalent to murder, being the murder of the soul. When Pedro II issued his harsh edict against the Cathari of Aragon, he claimed that he was actuated by zeal for the public welfare and a desire to obey the canons of the Church. There was no order in the canons that heretics should be burnt to death; but otherwise, Pedro's appeal to Canon law was justified: and besides the canons, there were the various edicts of ecclesiastical councils during the century, all of them calling upon the secular authority to use its utmost efforts towards the eradication of heresy.

It has been urged that the attitude adopted by the Church was a most unwilling attitude, forced upon it by influences too powerful to resist, that the main motive power of persecution came not from the Church, but from the lay authority and from public opinion. The theory is advanced that during the period, roughly from 1000 to 1150, when the position of the heretic was a matter of legal uncertainty, the clergy opposed the violence evinced against heretics, and in eventually yielding they submitted to the strength of a custom which constituted a sort of *jus non scriptum*. But there is not much force in this plea. To acquiesce in a *jus non scriptum* argues either indifference or impotence: and the Church in the eleventh and twelfth centuries was neither indifferent nor impotent. Nor is the opposition of the clergy to mob violence an argument to the point. A dislike for mob law and lynching does not necessarily betoken disapproval of capital punishment. It is true—and this is very important—that spontaneously, without any direct incitement from the clergy, the people regarded the heretic with intense abhorrence. We ought probably to add that in the absence of written law on the subject there was a rather vague idea, shared by the mob and their rulers, that not only death, but a particularly terrible kind of death, was an appropriate punishment for the heretic—this idea being perhaps derived from the fact that Roman law had at different times meted out this doom for certain kinds of heretics, particularly Manichaeans, and other offenders, such as sorcerers and witches. It is true also that the heretics upon whom the mob turned were generally Manichaean. Yet no one who has any knowledge of the position of the mediaeval Church can honestly maintain on these grounds that the Church had no responsibility for the rigour displayed towards the heretic. The heretic was regarded as an offender against society, because it was a Christian society. Heresy, being error in the faith, was investigated and recognized by the Church. The clergy, not the mob, discovered the heresy and the heretic; for such discovery could not be made without theological knowledge, of which the mob were ignorant. And such knowledge as they possessed, were it reasoned understanding or merely half-assimilated fragments of doctrine, was derived solely from clerical instruction. It was difficult for any sort of knowledge to come from any other source. Heresy was regarded as dangerous to the community, because, to begin with, the Church had found it dangerous to itself. The intellectual and spiritual atmosphere with which Christendom was permeated was of the Church's making. The attempt, therefore, to absolve the Church from responsibility for the measures taken against heresy in these centuries—by whomsoever they were taken—involves a wholly erroneous, indeed an absurd, under-estimate of the authority of the Church.

In 1198 there came to the papal throne perhaps the greatest of the whole pontifical line, Lothario Conti, Innocent III. High in resolve to strengthen Church and Papacy, he at once gave his attention to the problem of heresy. But though zealous, in some respects he showed a commendable moderation. He was anxious that the innocent should not be confounded with the guilty in the impetuosity of the perfervid clerk or the impatience of the mob; and for the first ten years of his pontificate he made trial of a pacific programme. But in one part of Christendom the problem of heresy had by this time become acute. In the lands of the Count of Toulouse, Catharism was as rampant as were clerical abuses. The pleasure-loving, prosperous inhabitants of Provence, of Narbonne, of Albi felt the authority of the Church to be an obnoxious incubus upon their worldliness, their careless independence. The clergy were hated and despised. The troubadour made pleasant ridicule of the sacraments and every doctrine of the Church, however sacred. The death-bed repentance scheme of the Catharan system, its denial of a purgatory and a hell, were popular. Still more so was the pretext afforded by its anti-sacerdotal precepts for despoiling the Church. So the nobles and the rich *bourgeoisie* and merchants received heretics into their houses, clothed them and fed them, while they were exempted from taxes. So great was the hold of heresy in his lands, that Count Raymond V of Toulouse declared himself to be wholly unable to resist it. His successor, Raymond VI, had no wish to resist it, being of the same stuff as his people and seeing no call to disturb them at the bidding of priests. Thus when a Council at Montpellier in 1195 anathematized all princes failing to enforce the Church's decrees against heretics, he paid no heed.

A couple of months after his accession Innocent III sent two commissioners into Languedoc, one of them being subsequently entrusted with legatine powers, to tackle a situation so serious that the whole of that country seemed on the point of slipping away from its allegiance to the Catholic faith and communion. They were instructed that obdurate heretics were to be banished, their property confiscated; and the secular authority was to see to it that their measures were carried out under pain of interdict. The efforts of these two commissioners were entirely fruitless. In 1204 their successors were entrusted with increased authority, which gave them a complete dictatorship over the ecclesiastical dignitaries of Languedoc, who were bitterly reviled for their incapacity. Yet neither these measures nor lavish bribes to secular rulers proved efficacious, and even the iron resolution of the commissioners, Pierre de Castelnau and Arnaud of Citeaux, was breaking down beneath the weight of persistent failure, when a certain Spaniard, Diego de Arzevedo, Bishop of Osma, suggested to the legates the scheme of an evangelistic enterprise. This was adopted, and barefooted missionaries were sent forth to re-convert the erring by simple preaching and exhortation. Among the preachers was St. Dominic himself. This laudable scheme also failed. There is a legend that Dominic, stung by his ill-success, predicted what the upshot of such deplorable obduracy must eventually be There was a saying in Spain, he quoted, that a beating may work where a blessing won't. The towers of the cities of the fair land would have to be laid low, its people reduced to servitude. The actual signal for a complete reversal of policy was the murder of Pierre de Castelnau in circumstances which recall the murder of Becket. The legate had exasperated the Count of Toulouse; one of the latter's knights slew the priest. Innocent called for vengeance upon the blood-guilty Count; and the Albigensian Crusade, which Innocent had ere this been preaching in vain to Philip Augustus of France, was the immediate consequence. The first crusading army, an international force, assembled at Lyons in June 1209. The ensuing wars are memorable for the men who took part in them—Pedro of Aragon, the zealous catholic, now intervening on behalf of Count Raymond and perishing on the field of Muret, Simon de Montfort, the "athlete of Christ"! Never was there Christian warrior purer in his motives than Simon, more whole-hearted in his enthusiasm, or more utterly inhuman in his fanaticism. These wars are also memorable for their political issues and consequences. From the outset purely political interests were intermixed with the religious. The great nobles who led the forces of the Cross united with their pious zeal an at least equally genuine and powerful hatred and jealousy of the rich and bountiful southern land which harboured a culture so different from their own, more Saracen than European. The wars were wars of the north against the south, of one civilization against another. The astute and calculating Philip Augustus seized with avidity the opportunity of bringing under his direct control a province of France, which had been practically an independent kingdom; and the crusade is, therefore, of first rate importance as a big contribution to the unification of the French kingdom.

If to many who took part in them the original purpose of these religious wars was altogether subsidiary, that purpose was none the less most horribly accomplished. The peculiar civilization of Languedoc was blotted out, its beauty and fragrance being utterly extinguished by the onslaught of the crusaders. With the civilization went the heresy that it had harboured. Catharism indeed continued to exist in the devastated region, but all its vital power of expansion had been destroyed when the conditions that fostered it vanished. The Albigensian wars were the most successful attempt to extirpate heresy known in history. They were successful because they were utterly ruthless and included wholesale massacres. When the town of

Béziers fell, it is said that twenty thousand of its inhabitants were slaughtered. There were good catholics as well as Cathari among the populace of the place; but the story goes that when Arnaud of Citeaux was asked whether the catholics were to be spared, in his anxiety lest a single heretic should escape by pretending orthodoxy, he replied, "Kill them all, for God knows His own."

When the crusaders appeared in Languedoc, toleration vanished out of western Christendom. There was no asylum left where the heretic could feel assured of safety from the persecutor. The power of the Church against the disobedient had been mightily asserted. The ruler who had dared to disregard her order to purify his land of its contaminators had been brought low. From every country the papacy had been able to bring together doughty warriors to uphold the unity of the faith by spilling the blood of the perverse wanderers from the fold. The policy of force had been triumphantly vindicated by the amplitude of its success.

68. SCENES FROM THE LIFE OF ST. FRANCIS OF ASSISI [1]

St. Francis of Assisi is perhaps the most famous saint of the Middle Ages, and so great was his religious fervor and so pure was his life after his conversion that very few Protestants are bold enough to refer to him as simply Francis of Assisi. Much has naturally been written about him. We possess valuable accounts by contemporary eye-witnesses. It is doubtful, however, whether any description of his life and character, no matter in what language, is more illuminating to the modern reader in America than the eloquent story by Sabatier, the eminent French writer, whose Life of St. Francis of Assisi *is based on much careful study of the original sources and of the whole environment in which the saint was reared and in which he began his work as reformer. The extracts given below describe how there occurred in his life the great metamorphosis commonly called his conversion.*

Assisi is to-day very much what it was six or seven hundred years ago. The feudal castle is in ruins, but the aspect of the city is just the same. Its long-deserted streets, bordered by ancient houses, lie in terraces halfway up the steep hill-side. Above it Mount Subasio proudly towers, at its feet lies outspread all the Umbrian plain from Perugia to Spoleto. The crowded houses clamber up the rocks like children a-tiptoe to see all that is to be

[1] P. Sabatier, *Life of St. Francis of Assisi,* translated by Louise S. Houghton. New York, Charles Scribner's Sons, 1928, pp. 2–3, 3–6, 7–8, 9–11, 12–13, 13–15, 17–20, 21–24, 25–27, 53–56, 57–61, 61–62, 62–63, 64, 65–66, 67–68, 68–70. Used by permission of Charles Scribner's Sons.

seen; they succeed so well that every window gives the whole panorama set in its frame of rounded hills, from whose summits castles and villages stand sharply out against a sky of incomparable purity.

These simple dwellings contain no more than five or six little rooms, but the rosy hues of the stone of which they are built give them a wonderfully cheerful air. The one in which, according to the story, St. Francis was born has almost entirely disappeared, to make room for a church; but the street is so modest, and all that remains of the *palazzo dei genitori di San Francesco* is so precisely like the neighboring houses that the tradition must be correct. Francis entered into glory in his lifetime; it would be surprising if a sort of worship had not from the first been centred around the house in which he saw the light and where he passed the first twenty-five years of his life.

He was born about 1182. The biographies have preserved to us few details about his parents. His father, Pietro Bernardone, was a wealthy cloth-merchant. We know how different was the life of the merchants of that period from what it is to-day. A great portion of their time was spent in extensive journeys for the purchase of goods. Such tours were little short of expeditions. The roads being insecure, a strong escort was needed for the journey to those famous fairs where, for long weeks at a time, merchants from the most remote parts of Europe were gathered together.

. . . .

Bernardone often made these long journeys; he went even as far as France, and by this we must surely understand Northern France, and particularly Champagne, which was the seat of commercial exchange between Northern and Southern Europe.

He was there at the very time of his son's birth. The mother, presenting the child at the font of San Rufino, had him baptized by the name of John, but the father on his return chose to call him Francis. Had he already determined on the education he was to give the child; did he name him thus because he even then intended to bring him up after the French fashion, to make a little Frenchman of him? It is by no means improbable. Perhaps, indeed, the name was only a sort of grateful homage tendered by the Assisan burgher to his noble clients beyond the Alps. However this may be, the child was taught to speak French, and always had a special fondness for both the language and the country.

These facts about Bernardone are of real importance; they reveal the influences in the midst of which Francis grew up. Merchants, indeed, play a considerable part in the religious movements of the thirteenth century. Their calling in some sense forced them to become colporters of ideas. What else could they do, on arriving in a country, but answer those who asked for news? And the news most eagerly looked for was religious news, for men's minds were turned upon very different subjects then from now. They accommodated themselves to the popular wish, observing, hearkening everywhere, keeping eyes and ears open, glad to find anything to tell; and little by little many of them became active propagandists of ideas concerning which at first they had been simply curious.

The importance of the part thus played by the merchants as they came and went, everywhere sowing the new ideas which they had gathered up in their travels, has not been put in a clear enough light; they were often, unconsciously and quite involuntarily, the carriers of ideas of all kinds, especially of heresy and rebellion. It was they who made the success of the Waldenses, the Albigenses, the Humiliati, and many other sects.

Thus Bernardone, without dreaming of such a thing, became the artisan of his son's religious vocation. The tales which he brought home from his travels seemed at first, perhaps, not to have aroused the child's attention, but they were like germs a long time buried, which suddenly, under a warm ray of sunlight, bring forth unlooked-for fruit.

The boy's education was not carried very far; the school was in those days overshadowed by the church. The priests of San Giorgio were his teachers, and taught him a little Latin. This language was spoken in Umbria until toward the middle of the thirteenth century; every one understood it and spoke it a little; it was still the language of sermons and of political deliberations.

He learned also to write, but with less success; all through his life we see him take up the pen only on rare occasions, and for but a few words. The autograph of Sacro-Convento, which appears to be entirely authentic, shows extreme awkwardness; in general he dictated, signing his letters by a simple *τ*, the symbol of the cross of Jesus.

That part of his education which was destined to have most influence upon his life was the French language, which he perhaps spoke in his own family. It has been rightly said that to know two languages is to have two souls; in learning that of France the boy felt his heart thrill to the melody of its youthful poetry, and his imagination was mysteriously stirred with dreams of imitating the exploits of the French cavaliers.

. . . .

His father's profession and the possibly noble origin of his mother raised him almost to the level of the titled families of the country; money, which he spent with both hands, made him welcome among them. Well pleased to enjoy themselves at his expense, the young nobles paid him a sort of court. As to Bernardone, he was too happy to see his son associating with them to be niggardly as to the means. He was miserly, as the course of this history will show, but his pride and self-conceit exceeded his avarice.

Pica, his wife, gentle and modest creature, concerning whom the biographers have been only too laconic, saw all this, and mourned over it in silence, but though weak as mothers are, she would not despair of her son, and when the neighbors told her of Francis's escapades, she would calmly reply, "What are you thinking about? I am very sure that, if it pleases God, he will become a good Christian." The words were natural enough from a mother's lips, but later on they were held to have been truly prophetic.

. . . .

At this very time the troubadours were roaming over the towns of Northern Italy and bringing brilliant festivities and especially Courts of Love into vogue. If they worked upon the passions, they also made appeal to feelings of courtesy and delicacy; it was this that saved Francis. In the midst of his excesses he was always refined and considerate, carefully abstaining from every base or indecent utterance. Already his chief aspiration was to rise above the commonplace. Tortured with the desire for that which is far off and high, he had conceived a sort of passion for chivalry, and fancying that dissipation was one of the distinguishing features of nobility, he had thrown himself into it with all his soul.

But he who, at twenty, goes from pleasure to pleasure with the heart not absolutely closed to good, must now and then, at some turning of the road, become aware that there are hungry folk, who could live a month on what he spends in a few hours on frivolity. Francis saw them, and with his impressionable nature for the moment forgot everything else. In thought he put himself in their place, and it sometimes happened that he gave them all the money he had about him and even his clothes.

One day he was busy with some customers in his father's shop, when a man came in, begging for charity in the name of God. Losing his patience Francis sharply turned him away; but quickly reproaching himself for his harshness he thought, "What would I not have done if this man had asked something of me in the name of a count or a baron? What ought I not to have done when he came in the name of God? I am no better than a clown!" Leaving his customers he ran after the beggar.

Bernardone had been well pleased with his son's commercial aptitude in the early days when the young man was first in his father's employ. Francis was only too proficient in spending money; he at least knew well how to make it. But this satisfaction did not last long. Francis's bad companions were exercising over him a most pernicious influence. The time came when he could no longer endure to be separated from them; if he heard their call, nothing could keep him, he would leave everything and go after them.

All this time political events were hurrying on in Umbria and Italy; after a formidable struggle the allied republics had forced the empire to recognize them. By the immortal victory of Legnano (May 29, 1176) and the Peace of Constance (June 25, 1183) the Lombard League had wrested from Frederick Barbarossa almost all the prerogatives of power; little was left to the emperor but insignia and outward show.

From one end of the Peninsula to the other visions of liberty were making hearts beat high. For an instant it seemed as if all Italy was about to regain consciousness of its unity, was about to rise up as one man and hurl the foreigner from its borders; but the rivalries of the cities were too strong for them to see that local liberty without a common independence is precarious and illusory.

. . . .

Perugia was at this time at the apogee of its power, and had already made many efforts to reduce Assisi to submission. It . . . declared war upon Assisi . . . in 1202. An encounter took place in the plain about halfway between the two cities, not far from Ponte San Giovanni. Assisi was defeated, and Francis, who was in the ranks, was made prisoner.

The treachery of the nobles had not been universal; a few had fought with the people. It was with them and not with the *popolani* that Francis, in consideration of the nobility of his manners, passed the time of his captivity, which lasted an entire year. He greatly astonished his companions by his lightness of heart. Very often they thought him almost crazy. Instead of passing his time in wailing and cursing he made plans for the future, about which he was glad to talk to any one who came along. To his fancy life was what the songs of the troubadours had painted it; he dreamed of glorious adventures, and always ended by saying: "You will see that one day I shall be adored by the whole world."

. . . .

A compromise was finally arrived at between the counts and the people of Assisi. In November, 1203, the arbitrators designated by the two parties announced their decision. The commons of Assisi were to repair in a certain measure the damage done to the lords, and the latter agreed, on their part, to make no further alliances without authorization of the commons. Rural serfage was maintained, which proves that the revolution had been directed by the burghers, and for their own profit. Ten years more were not, however, to elapse before the common people also would succeed in achieving liberty. In this cause we shall again see Francis fighting on the side of the oppressed, earning the title of Patriarch of religious democracy which has been accorded him by one of his compatriots.

The agreement being made the prisoners detained at Perugia were released, and Francis returned to Assisi. He was twenty-two years old.

. . . .

On his return to Assisi Francis at once resumed his former mode of life; perhaps he even tried in some degree to make up for lost time. Fêtes, games, festivals, and dissipations began again. He did his part in them so well that he soon fell gravely ill. For long weeks he looked death so closely in the face that the physical crisis brought about a moral one.

. . . .

By a holy violence he was to arrive at last at a pure and virile faith; but the road to this point is long, and sown thick with obstacles, and at the moment at which we have arrived he had not yet entered upon it, he did not even suspect its existence; all he knew was that pleasure leads to nothingness, to satiety and self-contempt.

He knew this, and yet he was about to throw himself once more into a life of pleasure. The body is so weak, so prone to return to the old paths, that it seeks them of itself, the moment an energetic will does not stop it. Though no longer under any illusion with respect to it, Francis returned to his former life. Was he trying to divert his mind, to forget that day of bitter thought? We might suppose so, seeing the ardor with which he threw himself into his new projects.

An opportunity offered itself for him to realize his dreams of glory. A knight of Assisi, perhaps one of those who had been in captivity with him at Perugia, was preparing to go to Apulia under orders from Count Gentile. The latter was to join Gaultier de Brienne, who was in the south of Italy fighting on the side of Innocent III. Gaultier's renown was immense all through the Peninsula; he was held to be one of the most gallant knights of the time. Francis's heart bounded with joy; it seemed to him that at the side of such a hero he should soon cover himself with glory. His departure was decided upon, and he gave himself up, without reserve, to his joy.

He made his preparations with ostentatious prodigality. His equipment, of a princely luxury, soon became the universal subject of conversation. It was all the more talked about because the chief of the expedition, ruined perhaps by the revolution of 1202 or by the expenses of a long captivity, was constrained to order things much more modestly. But with Francis kindliness was much stronger than love of display. He gave his sumptuous clothing to a poor knight. The biographies do not say whether or not it was to the very one whom he was to accompany. To see him running hither and thither in all the bustle of preparation one would have thought him the son of a great lord. His companions were doubtless not slow to feel chafed by his ways and to promise themselves to make him cruelly expiate them. As for him, he perceived nothing of the jealousies which he was exciting, and night and day he thought only of his future glory. In his dreams he seemed to see his parents' house completely transformed. Instead of bales of cloth he saw there only gleaming bucklers hanging on the walls, and arms of all kinds as in a seigniorial castle. He saw himself there, beside a noble and beautiful bride, and he never suspected that in this vision there was any presage of the future which was reserved for him. Never had any one seen him so communicative, so radiant; and when he was asked for the hundredth time whence came all this joy, he would reply with surprising assurance: "I know that I shall become a great prince."

The day of departure arrived at last. Francis on horseback, the little buckler of a page on his arm, bade adieu to his natal city with joy, and with the little troop took the road to Spoleto which winds around the base of Mount Subasio.

What happened next? The documents do not say. They confine themselves to reporting that that very evening Francis had a vision which decided him to return to Assisi. Perhaps it would not be far from the truth to conjecture that once fairly on the way the young nobles took their revenge on the son of Bernardone for his airs as of a future prince. At twenty years one hardly pardons things like these. If, as we are often assured, there is a pleasure unsuspected by the profane in getting even with a stranger, it must be an almost divine delight to get even with a young coxcomb upon whom one has to exercise so righteous a vengeance.

Arriving at Spoleto, Francis took to his bed. A fever was consuming him; in a few hours he had seen all his dreams crumble away. The very next day he took the road back to Assisi.

So unexpected a return made a great stir in the little city, and was a cruel blow to his parents. As for him, he doubled his charities to the poor, and sought to keep aloof from society, but his old companions came flocking about him from all quarters, hoping to find in him once more the tireless purveyor of their idle wants. He let them have their way.

Nevertheless a great change had taken place in him. Neither pleasures nor work could long hold him; he spent a portion of his days in long country rambles, often accompanied by a friend most different from those whom until now we have seen about him.

. . . .

Often Francis directed his steps to a grotto in the country near Assisi, which he entered alone. This rocky cave concealed in the midst of the olive trees became for faithful Franciscans that which Gethsemane is for Christians. Here Francis relieved his overcharged heart by heavy groans. Sometimes, seized with a real horror for the disorders of his youth, he would implore mercy, but the greater part of the time his face was turned toward the future; feverishly he sought for that higher truth to which he longed to dedicate himself, that pearl of great price of which the gospel speaks: "Whosoever seeks, finds; he who asks, receives; and to him who knocks, it shall be opened."

When he came out after long hours of seclusion the pallor of his countenance, the painful tension of his features told plainly enough of the intensity of his asking and the violence of his knocks.

The inward man, to borrow the language of the mystics, was not yet formed in him, but it needed only the occasion to bring about the final break with the past. The occasion soon presented itself.

His friends were making continual efforts to induce him to take up his old habits again. One day he invited them all to a sumptuous banquet. They thought they had conquered, and as in old times they proclaimed him king of the revels. The feast was prolonged far into the night, and at its close the guests rushed out into the streets, which they filled with song and uproar. Suddenly they perceived that Francis was no longer with them. After long searching they at last discovered him far behind them, still holding in his hand his sceptre of king of misrule, but plunged in so profound a reverie that he seemed to be riveted to the ground and unconscious of all that was going on.

"What is the matter with you?" they cried, bustling about him as if to awaken him.

"Don't you see that he is thinking of taking a wife?" said one.

"Yes," answered Francis, arousing himself and looking at them with a smile which they did not recognize.

"I am thinking of taking a wife more beautiful, more rich, more pure than you could ever imagine."

This reply marks a decisive stage in his inner life. By it he cut the last links which bound him to trivial pleasures. It remains for us to see through what struggles he was to give himself to God, after having torn himself free from the world. His friends probably understood nothing of all that had taken place, but he had become aware of the abyss that was opening between them and him. They soon accepted the situation.

As for himself, no longer having any reason for caution, he gave himself up more than ever to his passion for solitude. If he often wept over his past dissipations and wondered how he could have lived so long without tasting the bitterness of the dregs of the enchanted cup, he never allowed himself to be overwhelmed with vain regrets.

The poor had remained faithful to him. They gave him an admiration of which he knew himself to be unworthy, yet which had for him an infinite sweetness. The future grew bright to him in the light of their gratitude, of the timid, trembling affection which they dared not utter but which his heart revealed to him; this worship which he does not deserve to-day he will deserve to-morrow, at least he promises himself to do all he can to deserve it.

To understand these feelings one must understand the condition of the poor of a place like Assisi. In an agricultural country poverty does not, as elsewhere, almost inevitably involve moral destitution, that degeneration of the entire human being which renders charity so difficult. Most of the poor persons whom Francis knew were in straits because of war, of bad harvests, or of illness. In such cases material succor is but a small part. Sympathy is the thing needed above all. Francis had treasures of it to lavish upon them.

He was well requited. All sorrows are sisters; a secret intelligence establishes itself between troubled hearts, however diverse their griefs. The poor people felt that their friend also suffered; they did not precisely know with what, but they forgot their own sorrows in pitying their benefactor. Suffering is the true cement of love. For men to love each other truly, they must have shed tears together.

. . . .

About this time he made a pilgrimage to Rome, whether to ask counsel of his friends, whether as a penance imposed by his confessor, or from a mere impulse, no one knows. Perhaps he thought that in a visit to the *Holy Apostles,* as people said then, he should find the answers to all the questions which he was asking himself.

At any rate he went. It is hardly probable that he received from the visit any religious influence, for his biographers relate the pained surprise which he experienced when he saw in Saint Peter's how meagre were the offerings of pilgrims. He wanted to give everything to the prince of the apostles, and emptying his purse he threw its entire contents upon the tomb.

This journey was marked by a more important incident. Many a time when succoring the poor he had asked himself if he himself was able to endure poverty; no one knows the weight of a burden until he has carried it, at least for a moment, upon his own shoulders. He desired to know what it is like to have nothing, and to depend for bread upon the charity or the caprice of the passer-by.

There were swarms of beggars crowding the Piazza before the great basilica. He borrowed the rags of one of them, lending him his garment in exchange, and a whole day he stood there, fasting, with outstretched hand. The act was a great victory, the triumph of compassion over natural pride. Returning to Assisi, he doubled his kindnesses to those of whom he had truly the right to call himself the brother. With such sentiments he could not long escape the influence of the Church.

On all the roadsides in the environs of the city there were then, as now, numerous chapels. Very often he must have heard mass in these rustic sanctuaries, alone with the celebrant. Recognizing the tendency of simple natures to bring home to themselves everything that they hear, it is easy to understand his emotion and agitation when the priest, turning toward him, would read the gospel for the day. The Christian ideal was revealed to him, bringing an answer to his secret anxieties. And when, a few moments later, he would plunge into the forest, all his thoughts would be with the poor carpenter of Nazareth, who placed himself in this path, saying to him, even to him, "Follow thou me."

Nearly two years had passed since the day when he felt the first shock; a life of renunciation appeared to him as the goal of his efforts, but he felt that his spiritual novitiate was not yet ended. He suddenly experienced a bitter assurance of the fact.

He was riding on horseback one day, his mind more than ever possessed with the desire to lead a life of absolute devotion, when at a turn of the road he found himself face to face with a leper. The frightful malady had always inspired in him an invincible repulsion. He could not control a movement of horror, and by instinct he turned his horse in another direction.

If the shock had been severe, the defeat was complete. He reproached himself bitterly. To cherish such fine projects and show himself so cowardly! Was the knight of Christ then going to give up his arms? He retraced his steps and springing from his horse he gave to the astounded sufferer all the money that he had; then kissed his hand as he would have done to a priest. This new victory, as he himself saw, marked an era in his spiritual life.

It is far indeed from hatred of evil to love of good. Those are more numerous than we think who, after severe experience, have renounced what the ancient liturgies call the world, with its pomps and lusts; but the greater number of them have not at the bottom of their hearts the smallest grain of pure love. In vulgar souls disillusion leaves only a frightful egoism.

This victory of Francis had been so sudden that he desired to complete it; a few days later he went to the lazaretto. One can imagine the stupefaction of these wretches at the entrance of the brilliant cavalier. If in our days a visit to the sick in our hospitals is a real event awaited with feverish impatience, what must not have been the appearance of Francis among these poor recluses? One must have seen sufferers thus abandoned, to understand what joy may be given by an affectionate word, sometimes even a simple glance.

Moved and transported, Francis felt his whole being vibrate with unfamiliar sensations. For the first time he heard the unspeakable accents of a gratitude which cannot find words burning enough to express itself, which admires and adores the benefactor almost like an angel from heaven.

. . . .

Since his abrupt return from Spoleto, life in his father's house had become daily more difficult. Bernardone's self-love had received from his son's discomfiture such a wound as with commonplace men is never healed. He might provide, without counting it, money to be swallowed up in dissipation, that so his son might stand on an equal footing with the young nobles; he could never resign himself to see him giving with lavish hands to every beggar in the streets.

Francis, continually plunged in reverie and spending his days in lonely wanderings in the fields, was no longer of the least use to his father. Months passed, and the distance between the two men grew ever wider; and the gentle and loving Pica could do nothing to prevent a rupture which from this time appeared to be inevitable. Francis soon came to feel only one desire, to flee from the abode where, in the place of love, he found only reproaches, upbraidings, anguish.

The faithful confidant of his earlier struggles had been obliged to leave him, and this absolute solitude weighed heavily upon his warm and loving heart. He did what he could to escape from it, but no one understood him. The ideas which he was beginning timidly to express evoked from those to whom he spoke only mocking smiles or the head-shakings which men sure that they are right bestow upon him who is marching straight to madness. He even went to open his mind to the bishop, but the latter understood no more than others his vague, incoherent plans, filled with ideas impossible to realize and possibly subversive. It was thus that in spite of himself Francis was led to ask nothing of men, but to raise himself by prayer to intuitive knowledge of the divine will. The doors of houses and of hearts were alike closing upon him, but the interior voice was about to speak out with irresistible force and make itself forever obeyed.

Among the numerous chapels in the suburbs of Assisi there was one which he particularly loved, that of St. Damian. It was reached by a few minutes' walk over a stony path, almost trackless, under olive trees, amid odors of lavender and rosemary. Standing on the top of a hillock, the entire plain is visible from it, through a curtain of cypresses and pines which seem to be trying to hide the humble hermitage and set up an ideal barrier between it and the world.

Served by a poor priest who had scarcely the wherewithal for necessary food, the sanctuary was falling into ruin. There was nothing in the interior but a simple altar of masonry, and by way of reredos one of those byzantine crucifixes still so numerous in Italy, where through the work of the artists of the time has come down to us something of the terrors which agitated the twelfth century. In general the Crucified One, frightfully lacerated, with bleeding wounds, appears to seek to inspire only grief and compunction; that of St. Damian, on the contrary, has an expression of inexpressible calm and gentleness; instead of closing the eyelids in eternal surrender to the weight of suffering, it looks down in self-forgetfulness, and its pure, clear gaze says, not "I suffer," but, "Come unto me."

One day Francis was praying before the poor altar: "Great and glorious God, and thou, Lord Jesus, I pray ye, shed abroad your light in the darkness of my mind. . . . Be found of me, Lord, so that in all things I may act only in accordance with thy holy will."

Thus he prayed in his heart, and behold, little by little it seemed to him that his gaze could not detach itself from that of Jesus; he felt something marvellous taking place in and around him. The sacred victim took on life, and in the outward silence he was aware of a voice which softly stole into the very depths of his heart, speaking to him an ineffable language. Jesus accepted his oblation. Jesus desired his labor, his life, all his being, and the heart of the poor solitary was already bathed in light and strength.

This vision marks the final triumph of Francis. His union with Christ is consummated; from this time he can exclaim with the mystics of every age, "My beloved is mine, and I am this."

But instead of giving himself up to transports of contemplation he at once asks himself how he may repay to Jesus love for love, in what action he shall employ this life which he has just offered to him. He had not long to seek. We have seen that the chapel where his spiritual espousals had just been celebrated was threatened with ruin. He believed that to repair it was the work assigned to him.

From that day the remembrance of the Crucified One, the thought of the love which had triumphed in immolating itself, became the very centre of his religious life and as it were the soul of his soul. For the first time, no doubt, Francis had been brought into direct, personal, intimate contact with Jesus Christ.

. . . .

From that time his way was plain before him. Coming out from the sanctuary, he gave the priest all the money he had about him to keep a lamp always burning, and with a ravished heart he returned to Assisi. He had decided to quit his father's house and undertake the restoration of the chapel, after having broken the last ties that bound him to the past. A horse and a few pieces of gayly colored stuffs were all that he possessed. Arrived at home he made a packet of the stuffs, and mounting his horse he set out for Foligno. This city was then as now the most important commercial town of all the region. Its fairs attracted the whole population of Umbria and the Sabines. Bernardone had often taken his son there, and Francis speedily succeeded in selling all he had brought. He even parted with his horse, and full of joy set out upon the road to Assisi.

This act was to him most important; it marked his final rupture with the past; from this day on his life was to be in all points the opposite of what it had been; the Crucified had given himself to him; he on his side had given himself to the Crucified without reserve or return. To uncertainty, disquietude of soul, anguish, longing for an unknown good, bitter regrets, had succeeded a delicious calm, the ecstasy of the lost child who finds his mother, and forgets in a moment the torture of his heart.

From Foligno he returned direct to St. Damian; it was not necessary to pass through the city, and he was in haste to put his projects into execution.

The poor priest was surprised enough when Francis handed over to him the whole product of his sale. He doubtless thought that a passing quarrel had occurred between Bernardone and his son, and for greater prudence refused the gift; but Francis so insisted upon remaining with him that he finally gave him leave to do so. As to the money, now become useless, Francis cast it as a worthless object upon a window-seat in the chapel.

Meanwhile Bernardone, disturbed by his son's failure to return, sought for him in all quarters, and was not long in learning of his presence at St. Damian. In a moment he perceived that Francis was lost to him. Resolved to try every means, he collected a few neighbors, and furious with rage hastened to the hermitage to snatch him away, if need were, by main force.

But Francis knew his father's violence. When he heard the shouts of those who were in pursuit of him he felt his courage fail and hurried to a hiding-place which he had prepared for himself for precisely such an emergency. Bernardone, no doubt ill seconded in the search, ransacked every corner, but was obliged at last to return to Assisi without his son. Francis remained hidden for long days, weeping and groaning, imploring God to show him the path he ought to follow. Notwithstanding his fears he had an infinite joy at heart, and at no price would he have turned back.

This seclusion could not last long. Francis perceived this, and told himself that for a newly made knight of the Christ he was cutting a very pitiful figure. Arming himself, therefore, with courage, he went one day to the city to present himself before his father and make known to him his resolution.

It is easy to imagine the changes wrought in his appearance by these few weeks of seclusion, passed much of them in mental anguish. When he appeared, pale, cadaverous, his clothes in tatters, upon what is now the Piazza Nuova, where hundreds of children play all day long, he was greeted with a great shout, *"Pazzo, Pazzo!"* (A madman! a madman!) *"Un pazzo ne fa cento"* (One madman makes a hundred more), says the proverb, but one must have seen the delirious excitement of the street children of Italy at the sight of a madman to gain an idea how true it is. The moment the magic cry resounds they rush into the street with frightful din, and while their parents look on from the windows, they surround the unhappy sufferer with wild dances mingled with songs, shouts, and savage howls. They throw stones at him, fling mud upon him, blindfold him; if he flies into a rage, they double their insults; if he weeps or begs for pity, they repeat his cries and mimic his sobs and supplications without respite and without mercy.

Bernardone soon heard the clamor which filled the narrow streets, and went out to enjoy the show; suddenly he thought he heard his own name and that of his son, and bursting with shame and rage he perceived Francis. Throwing himself upon him, as if to throttle him, he dragged him into the house and cast him, half dead, into a dark closet. Threats, bad usage, everything was brought to bear to change the prisoner's resolves, but all in vain. At last, wearied out and desperate, he left him in peace, though not without having firmly bound him.

A few days after he was obliged to be absent for a short time. Pica, his wife, understood only too well his grievances against Francis, but feeling that violence would be of no avail she resolved to try gentleness. It was all in vain. Then, not being able longer to see him thus tortured, she set him at liberty.

He returned straight to St. Damian.

Bernardone, on his return, went so far as to strike Pica in punishment for her weakness. Then, unable to tolerate the thought of seeing his son the jest of the whole city, he tried to procure his expulsion from the territory of Assisi. Going to St. Damian he summoned him to leave the country. This time Francis did not try to hide. Boldly presenting himself before his father, he declared to him that not only would nothing induce him to abandon his resolutions, but that, moreover, having become the servant of Christ, he had no longer to receive orders from him. As Bernardone launched out into invective, reproaching him with the enormous sums which he had cost him, Francis showed him by a gesture the money which he had brought back from the sale at Foligno lying on the window-ledge. The father greedily seized it and went away, resolving to appeal to the magistrates.

The consuls summoned Francis to appear before them, but he replied simply that as servant of the Church he did not come under their jurisdiction. Glad of this response, which relieved them of a delicate dilemma, they referred the complainant to the diocesan authorities.

The matter took on another aspect before the ecclesiastical tribunal; it was idle to dream of asking the bishop to pronounce a sentence of banishment, since it was his part to preserve the liberty of the clerics. Bernardone could do no more than disinherit his son, or at least induce him of his own accord to renounce all claim upon his inheritance. This was not difficult.

When called upon to appear before the episcopal tribunal Francis experienced a lively joy; his mystical espousals to the Crucified One were now to receive a sort of official consecration. To this Jesus, whom he had so often blasphemed and betrayed by word and conduct, he would now be able with equal publicity to promise obedience and fidelity.

. . . .

The bishop first set forth the case, and advised Francis to simply give up all his property. To the great surprise of the crowd the latter, instead of replying, retired to a room in the bishop's palace, and immediately reappeared absolutely naked, holding in his hand the packet into which he had rolled his clothes; these he laid down before the bishop with the little money that he still had kept, saying: "Listen, all of you, and understand it well; until this time I have called Pietro Bernardone my father, but now I desire to serve God. This is why I return to him this money, for which he has given himself so much trouble, as well as my clothing, and all that I have had from him, for from henceforth I desire to say nothing else than *'Our Father, who art in heaven.'*"

A long murmur arose from the crowd when Bernardone was seen to gather up and carry off the clothing without the least evidence of compassion, while the bishop was fain to take under his mantle the poor Francis, who was trembling with emotion and cold.

. . . .

After emotions such as he had just experienced he felt the need of being alone, of realizing his joy, of singing the liberty he had finally achieved along all the lines where once he had so deeply suffered, so ardently struggled. He would not, therefore, return immediately to St. Damian. Leaving the city by the nearest gate, he plunged into the deserted paths which climb the sides of Mount Subasio.

It was the early spring. Here and there were still great drifts of snow, but under the ardor of the March sun winter seemed to own itself vanquished. In the midst of this mysterious and bewildering harmony the heart of Francis felt a delicious thrill, all his being was calmed and uplifted, the soul of things caressed him gently and shed upon him peace. An unwonted happiness swept over him; he made the forest to resound with his hymns of praise. . . .

Not far away was a monastery. He entered and offered his services. In those solitudes, peopled often by such undesirable neighbors, people were suspicious. The monks permitted him to make himself useful in the kitchen, but they gave him nothing to cover himself with and hardly anything to eat. There was nothing for it but to go away; he directed his footsteps toward Gubbio, where he knew that he should find a friend. Perhaps this was he who had been his confidant on his return from Spoleto. However this may be, he received from him a tunic, and a few days after set out to return to his dear St. Damian.

. . . .

During this time the poor priest of St. Damian felt his heart swelling with love for this companion who had at first caused him such embarrassment, and he strove to prepare for him his favorite dishes. Francis so perceived it. His delicacy took alarm at the expense which he caused his friend, and, thanking him, he resolved to beg his food from door to door.

It was not an easy task. The first time, when at the end of his round he glanced at the broken food in his wallet, he felt his courage fail him. But the thought of being so soon unfaithful to the spouse to whom he had plighted his faith made his blood run cold with shame and gave him strength to eat ravenously.

. . . .

In the spring of 1208 he finished the restoration of St. Damian; he had been aided by all people of good will, setting the example of work and above all of joy, cheering everybody by his songs and his projects for the future. He spoke with such enthusiasm and contagious warmth of the transformation of his dear chapel, of the grace which God would accord to those who should come there to pray, that later on it was believed that he had spoken of Clara and her holy maidens who were to retire to this place four years later.

This success soon inspired him with the idea of repairing the other sanctuaries in the suburbs of Assisi. Those which had struck him by their state of decay were St. Peter and Santa Maria, of the *Portiuncula,* called also Santa Maria degli Angeli. The former is not otherwise mentioned in his biographies. As to the second, it was to become the true cradle of the Franciscan movement.

This chapel, still standing at the present day after escaping revolutions and earthquakes, is a true Bethel, one of those rare spots in the world on which rests the mystic ladder which joins heaven to earth; there were dreamed some of the noblest dreams which have soothed the pains of humanity. It is not to Assisi in its marvellous basilica that one must go to divine and comprehend St. Francis; he must turn his steps to Santa Maria degli Angeli at the hours when the stated prayers cease, at the moment when the evening shadows lengthen, when all the fripperies of worship disappear in the obscurity, when all the nation seems to collect itself to listen to the chime of the distant church bells.

. . . .

One day, it was probably February 24, 1209, the festival of St. Matthias, mass was being celebrated at the Portiuncula. When the priest turned toward him to read the words of Jesus, Francis felt himself overpowered with a profound agitation. He no longer saw the priest; it was Jesus, the Crucified One of St. Damian, who was speaking: "Wherever ye go, preach, saying, 'The kingdom of heaven is at hand. Heal the sick, cleanse the lepers, cast out devils. Freely ye have received, freely give. Provide neither silver nor gold nor brass in your purses, neither scrip nor two coats, nor shoes nor staff, for the laborer is worthy of his meat.' "

These words burst upon him like a revelation, like the answer of Heaven to his sighs and anxieties.

"This is what I want," he cried, "this is what I was seeking; from this day forth I shall set myself with all my strength to put it in practice." Immediately throwing aside his stick, his scrip, his purse, his shoes, he determined immediately to obey, observing to the letter the precepts of the apostolic life.

It is quite possible that some allegorizing tendencies have had some influence upon this narrative. The long struggle through which Francis passed before becoming the apostle of the new times assuredly came to a crisis in the scene at Portiuncula; but we have already seen how slow was the interior travail which prepared for it.

The revelation of Francis was in his heart; the sacred fire which he was to communicate to the souls of others came from within his own, but the best causes need a standard. Before the shabby altar of the Portiuncula he had perceived the banner of poverty, sacrifice, and love, he would carry it to the assault of every fortress of sin; under its shadow, a true knight of Christ, he would marshal all the valiant warriors of a spiritual strife.

69. THE STORY OF ST. FRANCIS AND THE WOLF OF GUBBIO [1]

As the fame of St. Francis grew, many wondrous tales were told of the miracles that he had performed. One of the most charming of these is the story of his conversion of the Wolf of Gubbio.

Of the Most Holy Miracle of St. Francis in Taming the Wolf of Gubbio.

At the time when St. Francis was living in the city of Gubbio, a large wolf appeared in the neighbourhood, so terrible and so fierce, that he not only devoured other animals, but made a prey of men also; and since he often approached the town, all the people were in great alarm, and used to go about armed, as if going to battle. Notwithstanding these precautions, if any of the inhabitants ever met him alone, he was sure to be devoured, as all defence was useless: and, through fear of the wolf, they dared not go beyond the city walls. St. Francis, feeling great compassion for the people of Gubbio, resolved to go and meet the wolf, though all advised him not to do so. Making the sign of the holy cross, and putting all his confidence in God, he went forth from the city, taking his brethren with him; but these fearing to go any farther, St. Francis bent his steps alone toward the spot where the wolf was known to be, while many people followed at a distance, and witnessed the miracle. The wolf, seeing all this multitude, ran towards St. Francis with his jaws wide open. As he approached, the saint, making the sign of the cross, cried out: "Come hither, brother wolf; I command thee, in the name of Christ, neither to harm me nor anybody else." Marvellous to tell, no sooner had St. Francis made the sign of the cross, than the terrible wolf, closing his jaws, stopped running, and coming up to St. Francis, lay down at his feet, as meekly as a lamb. And the saint thus addressed him: "Brother wolf, thou hast done much evil in this land, destroying and killing the creatures of God without his permission; yea, not animals only hast thou destroyed, but thou hast even dared to devour men, made after the image of God; for which thing thou art worthy of being hanged like a robber and a murderer. All men cry out against thee, the dogs pursue thee, and all the inhabitants of this city are thy enemies; but I will make peace between them and thee, O brother wolf, if so be thou no more offend them, and they shall forgive thee all thy past offences, and

[1] *The Little Flowers of Saint Francis of Assisi.* In the first English translation revised and emended by Dom Roger Huddleston with an introduction by Arthur Livingston. Printed for the Limited Editions Club. New York, 1930, pp. 56–59. Used by permission of Burns, Oates & Washbourne, Ltd.

neither men nor dogs shall pursue thee any more." Having listened to these words, the wolf bowed his head, and, by the movements of his body, his tail, and his eyes, made signs that he agreed to what St. Francis said. On this St. Francis added: "As thou art willing to make this peace, I promise thee that thou shalt be fed every day by the inhabitants of this land so long as thou shalt live among them; thou shalt no longer suffer hunger, as it is hunger which has made thee do so much evil; but if I obtain all this for thee, thou must promise, on thy side, never again to attack any animal or human being: dost thou make this promise?" Then the wolf, bowing his head, made a sign that he consented. Said St. Francis again: "Brother wolf, wilt thou pledge thy faith that I may trust to this thy promise?" And putting out his hand he received the pledge of the wolf; for the latter lifted up his paw and placed it familiarly in the hand of St. Francis, giving him thereby the only pledge which was in his power. Then said St. Francis, addressing him again: "Brother wolf, I command thee, in the name of Christ, to follow me immediately, without hesitation or doubting, that we may go together to ratify this peace which we have concluded in the name of God"; and the wolf, obeying him, walked by his side as meekly as a lamb, to the great astonishment of all the people. Now, the news of this most wonderful miracle spreading quickly through the town, all the inhabitants, both men and women, small and great, young and old, flocked to the market-place to see St. Francis and the wolf. All the people being assembled, the saint got up to preach, saying, amongst other things, how for our sins God permits such calamities, and how much greater and more dangerous are the flames of hell, which last forever, than the rage of a wolf, which can kill the body only; and how much we ought to dread the jaws of hell, if the jaws of so small an animal as a wolf can make a whole city tremble through fear. The sermon being ended, St. Francis added these words: "Listen, my brethren: the wolf who is here before you has promised and pledged his faith that he consents to make peace with you all, and no more to offend you in aught, and you must promise to give him each day his necessary food; to which, if you consent, I promise in his name that he will most faithfully observe the compact." Then all the people promised with one voice to feed the wolf to the end of his days; and St. Francis, addressing the latter, said again: "And thou, brother wolf, dost thou promise to keep the compact, and never again to offend either man or beast, or any other creature?" And the wolf knelt down, bowing his head, and, by the motions of his tail and of his ears, endeavoured to show that he was willing, as far as was in his power, to hold to the compact. Then St. Francis continued: "Brother wolf, as thou gavest me a pledge of this thy promise when we were outside the town, so now I will that thou renew it in the sight of all this people, and assure me that I have done well to promise in thy name"; and the wolf, lifting up his paw placed it in the hand of St. Francis. Now this event caused great joy in all the people, and a great devotion towards St. Francis, both because of the novelty of the miracle, and because of the peace which had been concluded with the wolf; and they lifted up their voices to heaven, praising and blessing God, who had sent them St. Francis, through whose merits they had been delivered from such a savage beast. The wolf lived two years at Gubbio; he went familiarly from door to door without harming anyone, and all the people received him courteously, feeding him with great pleasure, and no dog barked at him as he went about. At last, after two years, he died of old age, and the people of Gubbio mourned his loss greatly; for when they saw him going about so gently amongst them all, he reminded them of the virtue and sanctity of St. Francis.

70. *PHILIP AUGUSTUS AND THE GROWTH OF ROYAL POWER IN FRANCE* [1]

Philip II, generally surnamed Augustus, because of his illustrious reign and his successful attempt to increase the power of the French monarchy, did more for the growth of royal absolutism in France than any of his predecessors. The story of his reign as told in Kitchin's History of France *enables us to see how he utilized various events and circumstances to complete the task he took upon himself—"the work of building up, stone by stone, the great edifice of monarchy."*

Philip Augustus was fifteen years old, when he began to reign alone: yet, boy though he was, he never for a moment swerved from his course, or made a false step in it. Coming so young to his crown, he grasped with all a boy's eagerness at the dignity of his royal name; and being proud of disposition and not without a tendency to romance, he at once set his kingship in his own mind far above all, even the greatest of his neighbours; while at the same time he pleased his imagination with dreams of the restoration of a Caroling realm, to which his attention was specially called by his first marriage; he deemed himself destined to recover the whole breadth of the Empire of Charles the Great. There is a story, which may well be true, to the effect that when he was scarcely twenty years old, his courtiers saw him gnawing a green bough, and glaring about him wildly. One of them asked him boldly what he was thinking of; and he replied, "I am wondering whether God will grant me or my heirs grace to raise

[1] G. W. Kitchin, *A History of France,* Vol. I. Oxford, Clarendon Press, 1899, pp. 285–290, 293–295, 298–300, 307–309, 325–327.

France once more to the height she reached in the days of Charlemagne!" For forty-three years he pursued this end, and brought to bear on it a cold pertinacity, a freedom from uneasy scruples, a clear sagacity in conceiving crafty plans, and constancy in carrying them out. No wonder that his reign is an epoch in the history of French monarchy, and that he succeeded in raising the royal power far above the highest level it had hitherto reached.

When Louis "the Fat" died in 1137, he had taken good care not to allow the unity of the kingdom to be weakened by those grants to younger sons, which so often had undone the work of a lifetime: he left, in substance, all the royal domain to his successor, Louis the Young. Fortunately for the monarchy, this weak prince left only one son, and had therefore no temptation to divide his territories; and Philip Augustus succeeded to all the power, which had been painfully gathered together by his grandfather. The kingly office at this moment was regarded by men as a power distinct from feudalism, and as only partly territorial. The King was not merely the head-baron of the system; he was possessor of a real, if indefinite, claim on the respect of mankind, as one solemnly consecrated to his office, and inheritor in a dim way of the ancient conception of kingship; he was felt to be the brother of the kings of England and Normandy, and of those of Spain; as something between Pope and Emperor on the one side, and the independent and powerful Dukes (as of Burgundy or Flanders) on the other. His was an independent and general power, with claims on the allegiance of all France, the centre round which the unity of the nation was already beginning to form.

The first act of the young King's reign was a sad one. Glad to taste the pleasures of power, and urged to it by his clergy, Philip marked the opening of his career by a violent attack on the Jews, whom his weaker and more humane father had spared. They were all banished the realm in 1182. Other like acts followed. An edict was issued which punished profane swearing with death; the Paterins also, an obscure sect, who "ventured to attempt a reform of morals as well as of dogma," were hunted down and burnt, "passing"—so ran the formula—"from the short temporal flames to the eternal flames that awaited them."

Even in his father's life-time, Philip had shown his kinsfolk that he could and would act for himself. Alice the Queen and her four brothers had formed a sort of council, in whose hands the old King left the care of all things. But Philip had gone to Philip of Alsace, Count of Flanders, and, without asking leave of any one, had married Isabella of Hainault, his niece, by which step he allied himself with the older dynasty. No sooner was the old king gone than almost all the great vassals, including the Count of Flanders, himself, attacked the youthful king. But he was helped by Henry Courtmantel, son of Henry of England, and held his own, till winter brought rest. Henry of England then interfered in hopes of peace. Philip, in right of his wife, claimed the succession of her mother Elizabeth of Vermandois, who had just died; he was persuaded to content himself with Amiens and some lesser concessions. Amiens had been held as fief under its bishop; and when that churchman claimed homage from Philip Augustus, the proud boy answered haughtily that he, as King, "neither could nor ought to pay homage to any man":—and claimed for monarchy a lofty superiority over feudalism.

Yet did he not disdain the aid that feudalism brought him: he accepted the homage of Henry of England, and such help as that great vassal, well-nigh worn out with war and the turbulence of his sons, could give. These four sons of his, Henry Courtmantel, Richard Coeur de Lion, Geoffrey, and John, had done all they could to destroy their father's power and happiness; and in the end they succeeded in ruining their own fortunes. They kept up great state and court, with many followers; but having neither money nor estates with which to reward these hangers-on, they were tempted, even against their own true interests, to struggle for whatever they could get. Thanks to this, the French monarchy was enabled to rise above all its dangers. Henry Courtmantel died; so also Geoffrey, leaving a posthumous son, Arthur, whose name recalled to the Bretons their great hero, and towards whom they seemed to be drawn by all the force of their romantic and imaginative nature.

Philip now embarked in a series of wars. First, in 1185, he waged successful warfare against his old friend, the Count of Flanders; successful so far that the Count, although he had on the whole the best of the fighting, ceded to the King the county of Vermandois, and confirmed him in possession of Amiens. Success tempted the young King to go on; he was no sooner clear of the Flemish count than he fell on Hugh III, Duke of Burgundy (A. D. 1185–1186). Hugh appealed to Frederick Barbarossa, whose vassal he was for part of his lands; but as the Duchy of Burgundy was no part of the ancient Kingdom of Burgundy, nor was held under the Empire, Frederick refused to interfere on another man's ground. Philip relieved Vergy, besieged by the duke, and encouraged the Burgundian bishops to carry their grievances before him, raising the remarkable plea that all churches held direct from the Crown, even though they were within the borders of the greatest fiefs. He then took Châtillon-on-Seine, and was moving forwards when Hugh met him with submission. The young king exacted severe conditions, to which the great vassal submitted; then, with a prudence remarkable for his years, and possibly with some of the generosity of youth, he remitted them all. He was content to have shown his power, and not less content to secure the friendship of so strong a neighbour:

he also foresaw a still harder task before him, and desired to make his eastern frontier quiet and secure.

And now began the many restless years which lay between the French King and the attainment of his great desire, the subjection of Normandy. In 1186 we have the first of a long series of discussions under the "Elm of Conferences" between Trie and Gisors: all went peacefully awhile; but things were in such a state that pretexts for war were never wanting. Richard Coeur de Lion had attacked Raymond V of Toulouse, who called for help on the French King as his lord—a great change from the older attitude of the southern states. Next Philip claimed the restitution of Gisors and the Vexin, which had passed to the other side when Margaret married Henry Courtmantel. When he died and she married again, the French King, with no small show of justice, claimed them as having lapsed to him by her second marriage. There was a third dispute as to the lordship over Brittany, where the duke, Geoffrey Plantagenet, was dead; as his widow gave birth to a boy, Arthur, this point was thereby settled for a while. Lastly, Philip pushed on the marriage of his sister Alix to Richard, who was still at variance with Henry: he seemed eager for open war with the veteran of England. But conference followed conference under the ancient elm, truce followed truce: for the old King could not trust his sons or his followers, nor did Philip feel quite sure as to the fidelity of his comrades. War however at last began. Philip attacked Aquitaine, which was under Richard's care; the impetuous prince was false to his father, and seemed likely to go over to his enemy. Then Henry made peace for two years, on terms favourable to Philip; and Richard hastened into the French King's camp, where he became so friendly with him that they drank of the same cup, lodged in the same tent, even slept in the same bed.

And now came terrible news from the East. The Christians had grown even weaker; till at last, in 1187, Saladin met them in the Tiberiad, and defeated them utterly after a two days' battle. The true cross, Guy of Lusignan, the titular Prince of Antioch, the Grand Masters of the Temple and of St. John, all fell into the victor's hands. He swept on over the powerless land, and Jerusalem lay prostrate before him: nothing was left to the Christians save Tyre, Antioch, and Tripoli. When these sore tidings reached the West, all men stood still and held their breath. The Pope, Urban III, died of grief: war, pillage, debauchery, crime, suddenly ceased: "Verily we are guilty by reason of our brother," was the thought in every heart; and the danger was brought home to all minds by the descent of a vast host of Arabs on the Spanish coast. The voices of the new Pope, Clement III, and of William, Archbishop of Tyre, broke the silence; the Kings of France and England once more met at Gisors; they embraced and took the cross.

Richard joined them; as did a crowd of great princes and barons. The Emperor Frederick Barbarossa did the same.

Yet even then Philip and Henry could not be still. War began again in 1188; but now Henry's strength was gone. His barons deserted him, his sons betrayed him; he was compelled to make a shameful peace, to declare himself Philip's liegeman in full, to yield Berri, a Duchy lying south of the Loire below Orleans, and to promise pardon to all who had betrayed him. We are told that he asked to see the list of those whom he was thus compelled to pardon; and that when he saw the first name, the name of his favourite son John, for whom he had done and suffered so much, his heart broke; and with a bitter curse on all his children, he lay down and died.

Henceforth the power of the House of Anjou receded, and the lordship over France was assured to the house of Capet.

And now the great princes of Europe began to think seriously of their vow. The brave old Emperor, Frederick Barbarossa, took the land route; passed safely through the snares of Constantinople, and led his army unscathed over the worst part of the march; took Iconium, and was pushing on, when, in crossing some little river, he was by a trivial accident swept away and drowned. His Germans fell into despair; the Duke of Swabia, who took the command, brought only about five thousand men through to the camp under the walls of Ptolemais (Acre.)

[*A brief account of the Third Crusade and of rivalry and warfare between Philip and Richard follows.*]

When tidings of Richard's death came to Philip, he must have felt that the moment for which he had waited so long was come at last. Against the experience and sagacity of Henry II he had been able to do but little; though even from him he wrested something: and Richard's heroism and warlike ability had been at least a match for his cold and cautious antagonist. Now there remained of all the Plantagenets only young Arthur of Brittany, who might be more useful than dangerous, and John, the great King's last and feeblest son. According to the popular belief, the evil spirit that possessed him was the demon of cowardice and sloth, of luxury and self-indulgence; weakest and worst of all the race, he was destined to degrade himself before the French King, before his barons, before the Pope. Whatever he touched, he spoilt.

While England and Normandy at once declared for John, despising the Breton Arthur, Anjou, Maine, Poitou, Touraine, raised Arthur's banner, and, feeling themselves unable to stand alone, put themselves under Philip's protection. The wily King suggested that a fair division would be, the French provinces for Arthur, and England for John. But John was not prepared to accept England as his home; he was as little English as his brother. War broke out at once, Philip desiring nothing so much. In the name of Arthur he swept across Brittany, and every town he took he at once dismantled, to the dismay of Arthur's party. He soon felt that he could not secure his gains so long as he remained at variance with the Church; consequently, he made peace with John, retaining Evreux and some strong places in Berri, agreeing to marry his son, Louis, to John's niece, Blanche, and abandoning altogether the defenceless Arthur to his fate. Philip's quarrel with the Church was on the old lines, the old struggle as to matters of divorce and marriage. He had taken a great dislike to his bride, Ingeborg of Denmark, and had made obsequious bishops dissolve his marriage with her soon after the wedding-day. The poor young Dane, who knew no word of French, was told by signs that Philip had divorced her; and in her grief and anger she appealed to Rome. In the chair of the Pontiffs sat Innocent III, ever ready to interfere, only too glad when the passions of kings gave him so good a reason for interference. For Philip had not only sent Ingeborg away, but had taken to wife the beautiful Agnes of Meran, whose misfortunes form one of the romances of the age. The Pope at once threatened Philip with excommunication, and the kingdom with an Interdict; and, in 1200, this curse was laid on the unoffending people. It is true that it did not directly punish the offender; still, it reached him by oppressing his subjects; their discontent would be certain after a while to compel him to yield. Philip fought vigorously against this foreign interference: his pride and passion were alike engaged in the struggle. Still, he was too clear-sighted not to see that he must be the loser; and therefore, even after a council had been called at Soissons to judge the case, he did not stay for the sentence, but took again his Danish wife, and left the town. He treated her with no affection, and with the scantiest courtesy: still the Pope had won; Philip was restored to clerical favour, and the cloud gathering over his fortunes melted away. The time had not yet quite come when he could brave the imperious Pope; nor was his cause in itself sufficiently strong and good to enlist the hearts of his great vassals, the goodwill of his clergy, and to neutralise the distress arising to the people from the Interdict.

. . . .

Philip Augustus was endowed with a cold clear mind and a keen sense of his royal dignity, which easily discerned the great value of the law to him as an instrument for advancing his high pretensions. If it is true that the greatest men have a passion for justice, it is equally true that great kings are irresistibly attracted towards the law; and Philip with his delight in the newly revived Roman law may well be compared to Edward I, "the Justinian of England." In the Roman Law the royal claims found a sanction before which all society was willing to bow. Law and the lawyers became the strongest supporters of the monarchy, and stood it in good stead when it resisted the claims of Papal power; for the law was a double-edged sword, with which the King could smite both Pope and Feudalism. By the side of this great engine of government, the Civil Law, grew up an analogous ecclesiastical code, the Canon Law, which regulated the relations of churchmen among themselves, and ruled their dealings with the laity. As the Civil Law strengthened the claims of Kings, so did the Canon Law those of Popes. The struggle between them was sharp and lasted long.

At this same time Northern and Southern France alike, as well as Germany, teemed with noble growths of poetry. On the Frankish hills grew the epic: on the sunny slopes of the south flowered the lyrical poems of the troubadours. The Northern poets told of Arthur and Charlemagne: the old half-mystical tales grew into chivalric epics; and men, consciously or not, took them as motives and guides. It was not difficult in that young age of chivalry and of crusading adventure for men to feel that life was an acted epic. Philip Augustus himself yearned to raise his kingly state to the level of the Empire of Charles the Great.

And indeed we are coming to the heroic period of his reign, when the Norman campaigns brought out all the king's higher qualities, and gave him a high place in history.

In 1202 the luckless Arthur, who had placed his hands between those of Philip, swearing fealty for all his lands, and all his claims, fell after a disastrous battle into the hands of his uncle, King John, and was carried captive to Rouen tower.

And there he disappeared. How, no man knows to this day: but all men at that time agreed in suspecting that John, who was fully capable of such things, took the boy in a boat, stabbed him, and threw his dead body into the Seine. Murderer or not, John, like his father Henry in the case of Becket, had a far worse foe in the dead than the living prince had been. All Europe was aroused. The Bretons rose at once; the boy was their Arthur, faint shadow of their ancient hero, and they had hoped to become a great people under him. Philip arose as the avenger, with justice and interest alike calling him on, and helping his steps. Anjou and Brittany attacked the Norman frontier from the south: Philip entered Poitou, where all men rallied to his banner. John still lay at Rouen, and made no sign, spending his days either at table or in bed.

Philip soon saw that he could do better farther north, and made ready to reach the heart of John's power in Normandy.

The great fortress of Château Gaillard lay across his path; it must first fall before Rouen could be reached. . . .

[*The account of Philip's capture of this strategic fortress follows.*]

At last, on March 6, 1204, after a five months' siege, the great tower, the last defence, was given up into Philip's hands. It is said, and it illustrates the character of feudal warfare, that before the actual assault of the place only four English knights had been slain. There were but one hundred and eighty fighting men left in Château Gaillard when Philip entered in.

This one success decided all. The Norman towns knew that there was no help from John; and that if Château Gaillard could not withstand Philip, no other stronghold could do so. The rest of his march was a continual triumph. Falaise resisted, strong as it was, only seven days. Caen, Bayeux, Lisieux, threw open their gates. Guy de Thouars, Governor of Brittany, took Mont St. Michel and Avranches, and then joined Philip at Caen. Thence the French King moved on to Rouen. Even there, with a braver prince, resistance had been possible; for Rouen was strong, and hated the French. But what could be done for such a creature as King John? The city capitulated on honourable terms; and Normandy at last became a part of the kingdom of France. Brittany had already given herself up to the avenger of Arthur. For a while the Normans were restless under the stranger, as they deemed the French King. As however Philip was as wise in peace as he was skilful in war, Normandy before long became thoroughly reconciled to her new lord.

Poitou, Touraine, and Anjou fell at the conqueror's feet. Thouars and Niort held out for John; Rochelle on the coast alone gave him entry into France.

The campaign of 1203, 1204, was of vast use to the royal power. The King with one hand held the Normans down, while with the other he pushed back the haughty and menacing Pope. All the country folk, wherever he passed, declared for him; he rose far above all rivalry, and made the kingdom of France real in the eyes of men. Not content with these material gains, he summoned King John to undergo the judgment of his peers, on the charge of carrying off Isabella, the betrothed of Hugh de la Marche. But the "King of England" could not permit the "Duke of Normandy" to appear: John was willing to retain his substantial advantages where he was King, and to let judgment go by default where he was vassal. So his continental possessions were confiscated for his disobedience to his suzerain's summons, and King Philip was able to give his conquests the appearance of legal right. Though it is not known what peers met to give this judgment, from this time the "twelve Peers of France" seem to emerge more clearly out of the mists of time. Probably those sturdy chieftains, who, like Eudes of Burgundy, promised under their hand and seal to stand by the King against the terrors of a Papal war, formed the Court of Peers. They were certain, when they had given such a proof of confidence and devotion, to take care that Philip's interests suffered no harm. Faithful to the strong feeling, which has been already noticed, that the French Court was the rightful successor of that of Charles the Great, the number twelve had been chosen; six laymen, six ecclesiastics: the great vassals of the realm were thus grouped round the royal power, and lent it fresh dignity, while it also gave a sanction of right and justice to its acts.

. . . .

As we have drawn out the story of his reign we have noted the chief characteristics of his mind: his coolness and patience; no eager ambition or restlessness, but an aim taken with a steady hand and a farseeing eye. His ruling quality was pride, a noble pride in being King; and a firmness and dignity in asserting and fulfilling his ideal of the kingly place. With him coolness was also coldness; he was at no time a genial or friendly man. And with coldness went not unnaturally a want of generosity of character, which sometimes descended into trickiness, cunning, or deceit, as when he tried to get Pope Celestin to release him from his promise to King Richard, or when he tempted away from the old King Henry II his undutiful sons. Such a man could well conceal his feelings, nurture secret anger, wait, dissembling fairly, for occasions of requital, if not of revenge. He was a great captain rather than a gallant soldier. His nature was far from being cowardly, and he knew that a King's armour was good and sound; but he had none of that heat of courage which in those days made heroes, and which burnt so high in King Richard. He was eminent as an engineer in war: his skill conduced greatly to the capture of Château Gaillard; he laboured strenuously to strengthen the fortifications of his chief cities. In general he was fair-minded, and kinglike in his respect for justice. It was noticed of him that he gave full compensation to those whose houses he destroyed when he fortified Paris; a stretch of just dealing hardly credible in those days. His political sagacity was perhaps the most remarkable quality in his character He succeeded, even in very critical times, in keeping the greater lords faithful to his crown. He divided the Royal Domain into bailliages and prévotés, and on leaving France for the Crusade, commanded the Regents to hold four assizes of the Royal Court every year. He is thus the founder of the administrative system, whereby the French kings collected their taxes, mustered their armies, and administered justice in the provinces; for the baillies and provosts were tax collectors, army officials, and judges in one. He is thus too the first to provide for regular sessions of the Royal Court. He took pleasure in and presided over their assemblies; he began the shadowy greatness of the Court of Peers; he passed successfully through the great peril of several trials of strength with the Pope, yielding where no political question was involved, as in the case of Ingeborg, but standing firm, defiantly firm, when the royal prerogative was attacked. The greatest Pope of the century gave way before him. He checked the pretensions of the spiritual tribunals, marking out clearly the relations of the barons and the Church; and he braved the threat of an interdict firmly and successfully, when he felt it his duty to coerce the Bishops of Orleans and Auxerre, who were minded to be contumacious before the royal power; he succeeded in making feudal privilege and power spring largely from himself. He saw the importance of his cities, and encouraged their growth and independence, as we have seen at the battle of Bouvines. Paris, his capital, he especially cherished; paved her chief streets, which up to that time had been common sewers, muddy, ill-smelling, and pestilential; he new-walled the town, giving it more room to grow, had good houses built, and set up excellent markets.

Whether himself learned or not, he was fully aware of the uses of learning; he encouraged and expanded the University of Paris; he loved the literature of his day; its romances of Alexander, and Arthur, and "Kallemain."

Religion of a kind was an element in his character: a religion that had no weakness in it. His cold nature allowed him to favour persecutions: they were not distasteful to him, and they kept Rome in good humour. Innocent was not likely to push a strong man hard, when that strong man was also vigorous in repressing Jew and heretic. On the other hand, Philip's religion, mixed up throughout with his own interests, never overbore his cool judgment, or led him to pay deference to the Church, if she encroached on his prerogative.

In sum, the King's character, though it falls far short of greatness, and though very deficient in those qualities which ensure our goodwill and affection, was in a remarkable degree fitted for the work he set before him,—the work of building up, stone by stone, the great edifice of Monarchy.

71. ST. LOUIS[1]

Joinville was a French chronicler, born about the year 1225. In 1248 he accompanied King Louis IX (St. Louis) of France, and returned to France in the year 1254. He wrote a chronicle about the career of the monarch whom he nobly served and whom he knew intimately. The title of this chronicle is usually translated as Memoirs, *or* St. Louis, King of France. *It was completed in the year 1309, when the author was about eighty-five years old, and it covers events that occurred mostly about fifty years before the time of writing. The conversations reported by him are therefore not absolutely accurate, and some of the minor details may need a slight correction, but Joinville speaks as an eye-witness and writes with an air of authority and remarkable ability, so that*

[1] The Sire de Joinville, *Saint Louis, King of France.* Translated by James Hutton. New York, Scribner, Welford, and Co., 1869, pp. 3–8; 10–11; 199–200; 203–204; 206.

we owe much to him. Particularly valuable is the description he gives of the French king and of his rule.

In the name of Almighty God, I, John, Sire de Joinville, Seneschal of Champagne, cause to be written the life of our sainted Louis, what I saw and heard for the space of six years that I was in his company in the pilgrimage over the sea, and since we returned from it. And before I recount to you his great exploits and feats of arms, I will tell you what I saw and heard of his holy words and sage teachings, that they may be found in their order for the edification of those who shall hear them. This holy man loved God with all his heart, and imitated His works; which appeared in this that, as God died for the love He had for His people, he also several times perilled his life for the love he had for his people, when he could have done otherwise had he wished, as you will hear by-and-bye. The love he had for his people was shown in what he said to his eldest son during a sore sickness which he had at Fontainebleau.

"Fair son," said he, "I pray you make yourself beloved by the people of your kingdom; for, truly, I would rather that a Scotsman should come from Scotland and govern the people justly and loyally, than that you should govern badly in the sight of all."

The saint loved truth to such a degree, that even with the Saracens he would not draw back from what he had promised them, as you will bear by-and-bye. As to his palate, he was so indifferent, that never in my life did I hear him ask for any particular dish, as many rich men do, but he ate contentedly of what his cooks served up to him. He was measured in his speech, for never in my life did I hear him speak ill of any one, nor did I ever hear him name the devil, a name widely spread through the realm, which cannot, I think, be pleasing to God. He diluted his wine by measure, according as he saw the wine would bear it. He asked me in Cyprus why I put no water into my wine; and I answered him the reason was because the physicians had told me that I had a large head and a cold stomach, and therefore need not fear becoming intoxicated. He replied that they deceived me, for if I did not learn in my youth to dilute my wine, and wished to do it in my old age, I should be attacked with gout and pains of the stomach, so that I should never have health; and if in my old age I drank wine by itself, I should become intoxicated every evening, and it was a sorry thing for a man of worth to get drunk.

He asked me if I wished to be honoured in this world and enter Paradise through death. I answered, yes; and he said to me, "Keep yourself, then, from doing or saying anything wittingly which if all the world knew you could not avow it, and say, 'I did this, I said that.'"

He told me to refrain from contradicting or gainsaying anything that was said in my presence, provided there would be no sin or hurt in my remaining silent, because hard words engender strifes which have cost the lives of thousands.

He used to say that a man ought so to dress and equip his person, that the greybeards of the day should not be able to say that it was overdone, nor the young men, that there was something wanting. This was recalled to my mind by the father of the king who now reigns, in alluding to the embroidered coats-of-arms which are fashioned nowadays. I made answer to him that never, in the voyage over the sea I made, did I see embroidered coats-of-arms, either on the king, or on anyone else. And he told me that he had coats embroidered with his arms which had cost him 800 livres parisis. I replied that he would have made a better use of them had he bestowed them for the love of God, and had made his coats of good taffety (*cendal*), ornamented with his arms, as his father used to do.

The sainted king was at Corbeil one Whitsuntide, with eighty knights in his company. After dinner the king went down into the meadow below the chapel, and spoke at the gateway to the Count of Brittany, the father of the present duke, whom God preserve! Master Robert de Sorbon came in quest of me, and taking hold of the end of my mantle, led me to the king, and all the other knights came after us.

Then I asked Master Robert, "Master Robert, what do you want with me?"

And he said to me, "If the king were to sit down in this meadow, and you were to seat yourself on a bench above him, I wish to ask you if you would be worthy of blame?"

I answered him, yes.

He continued: "Then You do a thing much to be blamed, seeing that you are more magnificently dressed than the king; for you attire yourself in furs of different colours and in green cloth, which the king does not do."

I made him answer: "Master Robert, with your permission, I do nothing to be blamed if I clothe myself in furs of different colours and in green cloth, for it is the dress left me by my father and my mother. On the contrary, it is you who are to blame, for you are the son of a *villain* father and a *villain* mother, and you have abandoned the dress of your father and your mother, and clothe yourself in richer camlet than the king." Then I took the flap of his surcoat and that of the king's surcoat, and said, "See, now, if I speak the truth."

Whereupon the king undertook, with all his might, to defend Master Robert.

Some short time afterwards, my lord the king summoned Monseigneur Philip, the father of the present king, and King Thibaud, and sat down at the door of his oratory, and, placing his hand on the ground, said:

"Sit down here, quite close to me, so that no one may hear us."

"Ah, sire," replied they, "we dare not sit so close to you."

Then he said to me, "Seneschal, sit down here."

I did so, and so close to him that my robe touched his. And he made them sit down next to me, and said to them:

"You did very wrong, you my sons, in not doing at once what I commanded you; take care that does not happen again."

And they said they would never again do so.

Then he said to me that he had called us to him that he might confess to me that he was wrong in defending Master Robert against me.

"But," he added, "I saw he was so taken aback, that he much needed help from me. For all that, do not you regard what I may have said in defence of Master Robert; for, as the seneschal asserted, you ought to dress well and becomingly, because your wives will love you the more, and your people will value you the more. For, as the sage remarks, we ought so to adorn ourselves in apparel and armour that the greybeards of this age shall not be able to say that we have done too much, nor the young men of this age that we have not done enough."

He told me that Bishop William of Paris had related to him how that a great master in theology once came to him and said that he wished to speak to him. The bishop replied:

"Master, say whatever you wish to say." And when the master was about to speak to the bishop, he began to weep very bitterly; so the bishop said to him: "Master, speak. Do not be down-hearted, for no one can sin so much that God cannot forgive yet more."

"I tell you, sir," said the master, "that I cannot but weep; for I look upon myself as an infidel, because I cannot bring my heart to believe in the sacrament of the altar, as it is taught by the holy Church; and yet I know right well that it is one of the temptations of the enemy."

"Master," said the bishop, "tell me, when the enemy sends you this temptation, is it pleasing to you?"

To which the master made answer:

"Sir, on the contrary, it annoys me as much as anything can annoy me."

"Now, I ask you," continued the bishop, "would you accept gold or silver on condition that you should utter with your lips something against the sacrament of the altar, or against the other holy sacraments of the Church?"

"I, sir!" exclaimed the master. "Know that there is nothing in the world that I would accept on that condition. I would rather that they tore all my limbs out of my body than say anything of the kind."

"I will now say something else to you," the bishop observed. "You are aware that the King of France is at war with the King of England; and you are also aware that the castle which is nearest to the frontier between the two is La Rochelle, in Poitou. Now, then. I therefore ask you one question: if the king of France entrusted you with the custody of the La Rochelle, which is on the frontier, and had consigned to me the keeping of the castle of Laon, which is in the heart of France, and in a land at peace, to whom ought the king to be most grateful at the end of his war—to you, who had guarded La Rochelle without losing it, or to me, who had guarded Laon?"

"In heaven's name, sir," cried the master, "it would be to me, who had guarded La Rochelle without losing it."

"Master," resumed the bishop, "I tell you that my heart is like the castle of Laon, for I have no temptation or doubt touching the sacrament of the altar. Wherefore I say to you that for once God is pleased with me because I believe steadfastly and in peace, He is pleased four times with you, because you keep your heart for Him in the war of tribulation, and have such good-will towards him that for no earthly good, nor for any hurt that could be done to your body, would you forsake Him. I tell you, therefore, to be quite at your ease, for that your state under these circumstances is more pleasing to our Lord than my own."

When the master heard that, he knelt down before the bishop, and was well content.

. . . .

The king governed his land rightly and loyally, and according to God, as you will learn hereafter. He had his work regulated in such a manner, that Monseigneur de Nesle, and the good Count de Soissons, and the rest of us who were about his person, after attending mass, went to hear the pleadings at the gateway, now called the Court of Requests; and when he returned from church he sent for us, and seating himself at the foot of his bed, he made us sit down around him, and asked us if there were any cases to dispose of which could not be disposed of without him. We mentioned such to him and he commanded that they should be brought before him, and asked them: "Why do you not take what my people offer you?" And they would say: "Sire, it is because they offer too little." Then he would answer them: "You would do well to take what they wish you to take." Thus the holy man exerted himself with all his might to put them in the path of justice and reason.

Many a time it happened that in summer time he would go and sit down in the wood at Vincennes, with his back to an oak, and make us take our seats around him. And all those who had complaints to make came to him without hindrance from ushers or other folk. Then he asked them with his own lips: "Is there any one here who has a cause?" Those who had a cause stood up, when he would say to them: "Silence all, and you shall be dispatched one after the other." Then he would call Monseigneur de Fontaines or Monseigneur Geoffrey de Villette, and would say to one of them: "Dispose of this case for me." When he saw anything to amend in the words of those who spoke for others, he would correct it with his own lips. Sometimes in summer I have seen him, in order to administer justice to the people, come into the garden of Paris dressed in a camlet coat, a surcoat of woollen stuff (*tyreteinnes*) without sleeves, a mantle of black taffety (*cendal*) round his neck, his hair well combed and without coif, a hat with white peacock's feathers on his head. Carpets were spread for us to sit down upon around him, and all the people who had business to dispatch stood about in front of him. Then he would have it dispatched in the same manner as I have already described in the wood of Vincennes.

The king's loyalty was shown in the affair of Monseigneur de Trie, who brought to the holy man a charter which affirmed that the king had conferred upon the heirs of the Countess of Boulogne, the last who died, the county of Dammartin, in Gouelle. The seal of the charter was broken, so that there only remained one half of the legs of the king's figure on the seal, and the stool on which his feet rested. He showed it to all of us who were of his council, and said that we must help him with our advice. We all of us answered, without anyone dissenting, that he was in no way bound to execute the charter. Then he told John Sarrazin, his chamberlain, to hand him the letter which he had asked of him. And when he had got the letter he said to us: "Sirs, this is the seal which I used before I went across the sea, and you may see clearly from this that the impression on the broken seal is similar to the seal that is entire. Therefore, I dare not with a clear conscience hold back the said county." Then he called for Monseigneur de Trie, and said to him, "I make over the county to you."

. . . .

I will speak to you now of his wisdom. Upon one occasion it was declared that there was no one in his council as wise as himself. And it appeared in this that of himself, without consulting anyone, and off-hand, as I have heard, he replied to all the prelates of France, touching a request they made to him to this effect:

Bishop Guy, of Auxerre, spoke to him in the name of all. "Sire," said he, "these archbishops and bishops who are here have commissioned me to tell you that Christianity is decaying and perishing in your hands, and that it will decay still further if you do not see to it, because no one now-a-days has any fear of an excommunication. We require of you, therefore, sire, that you command your bailiffs and sergeants that they constrain those who have been excommunicated for a year and a day to render satisfaction to the Church." And the king replied to them of himself, without consultation, that he would be quite willing to command his bailiffs and sergeants to constrain the excommunicated, as they requested of him, provided they would give him cognizance of the sentence, to decide if it were just or not. Then they consulted together, and answered the king that they would not give him cognizance of what belonged to the ecclesiastical court. The king thereupon replied in turn that he would not give them cognizance of what belonged to himself, nor would he command his sergeants to constrain the excommunicated to seek absolution, whether they were in the right or in the wrong. "For, if I did so, I should act contrary to God's will and justice. And I will give you, as an example, the Count of Brittany, whom the Bishops of Brittany kept for seven years under excommunication, when he obtained absolution from the court of Rome, and had I constrained him at the end of one year, I should have done so wrongfully."

. . . .

No man in the world ever worked harder to make peace between his subjects, especially between powerful neighbors and the princes of the realm, for example, between the Count of Châlons, uncle of the Seigneur de Joinville, and his son, the Count of Burgundy, who were at war with one another when we returned from beyond sea. To make peace between father and son, he sent his own counsellors into Burgundy, and at his own charges, and through his intervention peace was concluded between father and son. At a later period there was great contest between King Thibaud of Champagne, second of that name, and Count John of Châlons and the Count of Burgundy, his son, for the Abbey of Luxeuil. To allay this strife Monseigneur the King dispatched Monseigneur Gewaise d' Escraines, who was at that time mastercook of France, and by his means he reconciled them.

. . . .

The king was such a bountiful almoner that wherever he went through his kingdom, he made donations to poor churches, lazaretti, townhalls, hospitals, and men and women of gentle blood reduced to poverty. Every day he fed a multitude of poor people, without reckoning those who dined in his chamber; and many a time I have seen him cut bread for them and pour them out drink.

72. THE ORIGIN AND DEVELOPMENT OF THE ENGLISH PARLIAMENT[1]

The origin and early development of the English parliament seemed not so very different for a time from the history of similar bodies on the Continent, nor did it appear to have more than national significance. Afterward, however, particularly in the nineteenth century, the English parliament assumed an importance far beyond the promise it gave in the Middle Ages. This is one of the reasons why a rather lengthy discussion, such as the one that follows here, may be of use to students of general European history.

The word "parliament" originally meant a talk. In its Latin form it is applied by monastic statutes of the thirteenth century to the talk held by monks in their cloisters after dinner, talk which the statutes condemn as unedifying. A little later on the term was used to describe solemn conferences such as that held in 1245 between Louis IX of France and Pope Innocent IV. When our Henry III summoned a council or conference of great men to discuss grievances he was said by a contemporary chronicler to hold a parliament. The word struck root in England, and was soon applied regularly to the national assemblies which were summoned from time to time by Henry's great successor, Edward I, and which took something like definite shape in what was afterwards called the "model parliament" of 1295. The word, as we have seen, signified at first the talk itself, the conference held, not the persons holding it. By degrees it was transferred to the body of persons assembled for conference, just as the word "conference" itself has a double meaning. When Edward I was holding his parliaments institutions of the same kind were growing up in France. But the body which in France bore the same name as the English parliament had a different history and a different fate. The French "parlement" became a judicial institution, though it claimed to have a share in the making of laws.

The history of the English parliament may be roughly divided into four great periods: the period of the mediæval parliaments, of which the parliament of 1295 became the model and type; the period of the Tudors and Stuarts, having for its central portion the time of conflict between king and parliament, between prerogative and privilege; the period between the Revolution of 1688 and the Reform Act of 1832; and the modern period which began in 1832.

[1] Sir Courtenay Ilbert, *Parliament: Its History, Constitution and Practice.* London, Williams and Norgate, New York, Henry Holt, 1917, pp. 7–25. Used by permission of Henry Holt and Company, publishers.

Let us try and trace, in broad outline, the elements out of which the parliament of 1295 grew up, and the main stages through which its development passed.

It had always been regarded in England as a principle that in grave and important matters, such as the making of laws, the king ought not to act without counsel and consent. The counsel and consent which the Saxon kings sought was that of their wise men, and the "Witenagemot" of English constitutional history was a meeting of these wise men. It seems, says Maitland, to have been a very unstable and indefinite body. It was an assembly of the great folk. When there was a strong king it was much in his power to say how the assembly should be constituted and whom he would summon. When the king was weak the assembly was apt to be anarchical. The Saxon witenagemot was not numerous. Small men, especially if they lived at a distance, could not come. Great men often would not come. The institution was not much of a safeguard against oppression. Still it was an important fact that, on the eve of the Norman conquest, no English king had taken on himself to legislate or tax without the counsel and consent of a national assembly, an assembly of the wise, that is, of the great.

The Norman conquest made a great break in English institutions, but not so great as was at one time supposed. In the first place William the Conqueror had to build with English materials and on English foundations. In the next place English institutions had, during the reign of Edward the Confessor, been rapidly approximating to the continental type. What William did was to emphasize, rather than to introduce, certain principles of what was afterwards vaguely described as the "feudal system," and to adapt them to his own purposes. He insisted on the principle that all land in the country was ultimately held of the king. There were to be no full owners of land under him, only holders or tenants. He insisted on the principle that every landholder in the country owed direct allegiance to the king. The landholder might hold his land under, and owe allegiance to, another lord, but his oath of allegiance to that lord was qualified by his allegiance to the king. And, in portioning out the English soil among the motley band of adventurers who had followed him and whom he had to reward for their share in his raid, he tried to break the strength of the greater men by scattering their estates over different parts of England, and by mixing up with them smaller men, who held their land, not under any intermediate lord, but directly under the king. He did not wholly succeed, as he and those after him found to their cost. But the existence, by the side of the greater lords, of a number of comparatively small landholders, who also held their land directly from the king, had an important bearing on the development of parliament. The Norman kings were despots, untrammelled by any constitutional restrictions, and controlled only by the resistance of powerful and turbulent subjects. But there were the traditions of better things past; there were the charters, often broken but always there, by the help of which kings with doubtful titles obtained succession, and in which they promised to observe those traditions; and there was a feeling that, apart from these promises, it was prudent and politic to obtain an expression of counsel and consent, if it could be obtained. "Thrice a year," says the Saxon chronicle of the Conqueror, "King William wore his crown every year he was in England; at Easter he wore it at Winchester, at Pentecost at Westminster, and at Christmas at Gloucester; and at these times all the men of England were with him—archbishops, bishops and abbots, earls, thegns and knights." "All the men of England." What did this mean? To the Saxon chronicler it probably meant the men who counted, the wise and great, the men who might have been expected to attend a witenagemot. But William's court was a feudal court, and from the Norman point of view perhaps it was an assembly of the king's tenants in chief. These, however, were numerous, and many of them were small men, so that probably only a select few were summoned. Courts or great councils of the same kind were held under the later Norman kings, but we know little about their composition or functions. All that can be said with safety is that the few legislative acts of this period were done with the counsel and consent of the great men.

What we have to watch is the transformation of the body whose counsel and consent is required from a merely feudal body, a body of great vassals or tenants in chief, to a body more representative of the nation at large.

Henry II did something when he imposed a tax on movables, the Saladin tithe of 1188, and had it assessed by a jury of neighbours, a jury in some sense representative of the taxpayer and of the parish in which he lived, and thus brought into connection the ideas of taxation and representation.

The Great Charter of 1215 declared that exceptional feudal aids were not to be levied without the common counsel of the realm. But this counsel was to be given by an assembly consisting of prelates and great lords summoned singly, and of tenants in chief summoned collectively through the sheriffs. So it was still a feudal assembly.

A further step was taken when, in 1254, at a time when Henry III was in great need of money, each sheriff was required to send four knights from his county to consider what aid they would give the king in his great necessity. For these knights represented, not the tenants in chief, but all the free men of their county. They were representatives of counties.

Eleven years later, in 1265, Simon de Montfort summoned to his famous parliament representatives, not merely of counties, but also of cities and boroughs.

Edward I held several great assemblies, which were usually called parliaments, and which made some great laws, but some of these laws were made without the assent of representatives of the commons.

The model parliament, which settled the general type for all future times, was held in 1295. To this parliament King Edward summoned separately the two archbishops, all the bishops, the greater abbots, seven earls and forty-one barons. The archbishops and bishops were directed to bring the heads of their cathedral chapters, their archdeacons, one proctor for the clergy of each cathedral, and two proctors for the clergy of each diocese. Every sheriff was directed to cause two knights of each shire, two citizens of each city, and two burgesses of each borough, to be elected.

Two points should be specially noticed about the constitution of this parliament.

In the first place it was not a feudal court, nor a meeting of the king's tenants, but a national assembly. Edward had suffered much in his father's time from the great barons, who had made him prisoner at the battle of Lewes, and he wished to draw counsel and help from other quarters. His parliament was intended to represent the three great estates or classes into which medieval society might be roughly divided, the clergy, the barons, and the commons; those who pray, those who fight and those who work, as Maitland puts it. The same idea underlay the States General which were coming into existence about the same time in France, and which met, at intervals, during many centuries. After an interval of 175 years the three estates of France were for the last time summoned to meet as separate bodies in 1789, but were at once merged in the national assembly which began the French Revolution.

The idea of the three estates was never realized in England. The clause by which archbishops and bishops were directed to bring with them representatives of their clergy, a clause still remaining in the writ by which they are summoned at the present day, was persistently ignored. The clergy as a body preferred to stand aloof, to meet in their own clerical assemblies or convocations, and to settle there what contribution they would make to the king's needs. The archbishops, bishops and greater abbots attended, as they had attended the great councils of previous kings. But then they were not merely clerics, they were great feudal lords and great holders of land.

The knights of the shires were drawn from the same class as the greater barons. The word "baron" originally meant simply "man," and for some time there was much uncertainty as to who should be treated as a man so great as to be entitled to a separate summons, and who should be left to be represented, like other freemen of the lesser sort, by the knights of the shires. The title of baron came eventually to be confined to the greater men who were summoned separately. The knights who represented the shires, when they came to Westminster, mingled themselves with the representatives of the cities and boroughs. In the time of Edward III there was a risk of the merchants being consulted as a separate class for the purpose of taxation, but this risk was avoided. If things had fallen out somewhat differently the English parliament might have sat as three separate houses, as in France, or might have been grouped in a single house, as in Scotland, or might have formed four houses, as in Sweden. But the inferior clergy abstained from attendance, the greater clergy, the spiritual lords, sat with the lay or temporal lords, and the knights of the shires threw in their lot with the citizens and burgesses. Thus parliament became an assembly, not of three estates, but of two houses, the house consisting of the lords spiritual and temporal, and the house representing the commons, the house of lords and the house of commons.

The other point to be noticed is that parliament was an expansion, for temporary purposes, of the king's continuous council. The Norman and Plantagenet kings, like other kings, needed continuous assistance, both for domestic and ceremonial purposes, and for the business of government, such as the administration of justice, and the collection and expenditure of revenue. The courts or councils composed of the men on whom the king most relied for this assistance bore various names, varied in number, and exercised varying functions. As the work of government increased and specialized, these nebulous bodies split up into more coherent parts, with more definite functions, and out of them grew the king's courts of justice and the great departments of the central government. When the king held his great assemblies it was necessary that he should have about him the men on whom he was accustomed to place special reliance for advice and assistance. Accordingly there was summoned by name to the parliament of 1295 men who were not earls or barons, but were members of the king's council, and in particular the king's judges. And to this day the judges of the supreme court are summoned to parliament, and some of them take their seats in the house of lords when the king opens parliament.

The fact that the mediæval parliament was an expansion of the king's council explains the nature of the business which it had to transact. The immediate cause of summoning a parliament was usually want of money. The king had incurred, or was about to incur, expenses which he could not meet out of his ordinary resources, such as the revenues of his domain and the usual feudal dues. He summoned a parliament and, through his chancellor or some other minister, explained what he wanted and why he wanted it. The king's speech might touch on other great matters about which he might need advice or approval, but money was the gist. On the other hand the king's subjects had grievances for which they desired redress. The grievances would be of different kinds, breach of old customs, failure to observe charters or laws, oppression by the king's officers or by great men, maladministration of justice, difficulties in the way of settling private disputes, and so forth. For the redress of these grievances petitions were presented, petitions which in their multifarious character were not unlike the statements of grievances presented to the national assembly on the eve of the French Revolution. The petitions were to the king in parliament or to the king in his council, and parliament was the petitioning body, the body by or through whom the petitions were presented. The remedies required would be classified in modern language as judicial, legislative or administrative. But in the thirteenth century these distinctions had not been clearly drawn. A statute made by Edward I in his parliament of 1292, known as the Statute of Waste, and based on a petition presented to him in that parliament, supplies a good illustration of the way in which judicial, legislative and administrative remedies might be combined. The statute begins with a long story showing how Gawin Butler brought a complaint before the king's justices about waste done to his land, but died before obtaining judgment; how his brother and heir, William, who was under age and a ward of the king, sought to continue the proceedings; and how the justices differed in opinion as to whether he was entitled to do so. Thereupon the king, in his full parliament, by his common council or by general consent (for the Latin phrase wavers between the two meanings of "council" and "counsel") ordains that all heirs may have an action by writ of waste for waste done in the time of their ancestors, and the king himself commands his justices to give judgment accordingly. Here the king acts partly in his legislative capacity, laying down a general rule, partly in his judicial capacity, as having power to review and control the proceedings of his justices, and partly in an administrative capacity as guardian of an infant heir.

At the beginning of each parliament the king, or his great council on his behalf, appointed persons to receive and to try these petitions, that is to say to sort them out, to consider what remedy, if any, each petition required, and to devise an appropriate form of remedy. The triers or auditors of petitions were really committees of the king's council. Until near the close of the nineteenth century receivers and triers of petitions from England, Scotland and Gascony respectively (for Edward I ruled in Gascony as well as England) were appointed at the beginning of each parliament by an entry in the lords journals. But their functions had ceased for many centuries.

The sittings of an early Plantagenet parliament did not extend over many days. Travelling was difficult, dangerous and costly; members could not afford to stay long away from their homes. The main object of the meeting was usually to strike a bargain between the king and his subjects. The king wanted a grant of money, and it was made a condition of the grant that certain grievances, about which petitions had been presented, should be redressed. When an agreement had been arrived at as to how much money should be granted and on what terms, the commoners and most of the lords went their ways, leaving the king's advisers, the members of his council, to devise and work out, by means of legislation or otherwise, such remedies as might be considered appropriate and advisable.

It is to the Plantagenet period that we owe the most picturesque of our parliamentary ceremonials, those which attend the opening of parliament and the signification of the royal assent to Acts. And we ought to think of the Plantagenet parliament as something like an oriental durbar, such as was held by the late Amir of Afghanistan, with the king sitting on his throne, attended by his courtiers and great chiefs, hearing the complaints of his subjects and determining whether and how they should be met.

Of the changes in the composition of parliament which took place during this period something will be said later on, but a few words must be said here about the changes in its powers and functions, specially with respect to the two main branches of its business, taxation and legislation.

Before the end of the fourteenth century parliament had established two principles of taxation. In the first place they had taken away the power of the king to impose direct taxes without their consent, and had restricted his power to impose indirect taxes without their consent to such taxes as might be justified under the customs recognized by the Great Charter. In the second place parliament had acquired the right to impose taxes, direct and indirect, of all kinds. In imposing these taxes they did not care to go beyond the immediate needs of the case. Hence the necessity for frequent parliaments.

According to the theory of the three estates, each estate would tax itself separately, and this theory was at first observed. The clergy granted their subsidies, not in parliament, but in convocation, and continued to do so, in theory at least, until after the Restoration of 1660. But long before this time they had agreed to grant or submit to taxes corresponding to those imposed on the laity. At a much earlier date, before the end of the fourteenth century, the lords and commons, instead of making separate grants, agreed to join in a common grant. And, as the bulk of the burden fell upon the commons, they adopted a formula which placed the commons in the foreground. The grant was made by the commons, with the consent of the lords spiritual and temporal. This formula appeared in 1395, and became the rule. In 1407, eight years after Henry IV came to the throne, he assented to the important principle that money grants were to be initiated by the house of commons, were not to be reported to the king until both houses were agreed, and were to be reported by the Speaker of the commons house. This rule is strictly observed at the present day. When a money bill, such as the finance bill for the year or the appropriation bill, has been passed by the house of commons and agreed to by the house of lords it is, unlike all other bills, returned to the house of commons. On the day for signifying the royal assent the clerk of the house of commons takes it up to the bar of the house of lords, then hands it to the Speaker, who delivers it with his own hand to the officer charged with signifying the king's assent, the clerk of parliaments.

Ever since the reign of Henry VII the enacting formula of Acts of Parliament has run thus—

"Be it enacted by the king's (or queen's) most excellent majesty by and with the advice and consent of the lords spiritual and temporal, and commons, in this present parliament assembled, and by the authority of the same, as follows." This formula grew into shape in what has been called above the mediæval period of parliament. At the beginning of this period the king made laws with the requisite advice and consent. One important early Act was expressed to be made at the instance of the great men. Later on the concurrence of the whole parliament, including the commons, became essential. But the commons usually appear at first in a subordinate position. Throughout the fourteenth century the kind of form most usually adopted is that a statute is made with the assent of the earls, prelates and barons and at the request of the knights of the shires and commons in parliament assembled. The commons appear as petitioners for laws rather than as legislators. And this is in fact what they were. They presented their petitions, which might ask for amendment or clearer declaration of the law. It was for the king, with the aid of those more intimately in his counsels, to determine whether legislation was required and if so what form it should assume. Throughout the fourteenth century there was much risk that, even if the making of a law were granted, the law, when made, would not correspond to the petition on which it was based. The statute was not drawn up until after the parliament was dissolved, its form was settled by the king's council, and there were many complaints about the variance between petitions and statutes. At last in 1414, soon after the accession of Henry V, the king conceded the point for which the commons had repeatedly pressed. The commons prayed "that there never be no law made and engrossed as statute and law neither by additions nor discriminations by no manner of term or terms which should change the sentence and the intent asked." And the king in reply granted that from henceforth "nothing be enacted to the petition of the commons contrary to their asking, whereby they should be bound without their assent." This concession led to an important change in the method of framing statutes. It became the practice to send up to the king, not a petition, but a bill drawn in the form of a statute, so that the king was left no alternative beyond assent or dissent. Legislation by bill took the place of legislation on petition. This practice became settled about the end of the reign of Henry VI.

The changes in practice were reflected by changes in the legislative formula. Statutes were expressed to be made by the advice and consent of the lords and the commons, thus putting the two houses on an equal footing. And before the middle of the fifteenth century a significant addition was made to the formula. Statutes were expressed to be made, not only with the advice and consent of the lords and commons in parliament, but "by the authority of the same." This was an admission that the statute derived its authority from the whole parliament. The two houses had become not merely an advising, consenting, or petitioning body, but a legislative authority.

The power to refuse assent to legislation still remained, and it was often exercised until a much later date. It was signified in a courteous form— "The king will consider."

The political power of parliament grew rapidly in the fourteenth and fifteenth centuries. In 1327 a parliament which had been summoned in the name of Edward II resolved, in summary fashion, on his deposition and forced him to resign. But the proceedings on the deposition of Richard II were more formal. Richard was forced to summon a parliament, and then to execute a deed of resignation. The parliament assembled in Westminster Hall, which Richard had rebuilt, and which stood then much as it stands now. Parliament accepted his resignation and went on, by further resolutions, to declare that he was deposed and to resolve that Henry of Lancaster should be king in his place. A parliament which could thus make and unmake kings was a formidable body. The Lancastrian kings, it had been said, were kings by Act of Parliament; they meant to rule and did rule by means of parliament. In the quarrels of the seventeenth century between king and commons men looked back to the Lancastrian period as the golden age of parliament, and precedents from that period were freely quoted for parliamentary use. But in the fifteenth century the times were not ripe for parliamentary government. The powers of parliament fell into the hands of turbulent nobles. Henry V was a famous and capable warrior. But Henry VI began his reign as an infant, and ended it as an idiot; he was ruled by unscrupulous uncles and a termagant queen; and the bloody faction fights known as the Wars of the Roses brought the Plantagenet dynasty to a close, weeded out the older nobility, and cleared the way for a new form of monarchy.

73. *WRITS OF SUMMONS TO PARLIAMENT*[1]

Sept. 30—Oct. 3, 1295

The parliament convoked in 1295 by Edward I is commonly referred to as the model parliament, because it was the first parliament in which all the three estates were represented. Not only the members of the first estate (the clergy) and the second estate (the nobility), but also two knights from each county and two sheriffs from each city or borough were summoned to appear. The writs below are among those that were sent out to the respective members of the three estates.

Summons of the Clergy

The King to the venerable father in Christ Robert, by the same grace archbishop of Canterbury, primate of all England, greeting. As a most just law, established by the careful providence of sacred princes, exhorts and decrees that what affects all, by all should be approved, so also, very evidently should common danger be met by means provided in common. You know sufficiently well, and it is now, as we believe, divulged through all regions of the world, how the king of France fraudulently and craftily deprives us of our land of Gascony, by withholding it unjustly from us. Now, however, not satisfied with the before-mentioned fraud and injustice, having gathered together for the conquest of our kingdom a very great fleet, and an abounding multitude of warriors, with which he has made a hostile attack on our kingdom and the inhabitants of the same kingdom, he now proposes to destroy the English language altogether from the earth, if his power should correspond to the detestable proposition of the contemplated injustice, which God forbid. Because, therefore, darts seen beforehand do less injury, and your interest especially, as that of the rest of the citizens of the same realm, is concerned in this affair, we command you, strictly enjoining you in the fidelity and love in which you are bound to us, that on the Lord's day next after the feast of St. Martin, in the approaching winter, you be present in person at Westminster; citing beforehand [præmunientes] the dean and chapter of your church, the archdeacons and all the clergy of your diocese, causing the same dean and archdeacons in their own persons, and the said chapter by one suitable proctor, and the said clergy by two, to be present along with you, having full and sufficient power from the same chapter and clergy, to consider, ordain and provide,

[1] From G. B. Adams and H. M. Stephens, *Select Documents of English Constitutional History.* New York, Macmillan and Co., 1927, pp. 82–84. By permission of The Macmillan Company, publishers.

along with us and with the rest of the prelates and principal men and other inhabitants of our kingdom, how the dangers and threatened evils of this kind are to be met. Witness the king at Wangham, the thirtieth day of September.

Identical summonses were sent out to the two archbishops and eighteen bishops, and, with the omission of the last paragraph, to seventy abbots.

Summons of the Barons

The king to his beloved and faithful relative, Edmund, Earl of Cornwall, greeting. Because we wish to have a consultation and meeting with you and with the rest of the principal men of our kingdom, as to provision for remedies against the dangers which in these days are threatening our whole kingdom; we command you, strictly enjoining you in the fidelity and love in which you are bound to us, that on the Lord's day next after the feast of St. Martin, in the approaching winter, you be present in person at Westminster, for considering, ordaining and doing along with us and with the prelates, and the rest of the principal men and other inhabitants of our kingdom, as may be necessary for meeting dangers of this kind.

Witness the king at Canterbury, the first of October.

Similar summonses were sent to seven earls and forty-one barons.

Summonses of Representatives of the Counties and Boroughs

The king to the sheriff of Northamptonshire. Since we intend to have a consultation and meeting with the earls, barons and other principal men of our kingdom with regard to providing remedies against the dangers which are in these days threatening the same kingdom; and on that account have commanded them to be with us on the Lord's day next after the feast of St. Martin in the approaching winter, at Westminster, to consider, ordain, and do as may be necessary for the avoidance of these dangers; we strictly require you to cause two knights from the aforesaid county, two citizens from each city in the same county, and two burgesses from each borough, of those who are especially discreet and capable of laboring, to be elected without delay, and to cause them to come to us at the aforesaid time and place.

Moreover, the said knights are to have full and sufficient power for themselves and for the community of the aforesaid county, and the said citizens and burgesses for themselves and the communities of the aforesaid cities and boroughs separately, then and there for doing what shall then be ordained according to the common counsel in the premises; so that the aforesaid business shall not remain unfinished in any way for defect of this power. And you shall have there the names of the knights, citizens and burgesses and this writ.

Witness the king at Canterbury on the third day of October.

Identical summonses were sent to the sheriffs of each county.

74. *THE CAUSES OF THE HUNDRED YEARS' WAR IN FRENCH AND ENGLISH SCHOOL TEXTBOOKS* [1]

It is surprising how much disagreement there is among historians on the causes of war. Around the origins of the World War a great controversy has raged; around the origins of the Franco-Prussian War of 1870–1871 a smaller one. On the responsibilities for the American Civil War there is still wide difference of opinion. Even in regard to a struggle as remote as the Hundred Years' War between France and England historians, as the following selection shows, find it difficult to keep their sympathies in check.

For centuries England and France were intermittently engaged in deadly warfare. Does the story of that warfare in the French textbooks tend to develop a bias against England? This question can be answered in part by examining the textbook treatment of such great crises in that warfare as the Hundred Years' War, the Seven Years' War, the Napoleonic Wars. Thus, perchance, we can discover whether the ghost of past hatreds still haunts and disturbs present friendships.

The Hundred Years' War began in 1337, when Edward III of England claimed the throne of France, and lasted until 1453. The responsibility for causing it, the writers of the French textbooks place squarely on the shoulders of England and England's king: their general opinion is that it was brought on by Edward's ambition. According to one writer the English had never sincerely renounced those provinces which they had once controlled in France and which they had later been forced to give up to the French king, Philip Augustus. They simply sought an occasion for attack.

That occasion offered itself when Edward III claimed the French throne. The main line of French kings, the Capetian, had come to an end. Two relatives of the late king claimed the throne, Philip of Valois and Edward. Edward claimed succession through his mother. Certain of the textbook writers make the point that Edward was debarred by reason of the Salic law, which is supposed to have excluded women from succession to the

[1] Jonathan F. Scott, *The Menace of Nationalism in Education.* London, George Allen & Unwin, 1926, pp. 38–41; 161–164. Used by permission.

throne of France, as well as succession through the female line. An assembly of nobles and lawyers chose Philip, who then succeeded to the throne. "Edward the Third, furious at having been excluded from the throne, did not despair of seizing it by force." One textbook, very elementary, avoiding details, sums the whole matter up thus: "In the reign of Philip VI of Valois, the king of England, Edward III, resolved to conquer France, and began the Hundred Years' War."

On the whole the French point of view is fairly well justified. Professor A. L. Cross, who, being an American, starts with no nationalistic bias on the question of the Hundred Years' War, summarizing the results of impartial historical research, states that Edward's claim was a mere pretext. "The peers of France decided in favour of Philip, son of Charles of Valois." But Professor Cross also points out that Philip irritated the king of England by encroaching on the Duchy of Guyenne, a possession of the English ruler in France. Furthermore, Philip aided the Scots, at that time warring with the pugnacious Edward. These causes of conflict do not justify Edward's invasion; they simply make it appear less unjustifiable. And these mitigating circumstances the representative French school books, to which I have referred, fail to mention.

Furthermore, it is generally recognized by scholars that the Salic law did not in actuality exclude succession through the female line. The French nobles and lawyers naturally did not desire a foreign prince called in to rule over them. They pretended to find legal justification in this old law of the Salian Franks. Pagès, the author of a little historical text much used in French schools, frankly acknowledges this:

"Edward III, duke of Guyenne and king of England, was the nearest heir of Charles IV; his mother was a daughter of Philip the Fair. But the nobles, who preferred Philip VI, declared that women had no right to the throne. Later they called this new custom the Salic law, because they pretended to have found it among the old laws of one of the Frankish peoples, the Salian Franks."

The story of the Hundred Years' War in these books is such as to fire the imagination of the children who read it. The English invaders swarm into France, pillage the cottages, ravage the fields, massacre the peasants. French knights in armour yield to English bowmen at Crécy and Poitiers. The French hero, "Grand Ferré," is attacked on his death-bed by twelve English soldiers. "Brigands," shouts the giant, "you have come to take me while I am in bed, but even so you will not capture me," and jumping from his couch he seizes an axe, falls on the assassins, kills seven of them and puts the rest to flight. Then, falling back on his couch, he dies.

In spite of such exploits the French, disorganized, quarrelling among themselves, yield almost everywhere to the "cruel and insolent" invader.

But *in extremis* patriotism is born. Never before in French history had it definitely surmounted local feeling. Now hatred of the foreigner unites the people. The Maid of Orleans rallies the French, draws them together, and drives out the foreigner. But she herself is captured by the English and burned at the stake. As she dies, the English, ashamed and frightened at their crime, cry out: "We are lost. We have burned a saint."

Inevitably the narrative of the Hundred Years' War becomes to the French child something more than a romantic tale of knights in armour, bowmen and heroes, as it might appear, for example, to some American children, or a weary catalogue of events and dates as it might seem to others. It is part of his country's struggle for freedom; as such it excites his sympathies and develops his animosities. It is easy for a bias against England to bud.

. . . .

Regarding the causes of the Hundred Years' War, the usual interpretation of the English textbook writers is decidedly different from that of the French. The French writers emphasize the ambitions of Edward III of England, stressing his aggressive aims, pointing out that his claim to the French throne was a mere pretext for conquest. Of the aid that the French king was giving the Scots, who were at war with the English, of the encroachments of the French king on the English possessions in France, the authors of those French textbooks that I have examined say nothing.

Yet these latter are precisely the points that certain English writers of textbooks emphasize. Thus the author of a book in the series *Highroads of History* says: "The French kings cast longing eyes on the fair lands which still remained in the hands of the English, and constantly strove to win them back. They kept nibbling at the frontier, and by the time Edward III came to the throne they had seized a number of towns, which they refused to give up. This was the chief cause of the long struggle known in history as the Hundred Years' War." Professor Prothero gives four principal causes of the war: (1) The French encroachments on Gascony; (2) the alliance between France and Scotland, resulting in French aid to the Scots; (3) the desire of the English king to secure alliance with the Flemings, "who, being great weavers of cloth, were good customers of the English wool merchants"; and (4) the rivalry between England and France for the command of the Channel. "But," he concludes, "the independence of Flanders and the command of the Channel were only minor causes of the war. The chief reasons for it were Edward's desire to keep hold of Gascony and his wish to prevent the French from sending aid to the Scots."

There is, however, a certain amount of frank criticism of Edward and the English for their part in causing the war. While some writers make no comment on the question of the validity of Edward's claim to the French throne, others outspokenly call it a pretext. "As usual," says one writer, "most people believed exactly what they wished to believe. In these enlightened days, however, when we look at the matter calmly and without prejudice, we, as fair-minded Englishmen, must admit that Edward's title was a very flimsy one." "It is possible that he may have believed in his claim," writes the author of one of the books in that objectively written series, *The Way of History,* "but it is more likely that he merely knew his kingdom was rich and strong, and hoped to make himself still more powerful by means of a successful war." Arnold Forster sums up the whole question of the causes of the war by saying: "It matters little nowadays what were the rights or the wrongs of the quarrel. Both sides were ready for the fight, and if one excuse had not been enough, they would soon have found another."

Clearly the English historical texts, in interpreting the causes of the Hundred Years' War, present no uniform front of nationalism. Yet there is a nationalistic bias in certain of them, of which their authors are probably unconscious. These texts stress the provocations under which Edward III laboured: French encroachments on Gascony, French aid to the Scots, French attempts to crush the Flemings. But they make little or nothing of the ambitious motives of Edward in undertaking what was primarily a war of conquest. In other texts, however, the treatment of this ancient struggle between England and France reveals no nationalistic emphasis whatsoever.[1]

75. *THE REBELLION OF JACOB VAN ARTEVELDE*[2]

At the outbreak of the Hundred Years' War, Philip VI of France was considering how he might assist the Christians in the Near East against the Mohammedans. When King Edward III of England heard of this, he reasoned that an opportunity would be offered him of wresting from the French monarch some parts of France. He was being egged on by Robert of Artois,

[1] Professor Ramsay Muir, writing of Edward III and the Black Prince, says: "Edward III, who founded the most noble order of Knights of the Garter in honour of the fair Countess of Salisbury, thought nothing of breaking his pledged word to the burgesses of Parliament, and was only with difficulty persuaded by the implorings of his queen to spare the lives of the merchants of Calais who came out from the besieged city to beg his mercy. His son, the Black Prince, the most gallant and chivalrous knight of his age, . . . saw nothing unchivalrous in ordering the cold-blooded massacre of three thousand men, women and children of Limoges, who had angered him by defending their city."—*Short History of the British Commonwealth,* Part I, p. 123.

[2] *Chronicles of England, France, Spain, and adjoining Countries,* by John Froissart. Translated by Thomas Johnes, 4 volumes. New York, Leavitt and Allen, 1847. The selection reproduced here is Vol. I, chapters 28 and 29, pp. 29–31. Minor corrections have been made by A. Hyma.

a fugitive from France and a bitter enemy of Philip VI. Furthermore, Count Louis of Flanders, who was hated by his rebellious subjects and owed his throne to the friendship of Philip VI, had offended Edward III by molesting English merchants in Flanders. The English monarch, therefore, sympathized with the Flemings who were trying to overthrow the rule of their count. He simultaneously sought to diminish the influence exerted by the French king in Flanders. In this attempt he was aided by the rebellion of Jacob van Artevelde, which is the subject of the following discourse by Froissart.

Froissart was born in Valenciennes (which in the Middle Ages belonged to the Low Countries but now is situated in northern France) in 1337. He was for a time secretary of Philippa of Hainault, one of the seventeen little states that constituted the Low Countries or Netherlands; afterward he served the Black Prince, the eldest son of Edward III, who won the Battle of Crécy, and whom he attended in 1366.

At the time when nothing but this crusade was talked of, the lord Robert d'Artois was in England, very near the king's person, whom he was continually advising to make war upon the king of France for wrongfully withholding his inheritance. The king held many councils upon this subject, and consulted with his most special and privy councillors by what means he could obtain his right, for he would gladly amend himself if he knew how. The question was argued, supposing he should demand his right, and it was refused, as it was probable it would be, and he afterwards to sit quiet and not support his claim, he would be more blamed than if he had never moved in it. He saw clearly that it was impossible for him, and all the force he could bring from his own country, to subdue such a great kingdom as that of France, if he did not obtain powerful friends and assistance in the empire, and in other parts, by means of his money; he therefore frequently demanded of his privy council what opinion they had on this subject.

They at length gave this as their unanimous answer: "Dear sir, the question is of such importance, that we dare not advise you definitely upon it, but recommend to you, dear sir, to send embassadors sufficiently instructed to the gallant earl of Hainault, whose daughter you have married, and to lord John, his brother, who has before so valiantly assisted you, to entreat their lordships to advise you how to act, for in such a matter they are better informed than we can be: if they agree with you in opinion, they will give you counsel who are the lords most able to assist you, and also point out the most proper means of gaining them to your interest." The king agreed to this proposal, and entreated the bishop of Lincoln to undertake this journey through affection to him, and desired two knights bannerets, and two counsellors learned in the law, to accompany him on the embassy. They set out as soon as they could, embarked and landed at Dunkirk; whence they rode through Flanders to Valenciennes, where they found William, earl of Hainault, so sorely afflicted with the gout and gravel that he could not move. The lord John, his brother, was there also, by whom they were much feasted: and to them they explained the object of their mission. Upon which the gallant earl said: "I vow to God, if the king can succeed in this, I shall be much rejoiced; for as you may easily imagine, I feel more interested for him who has married my daughter than for king Philip, who has never done anything for me although I am married to his sister. He also prevented, clandestinely, the marriage of the young duke of Brabant with my daughter; on which account I will not fail my dearly beloved son, the king of England, in any respect, if his council should advise the undertaking of it. I will also give him every aid, as will John, my brother, now present, who has before assisted him. But know, that you must seek for other supporters more powerful than we are, for Hainault is too small a territory to measure itself with the kingdom of France, and England lies too far off to be of help to it."

"Certainly, sir, you have given us very excellent advice, and testified great love and good will, for which, in the name of our lord and king, I return you my thanks," replied the bishop of Lincoln; "but, dear sir, tell us the names of those lords that you think can best help our master, that we may report them to him."

"Upon my soul," replied the earl, "I cannot think of any lords, that can so powerfully assist him as the duke of Brabant, his cousin-german, the bishop of Liége, the duke of Gueldres, who married his sister, the archbishop of Cologne, the marquis of Juliers, sir Arnold de Bacqueghen, and the lord of Fauquemont: these are the lords that can, in a short time, furnish greater numbers of men-at-arms than any I know; they are very warlike themselves, and, if they choose, can easily make up ten thousand men completely armed and equipped; but you must give them money beforehand, for they are men who love to gain wealth. If by your means the king, my son-in-law and your lord, could ally himself with the lords whom I have just mentioned, and were on this side of the sea, he might pass the river Oise to seek king Philip, and offer him battle."

The embassadors returned to London with the answer they had received, which, when king Edward heard it, gave him much pleasure and comfort. News of what was going forward was soon carried to France, and by degrees magnified, so that King Philip grew very indifferent to this crusade which had been preached, and of which he had undertaken to be the chief. He countermanded his officers (who were making very great preparations,) and gave them directions not to proceed further, until he should see upon what footing the king of England meant to act, as he was incessantly employed in assembling men-at-arms.

The king of England ordered ten knights bannerets, and forty knights bachelors, in company with the bishop of Lincoln, who was a right valiant man, to cross the sea, and to go straight to Valenciennes, to treat with those lords of the empire, whom the earl of Hainault had named, and to act as he and his brother John might advise. When they were arrived at Valenciennes, all were emulous of the state they should hold, and spared no expenses; for if the king of England had been there in person, they could not have done more, by which they gained great renown and reputation. There were among them many young knights bachelors, who had one of their eyes covered with a piece of cloth so that they could not see with it. It was said they had made a vow to some ladies in their country, that they would never use but one eye until they had personally performed some deeds of arms in France; nor would they make any reply to whatever questions were asked them; so that all marvelled at their strange demeanor. After they had been sufficiently feasted and honored at Valenciennes, the bishop of Lincoln and the greater number of them drew toward the duke of Brabant, by the advice of the earl of Hainault. The duke treated them magnificently, and agreed afterwards to promise his support and assistance to the king of England, to whom he was cousin-german, with all the means in his power, and to allow him to enter and quit his territories, armed or disarmed, as often as he pleased. He had also promised, by the advice of his council, and for a round sum of florins, that if the king of England, his cousin, would defy the king of France, and enter his territories with a sufficient force, and could obtain the aid of the lords before mentioned, he would defy him also, and join him with a thousand armed men.

The embassadors then returned to Valenciennes; by their negotiations and gold, they prevailed upon the duke of Gueldres, brother-in-law to King Edward, the marquis of Juliers for himself, and for the archbishop of Cologne, and his brother Waleran, and the lord of Fauquemont, to come to Valenciennes, to treat with them before the earl of Hainault, who was unable to ride on horseback; and before his brother John. They managed matters so well, by a plentiful distribution of florins among the principals and others, that they agreed to defy the king of France, and to go with the king of England whenever and wherever he pleased, and that each would serve him with a certain number of men-at-arms with helmets surmounted with crests. Now is the time come when we must speak of lances, swords, and coats of mail; and I inform you, that the above named lords promised the embassadors from England, that they would ally themselves with the lords on the other side of the Rhine, who had the power to bring a large number of men-at-arms, but they must first be furnished with the means to fix them. These lords from Germany then took their leave, and departed to their own country; the English lords remained some little time longer with the earl of Hainault. They sent many messages to Raoul, bishop of Liége, and would most willingly have drawn him over to their own party; but he would do nothing against the king of France, whose liegeman he was, and to whom he had sworn fealty. The king of Bohemia was not sent to, because they knew he was so connected with the king of France, by the marriage of John, duke of Normandy, with the lady Bona, daughter of that king, that he would never act against him.

During these times of which I am speaking, there were great dissensions between the count of Flanders and the Flemings; for they would not obey him; nor could he venture to remain in Flanders without great danger to himself.

There was in Ghent a man that had formerly been a brewer of metheglin, called Jacob Van Artevelde, who had gained so much popular favor and power over the Flemings, that everything was done according to his will. He commanded in all Flanders, from one end to another, with such authority, that no one dared to contradict his orders. Whenever he went out into the city of Ghent, he was attended by three or four-score armed men on foot, among whom were two or three that were in his secrets; if he met any man whom he hated or suspected, he was instantly killed; for he had ordered those who were in his confidence to remark whenever he should make a particular sign on meeting any person, and to murder him directly without fail, or waiting further orders, of whatever rank he might be. This happened very frequently; so that many principal men were killed; and he was so dreaded, that no one dared to speak against his actions, or scarce to contradict him, but all were forced to entertain him handsomely.

When his companions before mentioned had conducted him to his hotel, each went home to his dinner, and immediately after returned to the street before his house, where they remained making a noise and brawling, until he pleased to come out and go round the town, to pass his time and amuse himself; and thus was he escorted until he chose to go to supper. Each of these soldiers had four Flemish groats a day, as wages, and for his expenses, which he had paid to him very regularly every week. He had also in every town and castlewick, through Flanders, sergeants and soldiers in his pay, to execute his orders, and serve him as spies, to find out if any were inclined to rebel against him, and to give him information. The instant he knew of any such thing in a town, he was banished or killed without delay, and none were so great as to be exempted, for so early did he take such measures to guard himself. At the same time he banished all the most powerful knights and esquires from Flanders, and such citizens from the principal towns as he thought were in the least favorable to the count; seized one half of their rents, giving the other moiety for the dower of their wives and support of their children. Those that were banished, of which the number was very considerable, resided for the most part at St. Omar, and were called *les avolez*. To speak the truth, there never was in Flanders, or in any other country, count, duke, or prince, who had such perfect command as Jacob Van Artevelde. He collected the rents, the duties on wines, and other taxes belonging to the count, though they were the count's lawful revenue, in whatever part of the country of Flanders he might reside; he raised also extraordinary subsidies, which he spent and gave away, without rendering account to any one. When he said he was in want of money, he was immediately believed—and well it was for them who did believe him—for it was perilous to contradict him; and if he wished to borrow money of any of the citizens, there was no one who dared to refuse him.

The embassadors from England, and who kept such honorable state at Valenciennes, as you have before heard, thought among themselves, that it would give their king great comfort and assistance in what he was anxious to undertake, if they could get the aid of the Flemings, who at that time were ill with the king of France, and with the count their lord. They consulted the Count of Hainault on the subject; who told them, that, in truth, it would be the greatest support they could get; but he did not see how it could be obtained, unless they previously could win the friendship of Jacob Van Artevelde, . . . and great favor in the city, particularly with an old knight who lived in Ghent, where he was much beloved; he was called my lord le Courtisien, was a banneret, and was looked upon as the most gallant knight and warlike man in all Flanders, who had served his lords right valiantly. This lord having kept company with the English lords, and much honored them (and every loyal knight should honor strangers), he was criminally accused to the king of France for these distinctions he had paid the English, who instantly sent an order to the count of Flanders, commanding him by some means or other to get hold of this knight, and to cut off his head. The count, who dared not refuse obedience to this command, managed so that Courtisien, coming to the place which he had appointed, was immediately arrested and beheaded. This caused infinite grief to many, for he was much beloved by the gentry of the country, and it created much ill will against the count. The English lords were so active in Flanders, that Jacob Van Artevelde assembled several times the chiefs of the principal cities to confer with them on the business they were come about, as well as on the franchises and friendship which the king of England offered to them. The matter being fully discussed, was brought to this conclusion; the chiefs of the principal towns gave their consent that the king of England and his army might pass through Flanders whenever he pleased; but as they were so much obliged to the king of France, they could not annoy him, or enter his kingdom, without suffering too heavy a penalty in a large sum of florins, and entreated the embassadors to be satisfied with this answer for the present. They returned to Valenciennes much pleased with what they had done. They frequently informed the king, their master, how things were going; and he sent them large sums of money, as well for their own expenses, as to distribute among the lords of Germany, who did not wish for anything more agreeable.

76. *THE BATTLE OF CRÉCY*[1]

At the age of twenty Froissart began to write down an account of numerous happenings in the Hundred Years' War, to many of which he was an eyewitness. He was well qualified to describe the arrangement of the English and French armies, and his narrative of the most important battles is of considerable value, although not all the minute details are correct. His description of the Battle of Crécy, reproduced below, is an example of his work as chronicler.

The king of England, as I have mentioned before, encamped Friday in the plain; for he found the country abounding in provisions; but, if they should have failed, he had plenty in the carriages which attended on him. The army set about furbishing and repairing their armor; and the king gave a supper that evening to the earls and barons of his army, where they made good cheer. On their taking leave, the king remained alone, with the lords of his bed-chamber: he retired into his oratory, and, falling on his knees before the altar, prayed to God, that, if he should combat his enemies on the morrow, he might come off with honor. About midnight he went to bed; and, rising early the next day, he and the prince of Wales heard mass, and communicated. The greater part of his army did the same, confessed, and made proper preparations. After mass, the king ordered his men to arm themselves, and assemble on the ground he had before fixed on. He had inclosed a large park near a wood, on the rear of his army, in which he placed all his baggage-wagons and horses; and this park had but one entrance: his men-at-arms and archers remained on foot.

The king afterwards ordered, through his constable and his two marshals,

[1] *Chronicles of England, France, Spain, and the adjoining Countries,* by John Froissart. Translated by Thomas Johnes, 4 volumes. New York, Leavitt and Allen, 1847. The selection reproduced here is Vol. I, chapters 127–131, pp. 80–83.

that the army should be divided into three battalions. In the first, he placed the young prince of Wales, and with him the earls of Warwick and Oxford, Sir Godfrey de Harcourt, The Lord Reginald Cobham, Lord Thomas Holland, Lord Stafford, Lord Mauley, the Lord Delaware, Sir John Chandos, Lord Bartholomew Burgherst, Lord Robert Neville, Lord Thomas Clifford, the Lord Bourchier, the Lord Latimer, and many other knights and squires whom I cannot name. There might be, in this first division, about eight hundred men-at-arms, two thousand archers, and a thousand Welshmen. They advanced in regular order to their ground, each lord under his banner and pennon, and in the centre of his men. In the second battalion were the Earl of Northampton, the Earl of Arundel, the Lords Roos, Willoughby, Basset, Saint Albans, Sir Lewis Tufton, Lord Multon, the Lord Lascels, and many others; amounting in the whole, to about eight hundred men-at-arms, and twelve hundred archers. The third battalion was commanded by the king, and was composed of about seven hundred men-at-arms, and two thousand archers.

The king then mounted a small palfrey, having a white wand in his hand, and attended by his two marshals on each side of him: he rode a foot's pace through all the ranks, encouraging and entreating the army, that they would guard his honor and defend his right. He spoke this so sweetly, and with such a cheerful countenance, that all who had been dispirited were directly comforted by seeing and hearing him. When he had thus visited all the battalions, it was near ten o'clock: he retired to his own division, and ordered them all to eat heartily, and drink a glass after. They ate and drank at their ease; and, having packed up pots, barrels, etc., in the carts, they returned to their battalions, according to the marshals' orders, and seated themselves on the ground, placing their helmets and bows before them, that they might be the fresher when their enemies should arrive.

That same Saturday, the king of France rose betimes, and heard mass in the monastery of St. Peter's in Abbeville, where he was lodged: having ordered his army to do the same, he left that town after sunrise. When he had marched about two leagues from Abbeville, and was approaching the enemy, he was advised to form his army in order of battle, and to let those on foot march forward, that they might not be trampled on by the horses. The king, upon this, sent off four knights, the Lord Moyne of Bastleberg, the Lord of Noyers, the Lord of Beaujeu, and the Lord of Aubigny, who rode so near to the English that they could clearly distinguish their position. The English plainly perceived they were come to reconnoitre them: however, they took no notice of it, but suffered them to return unmolested. When the king of France saw them coming back, he halted his army; and the knights, pushing through the crowds, came near the king, who said to them. "My lords, what news?" They looked at each other, without opening their mouths; for neither chose to speak first. At last, the king addressed himself to the Lord Moyne, who was attached to the king of Bohemia, and had performed very many gallant deeds, so that he was esteemed one of the most valiant knights in Christendom. The Lord Moyne said, "Sir, I will speak, since it pleases you to order me, but under the correction of my companions. We have advanced far enough to reconnoitre your enemies. Know, then, that they are drawn up in three battalions, and are waiting for you. I would advise, for my part, (submitting, however, to better counsel,) that you halt your army here, and quarter them for the night; for before the rear shall come up, and the army be properly drawn out, it will be very late, your men will be tired and in disorder, while they will find your enemies fresh and properly arrayed. On the morrow, you may draw up your army more at your ease, and may reconnoitre at leisure on what part it will be most advantageous to begin the attack; for, be assured they will wait for you." The king commanded that it should so be done: and the two marshals rode, one toward the front, and the other to the rear, crying out, "Halt banners, in the name of God and St. Denis." Those that were in the front halted; but those behind said they would not halt, until they were as forward as the front. When the front perceived the rear pressing on, they pushed forward; and neither the king nor the marshals could stop them, but they marched without any order until they came in sight of their enemies. As soon as the foremost rank saw them, they fell back at once, in great disorder, which alarmed those in the rear, who thought they had been fighting. There was then space and room enough for them to have passed forward, had they been willing so to do: some did so, but others remained shy. All the roads between Abbeville and Crécy were covered with common people, who, when they were come within three leagues of their enemies, drew their swords, bawling out, "Kill, kill"; and with them were many great lords that were eager to make show of their courage. There is no man, unless he had been present, that can imagine, or describe truly, the confusion of that day; especially the bad management and disorder of the French, whose troops were out of number. What I know, and shall relate in this book, I have learnt chiefly from the English, who had well observed the confusion they were in, and from those attached to Sir John of Hainault, who was always near the person of the king of France.

The English, who were drawn up in three divisions, and seated on the ground, on seeing their enemies advance, rose undauntedly up, and fell into their ranks. That of the prince was first to do so, whose archers were formed in the manner of a portcullis, or harrow, and the men-at-arms in the rear. The earls of Northampton and Arundel, who commanded the second division, had posted themselves in good order on his wing, to assist and succor the prince, if necessary.

You must know, that these kings, earls, barons and lords of France, did not advance in any regular order, but one after the other, or any way most pleasing to themselves. As soon as the king of France came in sight of the English, his blood began to boil, and he cried out to his marshals, "Order the Genoese forward, and begin the battle, in the name of God and St. Denis." There were about fifteen thousand Genoese cross-bowmen; but they were quite fatigued, having marched on foot that day six leagues, completely armed, and with their cross-bows. They told the constable, they were not in a fit condition to do any great things that day in battle. The count of Alençon hearing this, said, "This is what one gets by employing such scoundrels, who fall off when there is any need for them." During this time a heavy rain fell, accompanied by thunder and a very terrible eclipse of the sun; and before this rain a great flight of crows hovered in the air over all those battalions, making a loud noise. Shortly afterwards it cleared up, and the sun shone very bright; but the Frenchmen had it in their faces, and the English in their backs. When the Genoese were somewhat in order, and approached the English, they set up a loud shout, in order to frighten them; but they remained quite still, and did not seem to attend to it. They then set up a second shout, and advanced a little forward; but the English never moved.

They hooted a third time, advancing with their cross-bows presented, and began to shoot. The English archers then advanced one step forward, and shot their arrows with such force and quickness, that it seemed as if it snowed. When the Genoese felt these arrows, which pierced their arms, heads, and through their armor, some of them cut the strings of their cross-bows, others flung them on the ground, and all turned about and retreated quite discomfited. The French had a large body of men-at-arms on horseback, richly dressed, to support the Genoese. The king of France, seeing them thus fall back, cried out, "Kill me those scoundrels; for they stop up our road, without any reason." You would then have seen the above mentioned men-at-arms lay about them, killing all they could of these runaways.

The English continued shooting as vigorously and quickly as before; some of their arrows fell among the horsemen, who were sumptuously equipped, and, killing and wounding many, made them caper and fall among the Genoese, so that they were in such confusion they could never rally again. In the English army there were some Cornish and Welshmen on foot, who had armed themselves with large knives: these advancing through the ranks of the men-at-arms and archers, who made way for them, came upon the French when they were in this danger, and, falling upon earls, barons, knights and squires, slew many, at which the king of England was afterwards much exasperated. The valiant king of Bohemia was slain there. He was called Charles of Luxemburg; for he was the son of the gallant king and emperor, Henry of Luxemburg: having heard the order of the battle, he inquired where his son, the lord Charles, was: his attendants answered, that they did not know, but believed he was fighting. The king said to them; "Gentlemen, you are all my people, my friends and brethren at arms this day: therefore, as I am blind, I request of you to lead me so far into the engagement that I may strike one stroke with my sword." The knights replied, they would directly lead him forward; and in order that they might not lose him in the crowd, they fastened all the reins of their horses together, and put the king at their head, that he might gratify his wish, and advanced towards the enemy. The lord Charles of Bohemia, who already signed his name as king of Germany, and bore the arms, had come in good order to the engagement; but when he perceived that it was likely to turn out against the French, he departed. and I do not know what road he took. The king, his father, had rode in among the enemy, and made good use of his sword; for he and his companions had fought most gallantly. They had advanced so far that they were all slain; and on the morrow they were found on the ground, with their horses all tied together.

The count of Alençon advanced in regular order upon the English, to fight with them; as did the count of Flanders, in another part. These two lords, with their detachments, coasting, as it were, the archers, came to the prince's battalion, where they fought valiantly for a length of time. The king of France was eager to march to the place where he saw their banners displayed, but there was a hedge of archers before him. He had that day made a present of a handsome black horse to Sir John of Hainault, who had mounted on it a knight of his, called Sir John de Fusselles, that bore his banner; which horse ran off with him, and forced his way through the English army, and, when about to return, stumbled and fell into a ditch and severely wounded him: he would have been dead, if his page had not followed him round the battalions, and found him unable to rise: he had not, however, any other hindrance than from his horse; for the English did not quit the ranks that day to make prisoners. The page alighted, and raised him up; he did not return the way he came, as he would have found it difficult from the crowd. This battle, which was fought on the Saturday between la Broyes and Crécy, was very murderous and cruel; and many gallant deeds of arms were performed that were never known. Toward evening, many knights and squires of the French had lost their masters: they wandered up and down the plain, attacking the English in small parties: they were soon destroyed; for the English had determined that day to give no quarter, or hear of ransom from any one.

Early in the day, some French, Germans, and Savoyards, had broken through the archers of the prince's battalion, and had engaged with the men-at-arms; upon which the second battalion came to his aid, and it was time, for otherwise he would have been hard pressed. The first division, seeing the danger they were in, sent a knight in great haste to the king of England, who was posted upon an eminence, near a windmill. On the knight's arrival, he said, "Sir, the earl of Warwick, the lord Reginald Cobham, and the others who are about your son, are vigorously attacked by the French; and they entreat that you would come to their assistance with your battalion, for, if their numbers should increase, they fear he will have too much to do." The king replied, "Is my son dead, unhorsed, or so badly wounded that he cannot support himself?" "Nothing of the sort, thank God," rejoined the knight; "but he is in so hot an engagement that he has great need of your help." The king answered, "Now, Sir Thomas, return back to those that sent you, and tell them from me, not to send again for me this day, or expect that I shall come, let what will happen, as long as my son has life; and say, that I command them to let the boy win his spurs; for I am determined, if it please God, that all the glory and honor of this day shall be given to him, and to those into whose care I have intrusted him." The knight returned to his lords, and related the king's answer, which mightily encouraged them, and made them repent they had ever sent such a message.

It is a certain fact, that Sir Godfrey de Harcourt, who was in the prince's battalion, having been told by some of the English, that they had seen the banner of his brother engaged in the battle against him, was exceedingly anxious to save him; but he was too late, for he was left dead on the field, and so was the earl of Aumarle his nephew. On the other hand, the counts of Alençon and of Flanders were fighting lustily under their banners, and with their own people; but they could not resist the force of the English, and were there slain, as well as many other knights and squires that were attending on or accompanying them. The earl of Blois, nephew to the king of France, and the duke of Lorraine, his brother-in-law, with their troops, made a gallant defence; but they were surrounded by a troop of English and Welsh, and slain in spite of their prowess. The earl of St. Pol and the earl of Auxerre were also killed, as well as many others. Late after vespers, the king of France had not more about him than sixty men, every one included. Sir John of Hainault, who was of the number, had once remounted the king; for his horse had been killed under him by an arrow: he said to the king, "Sir, retreat while you have an opportunity, and do not expose yourself so simply: if you have lost this battle, another time you will be the conqueror." After he had said this, he took the bridle of the king's horse, and led him off by force; for he had before entreated of him to retire. The king rode on until he came to the castle of la Broyes, where he found the gates shut, for it was very dark. The king ordered the governor of it to be summoned: he came upon the battlements, and asked who it was that called at such an hour? The king answered, "Open, open, governor; it is the fortune of France." The governor, hearing the king's voice, immediately descended, opened the gate, and let down the bridge. The king and his company entered the castle; but he had only with him five barons, Sir John of Hainault, the lord Charles of Montmorency, the lord of Beaujeu, the lord of Aubigny, and the lord of Montfort. The king would not bury himself in such a place as that, but, having taken some refreshments, set out again with his attendants about midnight, and rode on, under the direction of guides who were well acquainted with the country, until, about daybreak, he came to Amiens, where he halted. This Saturday the English never quitted their ranks in pursuit of any one, but remained on the field, guarding their position, and defending themselves against all who attacked them. The battle was ended at the hour of vespers.

When, on the Saturday night, the English heard no more hooting or shouting, nor any more crying out to particuluar lords or their banners, they looked upon the field as their own, and their enemies as beaten. They made great fires, and lighted torches because of the obscurity of the night. King Edward then came down from his post, who all that day had not put on his helmet, and, with his whole battalion, advanced to the Prince of Wales, whom he embraced in his arms and kissed, and said, "Sweet son, God give you good perseverance: you are my son, for most loyally have you acquitted yourself this day: you are worthy to be a sovereign." The prince bowed down very low, and humbled himself, giving all the honor to the king his father. The English, during the night, made frequent thanksgivings to the Lord, for the happy issue of the day, and without rioting; for the king had forbidden all riot or noise. On the Sunday morning, there was so great a fog that one could scarcely see the distance of half an acre. The king ordered a detachment from the army, under the command of the two marshals, consisting of about five hundred lances and two thousand archers, to make an excursion, and see if there were any bodies of French collected together. The quota of troops from Rouen and Beauvais, had, this Sunday morning, left Abbeville and St. Ricquier in Ponthieu, to join the French army, and were ignorant of the defeat of the preceding evening: they met this detachment, and, thinking they must be French, hastened to join them.

As soon as the English found who they were, they fell upon them; and there was a sharp engagement; but the French soon turned their backs, and fled in great disorder. There were slain in this fight in the open fields, under hedges and bushes, upward of seven thousand; and had it been clear weather, not one soul would have escaped.

A little time afterwards, this same party fell in with the archbishop of Rouen and the great prior of France, who were also ignorant of the discomfiture of the French: for they had been informed that the king was not to fight before Sunday. Here began a fresh battle: for those two lords were well attended by good men-at-arms; however, they could not withstand the English, but were almost all slain, with the two chiefs who commanded them; very few escaping. In the course of the morning, the English found many Frenchmen who had lost their road on the Saturday, and had lain in the open fields, not knowing what was become of the king, or their own leaders. The English put to the sword all they met: and it has been assured to me for fact, that of foot soldiers, sent from the cities, towns and municipalities, there were slain, this Sunday morning, four times as many as in the battle of Saturday.

This detachment, which had been sent to look after the French, returned as the king was coming from mass, and related to him all that they had seen and met with. After he had been assured by them that there was not any appearance of the French collecting another army, he sent to have the numbers and condition of the dead examined.

He ordered on this business, Lord Reginald Cobham, Lord Stafford, and three heralds to examine their arms, and two secretaries to write down all the names. They took much pains to examine all the dead, and were the whole day in the field of battle, not returning but just as the king was sitting down to supper. They made to him a very circumstantial report of all they had observed, and said, they had found eighty banners, the bodies of eleven princes, twelve hundred knights, and about thirty thousand common men.

The English halted there that day, and on the Monday morning prepared to march off. The king ordered the bodies of the principal knights to be taken from the ground, and carried to the monastery of Montenay, which was hard by, there to be interred in consecrated ground. He had it proclaimed in the neighborhood, that he should grant a truce for three days, in order that the dead might be buried. He then marched on, passing by Montreuil-sur-Mer.

His marshals made an excursion as far as Hesdin, and burnt Vaubain and Serain; but they could make nothing of the castle, as it was too strong and well guarded. They lay that Monday night upon the banks of the Canche, near Blangy. The next day they rode toward Boulogne, and burnt the towns of St. Josse and Neufchatel: they did the same to Estaples, in the country of the Boulonois. The whole army passed through the forest of Hardelou, and the country of the Boulonois, and came to the large town of Wisant, where the king, prince, and all the English lodged; and having refreshed themselves there one whole day, they came, on the Thursday, before the strong town of Calais.

77. THE BLACK DEATH[1]

Boccaccio was the author of a book of tales called The Decameron, *in which he not only rehearsed old stories but also added new material, describing the men and women of the fourteenth century. Hence his book is known as an important source of the civilization of the period in which he flourished. Particularly valuable is his account of the Black Death, given below.*

In the year then of our Lord 1348, there happened at Florence, the finest city in all Italy, a most terrible plague; which, whether owing to the influence of the planets, or that it was sent from God as a just punishment for our sins, had broken out some years before in the Levant, and after passing from place to place, and making incredible havoc all the way, had now reached the west. There, spite of all the means that art and human foresight could suggest, such as keeping the city clear from filth, the exclusion of all suspected persons, and the publication of copious instructions for the preservation of health; and notwithstanding manifold humble supplications offered to God in processions and otherwise; it began to show itself in the spring of the aforesaid year, in a sad and wonderful manner. Unlike what had been seen in the east, where bleeding from the nose is the fatal prognostic, here there appeared certain tumours in the groin or under the armpits, some as big as a small apple, others as an egg; and afterwards purple spots in most parts of the body; in some cases large and but few in number, in others smaller and more numerous, both sorts the usual messengers of death. To the cure of this malady, neither medical knowledge nor the power of drugs was of any effect; whether because the disease was in its own nature mortal, or that the physicians (the number of whom, taking quacks and women pretenders into the account, was grown very great), could form no just idea of the cause, nor consequently devise a true method of cure; whichever was the reason, few escaped; but nearly all died the third day from the first appearance of the symptoms, some sooner, some later, without any fever or other accessory symptoms. What gave the more virulence to this plague was that, by being communicated from the sick to the hale, it spread daily, like fire when it comes in contact with large masses of combustibles. Nor was it caught only by conversing with, or coming near the sick, but even by touching their clothes, or anything that they had before touched. It is wonderful what I am going to mention, and had I not seen it with my own eyes, and were there not many witnesses to attest it besides myself, I should never venture to relate it, however worthy it were of be-

[1] G. Boccaccio, *The Decameron,* The Introduction. Bohn's edition.

lief. Such, I say, was the quality of the pestilential matter, as to pass not only from man to man, but, what is more strange, it has been often known, that anything belonging to the infected, if touched by any other creature, would certainly infect, and even kill that creature in a short space of time. One instance of the kind I took particular notice of: the rags of a poor man, just dead, had been thrown into the street; two hogs came up, and after rooting amongst the rags and shaking them about in their mouths, in less than an hour they both turned round and died on the spot.

These facts, and others of the like sort, occasioned various fears and devices amongst those who survived, all tending to the same uncharitable and cruel end, which was, to avoid the sick and everything that had been near them, expecting by that means to save themselves. And some holding it best to live temperately, and to avoid excesses of all kinds, made parties and shut themselves up from the rest of the world, eating and drinking moderately of the best, and diverting themselves with music, and such other entertainments as they might have within doors, never listening to anything from without to make them uneasy. Others maintained free living to be a better preservative, and would baulk no passion or appetite they wished to gratify, drinking and revelling incessantly from tavern to tavern, or in private houses (which were frequently found deserted by the owners, and, therefore, common to every one), yet strenuously avoiding, with all this brutal indulgence, to come near the infected. And such, at that time, was the public distress, that the laws, human and divine, were no more regarded; for the officers to put them in force being either dead, sick, or in want of persons to assist them, every one did just as he pleased. A third sort of people chose a method between these two, not confining themselves to rules of diet like the former, and yet avoiding the intemperance of the latter; but eating and drinking what their appetites required, they walked everywhere with odours and nosegays to smell to, as holding it best to corroborate the brain, for the whole atmosphere seemed to them tainted with the stench of dead bodies, arising partly from the distemper itself and partly from the fermenting of medicines within them. Others, with less humanity, but perchance, as they supposed, with more security from danger, decided that the only remedy for the pestilence was to avoid it; persuaded, therefore, of this, and taking care for themselves only, men and women in great numbers left the city, their houses, relations and effects, and fled to the country, as if the wrath of God had been restrained to visit those only within the walls of the city, or else concluding that none ought to stay in a place thus doomed to destruction.

Thus divided as they were in their views, neither did all die, nor all escape; but falling sick indifferently, as well those of one as of another opinion, they who first set the example by forsaking others now languished themselves without pity. I pass over the little regard that citizens and relations showed to each other, for their terror was such that a brother even fled from his brother, a wife from her husband, and, what is more uncommon, a parent from his own child. Hence, numbers that fell sick could have no help but what the charity of friends, who were very few, or the avarice of servants supplied; and even these were scarce and at extravagant wages, and so little used to the business that they were fit only to reach what was called for, and observe when their employers died, and this desire of getting money often cost them their lives.

78. WYCLIFFE AND THE PEASANTS' RISING OF 1381 OF ENGLAND[1]

Much has been said and written about Wycliffe as a religious reformer, but it is interesting to note that this scholar, although far removed from the common people, exerted considerable influence upon them through his doctrine of "dominion": Since all things belonged to God and since all men held of him directly, all things must be held in common by the righteous. In other words, he favored in a limited sense the theory of communism. Large numbers of men from many different walks of life came to Oxford, where he taught, to get in touch with him, and from Oxford they returned to their respective communities, spreading the doctrine of common possession wherever they went. Wycliffe himself after 1375 lost practically all interest in his doctrine about property. Nevertheless his followers continued to preach it, so that Wycliffe in a certain sense was a cause of the Peasants' Revolt, which broke out in England in the year 1381.

It will be seen that when that event [the Peasants' Rising of 1381] took place the process of commuting villein services for money rents was going on fast, but not quite so fast as the serfs themselves wished, now that they were possessed by the idea of man's right to freedom. But the release from forced service was not the only question at issue between lords and villeins, nor did the latter consider themselves wholly free when such services had been commuted. The lord possessed other rights over the person of the villein and his family, rights varying in different counties and different manors, varying even from farm to farm on the same manor, rights that were often petty, but so multitudinous as to be exasperating, and so humiliating that they were incompatible with the new ideal. One villein must pay a fine to

[1] George Macaulay Trevelyan, *England in the Age of Wycliffe*. London, Longmans, Green and Co., 1912, pp. 194-202. Used by permission.

the lord when he gave his daughter in marriage, another must have his corn ground at the lord's mill only, and pay a high price to the monopolist miller. It was little grievances like these, which in old France mounted up to such a sum of wrong that the great Revolution was the result. It was not service on the lord's demesne, but the enormous multiplication of small seigniorial dues and taxes that caused the "culbute générale" in 1789. In England they had always been a less prominent feature, and in the course of the fifteenth century they disappeared, or survived only in the "innocuous curiosities of copyhold." But in the fourteenth century they were an additional goad in the side of the vexed peasant.

Two principal marks of serfdom were specially grievous. The villein might not plead in court against his lord; he had therefore no protection from the justice of his country against the man with whom he had most dealings. Above all, the villein could not sell his land or leave his farm without permission. In these days of dear labour, his lord was unusually anxious to keep him on the manor, while he himself was often willing to desert his unprofitable farm and better himself elsewhere as a landless labourer; but even if his services on the demesne had been commuted, he was still a serf "bound to the soil." The economic condition of affairs must have lent special bitterness to this incident of serfdom. The social questions of the period cannot be understood, unless we remember that in 1381 more than half the people of England did not possess the privileges which Magna Charta secured to every "freeman."

All great revolutions in the affairs of mankind have in them a mysterious element. Neither the philosopher nor the historian can fully explain the inspiration which suddenly moves a nation or a class, long sunk in mediocrity or servitude, to flash out for a space before the eyes of the world in all the splendour of human energy. The wind bloweth where it listeth. No one can account for the age of Pericles or for the age of Elizabeth, for the Jesuits, for Calvinism, for the French Revolution. We can tell their occasion, but not their cause. Sometimes a crisis calls for movement, and no movement comes. Why on some occasions there is an outburst, is in each case a mystery. It is the modest task of the historian to relate the circumstances under which a movement occurred, and to describe the speculative or religious forms in which the ideas of the movement were presented. More he cannot do.

We have already set out the economic and social conditions of the Rising. It remains to indicate the ideas by which it was inspired. In that age revolutionary theories were as naturally religious as in the eighteenth century they were naturally irreligious. And so we find in this case. The idea of personal freedom was, in the first instance, brought before the peasant by the commutation of praedial service for economic reasons; and but for this occurrence it might, for all we can tell, have slumbered yet another century. But this idea, once awakened, was immediately discovered to be in accordance with the teaching of Christianity. Complete slavery had long been opposed by the Church, but the Abbots and Bishops who held manors all over the country had not yet seen any incompatibility between Christian brotherhood and the status of the villein. But the peasantry and their humbler religious pastors saw it for themselves. Besides the levelling and democratic tendencies of the Christian spirit, the belief in a common origin from Adam and Eve, not then shaken or allegorised by scientific criticism, was a very real and valid argument against hereditary serfdom. Indeed it is hard to see how the lords, basing their claims on inheritance only, and not on general utility, could logically escape the difficulty. At any rate the famous catchword,

> When Adam delved and Evé span
> Who was then a gentleman?

seems to have corresponded in importance and popularity to "Liberté, Egalité, Fraternité."

Those who stirred up these Christian aspirations towards an ideal of more perfect freedom and equality, were the religious persons who were most directly in touch with the labouring classes. Like some parish priests at the beginning of the French Revolution, many of the poorer English clergy were instigators of rebellion. John Ball, the principal agitator, was a chaplain, and a religious zealot. In the character of prophet he had for twenty years been going round the country. Church and State he alike attacked, but laid most stress on the iniquity of serfage. He had begun his career as a radical long before John Wycliffe was of any great importance in the world of politics and religion. In so far as he had any connection with the reformer, it was not as follower but as precursor. It was said that he adopted, in the last year of his life, Wycliffe's new heresy on the Eucharist. Otherwise he is himself responsible for the good and evil he did. He had once been a priest somewhere in the North, but finally became an agitator in London and its neighbourhood, where Sudbury, first as Bishop of London, and then as Metropolitan, had repeatedly to adopt repressive measures against him.

"He was accustomed," says Froissart, "every Sunday after Mass, as the people were coming out of the church, to preach to them in the market-place and assemble a crowd around him, to whom he would say, 'My good friends, things cannot go well in England, nor ever will until everything shall be in common; when there shall be neither vassal nor lord and all distinctions levelled, when the lords shall be no more masters than ourselves. How ill have they used us? And for what reason do they thus hold us in bondage? Are we not all descended from the same parents, Adam and Eve? And what can they show or what reason give, why they should be more masters than ourselves? except perhaps in making us labour and work for them to spend. They are clothed in velvets and rich stuffs, ornamented with ermine and other furs, while we are forced to wear poor cloth. They have handsome seats and manors, when we must brave the wind and rain in our labours in the field; but it is from our labour they have wherewith to support their pomp. We are called slaves, and if we do not perform our services we are beaten.' " Such, in spirit, was John Ball's agitation. But the report is that of a prejudiced person in full sympathy with the upper classes, and shocked by the startling horrors of the Rising. It may be questioned how much stress was really laid by the agitators on the project of "having all things in common." When the Rising took place, no such request was put forward. Personal freedom, and the commutation of all services for a rent of 4d. an acre, were the very practical demands then made. When this had been granted, most of the rebels went home; even those who stayed, produced no scheme of speculative communism, but confined their further demands, at most, to disendowment of the Church, free use of forests, abolition of game-laws and of outlawry. The attempt to picture the Rising as a communistic movement ignores the plainest facts. It was, as far as the bulk of the peasantry was concerned, a rising to secure freedom from the various degrees and forms of servitude that still oppressed them severally. Whenever there is a labour movement, a few will always be communists, and the conservative classes will always give unfair prominence to the extreme idea.

The itinerant friars, with their direct and powerful influence on both poor and rich, were thought to have an active share in the fermentation that led to the risings. They were loudly accused by the Lollards of setting class against class. Probably the friar on his rounds was urged by self-interest to keep up his popularity, and often by genuine feelings to protest against oppression and serfdom. He had imbibed in his convent a theoretical prejudice against property. Langland declares that the friars preached communism to the vulgar, with arguments drawn from the proverbial learning of their order.

> They preach men of Plato and prove it by Seneca,
> That all things under Heaven ought to be in common;
> And yet he lieth, as I live, that to the unlearned so preacheth.

Besides the friars, there was another body of friends of the people who at the time of the Rising were just coming into prominence. Wycliffe's Poor Priests cannot at this time have been, and probably never were, at work all over England. Neither had this missionary movement yet been organised as regularly as it afterwards was. But it seems clear that men, drawing some of their doctrines from the great Oxford reformer, were already perambulating the country. It would, indeed, be remarkable if at a period of such fierce social agitation, and such desperate religious controversy, the theories of the most famous thinker of the time had not been carried far and wide in the mouths of enthusiasts, and more or less travestied in the process. What these theories were on religion, and on Church property, we have already seen. But it is the doctrine of Wycliffe with regard to secular property, that specially concerns the story of the Peasants' Rising. Ten years before that event he had expounded his famous theory of "dominion." All things, he said, belonged to God, and all men held of him directly. Only the good could hold property of him truly, and every good man possessed all things. The bad possessed nothing, although they seemed to possess. Hence he argued in favour of communism. All things must be held in common by the righteous, for all the righteous possess all. After this curious metaphysical juggle, he makes a right about face, and states that in practical life the good must leave the bad in possession, that a wicked master must be obeyed, and that resistance and revolution are justified by God only under certain strictly limited conditions. The practical application of his theory, as regards secular society, was quite conservative, for he did not apply it at all. But the mere fact that the great schoolman had given his blessings to the theory of communism was welcome news to agitators throughout the country. To Oxford, men of all sorts and all classes congregated, and from Oxford they spread over England, each with his own version of intellectual discoveries made there. Such was the Clarendon Press of the period, and it is impossible to tell how many different versions or travesties of the "De Dominio Civili" it supplied.

Meanwhile Wycliffe himself went on his way, became more and more interested in Church affairs, lost all interest in his old theories about possession, and as he became more revolutionary in religion, became more conservative in social and political questions. He exalted the power of the King and the temporal lords, in order to forge a weapon with which to strike down the Church. His theory, as he stated it over and over again both before and after the Rising, was that temporal lords had a right to their property, but that Churchmen had no right to theirs, because they ought to live in evangelical poverty on the alms of the faithful. This strict contrast between clerical and lay property is the most marked feature of his writings from 1377 onwards. Of communism we hear not another word. If before 1381 he himself sent out any Poor Priests, he sent them to preach this doctrine, and not communism, or revolt of any sort against lay lordship. But, as was only natural, popular missionaries, drawn from the people, speaking to the people and depending on the people for alms, were influenced by popular ideas. They failed to make Wycliffe's distinction between secular and clerical property. He meant them to preach against the payment of tithes, and they condemned the performances of villein services as well; he meant them to denounce the riches of a corrupt Church, and they introduced into their anathemas the riches of a corrupt aristocracy. A hostile satirist thus speaks of their double influence—

> All stipends they forbid to give
> And tithes whereon poor curates live.
> From sinful lords their dues they take;
> Bid serfs their services forsake.

Such men were firebrands, and they set light to one stack more than Wycliffe wished. But they were most of them not the real Wycliffite missionaries. The Lollards who were brought to trial by the Church for spreading his heretical doctrines, were in no single case accused of having had hand or part in the Peasants' Rising. Similarly the indictments of the rebels contain no hint of heresy. The rebellion was not a Lollard movement, although some of the agitators were influenced by some of Wycliffe's ideas, and at Smithfield Wat Tyler is said to have demanded disendowment of the Church. It is not unlikely that some of the Poor Priests entered zealously into the movement for abolishing serfage.

Wycliffe's own view of the proper relations between master and servant he expressed so clearly that no doubt whatever can remain on the subject. He continually emphasised the rights of property and the duty of performing services even to sinful lords. It was part of his regular moral teaching to exhort all Christians to render legal dues without question of their equity. His own theory of Dominion, so dangerous to the proprietary rights of the wicked, remained stillborn in the "De Dominio Civili," and made no appearance in his later Latin works, or in any of his English tracts. Popular preachers were exhorting the villeins to withdraw their services from their masters because of the wickedness of the upper classes. This plea of moral reprobation, which can be traced in the speeches and messages that fomented the Rising, was in accordance with the general tenor of Wycliffe's old theory. But, now that it had become a practical question, he denounced it unmistakably, together with any crude and levelling inferences from the notion of Christian brotherhood.

"The fiend," he says, "moveth some men to say that Christen men should not be servants or thralls to heathen lords, sith they ben false to God and less worthy than Christen men; neither to Christen lords, for they ben brethren in kind, and Jesu Christ bought Christen men on the Cross and made them free. But against this heresy Paul writeth in God's law." "But yet," he goes on, "some men that ben out of charity, slander Poor Priests with this error, that servants or tenants may lawfully withhold rents or services from their lords, when lords ben openly wicked in their living."

But while Wycliffe thus made his position clear as to violent and illegal remedies, and did at least something to counteract any effect which his early academical speculations might have had on society, he was not afraid to vow his sympathy with the serfs' demand for freedom, and his anger at their oppression by the upper class:—

"Strifes, contests and debates ben used in our land, for lords striven with their tenants to bring them in thraldom more than they shoulden by reason and charity. Also lords many times do wrongs to poor men by extortions and unreasonable amercements and unreasonable taxes, and take poor men's goods and payen not therefore but with sticks (tallies), and despisen them and menace and sometimes beat them when they ask their pay. And thus lords devour poor men's goods in gluttony and waste and pride, and they perish for mischief and hunger and thirst and cold, and their children also. And if their rent be not readily paid their beasts ben distressed, and they pursued without mercy, though they ben never so poor and needy. . . . And so in a manner they eat and drink poor men's flesh and blood, and ben manquellers, as God complaineth by his prophets." Wycliffe was one of the very few men who could see both the rights of the lords and the wrongs of the peasants. This large view of the social problems of the day enabled him, immediately after the rising was over, to speak of that astounding event with great moderation and breadth of view. At the time when all the upper classes thought of nothing but revenge, he had the courage to make the characteristic proposal that the Church property should be given to the secular lords, in order to enable them at once to relieve the poor of the burdens that had caused the outbreak.

79. THE TRIAL OF JEANNE D'ARC. EXTRACTS[1]

Captured by the Burgundians, Jeanne d'Arc was turned over to the English. The English accused her of heresy and witchcraft and she was tried on these charges. Her judges were Frenchmen, members of the clergy and university professors. Condemned to death as a result of the trial she was burned at the stake in 1431.

In the Name of the Lord, Amen

Here begin the Proceedings in Matter of Faith against a Dead Woman, Jeanne, commonly known as The Maid.

[1] *The Trial of Jeanne d'Arc.* A Complete Translation of the Text of the Original Documents with an Introduction by W. P. Barrett. London, George Routledge and Sons, Ltd., 1931 (Broadway Medieval Library, edited by G. G. Coulton and Eileen Power), pp. 19–21; 54–58; 70–72; 73–74; 327–329. Used by permission of Gotham House, Inc.

To all those who shall see these present letters or public instrument, Pierre, by divine mercy Bishop of Beauvais, and brother Jean Le Maistre, of the order of Preaching brothers, deputy in the diocese of Rouen, and especially appointed in this trial to the office of the pious and venerable master Jean Graverent of the same order, renowned doctor of theology, by apostolic authority Inquisitor of the Faith and of Heretical Error in all the kingdom of France: greeting in the author and consummator of the faith, Our Lord Jesus Christ.

It has pleased divine Providence that a woman of the name of Jeanne, commonly called *The Maid,* should be taken and apprehended by famous warriors within the boundaries and limits of our diocese and jurisdiction. The reputation of this woman had already gone forth into many parts: how, wholly forgetful of womanly honesty, and having thrown off the bonds of shame, careless of all the modesty of womankind, she wore with an astonishing and monstrous brazenness, immodest garments belonging to the male sex; how, moreover, her presumptuousness had grown until she was not afraid to perform, to speak, and to disseminate many things contrary to the Catholic faith and hurtful to the articles of the orthodox belief. And by so doing, as well in our diocese as in several other districts of this kingdom, she was said to be guilty of no inconsiderable offences. These things having come to the knowledge of our mother the University of Paris, and of brother Martin Billorin, vicar-general of the lord Inquisitor of Heretical Error, they immediately summoned the illustrious prince, the Duke of Burgundy and the noble lord Jean de Luxembourg, who at this time held the said woman in their power and authority, in the name of the vicar-general above-mentioned, and under penalty of law, to surrender and despatch to us, as ordinary judge, the woman so defamed and suspected of heresy.

We, the said Bishop, according to our pastoral office, desirous of promoting with all our might the exaltation and increase of the Christian faith, did resolve to institute a proper inquiry into these facts so commonly known, and so far as law and reason should persuade us, to proceed with mature deliberation to such further decisions as were incumbent upon us. We required the said prince and the said lord Jean also, under penalties of law, to surrender for trial the said woman to our spiritual jurisdiction: whilst the very serene and most Christian prince, our lord the King of France and England, summoned them to the same effect. Finally, the most illustrious lord Duke of Burgundy and the lord Jean de Luxembourg graciously consenting to these demands, and solicitous in their catholic souls of the accomplishment of what appeared to them as helpful to the growth of the faith, surrendered and despatched the woman to our lord the King and his commissioners. Thereafter the King in his providence, burning with a desire to succour the orthodox faith, surrendered this woman to us, that we might hold a complete inquiry into her acts and sayings before proceeding further, according to the ecclesiastical laws. When that was done, we requested the distinguished and notable chapter of the church of Rouen, charged with the administration of all spiritual jurisdiction in the vacancy of the archiepiscopal seat, to grant to us territory in the town of Rouen for us to make this inquiry: which was graciously and freely given. But before preferring any further charge against this woman we held it wise to consult, with prolonged and mature deliberation, the opinion of experienced authorities in canon and civil law, of which, by God's grace, the number in the town of Rouen was considerable.

. . . .

Whereupon the distinguished professor of sacred theology, master Jean Beaupère, at our order and command questioned the said Jeanne as follows.

And first he exhorted her to answer truly, as she had sworn, what he should ask her. To which she replied: "You may well ask me such things, that to some I shall answer truly, and to others I shall not." And she added, "If you were well informed about me, you would wish me to be out of your hands. I have done nothing except by revelation."

Asked how old she was when she left her father's house, she said she could not vouch for her age.

Asked if in her youth she had learned any craft, she said yes, to sew and spin: and in sewing and spinning she feared no woman in Rouen. And moreover she confessed that for dread of the Burgundians she left her father's house and went to the town of Neufchâteau, in Lorraine, to the house of a certain woman called *La Rousse,* where she stayed about a fortnight. She added too, that as long as she was at home with her father, she saw to the ordinary domestic tasks; and that she did not go to the fields to look after the sheep and other animals.

Asked if she confessed her sins once a year, she said yes, to her own curé; and when he was prevented she confessed to another priest, with his permission. Sometimes, too, twice or thrice perhaps she confessed to mendicant friars: but that was in the town of Neufchâteau. And she received the sacrament of the Eucharist at Easter.

Asked if, at other feasts than Easter, she received the said sacrament of the Eucharist, she told the interrogator to continue to the next question. Afterwards she declared that at the age of thirteen she had a voice from God to help her and guide her. And the first time she was much afraid. And this voice came towards noon, in summer, in her father's garden: and the said Jeanne had [not] fasted on the preceding day. She heard the voice on her right, in the direction of the church; and she seldom heard it without a light. This light came from the same side as the voice, and generally there was a great light. When she came to France she often heard the voice.

Asked how she could see the light of which she spoke, since it was at the side, she made no reply, and went on to other things. She said that if she was in a wood she easily heard the voices come to her. It seemed to her a worthy voice, and she believed it was sent from God; when she heard the voice a third time she knew that it was the voice of an angel. She said also that this voice always protected her well and that she understood it well.

Asked what instruction this voice gave her for salvation of her soul: she said it taught her to be good and to go to church often; and it told her that she must come to France. And, Jeanne added, Beaupère would not learn from her, this time, in what form that voice appeared to her. She further said that this voice told her once or twice a week that she should leave and come to France, and that her father knew nothing of her leaving. She said that the voice told her to come, and she could no longer stay where she was; and the voice told her again that she should raise the siege of the city of Orleans. She said moreover that the voice told her that, she, Jeanne, should go to Robert de Baudricourt, in the town of Vaucouleurs of which he was captain, and he would provide an escort for her. And the said Jeanne answered that she was a poor maid, knowing nothing of riding or fighting. She said she went to an uncle of hers, and told him she wanted to stay with him for some time; and she stayed there about eight days. And she told her uncle she must go to the said town of Vaucouleurs, and so her uncle took her.

Then she said that when she reached Vaucouleurs she easily recognized Robert de Baudricourt, although she had never seen him before; and she knew him through her voice, for the voice had told her it was he. And the said Jeanne told Robert she must come to France. The said Robert twice refused to hear her and repulsed her; the third time he listened to her and gave her an escort. And the voice had told her that it would be so.

Then she declared that the duke of Lorraine ordered that she should be taken to him; and she went to him and told him she wished to go to France. And the duke questioned her about the recovery of his health; but she said she knew nothing about that; and she spoke to him little concerning her journey. She told the duke nevertheless to send his son and some men to escort her to France, and she would pray to God for his health. She visited him with a safe conduct and returned to the town of Vaucouleurs.

She declared that, on her departure from Vaucouleurs, she wore the habit of a man, and carried a sword which Robert de Baudricourt had given her, but no other arms; and accompanied by a knight, a squire, and four servants, she reached the town of Saint Urbain, where she slept in an abbey.

She said that on her journey she passed through Auxerre, and she heard

Mass in the principal church there; and from that time she frequently heard her voices, including the one already mentioned.

Required to say by what advice she took to man's dress, she several times refused to answer. Finally she answered that she charged no one with that; and several times she answered variously.

She said that Robert de Baudricourt had sworn those who accompanied her to conduct her well and safely. "Go," said Robert to Jeanne, as she departed, "Go, and come what may."

Jeanne said furthermore that she knows very well that God loves the duke of Orleans; and so she had more revelations concerning him than any man alive, except him whom she calls her king. She said also that it was altogether necessary to change her women's clothes for men's. She believed that her counsel said well.

She said that she sent to the English at Orleans letters telling them to depart, as shown in the copy of the letters which had been read to her in this town of Rouen, except two or three words in the copy: for example, where in this copy it read *Surrender to the Maid* it should read *Surrender to the King*. There are also these words, *body for body* and *chieftain of war,* which were not in the original letters.

After this the said Jeanne told that she went without hindrance to him whom she calls her king. And when she had arrived at Ste. Catherine de Fierbois, then she sent first to Chinon, where he who she calls her king was. She reached Chinon towards noon and lodged at an inn; and after dinner she went to him whom she calls king, who was at the castle. She said that when she entered her king's room she recognized him among many others by the counsel of her voice, which revealed him to her. She told him she wanted to make war on the English.

Asked whether, when the voice showed her her king, there was no light, she answered: "Pass on to the next question." Asked if she saw no angel above the king, she answered: "Spare me that. Continue." She said also that before the king put her to work he had several apparitions and beautiful revelations.

Asked what revelations and apparitions the king had, she answered: "I will not tell you. It is not now the time to tell you; but send to the king and he will tell you."

Then Jeanne said that her voice had promised her that as soon as she should come to the king he would receive her. She said also that those of her party knew well that the voice was sent to Jeanne from God, and they saw and knew this voice. She said further that her king and several others heard and saw the voices which came to the said Jeanne; and there were present Charles de Bourbon, and two or three others.

Then Jeanne said that there is not a day when she does not hear this voice; and she has much need of it. She said she never asked of it any final reward but the salvation of her soul. The voice told her to remain at Saint-Denis in France, and the said Jeanne wished to remain; but against her will the lords took her away. However, if she had not been wounded, she would not have left; she was wounded in the trenches before Paris, after she left Saint-Denis; but recovered in five days. Further she confessed that she caused an assault to be made before Paris.

And when she was asked if that day were a feast day, she answered she thought it certainly was.

Asked if she thought it was a good thing to do, she answered: "Pass on." When this was over, as it appeared to us sufficient for one day, we postponed the affair until the following Saturday, at eight o'clock in the morning.

. . . .

Asked if God ordered her to wear a man's dress, she answered that the dress is a small, nay, the least thing. Nor did she put on man's dress by the advice of any man whatsoever; she did not put it on, nor did she do aught, but by the command of God and the angels.

Asked whether it seemed to her that this command to assume male attire was lawful, she answered: "Everything I have done is at God's command; and if He had ordered me to assume a different habit, I should have done it, because it would have been His command."

Asked if she did it at the order of Robert de Baudricourt she said no.

Asked if she thought she had done well to take man's dress, she answered that everything she did at God's command she thought well done, and hoped for good warrant and succour in it.

Asked if, in this particular case, by taking man's dress, she thought she had done well, she answered that she had done nothing in the world but by God's commands.

Asked whether, when she saw the voice coming to her, there was a light, she answered that there was a great deal of light on all sides, as was most fitting. She added to the examiner that not all the light came to him alone!

Asked whether there was an angel over her king's head, when she saw him for the first time, she answered: "By Our Lady! if there was, I do not know and did not see it."

Asked if there was a light, she answered: "There were three hundred knights and fifty torches, without counting the spiritual light, and I have seldom had revelations but there is a light."

Asked how the king gave credence to her words, she answered that he had good signs, and through the clergy.

Asked what revelations the king had, she answered: "You will not learn from me this year." She said that for three weeks she was examined by the clergy, at Chinon and Poitiers; and her king had a sign touching of her mission before he believed in her. The clergy of her party held that there was nothing but good in her mission.

Asked if she had been to Ste. Catherine de Fierbois, she answered yes; and there she heard Masses three times on the same day; and then went to Chinon. She said she sent letters to her king, to the effect that she was sending to find out if she should enter the town where her king was; and that she had journeyed a good hundred and fifty leagues to come to his aid, and that she knew many things to his advantage. And she thought these letters said she would be able to recognize the king among all others. She said she had a sword which she took to the town of Vaucouleurs. She added that when she was at Tours or Chinon she sent for a sword which was in the church of Ste. Catherine de Fierbois, behind the altar; and immediately it was found there all rusted over.

Asked how she knew that this sword was there, she answered that the sword was in the ground, rusted over, and upon it were five crosses; and she knew it was there through her voices, and she had never seen the man who fetched it. She wrote to the clergy of the place asking if it was their pleasure that she should have the sword, and they sent it to her. Nor was it buried deep behind the altar, but she believed she wrote saying it was behind. She added that as soon as the sword was found the priests rubbed it, and the rust fell off at once without effort; a merchant, an armourer of Tours, fetched it. The local priests gave her a scabbard, as did those of Tours also; they made two in all, one of crimson velvet, in French *de velous vermeil,* and the other of cloth of gold. She herself had another made of very strong leather. She added that when she was captured she had not this sword with her.

She said also that she carried it continually from the time she obtained it until her departure from St. Denis, after the assault on Paris.

. . . .

Asked what force her king gave her when he set her to work, she answered that he gave her 10 or 12,000 men; and she went first to Orleans, to the fortress of Saint-Loup, and then to the fortress of the Bridge.

Asked to which fortress she ordered her men to retire, she says she does not remember. She added that she was confident of raising the siege of Orleans, for it had been revealed to her, and she had told the king so before going there.

Asked whether, when the assault was to be made, she did not tell her men that she would receive arrows, crossbolts and stones hurled by catapults or cannons, she answered no; there were a hundred wounded, or more. But she had indeed told her men not to fear and they would raise the siege. She said also that at the assault upon the fortress of the Bridge she was wounded in the neck by an arrow or crossbolt; but she received great comfort from St. Margaret, and was better in a fortnight. But she did not on account of that give up her riding or work.

Asked if she knew beforehand that she would be wounded, she answered that she did indeed, and she had told her king so; but that notwithstanding she would not give up her work. And it was revealed to her by the voices of the two saints, namely the blessed Catherine and Margaret. She added that she herself was the first to plant the ladder against the said fortress of the Bridge; and as she was raising the ladder she was wounded in the neck with the crossbolt, as she had said.

. . . .

Afterwards towards nine o'clock in the morning of the same day we the said judges repaired to the Old Market of Rouen, near the church of St. Sauveur, in the presence of and assisted by the reverend fathers in Christ the lord bishops of Thérouanne and of Noyon, masters Jean de Châtillon, André Marguerie, Nicolas de Venderès, Raoul Roussel, Denis Gastinel, Guillaume Le Boucher, Jean Alespée, Pierre Houdenc, William Haiton, the prior of Longueville, Pierre Maurice and many other lords, masters and clergy. The said Jeanne was led before us in view of a great multitude of people assembled in this place; she was placed upon a scaffold or platform. For her salutary admonition and the edification of the people a solemn sermon was delivered by the distinguished doctor of theology, master Nicolas Midi. He took as his text the words of the Apostle in the twelfth chapter of the first Epistle to the Corinthians. "Si quid patitur unum membrum, compatiuntur alia membra. . . . Whether one member suffer, all the members suffer with it."

When this sermon was over we once more admonished Jeanne to look to the salvation of her soul, to reflect on her misdeeds and to repent and show true contrition for them. We exhorted her to believe the counsel of the clergy and notable persons who instructed and taught her things concerning her salvation, and especially of the two venerable Preaching brothers who were then standing near her, and whom we had appointed to instruct her continually and zealously to her salutary admonitions and profitable counsels. Finally we the bishop and vicar aforesaid, having regard to what has gone before, in which it is manifest that this woman had in her obstinate rashness never truly abandoned her errors and abominable crimes; but rather that she had shown herself infinitely more damnable by the diabolical malice of her obstinacy in the false simulation of contrition, penitence and correction, and by the perjury of God's holy name and the blasphemy of

His saints: that she had by such means declared herself obstinate, incorrigible, a heretic, relapsed in heresy, altogether unworthy of grace and of the communion which in our earlier sentence we had mercifully offered her. In view of all the things to be considered in this matter, and after mature deliberation and counsel with many learned persons, we proceeded to the final sentence in these terms:

"In the name of the Lord, amen. As often as the poisonous virus of heresy obstinately attaches itself to a member of the Church and transforms him into a limb of Satan, most diligent care must be taken to prevent the foul contagion of this pernicious leprosy from spreading to other parts of the mystic body of Christ. The decrees of the holy Fathers have laid down that hardened heretics must be separated from the midst of the just rather than permit such pernicious vipers to lodge in the bosom of Our Holy Mother Church, to the great peril of the rest. Therefore, we, Pierre by divine mercy bishop of Beauvais and brother Jean Le Maistre, vicar of the renowned doctor Jean Graverent, the Inquisitor of Heretical Error and especially appointed by him in this case, both competent judges in this trial, have declared by a just judgment that you, Jeanne, commonly called *The Maid,* have fallen into divers errors and crimes of schism, idolatry, invocation of demons and many other misdeeds. Nevertheless, since the Church never closes her bosom to the wanderer who returns, esteeming that with a pure spirit and unfeigned faith you had cut yourself off from these errors and crimes because on a certain day you renounced them, swore in public, vowed and promised never to return to the said errors or heresy under any influence or in any manner whatever; but rather to remain indissolubly in the unity of the Catholic Church and the communion of the Roman pontiff, as is proven at greater length in the formula signed by your own hand. Since subsequently, after this abjuration of your errors the author of schism and heresy has arisen in your heart which he has seduced and since you are fallen again— O, sorrow!—into these errors and crimes as the dog returns to his vomit, as it is sufficiently and manifestly clear from your willing confessions and statements, we have concluded in most celebrated decisions that the denial of your previous inventions and errors was merely verbal. *Therefore* we declare that you are fallen again into your former errors and under the sentence of ex-communication which you originally incurred we decree that you are a relapsed heretic; and by this sentence which we deliver in writing and pronounce from this tribunal, we denounce you as a rotten member, which, so that you shall not infect the other members of Christ, must be cast out of the unity of the Church, cut off from her body, and given over to the secular power: we cast you off, separate and abandon you, praying this same secular power on this side of death and the mutilation of your limbs, to moderate its judgment towards you, and if true signs of repentance appear in you to permit the sacrament of penance to be administered to you."

80. THE QUARREL BETWEEN POPE BONIFACE VIII AND PHILIP IV OF FRANCE[1]

In the period from 1050 to 1250 there occurred a long and bitter contest for political supremacy between the Hohenstaufen emperors of the Holy Roman Empire and the papacy. When this struggle was ended, the pope emerged as victor. Frederick II was the last member of his house to raise his head against the papacy. He was succeeded in 1250 by his son Conrad IV, who died in 1254, leaving an infant of two as his heir. Hereupon Pope Innocent IV grasped the opportunity of driving the Hohenstaufens out of Italy. He invited Charles of Anjou, a brother of King Louis IX of France, to become king of Sicily. Charles was not loath to accept the invitation, and in the year 1268 the son of Conrad IV was executed in Naples. But now the house of Anjou, which owed its crown to the papacy, took over the rôle formerly played by the Hohenstaufens in attacking the papacy. Before long the royal house of France grew so powerful that it accomplished what neither Henry IV nor Frederick II had been able to do, namely, to defeat the papacy and then to keep it under supervision for the space of seventy years, the period of the Babylonian Captivity, when the popes resided on the bank of the Rhône instead of the Tiber.

The conflict between the French monarchy and the papacy which was to lead to the Babylonian Captivity opens with a bitter quarrel between Pope Boniface VIII and King Philip IV of France.

The French monarch took up the war against ecclesiastical supremacy, in which the Hohenstaufens, after having shaken the foundations of the Papacy, had perished. This event grew into one of the most important revolutions of the ecclesiastical and political world. For during the entire Middle Ages France had been the asylum and the most faithful defender of the Papacy; it had effected the downfall of the Hohenstaufens; its influence had supplanted German influence both in Italy and Rome. When the popes, however, raised the royal house of France to the throne of Italy and made it the protector of the Church, their weakness was punished by the ever-recurring law which transforms protectors into conquerors. With Charles

[1] Ferdinand Gregorovius, *History of the City of Rome in the Middle Ages*. Translated from the Fourth German Edition by Annie Hamilton. Second edition revised. 8 vols. London, George Bell and Sons. Vol. V, Part II., 1897, pp. 570–597 (Condensed). Used by permission.

of Anjou, the Papacy was gradually conquered by France, until the sacred chair was removed to the shores of the Rhone, and was occupied solely by Frenchmen for a space of seventy years. The collision between the spiritual claims of Rome and the national pride of France was rendered unavoidable, when Boniface VIII, in an age of advanced civilisation, sought to turn the principles of papal universal supremacy against the protectorate of France. The German empire was defeated by the popes because it did not rest on practical grounds; but the quarrel between the King of France and the Pope was a war of the law of the Church, on the soil of a national monarchy defended by the estates of the realm. The tedious reaction of the political spirit against this European ecclesiastical law, which penetrated all civil and economic relations, is, upon the whole, the chief motive of the history of the Middle Ages. It appears in every period under different forms and names, more especially as the quarrel for investitures and the war with the Hohenstaufens; it was afterwards continued in the Reformation, later in the French Revolution, and is still evident in the concordats of the latest times and in the oppositions of our own days.

Philip le Bel, grandson of that Lewis IX whom Boniface VIII in 1297 had himself received among the saints of the Church, reigned in France at this time. He was a prince of talent and ambition, an unscrupulous despot, but one of the founders of the French monarchy. A man such as he was eminently qualified to encounter the exasperating arrogance of a Boniface VIII. The Pope's interference in the war between France and England, in which he hoped to act as judge, the investitures and the tithes demanded, brought Philip into collision with the Roman Curia. Boniface issued his bull, *Clericis Laicos,* mainly to protect the immunity of the churches, and by this bull he solemnly forbade all clergy and religious bodies to make gifts, or to pay taxes, to laymen without permission from the Pope. This bull struck severely at King Philip, who required tribute from his clergy for his wars in Flanders and England, and who in his financial distress had been reduced to issue base money in the most shameless way. He replied by forbidding money to be sent from France, an order which dealt a no less severe blow to Rome.

When the Pope yielded and the storm was consequently appeased, a more severe tempest broke forth in 1301. It was caused by the controversies between spiritual and temporal rights, and by the administration of vacant benefices, which the French crown claimed as regalia. The papal legate was imprisoned and put on his trial; a parliament approved the high-handed conduct of the King, and Boniface consequently addressed a bull to Philip, on Dec. 5, which set France in complete uproar. He reproved the King for his attacks on the rights of the Church, explained that the pope had received from God absolute power over kings and kingdoms, warned him to disabuse his mind of the idea that he had no superior over him, admonished him to dismiss his evil counsellors, and invited the French clergy to a Council in Rome on November 1, 1302, where sentence would be passed as to whether the King was right or wrong. A storm of indignation rose at the French court. The jurisconsults, among them Peter Flotte and William of Nogaret, excited the King by speeches and also perhaps by papal letters which had been forged. It was asserted that Boniface presumed to treat free France as a vassal state. The papal bull was publicly burnt at Notre Dame in Paris on February 11, 1302, and its destruction publicly proclaimed by heralds amid the braying of trumpets. The first flame which consumed a papal bull was a historic event. The legate was banished with insult; a royal edict, as in the days of Frederick II, forbade the clergy to travel to Council; a parliament of the three states assembled at Notre Dame on April 10, and confirmed these decrees, and the bishops, who had already assumed a submissive attitude towards the King, willingly or otherwise bowed to his commands. It was the first time that the clergy of a country deserted the pope and stood by the prince. When Boniface received the letter in which the Gallican Church opposed his assertion that the pope stood above the king even in temporal matters, and which implored him to release the clergy from their journey to Rome, he recognised that an abyss was opening before him. But he could no longer draw back without morally destroying the papal power in the eyes of the world. He must try to break the French monarchy which was becoming united, as his predecessors had broken the empire of the Hohenstaufens which was growing absolute.

At the Council of the Lateran in November, where only a few of the French clergy appeared, Boniface issued the bull *Unam Sanctam*. In this writing he embodied all the principles of his predecessors respecting the Divine authority of the Papacy, and all that the popes had acquired in a long course of centuries down to himself, in the following foolhardy speech. "We declare," it says, "that it is necessary to salvation that every human creature should be subject to the Roman pope." This dogma he placed as a crown on the structure of the Roman hierarchy, which towered to the skies. But the proclamation of the papal judicial authority in the mouth of Boniface VIII was merely a powerless phrase, although the same view was repeated in the Avignonese period, and called forth a storm of investigation in the sphere of theology and jurisprudence, which is not ended even at the present day. When the attempt at reconciliation failed and the Pope threatened excommunication, Philip made use of the estates of the realm to wage war upon his enemy; the first genuine parliament of France overthrew the arrogant Papacy. It met in the Louvre on June 13, 1303. The foremost nobles came forward as accusers of the Pope. The charges, which they brought against a man of more than eighty, were for the most part too absurd to be other than the explosions of hatred, but the fact that a national parliament indicted a pope, and appealed from him to a General Council, was serious and fruitful of consequences. A few years before two cardinals had cited the same pope before a Council; the representative of a great Catholic nation now adopted the same course, and thus the power to which Frederick II had first appealed was evoked against the principle of papal omnipotence. The whole of France in all its spiritual and secular corporations repeated the appeal.

Boniface beheld the approach of a terrible catastrophe. He did not lose courage, but in his infatuation deceived himself concerning the limits of the papal power. Nothing but his own fall, nothing but the defeat of the Papacy, which his immediate successors were obliged to recognise as an accomplished fact, enlightened the world on the subject. The Papacy suffered because it was incapable of rallying Italy round itself and of realising the Guelf theory. The great national policy of Alexander and Innocent III had been surrendered by the popes. In order to overthrow the Hohenstaufens they had summoned foreign princes into Italy, but had not been able to solve the differences between Guelfs and Ghibellines. The political ideal of the Curia was not rooted in the soil of Italy. To a large section of the Italians the Guelf idea appeared as a revolutionary novelty; they had never had any respect for the Papacy because they surveyed it from too short a distance. . . .

When the emperors wished to overthrow popes, their enemies, they came in their own capacity as Roman imperators with an army and made open war. The King of France possessed no such title to enter on a campaign against a pope; he resorted to a dishonourable expedient in order to silence his opponent. The attack on Boniface VIII in his ancestral town of Anagni, executed by mercenaries of a foreign despot, and in concert with Latin barons, his fellow-conspirators, was an act unheard of in the history of the popes. The exiled members of the house of Colonna had been received by Philip at his court; they fanned his wrath and he utilised their desire for revenge for his own purposes. Some time in February 1303 the plan was conceived of taking the Pope a prisoner and bringing him before a Council in Lyons. Guillaume de Nogaret of Toulouse, a doctor of law, and formerly a professor at Montpellier, undertook the execution of the design. On March 12 a meeting was held in the Louvre, in which some prelates also took part, and Nogaret brought before them the accusations against the Pope. Soon afterwards the minister journeyed to Italy with full powers from the King, who authorised his undertaking in general terms. The scheme was discussed with Sciarra at the castle of Staggia near Poggibonzi, which belonged to a Florentine banker, Musciatto, one of the conspirators. The agents were provided with letters of exchange on the house of Peruzzi, and no money was spared to bribe both friends and foes of the unsuspecting Pope, while

Nogaret assumed the demeanour of an envoy sent to negotiate with him.

The French minister sought, although in vain, to draw the King of Naples into the conspiracy, and equally fruitless were the exertions of his agents among the Romans. But his gold made its way into the fortresses of the Campagna. Above all, Nogaret won to his side Raynald of Supino, the captain of Ferentino, from whom the nephew of the Pope had wrested the fortress of Trevi and other property. Almost the whole of Latium took part in the conspiracy. . . .

Raynald of Supino, captain of Ferentino, some other barons, Nogaret and Sciarra collected troops in Sculcola. The unsuspecting Pope was at Anagni with several cardinals. He had taken the oath of purgation in public consistory on August 15. On September 8 he intended to pronounce Philip's excommunication and deposition in the same cathedral from which Alexander III had excommunicated Frederick I and Gregory IX Frederick II. The conspirators, therefore, hastened to silence him before he should pronounce the bull. They left Sculcola on the night of September 6, and in the dawn of morning entered the gates of Anagni, which had been opened to them, unfolding the banner of France with the cry: "Death to Pope Boniface! Long live King Philip!" Adenulf with the city militia immediately joined them, and Nogaret explained to the people that he had come to invite the Pope to a Council.

The clash of arms aroused the old man in his palace, the approaches to which were kept barred by his nephew Count Peter. The enemy did not succeed in reaching the cathedral, with which the papal palace was connected, until they had taken by assault Peter's house and the houses of three cardinals, the Penitentiary Gentilis, Francesco Gaetani, and Peter the Spaniard. The nephews manfully defended the palace and Boniface strove to gain time by negotiation. Sciarra accorded him a nine hours' delay for the acceptance of dishonouring conditions, among which were his abdication and the immediate restoration of the house of Colonna. These articles were declined and the storm was renewed. In order to reach the palace the besiegers set fire to the doors of the cathedral; the Pope, who had in vain summoned the people of Anagni to his rescue, soon found himself alone; his servants fled or deserted to the enemy; the cardinals disappeared, with the exception of Nicholas Boccasini of Ostia and Peter the Spaniard. The nephews laid down their arms; they were taken as prisoners to the house of Adenulf. Cardinal Francesco alone and the Count of Fundi succeeded in escaping in disguise.

When Nogaret and Sciarra, one the representative of the hatred of his King, the other the avenger of his ill-used house, made their way across the corpses of the slain (amongst whom was a bishop) to the palace, part of which was in flames, they found themselves in the presence of an old man clad in pontifical vestments, the tiara on his head, seated upon a throne, and bowed over a gold cross which he held in his hands. He was resolved to die as Pope. His venerable age and his majestic silence disarmed the men for an instant, then with yells they demanded his degradation, declared that they would carry him in chains to Lyons to be deposed, and allowed themselves to descend to insults, which he bore with magnanimity. The wild Sciarra seized him by the arm, dragged him from the throne, and would have thrust his dagger in his breast. Nogaret held his companion back by force. The ferocity, the excitement, the terror and despair knew no bounds; moderation, however, finally triumphed over passion. In strict imprisonment, under the custody of Raynald of Supino, Boniface was confined in the palace, while mercenaries as well as citizens sacked his treasures, which were believed inexhaustible, the cathedral, and also the houses of his nephews.

The almost inexplicable success of the attack shows how defenceless the Pope had become in his own country. His native city abandoned him to a hostile gang, which beside Nogaret and two French servants consisted solely of Italians. "O miserable Anagni," cried Boniface's impotent successor a year later, "that thou shouldst have allowed such a deed to be committed within thee! May neither dew nor rain fall upon thee! May it fall on other mountains and pass thee by, since under thy eyes, and although thou couldst have defended him, the hero fell, and he who was girded with power was vanquished!"

During three days Boniface, refusing in his pain or suspicion all nourishment, remained under the swords of his enemies, who seemed uncertain what to do, since their prisoner, contemptuous of death, refused to yield to their demands. Soon after followed a sudden change in his favour. On the news of the occurrence the friends of the Gaetani in the Campagna seized arms, while the barons of Latium, who had been oppressed by the Pope and his nephews, tried to reoccupy the districts which they had sold. The conspirators had not been able to win the city of Rome to their side, although it was filled with tumult indescribable, and thoughtful citizens were sensible of the insult suffered by the Pope. On Monday, September 10, Cardinal Luca Fieschi appeared at Anagni, rode through the streets, and summoned the already repentant people to avenge the outrage. He was answered with the cry, "Death to the traitors," and the same crowd which had so shamefully deserted Boniface, now, burning with indignation, stormed the palace where he sat imprisoned. The French banner was torn down, the prisoners were set free. Nogaret and Sciarra escaped to Ferentino.

The Pope, released when too late, addressed the people from the steps of the palace. In a moment of magnanimous emotion, he forgave all who had ill-treated him. He left his ungrateful birthplace on Friday, September 14, escorted by armed men, to betake himself to Rome. It is said that the Colonna attempted an attack on the way, but were repulsed. Rome sent aid, although, if only four hundred horsemen came to meet Boniface, we may see how lukewarm was the feeling in the city. Cardinal Matthew and Jacopo Orsini led the band, less perhaps with the object of affording the Pope assistance, than of securing his person. The Orsini were now in power in Rome, where they also occupied the Senate. As Boniface reached the city after a three days' journey, the people received him with signs of reverence; he spent the night in the Lateran, where he remained two days, and then advanced in procession to S. Peter's, where the old man in despair shut himself up in the chambers of the Vatican.

His excitement approached frenzy. Revenge was his fixed idea. He would summon a great Council to crush King Philip, as Innocent IV by a Council had formerly crushed Frederick II. Nevertheless, after his humiliation he was merely a phantom whom no one feared. He surveyed those who surrounded him with growing distrust; if he was forced to pardon Cardinal Napoleon, who was pointed out as one of the conspirators, his forgiveness only shows that he had lost his freedom. The Orsini kept watch over him with the eyes of an Argus, and began to dictate laws to him. They kept S. Angelo, as well as the Borgo, filled with armed men. They either feared excesses from the Pope's despair, or were so ungrateful as to extract profit from his misfortunes. The city was in a state of wild excitement, and divided into parties for and against the Pope, for and against the Orsini and Colonna. The Senators, incapable of maintaining order, resigned their offices into the hands of the people. Boniface summoned Charles of Naples to his aid; the Orsini, however, suppressed his letters. He desired to go to the Lateran, a quarter of the city ruled by the Anibaldi, a family who hated the Orsini and had no love for the Colonna. He was forbidden to leave the Vatican, and now recognised that he was a prisoner in the hands of the Orsini.

The days which the unfortunate Pope passed in the Vatican were beyond measure terrible. Frantic bitterness on account of his ill-treatment, and feelings of powerlessness, suspicion, fear, revenge and friendless loneliness tortured his passionate spirit. The spectre from the tower of Fumone stood before his excited imagination in these dark hours. If, in the shock of the reaction of his circumstances, the mind of so high-spirited a man broke its bounds and became the victim of delusions, it was but natural. It was reported that he shut himself up in his room, refused food, beat his head in frenzy against the wall, and was at last found dead upon his bed. The enemies of Boniface VIII took pleasure in painting his death in the darkest colours, and even moderate opponents saw in his fall the judgment of God on the arrogance of the mighty. A papal historian, who was probably in

Rome at the time of Boniface's death, says, "He died on the thirty-fifth day of his imprisonment; he was out of his mind; he believed that every one who came near him would take him to prison." The simple words reveal a juster measure of truth than the more dramatic descriptions of other narrators. Boniface VIII died, eighty-six years old, on October 11, 1303, and was buried in a chapel which he himself had built in a crypt of the Vatican.

Seldom had a pope had so many enemies, so few friends; seldom have contemporaries and after generations disputed more violently over his character. If judgment has been coloured by party passion, the opinon on the whole, nevertheless, remains fixed that Boniface VIII was a highly-gifted man of despotic nature. He was devoid of every spiritual virtue, was of passionate temper, violent, faithless, unscrupulous, unforgiving, filled with ambition and lust of worldly power. His contemporaries already called him "the great-hearted sinner," and he cannot be more fittingly described. The spirit of the age overthrew him as it had overthrown Frederick II. He strove after a goal, which had already become fantastic; he was the last pope who boldly conceived the thought of an all-ruling hierarchy, as Gregory VII, and Innocent III had conceived it. Boniface VIII, however, was only an unfortunate reminiscence of these popes. He was a man who achieved nothing great, whose high-aimed endeavours excited, instead of admiration, merely an ironical smile. He could not maintain himself at the summit of the Papacy. The scene in Anagni, so narrow and petty as compared with the earlier struggles of the Church against the empire, is in the history of the popes a battlefield, such as that of Benevento or Tagliacozzo, where with insignificant means and amid insignificant circumstances the result of tedious trials were decided. The tomb of Boniface VIII is the gravestone of the mediaeval Papacy, which was buried with him by forces of the age. We may still see the monument in the crypt of the Vatican, where the stone figure of the Pope lies on the sarcophagus, the two-fold tiara on his head, with strong and handsome countenance and royal mien.

81. THE POPES AT AVIGNON [1]

Ludwig Pastor is unquestionably the greatest authority on the history of the papacy. Fortunately his celebrated work on this subject has been translated in part into the English language. The author is a Roman Catholic and occasionally he presents an account from the standpoint of that church. He does not, however, indulge in misrepresentation of the facts. His discussion

[1] Ludwig Pastor, *The History of the Popes, from the Close of the Middle Ages.* Translated from the German, and edited by Frederick Ignatius Antrobus. Vol. I. London, John Hodges. 1891, pp. 57–70. Used by permission of Kegan Paul, Trench, Trubner & Co., Ltd.

of the papacy at Avignon is an interesting example of his work. It is the fruit of laborious research and thoughtful analysis.

The disastrous struggle between the highest powers of Christendom, which began in the eleventh century and reached its climax in the thirteenth, was decided, apparently to the advantage of the Papacy, by the tragical downfall of the house of Hohenstaufen. But the overthrow of the Empire also shook the temporal position of the Popes, who were now more and more compelled to ally themselves closely with France. In the warfare with the Emperors, the Papacy had already sought protection and had found refuge in that kingdom in critical times. The sojourn of the Popes in France had, however, been only transitory. The most sacred traditions, and a history going back for more than a thousand years, seemed to have bound the highest ecclesiastical dignity so closely to Italy and to Rome that, in the eleventh, twelfth, and thirteenth centuries, the idea that a Pope could be crowned anywhere but in the Eternal City, or could fix his residence for the whole duration of his Pontificate out of Italy, would have been looked upon as an impossibility.

A change came over this state of things in the time of Clement V. (1305-1314), a native of Gascony. Fearing for the independence of the Ecclesiastical power amid the party struggles by which Italy was torn, and yielding to the influence of Philip the Fair, the strong-handed oppressor of Boniface VIII, he remained in France and never set foot in Rome. His successor, John XXII, also a Gascon, was elected, after prolonged and stormy discussions, in 1316, when the Holy See had been for two years vacant. He took up his permanent abode at Avignon, where he was only separated by the Rhone from the territory of the French King. Clement V had lived as a guest in the Dominican Monastery at Avignon, but John XXII set up a magnificent establishment there. The essential character of that new epoch in the history of the Papacy, which begins with Clement V and John XXII, consists in the lasting separation from the traditional home of the Holy See and from the Italian soil, which brought the Popes into such pernicious dependence on France and seriously endangered the universal nature of their position.

"O good beginning!
To what a vile conclusion must Thou stoop."

The words of the great Italian poet are not exaggerated, for the Avignon Popes, without exception, were all more or less dependent on France. Frenchmen themselves, and surrounded by a College of Cardinals in which the French element predominated, they gave a French character to the government of the Church. This character was at variance with the principle of universality inherent in it and in the Papacy. The Church had always been the representative of this principle in contradistinction to that of isolated nationalities, and it was the high office of the Pope, as her Supreme Head, to be the common Father of all nations. This universality was in a great degree the secret of the power and influence of the Mediaeval Popes.

The migration to France, the creation of a preponderance of French Cardinals, and the consequent election of seven French Popes in succession, necessarily compromised the position of the Papacy in the eyes of the world, creating a suspicion that the highest spiritual power had become the tool of France. This suspicion, though in many cases unfounded, weakened the general confidence in the Head of the Church, and awakened in the other nations a feeling of antagonism to the ecclesiastical authority which had become French. The bonds which united the States of the Church to the Apostolic See were gradually loosened, and the arbitrary proceedings of the Court at Avignon, which was too often swayed by personal and family interests, accelerated the process of dissolution. The worst apprehensions for the future were entertained.

The dark points of the Avignon period have certainly been greatly exaggerated. The assertion that the Government of the Avignon Popes was wholly ruled by the "will and pleasure of the Kings of France," is, in this general sense, unjust. The Popes of those days were not all so weak as Clement V, who submitted the draft of the Bull, by which he called on the Princes of Europe to imprison the Templars, to the French King. Moreover, even this Pope, the least independent of the fourteenth century Pontiffs, for many years offered a passive resistance to the wishes of France, and a writer, who has thoroughly studied the period, emphatically asserts that only for a few years of the Pontificate of Clement V was the idea so long associated with the "Babylonian Captivity" of the Popes fully realized. The extension of this epithet to the whole of the Avignon sojourn is an unfair exaggeration. The eager censors of the dependence into which the Avignon Popes sank, draw attention to the political action of the Holy See during this period so exclusively, that hardly any place is left for its labours in the cause of religion. A very partial picture is thus drawn, wherein the noble efforts of these much abused Pontiffs for the conversion of heathen nations become almost imperceptible in the dim background. Their labours for the propagation of Christianity in India, China, Egypt, Nubia, Abyssinia, Barbary, and Morocco have been very imperfectly appreciated. The earliest of the Avignon Popes, Clement V and John XXII, gave the greatest attention to Eastern affairs, and were the originators of a series of grand creations, from which the best results were to be expected. Their successors were chiefly occupied in the maintenance and preservation of the works established by the wisdom of their predecessors, yet in the time of Clement VI an effort was made to extend the sphere of the Church even to the furthest limits of Eastern Asia. The unwearied assiduity of the Avignon Popes in taking advantage of every favourable event in the East, from the Crimea to China, to promote the spread of Christianity by sending out missions and founding Bishoprics, is all the more admirable because of the great difficulties with which the Papacy was at that time beset. . . .

With the most ample recognition of the worldwide activity of the French Popes, it cannot be denied that the effects of the transfer of the Holy See from its natural and historical home were disastrous. Torn from its proper abode, the Papacy, notwithstanding the individual greatness of some of the Avignon Pontiffs, could not maintain its former dignity. The freedom and independence of the highest tribunal in Christendom, which, according to Innocent III, was bound to protect all rights, was endangered, now that the supreme direction of the Church was so much under the influence of a nation so deeply imbued with its own spirit, and possessing so little of the universal. That France should obtain exclusive possession of the highest spiritual authority was a thing contrary both to the office of the Papacy and the very being of the Church.

This dependence on the power of a Prince, who in former times had often been rebuked by Rome, was in strange contradiction with the supremacy claimed by the Popes. By this subjection and by its worldliness, the Avignon Papacy aroused an opposition which, though it might for a moment be overborne while it leant on the crumbling power of the Empire, yet moved men's minds so deeply that its effects were not effaced for several centuries. Its downfall is most closely connected with this opposition, which was manifested, not only in the bitter accusations of its political and clerical enemies, but even also in the letters of its devoted friend St. Catherine, which are full of entreaties, complaints, and denunciations. The Papal Government, founded as it was on the principle of authority, built up in independence of the Empire, and gaining strength in proportion to the decay of that power, was unable to offer any adequate resistance to this twofold stream of political and religious antagonism. The catastrophe of the great Schism was the immediate consequence of the false position now occupied by the Papacy.

The disastrous effects produced by the residence of the Popes at Avignon were at first chiefly felt in Italy. Hardly ever has a country fallen into such anarchy as did the Italian peninsula, when bereft of her principle of unity by the unfortunate decision of Clement V to fix his abode in France. Torn to pieces by irreconcilable parties, the land, which had been fitly termed the garden of Europe, was now a scene of desolation. It will easily be understood that all Italian hearts were filled with bitter longings, a regret which found voice in continual protests against the Gallicized Papacy. The author of the Divine Comedy sharply reproved the "Supreme Pastor of the West" for this alliance between the Papacy and the French monarchy. On the death of Clement V, when the Cardinals assembled in conclave at Carpentras, Dante came forward as the exponent of the public feeling which demanded the return of the Papal Throne to Rome. In a severe letter addressed to the Italian Cardinals he says: "You, the chiefs of the Church militant, have neglected to guide the chariot of the Bride of the Crucified One along the path so clearly marked out for her. Like that false charioteer Phaeton, you have left the right track and though it was your office to lead the hosts safely through the wilderness, you have dragged them after you into the abyss. But one remedy now remains: you, who have been the authors of all this confusion, must go forth manfully with one heart and one soul into the fray in defence of the Bride of Christ whose seat is in Rome, of Italy, in short of the whole band of pilgrims on earth. This you must do, and then returning in triumph from the battle-field, on which the eyes of the world are fixed, you shall hear the song 'Glory to God in the Highest'; and the disgrace of the covetous Gascons, striving to rob the Latins of their renown, shall serve as a warning to all future ages."

Petrarch judges the French Popes with the greatest severity. In theory he condemns every one, worthy or unworthy, who lived at Avignon. No expression is too strong when he speaks of this city, which he compares to the Babylon of the Apocalypse. In one of his poems he calls it "the fountain of anguish, the dwelling-place of wrath, the school of errors, the temple of heresy, once Rome, now the false guilt-laden Babylon, the forge of lies, the horrible prison, the hell upon earth." In a whole series of letters, which, however, he took care to keep to himself, he pours forth the vials of his wrath on the city, which had drawn the Popes away from sacred Rome. He even uses the peaceful sonnet, in which he had formerly been wont to express only the bliss and the pain of love, to fulminate, like a prophet of the Old Testament, against the doings of the unholy city. It would be, however, a great mistake to consider his picture of the wickedness of Avignon and the corruption of the Church, painted with true Italian fervour, as strictly trustworthy and accurate. Petrarch here speaks as a poet and as a fiery, enthusiastic, Roman patriot. His judgments are often intemperate and unjust. His own life was not such as to give him the right to come forward as a preacher of morals. Passing over his other failings, we need here only allude to his excessive greed for benefices. This passion has much to do with his bitterness against Avignon and the Papal Court. We are led to suspect that there were many unsuccessful suits. Petrarch did nothing towards the amendment of this evil world; the work of reformation was in his own case begun very late. He was a dreamer, who contented himself with theories, and in practice eschewed all improvements which demanded any greater effort than that of declamation.

The unmitigated condemnation of the Avignon Popes must have been based in great measure on Petrarch's unjust representations, to which, in later times and without examination, an undue historical importance has been attached. He is often supposed to be a determined adversary of the Papacy; but this is a complete mistake. He never for a moment questioned its divine institution. We have already said that he was outwardly on the best terms with almost all the Popes of his time, and received from them many favours. They took his frequent and earnest exhortations to leave Avignon and return to desolate Rome as mere poetical rhapsodies, and in fact they were nothing more. If Petrarch himself, though a Roman citizen, kept aloof from Rome; if, though nominally an Italian patriot, he fixed his abode for many years, from motives of convenience, or in quest of preferment, in that very Avignon which he had bitterly reproached the Popes for choosing, and which he had called the most loathsome place in the world, must not the Babylonish poison have eaten deeply into his heart? How much easier it would have been for Petrarch to have returned to Rome than it was for the Popes, fettered as they were by so many political considerations!

But however much we may question Petrarch's right to find fault with the moral delinquencies of the Court at Avignon; however much we may, in many respects, modify the picture he paints of it, no impartial inquirer can deny that it was pervaded by a deplorable worldliness. For this melancholy fact we have testimony more trustworthy than the rhetorical descriptions of the Italian poet. Yet it must in justice be borne in mind that the influx of thousands of strangers into the little French provincial town, so suddenly raised to the position of capital of the world, had produced all the evils which appertain to densely populated places. Moreover, even if we are to believe all the angry assertions of contemporaries as to the corruption prevailing in Avignon, evidence is not wanting, on the other hand, of ardent yearnings for a life conformable to the precepts of the Gospel.

Side by side with the profligacy which was the characteristic of the age, and, therefore, prominent in its history, there were still to be found scattered in various places many homes of quiet and devout contemplation. Thence went forth an influence, winning noble souls to a higher ideal of existence, and gently, but perseveringly, striving by means of self-denial and persuasion, to allay the passionate feuds of parties and disentangle their intrigues. As this higher life only manifested itself here and there, history passes it by; it is dealt with in commonplace phrases, judged, or rather misjudged, by the measure of the later movements of the sixteenth century, as if they formed a canon for the historical investigation of all religious phenomena. At no time were there wanting good and earnest men, who were doing their utmost in their own circle to stem the tide of corruption, and exerting a salutary influence on their age and surroundings. It would be most unjust to the champions of the Papal rights to suppose that, because they maintained the monarchy of the Pope and his right to both swords, they were ready to sanction that which was evil at Avignon, or condone tyrannous abuses. In the highest circles there were men of the ancient stamp with the strictest views of life. Alvaro Pelayo praised the Cardinal Legate Martin, who went to Denmark poor and returned poor, and the Legate Gaufridus who, when sent to Aquitaine, bought his own fish and would not accept even wooden platters. He wished Bishops and Popes not to have smart pages about them, and not to promote undeserving relations. He prayed that all simoniacal practices should be abolished, that the Roman Church should be a mother, not a sovereign, and that the Pope should consider himself not a lord, but a servant, a steward, a labourer. These men, who looked on Louis of Bavaria as a tyrant, were not on that account disposed to give the Pope a free pass. While energetically asserting his rights and those of the Church and the Bishops, they also insisted on the accompanying duties with a plainness of speech, which we miss in later ages, together with the magnanimity shown by those who suffered it.

The removal of the Holy See to Avignon was most disastrous to the *Eternal City,* which thereby lost, not only her historic position as the Capital of Christendom, but also the material benefits which the presence of the Popes conferred on the community at large, and on many of the individual inhabitants. While the Popes resided in Rome and its neighbourhood, they were able, for longer or shorter periods, to maintain order and peace between Barons and Burghers. Their Court and the influx of strangers which it attracted, brought great wealth into the City, and when the Pontiff was in their midst, the Romans could easily attain to lucrative ecclesiastical positions. This state of things was now completely changed. Rome, thrown upon herself, was in her interior resources inferior to all the considerable cities of central Italy. She became a prey to increasing isolation and anarchy. The longer the absence of the Popes continued, the greater was the desolation. The Churches were so dilapidated and neglected that in St. Peter's and the Lateran cattle were grazing even to the foot of the altar. Many sacred edifices were roofless, and others almost in ruins. The monuments of heathen antiquity fared even worse than those of Christian Rome, and were mercilessly destroyed. A Legate sold the marble blocks of the Colosseum to be burned for lime. The materials of the ancient edifices were even carried out of the City. In the archives regarding the construction of the Cathedral of Orvieto are a number of documents, which show that the overseers of the work brought a great deal of the marble employed from Rome, that they sent agents there almost more frequently than to Carrara, and that they repeatedly received presents of great blocks of marble, especially from the families of the Orsini and Savelli. The only public work executed in Rome during the Avignon period was the construction of the marble steps leading up to the Church of St. Maria Ara Coeli. The remarkable development of art which had been going on during the latter half of the thirteenth century was suddenly arrested. The school of the Cosmati came to an end; the influence of Giotto had vanished. Avignon became in this respect a dangerous rival to the Eternal City, for even in their exile the Popes did not forget the fine arts. Death alone hindered Giotto from accepting the flattering invitation of Benedict XII, and in 1338–39 the Pope summoned in his stead the celebrated painter, Simone Martini of Siena, to adorn his Cathedral and his Palace; the interesting but long-neglected frescoes of this artist are now, alas! in a melancholy condition. The bereaved City fared almost as ill in regard to literature as to art. The consequences of this state of things, which then passed unperceived, made themselves felt at a later period. The triumph of the Renaissance in Rome would have been neither so rapid nor so complete, but for the state of barbarism into which the City had fallen when deprived of the Pope.

82. *MARSILIUS (MARSIGLIO) OF PADUA AND THE PAPACY* [1]

In the long contest between the papacy and the rulers of France, England, and the Holy Roman Empire much of the fighting was done with the pen. Not only were numerous letters written and papal bulls issued but also books were composed. Perhaps the most famous of the latter was a work by Marsilius of Padua, who in 1324 penned the Defensor Pacis, *or* Defender of the Peace, *in which he boldly attacked the papacy. At this time the emperor of the Holy Roman Empire was Louis or Lewis the Bavarian, the enemy of Pope John XXII. He was favorably impressed by the arguments adduced by Marsilius of Padua, and, as Creighton tells us in the following passage, he actually attempted to enforce them. Creighton also gives us a masterful analysis of the* Defensor Pacis, *which in some respects clarifies the views of the writer and even surpasses the original document.*

Marsiglio was an Italian, who, in the politics of his own city, had gained a comprehensive grasp of principles, and whose mind had matured by the

[1] M. Creighton, *A History of the Papacy from the Great Schism to the Sack of Rome,* Vol. I. London and New York, Longmans, Green, and Co., 1907, pp. 41–47. Used by permission.

study of Aristotle. John of Jandun, a Frenchman, was Marsiglio's friend, and both held high positions in the University of Paris, which they suddenly quitted in 1327, sought out Lewis [of Bavaria], and placed their learning at his disposal for an attack upon the Pope. It was strange that scholars and theorists should come forward merely on theoretical grounds to enter into a contest which in no way affected themselves. They proposed to Lewis a serious undertaking—that the Empire, as such, should enter into a controversy on abstract questions with the Pope. The Papacy was the source of orthodoxy, the centre of learning; rude soldiers before this had answered its claims by deeds, but Lewis was asked to meet the Pope with his own weapons. Marsiglio urged that John XXII had already laid himself open to the charge of heresy; his decision about the friars was in contradiction to the opinion of his predecessors; unless the Papal autocracy were to be absolutely admitted, it was the Emperor's duty to check an erring Pope. For a time Lewis hesitated; then he accepted Marsiglio's proposal, and appealed to Christendom to support him in his position.

The great work of Marsiglio, the "Defensor Pacis," was already written, when first he sought Lewis, and was at once published in explanation of the principles on which Lewis acted. The title of the work was skilfully chosen; it marked out the Pope as the originator of the troubles, discords, and wars which a pacific Emperor wished to check. The work itself is a keen, bold, and clear assertion of the rights of the State as against the Church. Following in the steps of Aristotle's "Politics," Marsiglio traces the origin of government and of law. Civil society is a community for the purpose of common life; in such community there are various classes with various occupations; the occupation of the priestly class is "to teach and discipline men in things which, according to the Gospel, ought to be believed, done, or omitted to obtain eternal salvation." The regulator of the community is the judicial or governing class, whose object is to enforce the laws. Law is defined as "knowledge of what is just or useful, concerning the observance of which a coercive precept has been issued." The legislator is "the people or community of the citizens, or the majority of them, determining, by their choice or will, expressed by word in a general assembly, that anything should be done or omitted regarding man's civil acts under pain of temporal punishment." This legislative power is the source of the authority of the prince or ruler, whose duty it is to observe the laws and compel others to observe them. If the prince set himself above the laws, he ought to be corrected by the legislative power which he represents.

This system of civil life is disturbed by the interference of the spiritual authority, especially of the Pope, with the due execution of the laws, and with the authority of the prince. The Papal claims rest on the supposed descent to Christ's representatives of the plenitude of Christ's power; but this carries with it no coercive jurisdiction (jurisdictio coactiva) by which they may exact penalties or interfere in temporal affairs. It is their claim to this coercive jurisdiction that destroys civil government and causes universal disorder.

To trace this point more fully Marsiglio proceeds to examine the relations of the priesthood towards the community. The Church is the community of all who believe in Christ; for all, priests and laity alike, are "Churchmen," because Christ redeemed them with His Blood. So far as a priest possesses worldly goods or engages in worldly matters, he is under the same laws as the rest of the community. The priesthood can have no authority except what was given by Christ, and the question to be considered is not what power Christ could have given them, but what He actually gave. We find that Christ did not Himself exercise coercive jurisdiction, and did not confer it on the Apostles, but warned them by example, advice and precept to abstain from using it; moreover, Christ submitted Himself to the coercive jurisdiction of temporal princes. Hence no priest has any judicial or coercive power unless it be given him by the legislator; his priestly authority, which he derives from Christ, is to preach the doctrine and administer the sacraments of Christ. To pronounce excommunication does not belong to an individual priest, but to the community of believers or their representatives. The priest is the minister of God's law, but has no power to compel men to accept or obey it; only as physicians care for the health of the body, so do priests, by wise advice and warning, operate on the soul. It may be objected that, at least in question of heresy, the priesthood has to judge and punish: really, however, the judge of heresy is Christ, and the punishment is inflicted in another world; the priest judges in Christ's stead in this world, and must warn and terrify offenders by the thoughts of future punishment. The civil power punishes heresy only so far as heresy subverts the law.

Marsiglio next subjects to criticism the doctrine of the Papal supremacy. Priests as such are all equal: S. Peter had no authority over the other Apostles, no power of punishment or jurisdiction. Moreover, the legend that S. Peter was the first Bishop of Rome rests on no Scriptural authority, and has no historical evidence. The appointment and deprivation of ecclesiastics belong to the community of the faithful, as is shown by the appointment of the first deacons recorded in the Acts of the Apostles. This authority of the community is now vested in the princes, and the appointment of good priests is a matter which concerns the well-being of the State.

The Catholic faith is one, and rests on Scripture only, so that decretals and decrees of Popes and Cardinals are not necessary for salvation. When doubts arise about the meaning of Scripture, they can be settled only by a general council of the faithful, in which laity and clergy alike have seats. The summoning of such a council belongs to the supreme legislative power, and only a council can pronounce excommunication or interdict upon princes or peoples. The authority of the Roman bishop over other bishops is necessary to give a head to the Church and a president to its councils; but the Roman bishop has no power of coercion beyond what a council offers.

The existing theory of the primacy of the Pope sprang from the respect originally paid to the Bishop of Rome, which has been extended, partly by unfounded claims of scriptural right, partly by the grants of princes, especially by the donation of Constantine. The Papal primacy has corrupted the Church; for the Pope, through the plenitude of his power, interferes with elections, sets aside the rights of chapters, and appoints bishops who cannot speak the language of the people over whom they are set as shepherds, and who simply aim at gathering money from their flocks. Generally speaking, the bishops cannot preach, nor have they knowledge to refute heresies; and the inferior clergy are as ignorant as their superiors. Lawyers, not theologians, fill the Papal Court; ecclesiastical order is everywhere overthrown by the dispensations from episcopal control which the Pope readily grants to monks and friars. Simony abounds, and on all sides may be seen the proofs that the plenitude of the Papal power is the root of corruption in the Church.

Moreover the Papacy has put forth claims against the temporal power, especially against the Empire. This arises from the fact that the Pope crowned the Emperor, and a reverence at first voluntary has gradually been regarded as a right. Papal recognition has been considered necessary to complete the authority bestowed on the Emperor by election. But this is entirely unfounded; the right conferred by election needs no supplement, and the claims of the Papacy have simply been advanced owing to the frequency of disputed elections and vacancies in the Empire. The Papal claims and the exercise of Papal power in temporal matters have plunged Italy and Germany into discord, and it is the duty of all men, especially of kings and rulers, to check the abuse of this usurped authority.

This remarkable work of Marsiglio stands on the very threshold of modern history as a clear forecast of the ideas which were to regulate the future progress of Europe. The conceptions of the sovereignty of the people, and of the official position of the ruler, mark the development of European politics up to our own day. The general relations between Church and State, which Marsiglio foreshadowed, were those which the Reformation established in countries where it prevailed. In the clear definition of the limits of ecclesiastical authority, and in his assertion of the dignity of the individual believer, Marsiglio's ideas still remained unrealized. It is a wonderful testimony to the vigour of Italian civic life that the political experience gleaned at Padua ran so readily into the form provided by a study of Aristotle's "Politics," and produced results so clear, so bold, and so systematic. It is the scientific character of the "Defensor Pacis" that marks it as especially important, and sets it far beyond the other political writings of the next two centuries. It was calculated to produce a powerful impression on men's minds, and remained as a great storehouse for the writers of the next century. The ease with which the conciliar movement won its way to general acceptance throughout Christendom must be attributed in great measure to the dissemination of Marsiglio's principles. Pope Clement VI declared that he had never read a more pestilent heretic; and Gregory XI found that the opinions of Wyclif were only slightly changed from those of Marsiglio. If Wyclif had been as clear and as systematic as Marsiglio, his influence on his contemporaries would have been far greater and his teaching would not have lent itself to so much misunderstanding.

It was Marsiglio's misfortune that he was allied to a cause which had not a leader strong enough to give adequate expression to the principles which the genius of Marsiglio supplied. The traditions of the past still determined the steps of Lewis; in 1327 he marched into Italy and was elected Emperor by the people of Rome. The old rights of the Roman Republic were set up against those of the Pope, and the Imperial crown was placed on the head of Lewis by Sciarra Colonna, who struck the deadly blow against Boniface VIII at Anagni. Nor was this enough. The Minorites from the pulpits denounced John XXII as a heretic, and Rome, which had made an Emperor, was willing to go further and also make a Pope. John XXII was deposed; a friar was elected Pope by the clergy and laity of Rome, and took the name of Nicolas V. Lewis had no means of combating the fictions on which the Papal power was founded save by setting against them a fiction still more ludicrous. The claim of the citizens of Rome to appoint the temporal and spiritual heads of Christendom was more monstrous than that of the Pope to determine the election of the Emperor. The mediaeval theory might be untenable, but the attempt to overthrow it by a revival of classical usage was absurd. The last struggle which had so long raged between Empire and Papacy ended in an empty theatrical display.

83. BEGINNING OF THE GREAT WESTERN SCHISM [1]

While Christendom was still breathing a sigh of relief over the return of the Papacy from Avignon to Rome it was plunged into new distress by the Great Western Schism. This Schism, or breach in the Church, was the result of the election of two Popes, one of whom remained at Rome while the other went back to Avignon. Christian peoples were divided and uncertain as to which was the rightful Pontiff; and remedies for the unhappy situation were desperately sought. Finally, in 1409, a great Church Council was held at Pisa to settle the problem. But the Council of Pisa only made matters worse, for it chose a third man as Pope without securing the abdication of the other two. So instead of two claimants to the Papal throne there were now three.

The beginning of the Great Western Schism is graphically described by Henry Hart Milman (1791–1868) in his History of Latin Christianity, *first published in 1855. Of this book it has been said that its "shortcomings and minor inaccuracies are amply compensated by qualities till then rare in ecclesiastical historians—liberality, candour, sympathy, and catholic appreciation of every estimable quality in every person or party—which not only contributed an especial charm to the work, but may be said to have permanently raised the standard of ecclesiastical history"* (Dictionary of National Biography, *vol. XIII, p. 450*).

Gregory XI had hardly expired when Rome burst out into a furious tumult. A Roman Pope, at least an Italian Pope, was the universal outcry. The Conclave must be overawed; the hateful domination of a foreign, a French Pontiff must be broken up, and forever. This was not unforeseen. Before his death Gregory XI had issued a Bull, conferring the amplest powers on the Cardinals to choose, according to their wisdom, the time and the place for the election. It manifestly contemplated their retreat from the turbulent streets of Rome to some place where their deliberations would not be overborne, and the predominant French interest would maintain its superiority. On the other hand there were serious and not groundless apprehensions that the fierce Breton and Gascon bands, at the command of the French Cardinals, might dictate to the Conclave. The Romans not only armed their civic troops, but sent to Tivoli, Velletri, and the neighboring cities; a strong force was mustered to keep the foreigners in check. Throughout the interval between the funeral of Gregory and the opening of the Conclave, the Cardinals were either too jealously watched, or thought

[1] Henry H. Milman, *History of Latin Christianity.* 8 Vols. New York, Sheldon and Co., 1862, Vol. VII, pp. 228–245.

it imprudent to attempt flight. Sixteen Cardinals were present at Rome, one Spaniard, eleven French, four Italians. The ordinary measures were taken for opening the Conclave in the palace near St. Peter's. Five Romans, two ecclesiastics and three laymen, and three Frenchmen were appointed to wait upon and to guard the Conclave. The Bishop of Marseilles represented the great Chamberlain, who holds the supreme authority during the vacancy of the Popedom. The Chamberlain the Archbishop of Arles, brother of the Cardinal of Limoges, had withdrawn into the Castle of St. Angelo, to secure his own person, and to occupy that important fortress.

The nine solemn days fully elapsed, on the 7th of April they assembled for the Conclave. At that instant (inauspicious omen!) a terrible flash of lightning, followed by a stunning peal of thunder, struck through the hall, burning and splitting some of the furniture. The Hall of Conclave was crowded by a fierce rabble, who refused to retire. After about an hour's strife, the Bishop of Marseilles, by threats, by persuasion, or by entreaty, had expelled all but about forty wild men, armed to the teeth. These ruffians rudely and insolently searched the whole building; they looked under the beds, they examined the places of retreat. They would satisfy themselves whether any armed men were concealed, whether there was any hole, or even drain through which the Cardinals could escape. All the time they shouted, "A Roman Pope! we will have a Roman Pope!" Those without echoed back the savage yell. Before long appeared two ecclesiastics, announcing themselves as delegated by the commonalty of Rome; they demanded to speak with the Cardinals. The Cardinals dared not refuse. The Romans represented, in firm but not disrespectful language, that for seventy years the holy Roman people had been without their pastor, the supreme head of Christendom. In Rome were many noble and wise ecclesiastics equal to govern the Church: if not in Rome, there were such men in Italy. They intimated that so great was the fury and determination of the people, that if the Conclave should resist, there might be a general massacre, in which probably they themselves, assuredly the Cardinals, would perish. The Cardinals might hear from every quarter around them the cry, "A Roman Pope! if not a Roman, an Italian!" The Cardinals replied, that such aged and reverend men must know the rules of the Conclave; that no election could be by requisition, favor, fear, or tumult, but by the interposition of the Holy Ghost. To reiterated persuasions and menaces they only said, "We are in your power; you may kill us, but we must act according to God's ordinance. Tomorrow we celebrate the Mass for the descent of the Holy Ghost; as the Holy Ghost directs, so shall we do." Some of the French uttered words which sounded like defiance. The populace cried, "If ye persist to do despite to Christ, if we have not a Roman Pope, we will hew these Cardinals and Frenchmen in pieces." At length the Bishop of Marseilles was able entirely to clear the hall. The Cardinals sat down to a plentiful repast; the doors were finally closed. But all the night through they heard in the streets the unceasing clamor, "A Roman Pope, a Roman Pope!" Towards the morning the tumult became more fierce and dense. Strange men had burst into the belfry of St. Peter's; the clanging bells tolled as if all Rome was on fire.

Within the Conclave the tumult, if less loud and clamorous, was hardly less general. The confusion without and terror within did not allay the angry rivalry, or suspend that subtle play of policy peculiar to the form of election. The French interest was divided; within this circle there was another circle. The single diocese of Limoges, favored as it had been by more than one Pope, had almost strength to dictate to the Conclave. The Limousins put forward the Cardinal de St. Eustache. Against these the leader was the Cardinal Robert of Geneva, whose fierce and haughty demeanor and sanguinary acts as Legate had brought so much of its unpopularity on the administration of Gregory XI. With Robert were the four Italians and three French Cardinals. Rather than a Limousin, Robert would even consent to an Italian. They on the one side, the Limousins on the other, had met secretly before the Conclave: the eight had sworn not on any account to submit to the election of a traitorous Limousin.

All the sleepless night the Cardinals might hear the din at the gate, the yells of the people, the tolling of the bells. There was constant passing and repassing from each other's chambers, intrigues, altercations, manoeuvres, proposals advanced and rejected, promises of support given and withdrawn. Many names were put up. Of the Romans within the Conclave two only were named, the old Cardinal of St. Peter's, the Cardinal Jacobo Orsini. The Limousins advanced in turn almost every one of their faction; no one but himself thought of Robert of Geneva.

In the morning the disturbance without waxed more terrible. A vain attempt was made to address the populace by the three Cardinal Priors; they were driven from the windows with loud derisive shouts, "A Roman! A Roman!" For now the alternative of an Italian had been abandoned; a Roman, none but a Roman, would content the people. The madness of intoxication was added to the madness of popular fury. The rabble had broken open the Pope's cellar, and drunk his rich wines. In the Conclave the wildest projects were started. The Cardinal Orsini's was to dress up a Minorite Friar (probably a Spiritual) in the Papal robes, to show him to the people, and so for themselves to effect their escape to some safe place, and proceed to a legitimate election. The Cardinals, from honor or from fear, shrunk from this trick.

At length both parties seemed to concur. Each claimed credit for first advancing the name, which most afterwards repudiated, of the Archbishop of Bari, a man of repute for theologic and legal erudition, an Italian, but a subject of the Queen of Naples, who was also Countess of Provence. They came to the nomination. The Cardinal of Florence proposed the Cardinal of St. Peter's. The Cardinal of Limoges arose, "The Cardinal of St. Peter's is too old. The Cardinal of Florence is of a city at war with the Holy See. I reject the Cardinal of Milan as the subject of the Visconti, the most deadly enemy of the Church. The Cardinal Orsini is too young, and we must not yield to the clamor of the Romans. I vote for Bartholomew Prignani, Archbishop of Bari." All was acclamation; Orsini alone stood out: he aspired to be the Pope of the Romans.

But it was too late; the mob was thundering at the gates, menacing death to the Cardinals, if they had not immediately a Roman pontiff. The feeble defences sounded as if they were shattering down; the tramp of the populace was almost heard within the Hall. They forced or persuaded the aged Cardinal of St. Peter's to make a desperate effort to save their lives. He appeared at the window, hastily attired in what either was or seemed to be the Papal stole and mitre. There was a jubilant and triumphant cry, "We have a Roman Pope, the Cardinal of St. Peter's. Long live Rome! long live St. Peter!" The populace became even more frantic with joy than before with wrath. One band hastened to the Cardinal's palace, and according to the strange usage, broke in, threw the furniture into the streets, and sacked it from top to bottom. Those around the Hall of Conclave, aided by the connivance of some of the Cardinals' servants within, or by more violent efforts of their own, burst in in all quarters. The supposed Pope was surrounded by eager adorers; they were at his feet; they pressed his swollen, gouty hands till he shrieked from pain, and began to protest, in the strongest language, that he was not the Pope.

The indignation of the populace at this disappointment was aggravated by an unlucky confusion of names. The Archbishop was mistaken for John of Bari, of the bedchamber of the late Pope, a man of harsh manners and dissolute life, an object of general hatred. Five of the Cardinals, Robert of Geneva, Acquasparta, Viviers, Poitou, and De Verny, were seized in their attempt to steal away, and driven back, amid contemptuous hootings, by personal violence. Night came on again; the populace, having pillaged all the provisions in the Conclave, grew weary of their own excesses. The Cardinals fled on all sides. Four left the city; Orsini and St. Eustache escaped to Vicovaro, Robert of Geneva to Zagarolo, St. Angelo to Guardia; six, Limoges, D'Aigrefeuille, Poitou, Viviers, Brittany, and Marmoutiers, to the Castle of St. Angelo; Florence, Milan, Montmayeur, Glandève, and Luna, to their own strong fortresses.

The Pope lay concealed in the Vatican. In the morning the five Cardinals in Rome assembled round him. A message was sent to the Bannerets of

Rome, announcing his election. The six Cardinals in St. Angelo were summoned; they were hardly persuaded to leave their place of security; but without their presence the Archbishop would not declare his assent to his elevation. The Cardinal of Florence, as Dean, presented the Pope Elect to the Sacred College, and discoursed on the text, "Such ought he to be, an undefiled High Priest." The Archbishop began a long harangue, "Fear and trembling have come upon me, the horror of great darkness." The Cardinal of Florence cut short the ill-timed sermon, demanding whether he accepted the Pontificate. The Archbishop gave his assent; he took the name of Urban VI. Te Deum was intoned; he was lifted to the throne. The fugitives returned to Rome. Urban VI was crowned on Easter Day, in the Church of St. John Lateran. All the Cardinals were present at the august ceremony. They announced the election of Urban VI to their brethren who had remained in Avignon. Urban himself addressed the usual encyclic letters, proclaiming his elevation, to all the Prelates in Christendom.

None but He who could read the hearts of men could determine how far the nomination of the Archbishop of Bari was free and uncontrolled by the terrors of the raging populace; but the acknowledgement of Urban VI by all the Cardinals, at his inauguration in the holy office—their assistance at his coronation without protest, when some at least might have been safe beyond the walls of Rome—their acceptance of honors, as by the Cardinals of Limoges, Poitou, and Aigrefeuille—the homage of all—might seem to annul all possible irregularity in the election, to confirm irrefragably the legitimacy of his title.

Not many days had passed, when the Cardinals began to look with dismay and bitter repentance on their own work. "In Urban VI," said a writer of these times (on the side of Urban as rightful Pontiff), "was verified the proverb— None is so insolent as a low man suddenly raised to power." The high-born, haughty, luxurious Prelates, both French and Italian, found that they had set over themselves a master resolved not only to redress the flagrant and inveterate abuses of the College and of the Hierarchy, but also to force on his reforms in the most hasty and insulting way. He did the harshest things in the harshest manner.

The Archbishop of Bari, of mean birth, had risen by the virtues of a monk. He was studious, austere, humble, a diligent reader of the Bible, master of the canon law, rigid in his fasts; he wore hair-cloth next his skin. His time was divided between study, prayer, and business, for which he had great aptitude. From the poor bishopric of Acherontia he had been promoted to the archbishopric of Bari, and had presided over the Papal Chancery in Avignon. The monk broke out at once on his elevation in the utmost rudeness and rigor, but the humility changed to the most offensive haughtiness. Almost his first act was a public rebuke in his chapel to all the Bishops present for their desertion of their dioceses. He called them perjured traitors. The Bishop of Pampeluna boldly repelled the charge; he was at Rome, he said, on the affairs of his see. In the full Consistory Urban preached on the text "I am the good Shepherd," and inveighed in a manner not to be mistaken against the wealth and luxury of the Cardinals. Their voluptuous banquets were notorious (Petrarch had declaimed against them). The Pope threatened a sumptuary law, that they should have but one dish at their table: it was the rule of his own Order. He was determined to extirpate simony. A Cardinal who should receive presents he menaced with excommunication. He affected to despise wealth. "Thy money perish with thee!" he said to a collector of the Papal revenue. He disdained to conceal the most unpopular schemes; he declared his intention not to leave Rome. To the petition of the Bannerets of Rome for a promotion of Cardinals, he openly avowed his design to make so large a nomination that the Italians should resume their ascendency over the Ultramontanes. The Cardinal of Geneva turned pale, and left the Consistory. Urban declared himself determined to do equal justice between man and man, between the Kings of France and England. The French Cardinals, and those in the pay of France, heard this with great indignation.

The manners of Urban were even more offensive than his acts. "Hold your tongue!" "You have talked long enough!" were his common phrases to his mitred counsellors. He called the Cardinal Orsini a fool. He charged the Cardinal of St. Marcellus (of Amiens), on his return from his legation in Tuscany, with having robbed the treasures of the Church. The charge was not less insulting for its justice. The Cardinal of Amiens, instead of allaying the feuds of France and England, which it was his holy mission to allay, had inflamed them in order to glut his own insatiable avarice by draining the wealth of both countries in the Pope's name. "As Archbishop of Bari, you lie," was the reply of the high-born Frenchman. On one occasion such high words passed with the Cardinal of Limoges, that but for the interposition of another Cardinal the Pope would have rushed on him, and there had been a personal conflict.

Such were among the stories of the time. Friends and foes agree in attributing the schism, at least the immediate schism, to the imprudent zeal, the imperiousness, the ungovernable temper of Pope Urban. The Cardinals among themselves talked of him as mad; they began to murmur that it was a compulsory, therefore invalid, election.

The French Cardinals were now at Anagni: they were joined by the Cardinal of Amiens, who had taken no part in the election, but who was burning under the insulting words of the Pope, perhaps not too eager to render an account of his legation. The Pope retired to Tivoli; he summoned the Cardinals to that city. They answered that they had gone to large expenses in laying in provisions and making preparations for their residence in Anagni; they had no means to supply a second sojourn in Tivoli. The Pope, with his four Italian Cardinals, passed two important acts as Sovereign Pontiff. He confirmed the election of Wenceslaus, son of Charles IV, to the Empire; he completed the treaty with Florence by which the Republic paid a large sum to the See of Rome. The amount was 70,000 florins in the course of the year, 180,000 in four years, for the expenses of the war. They were relieved from ecclesiastical censures, under which this enlightened Republic, though Italian, trembled, even from a Pope of doubtful title. Their awe showed perhaps the weakness and dissensions in Florence rather than the Papal power.

The Cardinals at Anagni sent a summons to their brethren inviting them to share in their counsels concerning the compulsory election of the successor to Gregory XI. Already the opinions of great legists had been taken; some of them, that of the famous Baldus, may still be read. He was in favor of the validity of the election.

But grave legal arguments and ecclesiastical logic were not to decide a contest which had stirred so deeply the passions and interests of two great factions. France and Italy were at strife for the Popedom. The Ultramontane Cardinals would not tamely abandon a power which had given them rank, wealth, luxury, virtually the spiritual supremacy of the world, for seventy years. Italy, Rome, would not forego the golden opportunity of resuming the long-lost authority. On the 9th August the Cardinals at Anagni publicly declared, they announced in encyclic letters addressed to the faithful in all Christendom, that the election of Urban VI was carried by force and the fear of death; that through the same force and fear he had been inaugurated, enthroned, and crowned; that he was an apostate, an accursed Antichrist. They pronounced him a tyrannical usurper of the Popedom, a wolf that had stolen into the fold. They called upon him to descend at once from the throne which he occupied without canonical title; if repentant, he might find mercy; if he persisted, he would provoke the indignation of God, of the Apostles St. Peter and St. Paul, and all the Saints, for his violation of the Spouse of Christ, the common Mother of the Faithful. It was signed by thirteen Cardinals. The more pious and devout were shocked at this avowal of cowardice; Cardinals who would not be martyrs in the cause of truth and of spiritual freedom condemned themselves.

But letters and appeals to the judgment of the world, and awful maledictions, were not their only resources. The fierce Breton bands were used to march and to be indulged in their worst excesses under the banner of the Cardinal of Geneva. As Ultramontanists it was their interest, their inclination, to espouse the Ultramontane cause. They arrayed themselves to advance and join the Cardinals at Anagni. The Romans rose to oppose them; a fight took place near the Ponte Salario, three hundred Romans lay dead on the field.

Urban VI was as blind to cautious temporal as to cautious ecclesiastical policy. Every act of the Pope raised him up new enemies. Joanna, Queen of Naples, had hailed the elevation of her subject the Archbishop of Bari. Naples had been brilliantly illuminated. Shiploads of fruit and wines, and the more solid gift of 20,000 florins, had been her oblations to the Pope. Her husband, Otho of Brunswick, had gone to Rome to pay his personal homage. His object was to determine in his own favor the succession to the realm. The reception of Otho was cold and repulsive; he returned in disgust. The Queen eagerly listened to suspicions, skilfully awakened, that Urban meditated the resumption of the fief of Naples, and its grant to the rival House of Hungary. She became the sworn ally of the Cardinals at Anagni. Honorato Gaetani, Count of Fondi, one of the most turbulent barons of the land, demanded of the Pontiff 20,000 florins advanced on loan to Gregory XI. Urban not only rejected the claim, declaring it a personal debt of the late Pope, not of the Holy See, he also deprived Gaetani of his fief, and granted it to his mortal enemy, the Count San Severino. Gaetani began immediately to seize the adjacent castles in Campania, and invited the Cardinals to his stronghold at Fondi. The Archbishop of Arles, Chamberlain of the late Pope, leaving the Castle of St. Angelo under the guard of a commander who long refused all orders from Pope Urban, brought to Anagni the jewels and ornaments of the Papacy, which had been carried for security to St. Angelo. The Prefect of the city, De Vico, Lord of Viterbo, had been won over by the Cardinal of Amiens.

The four Italian Cardinals still adhered to Pope Urban. They labored hard to mediate between the conflicting parties. Conferences were held at Zagarolo and other places; when the French Cardinals had retired to Fondi, the Italians took up their quarters at Subiaco. The Cardinal of St. Peter's, worn out with age and trouble, withdrew to Rome, and soon after died. He left a testamentary document declaring the validity of the election of Urban. The French Cardinals had declared the election void; they were debating the next step. Some suggested the appointment of a coadjutor. They were now sure of the support of the King of France, who would not easily surrender his influence over a Pope at Avignon, and of the Queen of Naples, estranged by the pride of Urban, and secretly stimulated by the Cardinal Orsini, who had not forgiven his own loss of the tiara. Yet even now they seemed to shrink from the creation of an Antipope. Urban precipitated and made inevitable this disastrous event. He was now alone; the Cardinals of St. Peter's was dead; Florence, Milan, and the Orsini stood aloof; they seemed only to await to be thrown off by Urban, to join the adverse faction. Urban at first declared his intention to create nine Cardinals; he proceeded at once, and without warning, to create twenty-six. By this step the French and Italian Cardinals together were now but an insignificant minority. They were instantly one. All must be risked, or all lost.

On September 20, at Fondi, Robert of Geneva was elected Pope in the presence of all the Cardinals (except St. Peter's) who had chosen, inaugurated, enthroned, and for a time obeyed Urban VI. The Italians refused to give their suffrages, but entered no protest. They retired into their castles, and remained aloof from the schism. Orsini died before long at Tagliacozzo. The qualifications which, according to his partial biographer, recommended the Cardinal of Geneva, were rather those of a successor to John Hawkwood or to a Duke of Milan, than of the Apostles. Extraordinary activity of body and endurance of fatigue, courage which would hazard his life to put down the intrusive Pope, sagacity and experience in the temporal affairs of the Church; high birth, through which he was allied with most of the royal and princely houses of Europe: of austerity, devotion, learning, holiness, charity, not a word. He took the name of Clement VII: the Italians bitterly taunted the mockery of this name, assumed by the Captain of the Breton Free Companies—by the author, it was believed, of the massacre at Cesena.

So began the Schism which divided Western Christendom for thirty-eight years. Italy, excepting the kingdom of Joanna of Naples, adhered to her native Pontiff; Germany and Bohemia to the Pontiff who had recognized King Wenceslaus as Emperor; England to the Pontiff hostile to France; Hungary to the Pontiff who might support her pretensions to Naples; Poland and the Northern Kingdoms, with Portugal, espoused the same cause. France at first stood almost alone in support of her subject, of a Pope at Avignon instead of at Rome. Scotland only was with Clement, because England was with Urban. So Flanders was with Urban because France was with Clement. The uncommon abilities of Peter di Luna, the Spanish Cardinal (afterwards better known under a higher title), detached successively the Spanish kingdoms, Castile, Arragon, and Navarre, from allegiance to Pope Urban.

84. THE COUNCIL OF CONSTANCE [1]

The Great Schism to which we have just referred lasted from 1378 to 1417. In the latter year it was ended by the Council of Constance, which deposed Popes John XXIII, Gregory XII, and Benedict XIII, and elected

[1] M. Creighton, *A History of the Papacy from the Great Schism to the Sack of Rome,* Vol. I. London and New York, Longmans, Green, and Co., 1907, pp. 299–308. Used by permission.

in their place Martin V. The schism had been one of the chief causes of the criticism hurled at the papacy and the Church in general, and it was widely felt that only a great church council could restore the Roman Catholic Church to its former purity. Pious reformers as well as civil authorities had long insisted on the need of such a council, particularly since the papacy had temporarily ceased to maintain high standards and to exercise centralized authority. Some of the reasons why the Council of Constance was convoked and a description of how the assembly began its work have been ably presented in the following selection by M. Creighton.

At the time of the assembling of the Council of Constance there was a widespread and serious desire throughout Europe for a reformation of the ecclesiastical abuses which the Schism had forced into such luxuriant growth; not only was unity to be restored to the headship of the Church, but a remedy must also be found for the evils which beset the entire body. The gross extortions of the Pope and Curia must be checked and their occasion done away with. The Papal invasion of ecclesiastical patronage all over Christendom must be stopped. The ordinary machinery of Church government, which had been weakened by the constant interference of the Pope, must be again restored. The clergy, whose knowledge, morality and zeal had all declined, must be brought back to discipline, so that their waning influence over earnest men might be re-established.

If we would understand aright the force of the feelings that made the Papacy hateful, till the hatred broke out into open revolt, it is worth while to gather a few of the impassioned utterances of this time. Dietrich Vrie, a German monk who went to Constance, in a Latin poem more remarkable for its vigour than its grace, puts the following language into the mouth of the disconsolate Church:

"The Pope, once the wonder of the world, has fallen, and with him fell the heavenly temples, my members. Now is the reign of Simon Magus, and the riches of this world prevent just judgment. The Papal Court nourishes every kind of scandal, and turns God's houses into a market. The sacraments are basely sold; the rich is honoured, the poor is despised, he who gives most is best received. Golden was the first age of the Papal Court; then came the baser age of silver; next the iron age long set its yoke on the stubborn neck. Then came the age of clay. Could aught be worse? Aye, dung; and in dung sits the Papal Court. All things are degenerate; the Papal Court is rotten; the Pope himself, head of all wickedness, plots every kind of disgraceful scheme, and, while absolving others, hurries himself to death."

Vrie's "History of the Council of Constance" begins with a denunciation of the simony, the avarice, the ambition, and the luxury of the Pope, the bishops, and the entire clergy: "What shall I say of their luxury when the facts themselves cry out most openly on the shameless life of prelates and priests! They spare neither condition nor sex; maidens and married men and those living in the world are all alike to them." "Benefices," he complains, "which ought to provide alms for the poor have become the patrimony of the rich. One holds eighteen, another twenty, a third twenty-four; while the poor man is despised, his knowledge and his holy life are of no account. An infant newly born is provided by his careful parents with ecclesiastical benefices. 'We will hand him over,' say they, 'to such a bishop who is our friend, or whom we have served, that we may be enriched from the goods of the Lord, and our inheritance be not divided amongst so many children.' Another is nurtured with more than fatherly affection by some dean or provost, that he may succeed him—is nurtured in luxury and sin. Another, perhaps the son of a prince, is worthy of an archdeaconry, much more so if he be a bishop's nephew. Another eagerly seeks a place on every side, flatters, cringes, dissembles, nay, does not blush to beg, crawling on hands and knees, provided that by any guile he may creep into the patrimony of the Crucified One."

If these utterances of Vrie be thought rhetorical, the more sober spirit of Nicolas de Clémanges, Doctor of the University of Paris and Secretary to Benedict XIII, gives no very different account. "Now-a-days in undertaking a cure of souls no mention is made of Divine services, of the salvation or edification of those entrusted to the priest's care; the only question is about the revenue. Nor do men count the revenue to be the value of the benefice to one who is resident and serves the Church, but what it will yield to one who is far away and perhaps never intends to visit it. No one obtains a benefice however great his merit without constant and repeated asking for it. The Popes in their desire for money have drawn all manner of elections into their own hands, and appoint ignorant and useless men, provided they are rich and can afford to pay large sums. The rights of bishops and patrons are set at naught; grants of benefices in expectancy are given to men who come from the plough and do not know A from B. The claims of the Popes for first-fruits, or the first year's revenue on presentation to a benefice, and other dues have become intolerable. Papal collectors devastate the land, and excommunicate or suspend those who do not satisfy their demands; hence churches fall into ruins, and the church plate is sold; priests leave their benefices and take to secular occupations. Ecclesiastical causes are drawn into the Papal Court on every kind of pretext, and judgment is given in favour of those who pay the most. The Papal Curia alone is rich, and benefices are heaped on Cardinals who devour their revenues in luxury and neglect their duties."

In this state of things, Clémanges proceeds, the chief care of the clergy is of their pockets, not of their flocks. "They strive, scold, litigate, and would endure with greater calmness the loss of ten thousand souls than of ten thousand shillings. If by chance there arise a pastor who does not walk in this way, who despises money, or condemns avarice, or does not wring gold justly or unjustly from his people, but strives by wholesome exhortation to benefit their souls, and meditates on the law of God more than the laws of men, forthwith the teeth of all are whetted against him. They cry out that he is entirely senseless and unworthy of the priesthood; he is ignorant of the law and does not know how to defend his rights, or rule his people, or restrain them by canonical censures; he knows nothing save idle preaching which is more fitting for friars who have none of the cares of temporal administration. The study of Holy Writ and its professors are openly turned to ridicule, especially by the Popes, who set up their traditions far above the Divine commands. The sacred and noble duty of preaching is held so cheap among them that they count nothing less befitting their dignity."

"Episcopal jurisdiction is useless. Priests condemned for theft, homicide, rape, sacrilege, or any other serious offence are only condemned to imprisonment on a diet of bread and water, and are imprisoned only till they have paid enough money, when they walk away scot free. On the other hand, the Episcopal jurisdiction is eagerly extended over harmless rustics, and summoners scour the land to pry out offences against canon law, for which the luckless victims are harassed by a protracted process and are driven to pay heavy fines to escape. Bishops do not hesitate to sell to priests licenses to keep concubines. No care is taken to ordain proper persons to the priesthood. Men who are lazy and do not choose to work, but who wish to live in idleness, fly to the priesthood; as priests, they frequent brothels and taverns, and spend their time in drinking, revelling, and gambling, fight and brawl in their cups, and with their polluted lips blaspheme the name of God and the saints, and from the embraces of prostitutes hurry to the altar." Bishops are rarely resident in their sees and are generally engaged in political or temporal pursuits; yet they are of such a character that their absence is better than their presence. Chapters and their canons are no better than bishops. Monks are undisciplined and dissolute, idle and good for nothing. The Friars, on the other hand, are active enough, but active only in rapacity and voluptuousness. Nunneries are so sunk in shame, so openly given to evil, that it is scarcely possible to speak of them. Clémanges admits that there are some good men among the clergy, but "scarcely one in a thousand sincerely does what his profession requires." The Schism is the scourge of God on these abuses, and unless a reformation be wrought worse ills will follow and the Church will be destroyed.

Denunciations to the same effect might be quoted from writers of almost every land. Lamentations over the corruptions of the Church were not confined to a few enthusiasts; men of high ecclesiastical position and of undoubted orthodoxy spoke openly of the abuses which everywhere prevailed. It was not wonderful that heresy spread, that the doctrines of Wyclif and Hus made many converts. Men went to Constance with three aims in view —to restore the unity of the Church; to reform it in head and members; and to purge it of erroneous doctrines. These objects were to be attained by means of a General Council, though the exact scope of its power was yet to be determined. The foundation of the Council's authority was the theory that the plenitude of ecclesiastical power vested in the universal Church, whose Head was Christ, and of which the Pope was the chief minister. The executive power in the Church rested generally with the Pope; but a Council had a concurrent jurisdiction in all important matters, a corrective power in case of abuses, and a power of removing the Pope in case of necessity. For these purposes a Council had a power of compulsion and of punishment against a Pope. Such was the general result of the teaching of the Parisian theologians which had been turned into practice by the Council of Pisa.

But the Parisian theologians did not wish to push these principles too far. In practice they only aimed at rescuing the Papal primacy from the evils of the Schism, restoring its unity, regulating its powers, and then reinstating it in its former position. There was a school of German reformers who had a more ideal system before their eyes, who aimed at diminishing the plenitude of the Papal primacy, and making it depend on the recognition of the Church. Their views are fully expressed in a treatise written in 1410, most probably the work of Dietrich of Niem, who well knew the ways of the Roman Curia: "About the means of unity and reforming the Church." Beginning from the Creed, the writer asserts his belief in "one Catholic and Apostolic Church." The Catholic Church consists of all who believe in Christ, who is its only Head, and it can never err; the Apostolic Church is a particular and private Church, consisting of Pope, Cardinals, and prelates; its head is supposed to be the Pope, and it can err. The Catholic Church cannot be divided; but for the sake of its members we must labour for the unity of the Apostolic Church, which stands to the Catholic Church as a genus to species. As the object of all society is the common good, a Pope can have no rights as against the well-being of the Church. The Papal primacy has been won by guile, and fraud, and usurpation; but the idea that a Pope cannot be judged by any is contrary alike to reason and Scripture. The Pope is a man, born of man, subject to sin, a few days ago a peasant's son; how is he to become impeccable and infallible? He is bound to resign or even to die if the common good should require it. The unity of the Church must be secured by the abdication of two of the three Popes, or, if it be necessary, by the compulsory abdication of all of them. Union with a particular Pope is no part of the faith of the Catholic Church, nor is it necessary for salvation; rather, Popes contending for their private goods are in mortal sin, and have no claim on the allegiance of Christians.

A General Council represents the universal Church; and when the question to be settled is the resignation of a Pope, it does not belong to the Pope to summon the Council, but to prelates and princes who represent the community. The Pope is bound to obey such a Council, which can make new laws and rescind old ones. The Council must make a general reform in the Church, must sweep away simony, and amend the ways of Pope, Cardinals, prelates, and other clergy. For this purpose it must limit the power of the Pope who has invaded the rights of Bishops, drawn all matters to the Curia, and overthrown the original constitution of the Church. The authority of the Pope must be reduced to its ancient limits, the abuses of the Cardinals must be checked, and the prelates and clergy purified. The writer of this treatise admits that there are many difficulties in the way—difficulties arising from self-interest and conservative prejudice. A Council can only succeed if supported by the Emperor who holds from God a power over the bodies of all men. The work concludes with defining the business of the Council to be: (1) the reincorporation of the members of the universal Church, (2) the establishment of one undoubted and good Pope, (3) limitation of the Papal power, (4) restoration of the ancient rights of the primitive Church, (5) provisions concerning Pope and Cardinals which may prevent future schism, and finally (6) the removal of all abuses in the government of the Church.

Such was the large plan of the reforming party in Germany. It was to be decided in the Council assembled at Constance how much of it should be carried into actual effect.

. . . .

The quiet city of Constance was now to be the centre of European politics; for the Council held in it was looked upon as a congress rather than a synod. Every nation in Europe felt itself more or less helpless, and in need of assistance. Italy was in a condition of hopeless confusion; the Greek Empire was in its decrepitude menaced by the Turks, whom Hungary also had just reason to dread; Bohemia was torn by civil and religious discord; the Empire was feeble and divided; in France, the madness of King Charles VI gave an opportunity to the bloody feuds of the Burgundians and Armagnacs; England had gathered strength a little under Henry IV, but was disturbed by the Lollards, and was on the brink of war with France.

Europe was hopelessly distracted, and longed to realise its unity in some worthy work. The disunion of the ecclesiastical system was a symbol of the civil discord which everywhere prevailed. Men looked back longingly upon a more peaceful past, and Sigismund's appeal to old traditions met with a ready answer. The Council of Pisa had been an assemblage of prelates; through Sigismund's participation the Council of Constance became the meeting place of all the national interests of Christendom. Slowly but sincerely all the wisest in Europe prepared to set their faces towards Constance.

Men did not assemble at once. Till the last there had been doubts whether the Pope would come. In June came the Bishop of Augsburg and the Count of Nellenburg to make preparations on Sigismund's part; it was not till August 12 that the Cardinal of Viviers arrived on behalf of the Pope, and preparations were made in earnest. The magistrates and citizens of Constance set themselves diligently to work to provide lodgings, lay up stores of provisions, take measures for the safety and order of the city, and make all the numerous changes which were necessary to enable them to fulfil the honourable duty which had fallen upon them. At first, however, prelates arrived slowly, chiefly from Italy, in obedience to the Pope. On November 1, owing to the scanty attendance, John deferred the opening of the Council till the 3rd, and in so doing pronounced the Council to be a continuation of the Council of Pisa. On November 3, the opening was again deferred till the 5th, when the Pope with fifteen Cardinals, two Patriarchs, twenty-three Archbishops, and a good number of other prelates, solemnly opened the Council by a service in the cathedral, after which the first session was fixed for the 16th.

Now that the Council had begun, arrivals became more frequent, still chiefly from Italy, whence the good news of the recovery of Rome filled the Pope's heart with joy. Meanwhile the theologians were busy in drawing up proposals for the procedure of the Council. They suggested that proctors and promoters be appointed as at Pisa, who should lay matters before the Council; besides them was to be chosen a number of doctors who between the sessions should receive suggestions and determine the form in which business should be brought forward. It was generally agreed that the first question should be the restoration of the unity of the Church by procuring, if possible, the abdication of Gregory XII and Benedict XIII. At the first session on November 16, John XXIII preached a sermon on the text, "Speak ye every man the truth"; after which a Bull was read detailing the circumstances of the summoning of the Council, and its connexion with the Councils of Pisa and Rome, exhorting the members to root out the errors of Wyclif and reform the Church, and promising to all entire freedom of consultation and action. Nothing more was done that day. As yet the Pope and the Council were watching each other, and no one was ready to take a decided step. Those amongst the Germans and Italians who wished something to be done were waiting for the French and English prelates to lead them.

85. *THE IMITATION OF CHRIST*[1]

[*Introduction by Albert Hyma*]

Among all the books ever written in Europe and America, none have enjoyed such a wide circulation as De Imitatione Christi, *or* The Imitation of Christ. *According to the catalogue of the British Museum, the* Imitation *has been for four hundred years next to the Bible the most widely read book in the world. "After the Gospel," writes one prominent Catholic scholar in America, "the* Imitation *undoubtedly is the book that reflects with the greatest perfection the light which Jesus Christ brought us down from heaven. . . . Nowhere else do we find the same doctrine inculcated with a more persuasive eloquence than in the unpretending little volume that all of us have a hundred times perused."*

John Wesley wrote in the preface of the edition he edited himself: "Such is the strength, spirit, and weight of every sentence that it is scarce possible, without injury to the sense, to add or diminish anything. . . . A serious mind will never be sated with it, though it were read a thousand times over; for those general principles are the seeds of meditation, and the stores they contain are never exhausted. And herein it greatly resembles the Holy Scriptures, that under the plainest words, there is divine hidden virtue, continually flowing into the soul of a pious and attentive reader, and by the blessing of God transforming it into His image."

Milman, in his History of Latin Christianity, *testifies that "in one remarkable book was gathered and concentrated all that was elevating, passionate, profoundly pious, in all the older mystics. Gerson, Ruysbroeck, Tauler, all who addressed the heart in later times, were summed up, and brought into one circle of light and heat, in the one single volume, the* Imitation of Christ. *That this book supplies some imperious want in the Christianity of mankind, that it supplied it with a fullness and felicity which left nothing, at this period of Christianity, to be desired, its boundless popularity is the one unanswerable testimony. . . . The book absolutely and entirely supersedes and supplies the place of the spiritual teacher, the spiritual guide, comforter. According to its notion of Christian perfection, Christian perfection is attainable by its study and by the performance of its precepts; the soul needs no other mediator, at least no earthly mediator, for its union with the Lord."*

The author of the Imitation *was Thomas à Kempis (1379–1471), a German monk.*

[1] *The Imitation of Christ,* ed. by Albert Hyma. New York and London, The Century Co., pp. vii–viii, 3–5, 55–58.

Book I

Chapter I. Of the Imitation of Christ, and Contempt of all the Vanities of the World

"He that followeth me, walketh not in darkness," says the Lord.

These are the words of Christ, by which we are admonished how we ought to imitate his life and ways; if we would be truly enlightened, and be delivered from all blindness of heart.

Let therefore our most earnest study be, to meditate upon the life of Jesus Christ.

The teaching of Christ surpasses all the teachings of holy men, and he who has his spirit, will find therein the hidden manna.

But it happens that many who often hear the Gospel, yet feel but little longing after it, because they have not the spirit of Christ.

He, therefore, that would fully and with true wisdom understand the words of Christ, must strive to conform his whole life to that of Christ.

What does it profit you to dispute profoundly of the Trinity, if you lack humility and be displeasing to the Trinity?

Surely it is not deep words that make a man holy and just, but a virtuous life makes him dear to God.

I had rather feel contrition than understand the definition thereof.

If you knew the whole Bible by heart, and the sayings of all the philosophers, what would that profit you without the love of God and grace?

Vanity of vanities, all is vanity, save to love God and to serve him only.

This is the highest wisdom, by contempt of the world to reach forward to the heavenly kingdom.

It is vanity then to seek after perishable riches, and to trust in them.

It is also vanity to covet honors, and to lift up ourselves on high.

It is vanity to follow the desires of the flesh, and to labor for that which will afterward bring heavy punishment.

It is vanity to desire a long life, and to have little care for a good life.

It is vanity to take thought only for the present life, and not to look forward to those things which are to come.

It is vanity to love that which quickly passes away, and not to hasten thither where everlasting joy abides.

Call often to mind that proverb: "The eye is not satisfied with seeing, nor the ear with hearing."

Strive, therefore, to wean your heart from visible things, and turn yourself to the invisible.

For they who follow after their fleshly lusts, defile their conscience, and lose the favor of God. . . .

Book II

Chapter I. Of the Inward Life

"The Kingdom of God is within you," says the Lord.

Turn yourself with your whole heart to the Lord, and forsake this wretched world; and your soul will find rest.

Learn to despise outward things and to give yourself to things within; and you will see the Kingdom of God coming within you.

For the Kingdom of God is peace and joy in the Holy Ghost, which is not given to the wicked.

Christ will come to you and will show you this consolation, if you prepare for him a worthy mansion within you.

All his glory and beauty is from within, and there is his delight.

He frequently visits the inner man; sweet discourse, pleasant solace, much peace, familiarity exceedingly wonderful.

Go to, faithful soul, make ready your heart for this Bridegroom, that he may vouchsafe to come to you and dwell in you.

For thus he says: "If any man love me, he will keep my Commandments; and my Father will love him, and we will come to him and make our abode with him."

Make therefore room for Christ, and deny entrance to all others.

When you have Christ, you are rich, and you have enough.

He will be your provider and faithful watchmen in all things, so that it will not be necessary to trust in men.

For men soon change, and swiftly pass away, but Christ remains forever, and stands firmly by us till the end.

No great trust should be placed in a frail and mortal man, even when he is useful and dear to us; neither ought we to be grieved when sometimes he opposes and contradicts us.

Those who are on your side to-day, may be against you to-morrow; and they often turn around as the wind.

Put all your trust in God, and let him alone be your fear and your love.

He will answer for you, and will do what is best for you.

"Here you have no continuing city," and wherever you may be, you are a stranger and pilgrim; neither will you have any rest, unless you are firmly united with Christ.

Why do you here gaze about, since this is not the place of your rest?

In heaven ought to be your home, and all earthly things are to be looked upon as a passing show.

They all pass away and you alike with them.

Beware you cleave not to them, lest you be caught and perish.

Let your thought be on the Highest, and your prayer be continually directed to Christ.

If you cannot contemplate high and heavenly things, rest yourself in the passion of Christ, and dwell willingly in his sacred wounds.

For if you devoutly flee to the wounds and precious marks of Jesus, you will feel great comfort in tribulations; neither will you care for the slights of men, and will easily bear the words of detraction.

Christ was also in the world, despised of men, and when in greatest need, forsaken by friends and acquaintances, in the midst of slander.

Christ was willing to suffer and be despised; and dare you complain of any man?

Christ had adversaries and backbiters, and do you wish all men as your friends and benefactors?

Whence will your patience get its crown if no adversity befall you?

If you wish to suffer nothing, how will you be the friend of Christ?

Suffer with Christ and for Christ, if you desire to reign with Christ.

If you had but once perfectly entered into the inner life of Jesus, and had tasted a little of his ardent love, then you would not be anxious about your own convenience or inconvenience, but would rather rejoice at slander, because the love of Jesus makes a man despise himself.

A lover of Jesus, and inwardly true, and free from inordinate affections, can freely turn himself to God, and lift himself above himself in spirit, and rest fruitfully.

He who judges things as they are, not as they are said or esteemed to be, is truly wise, and taught more by God than by men.

He who knows how to walk, and to set little value upon outward things, neither requires places nor expects times for the performing of religious exercises.

The inward man quickly recollects himself, because he never pours out himself wholly to outward things.

He is not hindered by labor, nor by occupation necessary for the time being; but as things turn out, so he accommodates himself to them.

He who is well disposed, and well ordered within himself, does not care for the strange and perverse behavior of men.

A man is hindered and distracted in proportion as he draws matters to himself.

If it were well with you, and if you were well purified, all things would work out for your good and advancement.

For this cause many things displease and disturb you, that you are not yet perfectly dead to yourself, nor separated from all earthly things.

Nothing so defiles and entangles the heart of man as the foul longing for creatures.

If you refuse to be comforted outwardly, you will be able to contemplate heavenly things and frequently to rejoice inwardly.

86. THE EMOTIONAL CHARACTER OF LIFE AT THE CLOSE OF THE MIDDLE AGES[1]

One of the recent and most favorably received works on medieval society is The Waning of the Middle Ages *by Professor J. Huizinga of the University of Leyden. This book deals largely with the literary and artistic productions of northern France and the Low Countries in the fourteenth and fifteenth centuries, and it tells how these productions reflect the lives of various classes of people. The author has succeeded in admirably reproducing and recasting many rare and choice bits of information. His story opens with the selection given below.*

To the world when it was half a thousand years younger, the outlines of all things seemed more clearly marked than to us. The contrast between suffering and joy, between adversity and happiness, appeared more striking. All experience had yet to the minds of men the directness and absoluteness of the pleasure and pain of child-life. Every event, every action, was still embodied in expressive and solemn forms, which raised them to the dignity of a ritual. For it was not merely the great facts of birth, marriage and death which, by the sacredness of the sacrament, were raised to the rank of mysteries; incidents of less importance, like a journey, a task, a visit, were equally attended by a thousand formalities: benedictions, ceremonies, formulae.

Calamities and indigence were more afflicting than at present; it was more difficult to guard against them, and to find solace. Illness and health presented a more striking contrast; the cold and darkness of winter were more real evils. Honours and riches were relished with greater avidity and contrasted more vividly with surrounding misery. We, at the present day, can hardly understand the keenness with which a fur coat, a good fire on the hearth, a soft bed, a glass of wine, were formerly enjoyed.

Then, again, all things in life were of a proud or cruel publicity. Lepers sounded their rattles and went about in processions, beggars exhibited their deformity and their misery in churches. Every order and estate, every rank and profession, was distinguished by its costume. The great lords never moved about without a glorious display of arms and liveries, exciting fear and envy. Executions and other public acts of justice, hawking, marriages

[1] J. Huizinga, *The Waning of the Middle Ages*. London, Edward Arnold and Co., 1924, pp. 1–6. Used by permission.

and funerals, were all announced by cries and processions, songs and music. The lover wore the colours of his lady; companions the emblem of their confraternity; parties and servants the badges or blazon of their lords. Between town and country, too, the contrast was very marked. A medieval town did not lose itself in extensive suburbs of factories and villas; girded by its walls, it stood forth as a compact whole, bristling with innumerable turrets. However tall and threatening the houses of noblemen or merchants might be, in the aspect of the town the lofty masses of the churches always remained dominant.

The contrast between silence and sound, darkness and light, like that between summer and winter, was more strongly marked than it is in our lives. The modern town hardly knows silence or darkness in their purity, nor the effect of a solitary light or a single distant cry.

All things presenting themselves to the mind in violent contrasts and impressive forms, lent a tone of excitement and of passion to everyday life and tended to produce that perpetual oscillation between despair and distracted joy, between cruelty and pious tenderness which characterize life in the Middle Ages.

One sound rose ceaselessly above the noises of busy life and lifted all things unto a sphere of order and serenity: the sound of bells. The bells were in daily life like good spirits, which by their familiar voices, now called upon the citizens to mourn and now to rejoice, now warned them of danger and now exhorted them to piety. They were known by their names: big Jacqueline, or the bell Roland. Every one knew the difference in meaning of the various ways of ringing. However continuous the ringing of the bells, people would seem not to have become blunted to the effect of their sound.

Throughout the famous judicial duel between two citizens of Valenciennes, in 1455, the big bell, "which is hideous to hear," says Chastellain, never stopped ringing. What intoxication the pealing of the bells of all the churches, and of all the monasteries of Paris, must have produced, sounding from morning till evening, and even during the night, when a peace was concluded or a pope elected.

The frequent processions, too, were a continual source of pious agitation. When the times were evil, as they often were, processions were seen winding along, day after day, for weeks on end. In 1412 daily processions were ordered in Paris, to implore victory for the king, who had taken up the oriflamme against the Armagnacs. They lasted from May to July, and were formed by ever-varying orders and corporations, going always by new roads, and always carrying different relics. The Burgher of Paris calls them "the most touching processions in the memory of men." People looked on or followed, "weeping piteously, with many tears, in great devotion." All went barefooted and fasting, councillors of the Parlement as well as poorer citizens. Those who could afford it, carried a torch or a taper. A great many small children were always among them. Poor country-people of the environs of Paris came barefooted from afar to join the procession. And nearly every day the rain came down in torrents.

Then there were the entries of princes, arranged with all the resources of art and luxury belonging to the age. And, lastly, most frequent of all, one might almost say, uninterrupted, the executions. The cruel excitement and coarse compassion raised by an execution formed an important item in the spiritual food of the common people. They were spectacular plays with a moral. For horrible crimes the law invented atrocious punishments. At Brussels a young incendiary and murderer is placed in the centre of a circle of burning fagots and straw, and made fast to a stake by means of a chain running round an iron ring. He addresses touching words to the spectators, "and he so softened their hearts that every one burst into tears and his death was commended as the finest that was ever seen." During the Burgundian terror in Paris in 1411, one of the victims, Messire Mansart du Bois, being requested by the hangman, according to custom, to forgive him, is not only ready to do so with all his heart, but begs the executioner to embrace him. "There was a great multitude of people, who nearly all wept hot tears."

When the criminals were great lords, the common people had the satisfaction of seeing rigid justice done, and at the same time finding the inconstancy of fortune exemplified more strikingly than in any sermon or picture. The magistrate took care that nothing should be wanting to the effect of the spectacle: the condemned were conducted to the scaffold, dressed in the garb of their high estate. Jean de Montaigu, grand maître d'hôtel to the king, the victim of Jean sans Peur, is placed high on a cart, preceded by two trumpeters. He wears his robe of state, hood, cloak, and hose half red and half white, and his gold spurs, which are left on the feet of the beheaded and suspended corpse. By special order of Louis XI, the head of maître Oudart de Bussy, who had refused a seat in the Parlement, was dug up and exhibited in the market-place of Hesdin, covered with a scarlet hood lined with fur "selon la mode des conseillers de Parlement," with explanatory verses.

Rarer than processions and executions were the sermons of itinerant preachers, coming to shake people by their eloquence. The modern reader of newspapers can no longer conceive the violence of impression caused by the spoken word on an ignorant mind lacking mental food. The Franciscan friar Richard preached in Paris in 1429 during ten consecutive days. He began at five in the morning and spoke without a break till ten or eleven, for the most part in the cemetery of the Innocents. When, at the close of his tenth sermon, he announced that it was to be his last, because he had no permission to preach more, "great and small wept as touchingly and as bitterly as if they were watching their best friends being buried; and so did he." Thinking that he would preach once more at Saint Denis on the Sunday, the people flocked thither on Saturday evening, and passed the night in the open, to secure good seats.

Another Minorite friar, Antoine Fradin, whom the magistrate of Paris had forbidden to preach, because he inveighed against the bad government, is guarded night and day in the Cordeliers monastery, by women posted around the building, armed with ashes and stones. In all the towns where the famous Dominican preacher Vincent Ferrer is expected, the people, the magistrates, the lower clergy, and even prelates and bishops, set out to greet him with joyous songs. He journeys with a numerous and ever-increasing following of adherents, who every night make a circuit of the town in procession, with chants and flagellations. Officials are appointed to take charge of lodging and feeding these multitudes. A large number of priests of various religious orders accompany him everywhere, to assist him in celebrating mass and in confessing the faith. Also several notaries, to draw up, on the spot, deeds embodying the reconciliations which this holy preacher everywhere brings about. His pulpit has to be protected by a fence against the pressure of the congregation which wants to kiss his hand or habit. Work is at a stand-still all the time he preaches. He rarely fails to move his auditors to tears. When he spoke of the Last Judgment, of Hell, or of the Passion, both he and his hearers wept so copiously that he had to suspend his sermon till the sobbing had ceased. Malefactors threw themselves at his feet, before every one, confessing their great sins. One day, while he was preaching, he saw two persons, who had been condemned to death—a man and a woman—being led to execution. He begged to have the execution delayed, had them both placed under the pulpit, and went on with his sermon, preaching about their sins. After the sermon, only some bones were found in the place they had occupied, and the people were convinced that the word of the saint had consumed and saved them at the same time.

After Olivier Maillard had been preaching Lenten sermons at Orleans, the roofs of the houses surrounding the place whence he had addressed the people had been so damaged by the spectators who had climbed on to them, that the roofer sent in a bill for repairs extending over sixty-four days.

The diatribes of the preachers against dissoluteness and luxury produced violent excitement which was translated into action. Long before Savonarola started bonfires of "vanities" at Florence, to the irreparable loss of art, the custom of these holocausts of articles of luxury and amusement was prevalent both in France and in Italy. At the summons of a famous preacher, men and women would hasten to bring cards, dice, finery, ornaments, and burn them with great pomp. Renunciation of the sin of vanity in this way had taken a fixed and solemn form of public manifestation, in accordance with the tendency of the age to invent a style for everything.

All this general facility of emotions, of tears and spiritual upheavals, must be borne in mind in order to conceive fully how violent and high-strung was life at that period.

Public mourning still presented the outward appearance of a general calamity. At the funeral of Charles VII, the people are quite appalled on seeing the cortège of all the court dignitaries, "dressed in the deepest mourning, which was most pitiful to see; and because of the great sorrow and grief they exhibited for the death of their master, many tears were shed and lamentations uttered throughout the town." People were especially touched at the sight of six pages of the king mounted on horses quite covered with black velvet. One of the pages, according to the rumour, had neither eaten nor drunk for four days. "And God knows what doleful and piteous plaints they made, mourning for their master."

Solemnities of a political character also led to abundant weeping. An ambassador of the king of France repeatedly bursts into tears while addressing a courteous harangue to Philip the Good. At the meeting of the kings of France and of England at Ardres, at the reception of the dauphin at Brussels, at the departure of John of Coïmbre from the court of Burgundy, all the spectators weep hot tears. Chastellain describes the dauphin, the future Louis XI, during his voluntary exile in Brabant, as subject to frequent fits of weeping.

Unquestionably there is some exaggeration in these descriptions of the chroniclers. In describing the emotion caused by the addresses of the ambassadors at the peace congress at Arras, in 1435, Jean Germain, bishop of Chalons, makes the auditors throw themselves on the ground, sobbing and groaning. Things, of course, did not happen thus, but thus the bishop thought fit to represent them, and the palpable exaggeration reveals a foundation of truth. As with the sentimentalists of the eighteenth century, tears were considered fine and honourable. Even nowadays an indifferent spectator of a public procession sometimes feels himself suddenly moved to inexplicable tears. In an age filled with religious reverence for all pomp and grandeur, this propensity will appear altogether natural.

87. THE OPENING OF THE LAND ROUTES TO INDIA AND CHINA[1]

One phase of medieval history used to be somewhat neglected in many of the schools in this country as well as in Western Europe, namely, the opening

[1] Eileen Power, *The Opening of the Land Routes to Cathay,* in *Travel and Travellers of the Middle Ages,* edited by A. P. Newton. New York, Alfred A. Knopf, 1926, pp. 124–128, 136–138, 139–140, 141–142, 154–156. Used by permission of George Routledge & Sons, Ltd.

of the land routes from Europe to the Orient. The subject attracted little attention, partly because the sources were obscure and it was generally felt that there was practically no contact between East and West in the period from 1250 to 1350. We are very fortunate that recently a book appeared containing a chapter by Eileen Power on the topic just mentioned. Extracts from this chapter are given here.

The century lying between 1245 and 1345 is of unique importance in the history of medieval travel, because for a brief period it brought into contact the East and the West, the two centres of the civilized world; for during the Middle Ages it is true enough to say that the world had two centres, each of which thought that it was the only one, the great civilizations of India and China, proud and immemorially old, and the budding civilization of Christendom, then in all the vigour of its lusty youth.

In a sense, of course, they had always been in contact. Once before they had met and mingled, when Alexander took his Hellenism westward and left an ineffaceable mark upon the faces of the Buddhas of Northern India. Once again they had, as it were, looked at each other without meeting, when Chinese traders met the agents of Rome at the craggy city of Tashkurgan, called "the Stone Tower," and unrolled their bales of silk on the banks of the Yarkand River. And although all this had become a fairy tale to the men of the Middle Ages, they were still in contact with the East in the sense that they seasoned their dishes with spices from Ceylon and Java, set diamonds from Golconda in their rings, and carpets from Persia on their thrones, went splendidly clad in silks from China and played their interminable games of chess with ebony chessmen from Siam. But for all that a black and heavy curtain shut the East and the West from each other's sight.

For although the thriving merchants of Venice and Genoa and Pisa grew rich upon the Eastern trade, they knew it only at its termini, the ports of the Levant. From China and India merchandise could take two roads to the West. One was a land route across Central Asia, ending upon the shores of the Black Sea, or passing southward to Baghdad. But though the Greeks of Constantinople and Trebizond did an active trade in Eastern merchandise coming by this route, and though Italians were already beginning to frequent the Black Sea ports, it was impossible for them to go further along the trade routes, for all across Central Asia lay the Turks, blocking the road to the East. The other road was a sea road, separated from the Mediterranean by two land-vestibules, the vestibule of Persia and Syria, and the vestibule of Egypt. In Palestine and Syria the Christians still held a remnant of the Crusading States, with a valuable row of ports, and by treaty with the sultans at their backdoor they were allowed to journey a few miles inland to the busy cities of Aleppo and Damascus. But beyond this, to the great mart of Baghdad, the centre for the whole district, and along the trade routes to the Persian Gulf, they might not go. Here again the Turks stood in their path. In Egypt, too, their galleys came to Alexandria and did a great trade, but by what road the camels brought their loads and where the Nile boats took on board their cargoes, the Frankish merchants did not know, for once more the Turks blocked them. Islam, the hereditary foe of Christendom, lay like a wall between Europe and all the trade routes to the East.

But in the period which we have now to consider all this was changed. Italian merchants chaffered and Italian friars said Mass in the ports and cities of India and China, moved unhampered with their caravans on the great silk route across Central Asia, or passed through Persia to take ship on the long sea road. The East and the West for the first time came into direct contact from end to end. And if it be asked how this came about, the answer is an unexpected one—that it was the result of the conquests of a nomadic Mongol people from Central Asia of the same stock as the Turks, a people, moreover, which has come down in history with a reputation for unintelligent destruction equalled only by that of the Vandals. That people is best known under its medieval name of the Tartars.

The Tartar conquests began at the beginning of the thirteenth century, when Chinghiz Khan and his hordes came down from Mongolia and attacked the Chinese Empire, taking Peking in 1214 and by degrees, in the course of the next fifty years, extending their sway until they ruled almost the whole of Eastern Asia. They first turned westward in 1218 and the flood of conquest slowly spread right across Asia, over a large part of Russia, into Poland and Hungary, and all over Persia and part of Asia Minor, until by the death of Mangu Khan in 1259 one empire stretched from the Yellow River to the banks of the Danube, and from the Persian Gulf to Siberia. Nothing like it had ever been known in history before, for the Roman Empire was a mere midget in comparison, and nothing like it was to be known again until the great land empire of Russia in the nineteenth century. In the last half of the thirteenth century it broke up into four khanates. The Great Khan himself ruled from Cambaluc or Khanbalik (Peking) over the whole of China, Corea, Mongolia, Manchuria and Tibet, taking tribute also from Indo-China, Burma and Java. The Chagatai Khanate, with its capital at Almalik (Kulja), stretched over Central Asia, Turkestan and Afghanistan. The Kipchak Khanate, or the Golden Horde, with its capital at Sarai on the Volga, covered the country north of the Caucasus, Russia, and part of Siberia. The Persian Ilkhanate, with its capital at Tauris (Tabriz) held sway over Persia, Georgia, Armenia, and part of Asia Minor. Nevertheless, although thus divided, the Tartars were essentially one people, acknowledging the sway of the Great Khan at Peking and communicating with each other by messengers across the length and breadth of Asia.

The appearance of these wild horsemen, swift and savage beyond description, coming like an irresistible flood, a sort of terrible and overwhelming tidal wave, from the East at first struck horror into the soul of Europe, for it seemed as though they would continue their triumphant progress westward and ravage all Christendom to the sea. Twice they appeared, in 1222–3 and again in 1241. In 1238 Matthew tells how fear of them kept the people of Gothland and Friesland away from the Yarmouth herring fishery, and in 1241, when the Christian host was heavily defeated at Lignitz and they ravaged Poland, Silesia, and Hungary, the Emperor Frederick II called upon Henry III of England and other princes for common action against this new "Scourge of God." Horror and disgust and fear were the sentiments which they aroused.

But after 1241 the flood of conquest rolled back, and when next it rolled West again, it was seen to overwhelm not Christian kingdoms but the caliphates of Baghdad and Syria, establishing in the '50s Tartar for Muslim rule there, sacking Baghdad and extinguishing the Caliphate in 1258. For this reason this attitude of Europe began to undergo a change, and men saw in the Tartars not a menace to Christendom but a possible ally against a common enemy. As Europeans got to know more about the Tartars, they learned that they were tolerant to all creeds, Buddhist, Muhammadan, Jewish and Christian, having no very strongly marked beliefs of their own. They began also to learn that there were large groups of Nestorian Christians still scattered throughout Asia. Europeans who visited the Tartar camp at Karakorum brought back news of ladies of high rank, wives and mothers of khans, who professed the Christian faith. Rumours of the conversion now of the Great Khan himself in Cathay, now of one or other of the lesser khans in Persia or Russia, kept rising, and men repeated also the famous legend of Prester John. All these things, together with the indisputable fact that the Tartars had laid the Muslim power low all over Asia, began to present them to Western rulers in a totally new light. Gradually there took shape the dream of converting the Tartars to Christianity and then forming a great Tartar-Christian alliance which should smite Islam hip and thigh, reconquer Palestine and Egypt, and succeed where crusades from the West alone had failed.

From the middle of the thirteenth century, therefore, it is essential to remember that Europe was no longer shrinking in terror from the Tartars, but on the contrary was looking upon them as potential converts and allies. Embassies were continually setting out to one or other of the centres of their power, Sarai on the Volga, the new Persian capital of Tabriz, or distant

Cathay, from the Pope, or the King of France, or the King of England, with invitations to embrace Christianity and projects of alliance. Merchants also began to go thither to trade and Franciscan friars to preach, and by degrees a busy intercourse sprang up between East and West.

. . . .

There is no need to labour the effect of the tremendous mass of exact knowledge which the reports of Marco Polo brought to the enterprising mercantile world of Venice and Genoa, and to the hardly less enterprising ecclesiastical world which was still cherishing its great scheme of converting the Tartars. The two friars who first penetrated to Mongolia and the three merchants who first made the great tour to Cathay by land and back to Europe by sea were only pioneers of a widespread movement. For it was by now plain that the Tartar Empire had wrought one of the most startling revolutions in the history of the world up to that date by bringing into contact for the first time the two ends of the earth, Europe and the Far East. For the next fifty years or so, roughly between 1290 and 1340, a steady stream of travellers took the Eastern road. They had need, indeed, to find new trade routes, for the collapse of the Latin power in Palestine, culminating in the loss of Acre in 1291, was seriously interrupting the old. The term "trade routes" is used advisedly, for although some of the best travel books belonging to this period were written by missionaries, the real impetus to travel was given by trade, and the most frequent journeys to Persia, India and Cathay were made by merchants. These merchants now found themselves no longer mere clients at the closed gates of the East, loading their ships with goods brought to those termini by Muslim middlemen; they found that they could pass through the gates and themselves follow the trade routes. Direct access to the East was at last open to them, and it has been said with truth that "the unification of Asia by the Mongols was as important a fact for the commerce of the Middle Ages as the discovery of America for the men of the Renaissance. It was equivalent to the discovery of Asia."

What the Tartars in effect did was to throw open two out of the three great trade routes between East and West. One, the Egyptian road, remained in the hands of the Muslims and closed to Europeans, though the Venetian galleys still brought back their cargoes of spices and silk from the great terminus port of Alexandria. But the other two, the Persian-Syrian and long sea route and the Transasiatic land route were in the hands of the Tartars and were now thrown open. Marco Polo went by the latter and returned by the former.

Consider first the sea route to India, reached through the new Ilkhanate of Persia. During the Tartar period Persia resumed her historic role of antechamber to the East, which she had not played since the days of Alexander. The capital of Tartar Persia, Tabriz, or Tauris, soon outshone Baghdad as the chief mart of the district, and was visited and admired by all the great travellers of the age. "It is the best city in the world for merchandise," said Oderic of Pordenone, "and is worth more to the emperor than his whole kingdom is to the King of France." It had the initial advantage that it could be reached by caravan routes from two ports which were in Christian hands and thus did not incur, like Alexandria, the papal ban against trading with the infidel (not that Christian merchants took the ban very seriously). One of these ports was Lajazzo or Ayas, on the Gulf of Alexandretta in the kingdom of Little Armenia, from which Marco Polo started on his outward journey, and the other was Trebizond, on the southern shore of the Black Sea, the capital of an independent Greek state, from which he took ship on his way home. Coming from either of these ports to Tabriz, merchants could then follow the caravan route down to Ormuz at the mouth of the Persian Gulf, which was the chief port for the Indian trade at this period, and of which Marco Polo and other travellers have left admirable descriptions.

Very soon this Persian route almost ousted the Egyptian route as the vestibule between the Mediterranean and the Indian Ocean. The Mamluk sultans of Egypt imposed such heavy tolls at Alexandria that Indian merchandise increased 300% in price by the time it got to Europe; also they were apt to molest the Christian merchants and strictly forbade them the interior. But in Persia the Ilkhans pursued an enlightened policy, imposing low customs, protecting traders, policing the roads, establishing a regular system of posts, and allowing free passage everywhere. The Europeans were not slow to take advantage of the new facilities; we hear of an Italian merchant in Tabriz as early as 1264 (his will, made there in that year, survives and sets forth his stock of cloth from Venice, Germany and Flanders, pearls and sugar and chessmen from the East, saddles, cups, candlesticks and drinking glasses). At first the trade of the district fell mainly to the Genoese, and to this day the Turks of Asia Minor are wont to attribute to that enterprising people any ancient stone building whose origin is unknown. Marco Polo found them all powerful at Tabriz in 1294 and mentions that a Genoese company was already navigating the great inland Caspian Sea. But the Venetians began to compete with them early in the fourteenth century, and had an advantageous commercial treaty with the Ilkan in 1320 and a Consul in Tabriz in 1324. . . .

But it was not for the sake of Persia alone that the opening of the land route was epoch-making. Persia was only the antechamber; what was more important was that at Ormuz Europeans could now take ship and bear their gospel and their trade to India itself. In 1315 agents of the Genoese bank of Vivaldi (the same enterprising family which a quarter of a century before had sailed forth to find the road to India down the African coast and disappeared for ever) had trading stations on the Gujerat and Malabar coasts. European merchants regularly visited the great ports of the Gulf of Cambay and of Malabar and Coromandel, which were crowded with a mixed population of Christians, Hindus, Muslims and Chinese; for, as Heyd points out, the great age of the Tartars corresponds with the period of greatest activity in the political and commercial relations between India and China, and these ports, especially Calicut and Quilon, were among the richest in the world. Missionary activity was no less active here than in Persia. . . .

Moreover, although all travellers touched at an Indian port all did not stay there. For they could now take ship on one of the Chinese junks which came to Quilon and Malabar. . . .

Aboard one of these European travellers could sail on past Java and Sumatra and Indo-China to Cynkalan (Canton), or Zaiton by the route which Marco Polo took on his return journey, and many European travellers after 1290 came to China by this long sea route. Its disadvantage was that it was very slow (it took two years), and it was because the land route was much shorter and reputed to be safer that medieval opinion preferred the second of the two roads which the Tartars opened to the West.

This was the great caravan route across Central Asia, and it may be said with truth that if the Tartar conquest of Persia opened the road to India the Tartar conquest of Russia opened the road to China. The great overland silk route across Asia is one of the oldest and one of the most romantic trade routes in the world and its immense importance at this period can hardly be overestimated. Travellers could get by it to China in five or six months, travelling with the imperial posts, though çaravans naturally took longer. It could be reached from Trebizond or Lajazzo via Tabriz by making the golden journey to Merv, Bokhara and Samarcand along a caravan route which joined them; but from the beginning of the fourteenth century another route became much more important and that was the road which went from the Crimea by land or sea to Tana (Azov), then across the steppes to Astrakhan or to Sarai on the Volga, and by camel across the desert to Urgenje (near Khiva) on the Oxus, and so on to the Bokhara-Samarcand route, and straight across central Asia by one of the three great roads, the north Thian Shan (Pelu), the south Thian Shan (Nan-lu) or the north Kuenlun into China.

. . . .

History gives to the fifteenth century the name of the "Age of Discovery," because its discoveries were never lost. But are Vasco da Gama and Columbus himself more remarkable than Marco Polo, or than those half forgotten friars and wholly forgotten merchants, who took the land and sea roads to

India and Cathay in the century between 1245 and 1345? History, again, commonly represents the Tartars as mere barbarians, unintelligent and savage ravagers like the Huns, seeking to tear down the painfully reared civilization of Islam and the West, and the man in the street has gone even further than history; the phrase "to catch a Tartar" has become proverbial.

The truth is that popular opinion persists in remembering only the early onslaughts of the Tartars, the first period of destruction under the four Great Khans, Chinghiz, Ogotay, Kuyuk and Mangu (1206–57), and erects into an historical verdict the objurgations of Muslim or Christian writers like Ibnu'l-Athir and Matthew Paris, writing under the stress of the first invasions, and often enough writing from hearsay. The honest Matthew never saw a Tartar in his life, nor was Ibnu'l-Athir a witness of the horrors which he so vividly describes. It is true that the early invasions were orgies of the most barbarous slaughter, but is it fair to pass judgment on the Tartars on the witness of these alone? After all what were the Europeans of the day but descendants of those Germanic barbarians, whose first invasions were described, and deserved to be described, in precisely the same terms by the Roman provincials upon whom they fell? No conquering people can fairly be condemned on the period of its conquests and by the mouths of the conquered. It is in the subsequent period of settled government that it proves its true greatness or baseness, and few imperial nations of to-day would care for any other criterion. The Tartars deserve to be judged, not in their nomad state and in the first age of the invasions, but as they were when settled in their four great Khanates. They deserve to be judged as a people so tolerant that they welcomed the representatives of all religions, Christian friar, Buddhist lama, Jewish rabbi, Muslim doctor and Mongol medicine-man, equally at their courts, and were regarded by Christians not as "the worst enemies of human civilization" but as potential allies against Islam. The fact that the alliance did not eventuate was due not to the Tartars but to the internecine bickering of Christian Popes and monarchs. They deserve to be judged as the one political power under whom the Armenians, always from that day to this persecuted by the Turks and never from that day to this helped by the Christians, enjoyed a momentary tranquillity, a respite in the long crucifixion of their history. They deserve to be judged as the power whose policy towards commercial intercourse between nations was so enlightened that they welcomed traders, lowered dues and protected caravans and roads throughout their dominions, maintaining free intercourse over the length and breadth of Asia, so that Professor Beazley can with justice call this period "the age of the nomad peace" and Sir Henry Howorth, speaking of this marvellous bringing together of the peoples of West and East can write "I have no doubt myself . . . that the art of printing, the mariner's compass, firearms and a great many details of social life, were not discovered in Europe, but imported by means of Mongol influence from the furthest East."

88. THE TURKS AND THE TRADE ROUTES[1]

In the later Middle Ages there were three great trade routes connecting Europe with Asia. The northern route ran from India and China overland across Central Asia and branched out to Black Sea ports, Russian cities and the Baltic. The central route ran from China, India and the Spice Islands by sea to the northern end of the Persian gulf, then overland to Bagdad and thence to Mediterranean ports and elsewhere. The southern route, duplicating the central for the most part, went up the Red Sea instead of the Persian Gulf and thence by caravan to Cairo and Alexandria. It has been commonly assumed, as Professor Lybyer points out in the following selection, that the search for new routes to the Indies, which was a primary cause of the great maritime discoveries of early modern times, was itself caused principally by the closing or serious obstruction of the old trade routes by the Ottoman Turks. Professor Lybyer advances strong evidence tending to prove that this assumption is incorrect.

A generally prevalent view is expressed in the following three quotations put into print within the last 10 years in well-received books by reputable authors:

The old trade routes between Asia and Europe were effectually and permanently blocked by the Turkish conquests. . . . This is the explanation of that eager search for new routes which lay at the back of so many voyages of discovery in the fifteenth and sixteenth centuries.

The search for new routes to India that led Columbus to the discovery of the New World was caused by the advance westward of the Ottoman Turks and their interference with the old paths of commerce in the east.

The closing of the trade routes by the advance of the Ottoman Turks led traders to endeavor to find new channels and issued in the rounding of the Cape of Good Hope and the discovery of America.

A pamphlet printed privately within a year or two states that the Turks built, as it were, a wall across the old trade routes, and absolutely forced the western Europeans to seek other paths to the lands of silk and spices.

All of these statements express a firm belief that the closing or the serious

[1] Albert H. Lybyer, *The Influence of the Rise of the Ottoman Turks upon the Routes of Oriental Trade.* Reprinted from the Annual Report of the American Historical Association for 1914. Washington, 1916, Vol. I, pp. 125–133.

obstruction by the Ottoman Turks of the routes of oriental trade was the principal cause of the great maritime discoveries at the beginning of the modern age. It follows logically that the Turks, albeit unwittingly and negatively, belong among the greatest benefactors of mankind. But is this belief true? I formerly accepted it upon authority, but three or four years ago I noticed that it involves an anachronism. Obviously the Turks could not have caused the discoveries by obstructing the trade routes unless their obstruction antedated the discoveries. But the Turks had nothing to do with the two most important trade routes until they took Syria and Egypt in the winter of 1516 and 1517, while the greatest of the discoveries were made in 1487. 1492, and 1498, from 18 to 30 years before. The doubts raised by this serious anachronism have been justified by investigation. The Turks must be dethroned from their place beside Columbus.

The idea before us may be separated into simpler elements, which may be stated thus: The routes of oriental trade were closed (or permanently obstructed) before the year 1498; the closing of these routes caused (or strongly influenced) the great discoveries; the Turks closed (or were important agents in closing) the trade routes; therefore the Turks by closing the trade routes caused (or had a powerful influence upon) the great discoveries. Now, this chain of propositions hangs upon the first; if the routes of oriental trade were not closed (or permanently obstructed) before the year 1498, then the whole idea falls to pieces; the great discoveries were otherwise caused and the influence of the Turks, at least as far as closing the trade routes is concerned, is eliminated.

Now, it is very easy to show that the routes of oriental trade were neither closed nor permanently obstructed before or during the period of the great discoveries. Certain wares were produced only in the east. To reach the west they must pass along the trade routes of the Levant. If these routes had been closed the wares could not have come. But pepper, ginger, cloves, cinnamon, mace, nutmeg, rhubarb, and the like, never ceased to be obtainable in western Europe from the Roman times to the present. The trade routes, then, were never permanently closed. But perhaps they were closed at times, or permanently obstructed, so that spices and other products of the east became very difficult to get in western Europe. What would be the evidence of such a permanent obstruction? Obviously, a permanent elevation of prices If in the fourteenth and fifteenth centuries the advance of the Ottoman Turks or any other cause progressively obstructed oriental trade, the west would learn of it quite promptly by a progressive rise in the prices of oriental goods.

The extensive researches of Prof. Thorold Rogers and the Vicomte d'Avénel have put us in possession of much information about prices in England and France from the thirteenth to the nineteenth centuries. The averages of the items found for each 10 years by Rogers and for each 25 years by d'Avénel, give a very fair idea of the general fluctuations of prices. Now, what do these show as to the prices of pepper between the close of the Crusades and 1500, and particularly between 1453 and 1498, the capture of Constantinople by the Turks, and the arrival of Gama at Calicut? In England the price of a dozen pounds of pepper averaged 15s. 7d. in the fourteenth century, and 15s. 8d. in the fifteenth century. From 1451 to 1500 the average price was 15 shillings. From 1431 to 1480 the average was only 12s. 9d. It rose to 17s. between 1481 and 1490, but fell again to 13s. from 1491 to 1495. There was then on the whole, an actual decline in the price of pepper in England during the incubation of the great discoveries. In France the average price for a kilogram of pepper, as reduced to modern money by d'Avénel, was in the thirteenth century 6 fr., in the fourteenth century 11.12 fr., and in the fifteenth century only 4.17 fr. From 1450 to 1475 the price was 4.70 fr. and from 1475 to 1500 it was 4 fr. Thus, in France also the price of pepper declined at the time of the great discoveries. Prices of other spices and of home-grown commodities fluctuated in the two countries quite similarly to those of pepper. It is therefore clear that there was no permanent elevation in the prices of oriental products, and therefore there could have been no serious obstruction of the trade routes before the year 1500.

More direct evidence can be found than that of the price of pepper in England and France. The Venetian diarists, Marino Sanuto the Younger and Priuli who recorded the noteworthy events which came to their knowledge between 1496 and 1533, show that although succession disturbances of the Mameluke throne and the plague caused fluctuations of quantity, the old flow of oriental wares through Syria and Egypt was maintained unbroken down to 1502. In that year a new thing happened. The galleys from Beirut and Alexandria brought very few spices to Venice. In 1504 they brought none at all. The southern trade routes of the Levant had been emptied by the purchases of the Portuguese in India. Beginning with 1508, the Portuguese sent fleets to blockade the mouths of the Red Sea and the Persian Gulf. This seems to have been the first deliberate attempt on the part of anyone to stop permanently the passage of wares along any of the routes of oriental trade. It was not entirely successful. The Venetian galleys which continued to sail to the Levant usually found some spices. But the old certainty was gone, and the prices, low at Lisbon, were high at Beirut and Alexandria. The total quantity of spices which came by the old routes from the East to Europe was greatly reduced. Venice sent fewer ships to the Levant and thought it imprudent to build new galleys for the trade.

This was the situation when Selim I overthrew the Mameluke Sultans in 1516 and 1517. Instead of blocking the southern routes further, he took up the situation exactly where the Mamelukes had left it. He renewed the old treaties with Venice and the west, and took over the intention to crush the Portuguese naval power in the Indian Ocean by a fleet sent down the Red Sea. Except for the beginning of French participation in the Mediterranean trade, there was no marked change from this policy down to the time of Sanuto's death.

It has been shown that the main or southern routes of oriental trade through the Levant were never closed before the great discoveries, and that the Turks, after conquering Egypt and Syria, made no effort to close them. The main contention is established, then. The Turks did not cause the great discoveries by blocking the routes of oriental trade.

It is desirable to examine some lesser possibilities. Perhaps the acquisition by the Turks of the northern routes stimulated the great explorations, through causing fear that the Turks would some day control and close all the routes, and through diverting the energies of trading powers from the Mediterranean to the Atlantic. As for the first supposition, it lacks both probability and evidence. The Turks did not fight the Mamelukes before the war of 1485 to 1491, and then they were soundly beaten. Even in 1516 the outcome of the impending second war was believed to be uncertain. How, then, could westerners have expected that the Turks would one day close all the trade routes? Nor can I find the least evidence of such an expectation. The second supposition, that the Turks diverted the energies of Mediterranean trading powers so that they set out to seek new routes to India, is easily seen to be untenable. The governments of none of these, Venice, Genoa, Aragon, or Florence, had any part in the great discoveries. That was the work of the Atlantic powers, Portugal and Castile. Nor were the well-to-do citizens of the Mediterranean States more active. In 1291, or thereabouts, it is true, certain Genoese went out at the Straits of Gibraltar to seek a new way to the East Indies. But this was before there were any Ottoman Turks. No such expedition went forth from any Mediterranean port after the fall of Constantinople in 1453, of Trebizond in 1461, or of Kaffa in 1475. It becomes then impossible to discern any influence of the Turks through fear that they would close the oriental trade routes, or through the diversion by them of the large activities of Mediterranean cities.

One further line of possible influence of the Turks upon the great discoveries may be discussed. Christopher Columbus and John Cabot were Genoese by place of birth. Had not the northern regions of the Levant trade been reduced by the Turks, these men might have spent their lives in that trade, and never have become discoverers. But this is mere speculation. I believe that neither their own words nor those of their contemporary and later biographers express any consciousness of connection between their enterprises and the rise of the Turks. Columbus seems to have found his inspiration in Portugal and Cabot in Arabia. The same documents, I may say, fail also to reveal any thought in the minds of these men that the old trade routes were or were likely to become closed or seriously hindered. Similar things may be said by the way, of the documents that deal with Prince Henry the Navigator, of the histories of Turkey, and of Venetian writings and history, so far as I have been able to examine them.

It does not belong to this discussion to determine the true causes of the great discoveries, after the influence of the Turks has been eliminated. The intellect and enterprise of Renaissance Europe were adequate to the project and its execution. There is a negative bearing upon the argument, however, in the fact that Mr. Payne seeks to eliminate all effort to find a new route to the East Indies from the motives of Henry of Portugal, while M. Vignaud tries to do the same for Christopher Columbus. M. Vignaud would in fact postpone the date when even the Portuguese thought of the Eastern spice trade until the report of Covilham's journey to the east reached King John II, about the year 1490. In any case, two or three other motives, related to religion, crusading, conquest, and adventure, probably outweighed the seeking of spices in the minds of the great explorers and their royal supporters.

How did the legend of the great influence of the Turks upon the maritime discoveries originate? I have not been able to trace it back of Thorold Rogers, but does it not bear the marks of being a survival of the catastrophic theory in that particular phase which makes the fall of Constantinople the determining event of modern history? Deprived some time ago of the distinction of causing the Italian Renaissance and the German Reformation, this theory has maintained a while longer its hold upon the great discoveries and the desolation of the Levant. It must certainly give up the great discoveries. I think it must also surrender the desolation of the Levant, for the decay of the regions through which the old trade routes passed was probably caused less by the presence of the Turks than by the absence of trade, inevitably attracted away by the superior advantages of the cape route. The possibility of climatic change also deserves consideration.

Thorold Rogers appears to reveal his relation to the catastrophic theory when he asserts that "the fall of Constantinople beyond doubt stimulated research into the unknown oceans of the west and south." He affirms that before the Portuguese discoveries the Turks "appear to have blocked every passage but one," and that Selim I, by his conquest of Egypt, proceeded to "block the only remaining road." Most of these matters have been sufficiently dealt with. Prof. Rogers does not appear to have sought proof of his assertions outside of his own field of work. Within this, however, he thinks he has found confirmation of them in the rise of the prices of eastern wares in England for the decade 1451–1460 and the two decades 1521–1540. Aside from the obvious consideration that many elements enter into price fluctuations, such as weather conditions in the country of production, war and peace along the road and in the country of consumption, piracy and extortion, and monopolies and combinations, it would seem that Thorold Rogers has not considered his own figures with sufficient thoroughness. It is true that the price of pepper rose in England from 9s. 5d per dozen pounds between 1441 and 1450 to 13s. between 1451 and 1460. But it is also true that the former price was the lowest of all the 10-year averages, and that the latter price is well below the average for the fifteenth or any other century until much later. Again, the Wars of the Roses began in England in 1455. It is true also that 12 pounds of pepper averaged in England 16s. 2d. between 1501 and 1520, and 23s. 2d. between 1521 and 1540. But why did Prof. Rogers not observe that this was only part of the general rise of prices which is evident both in England and in France in the sixteenth century and which was almost certainly caused by the addition to the European stock of gold and silver from the Americas? Compare, for example, the price of pepper with that of wheat. For the first four 20-year periods of the sixteenth century the price, by Rogers's own tables, of a dozen pounds of pepper (pence being neglected) was 16, 23, 26, and 39 shillings; the price of a quarter of wheat was 6, 7½, 13, and 15 shillings. Pepper and wheat each rose in the fourth 10 years to about two and one-half times the price in the first 20 years. Surely Prof. Rogers would not have affirmed that the Turks raised the price of wheat in England. In the light of the whole scheme of prices it is not possible to affirm that the fall of Constantinople and the Turkish conquest of Egypt had any appreciable permanent effect upon the prices of oriental wares.

Thorold Rogers is led by this last error into several others. Being partly conscious of the anachronism of his catastrophic view, he strove to explain how the Turks could have raised the price of pepper by conquering Egypt 19 years after the cape had been turned. He concludes that the growth of Portuguese trade with the east was slow; that most of the oriental trade continued to come through Egypt; and that the Turks so burdened this trade with new exactions that the price of oriental wares was raised in the west. Truly a stupendous edifice of false fact erected by erroneous reasoning. It was shown above that the Turks put no new burdens on the oriental trade, and that after 1500 only a greatly reduced and uncertain part of the eastern wares came through Egypt and Syria. As for the rate of growth of the Portuguese trade, Gama took out 4 ships in 1497; Cabral, 13 in 1500; Nova, 4 in 1501 or 1502; Gama, 20 in 1502; Albuquerque, 9 in 1503; and after that from 12 to 15 Portuguese ships went every year. Perhaps one-third were lost, while others remained awhile to fight and explore, but the one-half or thereabouts which returned sufficed to supply western Europe with spices more abundantly than ever before. As for a last statement from Thorold Rogers to the effect that "the commercial decline of Venice, Genoa, Florence, and of the free German cities near the sources of the Danube and the Rhine, begins with the conquest of Egypt by the Turks," it needs but one correction. This may be made by striking out the words "the conquest of Egypt by the Turks" and substituting these: "The turning of the Cape of Good Hope by the Portuguese."

89. THE MOTIVES OF PRINCE HENRY THE NAVIGATOR[1]

More than half a century before Columbus discovered America Prince Henry (1394–1460), a younger son of the king of Portugal, was directing from his observatory on the coast of his native country the work of exploring the west coast of Africa, sending down one expedition after another. For his tireless interest in geographical study and his pioneer work in the field of exploration he has been surnamed "The Navigator."

Gomes Eannes de Azurara wrote an extended account of these expeditions, finishing his first draft in 1453. Azurara was at one time in charge of the library of the king of Portugal and in 1454 became royal chronicler. He was painstaking in collecting his material and reasonably accurate in his writing. His opinion of Prince Henry's motives, therefore, is of value to the student of history though it is obviously affected by current astrological beliefs. No one can ever know with certainty all the influences that impelled the Prince to carry on his self-appointed task.

In which five reasons appear why the Lord Infant was moved to command the search for the lands of Guinea.

We imagine that we know a matter when we are acquainted with the doer of it and the end for which he did it. And since in former chapters we have set forth the Lord Infant as the chief actor in these things, giving as clear an understanding of him as we could, it is meet that in this present chapter we should know his purpose in doing them. And you should note well that the noble spirit of this Prince, by a sort of natural constraint, was ever urging him both to begin and to carry out very great deeds. For which reason, after the taking of Ceuta he always kept ships well armed against the Infidel, both for war, and because he had also a wish to know the land

[1] Gomes Eannes de Azurara, *The Chronicle of the Discovery and Conquest of Guinea.* Translated by C. R. Beazley and Edgar Prestage. 2 Vols. London, Hakluyt Society Publications, Nos. 95 and 100, 1896 and 1899, vol. I, pp. 27–30.

that lay beyond the isles of Canary and that Cape called Bojador, for that up to his time, neither by writings, nor by the memory of man, was known with any certainty the nature of the land beyond that Cape. Some said indeed that Saint Brandan had passed that way; and there was another tale of two galleys rounding the Cape, which never returned. But this doth not appear at all likely to be true, for it is not to be presumed that if the said galleys went there, some other ships would not have endeavoured to learn what voyage they had made. And because the said Lord Infant wished to know the truth of this,—since it seemed to him that if he or some other lord did not endeavour to gain that knowledge, no mariners or merchants would ever dare to attempt it—(for it is clear that none of them ever trouble themselves to sail to a place where there is not a sure and certain hope of profit)—and seeing also that no other prince took any pains in this matter, he sent out his own ships against those parts, to have manifest certainty of them all. And to this he was stirred up by his zeal for the service of God and of the King Edward his Lord and brother, who then reigned. And this was the first reason of his action.

The second reason was that if there chanced to be in those lands some population of Christians, or some havens, into which it would be possible to sail without peril, many kinds of merchandise might be brought to this realm, which would find a ready market, and reasonably so, because no other people of these parts traded with them, nor yet people of any other that were known; and also the products of this realm might be taken there, which traffic would bring great profit to our countrymen.

The third reason was that, as it was said that the power of the Moors in that land of Africa was very much greater than was commonly supposed, and that there were no Christians among them, nor any other race of men; and because every wise man is obliged by natural prudence to wish for a knowledge of the power of his enemy; therefore the said Lord Infant exerted himself to cause this to be fully discovered, and to make it known determinately how far the power of those infidels extended.

The fourth reason was because during the one and thirty years that he had warred against the Moors, he had never found a Christian king, nor a lord outside this land, who for the love of our Lord Jesus Christ would aid him in the said war. Therefore he sought to know if there were in those parts any Christian princes, in whom the charity and the love of Christ was so ingrained that they would aid him against those enemies of the faith.

The fifth reason was his great desire to make increase in the faith of our Lord Jesus Christ and to bring to him all the souls that should be saved,—understanding that all the mystery of the Incarnation, Death, and Passion of our Lord Jesus Christ was for this sole end—namely the salvation of lost souls—whom the said Lord Infant by his travail and spending would fain bring into the true path. For he perceived that no better offering could be made unto the Lord than this; for if God promised to return one hundred goods for one, we may justly believe that for such great benefits, that is to say for so many souls as were saved by the efforts of this Lord, he will have so many hundreds of guerdons in the kingdom of God, by which his spirit may be glorified after this life in the celestial realm. For I that wrote this history saw so many men and women of those parts turned to the holy faith, that even if the Infant had been a heathen, their prayers would have been enough to have obtained his salvation. And not only did I see the first captives, but their children and grandchildren as true Christians as if the Divine grace breathed in them and imparted to them a clear knowledge of itself.

But over and above these five reasons I have a sixth that would seem to be the root from which all the others proceeded: and this is the inclination of the heavenly wheels. For, as I wrote not many days ago in a letter I sent to the Lord King, that although it be written that the wise man shall be Lord of the stars, and that the courses of the planets (according to the true estimate of the holy doctors) cannot cause the good man to stumble; yet it is manifest that they are bodies ordained in the secret counsels of our Lord God and run by a fixed measure, appointed to different ends, which are revealed to men by his grace, through whose influence bodies of the lower order are inclined to certain passions. And if it be a fact, speaking as a Catholic, that the contrary predestinations of the wheels of heaven can be avoided by natural judgment with the aid of a certain divine grace, much more does it stand to reason that those who are predestined to good fortune, by the help of this same grace, will not only follow their course but even add a greater increase to themselves. But here I wish to tell you how by the constraint of the influence of nature this glorious Prince was inclined to those actions of his. And that was because his ascendent was Aries, which is the house of Mars and exaltation of the sun, and his lord in the XIth house, in company of the sun. And because the said Mars was in Aquarius, which is the house of Saturn, and in the mansion of hope, it signified that this Lord should toil at high and mighty conquests, especially in seeking out things that were hidden from other men and secret, according to the nature of Saturn, in whose house he is. And the fact of his being accompanied by the sun, as I said, and the sun being in the house of Jupiter, signified that all his traffick and his conquests would be loyally carried out, according to the good pleasure of his king and lord.

90. *THE ITALIAN CITIES IN THE FOURTEENTH CENTURY* [1]

At the close of the Middle Ages no country in Europe was so wealthy and so highly developed intellectually as was the Italian peninsula. The following selection describes political conditions during the period in which Italy led Europe in many fields of human enterprise.

During the fourteenth century Pope and Emperor exercised only a secondary influence over Italian affairs. The destinies of Italy lay for the most part in the hands of the Italians themselves. It is the first great age of the despots. Della Scala in Verona, Visconti in Milan, Este in Ferrara, Gonzaga in Mantua, Carrara in Padua—all rose to greatness in the fourteenth century. It is also the age of the republics. Marsiglio of Padua preached the sovereignty of the people; and Rienzi tried to translate his doctrines into action. In Florence, Perugia, and Siena the nobility were excluded from political power, and the merchant classes reigned supreme. Florence began to extend her rule over neighbouring cities, while Perugia, as the champion of the Guelf cause in Umbria, "conquered in the Church's name, and took what she had conquered to herself." In the course of the fourteenth century Venice developed the most characteristic features of her constitution and emerged with undiminished forces from her long struggle with Genoa. The *condottiere* system was organized, and the disenfranchised nobility found fresh scope for their activity in the profession of arms. It is the age of Petrarch and Boccaccio, the prophets of humanism, of Arnolfo di Cambio, the Pisani and the Giotteschi who completed what has been called the heroic period of Italian art. It is a time when Italy cannot be treated as a whole. The true Italian history of the fourteenth century is written in a dozen varying forms in the records of each separate city-state.

Of all the Italian states none is at once so fascinating and so disappointing, so unique and so typical as Florence. Nowhere perhaps was there a truer or more abiding love of liberty than among the Florentines. Nowhere were there such men of genius or such possibilities of greatness. Yet with love of liberty and hatred of tyranny went an utter lack of discipline which rendered some form of tyranny inevitable. Guicciardini put his finger on the cause of at least half the ills of Florence when he said that she suffered from her passion for equality joined with the ambition of every family to be first. The thirteenth century had been marked by the rise to power of a wealthy middle class, organized in their trade guilds or arts, and popularly

[1] E. M. Jamison, C. M. Ady, K. D. Vernon, and C. Sanford Terry, *Italy, Mediaeval and Modern, A History*. Oxford, the Clarendon Press, 1917, pp. 165–183. Used by permission of the Oxford University Press.

known as the *Popolo Grasso*. In their wake came the *Popolo Minuto*, or members of the lesser arts, who were allowed a modicum of constitutional authority. The rise of the Popolo brought with it the ousting of the nobility from political life. From the promulgation of the Ordinances of Justice in 1293 the supreme magistracy in Florence consisted of the *Gonfaloniere di Justizia* and the six *Priori,* who held office for two months at a time and were drawn exclusively from members of the arts. No one who did not actually practise a trade was permitted to enrol himself in an art, and all families which numbered a knight among their members suffered under the political and civil disabilities of *Grandi*. The Florentine constitution showed the characteristic weaknesses of a democracy; it had a weak executive, a cumbersome system of representation, and a prejudice against great men. On the other hand, it suffered from many of the defects of an oligarchy. Florence was governed by a few wealthy families, acting in their own interests; and when the members of the *Popolo Grasso* quarrelled among themselves, there were at least three classes in the city ready to take advantage of the split in the government. The semi-enfranchised lesser arts, the disenfranchised nobility, and the unenfranchised artisans, all contributed to the political upheavals of fourteenth-century Florence.

Meanwhile the city was rapidly acquiring territory and rising to a foremost place among Italian states. San Miniato, Pistoia, Prato, Arezzo, Volterra, and San Gimignano, all bowed to the Florentine yoke in the course of the century; and during the supremacy of the Albizzi the boundaries of the Florentine state included Cortona and Montepulciano on the south, and Pisa, and Leghorn on the west. The subjugation of Pisa, the ancient rival of Florence, in 1406 was the crowning triumph of a long period of expansion. Florence, moreover, had constantly to defend herself against aspirants to supreme power in Italy. She bore the brunt of the resistance to Henry VII, and after his death her liberties were seriously threatened by Castruccio Castracani, Lord of Lucca, the leading Ghibelline in Tuscany. In 1340 Mastino della Scala, then at the height of his power in Verona, took possession of Lucca, and began to make his influence felt in Pisa and Arezzo. The time of Florence's gravest peril was, however, during the ascendancy of Gian Galeazzo Visconti. At the moment of his death in 1402 his armies were closing round the city, and Florence was saved by what seemed like a miracle.

These new acquisitions of territory and the menace to Florentine liberties from ambitious neighbours called for a strong and efficient government, capable of dealing effectively both with home and foreign politics. For this task the municipal constitution was wholly inadequate, and attempts were made to supplement its weakness by various forms of unofficial rule. Florence fell beneath the sway of would-be despots, both internal and external, of a political club and of a powerful family. All alike exercised an authority that was purely transitory, and all owed their fall partly to their own unbridled ambitions, partly to the Florentine passion for liberty which grew restive at the first suggestion of despotism.

On the expulsion of the Whites in 1301, Corso Donati, the leader of the Black party, was unquestionably the first man in Florence. For four years his supremacy was unchallenged, and he began to intrigue with the enemies of Florence in order to overthrow the Signoria and make himself lord of the city. But the Florentines got wind of the conspiracy and Corso Donati perished ignominiously in a street fight. As a means of defence against Castruccio Castracani, Florence commended herself to Charles of Calabria, the son of King Robert of Naples. Machiavelli's *History of Florence* records the death of Castruccio in 1328 with the following significant comment: "Fortune seldom fails to link one good with another: it happened at this time that Charles, Duke of Calabria and Lord of Florence, died at Naples; so that within a brief period the Florentines were freed from their fears of the one, and from the oppressions of the other." In September 1342, Walter de Brienne, the titular Duke of Athens, was appointed Lord of Florence for life amid the acclamations of the citizens. In July 1343, "the cry of Liberty being raised, the whole city ran to arms. . . . All the heads of the families, whether Grandi or Popolani, swore fidelity to one another and death to the Duke." The ten months' tyrant took refuge in flight, after being forced to sign his abdication.

During the greater part of the fourteenth century the chief power lay with the Parte Guelfa, a political club, with its own officers and organization, existing for the purpose of carrying out the proscription of Ghibellinism within Florence, and of keeping in touch with the Guelf faction throughout Italy. But in course of time the captains of the Parte Guelfa began to abuse their authority. They proscribed their personal enemies as Ghibellines, and acted in public matters as if they, and not the Signoria, were the heads of the Florentine state. In 1378 a new Signoria came into office bent on the downfall of the Parte Guelfa. This quarrel between the official and the unofficial government gave occasion to the rising of the Ciompi, the unenfranchised artisans of Florence. The city found itself in the throes of a social revolution, and when order was restored the predominance of the Parte Guelfa gave place to that of the Albizzi. From 1382 to 1434 Maso degli Albizzi and his son Rinaldo controlled Florentine politics. They supplied the element of strength and permanency which was lacking in the Signoria, while their trade connexions outside Florence gave them a special importance in foreign affairs. They took their full share in the literary and artistic activities of the Florentines, and made themselves even more popular outside the city than they were within its walls. Subject cities, such as Pisa, regarded the suzerainty of the Albizzi as infinitely preferable to that of the rival republic which had conquered them. Thus the Albizzi were despots in all that concerned the practical work of government, although in outward form they remained simple Florentine citizens. Florence had at last found a form of government which supplemented the defects of her constitution while respecting her democratic prejudices. When in 1434 the Albizzi were overthrown by the Medici, it was the family and not the system which was changed. Cosimo dei Medici and his descendants fulfilled all the functions of the Albizzi; their distinction lay in fulfilling them even more effectively.

The problems which beset other Italian cities did not differ materially from those of Florence. Civil strife, external enemies, and inadequate municipal constitutions were the main causes of the decline of Siena and Perugia in the fourteenth century. Philippe de Commines summed up the history of Siena when he said that "the city is always divided against herself and is governed more foolishly than any other city in Italy." Yet in the thirteenth century Siena was at the height of her prosperity. Her great noble families, such as the Salimbeni, the Tolomei, the Piccolomini, and the Malavolti, were both soldiers and merchants, who enriched the city by their commerce and defended her against her enemies. The strength of the civic spirit was manifested in Siena's clean, well-paved streets, in the beauty of her public buildings, and in her university with its professors chosen and paid by the republic. It was the rise to power of the burgher class, and subsequently of the artisans, which plunged the city into unending civil strife. She underwent at least three revolutions in the fourteenth century, and the quarrels between her five *Monti* or factions made Siena an easy prey to Gian Galeazzo Visconti in 1388. Finally, the recurrence of internal troubles, and the threat to her independence from the King of Naples in the fifteenth century, led to the depotism of Pandolfo Petrucci.

The golden age of Perugia lay like that of Siena in the latter half of the thirteenth and the beginning of the fourteenth centuries. This was the time of material progress, of the foundation of the university, of the growth of territory, and of great building activity. With the removal of the Papacy to Avignon, Perugia became the leader of the Guelf party in Umbria, and her power and independence were consequently increased. But after the peace which followed the departure of the Emperor Louis from Italy, a rupture between the classes took place. The compilation of the *Libro Rosso* or register of the nobles, in 1333, marked the beginning of class warfare, and of the subjection of the nobility to disabilities similar to those imposed by the Ordinances of Justice in Florence. From henceforth Perugia suffered from perpetual conflict; and it was her own internal weakness that caused her submission to the Church in 1371, and subsequently to the *condottiere,* Braccio. Towards the end of the fifteenth century a despotism was established in Perugia through the predominance of one of her leading nobles, Gian Paolo Baglioni.

In the vast majority of Italian cities the problem of government was solved, sooner or later, by the surrender of civic liberties into the hands of a despot. The Petrucci and the Baglioni came too late to save the situation in Siena and Perugia; but in the North Italian cities the despotism was established earlier, and with more permanent effect. It is not too much to say that every Italian despot based his authority primarily on popular consent. Supreme power was conferred on him by the citizens in order that he might perform certain definite functions. In many cases the depotism fell because it had forfeited popular favour, and had ceased to do the work for which it was created. On the other hand, the love of the citizens for their ruling family preserved the ascendancy of that family even when half the forces of Italy were bent upon its overthrow. Yet the element of force was not lacking. The despot was frequently a successful soldier, chosen because he could defend the city from her enemies or impose peace upon warring factions, while he sometimes won his election purely by conquest. The Signoria, or lordship of the city, was conferred by the citizens themselves, but the despot usually tried to render his position more secure by obtaining some external sanction for his authority in addition to popular election. He coveted the title of Imperial or Papal Vicar, and at a later stage he tried to obtain the investiture of his city, in order that he might hold it as a fief of the Papacy or the Empire.

The political theories which lie behind the Italian despotism are nowhere more clearly expressed than in Marsiglio of Padua's *Defensor Pacis*. This famous treatise was written in the University of Paris in 1324, but it breathes the atmosphere of the Italian city-state. The people as the source of all authority is the root principle of the *Defensor:* "the sole human legislator is the whole body of citizens or the majority of them." Next in importance is Marsiglio's insistence upon the concentration of executive power in the hands of a prince, who is the people's nominee and representative. He is the guardian of peace who gives the treatise its title. He alone has coercive jurisdiction in matters ecclesiastical and temporal. He is, in short, the modern state, efficient, all-absorbing, tyrannical. It has been said of Marsiglio that he put forward a theory of Church and State which was partly realized at the Reformation, partly in the revolutionary era, and of which part still awaits realization. Nevertheless the essentials of his theory could be seen in practical working in at least five North Italian cities within a few years of the publication of the *Defensor Pacis*.

Perhaps the most permanent effect of Henry VII's Italian expedition was the new importance which it gave to two budding despots, Matteo Visconti and Can Grande della Scala. While Henry lived, he singled them out for favour, and made them imperial vicars. At his death it fell to them to stem the tide of Ghibelline reaction, and in so doing to add to their own power and prestige. Can Grande is in many respects the most attractive of the Italian despots. A Trevisan poet described him at his death as "the fount of human justice, the fount of courtesy, the flower of Lombard knighthood." In him the man of ideas predominates over the mere politician, and his portrait is not marred by brutal or treacherous features. The permanent foundation of the Della Scala power in Verona dates from 1277, when Can Grande's father Alberto was made Captain of the People for life. His three sons succeeded him in that office, and in 1311 Can Grande became the supreme authority in Verona owing to the death of his elder brothers. The despotism did not replace the old municipal constitution, but was simply imposed upon it. Verona still had its councils, both executive and legislative, but all took an oath of fidelity to Can Grande, and he had power to alter and annul the statutes. Before his death his authority was extended over the neighbouring cities of Vicenza, Padua, Feltre, Belluno, and Treviso, under similar conditions. Thus Can Grande's state consisted in a federation of virtually self-governing municipalities, the sole link between them being the person of the despot. Can Grande owed much of his success to his qualities as a soldier. He had the power of inspiring devotion among his troops, and an instinct for discovering the weak spot in the enemy's position. Fatigue was unknown to him, and he was always the first to ford a stream or scale a wall. When he was not fighting, he worked off his energy in hunting and hawking. He was, moreover, a generous foe. He ruled his conquests well and wisely, and when a vanquished enemy fell into his hands he treated him with every courtesy. Above all, the despotism of Can Grande is distinguished by the splendours of his court. He encouraged great men of every kind to find a home in Verona, and laid himself out to be a model host. At one time, no less than twenty exiled Ghibelline princes took refuge with Can Grande. His court was thronged with scholars, musicians, sculptors, merchants, and the hospitality which he showed to Dante has given him a place in the seventeenth canto of the *Paradiso*. The highest point in the fortunes of the Della Scala was reached under his auspices. At his death in 1329 the glorious days of Verona were numbered, although it was not until 1387 that the Signoria fell before the rising power of Gian Galeazzo Visconti.

The supremacy of the Carrara in Padua dates from the year 1318, when the city was hard pressed by Can Grande, and the citizens agreed that the best means of self-preservation was to entrust the government to the care of a single man. Thereupon the Signoria was conferred on Jacopo da Carrara, one of the leading citizens, and successive members of his family were Lords of Padua until 1405. They ruled over a small state, hemmed in between powerful neighbours, and dangerously near to the Venetian lagoons. Thus they were engaged in a perpetual struggle for existence, and long wars and heavy taxation did not increase their popularity in Padua. Meanwhile the watchful eye of the Venetian Republic was always upon them. Venice protected the Carrara against Della Scala and Visconti, but when Francesco Carrara showed signs of too great independence she determined to sweep a possible rival from her path. She allowed Gian Galeazzo Visconti to conquer Padua in 1389, and although she helped to restore Francesco Novello in the following year, her motive for so doing was not love of the Carrara. In 1405 the Venetians entered the city, massacring every member of the ruling family whom they found, and the Paduans passed beneath the dominion of Venice with small signs of reluctance.

A more interesting and more durable example of a small despotism is that of the house of Gonzaga in Mantua. Lodovico Gonzaga wrested the supreme power from the hands of the rival family of Buonacolsi in 1328; and the dynasty which he established continued to flourish long after richer and more powerful Italian states had lost their independence. From very early days the Gonzaga were under the protection of the Empire. Lodovico held the title of Imperial Vicar, and in 1433 Gian Francesco II was made Marquis of Mantua by the Emperor Sigismund. This long-standing alliance was preserved in the sixteenth century. Charles V counted the Gonzaga princes among his most devoted friends, and in 1529 he brought them to the highest point of their greatness by raising Mantua into a duchy. The Lords of Mantua eked out their small resources by serving as soldiers of fortune in the Italian wars, but in spite of their poverty they soon won a great reputation in the sphere of art and letters. When Gian Francesco II persuaded Vittorino da Feltre to settle in Mantua as tutor to his children in 1425, the city became the most important educational centre in Italy. It was Vittorino's pupil, Lodovico Gonzaga, who decorated his capital under the guidance of Leo Battista Alberti, and through whom Mantegna came to Mantua, to live there for fifty years.

Azzo d'Este, the first Lord of Ferrara, died in 1212, and in Dante's day the Ferrarese Court was already famous as the resort of the troubadours of Provence. Thus the Este were by far the oldest of the Italian despots. The permanency of their rule in Ferrara is remarkable owing to the fact that their supremacy was disputed both by the Pope and the Venetians. Ferrara lay nominally within the States of the Church, and Venice had a trading colony in the city. So both the Papacy and the Venetian Republic looked upon the Este as rivals to their own power; and it seemed more than once as if the ruling family would be overthrown by these formidable adversaries. But the loyalty of their subjects proved stronger than all the forces which could be brought against them. Early in the fourteenth century Ferrara was obliged to open her gates to the papal armies; after a few years there was a rising in the city and the Este were recalled. In 1482 the Pope and Venice made a joint attack on Ferrara. The Este must have fallen had it not been for the gallant defence of the citizens, which kept the enemy at bay until help arrived from outside. The story of the house of Este in Ferrara goes far to prove the truth of Machiavelli's saying that a prince's best fortress is the love of the citizens.

Of all the Italian despots, Gian Galeazzo Visconti alone came within measurable distance of uniting Italy under his rule. At the time of his death his possessions extended over the whole of North Italy, from the frontiers of Piedmont to Padua and the March of Treviso. South of the Po he controlled the Via Emilia from Piacenza to Bologna, and established a protectorate over the Lords of Romagna. He crossed the Apennines and all but succeeded in reducing Florence to submission. His possession of Lucca, Pisa, and Piombino cut her off from the sea, while his occupation of Siena and Perugia blocked the two main roads to Rome. At this time the power of the Papacy was almost non-existent in Italy. Naples was in the throes of a succession war, and Venice had not yet turned her attention seriously towards the mainland. Everything seemed to favour Visconti's domination; and when he died in 1402 he was said to have mantle, sceptre, and diadem already prepared for his coronation as King of Italy.

The nature of Gian Galeazzo's rule was that of the typical Italian despot. It was an addition to, and not a substitute for, the forms of government already existing in the cities which acknowledged his authority. This federal character of the despotism explains both its rapid growth and its sudden collapse when the controlling hand was withdrawn. While Gian Galeazzo lived he brought peace, good government, and material prosperity to the Milanese state. Like Can Grande before him, he was a patron of art and letters. The University of Pavia owed much to his favour, and he won undying fame as the founder of the cathedral of Milan and the Certosa of Pavia. It is impossible to deny the benefits of Visconti rule, yet the history of the means by which they established their power is one long tale of crime and treachery. Matteo Visconti wormed himself into Henry VII's favour, intrigued with Guido della Torre against him, and ended by convincing Henry that the conspiracy was the work of Della Torre alone. Gian Galeazzo became sole ruler of Milan by murdering his uncle Bernabo. He used the Carrara to overthrow the Della Scala, and then, turning on his allies, he drove them from Padua. As a family the Visconti were remarkable, both for their ability and their unscrupulousness, in an age which produced many able and unscrupulous men. They were not a race of soldiers, but Gian Galeazzo's wealth and influence enabled him to command the flower of the Italian mercenary forces.

Two other characteristics of the Visconti despotism are worthy of notice.

Although they could not carry out Marsiglio of Padua's theory and deprive the Church of jurisdiction, the rulers of Milan contrived to unite spiritual and temporal authority in their own hands. The power of the Visconti began with Archbishop Otto in the thirteenth century, and Giovanni Visconti held both the Signoria and the archbishopric of Milan at the time of his death in 1354. Gian Galeazzo also endeavoured to increase his prestige by means of the marriage alliances which he formed with the chief European powers. His first wife was Isabella of France, the daughter of King John, who paid his ransom to the English with Visconti ducats. His sister became the bride of Lionel, Duke of Clarence, and his daughter, Valentina, married Louis, Duke of Orleans, thereby laying the foundations of the later French claims to Milan. In 1395 Gian Galeazzo realized a long-standing ambition and obtained the investiture of the Duchy of Milan from the Emperor Wenzel. The city despot had become a prince of the Empire.

While the chief Italian republics fell into the hands of despots, or wasted themselves in internal feuds, Venice alone attained to a form of government which was both constitutional and efficient, free and strong. In 1297 the famous *Serrata del Consiglio* restricted the governing class to certain families, members of which had already sat in the Grand Council. Thus birth became the chief qualification for citizenship, but, in spite of this limitation, there was practically no disaffection among the disenfranchised classes. The plebeians were content to hold important and lucrative posts in the civil service, and to prosper as merchants, realizing that the cares and responsibilities of state were on the shoulders of the nobility, while the fruits of good government belonged to all. When the discovery of the Tiepolo conspiracy in 1310 showed the need for some extraordinary body which could give an element of strength and secrecy to the constitution, the Council of Ten was created, "not a limb of the state but as it were a sword in her hand." The art of discipline which had been denied to the Florentines was carried to perfection among the Venetians. Entire devotion to the service of the Republic was demanded of all who held office, and no mercy was shown to failures. In 1355 the execution of the Doge, Marin Faliero, for conspiring to change the constitution, sent a thrill through Italy. "Those who are for a time Doges," wrote Petrarch, "I would warn to study the mirror set before their eyes, that they may see in it that they are leaders not lords, nay not even leaders, but honoured servants of the state."

The efficiency of the Venetian government contrasted sharply with that of Genoa; and herein lies the clue to the success of Venice in her struggle with the rival maritime republic. At the beginning of the fourteenth century the power of Genoa in the East was at least equal to that of Venice. The Venetians formed the backbone of the Latin Empire while Genoa stood by the Greeks. Thus the restoration of the Greek Empire in 1261 enabled the

Genoese to take a leading position at Constantinople, and to establish their famous colony at Galata. The Venetians, on the other hand, were forced to occupy the second place in commerce, and to feel that they were out of favour at the Imperial Court. In the course of the naval wars of the fourteenth century Genoa struck some hard blows at her adversary, chief among them being the destruction of the Venetian fleet at Sapienza in 1354, and the taking of Chioggia in 1371. Yet domestic feuds prevented Genoa from reaping the fruits of her victories, and the year before Sapienza she was obliged to acknowledge the suzerainty of the Visconti. Internal weakness robbed her of her maritime supremacy, while internal strength saved Venice even in that darkest hour when the banner of St. George of Genoa fluttered over the lagoons at Chioggia.

Throughout the fourteenth century the prosperity and trading activities of Venice increased steadily. Her merchants exported sugar to England and exchanged it for Boston wool, which was woven into cloth in Flanders, and so carried back in Venetian ships to Dalmatia and the Levant. In the course of the century the Fondaco de' Tedeschi in Venice was enlarged by the Republic, as the German merchants complained that it was impossible to see across the courtyard for the piles of merchandise that lay there. About the same time it was decided to add a new hall to the Doge's palace for meetings of the Grand Council. This was the beginning of that triumph of Venetian Gothic, the Palazzo Ducale as we know it today. While Venice was still primarily a maritime power, deriving her prosperity from Levantine trade, and recognized as the champion of Christianity against the growing power of the Turk, she was becoming increasingly occupied with mainland problems. The domination of the Della Scala taught her that a hostile power on the Italian mainland might deprive her of her food supply. It was a war with Mastino della Scala which laid the foundations of the Venetian *Terra Firma* by leaving her in possession of the March of Treviso. She fought with Hungary over Dalmatia, and alternately quarrelled with and protected her nearest neighbours, the Carrara of Padua. Her prosperity, her isolation, and her proud independence made her many enemies, and Italy must have appreciated the gibe of Nicholas, Bishop of Butrinto, who said that the Venetians looked upon themselves as a fifth element, belonging "neither to the Church nor to the Emperor, neither to the land nor to the sea." Yet the time was at hand when Venice could no longer stand aside from the main current of Italian politics. On the break-up of Gian Galeazzo Visconti's dominions she embarked in all seriousness on her career of conquest upon the mainland.

The rich and varied life of the city-states could not fail to engender a sense of patriotism among the Italians, which was increased by a consciousness of the superiority of their civilization over that of every other European country. A growing contempt for the foreigner is a characteristic of fourteenth-century Italy; and the abortive expeditions of Louis of Bavaria, John of Bohemia, and Charles IV helped to confirm the Italian point of view. Two men in particular gave expression to the national consciousness, and did their best to direct it towards the attainment of national unity. Both Petrarch and Rienzi found in the glories of ancient Rome their hope for the future of Italy. Petrarch's work for the revival of learning, and Rienzi's efforts to restore the Roman Republic were prompted by a common desire to make the great past live again. Both men were affected by the transference of the Papacy to Avignon. Rienzi spent his youth in Rome, and mourned over the city as a "grey-haired widow on a rudderless ship." His ambition was to restore to Rome that universal dominion which the departure of the popes had taken from her. Petrarch was the son of an exiled Florentine, who had made his home at Avignon, and his whole heart went out from "Babylon" to his native land. To him Italy was not only his unknown home, but also the home of Vergil and Cicero, those companions of his life of whom he loved to speak as "brother" and "father." "My longing to see Rome, deserted and merely the shadow of ancient Rome though she is," he wrote in 1334, "is scarcely to be believed."

91. WITH YOUNG ERASMUS IN THE CITY OF DEVENTER[1]

Desiderius Erasmus of Rotterdam is generally considered the most important humanist of the first three decades of the sixteenth century. When a boy, he spent about six years in the city of Deventer, a town located on the right bank of the river Yssel, which is an arm of the Rhine and flows northward into the Zuiderzee. This city was in the fourteenth and fifteenth centuries an important member of the celebrated Hanseatic League. When Erasmus arrived in this place about the year 1475, he was very fortunate to be able to attend the cathedral school and to live in a community which was in direct contact with many currents of civilization of a high order. The description of the city which follows is based on a careful study of numerous primary sources and would fit other cities in the Low Countries and adjoining regions during the close of the Middle Ages.

When one imagines oneself standing about the year 1475 on the right bank of the Yssel opposite the city of Deventer, one notes a striking contrast between the peaceful meadows and the thriving Hansa town across the water. Deventer has become a wealthy center of commerce. Its merchants

[1] Albert Hyma, *The Youth of Erasmus.* Ann Arbor, Mich., The University of Michigan Press, 1930, pp. 67–70.

have enabled the populace to build several stately churches, roomy monasteries, and splendid homes; and massive walls surmounted by heavy towers enhance the beauty of the scene as from a distance one gazes in admiration at the city. Along the bank of the river one sees a busy traffic, and numerous are the ships that are arriving and departing each day. Some of them are bringing wood from German forests and grain from Polish farms; others are loaded with stones hewn in the mountainous districts to the south. Some are carrying fish and some have a cargo of merchandise.

After crossing the river we enter the city and pass a number of workshops, where in a simple and rather primitive manner (from the viewpoint of a sophisticated inhabitant of a twentieth-century metropolis) all sorts of articles are manufactured. Everywhere the old craft guilds are still functioning, with their system of masters, journeymen, and apprentices. The streets are very narrow and one must use caution in passing the houses where the bakers have placed their products on "bread benches" in front of their shops, or where the manufacturers of leather goods, of furs, or of textiles have prepared similar exhibitions. The magistrates are very strict here; they take care that all articles have a proper weight. Occasionally they send an official to test the weights and measures and to weigh or examine the goods placed on sale.

In the center of the city is the market-square, named Brink. Here we can examine at leisure the architecture of the principal buildings. About one-third of them are still of wood, several with the upper story protruding over the lower. The majority have thatched roofs, but some are covered with tiles, and the number of tiled roofs is rapidly increasing, since the magistrates have warned against the danger of fire. There are also a few buildings covered with slate; these belong to the more wealthy burghers, usually merchants who have been eminently successful in various enterprises. Their homes are also distinguished by windows made of glass, but their less favored neighbors have to content themselves with panes of oiled paper, linen, or pigskin. Most houses are very low, leaving but seven or eight feet between the eaves and the street.

The color of most buildings is dark. Brown tar is commonly used, instead of paint, to protect the wood against the elements. The glaring contrast between the color of the tar and the yellow straw or the red tiles or the blue slate affects one rather unpleasantly. And so does the *ensemble* of the average group of houses on either side of the ordinary streets. They do not form a neat row, but nearly all stand apart from each other in a helter-skelter fashion. There is almost always at least a yard of space between the houses, "so that everybody can place a ladder upon his own lot."

It is evident that the knowledge of hygiene is not very widespread in the city, nor is cleanliness deemed a great virtue here. In some places the streets look most unsanitary, for many a burgher keeps a manure pile in his yard, not seldom in front of the house, where pigs, chickens, and children gleefully dig up the filthy dung. Pigs feel quite at home on the streets as well, for generally only a narrow strip in the center has been paved, while the market-square is also largely unpaved. The pavement is not smooth, since it consists of stones of all shapes and sizes. In some of the more narrow streets, named *stegen,* holes in the pavement have been filled with reeds or straw. Most lots have been inclosed by railings or fences, or they are marked off by ditches. Little poles in front of the lots indicate "how wide the street will have to remain," else greedy burghers might add part of the street to their property. The dirt which collects on the streets is taken away in little carts from time to time by officials, but the men do not come frequently. Many a time it is the rain which has to be relied upon in the cleaning of the streets.

The interior of the homes offers much food for wonder. Chimneys are few and so are stoves. In the center of each house still remains the time-honored fireplace, above which is seen a large round hole in the roof to let the smoke escape upward. This opening is covered when there is no fire, but in cold rainy weather it is sometimes difficult for the people to keep comfortable. Sleeping quarters are also rather unsanitary, particularly where beds have been placed in a room, or rather, a closet, where one sleeps all night behind closed doors without any ventilation whatsoever. As for bathing, that is a custom practically unheard of among the adult population. Children have to be bathed regularly, so the stolid burghers admit, but grown-ups merely need to change their underwear once in a fortnight; baths are entirely unnecessary.

And woe to the citizens when perchance a plague should visit the city. In the previous century such was no rare occurrence and who knows that another one is not due again in a few years? We, who know that in 1483 there will be a visitation which will once more sweep away hundreds of human lives within the city, feel duty-bound to warn the heedless burghers. But they reply that there is no remedy for contagious diseases. Nature must take its course; man is helpless against plagues and floods and earthquakes. which are sent by God, who alone knows the value of each human life.

There is much in the administration of justice, in the relation between social classes, in the municipal government, and in the realms of religion and education which we might criticize. Only we should discover to our chagrin that the burghers of Deventer could not appreciate our point of view. The possibility of social progress never seems to occur to them. It is true that in the fourteenth century Gerard Groote revealed many abuses existing in the Church and he found a warm response in the hearts of both clerics and laymen. The curriculum of the celebrated school attached to St.

Lebwin's Church has also undergone a marked transformation. There is a change going on in some directions, where it may have far-reaching effects. Elsewhere conditions must remain the same for centuries.

92. *THE NETHERLANDS IN THE FIFTEENTH CENTURY* [1]

In the fifteenth century the Netherlands, or Low Countries, was one of the most prosperous and highly civilized regions in the whole world. It is largely because afterward this collection of tiny states broke up into two separate units and because the southern provinces rapidly declined that comparatively little attention is usually paid to their history at the close of the Middle Ages. This is to be regretted, and it is hoped that a reading of passages like the following selection may help to correct wrong perspectives.

The Netherlands, or Low Countries, were a district including not only the territory which now forms the Kingdom of the Netherlands but also Belgium, Luxemburg, and a part of northern France. Strictly speaking, this district belonged partly to the Holy Roman Empire and partly to France, but during the course of the fifteenth century the seventeen tiny states which were collectively styled Netherlands became nearly independent of both the emperor and the French king.

At the opening of the fifteenth century most of the states, or provinces, had become subject to three foreign dynasties, namely, the houses of Wittelsbach (Bavarian), Luxemburg (Bohemian), and Burgundy. The Bavarian house ruled in Holland, Zeeland, and Hainault; the Bohemian house in Brabant, Limburg, and Luxemburg; while the duke of Burgundy had held Flanders since 1384 and was gradually extending his influence, to the detriment of the two rivals, who before long were to lose all their possessions in the Netherlands.

Greatest of all the dukes of Burgundy was Philip the Good (1419–67), who not only possessed the duchy of Burgundy and Franche-Comté, or the County of Burgundy, but inherited Flanders, Mechlin, and Artois from his grandmother Margaret; and Brabant, Limburg, and Antwerp from his cousin Philip. Through cunning, diplomacy, and force of arms he took possession of Limburg and Antwerp (1430), which were to a certain extent dependencies of Brabant; in the same manner he secured Holland, Zeeland, and Hainault (1433), and Luxemburg was added in 1451; Namur was bought from its count (1421) and the bishopric of Utrecht was given to David, his natural son (1456). Of the seventeen principalities which con-

[1] Albert Hyma, *The Youth of Erasmus*. Ann Arbor, Mich., The University of Michigan Press, 1930, pp. 13–20.

stituted the Netherlands, Philip actually possessed eleven, and he laid claim to Friesland, because the counts of Holland had for centuries regarded this district as a dependency of their country.

The reign of Philip the Good was of great importance in the history of the Netherlands. Gradually he increased his influence in the six districts which he himself could not occupy, so that by the end of his reign not only Utrecht, but also Gelderland and Liège formed little more than protectorates of the wily duke. His reign marked the end of feudalism in the Low Countries, for eleven separate principalities had been joined to form another "national state," controlled by one central government. Furthermore, Philip had withdrawn his possessions from the suzerainty of both the king of France and the emperor of the Holy Roman Empire. And what is still more significant, he had terminated the long series of social and political wars which had seriously hampered the expansion of trade and industry. There was only one task left for the duke of Burgundy, namely, the conquest of the territory between the Netherlands and the ancient duchy to the south.

Philip was not able to join the two great units, but when he passed away in 1467, his son, Charles the Bold (1467-77), firmly resolved to execute the plan and have himself crowned king besides. At first it seemed as if he would be successful, for the death of the Duke of Gelderland in 1473 enabled Charles to occupy this important duchy, and now he believed the time ripe for the creation of the kingdom of Burgundy. Had he not inherited the fairest provinces of the ancient kingdom of Lorraine, which once stretched all the way from the North Sea to the Mediterranean? In order to gain the good will of Emperor Frederick III he promised the hand of his only daughter, Mary, to the Emperor's son, Maximilian. In November, 1473, therefore, Charles was to be crowned king at Trier, but the day before the coronation the Emperor changed his mind and fled from the scene. King Louis XI of France, often named the "spider king," had informed the Emperor that Charles, his enemy, had no intention of keeping his promise. Against this cunning monarch the audacious but not highly intelligent duke was no match. He vainly attempted to increase his territories east of Burgundy, and in 1477 he was killed on the battle-field when fighting a Swiss army. At his death the French king pulled the whole duchy of Burgundy into his web, since Mary, Charles' heir, possessed neither soldiers nor finances with which to defend herself.

Shortly after the death of Charles the Bold his daughter married Maximilian, in accordance with the agreement between Charles and Frederick III. As archduke of Austria and prospective heir to all the Habsburg dominions, the bridegroom was expected to protect the Netherlands against the scheming "spider king." For the inhabitants of the Netherlands, however, the marriage was by no means an advantage. Maximilian and his successors remained true members of the illustrious house of Habsburg. The state so carefully constructed in the Low Countries by Philip the Good, even though it was enlarged later to include all the seventeen provinces, became and long remained a mere dependency of a great monarchy with its capital not in Brussels but in Vienna, and later in Madrid. The premature death of Charles the Bold and his lack of a capable successor were partly responsible for the subjection of the Netherlands to a number of monarchs who refused to identify their interests with those of the people in the Low Countries, and so it happened that the latter never formed a homogeneous state, not even in the reign of King William I (1815–30); and therefore a national consciousness did not develop in the country which gave birth to Erasmus [Holland] until it had separated from the southern provinces and rose against the king of Spain (1568–1648). Had Erasmus been born two hundred years later he would have felt quite differently about his native country.

The death of Charles the Bold ushered in a period of civil war in the Netherlands. Suddenly the hand of a powerful ruler had been withdrawn and now there was no longer a standing army to quell insurrection and party strife. The bishopric of Liège was the first to rise successfully against the rule of Mary. She granted to Louis of Bourbon, the bishop, complete independence, which the bishopric maintained until the close of the eighteenth century. Gelderland, however, was less fortunate, while the other provinces inherited by Mary agreed to accept her rule on condition that she sign a document named the "Great Privilege," which wrung many concessions from her, but did not revive the old feudal governments. The dukes and counts were gone, never to return.

In 1478 Mary bore a son, Philip the Fair, who afterward married Joanna of Spain, and who became the father of the powerful Charles V, the modern Charlemagne. The birth of Philip created great happiness in the Low Countries, for it was hoped that he would some day restore order in the distracted provinces. Maximilian successfully continued the war with France, and when, in 1481, he made an alliance with King Edward IV of England the French king was compelled to resort to defensive warfare. But in 1482 Mary died and once more the country faced a grave political crisis. Everywhere attempts were made to deprive Maximilian of power. Particularly in Flanders he was strongly resisted. The city of Ghent compelled him to surrender the reins of government to a council of regents, and six years later (1488) Ghent started a new revolution. Maximilian tried to call a meeting of the States-General in Bruges, but this city also was hostile to him. The guilds of Bruges closed their gates to the German army which Maximilian had ordered to suppress the insurgents. They occupied the market square, and the illustrious archduke, who since 1486 had also been King of the Romans, was imprisoned in a grocery store! He now lost even the title of Regent of Flanders, but, once set free, he hastened to mete out revenge to the burghers of Bruges and Ghent, who after stubborn resistance had to surrender to his rule. In 1492 Maximilian was master of Flanders, and Ghent had lost its independence.

In the northern provinces also much fighting occurred. Civil war, held in check by Philip the Good and Charles the Bold (1428–77), broke out anew as soon as Charles fell on the battle-field. The two factions which before 1428 had arrayed themselves against each other, namely, the *Hoekschen* and the *Kabeljauwschen,* now commenced another terrible war, causing widespread distress. The first-named party was opposed to the Burgundian house, while the other faction supported it. In Utrecht the bishop was defeated and it was not until 1483 that Bishop David, the son of Philip of Burgundy, was restored to power by Maximilian. In the former county of Holland a veritable guerilla war was waged. Two powerful noblemen fitted out an impregnable castle which formed a base of operations for plundering expeditions. Their fleet took Rotterdam in 1488 and their soldiers did untold damage in surrounding territory. . . . Then followed a very bad harvest in 1490, which aroused thousands of farmers to frenzy, for it was not so much the weather as the fighting which had brought the country near to famine. In 1491 and 1492 the roving peasants entered various cities, where they destroyed much valuable property. Near Leiden they were finally defeated by troops which had been sent from Germany.

For fifteen years (1477–92) the archduke of Austria had failed to restore order. It was indeed a pity for Holland that Charles the Bold had so recklessly thrown away his life. Whereas before the year 1477 the cities of Amsterdam, Leiden, Dordrecht, Haarlem, Rotterdam, and Gouda had just begun to rival the Hansa towns of northern Germany, the period of anarchy which followed the death of Charles witnessed the devastation of miles of fertile fields and the destruction of thousands of homes, paralyzing trade and undermining the foundations of prosperity. . . .

In 1492 the political crisis in the Low Countries had passed. Maximilian had finally achieved his purpose. The central government had been restored and the next year he could safely intrust the reins of political power to his son Philip the Fair, and direct his attention to affairs in the Holy Roman Empire, where he was soon to become Emperor himself. In 1493 he made peace with Charles VIII of France, who returned Franche-Comté and Artois to him, and in 1494 he embarked upon the conquest of Italy. In the Low Countries Philip the Fair was gladly hailed as Prince, and during the twelve years of his reign (1494–1506) the burghers of Flanders and Holland were content with their loss of political autonomy, for they had learned to appreciate order and prosperity more than self-government. They could now apply themselves to the task of making the Netherlands the emporium of the western world, the leader in scientific agriculture and the successful rival of Italy in the fields of commerce, industry, learning, and art.

Professor Henri Pirenne has shown that during the late medieval period (1000–1500 A. D.) the Low Countries were exceptionally prosperous. Throughout this middle region French monastic reforms, epics, and chivalry passed into Germany; and whatever ideas came from Germany to France traveled mostly by way of the Netherlands. It was here that intellectual as well as religious and commercial currents met and mingled; and from here they issued forth. The Flemish towns were the first in transalpine Europe to supplant the monasteries as chief seats of learning and art. Under the rule of the dukes of Burgundy, Bruges and Ghent became the wealthiest cities north of the Alps, not excepting Paris and London. In the middle of the fifteenth century the court at Bruges outshone even the court at Paris.

"The most brilliant court of Europe in the middle of the fifteenth century," says a noted French historian, "was that of Philip the Good, duke of Burgundy. No region was in fact so rich as the Netherlands, which belonged to him, and Philip was the most extravagant of all men. His reign was one long festival. His court, like that of the French kings after him, was a meeting place of the noblemen of his immense domains; they imitated his vices and dissipated their possessions through extravagant expenditures. . . . His court was a prefiguration of the court at Versailles. Everything was so arranged as to enhance the majesty of the prince. It was here that the etiquette of the Christian monarchies was invented or at least developed."

Like the despots of Florence, Milan, Verona, and Ferrara, the wealthy duke of Burgundy became a patron of learning and art. His famous library formed the nucleus of the Royal Library at Brussels. Dutch and Flemish musicians were the most renowned in all Europe, while in the field of printing the Netherlands achieved much. Some scholars still maintain that movable type was invented not by Gutenberg at Mainz, but by Dutch printers. At any rate, during the second half of the fifteenth century the number of printing-presses increased rapidly throughout the Netherlands.

The vernacular literatures, however, seemed to be subject to a process of stagnation; neither Flemish nor French productions rose above the level of the mediocre and banale. One can scarcely find a trace of patriotism in these writings, even though in France and Germany thousands of educated people displayed patriotic pride in cultivating their respective vernaculars. A national literature apparently could not thrive in the Netherlands. Only Latin, the universal language, was deemed worthy of those who knew how to write. This favor shown to Latin was a trait characteristic of the Burgundian Renaissance. "Like the language it employs," says Pirenne, "it is universal, and it responds to the essence of Belgian civilization. This level country, this territory open to all nations, this Burgundian state, could not live in isolation. In this region, toward which all European activity converged, the movement of ideas corresponded to the movement of merchandise and of capital. Just as Antwerp was the most cosmopolitan city of the sixteenth century, and Erasmus the most universal writer of his time, so the national character of the Low Countries, whenever they enjoyed a superior form of civilization, was original in that it was universal."

93. *THE HOLY ROMAN EMPIRE IN THE FOURTEENTH AND FIFTEENTH CENTURIES*[1]

Although the Holy Roman Empire reached its zenith as a political power in the eleventh century, it was at the close of the Middle Ages that this country led Europe in many fields of learning and industry. In this period its government underwent many important changes, which have been admirably portrayed in the following selection from the work of a leading German historian.

During the interregnum all the internal affairs of the Empire had fallen into such a state of disorder that the French writer, Charles de Luçon, who had sojourned some time on the Rhine, felt justified in speaking of "The end of Germany." Popular pressure, however, and the menacing attitude of the great Rhenish Leagues formed to oppose the usurpers obliged the electors to choose a sovereign worthy of the name.

With Rudolph of Hapsburg in 1273 began an attempt at re-establishment of the Empire. The new sovereign restored peace and order. He destroyed the power of the Bohemian king Ottocar, and, with the consent of the States, won back to his dominions Austria, which had been taken by the Czechs. Had the succession to the throne continued hereditary, Austria would have restored to the new kingly race all the domain that the Crown had lost, and thus Germany would again have become a united monarchy embracing all the various tribes. It was not in accordance, however, with the selfish ends of the electoral princes that there should be a strong central government and a united nation. After the death of Rudolph they inaugurated a shameful traffic of votes, and raised the feeble Adolphus

[1] J. Janssen, *History of the German People at the Close of the Middle Ages.* Translated from the German by M. A. Mitchell and A. M. Christie. Vol. II. St. Louis, Mo., B. Herder, 1896, pp. 117–135. Used by permission of Kegan Paul, Trench, Trubner & Co., Ltd.

of Nassau to the German throne. Adolphus was well-pleasing to them so long as he allowed himself to be used as a willing tool, but directly he began to assert his independence, and, supported by an army of mercenaries, declared his intention to "be King and to act as such," they feared that he meant to be a new Caesar and to subdue Germany. Thenceforward they began to plot his deposition. He seemed to them "quite evil-minded and contemptible." The princes then turned their minds to Albert, the son of Rudolph. "But in him they were even more deceived," says a chronicler of the times. Assisted by the burghers, who were anxious for the re-establishment of the unity of the Empire, and to whom he had appealed in 1301, Albert defied the electors, attacked their fortresses, obliged them to restore their ill-gotten possessions, and by removal of the duties opened up the Rhine to commerce.

In order to ensure the permanent loyalty of the burghers to the Crown, Albert did everything to advance the prosperity of the towns. He protected their foreign commerce, revived the corporations, and reformed the taxes, and was desirous of giving to the cities, through representatives at the Diet, a voice in the affairs of the nation. Such a measure would have exercised a far-reaching influence for good on the political constitution of the Empire; but base treachery interfered with all the great schemes of this King. He became the victim to a conspiracy of the princes, who employed the unfortunate Johann Parracida as their tool, and fell a martyr to the cause of the unification of the German Empire. After his assassination in 1308 the people longed in vain for "a powerful lord and king; a ruler who, with the sword of the great Charles, would cut the claws of those birds of prey the princes."

Albert's wise policy died with him, and all that he had tried to accomplish for the benefit of the Empire during his ten years' reign was lost to it. It is true that Henry of Luxemburg, his successor, somewhat revived the almost extinguished glory of the Empire by his expedition to Italy; but while he was seeking in Rome to recover the crown his power in Germany slipped away from him. After his death the double election of Louis of Bavaria and Frederick of Austria, brought about by the dissensions of the princes, paved the way for a new order of things. There was no longer any hope of re-establishment of the Empire on the old basis. The double reign of Louis and Frederick forms a period of transition between the united Empire and the State Confederation, which gained legal recognition in 1356 through the famous "Golden Bull" of Charles IV.

By the ordinances of the "Golden Bull" the right of electing the German King was made over to the seven electoral princes—viz. the three ecclesiastical dignitaries, the Archbishops of Mainz, Treves, and Cologne, and the four laymen, the Count Palatine of the Rhine, the Duke of Sachs Wittenberg, the Margrave of Brandenburg, and the King of Bohemia. This "Bull" also established the indivisibility of the electoral principalities and the right of primogeniture in the lay palatinates. It ensured to the electoral princes the royal privileges which they then enjoyed, such as the working of mines within their possessions, the coining of money, and the levying of taxes. It gave them judicial rights, by which no dependent of theirs could be cited before other tribunals than their own. Appeal to the Imperial Court was permitted only in case of denial of justice. Finally, it decided that an attempt made on the life of an electoral prince was as criminal as if made on the Emperor.

The fate of the Empire was thus delivered over to the seven electors, and the dominion placed in the hands of the princes. Already in the reign of Charles IV many of the electoral privileges were accorded to other princes.

In order to guard against the possible rebellion of the estates, especially those of the burghers and the nobility, against the threatened encroachment of princely power, the "Golden Bull" further enacted that no confederations should be allowed without the sanction of the sovereign princes. This prohibition, however, proved useless. When Charles IV in an unprecedented manner extorted large sums from the cities and delivered up to the electoral princes several imperial towns in pledge, the famous Suabian League was organised, and in a short time all the South German towns entered into an almost independent confederation with the view of insisting on a more general representation of the people in public affairs of government. The Rhenish, Franconian, and Bavarian towns joined the Suabian League. This was the last great effort to re-establish the Empire on the basis of more general representation, and to procure for the burghers a more prominent share in the administration.

"The League was formed," writes a contemporary chronicler, "in a spirit of greatness and liberality, for the benefit and advancement of the towns and provinces; but it was turned to a bad account. In the first great 'town war' in 1388 the power of the burghers succumbed to the superior might of the princes, and thenceforward the burgher element has always occupied a subordinate position in the government." "Under Wenceslaus," writes a chronicler, "the Holy Empire became weaker and weaker; there was no right or justice to be obtained, and the powerful might oppress the weak without fear of punishment. . . . Ruprecht, the successor of Wenceslaus, means well, but he has not the power to prevent wrong or to uphold right." In the year 1407 an honourable burgher wrote: "King Ruprecht is good and noble and would like to influence the princes, but I fear he cannot, for he is poor." In proof of the impoverished condition of the Empire we may quote from King Ruprecht's will, which directed that after his death his crown and other jewels were to be sold to pay his apothecary, smith, shoemaker, and painter in Heidelberg, and other poor people in Amberg and elsewhere.

Another chronicler writes: "After Ruprecht there came to the throne King Sigismund, who had many mighty lands of his own, and often said it was his desire to reform the Empire; but his heart was more with his own lands than with the Empire. Besides, he was not firm of will, today wishing this, tomorrow that. But the princes are more to blame than he: occupied with their strifes and jealousies, they think more of themselves than of the public good." Sigismund complained that "the crown is no longer a joy and a glory, but a burden almost too heavy to bear."

The change which the "Golden Bull" made in the electorates gradually extended to the other princely territories. The prelates, knights, and cities who before had acknowledged merely the protection and judicial or feudal rights of the princes were reduced to a kind of vassalage, and out of the fragments of dismembered territories the princes managed more and more to construct for themselves connected principalities.

The kingdom, once so united, seemed but a tangle of loose threads joined together by the frailest bonds. The King was little more than the steward of the kingdom, and the revenues were so reduced that in the time of Sigismund they amounted to only thirteen million florins.

And while the revenues were thus diminishing the change in the character of warfare which resulted from the invention of gunpowder had thrown the old feudal military organization into a pitiful condition. The Hussite wars left an indelible brand on Germany. At home private quarrels prevailed, and abroad the Empire inspired neither fear nor respect. A chronicler wrote: "The princes and rulers are making us the laughing-stocks of the world by their incessant quarrels. Incendiarism and pillage are laying waste the land. The princes are to blame that the Empire, once so mighty, has become powerless. In Italy and Germany there is no longer any respect for the Roman Emperor of the German nation."

Thus sings a Franconian poet of the time: "Thou wert once so proud, O beloved kingdom! Honoured and respected of all nations. Now art thou fallen, grovelling in the dust. Those who should protect thee live but to plunder. The princes are the plunderers of thy fame! Oh that an avenger of the people and the Empire might appear!"

For a short time after the accession of Albert II of Hapsburg there seemed once more hope that a ruler had arisen who would restore peace and justice to the nation, and compel the princes and petty powers to respect the rights of the people. In 1439 William Becker wrote: "I am not without hope. Albert is a powerful sovereign, experienced in war, indefatigably active, and well supplied with men and money."

No ruler who ever ascended the throne had inspired greater hopes than

Albert. The cities cherished the confidence that he would oppose the lawlessness and injustice of the princes and lords. The Council of Spires congratulated the cities on having a king of the Austrian House. Ambassadors who had visited the Court spoke of Albert as "a king possessing the true German spirit, and who would be favourable to the cities." All his contemporaries, even those opposed to Austria, spoke of his justice and energy.

In the plans for reform with regard to public peace and the better administration of justice which Albert proposed to the Diet at Nuremberg in the year 1438 he pointed out the most prominent matters which required political improvement. Ignoring petty personal differences, he proposed that, "for the sake of the general peace, the Empire should be divided into four districts, each district to be under the surveillance of a royal overseer." A judicious contemporary remarked that "should this plan be carried out, it would do much to strengthen the power of the King through those four governors, who would be responsible to him alone. The King's responsibility thus strengthened, the executive power to oppose evil-doers and to carry out the demands of justice being placed in his hands, he will be in a position to re-establish order where nothing but confusion reigns, and to make his kingdom and his people respected. He can turn his attention to reconquering the States which belonged to the Empire. What King Albert says, he means. I heard him say that, with the help of the people and the nobility, he would show the princes, by force of arms if need be, that the Empire must have one supreme ruler." Unhappily for Germany, premature death took Albert from his people in the second year of his reign.

Then followed the disastrous fifty years' reign of the cautious and hesitating Frederick III, in which both the internal politics and the foreign power of the Empire suffered. Under him the princes, particularly after being still further strengthened by their victory over the cities in 1450, were able to consolidate their dominion more and more firmly, to the great prejudice of the people. Frederick did not make the slightest attempt to punish the despisers of his name and honour, the powerful princes who, indifferent to the glory of the Empire, thought only of themselves and their own interests. The chronicler of Spires complained: "He was a useless emperor, who did not understand how to put down wars and disturbances in the provinces of the country. He remained quietly in his own land, and no further help could be obtained from him than what he could render through letters. During twenty-five years he did not once make his appearance in the kingdom, so that it was hardly understood that there was a ruler or a protector. It was not only his declared enemies who attacked the imperial power. The princes who professed to be friendly toward him did him quite as much harm by their acts of violence; for instance, that Margrave Albert Achilles of Hohenzollern, with his mystic utterances that no one could understand, who used to say that 'incendiarism is the ornament of war as the Magnificat is of the Vespers,' and whose favourite axiom with reference to his politics was, that he who does not confess will not be blamed." These mottoes seemed characteristic of the power of the princes.

Although the cities did not succeed in suppressing the usurpations of the sovereign princes, or in gaining recognition for the equal rights of the free cities, they remained sufficiently strong to prevent the Empire being broken up into a number of separate principalities and dominions. In them essentially was kept up the tradition of the oneness of the Empire and the union of all the tribes under one supreme sovereign.

Whereas under the feudal *régime* the fundamental idea of political life had been that of service rendered to a superior chief, in the later municipal constitution the brotherhood or union of guilds was the basis. According to this principle, all distinctions and rights are, as it were, the free expression of the sense of the community; all gradations of authority, from the highest to the lowest, are based on the willing submission of free citizens to rulers elected by themselves.

By adhesion to this principle the large cities managed by degrees to get the whole administration of their affairs into the hands of the citizens and the burgomasters and councils chosen by these. So long as they remained true to honour and love of independence the object of their ambition was to protect their free right to vote. During this glorious period the free cities were the centres of civilisation and commerce, and were patterns of good and orderly government; or, as Machiavelli expressed it, "They were the nerves of Germany."

Independent of all princely government, the so-called "Imperial" towns attained the highest political importance. Their progress was particularly marked in Suabia and the Rhine district, where, after the disolution of the dukedoms, no princely family had acquired a prominent position. In these provinces there were over a hundred of these imperial cities, the principal of which were Aix-la-Chapelle, Cologne on the Lower Rhine, Mainz, Spires, Worms, Frankfort on the Middle Rhine, Strasburg, Colmar, Basle on the Upper Rhine, Bern, Zürich in the interior of Switzerland, Schaffhausen, Constance, St. Gallen, Ueberlingen, Ravensberg on the Lake of Constance, Kempten, Kaufbeuren, Donaworth, Boffingen, Memmingen, Augsburg, Ulm, Rottweil in Upper Suabia, Reutlingen, Weil, Esslingen, Heilbronn, Wimpfen, Halle, Nordlingen in Lower Suabia.

In Franconia also the dukedom had been dissolved, but the number of powerful ecclesiastical principalities there prevented the development of the *Bürgerthum,* or civil government, which besides Nuremberg, could only boast of five smaller towns. The same state of things obtained in Westphalia, where there were only two imperial cities, Dortmund and Herford. In the three provinces of Austria, Brandenburg, and Bohemia there were none. In Bavaria, where the ancient ducal race had secured to itself the possession of a considerable district, Ratisbon was the only free city. In the remaining districts we may specially mention Lübeck, Bremen, Hamburg, and Goslar in Saxony; Erfurt, Muhlhausen, and Nordhausen in Thuringia; Cambria, Deventer, Nymwegen, and Groningen in the Netherlands; Metz, Toul, and Verdun in Lorraine.

As in each of these cities the constitution and forms of government had grown up out of the special needs of the particular city and in accordance with its distinctive character, each was found to have peculiar laws and institutions of its own. While the foundation of their liberties was one and the same, their local laws varied to suit existing circumstances. Their different constitutions were often not less artistic structures, in their way, than the cathedrals which they had erected within their walls.

In the twelfth and thirteenth centuries the municipal government was exclusively in the hands of the patrician classes. From the beginning of the fourteenth century, however, we find the trade guilds gradually getting admitted to a share in the government of the cities—in some cases this result being accomplished peacefully and quietly, while in others it was only brought about by violent and bloody struggles. Finally, however, both patricians and burghers were associated together in the guidance of public affairs, and the civil organisation established on a natural footing. In many of the towns—as, for instance, Ulm, Frankfort, and Nuremberg—the patricians took precedence of the burghers; but in most of them there grew up a so-called "Rule of the Guilds," which was the groundwork of the city constitutions. All citizens, even though having no trade, were obliged to belong to some guild; and the same rule prevailed with regard to the patricians, or at least they had to form somewhat similar societies among themselves.

After the war of the guilds, as before it, in cases, too, where the burgher classes took part in the choice of the councillors, the city council was independent of the district laws. Generally it had the right to fill vacancies in the corporation at discretion, or at least to choose from the candidates proposed. It was only in exceptionally important cases of legislation and taxation that a general assemblage of the citizens was called; as a rule the council had full executive power in all that concerned the safety, order, discipline, prosperity, and honour of the community. Business was executed either in full assembly or by special "officers" appointed for the different branches of affairs.

"In the interest of the honour, needs, and piety of the cities," a strict surveillance was maintained over commerce, exchange, and the prices of the necessaries of life, and constables were appointed for the supervision of buildings and the control of foreigners. One principal duty of the council was the management of the city economy. It determined the scale of the *indirect tax* on grain, meat, wine, &c., and from the fifteenth century onwards that of personal income-tax. It had the charge of all the expenses of the city; for instance, the preservation of its fortifications, buildings, roads, and bridges. The council paid particular attention to the armament of the city, and after the discovery of gunpowder we find it disposing of all useless arms. The arsenals were kept well supplied with ammunition, the tortresses prepared for the reception of artillery; powder mills and cannon foundries were established. In the wars of the Empire the condition of the artillery depended in a great measure on the cities. Military exhibitions were among the favourite amusements of the citizens on feast days and after working hours. After the recruiting of mercenaries became common the citizens formed volunteer regiments and marched beneath the flag of their town, which they held in veneration, branding as a coward anyone who deserted it.

This strong "burgher" stamp, however, was not confined to the "sovereign cities," but showed its mark also in those towns which were subject to the authority of some ecclesiastical or secular prince, and which not seldom equalled the others in power and influence. Among the latter we may note specially the episcopal cities of Magdeburg, Halberstadt, Hildesheim, Osnabrück, Minden, Paderborn, Münster, Soest, Treves, Coblenz, Passau, Freising, Würzburg, and Bamberg. Others such were Dantzic, Königsberg, Elbing, and Thorn, cities belonging to the Teutonic order; the Pomeranian towns Greifswalde and Stralsund; the Mecklenburg cities Rostock and Wismar; the Brandenburg cities Berlin, Brandenburg, and Frankfort-on-the-Oder; the Brunswick-Luneburg cities Luneburg, Brunswick, Gottingen, and Hanover; the Saxon cities Dresden, Meissen, Torgau, and Wittenburg; the Hessian towns Marburg and Cassel; the Bavarian towns Munich, Ingolstadt, Landshut, and Neuburg; and the Austrian cities Vienna, Grätz, Klagenfurt, and Innsbruck.

The provincial towns, as well as the imperial cities, possessed institutions and associations admirably suited to the social needs of the time. They also took a very prominent position in the framing of the constitution of the States.

The constitution of the provincial States, founded, like that of the cities, on the principles of unity, grew up chiefly out of the associations which the country towns and nobles and the prelates entered into in order to protect themselves against the princes. These unions secured to the people, up to the close of the fifteenth century, an extent of personal and civic liberty to which we scarcely find a parallel in any republic, ancient or modern. Thanks to them, the princes at that time enjoyed none of those privileges which came later to be looked upon as sovereign rights; none of that legislative prerogative which arbitrarily overrode legitimate rights; no influence over the courts of justice; no control of the taxes; no tyrannical authority under the mask of interest in the public weal; no right of enforcing military service. The decision also of war or peace did not legally rest in the hands of any single individual.

The right to take part in the general assembly was gradually conceded to all those who had possessions in land. Thus the prelates, the knights and nobles, and the cities came to be represented. These three orders were called Estates of the Land (*Stande des Landes*). In some districts, particularly in East Friesland and the Tyrol, the free peasants had also seats and votes in the assemblies. The first estate everywhere consisted of the prelates, the bishop, the superiors of cloisters and abbeys (in ecclesiastical districts canons took precedence).

Although representative government was not the root idea of the constitution, yet the States dealt with the affairs of their respective provinces, and called themselves "The representative Corporation of the Country."

As a rule, each prince on his accession was obliged to swear fidelity to all written and traditional customs, and it was only after he had conferred a charter of rights that fealty was pledged to him. Thus in 1506 Duke Albert IV of Bavaria directed that every prince's son or heir should, on receiving the vow of fealty, "secure to the State deputies of the prelates, nobles, and cities their freedom, ancient customs, and respected rights; and pledge himself not to interfere with them in any way." The formal clause, "The land and each inhabitant of it shall be undisturbed in his rights and customs," was a sure guarantee against all arbitrary legislation of the princes, without "counsel, knowledge, or will" of the Estates-General.

Not unfrequently the States formed leagues among themselves in order to compel the recognition of their rights before pledging fealty to a prince, or else to oblige him to keep his promises. Often they declared publicly their determination to stand by each other against anyone—the princes not excepted—who sought to rob them of their freedom or rights. The sovereign princes acknowledged, as is proved by many documents of the times, that the States had a right to refuse them obedience, and to defend themselves with arms in case their privileges were infringed. In 1471 Frederick, Duke of Brunswick-Luneberg, declared: "If (which God forbid) our prelates, subjects, or cities, either alone or collectively, be wronged by us or our heirs or successors, we authorise them individually or collectively to resist us, and arm themselves against us until they are righted, without restriction or protest."

In many districts courts were established to investigate differences between the sovereign princes and the States, and to "settle them peaceably or demand justice." The authority of the States was higher than that of the prince, and they had power to judge him, just as, according to imperial law, a court of the princes had power to impeach the King when he was false to his oath, and betrayed the privileges of the Empire. Should the prince resist the sentence, his subjects had a right to compel him by force of arms; but generally he yielded to the assembly, for he had not the necessary means for enforcing his will against theirs; he had no standing army, and no money at command; the nobility had control of the arms, and the prelates and the cities held the purse-strings.

The State authorities prevented evil advisers or enemies to the public good being near the princes, taking care that their counsellors should be persons independent of them, and intermediaries between the States and the sovereign power.

Usually the convocation of the States proceeded from the sovereign prince, who presided in person at the assembly, and very often took part in the deliberations. The States formed altogether a united body, although the deliberations were not everywhere conducted in the same manner. In some of the principalities the representatives of the prelates, nobles, and cities formed one body, while in others each class voted independently. Generally questions were decided by the voice of the majority, but often it required a unanimous vote to carry a measure. Sub-committees were often formed at the close of the session to see that the resolutions were carried out, particularly in the matter of money grants accorded to the sovereign by the consent of the deputies.

The levying of taxes was among the highest rights of the States; no prince had any prerogative in this matter. The consent of the Estates-General to the levying of a new tax, of whatever nature, must be "voluntary and uninfluenced." Taxation was only temporary, and for a specified purpose. Should the sovereign prince presume to impose an exceptional tax, the States had the "chartered" right to oppose it by force of arms.

The more luxurious and expensive the princely households became, the more onerous were the exactions; but in the same proportion the power of the States over the revenue and expenditure of the kingdom increased. Thus in Bavaria, in 1463, the laying out of the income derived from taxation was entrusted to them. The Dukes Johann and Sigmund declared in a charter: "The revenues collected shall be made over to those appointed by the States, and shall be by them distributed to the princes for the benefit of the States, the country, and the people." In order to prevent the depreciation of coin, the States kept the direction of the entire currency in their hands.

The more the princes were dependent on the States for the money supplies they were so greedy after, the more were the States able to strengthen themselves in other branches of administration. They took advantage of their power of levying taxes to secure the passage of a law preventing the princes, without their permission, from building dungeons or castles, from entering into any leagues, from declaring war or making peace. If they were not consulted on such occasions, they simply refused to vote the necessary assessments. In many cases the States acted as mediators or umpires in the strifes between their princes and foreign Powers. They were even called on to decide in cases of disputed succession to the throne, of regencies in case of minor heirs, and in cases of disputed inheritance between allied houses. Without the authority of the States no division of the Empire could be made, pledged, or hypothecated.

The authority of the States over the sovereign princes became so great that the French chronicler, Pierre Froissart, writing on the subject, said: "As the princes have brought the Emperor to a state of dependence, and allow him only certain superior rights, so in turn are they dependent on the pleasure of the States."

94. *MORALITY IN THE AGE OF THE RENAISSANCE*[1]

Perhaps the most widely read and most favorably reputed single volume on the Italian Renaissance is a work by Jacob Burckhardt, entitled, The Civilisation of the Renaissance in Italy. *The section devoted by the author to society and moral standards in Italy at the close of the Middle Ages throws welcome light on these subjects, inasmuch as many writers have discussed these matters without having acquired for themselves an adequate knowledge of the environment in which the leading humanists, artists, princes, and priests of Italy of the fifteenth century spent their lives.*

The relation of the various peoples of the earth to the supreme interests of life, to God, virtue, and immortality, may be investigated up to a certain point, but can never be compared to one another with absolute strictness and certainty. The more plainly in these matters our evidence seems to speak, the more carefully must we refrain from unqualified assumptions and rash generalisations.

This remark is especially true with regard to our judgment on questions of morality. It may be possible to indicate many contrasts and shades of difference among different nations, but to strike the balance of the whole is not given to human insight. The ultimate truth with respect to the char-

[1] J. Burckhardt, *The Civilisation of the Renaissance in Italy,* translated from the German by S. G. C. Middlemore. London, Swan Sonnenschein and Co., 1898, pp. 431–434, 435–440. Used by permission of George Allen & Unwin, Ltd., publishers.

acter, the conscience, and the guilt of a people remains forever a secret; if only for the reason that its defects have another side, where they reappear as peculiarities or even as virtues. We must leave those who find a pleasure in passing sweeping censures on whole nations, to do so as they like. The peoples of Europe can maltreat, but happily not judge one another. A great nation, interwoven by its civilisation, its achievements, and its fortunes with the whole life of the modern world, can afford to ignore both its advocates and its accusers. It lives on with or without the approval of theorists.

Accordingly, what here follows is no judgment, but rather a string of marginal notes, suggested by a study of the Italian Renaissance extending over some years. The value to be attached to them is all the more qualified as they mostly touch on the life of the upper classes, with respect to which we are far better informed in Italy than in any other country in Europe at that period. But though both fame and infamy sound louder here than elsewhere, we are not helped thereby in forming an adequate moral estimate of the people.

What eye can pierce the depths in which the character and fate of nations are determined?—in which that which is inborn and that which has been experienced combine to form a new whole and a fresh nature?—in which even those intellectual capacities, which at first sight we should take to be most original, are in fact evolved late and slowly? Who can tell if the Italian before the thirteenth century possessed that flexible activity and certainty in his whole being—that play of power in shaping whatever subject he dealt with in word or in form, which was peculiar to him later? And if no answer can be found to these questions, how can we possibly judge of the infinite and infinitely intricate channels through which character and intellect are incessantly pouring their influence one upon the other? A tribunal there is for each one of us, whose voice is our conscience; but let us have done with these generalities about nations. For the people that seems to be most sick the cure may be at hand; and one that appears to be healthy may bear within it the ripening germs of death, which the hour of danger will bring forth from their hiding-place.

At the beginning of the sixteenth century, when the civilisation of the Renaissance had reached its highest pitch, and at the same time the political ruin of the nation seemed inevitable, there were not wanting serious thinkers who saw a connexion between this ruin and the prevalent immorality. It was not one of those methodistical moralists who in every age think themselves called to declaim against the wickedness of the time, but it was Machiavelli, who, in one of his most well-considered works, said openly: "We Italians are irreligious and corrupt above others." Another man had perhaps said, "We are individually highly developed; we have outgrown the limits of morality and religion which were natural to us in our undeveloped state, and we despise outward law, because our rulers are illegitimate, and their judges and officers wicked men." Machiavelli adds, "because the Church and her representatives set us the worst example."

Shall we add also, "because the influence exercised by antiquity was in this respect unfavourable"? The statement can only be received with many qualifications. It may possibly be true of the humanists, especially as regards the profligacy of their lives. Of the rest it may perhaps be said with some approach to accuracy, that, after they became familiar with antiquity, they substituted for holiness—the Christian ideal of life—the cultus of historical greatness. We can understand, therefore, how easily they would be tempted to consider those faults and vices to be matters of indifference, in spite of which their heroes were great. They were probably scarcely conscious of this themselves, for if we are summoned to quote any statement of doctrine on this subject, we are again forced to appeal to humanists like Paolo Giovio, who excuses the perjury of Giangaleazzo Visconti, through which he was enabled to found an empire, by the example of Julius Caesar. The great Florentine historians and statesmen never stoop to these slavish quotations, and what seems antique in their deeds and their judgments is so because the nature of their political life necessarily fostered in them a mode of thought which has some analogy with that of antiquity.

Nevertheless, it cannot be denied that Italy at the beginning of the sixteenth century found itself in the midst of a grave moral crisis, out of which the best men saw hardly any escape.

Let us begin by saying a few words about that moral force which was then the strongest bulwark against evil. The highly gifted men of that day thought to find it in the sentiment of honour. This is that enigmatic mixture of conscience and egoism which often survives in the modern man after he has lost, whether by his own fault or not, faith, love, and hope. This sense of honour is compatible with much selfishness and great vices, and may be the victim of astonishing illusions; yet, nevertheless, all the noble elements that are left in the wreck of a character may gather around it, and from this fountain may draw new strength. It has become, in a far wider sense than is commonly believed, a decisive test of conduct in the minds of the cultivated Europeans of our own day, and many of those who yet hold faithfully by religion and morality are unconsciously guided by this feeling in the gravest decisions of their lives.

It lies without the limits of our task to show how the men of antiquity also experienced this feeling in a peculiar form, and how, afterwards, in the Middle Ages, a special sense of honour became the mark of a particular class. Nor can we here dispute with those who hold that conscience, rather than honour, is the motive power. It would indeed be better and nobler if it were so; but since it must be granted that even our worthier resolutions result from "a conscience more or less dimmed by selfishness," it is better to call the mixture by its right name. It is certainly not always easy, in treating of the Italian of this period, to distinguish this sense of honour from the passion for fame, into which, indeed, it easily passes. Yet the two sentiments are essentially different.

. . . .

A force which we must constantly take into account in judging of the morality of the more highly-developed Italian of this period, is that of the imagination. It gives to his virtues and vices a peculiar colour, and under its influence his unbridled egoism shows itself in its most terrible shape.

The force of his imagination explains, for example, the fact that he was the first gambler on a large scale in modern times. Pictures of future wealth and enjoyment rose in such life-like colours before his eyes, that he was ready to hazard everything to reach them. The Mohammedan nations would doubtless have anticipated him in this respect, had not the Koran, from the beginning, set up the prohibition against gambling as a chief safeguard of public morals, and directed the imagination of its followers to the search after buried treasures. In Italy, the passion for play reached an intensity which often threatened or altogether broke up the existence of the gambler. Florence had already, at the end of the fourteenth century, its Casanova—a certain Buonaccorso Pitti, who, in the course of his incessant journeys as merchant, political agent, diplomatist and professional gambler, won and lost sums so enormous that none but princes like the Dukes of Brabant, Bavaria, and Savoy, were able to compete with him. That great lottery-bank which was called the Court of Rome, accustomed people to a need of excitement, which found its satisfaction in games of hazard during the intervals between one intrigue and another. We read, for example, how Franceschetto Cybo, in two games with the Cardinal Raffaello Riario, lost no less than 14,000 ducats, and afterwards complained to the Pope that his opponent had cheated him. Italy has since that time been the home of the lottery.

It was to the imagination of the Italians that the peculiar character of their vengeance was due. The sense of justice was, indeed, one and the same throughout Europe, and any violation of it, so long as no punishment was inflicted, must have been felt in the same manner. But other nations, though they found it no easier to forgive, nevertheless forgot more easily, while the Italian imagination kept the picture of the wrong alive with frightful vividness. The fact that, according to the popular morality, the avenging of blood is a duty—a duty often performed in a way to make us shudder—gives to this passion a peculiar and still firmer basis. The government and the tribunals recognise its existence and justification, and only attempt to keep it within certain limits. Even among the peasantry, we read of Thyestean banquets and mutual assassination on the widest scale. Let us look at an instance.

In the district of Aquapendente three boys were watching cattle, and one of them said: "Let us find out the way how people are hung." While one was sitting on the shoulders of the other, and the third, after fastening the rope round the neck of the first, was tying it to an oak, a wolf came, and the two who were free ran away and left the other hanging. Afterwards they found him dead, and buried him. On the Sunday his father came to bring him bread, and one of the two confessed what had happened, and showed him the grave. The old man then killed him with a knife, cut him up, brought away the liver, and entertained the boy's father with it at home. After dinner, he told him whose liver it was. Hereupon began a series of reciprocal murders between the two families, and within a month thirty-six persons were killed, women as well as men.

And such "vendette," handed down from father to son, and extending to friends and distant relations, were not limited to the lower classes, but reached to the highest. The chronicles and novels of the period are full of such instances, especially of vengeance taken for the violation of women. The classic land for these feuds was Romagna, where the "vendetta" was interwoven with intrigues and party divisions of every conceivable sort. The popular legends present an awful picture of the savagery into which this brave and energetic people had relapsed. We are told, for instance, of a nobleman at Ravenna, who had got all his enemies together in a tower, and might have burned them; instead of which he let them out, embraced them, and entertained them sumptuously; whereupon shame drove them mad, and they conspired against him. Pious and saintly monks exhorted unceasingly to reconciliation, but they can scarcely have done more than restrain to a certain extent the feuds already established; their influence hardly prevented the growth of new ones. The novelists sometimes describe to us this effect of religion—how sentiments of generosity and forgiveness were suddenly awakened, and then again paralysed by the force of what had once been done and could never be undone. The Pope himself was not always lucky as a peacemaker. "Pope Paul II desired that the quarrel between Antonio Caffarello and the family of Alberino should cease, and ordered Giovanni Alberino and Antonio Caffarello to come before him, and bade them kiss one another, and promised them a fine of 2,000 ducats in case they renewed this strife, and two days after Antonio was stabbed by the same Giacomo Alberino, son of Giovanni, who had wounded him once before; and the Pope was full of anger, and confiscated the goods of Alberino, and destroyed his houses, and banished father and son from Rome." The oaths and ceremonies by which reconciled enemies attempted to guard themselves against a relapse, are sometimes utterly horrible. When the parties of the "Nove" and the "Popolari" met and kissed one another by twos in the cathedral at Siena on Christmas Eve, 1494, an oath was read by which all salvation in time and eternity was denied to the future violator of the treaty—"an oath more astonishing and dreadful than had ever been heard." The last consolations of religion in the hour of death were to turn to the damnation of the man who should break it. It is clear, however, that such a ceremony rather represents the despairing mood of the mediators than offers any real guarantee of peace, inasmuch as the truest reconciliation is just that one which has least need of it.

This personal need of vengeance felt by the cultivated and highly placed Italian, resting on the solid basis of an analogous popular custom, naturally displays itself under a thousand different aspects, and receives the unqualified approval of public opinion, as reflected in the works of the novelists. All are at one on the point, that, in the case of those injuries and insults for which Italian justice offered no redress, and all the more in the case of those against which no human law can ever adequately provide, each man is free to take the law into his own hands. Only there must be art in the vengeance, and the satisfaction must be compounded of the material injury and moral humiliation of the offender. A mere brutal, clumsy triumph of force was held by public opinion to be no satisfaction. The whole man with his sense of fame and of scorn, not only his fist, must be victorious.

The Italian of that time shrank, it is true, from no dissimulation in order to attain his ends, but was wholly free from hypocrisy in matters of principle. In these he attempted to deceive neither himself nor others. Accordingly, revenge was declared with perfect frankness to be a necessity of human nature. Cool-headed people declared that it was then most worthy of praise, when it was disengaged from passion, and worked simply from motives of expedience, "in order that other men may learn to leave us unharmed." Yet such instances must have formed only a small minority in comparison with those in which passion sought an outlet. This sort of revenge differs clearly from the avenging of blood, which has been already spoken of; while the latter keeps more or less within the limits of retaliation—the "jus talionis"—the former necessarily goes much farther, not only requiring the sanction of the sense of justice, but craving admiration, and even striving to get the laugh on its own side.

Here lies the reason why men were willing to wait so long for their revenge. A "bella vendetta" demanded as a rule a combination of circumstances for which it was necessary to wait patiently. The gradual ripening of such opportunities is described by the novelists with heartfelt delight.

There is no need to discuss the morality of actions in which plaintiff and judge are one and the same person. If this Italian thirst for vengeance is to be palliated at all, it must be by proving the existence of a corresponding national virtue, namely, gratitude. The same force of imagination which retains and magnifies wrong once suffered, might be expected also to keep alive the memory of kindness received. It is not possible, however, to prove this with regard to the nation as a whole, though traces of it may be seen in the Italian character of to-day. The gratitude shown by the inferior classes for kind treatment, and the good memory of the upper for politeness in social life, are instances of this.

This connexion between the imagination and the moral qualities of the Italian repeats itself continually. If, nevertheless, we find more cold calculation in cases where the Northerner rather follows his impulses, the reason is that individual development in Italy was not only more marked and earlier in point of time, but also far more frequent. Where this is the case in other countries, the results are also analogous. We find, for example, that the early emancipation of the young from domestic and paternal authority is common to North America with Italy. Later on, in the more generous natures, a tie of freer affection grows up between parents and children.

It is in fact a matter of extreme difficulty to judge fairly of other nations in the sphere of character and feeling. In these respects a people may be developed highly, and yet in a manner so strange that a foreigner is utterly unable to understand it. Perhaps all the nations of the West are in this point equally favoured.

95. *THE ARTISTIC RENAISSANCE*[1]

Though Giorgio Vasari (1511–1571) was both a painter and an architect, who went to Florence when he was thirteen years old and studied under Michelangelo and Andrea del Sarto, he is best known to us as a historian. His Lives of the Painters, Sculptors and Architects, *the book on which his reputation as a historian rests, was first published in 1550. Later research has shown that a number of his statements are inaccurate and that his judgments of the artists and their work, though usually discerning and shrewd, are*

[1] Giorgio Vasari, *The Lives of the Most Eminent Painters, Sculptors and Architects.* Translated by Mrs. Jonathan Foster, 5 vols. London, H. G. Bohn, 1850–1852. Vol. I, pp. 305–308; vol. II, pp. 384–385; vol. V, pp. 334–341 (condensed).

sometimes faulty. Nevertheless his book remains a most valuable source for the Renaissance of art in Italy.

Only brief extracts from Vasari's Lives *can be given here. Students who choose to dip into the book itself—and it is accessible in many libraries—will find it lively, entertaining and permeated with the spirit of the Renaissance.*

I. Sculpture and Painting of the Early Renaissance

Sculpture . . . at the first moment of its revival had some remains of excellence. Being once freed from the rude Byzantine manner, which was, indeed, so coarse that the works produced in it displayed more of the roughness of the raw material, than of the genius of the artist; those statues of theirs being wholly destitute of flexibility, attitude, or movement of any kind, and their draperies entirely without folds, so that they could scarcely be called statues—all this became gradually ameliorated, and when Giotto had improved the art of design, the figures of marble and stone improved also: those of Andrea Pisano, of his son Nino, and of his other disciples, were greatly superior to the statues that had preceded them; less rigid and stiff, displaying some approach to grace of attitude, and in all respects better. The works of the two Sienese masters, Agostino and Agnolo, may here be particularized, (by whom, as we have before related, the sepulchre of Guido, bishop of Arezzo, was constructed), and those of the Germans, by whom the façade of the cathedral of Orvieto was executed: upon the whole, therefore, sculpture was at this time perceived to make some little progress,—its figures received less rigid forms; the vestments were permitted to flow more freely; certain of the attitudes lost a portion of their stiffness, and some of the heads acquired more life and expression. There was, in short, a commencement of effort to reach the better path, but defects still remained in great numbers on every point; the art of design had not yet attained its perfection, nor were there many good models for the artists to imitate. All these impediments and difficulties considered, the masters of those days, and who have been placed by me in the first period, deserve all the praise and credit that can be awarded to their works, since it must not be forgotten that they had received no aid from those who preceded them, but had to find their way by their own efforts. Every beginning, moreover, however insignificant and humble in itself, is always to be accounted worthy of no small praise.

Nor had painting much better fortune during those times; but the devotion of the people called it more frequently into use, and it had more artists employed; by consequence, the progress made by it was more obvious than that of the two sister arts. Thus we have seen that the Greek, or Byzantine manner, first attacked by Cimabue, was afterwards entirely extinguished by the aid of Giotto, and there arose a new one, which I would fain call the manner of Giotto, since it was discovered by him, continued by his disciples, and finally honoured and imitated by all. By Giotto and his disciples, the hard angular lines by which every figure was girt and bound, the senseless and spiritless eyes, the long pointed feet planted upright on their extremities, the sharp formless hands, the absence of shadow, and every other monstrosity of those Byzantine painters, were done away with, as I have said; the heads received a better grace, and more softness of colour. Giotto himself, in particular, gave more easy attitudes to his figures; he made some approach to vivacity and spirit in his heads, and folded his draperies, which have more resemblance to reality than those of his predecessors; he discovered, to a certain extent, the necessity of foreshortening the figure, and began to give some intimation of the passions and affections, so that fear, hope, anger, and love were, in some sort, expressed by his faces. The early manner had been most harsh and rugged; that of Giotto became softer, more harmonious, and—if he did not give his eyes the limpidity and beauty of life, if he did not impart to them the speaking movement of reality, let the difficulties he had to encounter plead his excuse for this, as well as for the want of ease and flow in the hair and beards: or if his hands have not the articulations and muscles of nature, if his rude figures want the reality of life, let it be remembered that Giotto had never seen the works of any better master than he was himself. And let all reflect on the rectitude of judgment displayed by this artist in his paintings, at a time when art was in so poor a state; on the large amount of ability by which alone he could have produced the results secured; for none will deny that his figures perform the parts assigned to them, or that in all his works are found proofs of a just—if not a perfect—judgment, in matters pertaining to his art. The same quality is evinced by his successors, by Taddeo Gaddi, for example, whose colouring is distinguished by greater force, as well as more softness, whose figures have more spirit and movement, whose carnations are more lifelike, and his draperies more flowing. In Simon of Siena we mark increased facility in the composition of the stories. In Stefano the Ape (Stefano Schimmia), and in Tommaso his son, we see important ameliorations of the practice in design, as well as in the general treatment and harmony of colouring. By these masters the study of perspective, also, was promoted, to the great benefit of art. They displayed some fertility of invention, with softness and harmony of colouring, but adhered closely to the manner of Giotto. Not inferior to these in ability or practice were Spinello Aretino, Parri, his son, Jacopo di Casentino, Antonio Veneziano, Lippo, Gherardo Starnina, and the other masters who succeeded Giotto, and imitated his manner, outline, expression, and colour; these they perhaps improved, in some degree, but not to such an extent as to give the impression that they proposed to originate a new direction. He, therefore, who shall carefully consider this my discourse, will perceive that these three arts—Sculpture, Painting, and Architecture—have, up to the times here alluded to, been, so to speak, but roughly sketched out, and have wanted very much of their due perfection; insomuch, that if they had not made further progress, the slight improvements here enumerated would have availed but little, neither would they have merited to be held of much account. Nor would I have any to suppose me so dull of perception, or endowed with so little judgment, as not to perceive that the works of Giotto, of Andrea Pisano, of Nino, and all the rest, whom, because of their similitude of manner, I have placed together in the first part, could claim but a small amount of praise, if compared with those of their successors, or that I did not perceive this when I commended them. But, whoever will consider the character of the times in which these masters laboured, the dearth of artists, with the difficulty of obtaining any assistance of value, will admit—not only that they are beautiful, as I have said—but even that they are wonderful; and will doubtless take infinite pleasure in the examination of those first beginnings, those gleams of light and good which then began to be rekindled in the paintings and sculptures of the day.

II. The Mona Lisa of Leonardo da Vinci

For Francesco del Giocondo, Leonardo undertook to paint the portrait of Mona Lisa, his wife, but, after loitering over it for four years, he finally left it unfinished. This work is now in the possession of the King Francis of France, and is at Fontainebleau.[1] Whoever shall desire to see how far art can imitate nature, may do so to perfection in this head, wherein every peculiarity that could be depicted by the utmost subtlety of the pencil has been faithfully reproduced. The eyes have the lustrous brightness and moisture which is seen in life, and around them are those pale, red, and slightly livid circles, also proper to nature, with the lashes, which can only be copied, as these are, with the greatest difficulty; the eyebrows also are represented with the closest exactitude, where fuller and where more thinly set, with the separate hairs delineated as they issue from the skin, every turn being followed, and all the pores exhibited in a manner that could not be more natural than it is: the nose, with its beautiful and delicately roseate nostrils, might be easily believed to be alive; the mouth, admirable in its outline, has the lips uniting the rose-tints of their colour with that of the face, in the utmost perfection, and the carnation of the cheek does not appear to be painted. but truly of flesh and blood: he who looks

[1] It is now in the Gallery of the Louvre.

earnestly at the pit of the throat cannot but believe that he sees the beating of the pulses, and it may be truly said that this work is painted in a manner well calculated to make the boldest master tremble, and astonishes all who behold it, however well accustomed to the marvels of art. Mona Lisa was exceedingly beautiful, and while Leonardo was painting her portrait, he took the precaution of keeping someone constantly near her, to sing or play on instruments, or to jest and otherwise amuse her, to the end that she might continue cheerful, and so that her face might not exhibit the melancholy expression often imparted by painters to the likenesses they take. In this portrait of Leonardo's, on the contrary, there is so pleasing an expression, and a smile so sweet, that while looking at it one thinks it rather divine than human, and it has ever been esteemed a wonderful work, since life itself could exhibit no other appearance.

III. Michelangelo

Michelagnolo found his chief pleasure in the labours of art; all that he attempted, however difficult, proving successful, because nature had imparted to him the most admirable genius, and his application to those excellent studies of design was unremitting. For the greater exactitude, he made numerous dissections of the human frame, examining the anatomy of each part, the articulations of the joints, the various muscles, the nerves, the veins, and all the different minutiae of the human form. Nor of this only, but of animals, and more particularly of horses, which he delighted in, and kept for his pleasure, examining them so minutely in all their relations to art, that he knew more of them than do many whose sole business is the care of those animals. These labours enabled him to complete his works, whether of the pencil or chisel, with inimitable perfection, and to give them a grace, a beauty, and an animation, wherein (be it said without offence to any) he has surpassed even the antique. In his works he has overcome the difficulties of art, with so much facility, that no trace of labour appears in them, however great may be that which those who copy them find in the imitation of the same.

The genius of Michelagnolo was acknowledged in his lifetime, and not as happens in many cases, after his death only; and he was favoured, as we have seen, by Julius II, Leo X, Clement VII, Paul III, Julius III, Paul IV, and Pius IV; these Pontiffs having always desired to keep him near them, as indeed would Soliman, Emperor of the Turks, Francis, King of France, the Emperor Charles V, the Signoria of Venice, and lastly Duke Cosimo de' Medici: all very gladly have done, each of those monarchs and potentates having offered him the most honourable appointments, for the love of his great abilities. These things do not happen to any except men of the highest distinction, but in him all the three arts were found in such perfection, as God hath vouchsafed to no other master, ancient or modern, in all the many years that the sun has been turning round.

His powers of imagination were such that he was frequently compelled to abandon his purpose, because he could not express by the hand those grand and sublime ideas, which he had conceived in his mind, nay, he has spoiled and destroyed many works for this cause; and I know too that some short time before his death he burnt a large number of his designs, sketches, and cartoons, that none might see the labours he had endured, and the trials to which he had subjected his spirit, in his resolve not to fall short of perfection. I have myself secured some drawings by his hand, which were found in Florence, and are now in my book of designs and these, although they give evidence of his great genius, yet prove also that the hammer of Vulcan was necessary to bring Minerva from the head of Jupiter. He would make his figures of nine, ten, and even twelve heads long, for no other purpose than the research of a certain grace in putting the parts together which is not to be found in the natural form, and would say that the artist must have his measuring tools, not in the hand but in the eye, because the hands do but operate, it is the eye that judges; he pursued the same idea in architecture also.

None will marvel that Michelagnolo should be a lover of solitude, devoted as he was to Art, which demands the whole man, with all his thoughts, for herself. He who resigns his life to her may well disregard society, seeing that he is never alone nor without food for contemplation; and whoever shall attribute this love of solitude to caprice or eccentricity, does wrong; the man who would produce works of merit should be free from cares and anxieties, seeing that Art demands earnest consideration, loneliness, and quietude; she cannot permit wandering of the mind. Our artist did nevertheless prize the friendship of distinguished and learned men, he enjoyed the society of such at all convenient seasons, maintaining close intercourse with them, more especially with the illustrious Cardinal Ippolito de' Medici, who loved him greatly. Having heard that an Arab horse which he possessed was much admired for its beauty by Michelagnolo, the Cardinal sent it to him as a present, with ten mules, all laden with corn, and a servant to take care of those animals, which the master accepted very willingly. The most illustrious Cardinal Pole was also a very intimate friend of Michelagnolo, who delighted in the talents and virtue of that Prelate.

. . . .

In all things Michelagnolo was exceedingly moderate; ever intent upon his work during the period of youth, he contented himself with a little bread and wine, and at a later period, until he had finished the Chapel namely, it was his habit to take but a frugal refreshment at the close of his day's work; although rich, he lived like a poor man; rarely did any friend or other person eat at his table, and he would accept no presents, considering that he would be bound to any one who offered him such: his temperance kept him in constant activity, and he slept very little, frequently rising in the night because he could not sleep, and resuming his labours with the chisel.

For these occasions he had made himself a cap of pasteboard, in the centre of which he placed a candle, which thus gave him light without encumbering his hands. Vasari had often seen this cap; and, remarking that Michelagnolo did not use wax-lights, but candles made of unmixed goat's tallow, which are excellent, he sent the master four packets of the same, weighing forty pounds. His own servant presented them respectfully in the evening, but Michelagnolo refused to accept them; whereupon the man replied: "Messere, I have nearly broken my arms in bringing them from the bridge hither, and have no mind to carry them back; now, there is a heap of mud before your door which is thick enough to hold them upright, so I'll e'en stick them up there, and set them all a-light." But, hearing that, the master bade him lay down the candles, declaring that no such pranks should be played before his house.

He has told me that, in his youth, he frequently slept in his clothes, being wearied with his labours he had no mind to undress merely that he might have to dress again. Many have accused him of being avaricious, but they are mistaken; he has proved himself the contrary, whether as regards his works in art or other possessions.

. . . .

Michelagnolo had remarkable strength of memory, insomuch that, after having once seen a work of any other artist he would remember it so perfectly that, if it pleased him to make use of any portion thereof, he could do so in such a manner that none could perceive it. In his youth he was once supping with some painters his friends, when they amused themselves with trying who could best produce one of those figures without design and of intense ugliness, such as those who know nothing are wont to scratch on the walls. Here his memory came to his aid, he remembered precisely the sort of absurdity required, and which he had seen on a wall; this he reproduced as exactly as if he had had it before his eyes, surpassing all the painters around him: a very difficult thing for a man so accomplished in design, and so exclusively accustomed to the most elevated and finished works of mastery as was Michelagnolo.

He proved himself resentful, but with good reason, against those who had done him wrong, yet he never sought to avenge himself by any act of injury or violence; very orderly in all his proceedings, modest in his deportment, prudent and reasonable in discourse, usually earnest and serious, yet sometimes amusing, ingenious, and quick in reply; many of his remarks have been remembered and well merit to be repeated here, but I will add only a few of these recollections. A friend once speaking to him of death, remarked that Michelagnolo's constant labours for art, leaving him no repose, must needs make him think of it with great regret. "By no means," replied Michelagnolo, "for if life be a pleasure, yet, since death also is sent us by the hand of the same master, neither should that displease us."

. . . .

While Michelagnolo was concluding the Tomb of Julius II, he permitted a stone-cutter to execute a terminal figure, which he desired to put up in San Pietro in Vincola, directing him meanwhile by telling him daily, "Cut away here,"—"level there,"—"chisel this,"—"polish that," until the stone-cutter had made a figure before he was aware of it; but when he saw what was done, he stood lost in admiration of his work. "What dost thou think of it?" inquired Michelagnolo. "I think it very beautiful," returned the other, "and am much obliged to you." "And for what?" demanded the artist. "For having been the means of making known to me a talent which I did not think I possessed."

But now, to bring the matter to a conclusion, I will only add, that Michelagnolo had an excellent constitution, a spare form, and strong nerves. He was not robust as a child, and as a man he had two serious attacks of illness, but he was subject to no disease, and could endure much fatigue. It is true that infirmities assailed him in his old age, but for these he was carefully treated by his friend and physician, Messer Realdo Colombo. He was of middle height, the shoulders broad, and the whole form well-proportioned. In his latter years he constantly wore stockings of dog-skin for months together, and when these were removed, the skin of the leg sometimes came with them. Over his stockings he had boots of Cordovan leather, as a protection against the swelling of those limbs, to which he then became liable. His face was round, the brow square and ample, with seven direct lines in it; the temples projected much beyond the ears, which were somewhat large, and stood a little off from the cheeks; the nose was rather flattened, having been broken with a blow of the fist by Torrigiano, as we have related in the Life of that artist; the eyes were rather small than large, of a dark colour, mingled with blue and yellowish points; the eye-brows had but few hairs; the lips were thin, the lower somewhat the larger, and slightly projecting; the chin well-formed, and in fair proportion to the rest of the face; the hair black, mingled with grey, as was the beard, which was divided in the middle, and neither very thick nor very long.

This master, as I said at the beginning, was certainly sent on earth by God as an example for the men of our arts, to the end that they might profit by his walk in life, as well as learn from his works what a true and excellent artist ought to be. I, who have to thank God for an infinite amount of happiness, such as is rarely granted to those of our vocation, account it among the greatest of my blessings that I was born while Michelagnolo still lived, was found worthy to have him for my master, and being trusted by him, obtained him for my friend, as every one knows, and as the letters which he has written to me clearly prove. To his kindness for me I owe it that I have been able to write many things concerning him, which others could not have related, but which, being true, shall be recorded. Another privilege, and one of which he often reminded me, is, that I have been in the service of Duke Cosimo. "Thank God for this, Giorgio," has Michelagnolo said to me; "for to enable thee to build and paint, in execution of his thoughts and designs, he spares no expense, and this, as thou seest well, by the Lives thou hast written, is a thing which few artists have experienced."

96. SELECTIONS FROM PETRARCH'S LETTERS [1]

Petrarch (1304–1374) is often termed the first modern man, although such a statement is hazardous and debatable. We do know, however, that in many respects he consciously deviated from the intellectual standards of most of his contemporaries. He was one of the very first humanists, an enthusiastic admirer of classical civilization, a writer of great ability, and a scholar of no mean talent. One of his chief merits was his interest in human nature and natural sciences. On the other hand he by no means neglected the study of Christian writers who emphasized the value of spiritual as compared with material or physical things. This the student may gather from the selections below from his letters and a prose work entitled the Secret.

1. Letter to Thomas of Messina, dated Avignon, March 11, 1335(?)

You write to me of a certain old logician, who has been greatly excited by my letter as if I condemned his art. With a growl of rage he loudly

[1] This and the following selection are taken from *Petrarch, The First Modern Scholar and Man of Letters,* by James H. Robinson and Henry W. Rolfe, and are used by the courtesy of G. P. Putnam's Sons, Publishers, New York and London. They were reprinted in *The First Century of Italian Humanism* by Ferdinand Schevill. New York, F. S. Crofts and Co., 1928, pp. 14–19.

threatened to make war in turn upon our studies in a letter for which, you say, you have waited many months in vain. Do not wait any longer, for, believe me, it will never come. . . .

These logicians seek to cover their teachings with the splendor of Aristotle's name. They claim that Aristotle was wont to argue in the same way. . . . But they deceive themselves. Aristotle was a man of the most exalted genius, who not only discussed but wrote upon themes of the very highest importance. How can we otherwise explain so vast an array of his works, involving such prolonged labor and prepared with such supreme care? . . . Why is not the name of Aristotelians a source of shame to them rather than of satisfaction, for no one could be more utterly different from that great philosopher than a man who writes nothing, knows but little, and constantly indulges in much vain declamation? Who does not laugh at their trivial conclusions, with which they weary both themselves and others? They waste their whole lives in such contentions. . . . We find an example in the case of Diogenes, whom a contentious logician addressed as follows: "What I am, you are not." Upon Diogenes conceding this, the logician added: "But I am a man." As this was not denied, the poor quibbler triumphantly offered the deduction: "Therefore you are not a man." "The last statement is not true," Diogenes remarked, "but if you wish it to be true, begin with me in your major premise." . . .

On hearing such jibes as these, the logicians grow furious: "So you set yourself up to condemn logic," they cry. Far from it. I know well in what esteem it was held by that sturdy and virile sect of philosophers, the Stoics. I know that it is one of the Seven Liberal Arts, a ladder for those who are striving upwards. It stimulates the intellect, points the way to truth, shows us how to avoid fallacies, and, finally, if it accomplishes nothing else, makes us ready and quick-witted.

All this I freely admit. But because a road is proper for us to travel, it does not follow that we should linger on it forever. . . . Dialectic may form a portion of our road; it is certainly not our goal.

2. Letter to Dionisio of Borgo San Sepolcro, dated Malaucène, April 26, 1336

Today I made the ascent of the highest mountain in this region (*Vaucluse, France*) which is not improperly called Ventosum (*Windy*). My only motive was to see what so high an elevation had to offer. I have had the expedition in mind for many years; for, as you know, I have lived in this region from infancy, having been cast here by that fate which determines the affairs of men. Consequently the mountain, which is visible from a great distance, was ever before my eyes, and I conceived the plan of some time doing what I have at last accomplished today. (*On casting about for a companion he decides in favor of his younger brother, and the two attended by two servants to carry the luggage travel to the foot of the mountain where they pass the night. They begin the ascent in the morning.*)

The mountain is a very steep and almost inaccessible mass of stony soil. . . . It was a long day, the air fine. We enjoyed the advantage of vigor of mind and strength and agility of body and everything else essential to those engaged in such an undertaking, and so had no other difficulties to face than those of the region itself. We found an old shepherd in one of the mountain dales who tried at great length to dissuade us from the ascent, saying that some fifty years before he had, in the same ardor of youth, reached the summit, but had gotten for his pains nothing except fatigue and regret, and clothes and body torn by the rocks and briars. No one, so far as he or his companions knew, had ever tried the ascent before or after him. But his counsels increased rather than diminished our desire to proceed since youth is impatient of warnings. So the old man, finding that his efforts were in vain, went a little way with us and pointed out a rough path among the rocks, uttering many admonitions which he continued to send after us even after we had left him behind. Surrendering to him all such garments or other possessions as might prove burdensome to us, we made ready for the ascent and started off at a good pace. (*The difficulties of the climb are described in some detail, in spite of which the peak is at last scaled.*)

At first, owing to the unaccustomed quality of the air and to the effect of the great sweep of view spread out before me, I stood like one dazed. I beheld the clouds under our feet, and what I had read of Athos and Olympus seemed less incredible as I myself witnessed the same things from a mountain of less fame. I turned my eyes toward Italy, whither my heart most inclined. The Alps, rugged and snow-capped, seemed to rise close by. . . . I sighed, I must confess, for the skies of Italy, which I beheld rather with my mind than with my eyes. An inexpressible longing came over me to see once more my friend and my country. . . . (*On turning to the West*) I could see with the utmost clearness, off to the right, the mountains of the region about Lyons, and to the left the bay of Marseilles and the waters that lash the shores of Aigues Mortes, although all these places were so distant that it would require a journey of several days to reach them. Under our very eyes flowed the Rhone.

While I was thus dividing my thoughts, now turning my attention to some terrestrial object that lay before me, now raising my soul, as I had done my body, to higher planes, it occurred to me to look into my copy of St. Augustine's Confessions, a gift that I owe to your love and that I always have about me in memory of both the author and the giver. I opened the compact little volume with the intention of reading whatever came to hand, for I could happen upon nothing that would be otherwise than edifying and devout. Now it chanced that the tenth book presented itself. My brother, waiting to hear something of St. Augustine's from my lips, stood attentively by. I call him, and God too, to witness that where I first fixed my eyes it was written: "And men go about to wonder at the heights of the mountains and the mighty waves of the sea and the wide sweep of the rivers and the circuit of the ocean and the revolution of the stars, but themselves they consider not." I was abashed and, asking my brother who was anxious to hear more, not to annoy me, I closed the book, angry with myself that I should still be admiring earthly things who might long ago have learned from even the pagan philosophers that nothing is wonderful but the soul, which, when great itself, finds nothing great outside itself. Then in truth I was satisfied that I had seen enough of the mountain; I turned my inward eye upon myself, and from that time not a syllable fell from my lips until we reached the bottom again.

3. Letter to Pulice of Vicenza, dated Near Vicenza, May 13, 1351.

(*The writer recalls a recent visit at the house of his correspondent in Vicenza, on which occasion the conversation of the assembled company of scholars had swung to Cicero. To every one's surprise Petrarch had ventured to intersperse amidst abundant praises a few criticisms of the Roman author and orator and, to clinch his point, had fetched from among his baggage two letters to Cicero which he had had composed as literary exercises and in which he had enumerated Cicero's merits and demerits.*) These two (*letters*) you read while the others listened; and then the strife of words grew warmer. Some approved of what I had written, admitting that Cicero deserved my censure. But the old man stood his ground more stubbornly even than before. He was so blinded by love of his hero and by the brightness of his name that he preferred to praise him even when he was in the wrong; to embrace faults and virtues together rather than make any exceptions. He would not be thought to condemn anything at all in so great a man. So instead of answering our arguments he rang the changes again and again upon the splendor of Cicero's fame, letting authority usurp the place of reason. He would stretch out his hand and say imploringly, "Gently, I beg of you, gently with my Cicero." And when we asked him if he found it impossible to believe that Cicero had made mistakes, he would close his eyes and turn his face away and exclaim with a groan, as if he had been smitten, "Alas! alas! Is my beloved Cicero accused of doing wrong?" just as if he were speaking not of a man but of some god. I asked him accordingly whether in his opinion Tullius was a god or a man like others. "A god," he replied; and then realizing what he had said, he added, "a god of eloquence."

97. *EXTRACTS FROM PETRARCH'S "SECRET"* [1]

[*Introduction by Ferdinand Schevill*]

No work of Petrarch's shows as strikingly as this to what degree the great pioneer, often called the first modern man, continued to be held enthralled by medieval concepts. Without doubt Petrarch's novel literary and secular activities often overwhelmed him with a sense of guilt. In this dialogue Petrarch tries weakly to defend his position but yields point after point to the spirited Augustine, who reasserts every essential feature of the medieval faith touching the emptiness of our life on this earth.

S. Augustine. Every one knows, and the greatest philosophers are of the same opinion, that of all tremendous realities death is the most tremendous. So true is this that from of old its very name is terrible and dreadful to hear. Yet though so it is, it will not do that we hear that name lightly, or allow the remembrance of it to slip quickly from our mind. We must take time to realize it. We must meditate with attention thereon. We must picture to ourselves the effect of death on each part of our bodily frame, the cold extremities, the breast in the sweat of fever, the side throbbing with pain, the eyes sunken and weeping, the forehead pale and drawn, the teeth staring and discolored, the lips foaming, the tongue foul and motionless, the evil smell of the whole body, the horror of seeing the face utterly unlike itself—all these things will come to mind and, so to speak, be ready to one's hand, if one recalls what he has seen in any close observation of some deathbed which it has fallen to his lot to attend. . . . This is what I mean by letting the thought of death sink deeply into the soul. Falling in with the evil custom of our time, you probably never name the name of death, although nothing is more certain than the fact or more uncertain than the hour. . . .

(*Having brought Petrarch to acknowledge the need of thinking upon death, he continues his inquisition.*)

S. Augustine. . . . You are charmed with the very chains that are dragging you to your death and, what is most sad of all, you glory in them!

Petrarch. What may these chains be of which you speak?

[1] Petrarch's Secret or The Soul's Conflict with Passion. Three Dialogues between Petrarch and St. Augustine. Translated from the Latin by William H. Draper. Reprinted from *The First Century of Italian Humanism* by Ferdinand Schevill. New York, F. S. Crofts and Co., 1928, pp. 28–32.

S. Augustine. Love and glory.

Petrarch. Great Heavens! What is this I hear? You call these things chains? And you would break them from me if I would let you?

S. Augustine. Yes, I mean to try; but I doubt if I shall succeed.

Petrarch. (*He makes at considerable length a very noble defense of his love for Laura, who has inspired his verse and with whom his relationship has been pure and honorable.*)

S. Augustine. And now I shall deliver my sharpest thrust of all. In simple truth that woman, to whom you profess to owe everything, she, even she, has been your ruin.

Petrarch. Good Heavens! How do you think you will persuade me of that?

S. Augustine. She has detached your mind from the love of heavenly things and has inclined your heart to love the creature more than the creator: and that path alone leads sooner than any other to death. . . .

Petrarch. (*He gradually weakens.*) I cannot deny that what you say is true, and I see whither you are step by step leading me.

S. Augustine. To see it better still, lend me all your attention. Nothing so much leads a man to forget or despise God as the love of things temporal and most of all this passion that we call love. . . .

S. Augustine. (*The debate continues. Petrarch acknowledges himself beaten.*) One evil is left, to heal you of which I now will make a last endeavor.

Petrarch. Do so, most gentle father. For though I be not yet wholly set free from my burdens, nonetheless from a great part of them I feel a blessed release.

S. Augustine. Ambition still has too much hold on you. You seek too eagerly the praise of men and to leave behind you an undying name.

Petrarch. I freely confess it. I cannot beat down that passion in my soul. For it, as yet, I have found no cure.

S. Augustine. . . . Now I submit to you that reputation is nothing but talk about some one which many people pass from mouth to mouth.

Petrarch. I think your definition is a good one.

S. Augustine. It is then but a breath, a changing wind. And what should disgust you more, it is the breath of a crowd. (*The argument about glory derived from an earthly achievement continues and again poor Petrarch gets the worst of it.*)

Petrarch. Is it your wish, then, that I should put all my studies aside and renounce every ambition, or would you advise some middle course?

S. Augustine. I will never advise you to live wholly without ambition, but I would always urge you to put virtue before glory. You know that glory is in a sense the shadow of virtue. And therefore just as it is impossible that your body should not case a shadow when the sun is shining, so it is impossible also in the light of God Himself that virtues should exist and not cause the glory belonging to them to appear. . . . Here, therefore, is the rule for you to live by: follow after virtue and let glory take care of itself. . . .

And one thing more I beseech you to have in mind: look at the graves of those older than you, but whom nevertheless you have known. Look diligently and then rest assured that the same dwelling-place is also made ready for you. Thither are all of us traveling on. (*The argument ends, as it began, with the solemn facts of death and the grave.*)

98. SELECTION FROM THE DECAMERON [1]

Boccaccio was Petrarch's assistant and followed his master in making diligent search for the lost works of classical antiquity. He slavishly imitated their Latin, with the result that his Italian smacks too much of this language. However, he gained much from the reading of Greek and Latin tales. His own collection of tales, the celebrated Decameron, *written in Italian, is based on many classical as well as medieval sources. Furthermore, the author has freely drawn on his own experiences and the news he gathered from contemporaries.*

The Decameron. First Day, Novel II

At Paris there lived, as I have been told, a great merchant and worthy man called Jeannot, a dealer in silk and an intimate friend to a certain rich Jew, whose name was Abraham, a merchant also and a very honest man. Jeannot, being no stranger to Abraham's good and upright intentions, was greatly troubled that the soul of so wise and well-meaning a person should perish through his unbelief. He began, therefore, in the most friendly manner, to entreat him to renounce the errors of Judaism and embrace the truth of Christianity, which he might plainly see flourishing more and more, and as being the most wise and holy institution, gaining ground, whereas the religion of the Jews was dwindling to nothing. Abraham answered that he esteemed no religion like his own; he was born in it and in it he intended to live and die; nor could anything make him alter his resolution. All this did not hinder Jeannot from beginning the same arguments over again in a few days and setting forth for what reasons our religion ought to be preferred; and though the Jew was well read in his own law, yet, whether it was his regard for the man or that Jeannot had

[1] Reprinted from the edition in Bohn's Library.

the spirit of God upon his tongue, he began to be greatly pleased with his arguments; but continued obstinate, nevertheless, in his own creed, and would not suffer himself to be converted. Jeannot, on the other hand, was no less persevering in his earnest solicitations, insomuch that the Jew was overcome by them at last, and said: "Look you, Jeannot, you are very desirous I should become a Christian and I am so much disposed to do as you would have me, that I intend in the first place to go to Rome, to see him whom you call God's vicar on earth and to consider his ways a little and those of his brother cardinals. If they appear to me in such a light that I may be able to comprehend by them and by what you have said, that your religion is better than mine, as you would persuade me, I will then become a Christian; otherwise I will continue a Jew as I am."

When Jeannot heard this he was much troubled and said to himself: "I have lost all my labor, which I thought well bestowed, expecting to have converted this man; for should be go to Rome and see the wickedness of the clergy there, so far from turning Christian, were he one already, he would certainly again become a Jew." Then addressing Abraham, he said: "Nay, my friend, why should you be at the great trouble and expense of such a journey? Not to mention the dangers, both by sea and land, to which so rich a person as yourself must be exposed, do you think to find nobody here that can baptize you? Or if you have doubt and scruples, where will you meet with abler men than are here to clear them up for you and to answer such questions as you shall put to them?"

"I believe it is as you say," replied the Jew, "but the long and the short of the matter is that I am fully resolved, if you would have me do what you have so much solicited, to go thither, else I will in no wise comply."

Jeannot, seeing him determined, said: "God be with you!" and, supposing that he would never be a Christian after he had seen Rome, gave him over for lost. The Jew took horse and made the best of his way to Rome, where he was most honorably received by his brethren, the Jews; and, without saying a word of what he was come about, he began to look narrowly into the manner of living of the pope, the cardinals, and other prelates, and of the whole court; and from what he himself perceived, being a person of keen observation, and from what he gathered from others, he found that, from the highest to the lowest, they were given to all sorts of lewdness without the least shame or remorse; so that the only way to obtain anything considerable was by applying to prostitutes of every description. He observed, also, that they were generally drunkards and gluttons, and, like brutes, more solicitous about their bellies than anything else. Inquiring further, he found them all such lovers of money that they would not only buy and sell man's blood in general, but even the blood of Christians and sacred things of what kind soever, whether benefices or articles pertaining to the altar. These and other things, which I shall pass over, gave great offense to the Jew, who was a sober and modest person; and now thinking he had seen enough, he returned home.

As soon as Jeannot heard of his arrival he went to see him, thinking of nothing so little as of his conversion. They received one another with a great deal of pleasure and in a day or two, after the traveler had recovered from his fatigue, Jeannot began to inquire of him what he thought of the holy father, the cardinals, and the rest of the court. The Jew immediately answered: "To me it seems as if God was much kinder to them than they deserve; for, if I may be allowed to judge, I must be bold to tell you that I have neither seen sanctity, devotion or anything good in the clergy of Rome; but, on the contrary, luxury, avarice, gluttony, and worse than these, if worse things can be, are so much in fashion with all sorts of people that I should rather esteem the court of Rome to be a forge, if you will allow the expression, for diabolical operations than things divine; and, for all I can perceive, your supreme pastor, and consequently the rest, strive with their whole might and skill to overthrow the Christian religion and to drive it from off the face of the earth, even where they ought to be its chief succor and support. But as I do not see this come to pass which they so earnestly aim at; on the contrary, that your religion gains strength and becomes everyday more glorious, I plainly perceive that it is upheld by the Spirit of God, as the most true and holy of all. For which reason, though I have continued obstinate to your exhortations, now I declare to you that I will no longer defer being made a Christian. Let us go then to the church and do you take care that I be baptized according to the manner of your holy faith."

99. *LORENZO VALLA PROVES THE SO-CALLED DONATION OF CONSTANTINE TO BE A FORGERY*[1]

Lorenzo Valla was probably the most important of all the Italian humanists, and he has justly been described as the incarnation of the Renaissance in Italy. He thoroughly despised contemporary civilization, medieval Latin, and medieval scholasticism. Also, he bitterly attacked the papacy, particularly in the period from 1436 to 1447, when he was in the service of King Alphonso of Naples, the enemy of the pope. It was in that period that Valla composed a famous bit of historical criticism, called On the Donation of Constantine, *in which he exposed the old forgery intended to show that the pope owed his temporal power to the Emperor Constantine.*

[1] Reprinted from *The First Century of Italian Humanism* by Ferdinand Schevill. New York, F. S. Crofts and Co., 1928, pp. 53–57.

Extracts from the *Treatise of Lorenzo Valla on the Donation of Constantine.* Text and Translation into English by Christopher B. Coleman [*Introduction by Ferdinand Schevill*]

The so-called Donation of Constantine purported to record the gift of the western half of the Roman Empire by the first Christian emperor, Constantine the Great, to Pope Sylvester (314–336 A.D.*). The document, forged a little past the middle of the eighth century in the interest of the territorial aspirations of the papacy, was accepted as genuine till the fifteenth century and played a large part in the claim of the medieval popes to temporal supremacy over the sovereigns of Europe. Valla was not the first scholar to doubt its genuineness, but he was the first to demolish it utterly and publicly. When launching his attack in 1440, he was secretary to the King of Naples and pursued as his immediate end the undermining of the papal claim to suzerainty over his master.*

. . . I know that for a long time now men's ears are waiting to hear the offense with which I charge the Roman pontiffs. It is indeed an enormous one, due either to supine ignorance, or to gross avarice, . . . or to the pride of empire. For during some centuries now either they have not known that the Donation of Constantine is spurious and forged or else they themselves forged it; and their successors, walking in the same way of deceit as their elders, have defended as true what they knew to be false, dishonoring the majesty of the pontificate, the memory of ancient pontiffs, and the Christian religion. . . . The popes say the city of Rome is theirs, theirs the kingdom of Sicily and of Naples, the whole of Italy, the Gauls, the Spains, the Germans, the Britons, indeed the whole West. For all these are contained in the instrument of the Donation itself.

So all these are yours, supreme pontiff? And it is your purpose to recover them all? To despoil all kings and princes of the West of their cities or compel them to pay you a yearly tribute? Is that your plan? I, on the contrary, think it fairer to let the princes despoil you of all the empire you hold. For, as I shall show, that Donation whence the supreme pontiffs derive their right was known neither to Pope Sylvester nor to Emperor Constantine.

(*After discussing the inherent improbability of the surrender of the West by the emperor to the pope, he reviews the contemporary evidence and shows that it all tends to prove that the emperors, beginning with Constantine himself, continued to exercise rule over the West and that the popes did not exercise it.*)

Come now, was Pope Sylvester ever in possession? Who dispossessed him? For he did not have possession permanently nor did any of his successors, at least till Gregory the Great (*590–604* A. D.), and there is nothing to prove that Gregory had possession. One that is not in possession and can not prove that he has been dispossessed, certainly never did have possession; and if he says he did, he is mad. You see, I even prove that you are mad! Or if you be not, tell me who dislodged Sylvester? Did Constantine himself do it, or his sons, or Julian, or some other Caesar? Give the name of the expeller, give the date. From what place was the pope expelled first, whence next, and so in order? . . . Did he lose everything in a single day or gradually and by districts? . . .

(*He takes up the document in detail to show its historical and philological absurdities. The first paragraph he reviews contains a passage, according to which the emperor, "together with all our satraps and the whole senate and nobles also," declares it to be proper to endow the pope with every power and dignity because he represented God on earth.*)

O thou scoundrel, thou villian (*i.e., the forger*)! The Life of Sylvester (*a genuine document, let it be noted*), which you allege as your evidence, says that for a long time no one of senatorial rank was willing to accept the Christian religion and that Constantine was obliged to solicit the Roman poor with bribes to be baptized. And you venture to say that, within the first days, the senate, the nobles, the satraps, as though already Christians, together with the emperor passed decrees for the honoring of the Roman Church! What have satraps got to do with the case? Numskull, blockhead! Do emperors speak thus? Are Roman decrees drafted thus? Whoever heard of satraps in any Roman province?

(*The forger makes the blunder of speaking of Constantinople as a patriarchate of the Church.*)

How in the world . . . could one speak of Constantinople as one of the patriarchal sees, when it was not yet a patriarchate, nor a see, nor a Christian city, nor named Constantinople, nor founded, nor planned! For the concession was granted, so the document says, the third day after Emperor Constantine became a Christian. And at that time Byzantium, not Constantinople, occupied that site. . . .

(*Having demolished the document with his critical acumen, Valla declares that the popes, under the Donation, have become evil stewards.*)

Wherefore I declare and cry aloud . . . that in my time no one in the supreme pontificate has been either a faithful or prudent steward, but they have been so far from giving food to the household of God that they have devoured their income as food and a mere morsel of bread! The pope himself makes war on peaceable people and sows discord among states and princes. The pope both thirsts for the goods of others and drinks up his own. . . . Not only does he enrich himself at the expense of the empire . . .

but he enriches himself at the expense of even the Church and the Holy Spirit. . . . And when he is reminded of this by good people occasionally, he does not deny it but openly admits it and boasts that he is free to wrest from its occupants by any means whatever the patrimony given to the Church by Constantine. . . .

And so that he may recover the missing parts of the Donation, he spends money wickedly stolen from good people and supports armed forces, mounted and on foot, while Christ is dying of hunger in many thousands of paupers. Nor does he know, the unworthy reprobate, that while he works to deprive secular powers of what belongs to them, they in turn are either led by his bad example or driven by necessity . . . to make off with what belongs to the Church. And so there is no religion anywhere, no sanctity, no fear of God. And, what I shudder to mention, impious men pretend to find in the pope an excuse for all their crimes. . . .

If only I may see the time when the pope is the vicar of Christ alone and not of Caesar also! . . . Then the pope will be the Holy Father in fact as well as in name, Father of all, Father of the Church; nor will he stir up wars among Christians but those stirred up by others he, through his apostolic powers and papal majesty, will bring to an end.

100. THE COLLOQUIES OF ERASMUS[1]

The first collection was small and was composed at Paris in 1497, and intended for the perusal of his pupils. Erasmus had not planned to publish these colloquies, but when in 1518 Beatus Rhenanus, an Alsatian humanist, published them at Basel in November of that year, not even asking the author for his permission, Erasmus quickly revised them. His improved edition appeared at Basel in 1519, under the title of Formulas of Familiar Conversations by Erasmus of Rotterdam, useful not only for polishing a boy's Speech but for Building his Character. *A much larger edition followed in 1522, while the edition of 1524 was styled* Familiar Conversations. *Both were published by Froben. Further additions were made in the year 1524 and on several other occasions until the edition of March, 1533, completed the process. The Latin title was* Colloquia. *The earlier colloquies are the more interesting. Among later additions there were some very obscene passages, which reflected the influence of Italian humanism on Erasmus.*

The Colloquies *exerted enormous influence on the educated classes in the sixteenth century, being used very extensively as a textbook in Latin rhetoric*

[1] Reprinted from *Erasmus and the Humanists* by Albert Hyma. New York, F. S. Crofts and Co., 1930, pp. 36–55.

or composition. The author cleverly exposed in this work numerous abuses in church and state, as well as some superstitions. This is particularly noticeable in the colloquy entitled The Shipwreck.

I. *A Dialogue by Anthony and Adolph.*

The Shipwreck

A.[1] This is a dreadful story that you are telling. Is that sailing? God forbid that any such idea should come into my head.

B.[2] Indeed, what I have related is mere child's play compared with what you are about to hear.

A. I have heard more than enough of mishaps. I shudder while you narrate them, as though I myself were present at the danger.

B. Indeed, to me past struggles are pleasing. That night something happened which almost put the captain at his wits' end.

A. What I pray?

B. The moon was bright that night, and one of the sailors was standing in the topmast (for so it is called, I believe), keeping a lookout for land. A globe of fire appeared beside him. It is considered by sailors to be an evil omen if the fire be single, a good omen if it be double. In ancient times these were thought to be Castor and Pollux.

A. What have they to do with sailors? One of them was a horseman, the other a boxer.

B. Well, this is the view of the poets. The captain who was sitting at the helm began to speak. "Mate," said he (for sailors address each other in this manner), "do you see what is beside you?" "I see," he replied, "and I hope it may be lucky." Soon the fiery globe descended along the rigging and rolled to the captain.

A. Was he paralyzed with fear?

B. Sailors are accustomed to strange sights. The globe stopped there a while, then rolled along the side of the vessel and disappeared down through the middle of the deck. About noon the storm began to rage with great fury. Have you ever seen the Alps?

A. Yes, I have.

B. Those mountains are warts compared with the waves of the sea. When we were lifted up on the crest of a wave, we might have touched the moon with our fingers. As often as we went down between the billows, we seemed to be going directly to the infernal regions, the earth opening to receive us.

[1] A. stands for Anthony.
[2] B. stands for Adolph.

A. Madmen to trust themselves to the sea!

B. The sailors struggled in vain against the tempest, and at length the captain, quite pale, came toward us.

A. That pallor presages some great evil.

B. "Friends," says he, "I have lost control of my ship. The winds have conquered me, and nothing remains but to put our trust in God, and to prepare for the end."

A. A truly Scythian speech!

B. "But first," says he, "we shall relieve the ship of her cargo. Necessity, a stern mistress, commands this. It is better to save our lives, with the loss of our goods, than to perish along with our goods." The truth of this was evident to us; and many boxes of precious goods were thrown into the sea.

A. This was indeed a loss!

B. There was a certain Italian who had been upon an embassy to the king of Scotland; he had a box full of silver and gold, plates, rings, cloth, and silk garments.

A. Would he not settle with the sea?

B. No; he wished either to perish with his beloved wealth, or to be saved along with it; and so he refused.

A. What did the captain say?

B. "So far as we are concerned," says he, "you are welcome to perish with your goods; but it is not right that we should all be endangered for the sake of your box, and rather than that we will throw you headlong into the sea, along with your box."

A. A speech worthy of a sailor.

B. So the Italian also threw over his goods, with many an oath, regretting that he had trusted his life to so barbarous an element. A little later the winds, in no wise softened by our offerings, broke the rigging and tore the sails into shreds.

A. Too bad! Too bad!

B. Again the skipper approaches us.

A. With further information?

B. He greets us: "Friends, the time has come that everybody should commend himself to God and prepare for death." When some of the passengers who had some knowledge of the sea asked him how many hours he thought he could keep afloat, he said he could not say for certain, but that it would not be above three hours.

A. This news was more serious than the former.

B. With these words he ordered all ropes to be severed and the mast cut with a saw close to the deck, and to be thrown into the sea together with the spars.

A. Why?

B. Because the sails, being torn to pieces, were a burden rather than a help. All our hope was in the helm.

A. What were the passengers doing in the meantime?

B. There you might have seen a wretched spectacle. The sailors, singing *"SALVE, REGINA,"* implored the Virgin Mother, calling her star of the sea, queen of heaven, ruler of the world, harbor of safety, and flattering her with many other titles, which the Bible nowhere attributes to her.

A. What has she to do with the sea, who never sailed, so far as I know?

B. Venus formerly had the care of sailors, because she was supposed to have been born of the sea. Since she has ceased to care for them, the Virgin Mother has been substituted for her: as a mother and not as a virgin.

A. You are joking.

B. Some fell down upon the decks and worshipped the sea, pouring oil upon the waves, flattering them as we used to flatter an angry prince.

A. What did they say?

B. "O most merciful sea! O most generous sea! O most wealthy sea! Have pity, save us!" Many things of this sort they sang to the deaf sea.

A. Ridiculous superstition! What were the others doing?

B. Some were occupied with sea-sickness; but most of them offered vows. Among them was a certain Englishman, who promised mountains of gold to our Lady of Walsingham, if only he might reach land alive. Some promised much to the wood of the cross in a certain place; others to the same wood in another place. The same was done for the Virgin Mary, who reigns in many places; and they think the vow is of no avail, unless one names the place.

A. Absurd! As if the saints did not dwell in heaven.

B. Some vowed to be Carthusians. One promised to go to James of Compostella with bare head and feet, his body covered only with an iron coat of mail, and begging his food.

A. Did nobody mention Christopher?

B. I could not help laughing when I heard one with a loud voice (lest he should not be heard) promise Christopher in the high church at Paris, a mountain rather than a statue, a wax candle as big as he himself. While he was shouting this at the top of his voice, with now and then an additional emphasis, an acquaintance nudged him with his elbow and said, "Take care what you promise; for if you sell all your goods at auction, you will not be able to pay." Then said he in a lower voice, lest Christopher should hear: "Hold your tongue, fool; do you think I am in earnest? When once I reach land, I will not give him a tallow candle."

A. What a blockhead! I imagine he was a Hollander.

B. No, but he was a Zeelander.[1]

A. I am surprised that nobody thought of Paul the Apostle. He himself sailed, and when the ship was wrecked, leaped ashore; and he learned through misfortune to succor the unfortunate.

B. There was no mention of Paul.

A. Did they pray meanwhile?

B. Earnestly. One sang *"SALVE, REGINA,"* another the apostles' creed. Some had special prayers, like charms, against danger.

A. How religious men are in times of affliction! In prosperity neither God nor saint comes into our head. What were you doing all this time? Did you offer vows to none of the saints?

B. Not one.

A. Why not?

B. Because I do not bargain with the saints. For what else is it than a contract: "I will give this if you will do that; I will give you a wax candle, if I swim out of this; I will go to Rome, if you will save me."

A. But did you not implore the protection of some saint?

B. Not even that.

A. Why not?

B. Because Heaven is a large place. If I commend myself to some saint, St. Peter for example, who is most likely to hear me first of all, since he stands at the door; before he goes to God and explains my case I should have perished.

A. What did you do, then?

B. I went straight to the Father himself, saying: "Our Father who art in heaven." None of the saints hears sooner than He, nor gives more willingly what is asked.

A. But in the meanwhile did not your conscience cry out against you? Were you not afraid to call him Father whom you have offended with so many transgressions?

B. To tell the truth, my conscience did terrify me a little; but presently I gathered courage, thinking, there is no father so angry with his son, but, if he sees him in danger, in a river or a lake, would seize him by the hair and draw him out upon the bank. Among them all no one behaved more quietly than a certain woman who had a baby in her arms, which she was nursing.

A. What did she do?

B. She was the only one who did not shout or weep or promise. Embracing her child, she prayed silently. In the meantime the ship was struck by a big wave, and the captain, fearing lest it should go to pieces, bound it fore and aft with cables.

[1] Zeeland and Holland were Dutch counties.

A. What a miserable makeshift!

B. Then an aged priest, sixty years old, whose name was Adam, comes forward. Casting off his clothes even to his shirt and his leather stockings, he ordered that we should prepare ourselves in a similar manner for swimming; and standing thus in the middle of the ship he preached to us out of Gerson the five truths concerning the usefulness of confession, exhorting us all to prepare ourselves for life or death. There was also a Dominican to whom those who wished confessed.

A. What did you do?

B. Seeing that confusion reigned everywhere, I confessed silently to God, condemning my unrighteousness and imploring his mercy.

A. Where would you have gone, if you had died thus?

B. I left that to God as judge; nor was I disposed to be my own judge; yet in the meantime I was not without some hope. While these things were going on, the sailor returns to us weeping. "Let every one prepare himself," says he, "for the ship will not last a quarter of an hour." For it was badly broken, and the sea was rushing in. A little later the sailor informed us that he saw a church tower, and advised us to pray to the saint for aid, whoever might be the patron of that church. All fall upon their knees and pray to the unknown saint.

A. If you had called him by name perhaps he might have heard you.

B. He was unknown to us. Meanwhile the captain steers the ship, shattered as it was, and leaking at every seam, and evidently ready to fall to pieces, had it not been bound with cables.

A. A sad condition of affairs.

B. We came so near the shore that the inhabitants of the place saw our danger; and running in crowds to the beach, they held up their coats and put their hats upon lances, to attract our attention; and they raised their arms, to show that they were sorry for us.

A. I am anxious to know what happened.

B. The sea had already invaded the whole ship, so that we were likely to be no safer in the ship than in the sea.

A. Then you were obliged to flee to the holy anchor?

B. Nay, to the miserable one. The sailors bail out the boat and lower it into the sea. All attempt to crowd into it, and the sailors remonstrate vigorously, saying that the boat is not able to hold such a crowd; that each one should lay hold of whatever he could find and take to swimming. There was no opportunity for deliberation. One took an oar, another a boat-hook, another a tub, another a plank; and all took to the waves, each one resting upon his means of salvation.

A. In the meantime what became of that poor woman who alone did not cry out?

B. She reached land first.

A. How was that possible?

B. We placed her upon a wide board, and tied her on it so that she could not very well fall off. We gave her a paddle in her hand which she might use instead of an oar, and, wishing her well, we set her adrift, pushing her forward with a pole, so that she might float wide of the ship, from which there was danger. She held her baby with her left hand and paddled with her right.

A. What a courageous woman!

B. When nothing was left, some one pulled down a wooden image of the Virgin Mother, now rotten and hollowed out by the rats, and embracing it, began to swim.

A. Did the boat arrive safe?

B. They were the first ones to be lost.

A. How did that happen?

B. Before it could get clear of the ship it tipped and was overturned.

A. How badly managed! What then?

B. While watching the others I nearly perished myself.

A. How so?

B. Because nothing remained for me to swim upon.

A. Corks would have been of use there.

B. Just at this time I would rather have had some cheap cork than a golden candlestick. Finally, as I was looking about, it occurred to me that the stump of the mast would be of use to me; but as I could not get it out alone, I got a companion to help me. We both threw ourselves upon it and so committed ourselves to the sea, I upon the right end, he upon the left. While we were thus tossing about, the sea chaplain threw himself upon the middle, between our shoulders. He was a stout man. We cried out: "Who is this third man? He will cause us all to perish!" He, on the other hand, mildly replied: "Be of good cheer; there is room enough. God will be with us."

A. Why did he come so late?

B. He was to have been in the boat with the Dominican, for they all had great respect for him; but although they had confessed to one another on the ship, they had forgotten something (I know not what), wherefore they began confessing again at the ship's rail, and one laid his hand upon the other. Meanwhile the boat is turned over, as Adam himself told me.

A. What became of the Dominican?

B. He, the same one told me, implored the saints' help, put off his clothes and took to swimming all naked.

A. What saints did he invoke?

B. Dominic, Thomas, Vincent; but he relied most upon Catherine of Sens.

A. Did he say nothing of Christ?

B. Not a word, according to the priest.

A. He would have done better if he had not put off his holy cowl; with that off, how could Catherine of Sens recognize him? But go on about yourself.

B. While we were tossing about near the ship, which rolled hither and thither at the mercy of the waves, the helm broke the thigh of the man who held the left end of our float, and he was knocked off. The priest prayed for his eternal rest, and succeeded to his place, urging me to hold courageously to my end and move my feet actively. In the meanwhile we swallowed a great deal of salt water. Neptune had mixed for us not only a salt bath, but a salt drink. The priest, however, soon had a remedy for that.

A. What, I pray?

B. Every time a wave came toward us, he turned the back of his head to it with his mouth firmly closed.

A. You say he was a stout old man?

B. Swimming thus for some time we had made considerable progress when the priest, who was a man of unusual height, said: "Be of good cheer; I feel bottom." Not having dared to hope for such happiness, I replied: "We are yet too far from shore to hope to find bottom." "No," he said, "I feel the ground with my feet." "It is," I rejoined, "some of the boxes, perhaps, which the sea has thrown down here." "No," said he, "I plainly feel the earth by scratching with my toes." We swam on for some time longer, and he felt bottom again. "You must do," he said, "what you think is best. I will give you the whole mast and trust myself to the bottom"; and at the same time waiting for the waves to flow outward, he went forward as rapidly as he could. When the waves came again upon him, holding firmly to his knees with both hands he met the wave, sinking beneath it as sea-gulls and ducks are accustomed to do; and when the wave again receded he sprang up and ran. Seeing that this succeeded in his case, I did the same. Then some of the strongest of those who stood upon the beach, and those most used to the waves, fortified themselves against the force of the waves with long poles stretched between them, so that the outermost held out a pole to the swimmer; and when he had grasped it, the whole line moved shorewards and so he was drawn safely on dry land. Some were saved in this way.

A. How many?

B. Seven; but of these, two fainted with the heat, when placed before the fire.

A. How many were there in the ship?

B. Fifty-eight.

A. O cruel sea! At least it might have been content with the tithes, which suffice for the priests. Did it return so few out of so great a number?

B. We were surprisingly well treated by the people, who most cheerfully furnished us with everything, lodging, fire, food, clothes, and provisions for our homeward journey.

A. What people were they?

B. Hollanders.

A. No people are more civil, although they are surrounded with savage nations. You will not go to sea again, I take it?

B. Not if God keeps my mind sound.

A. And as for me, I would rather hear such tales than experience them.

II. *A Dialogue between Robert and William.*

The Inns

A.[1] Why do so many people stop at Lyons for two or three days? As for me, when I start upon a journey I do not rest until I reach my destination.

B.[2] Indeed, I wonder how any one can be got away from the place at all.

A. Why?

B. Because that is the place from which the companions of Ulysses could not have been drawn. The Sirens are there. No one is treated better in his own home than there at an inn.

A. What do they do?

B. The women are very handsome there, and one of them is always standing near the table to divert the guests with wit and fun. First the mistress of the house came to us, and bade us welcome. Then came the daughter, a fine woman, merry and charming, so that she might have amused Cato himself. Nor do they talk to their guests as if they were strangers, but as if they were old acquaintances.

A. Yes, I admit that French people are very civil.

B. But since they could not be present all the time (the business of the house had to be attended to and the other guests had to be greeted), a girl well supplied with jokes attended us during the whole meal. She was quite able to repay all the jesters in their own coin. She kept the stories going until the daughter returned. The mother, by the way, was somewhat elderly.

A. But what sort of fare did you have with all this? For the stomach is not filled with stories.

[1] A. stands for Robert.

[2] B. stands for William.

B. Fine! Indeed, I wonder how they can entertain guests so cheaply. Then too, after dinner they divert the guests with pleasant conversation, lest they should feel bored. It seemed to me that I was at home, not travelling.

A. How about the sleeping accommodations?

B. Even there we were attended by girls, laughing, romping and playing; they asked us if we had any soiled clothes, washed them for us and brought them back. What more can I say? We saw nothing but women and girls, except in the stables; and even there they burst in occasionally. They treat departing guests as affectionately as if they were all brothers or near relatives.

A. Very likely such manners suit the French; as for me, the customs of Germany please me more. They are more manly.

B. I never happened to visit Germany; so tell me how the Germans entertain a guest.

A. I cannot say what happens in all parts of Germany, but I will relate what I have seen. Upon the arrival of the guest nobody greets him, lest they should seem to court him for they consider that mean and unworthy of German dignity and gravity. When you have shouted yourself hoarse, finally someone puts his head out of the window of the stove-room (for they live there up to the middle of the summer), just as a snail pokes its head out of its shell. You have to ask him if you may be entertained there. If he says nothing, you understand that room will be made for you. To your inquiries, with a wave of his hand, he indicates where the stables are. There you are permitted to take care of your horse as you choose; for no servant lifts a finger. If the tavern is a large one, a servant will show you the stables and a rather inconvenient place for your horse. They keep the better places for the noblemen, who, as they pretend, are expected. If you find fault with anything, you are told at once that you are at liberty to hunt another tavern. In the cities it is difficult to get any hay, even a little, and it is almost as dear as oats. When your horse is provided for, you go just as you are to the stove-room, boots, baggage and mud. There is one room for all comers.

B. Among the French they take the guests to bed rooms, where they may change their clothes, bathe and warm themselves, or even take a nap, if they please.

A. Well, there is no such thing here. In the stove-room you take off your boots and put on slippers. If you like, you change your shirt; you hang your clothes, wet with rain, against the stove; and you sit by it yourself, in order to get dry. There is water ready if you care to wash your hands, but it is generally so dirty that you have to seek more water to wash off that ablution.

B. I cannot admire such manly people.

A. Even if you arrive at four in the afternoon, you cannot get your supper before nine, and sometimes ten.

B. Why is that?

A. They serve nothing until they see all the guests assembled, in order that the same effort may serve for all.

B. They have an eye to labor-saving.

A. You are right. And thus very often between eighty and a hundred persons are assembled in the same stove-room, footmen, horsemen, tradesmen, sailors, coachmen, farmers, boys, women, healthy people and sick people.

B. That is in truth a community.

A. One is combing his head, another wiping the perspiration from his face, another cleaning his winter shoes or boots, another reeks of garlic. What more could you desire? Here is no less confusion of tongue and of persons than there was once in the tower of Babel. But if they see a foreigner who shows some evidence of distinction in dress, they are all interested in him, and stare at him as if he were some animal from Africa. Even after they are at the table, they turn their heads to get a look, and neglect their meals rather than lose sight of him.

B. At Rome, Paris, and Venice there is no such gazing.

A. Remember, it is a mortal sin to call for anything. When the evening is far advanced and no more guests are expected, an old servant appears, with gray beard, cropped head, a savage look and shabby clothes.

B. It was necessary that such should be cup-bearers to the Roman Cardinals. . . .

A. Well, after all are seated, the grim servant comes out and counts his company. By and by he returns and sets before each guest a wooden dish and a spoon of the same kind of silver; then a glass and a little piece of bread. Each one polishes up his utensils in a leisurely way while the porridge is cooking. And thus they sit not uncommonly for upwards of an hour.

B. Does no guest call for food in the meantime?

A. No one who is acquainted with the temper of the country. At length wine is served, and wine that is far from being tasteless! Those who water their wine ought to drink no other kind, it is so thin and sharp. But if any guest wants better wine, offering to pay extra for it, they will give him a look as if they wished to murder him. If he insists upon it they answer that a great many counts and margraves have lodged there and none of them has complained of the quality of the wine; if it does not suit him, why then, let him go to another tavern, for they look upon their noblemen as the only men of importance, and exhibit their coats of arms everywhere. By this time the guests get a crust to throw to their barking stomachs. By and by the dishes come on in great array. The first usually consists of pieces of bread soaked in meat-broth, or, if it be fish-day, in a broth of herbs. After this comes another kind of broth, then some kind of warmed-up meat or salt fish. Again the porridge is brought on, then some more substantial food, until, when the stomach is well tamed, they serve up roast meat or boiled fish, which is not to be despised. But here they are sparing, and take the dishes away quickly. In this way they diversify the entertainment, like comedians who mix choruses with their scenes, taking care that the last act shall be the best.

B. This is indeed the mark of a good poet.

A. Moreover, it would be an unpardonable offense if anybody in the meantime should say: "Take away this dish; nobody cares for it." You must sit there through the prescribed time, which they measure, I suppose, with an hour-glass. At last, the bearded fellow, or the inn-keeper himself, who wears no better clothes than the servants, comes in and asks if there is anything wanted. Presently some better wine is brought in. They admire him the most who drinks the most; but although he is the greater consumer he pays no more than he who drinks least.

B. A curious people, indeed!

A. The result is that sometimes there are those who consume twice the value in wine of what they pay for the whole meal. But before I end my account of this entertainment, it is wonderful what a noise and confusion of voices arises, when all have begun to grow warm with drink. It is unnecessary to say that the riot is universal. So-called jesters thrust themselves in everywhere, and although there is no kind of human beings more despicable, yet you would scarcely believe how the Germans are pleased with them. They sing, shout, dance, and jump, so that the stove seems ready to fall. No one can hear another speak. But it seems to please them, and you are obliged to sit there, whether you will or not, until midnight.

A. Now you must finish the entertainment; for I am also worn out with the length of it.

B. Very well. When at last the cheese, which hardly pleases them unless rotten and full of worms, has been taken away, the bearded fellow appears, bearing a trencher on which are drawn with chalk some circles and semicircles, and he lays it upon the table, so silent, meanwhile, and sad, that you would say he was some Charon. Then they who comprehend the meaning of this lay down their money, one after another, until the trencher is filled. Then having observed who has contributed, he counts it silently; and if nothing is wanting he nods his head.

B. What if there should be too much?

A. Perhaps he would return it. As a matter of fact, this is sometimes done.

B. Does nobody ever complain about the counting as unjust?

A. Nobody who is prudent. For he would hear at once: "What sort of a fellow are you? You are paying no more than the others!"

B. This is certainly a frank kind of people you are telling about.

A. And if anybody, weary with his journey, asks to go to bed soon after supper, he is ordered to wait until the rest also go to bed.

B. I seem to see a Platonic city.

A. Then each is shown to his rest, and it is truly nothing more than a bed room; for there is nothing there but a bed, and nothing else that you can use or steal.

B. Is there cleanliness?

A. Just as at dinner; linen washed six months ago, perhaps.

B. In the meantime what had become of the horses?

A. They were treated according to the same method as the men.

B. But do you get the same accommodations everywhere?

A. Sometimes more courteous, sometimes harsher than I have told you; but on the whole it is as I have said.

B. How would you like me to tell you how guests are treated in that part of Italy which is called Lombardy, or in Spain, or in England and in Wales? For the English have assimilated in part the French and in part the German customs, being a mixture of these two nations. The Welsh boast that they are the original English.

A. I should like you to tell me, for I have never had occasion to see them.

B. At present I have not time, for the sailor told me to meet him at three o'clock, or I should be left behind; and he has my baggage. Some other time we shall have an opportunity of chatting to our hearts' content.

101. BROWNING'S CONCEPTION OF AN ITALIAN DESPOT OF THE RENAISSANCE

Robert Browning's poem, "My Last Duchess," takes the form of a monologue which the author places in the mouth of the Duke of Ferrara. The Duke speaks of his former wife to an envoy who has come to negotiate with the nobleman a new marriage. The poem is meant to reveal, but not too obviously, characteristics which Browning attributed to a certain type of Italian despot at the time of the Italian Renaissance. What those characteristics are the reader may determine for himself from the poem.

My Last Duchess

Ferrara

That's my last Duchess painted on the wall,
Looking as if she were alive. I call
That piece a wonder, now: Frà Pandolf's hand
Worked busily a day, and there she stands.
Will't please you sit and look at her? I said
"Frà Pandolf" by design, for never read
Strangers like you that pictured countenance,
The depth and passion of its earnest glance,
But to myself they turned (since none puts by
The curtain I have drawn for you, but I)
And seemed as they would ask me, if they durst,
How such a glance came there; so, not the first
Are you to turn and ask thus. Sir, 't was not
Her husband's presence only, called that spot
Of joy into the Duchess' cheek: perhaps
Frà Pandolf chanced to say, "Her mantle laps
Over my lady's wrist too much," or "Paint
Must never hope to reproduce the faint
Half-flush that dies along her throat:" such stuff
Was courtesy, she thought, and cause enough
For calling up that spot of joy. She had
A heart—how shall I say—too soon made glad,
Too easily impressed: she liked whate'er
She looked on, and her looks went everywhere.
Sir, 't was all one! My favor at her breast,
The dropping of the daylight in the West,
The bough of cherries some officious fool
Broke in the orchard for her, the white mule
She rode with round the terrace—all and each
Would draw from her alike the approving speech,
Or blush at least. She thanked men,—good! but thanked
Somehow—I know not how—as if she ranked
My gift of a nine-hundred-years-old name
With anybody's gift. Who'd stoop to blame
This sort of trifling? Even had you skill
In speech—(which I have not)—to make your will
Quite clear to such an one, and say, "Just this
Or that in you disgusts me; here you miss,

Or there exceed the mark"—and if she let
Herself be lessoned so, nor plainly set
Her wits to yours, forsooth, and made excuse,
—E'en then would be some stooping; and I choose
Never to stoop. Oh sir, she smiled, no doubt,
Whene'er I passed her; but who passed without
Much the same smile? This grew; I gave commands;
Then all smiles stopped together. There she stands
As if alive. Will't please you rise? We'll meet
The company below, then. I repeat,
The Count your master's known munificence
Is ample warrant that no just pretence
Of mine for dowry will be disallowed;
Though his fair daughter's self, as I avowed
At starting, is my object. Nay, we'll go
Together down, sir. Notice Neptune, though,
Taming a sea-horse, thought a rarity,
Which Claus of Innsbruck cast in bronze for me!

102. "THE PRINCE" BY MACHIAVELLI [1]

Machiavelli (1469–1527) was an able statesman, and served for fifteen years as secretary of the Chancery of Florence. In this capacity he learned a great deal about political theories in central Italy. He aimed at a new science of statesmanship, based not so much on views expressed by medieval authorities as on actual experience. Like many Italian humanists he was thoroughly pagan and greatly admired the Romans. He disliked Christianity, for he believed that it made men weak and humble. One of the princes in Italy whom he admired was the notorious Caesar Borgia, the hero of The Prince. *In this work Machiavelli carefully explained the qualities necessary for a successful ruler, such as he hoped Caesar Borgia would be, after he had formed a new state in central Italy. In the following excerpts he sets forth his opinions in no uncertain terms.*

Fifteenth Chapter

Concerning matters which enhance or diminish the reputation of a prince

It now remains to show how a prince should treat his subjects and friends, but since many have written on this point it may seem presumptuous for me to discuss it again, especially as I shall differ widely from the opinions of

[1] Nicolo Machiavelli, *The Prince*. The selections given in this volume have been translated by Albert Hyma.

others. My intention, however, is to present an exposition of practical value. Instead of depicting republics and principalities which never did nor can exist (as several others have done), I thought it better to describe them as they actually are. For the manner in which men now live is so different from that in which they ought to live, that one who deviates from the ordinary course of action and tries to do what he ought to do, is on the road to ruin while thinking that he is preserving his security; for he who wishes to lead a virtuous life will soon be overcome by the multitudinous forces of evil. Hence it is absolutely necessary for a prince who would hold his own to learn not to be good sometimes, and to use this knowledge according as the occasion demands.

Putting aside, therefore, imaginary situations and directing our attention to real conditions, I say that all men and especially princes (since they are placed in more responsible positions) are distinguished by some of the qualities which elicit praise or dishonor. For example, one is accounted liberal, another niggardly; [1] one is reputed generous, another rapacious; one cruel, another merciful; one faithless, another faithful; one effeminate and pusillanimous, another bold and courageous; one courteous and humane, another haughty and disdainful; one lewd, another chaste; one upright and sincere, another dishonest and deceitful; one stiff and reserved, another affable and pleasant; one grave, another frivolous; one religious, another irreligious; and so forth. I realize that every one will admit that a prince endowed with all the good qualities above mentioned would be deemed most praiseworthy, but since the frailty and perverseness of human nature is such that it is impossible for any man to put them all into practice, granted that he were in possession of them all, it is necessary for him to be so prudent as to avoid the ignominy of those vices which may deprive him of his state, and to take care not to commit others (which may not have such serious consequences), if he can possibly help it. But if this is not possible, he need not feel greatly disturbed nor feel uneasy in endeavoring to escape the calumny of those vices without which he could not keep his state. Upon due consideration it will be seen that some things which have the appearance of virtues would prove the ruin of the prince; and on the other hand, some other things which seem bad may bring him welfare and security.

Sixteenth Chapter

Concerning liberality and parsimony

To begin with the first of the above-named qualities, I say that it is well for a prince to be accounted liberal. Nevertheless, if this liberality is not ex-

[1] Machiavelli adds here a parenthesis concerning the Tuscan word for miserly or niggardly, which breaks the thread of the discourse and has therefore been omitted here.

ercized in such a manner as to bring him the reputation for liberality, it will harm him. For if he applies it with prudence and discretion, it will not become sufficiently known to the public and consequently he will not escape the reproach for the opposite. But in order to gain the reputation of being liberal, every sort of expense and munificence is required; so that a prince of such a disposition may squander his whole revenues in those extravagances, and in the end he will be obliged to oppress his subjects in resorting to heavy taxes and confiscations. This will soon make him odious to his own subjects and despised by every one else, when they see that he is reduced to poverty and distress; and since he has injured many and benefited few through his liberality, he will be exposed to the threat of ruin by the first reverse he meets. But what is worse, when he begins to realize his error and tries to correct it, he is thought guilty of the other extreme, and reproached with avarice.

A prince, therefore, who cannot make a show of liberality without peril to the safety of his state, ought not if he be wise to feel anxious to avoid the reputation of avarice. He will be esteemed liberal in due time, when his subjects note that he has improved his finances so much through husbanding the revenues that he is not only able to defend himself against any enemy but to invade the territory of others without oppressing his own subjects. In fact, all those will regard him as liberal from whom he has taken nothing, and they will be many; and those only will consider him miserly to whom he has not given so much as they had expected, and they will be few. We have seen no great things performed in our times except by those who have been deemed parsimonious; all others have failed in their attempts. Pope Julius II, having availed himself of a show of liberality in securing the papal office, almost immediately changed his tactics in order that he might be able to make war upon the king of France. He carried on several expensive wars without being required to levy any extraordinary tax upon his subjects. The present king of Spain [1] could never have succeeded in so many enterprises if he had sought to be reputed liberal.

. . . .

A prince should take care above all things to avoid the necessity of becoming odious and despised. Liberality leads to both. It is wiser, therefore, to submit to the reputation for avarice, which results in ignominy rather than hatred, than to reduce oneself through ostentation of liberality to the position of a tyrant, which will beget both infamy and hatred.

[1] Ferdinand of Aragon (1469–1516).

Seventeenth Chapter

Concerning cruelty and clemency, and whether it is better for a prince to be feared or loved

Proceeding to the other qualities mentioned above, I say that a prince should desire to be esteemed merciful. Nevertheless, he should take great care how he exercises his clemency. Caesar Borgia was accounted cruel, but his cruelty not only thoroughly reformed and united the Romagna, but restored peace within its borders and kept it firmly in allegiance to him. When properly considered, he was much more merciful than the Florentines, who, to avoid the reputation for cruelty, permitted Pistoia to be destroyed. A prince, therefore, ought not to be concerned about the reputation for cruelty, provided it is necessary to keep his subjects united and loyal. By making a few examples he will prove himself more merciful in the end than he who, by showing too much clemency, permits disorders to arise which result in murder and robbery. For these undermine the peace of the whole community, whereas legal executions extend only to individuals. . . .

Eighteenth Chapter

In how far princes should keep faith

Every one must confess that it is most praiseworthy in a prince to act with integrity and good faith rather than to have recourse to fraud. Nevertheless, experience has shown us that those princes of our own times who have done the greatest things have held their word of honor of little account; and by dint of craft and circumvention they have for the most part gotten the better of those who acted in good faith. It must be observed, therefore, that there are two ways of deciding any contest, the one by laws, the other by force. The former is proper to men, the latter to beasts. But since laws are not always sufficient to decide the contest, it becomes necessary sometimes to use force. A prince should, therefore, on certain occasions know how to resemble a beast as well as a man. . . .

Inasmuch as a prince must learn at times to act as a beast, he should make the lion and the fox his patterns. The lion does not have enough cunning to keep out of snares, and the fox lacks the necessary strength to cope with the wolf. Hence the prince must be a fox to locate the snares and a lion to terrify the wolves, and he that copies the lion only will not know how to proceed. A wise prince, therefore, should not keep his word if keeping it would be to his disadvantage and if the reasons for keeping it are no longer valid. This precept would not hold if men generally were good, but since they are bad and will not keep faith with you, you are not obliged to keep faith with them. A prince will never be in want of legitimate reasons for excusing his breach of faith. Of this numerous recent examples could be adduced, showing how many treaties and solemn promises have been perfidiously violated by princes; and those that have acted the part of the fox have always succeeded best in their affairs. . . . Among many examples I cannot pass over that of Pope Alexander VI, whose whole life was one continued imposition upon mankind. He neither did nor thought of anything else but how to deceive others; no man ever made stronger protestations of sincerity or took more solemn oaths to support them; no man observed them less. He was so well acquainted with the credulity of mankind that he always found new victims and succeeded in all his designs.

Therefore, it is not at all necessary for a prince to possess all the good qualities mentioned above, but it is most necessary to appear to possess them. I may even venture to affirm that to have them all and to practise them always is injurious, but that the appearance of having them is advantageous. . . . Let it then be the chief care of the prince to preserve himself and his state. Whatever the means are which he uses for this purpose, they will be deemed honorable. For the opinions of the vulgar are always determined by appearances and results; and since the world is chiefly composed of those who are called the vulgar, the voice of the few is seldom or never heeded. A certain prince (whom it is not well to name) talks about nothing but peace and good faith, though averse to both; and if he had favored the one or the other, he would long ago have lost both his reputation and his dominions.[1]

[1] This is Ferdinand of Aragon (1479–1516), who had acquired Naples and Navarre through perfidy and breach of faith.